# HANS EYSENCK

## Consensus and Controversy

*Essays in Honour of Hans Eysenck*

# Falmer International Master-Minds Challenged

*Psychology Series Editors: Drs Sohan and Celia Modgil*

# HANS EYSENCK.

## Consensus and Controversy

EDITED BY

## Sohan Modgil, PhD

Reader in Educational Research and Development
Brighton Polytechnic

AND

## Celia Modgil, PhD

Senior Lecturer in Educational Psychology
London University

CONCLUDING CHAPTER

BY

## Hans Eysenck

London University

The Falmer Press
A member of the Taylor & Francis Group
(Philadelphia and London)

**USA**    The Falmer Press, Taylor & Francis Inc., 242 Cherry Street, Philadelphia, PA 19106-1906

**UK**    The Falmer Press, Falmer House, Barcombe, Lewes, East Sussex, BN8 5DL

---

First published in 1986

**Library of Congress Cataloging in Publication Data**

Main entry under title:

Hans Eysenck: Consensus and Controversy.

(Falmer International Masterminds Challenge)
1. Psychology. 2. Social psychology. 3. Eysenck, H. J. (Hans Jurgen), 1916– . I. Modgil, Sohan. II. Modgil, Celia. III. Series.
BF121.H214 1986 150 86-11473
ISBN 1-85000-021-2

Jacket design by Caroline Archer

Typeset in 10/12 Times
by Imago Publishing Ltd., Thame, Oxon.

*Printed in Great Britain by Taylor & Francis (Printers) Ltd, Rankine Road, Basingstoke, Hants.*

# Contributors

Dr Sohan Modgil     and     Dr Celia Modgil
Brighton Polytechnic           University of London

Dr H. B. Gibson
(author of *Hans Eysenck: The Man and His Work*)

Professor Nicholas Martin
Dr Rosemary Jardine
Medical College of Virginia

Professor John Loehlin
University of Texas at Austin

Professor Paul Costa
Professor Robert McCrae
Baltimore City Hospitals

Dr Gordon Claridge
University of Oxford

Professor Arthur Jensen
University of California Berkeley

Professor Jerry Carlson
Dr Keith Widaman
University of California Riverside

Dr Chris Brand
University of Edinburgh

Dr John Ray
University of New South Wales

Professor Edward Erwin
University of Miami

Dr Paul Kline
University of Exeter

Dr Christopher Barbrack
Professor Cyril Franks
Rutgers, The State University of
   New Jersey

Professor Arnold Lazarus
Rutgers, The State University of
   New Jersey

Dr Glenn Wilson
University of London

Dr David Gilbert
University of Southern Illinois

Professor Charles Spielberger
University of South Florida

Professor Philip Burch
University of Leeds

Dr Carl Sargent
University of Cambridge

Dr David Nias
Dr Geoffrey Dean
University of London

Professor Hans Eysenck
University of London

# Acknowledgments

The undertaking of this volume in the *Falmer International Master-Minds Challenged Psychology Series* was only possible in collaboration with the numerous distinguished contributors herein. We are greatly indebted to them for demonstrating their trust by accepting our invitation to join forces to provide statements of how Eysenck's theory is seen in relation to particular areas.

The volume has been greatly enhanced by the recognition given to it by Hans Eysenck, who increased our confidence in the project by kindly agreeing to write the concluding chapter. We thank Professor Eysenck for his very kind and generous support and for his edifying contribution to the content.

We are further grateful to Falmer Press, a member of the Taylor and Francis group. We express our very sincere gratitude to Malcolm Clarkson, Managing Director, Falmer Press.

Sohan and Celia Modgil
June 1985

# Contents

In loving memory of
Piyare Lal Modgil

# Part I: Introduction

# 1. Hans Eysenck: Consensus and Controversy

SOHAN AND CELIA MODGIL

## INTRODUCTION

During the last forty years, Hans Eysenck's brilliant contribution to knowledge has been well-known world-wide. From its early transmission, his work has not been without its critics. Naturally, criticisms persist, although his work continues to be frequently acknowledged with great admiration in the channels of psychology. With such prolific work, it would seem justified to consider the discrepancies, the omissions, together with the various interpretations which have been and are currently being highlighted.

The publication of Eysenck's biography by Gibson (1981) has provided an excellent forerunner to a wider directed analysis of his work and its place in the evolution of psychology. Further, the Festschrift for Eysenck (Lynn, 1981), on the occasion of his sixty-fifth birthday with contributions from his past students and colleagues from the Institute of Psychiatry, London, together with others attracted by Eysenck's thinking, provides a review of the major contributions of Eysenck and his associates, ranging from the genetic and physiological foundations of personality to its clinical and social expressions.

## CONTINUING THE DEBATE: THE STRATEGY OF THE BOOK

The book has as its objective the evaluation of elements of Eysenck's work from the perspectives of a range of areas of psychology: behavioural genetics, personality, intelligence, social attitudes, psychotherapy and Freudian psychology, behaviour therapy, sexual and marital behaviour, smoking and health, astrology and parapsychology. It aims to provide in a single source the most recent 'crosscurrents and

1

crossfire', to begin to clarify the contribution of Eysenck to the evolution of the understanding of human behaviour.

The volume attempts to provide theoretical analysis supported by research on aspects of Eysenck's work, presented predominantly either positively or negatively by *pairs* of distinguished academics representing particular areas of knowledge. The *paired* contributions have been exchanged, through the editors, to provide an opportunity for both parties to refute the 'heart' of the opposing paper. This would perhaps go some way towards the prescription that what the study of human behaviour needs at this stage of its own development is a wide-ranging approach to the facts, furthering the hope that this growth will continue so as to include an openness to the evidence outside Eysenck's own framework.

Although axiomatic, it would be expedient to emphasize that the labelling 'predominantly positive' or 'predominantly negative' implies that the writer of the predominantly 'positive' chapter agrees in the *main* with the theory but is not in *entire* agreement, therefore being allowed some latitude towards disagreement. Likewise, 'negative' chapters mean that contributors *predominantly* but not *entirely* disagree with the theory, therefore permitting some latitude towards agreement. The interchange of chapters therefore produces points of consensus and of controversy.

The difficulties in this ambitious debate project are not minimized. Although every attempt has been made to achieve precision matching of pairs, in exceptional cases one of the contributors within a matched pair has followed a 'middle course'. This established itself as a 'contrasting' enough pair to lend itself to the debate format of the book.

Although the editors dictated the generic topics to be debated, the contributors were free to focus on any inherent aspect or specialization of their own. Again, however, the consequent interchange of the chapters allows formulation of points of consensus and of controversy, therefore retaining the thrust of the debate.

The choice of contributors was restricted to those who are objectively critical and who are knowledgeable about the theory. Some of the most publicized critics tend to have non-scientific axes to grind and their views and their polemics are well-known. The scholarly value of the book could be seriously damaged unless the contributors have the desire and the capacity for the kind of intellectual honesty needed to come to grips seriously with the scientific, psychological and social issues raised by the theory.

The following chapter by Gibson provides further initiation, and his introductory comments on the contents of the book are designed to stimulate and provoke the reader to engage in the debate.

## REFERENCES

Gibson, H. B. (1981) *Hans Eysenck: The Man and His Work,* London, Peter Owen.
Lynn, R. (Ed.) (1981) *Dimensions of Personality: Essays in Honour of Hans Eysenck,* Oxford, Pergamon Press.

# Part II: Introduction Chapter

# 2. Introductory Chapter

H. B. GIBSON

The idea of making Hans Eysenck's works the subject of a volume devoted to *Consensus and Controversy* is specially attractive, for of all living psychologists he is perhaps the most controversial figure. Again, because of the very wide scope of his writings, which embrace topics as diverse as intelligence, personality theory, social and political attitudes, Freudian theory, behaviour therapy and sexual behaviour, to mention but a few, here is an opportunity to bring together experts from a wide diversity of fields to discuss and debate Eysenck's contribution to their specialisms.

The Editors' intention has been to bring together a pair of disputants, 'predominantly positive' and 'predominantly negative' in their attitudes to Eysenck's contribution to each of the nine chosen fields. This intention was a highly ambitious one, and of course it has not been wholly achieved as we shall see. But although the formal structure of the volume has not attained a perfect balance, here we are provided with a rich feast of scholarship with varied individual approaches from different contributors who have been free to cast their chapters in whatever form they chose. Being invited to contribute an introductory chapter I take the same liberty, and I have had the advantage of having read the manuscripts of each of the eighteen chapters. Professor Eysenck will have the privilege of adding the concluding chapter when all is complete.

To comment that Eysenck is well-known for being a controversial psychologist is to risk the charge of mere banality. Some lesser writers have sought to advance their careers over a long period on the basis of a sustained campaign of criticizing and even vilifying him. Consequently, a few readers may be attracted to this volume in the hope of encountering an orgy of invective, perhaps sprinkled with four-letter words (I mean four-letter words such as 'dull', the worst swearword in the critics' armoury). Some may even hope for the quaint and alliterative baroque of political invective that has characterized Eysenck as 'a fascist and intellectual prostitute parading as a "professor of psychology"' (*Bulletin of the Progressive Intellectuals' Study Group*

3

(Birmingham), 1972). If this is their hope, then they will be disappointed, for these Birmingham 'intellectuals' are not represented here, and all controversy is conducted at quite a high level of academic discourse. As a privileged reader of the typescripts, I have noted that last-minute alterations have generally been in the direction of moderation of language and excision of ornate pejorative adjectives; for instance, one writer thought better of referring to Eysenck having a 'troglodytic' fixation on conditioning—now he is alleged just to have a fixation.

Some readers may regret the absence among the critics of thingummy and whatsisname who have offered themselves so persistently over the years as champions with their little slings against the Eysenckian Goliath. Other readers may be relieved that we are spared a repeat performance with sling-shot worn smooth with over-use. I think that we must applaud the great efforts that the Editors have made to bring together such a varied collection of commentators. It is a wide one, and among the eighteen contributions there is, of course, some unevenness in the standard of debate, as well as some variation in familiarity with Eysenck's writings.

The Editors' difficulty, as I see it, has been one of getting together a fair number of people who combine the various qualities of some personal eminence in their field, a sound knowledge of Eysenck's writings, and a critical detachment even to the point of sustaining an abrasive argument. To the 'outer barbarians' (those living without the educative influence of the Maudsley Commonwealth) it may seem that the Editors have just assembled a bunch of Eysenck's buddies to hold a party: but this is a phenomenon of perception encountered in psychophysics. If one is quite unfamiliar with a subject, important differences between stimuli are simply not perceived. To the barbarian the disputation among scholars seems pretty meaningless because to him they all appear to be saying much the same thing.

In this volume we have Gordon Claridge, recruited by the Editors to write a paper on Eysenck's contribution to the psychology of personality from a 'predominantly negative' point of view, worrying because he is being, he says, cast in the role of an 'Eysenck hit man'. He writes: 'I have always considered myself as veering more towards the sympathetic than towards the antipathetic pole of the love-hate-Eysenck dimension.' But there are few psychologists who know the Eysenckian theory of personality as thoroughly as he, and so Claridge is specially well qualified to identify and criticize weak points in that theory.

It is perhaps a pity that Charles Spielberger's appreciation of Eysenck's contribution to the 'Smoking and Health' controversy is not balanced by a more negative criticism, for the great body of the anti-smoking critics will not be appeased by Philip Burch's chapter.* But I have no hesitation in saying that we are privileged to have so distinguished a chapter from so eminent a scholar as Professor Burch. The anti-smoking establishment has a very vociferous and widely-publicized press anyway, so we really do not need to be concerned about appeasing the critics. Both Spielberger and Burch do a signal favour to scientific inquiry into the matter of smoking and health by their papers, which in their different ways applaud the role that Eysenck has played in the controversy.

Quite the same cannot be said for the chapters referring to 'Astrology and

---

*Editors' Footnote:* Professor Philip Burch accepted the invitation on the clear understanding that he would present a balanced perspective, that is, steer a 'middle' course. The Editors considered this to lend itself to a 'contrasting' enough pair to fit the debate format of the volume.

Parapsychology'. Many people will find it difficult to know what to make of the chapter by Sargent on 'Parapsychology and Astrology', astonishingly designated by him as 'the youthful sciences' (Babylon is fallen, is fallen, that great city!). But as a famous mediaeval cathedral has a tower that was deliberately flawed by the architect for fear of Heaven's jealous wrath against a creation that aimed to be too perfect, so among eighteen chapters we must allow a little amphigouri. On these topics one might have expected there to be no lack of critics of an *independent* status to provide the paired chapter to balance Sargent's extreme partiality; instead, we have Eysenck's co-author of *Astrology—Science or Superstition?*, David Nias, collaborating with Geoffrey Dean, editor of *Recent Advances in Natal Astrology*, providing the companion chapter. It might have been, therefore, that here we would have had a mere sciamachy among close associates of Eysenck, but in fact the Nias and Dean chapter is refreshingly critical, certainly as far as parapsychology is concerned. They cite the relevant studies so conspicuously omitted from Sargent's chapter, and openly discuss the issue of parapsychology's involvement with fraud and trickery. They make a serious effort to discuss the surprising fact of Eysenck's involvement with the whole area, an involvement that has surprised so many of those who take his work very seriously.

What is Eysenckian psychology? Basically it is the application of scientific method to the study of behaviour, and Eysenck focuses on human behaviour, for although he has always paid serious attention to experimental work with animals, to quote the title of one of his more popular books, *Psychology Is about People*. Indeed, the rat and the pigeon hardly get a look in throughout this volume. And what is the scientific method that is pursued in Eysenckian psychology? According to Thomas Huxley, 'Science is nothing but trained and organized common sense.' So do we have here a number of psychologists arguing about the application of common sense to the study of behaviour? The reader, who has his own ideas about what common sense consists of, must be the judge of how far this aim is fulfilled. For here we are concerned not with what is politically expedient, morally comfortable, aesthetically satisfying or even ethically justified; we are concerned with approximations to such truths as can be established by fallible men and women striving to come to grips with the reality of their time and with universals.

Eysenck himself has never been a 'comfortable' figure. His appetite for controversy has irked many people who appear to believe that the role of the scientist should be to provide convenient ammunition for the 'good guys' to use against the 'bad guys'. But the 'good guys' who seek convenient arguments and easy solutions will not always find them in Eysenckian psychology, in which inconvenient truths that cannot always be assimilated into a nice, smooth, 'progressive' policy, keep popping up and demanding answers in a most embarrassing way. As I have pointed out, the intention to divide the chapters of this book evenly between the 'predominantly positive' and 'predominantly negative' was not entirely fulfilled. The 'pro' chapters might have meant that the writers entirely agreed with Eysenck, but this is certainly not the case. The 'anti' chapters might have meant either that the writers believe that Eysenck talks through his hat, or that what he says is all very well to admit between specialists, but that it would be much better for us all socially, morally and for the sake of our peace of mind, if Eysenck would simply shut up. But insofar as there are 'anti' chapters, critics have taken neither of these views.

Because Eysenck has ventured into so many fields of psychology it stands to reason that he cannot be an outstanding expert in every one of them, and he makes this quite clear in his writings. In a volume such as this we have the opportunity to draw upon the expertise of many psychologists who have concentrated in depth on certain topics, and it is interesting to see how they have reacted to Eysenckian psychology in relation to those topics. In modern life experts tend all too often to work in their laboratories somewhat isolated from public understanding of what they are doing, and their findings are announced, sometimes in a garbled form, through the journalistic media. This sometimes leads to *ex cathedra* statements on scientific matters without the public having the ability to appreciate or assess the reality behind the statements. Eysenck is one of those who early in his career started to put psychology on the map and bring Everyman into the debates. His early books, *Uses and Abuses of Psychology*, *Sense and Nonsense in Psychology*, *Fact and Fiction in Psychology*, have had a tremendous influence. But as Donald Broadbent points out in introducing the *Festschrift* for Eysenck (Lynn, R. (Ed.) (1981) *Dimensions of Personality*), even if some of those people who were inspired by these books seriously to study psychology and related disciplines have later gone on to criticize Eysenck, the best of the critics have done so using the same principles of scientific reasoning that are basic to the Eysenckian approach. This volume is not just a book for specialists; the arguments raised by the protagonists can be continued by readers of widely different backgrounds, and they may very well disagree with both of the protagonists on some issues, and with Eysenck himself.

I am writing this introductory chapter without having seen Eysenck's concluding chapter, but I suspect that in some instances he will agree more with some of what is offered as 'predominantly negative' than with that which is supposed to be 'predominantly positive'. Indeed insofar as I am qualified to have a personal opinion, I find that some of the critics have come closest to what I understand Eysenck to mean. Eysenckian theory of personality has made great strides since the publication of *Dimensions of Personality* in 1947 because it has attracted so many men and women of outstanding ability and critical intelligence. Thus, without myself entering into the controversy over his theory of personality, with particular reference to the status of psychoticism, I think that Claridge ('predominantly negative' by intent) gets to the heart of the matter, and thereby advances the development of the theory, more than Costa and McCrae who confine themselves more to discussing and approving the descriptive aspects of the theory.

We may recall how Balak, King of Moab, hired Balaam to make a 'predominantly negative' judgment of the Israelites, in fact ritually to curse them. Balaam went upon his ass to perform this ceremony (interrupted on the way by the ass falling down before the Angel of the Lord); but although Balaam tried to perform the ceremony required of him three times, his message always turned out to be 'predominantly positive'—in fact he blessed their destiny, much to the chagrin of Balak and the Moabites. Now this may be said to have happened in certain cases in this volume, although I hope that no unkind reviewer will take the analogy further and suggest that the ass has had her say too.

There are just one or two who, invited to comment on the work of Hans Eysenck, have taken the line of, 'Blow what Eysenck has to say—but here's what me and my mates think on the topic, and here's a chance to publish it!' The majority have concentrated on Eysenck's writings rather than their own. In Arthur Jensen's brilliant and lucid chapter on 'The Theory of Intelligence' he refers us to over forty of Eysenck's publications, and to only one of his own. But even Kline, who refers to only three of Eysenck's publications and to fourteen of his own, is writing about psychoanalysis in a climate that has been substantially changed over the past thirty years by Eysenck's critique of the subject. Thirty years ago Kline would have been regarded by the psychoanalytic establishment not just as an extreme heretic, but as a monster determined to wreck the whole psychoanalytic movement by admitting the possibility (as he does) that psychoanalytic therapy is entirely ineffective. This would have put Kline in the dog-house in the 1950s, but it now seems that in the 1980s he can write with impunity and have no fear that a hit-squad will be sent out from the Tavvy to do him.

In this volume Spielberger refers to the fact that in his *Centennial* volume (in the *Centennial Psychology Series*) the papers that Eysenck selected as representing what he considered to be his most significant contributions were in the four areas of *personality*, *behaviour therapy*, *genetics* and *social psychology*. These four areas are certainly represented here, but perhaps the most outstanding of the more recent developments in his work is the advance he has made in the study of intelligence. This, of course, was the topic of the very first paper that he published in 1939 (slightly distorted by the additions from Burt's editorial pen!). The present volume begins with a most distinguished paper by Arthur Jensen, which describes Eysenck's progress over forty years and the increasing development of a biologically based theory of intelligence. This impressive paper, contributed by one of the world authorities on the subject, makes it clear that quite apart from Eysenck's contributions in all other areas of psychology he now stands as one of the most innovative and important theorists of intelligence. This is indeed remarkable, for up to about 1970 Eysenck had not initiated much research or published a great deal concerning intelligence. It is literally true that the research of Galton into the physiological basis of intelligence lay fallow for nearly 100 years for want of the technical hardware to advance it, and now in the late twentieth century Eysenck is in the forefront of those whose research and brilliant insights bid fair to achieve a revolution in the psychology of individual differences in intelligence.

No-one is going to read through this book like progressing through a nine-course European banquet. Rather, they are going to treat it like one form of Japanese banquet, where all the dishes are on the table, and one moves among them according to one's fancy. It would be pointless and indeed tedious if I were solemnly to discuss in turn each of the eighteen papers that have occupied so much of my reading time over recent weeks. Readers should be aware that the manner in which the papers were written has differed. Thus in some cases writer *A* has read and could respond to the chapter by *B*, and in some cases this has not been so. As I see it, in my capacity as writer of the introductory chapter I cannot do better than act as host at the feast, mentioning some of the highlights of some dishes, and even to neglect to mention others. The papers I do not mention are not necessarily of lower standard or of lesser importance, but I know quite well that each reader will first sample this, then make a meal of that, according to his individual fancy.

If readers first fancy a little vinegar in the dish, then let them turn to Arnold Lazarus for his views on 'Sterile Paradigms and the Realities of Clinical Practice'. They will find the sharpness of the dish offset by the more solid fare provided by Barbrack and Franks who inquire whether Eysenck is 'Anachronistic or Visionary'. They begin with a consideration of 'the question whether Eysenck has been influential in the development of behaviour therapy' which, they say, 'is the subject of disagreement'. This statement may surprise readers in the UK: personally in my inquiries among behaviour therapists in the UK when writing a biography of Eysenck

I encountered only one clinical psychologist of any experience who seriously maintained that Eysenck's work had been 'irrelevant' to the development of behaviour therapy. However, we must take the word of Barbrack and Franks that opinion is different in North America.

One of the difficulties we must face in assessing the value and relevance of these two chapters about behaviour therapy is the ambiguity about what constitutes the 'mainstream' of behaviour therapy. Thus, Barbrack and Franks express their opinion that in pursuing as his primary aim the search for a scientific model by which to explain behaviour 'Eysenck drove a wedge between himself and mainstream behaviour therapy.' When we come to Lazarus' chapter, however, we find a very different understanding of what constitutes behaviour therapy in North America, as we shall exemplify later. Barbrack and Franks go on to give a definition of behaviour therapy as accepted by the Association for Advancement of Behaviour Therapy that is so wide and vague that it might even be adopted by many disparate brands of psychotherapists, even with a Freudian tinge. Perhaps the reality is that the behaviour therapy movement, being launched as it was as an alternative to psychoanalytic therapy, has been too successful and has therefore become a bandwagon that all sorts of therapists have climbed upon, so there is in fact no 'mainstream' behaviour therapy at all.

Barbrack and Franks are at least at one with Eysenck in agreeing that their sort of behaviour therapy derives from *extensions* of Pavlovian-type conditioning. Lazarus bases much of his attack on treating Eysenck's work as though it were now hopelessly outmoded, and writes: 'Behaviour therapy has come a long way since Eysenck's (1959, 1960, 1964) first foray into the field, and I was curious to see what impact recent developments have had on his earlier thinking. The answer in two words is "zero impact".'

'There's glory for you! ... I meant (said Humpty Dumpty) "There's a nice knock-down argument for you!"'.

It is of interest to compare the reference lists given in the two papers in this debate. Although both parties give quite lengthy lists of published behaviour therapy literature, there is practically no correspondence between the lists—except for references to Eysenck's work. It seems that these protagonists operate in very separate necks of the woods of North America, and there is little converse between them. The fact that Eysenck is mentioned by both may be *ad hoc* to the topic of the debate, but it may be noted that Barbrack and Franks do not mention any of Lazarus' published work. So much for the 'mainstream' of behaviour therapy. Lazarus makes the usual criticism that Eysenck is not a practising clinician and 'non-therapists who lack clinical skills and who have not experienced the "battlefront conditions" of patient responsibility are likely to provide platitudes rather than pearls.' Barbrack and Franks bring forward a counter-argument which deserves very serious consideration and applies especially to behaviour therapy in the USA—that therapists in private practice are in the business of *selling* their services and are therefore perhaps not the people best fitted to assess whether their therapy is ineffective, or indeed, as Eysenck has unkindly suggested, in certain cases potentially harmful. They point out that 'Eysenck's advantage as an evaluator of therapy is that he is not a practitioner and has no financial investment in the outcomes of such evaluations.'

It is not for me to try to summarize the arguments of those discussing behaviour therapy in this book. My role as host at the feast is to comment on some of the salient points of difference, and sometimes express my puzzlement at some of the features presented. For instance, what are we to make of the following comment by Lazarus? 'On any bookshelf the volumes that are dog-eared from frequent reference by clinicians in search of pragmatic leads are not likely to bear the Eysenckian imprimatur.' Obviously he has done much research on the state of the books on his colleagues' bookshelves, but perhaps this finding tells us something about the nature of his colleagues. It accords oddly with the findings of Rushton, Endler and others who have done scholarly research over the years as to the frequency with which psychologists' names are cited in the SCI and SSCI. I think that the latter indices are probably a better guide than the Lazarus Dog-Ear Test.

For those who like the fine bold style of writing that characterizes Eysenck's work, let me recommend the strong meat offered by Martin and Jardine. With the coming of these authors Eysenck must look to his stylistic laurels! They triumphantly present the results of their large Australian study involving 3810 pairs of adult twins, writing with enormous self-confidence and having no false modesty in choosing the words to express their satisfaction with their study:

> The single most astonishing finding from this very powerful study is the complete lack of evidence for the effect of shared environmental factors in shaping variation in personality, and their relatively minor contribution to variation in social attitudes. . . . The conclusion is now so strong that we must suspect those who continue to espouse theories of individual differences in personality which centre on family environment and cultural influences, of motives other than scientific.

I do not think that Eysenck would go as far as this last sentence in his writing, whatever he might think privately. But as Martin and Jardine advance in triumph, one may think of them caparisoned in purple and gold, like the cohorts of the Assyrian, as they descend in ferocity upon the cowering rabble of the hapless environmentalists. They admit that 'outsiders' like myself cannot be expected entirely to appreciate the simple glory of their banners—the thirty-three tables that support their victorious advance (and I must agree):

> It may be difficult for the outsider to the field to appreciate how strikingly good are the fits of our simple models when consideration is given to the power with which they are tested and the many opportunities for them to fail should the assumptions on which they are based be false.

It is a pity that this challenging chapter was not available to John Loehlin when he wrote the companion chapter, for here would have been something most impressive to get his teeth into, in addition to the studies with which he deals. I predict that this chapter of Martin and Jardine will be, above all others in this book, the one that will provoke most comment and controversy.

And where does Eysenck come into all this work on behaviour genetics? It is to be noted that Martin and Jardine entitle their chapter 'Eysenck's Contributions to Behaviour Genetics', which is quite modest of them as the bulk of the chapter concerns their own work, and they might merely have assigned to Eysenck a role similar to that of John the Baptist. In behaviour genetics Eysenck tends to be the second author—as in his partnership with Lindon Eaves and Martin, apart from his earlier studies with Prell. But both of these chapters give due credit to Eysenck for the role he has played in facilitating behaviour genetic research by others. John Loehlin concludes that:

> Perhaps if Eysenck did not believe so firmly in the high heritability of his personality dimensions, all this would not have come to pass. If so, we who are interested in behaviour genetics would indeed

have been much the poorer. In that sense, I applaud his sturdy convictions. Long may they lead him forward!

Returning to the banquet spread before us, let us sample a dish with a provocative title. David Gilbert gives his critical chapter on 'Marriage and Sex' the subtitle, 'Limits of Monocular Vision'. Does Eysenck, like Nelson, view the field of sexual affairs with only one eye, and perhaps put his telescope to the blind eye sometimes? We are told that his approach to the understanding of marital satisfaction is similar to that of those researchers of *the first half of the century*, but contrary to the thinking of the vast majority of current ones—younger researchers like Gilbert, we presume, whom time the devourer of all things has not yet dulled.

Let us examine the inadequacy of Eysenck's research. According to Gilbert, Eysenck down-plays the *possibility* 'that whom one marries is a highly important determinant of one's MS (marital satisfaction).' If this were the case, I would have thought that his readers would laugh him to scorn. I did not myself get that impression from the Eysenck and Wakefield study cited. Gilbert discusses the methodology of Eysenck's research in a perfectly acceptable manner, but I failed to see, possibly because of my own advanced age and myopia, what he would see if he opened his other eye. Glenn Wilson, who provides the companion chapter, did not read all this or indeed any other publication of Gilbert's before he wrote his piece, nor apparently has Gilbert read anything of Wilson's. He and Wilson do not even seem to read the same literature, although they are discussing much the same topic, with a few exceptions. In fairness, it must be pointed out that Wilson's piece is a little-altered re-hash of his chapter published in 1981 in *Dimensions of Personality*, edited by Richard Lynn, and so Gilbert had the opportunity to read and comment on it some time ago, but they seem to inhabit rather different universes. Wilson seems more generally concerned with sex in all its splendours and miseries both within and outside marriage, and Gilbert more with the bread-and-butter issues that confront marriage guidance counsellors.

It is difficult for those who write on the topic of sex and marriage to avoid being unintentionally funny, for as Eysenck in his *Psychology Is about People* remarks, 'Neither tragedy nor beauty are the common coin of everyday sex, and thus laughter is the only antidote to tears. Why is sex funny? I think Bergson's theory of humour finds here one of the few places where it can be applied with impunity.' Glenn Wilson, in his quite extensive writings on the topic of sex, generally avoids the pitfalls by resort to a certain dry humour, but Gilbert's seriousness leads him to give the following subheading: 'DARING TO DO IT CORRECTLY'. But having raised our expectations, he fails to go on to discuss the 'missionary position'or anything like that. It is the researchers who must learn to do it correctly, according to a nine-point plan he proceeds to outline.

What spicy dish is there left for me to offer the reader? Christopher Brand (ostensibly positive) gives us 'The Psychological Bases of Political Attitudes and Interests', and John Ray (ostensibly negative) gives us 'Eysenck on Social Attitudes and Interests: An Historical Critique'. By now readers are tired of my telling them that most of the contributors in this book do not read the same books and journals: they only read Eysenck in common. Brand's chapter is something of a *tour de force* in what he sedulously avoids mentioning. He avoids reference to Eysenck's *Psychology of Politics*, although he does admit that Eysenck wrote something or other in the 1950s, and he admits to having looked at Adorno *et al.* (1950), and at Christie's attack on Eysenck's treatment of the personality of communists. His chapter is indeed something out of the ordinary. The tough-tender dimension is traced to *King Lear* (allegedly *via* William James). I think that he must refer to Edmund's speech to Cordelia's executioner:

> Know thou this, that men
> Are as the time is: to be tenderminded
> Does not become a sword.

But earlier King Lear has accused Cordelia of being 'so young and so untender'—not 'tough', mark you—for being 'un-tender' would imply being about the middle of the dimension, whereas her sisters feigned an extremity of tender-mindedness to flatter the old man. But what we should be concerned with is Eysenck's, not Shakespeare's, use of the term 'tender-mindedness', and for this we have to refer to *The Psychology of Politics*.

But John Ray takes a more traditional approach, and covers the ground that has been argued over for more than forty years. One point of his with which I must take issue, although I do not wish to get embroiled in the general argument, is his statement that:

> I think it behoves me to point out that there is a well-developed alternative theory to Eysenck's which, perhaps because it has largely been developed by economists and perhaps because it does not put Leftists in a particularly good light, seems virtually unknown among psychologists. This is the libertarian theory as spelt out in a vast range of publications including von Hayek (1944), von Mises (1949) and Friedman (1962). As two of the authors mentioned gained Nobel prizes for work they did in connection with this theory, it seems very strange to me that psychologists know so little of it.

Or do they? Eysenck specifically cites von Hayek (1960) as 'one of the few who has been looking at the T- or liberat end', and then he goes on to quote from von hayek. (This is in Eysenck's 'Ideology and the Study of Social Attitudes', in Eysenck and Wilson, 1978.) What is Ray getting at—and what is all this about psychologists having a Leftist prejudice? We have become accustomed to psychologists such as Eysenck, Glenn Wilson, Arthur Jensen, Uncle Tom Cobley and all being designated as Fascist Hyenas of the Right (yes, and John Ray, too, according to one of these 'Birmingham Intellectuals'!); now they are seen as being blinded by their Leftist views. Not that Ludwig von Mises is without Leftist connections; Oskar Lange of the Polish Politbureau proposed that a statue should be erected to him by the socialists for his advice on economic accounting in a socialist economy. As for the psychological motivation of 'economic man' as proposed by economists such as Milton Friedman, I think that we are getting a little outside the debate about political ideology and social attitudes.

Ray's major contention is that Eysenck has failed to establish the authoritarianism of the Left. In this he is curiously at one with Brand who maintains 'that Eysenck underestimated, if anything, the "authoritarianism" of the modern Left.' The only time that Eysenck underestimated the degree of their authoritarianism, to my knowledge, is when he got on a platform at the LSE naively expecting to give a lecture, instead of being punched on the nose. Would not Ray grant that this amounts to establishing Left authoritarianism *empirically*?

Before I leave this last interesting and exotic dish, I must comment on Brand's discussion of the nature of liberalism. I seem to detect an Eysenck-Hayek versus Brand disagreement. Is it that Brand has run his paper up the flagpole to see whether Eysenck will salute it or shoot it down? When Eysenck writes his concluding chapter we shall see. What really puzzles me about Brand's chapter is the number of unsupported statements he makes as though they were self-evident truths. That 'Left-wing and humanitarian views have tended to enjoy the support of the relatively clever and well-educated people in the twentieth century': sure they have, but have not relatively stupid and ill-educated people tended to support them just as frequently? Again: 'At least one source of the argument is that, in the sense that Eysenck has used the term, few people—at least few readers of psychology—are very eager to appear tough-minded.' Are they not? I would have thought the most elementary fact about a dimensional model of individual differences in personality, attitude and ideology was that a person is likely to be a bit of a nut and a nuisance all round if he is *at the extreme* of either end of any dimension. Again: 'Perhaps Eysenck's strongest disservice to his own cause was to try to contrive a psychology of politics without making much reference to intellectual differences and their expression in personality and values'; to which I can only say, 'Whew!', and invite you to tuck in, although you may not be able to swallow it all. What a pity that Brand and Ray do not read each other.

In picking here and there among the dishes, I fear that I may have been too critical, in attempting not to give this book too favourable a puff. I may have given the impression that, with a few notable exceptions, the 'pro' writers have made a more solid contribution than the 'anti'. I hasten to point out that I do not imply any deliberate bias on the part of the Editors who have had the very difficult job of recruiting in all twenty-four authors and trying to get their contributions finished and submitted not too many months after the proposed deadline. I know from my own experience in collecting material for the biography of Eysenck that while it is not too difficult to get material from those who are, on the whole, favourably disposed to him and his work, it is difficult indeed to get adequate cooperation from those less favourably disposed—that is, if we exclude the barely literate. This resulted in some unintended bias in the biography, and I am sure that the Editors of this volume have had to contend with the same sort of difficulty.

It is sometimes stated that although Eysenck is quite the most outstanding psychologist in Britain, his influence does not spread much beyond these islands. I think that the considerable contribution to this volume from writers in America gives quite a different picture. According to Costa and McCrae, 'In the United States he is most widely known as a personality theorist', but other contributions we have here from the USA show how extensive his influence has been there in other fields as well. All writers are naturally most aware of his influence in their own particular fields.

What Eysenck will make of all this in his own concluding chapter I cannot imagine. Many founders of important schools of thought have in the end sought to distance themselves from the work and the opinions of those they have inspired. Thus Karl Marx, somewhere in his later writings, declared that he was not a Marxist. I can only hope that Eysenck will not now declare that he is not an Eysenckian!

# Part III: Behavioural Genetics

# 3. Eysenck's Contributions to Behaviour Genetics

NICHOLAS MARTIN AND ROSEMARY JARDINE

Hans Eysenck has done more than anyone to promote the necessity for those interested in behaviour to take a serious interest in genetics. He has railed against the concept of the 'typical individual', arguing cogently that the best way to understand mechanisms is to study differences. This has long been recognized by geneticists. Thus, when Beadle and Ephrussi (1937) wished to understand the physiology of eye colour determination in *Drosophila*, they started with mutant individuals having eye colours different from normal (or 'wild type'). By crossing them in various configurations they were able to deduce the biochemical pathways responsible for eye colour. They later applied this paradigm to a much wider array of metabolic processes in the bread mould *Neurospora* (Beadle and Tatum, 1941), and in a short time others applied it to bacteria and their viruses. To this paradigm, which is but an extension of Mendel's experiments in his pea garden, can be attributed the scientific revolution which in only thirty years or so has revealed the structure of DNA, the mechanism of protein synthesis and now even the nucleotide sequences of genes responsible for major clinical disorders. Within two years or so, perhaps even by the time this book is published, we expect to know sequences for the genes responsible for Huntingdon's chorea and Duchenne's muscular dystrophy, an advance unimaginable even ten years ago.

The achievements of psychology and psychiatry in the same period can only be regarded as modest by comparison. Obviously the problems and the nature of the material are far less tractable than those to which geneticists have devoted their energies. But one cannot avoid the suspicion that it is the reluctance of many behavioural scientists either to analyze the causes of individual differences in the field, or to manipulate or control them in the laboratory, which is responsible for their discipline's indifferent performance in the post-war era. Too much sway has been held by those who have more allegiance to ideologies than to the scientific method. It is paradoxical that perhaps the greatest achievement of pre-war psychology, mental

**13**

testing theory, should have been subject to virulent and sustained attack in the past twenty years. Environmentalism untainted by biology has been the fashionable *Weltanschauung* during the lifetime of those aged less than forty. Many academics have preferred to engage in sterile semantic debates about 'whether IQ measures intelligence' or to advise governments on 'how to eliminate inequalities in educational achievement' than to undertake the more difficult tasks of measurement and openminded inquiry into the causes of individual differences.

In this bleak intellectual landscape perhaps no-one more than Eysenck has stood as vigorously against the tide of pop psychology and sociological pap. 'I have no faith in anything short of actual Measurement and the Rule of Three,' said Darwin, and neither has Eysenck, except perhaps that biometrical genetics might be added to the list. For, like Darwin, he has consistently been interested in the possibility that many of the observed differences in behaviour might be inherited and that from genetic studies might ultimately come an understanding of their physiological basis and their evolutionary significance.

Eysenck was early in the field with his own small twin studies of neuroticism and extraversion (Eysenck and Prell, 1951, 1956) which indicated that there was genetic variation for these personality traits. We shall not attempt to review his later contributions to the 'heritability of IQ debate' because these have been thoroughly aired elsewhere. It is arguably Eysenck's greatest contribution to behaviour genetics that he managed to interest professional geneticists, with backgrounds in plant and animal breeding, in the causes of variation in human behaviour. Most notably, Jinks and his students Eaves and Fulker started applying the methods of biometrical genetics to many of the measurements which Eysenck himself had developed (Jinks and Fulker, 1970; Eaves and Eysenck, 1974). The achievements of this synthesis have recently been summarized by Eaves and Young (1981) and by Fulker (1981). In the present chapter we report some new work, results of a study of personality and attitudes in 3810 pairs of twins, which owes its origins to Eysenck's earliest forays into the genetics of personality and which powerfully tests and vindicates his hypotheses.


## PREVIOUS WORK ON THE CAUSES OF INDIVIDUAL DIFFERENCES IN PERSONALITY AND ATTITUDES

The pioneering twin study of Newman *et al.* (1937) is often cited as indicating the lack of importance of genetic factors in variation in personality. Others have pointed out that this conclusion is neither supported by the data nor in agreement with the results from more recent studies. Certainly there is evidence for a substantial genetic component in variation in extraversion (Eysenck and Prell, 1956; Shields, 1962; Eaves and Eysenck, 1975), psychoticism (Eaves and Eysenck, 1977), neuroticism (Eysenck and Prell, 1951; Shields, 1962; Eaves and Eysenck, 1976a) and lie (Martin and Eysenck, 1976).

In a study of 837 twin pairs by Eaves and Eysenck (1975), it was found that variation in extraversion could be explained by the additive action of genes and individual environmental differences. There was no evidence for the importance of family environment. This simple genetic model has also been found to be appropriate for explaining variation in psychoticism (Eaves and Eysenck, 1977) and lie (Martin and Eysenck, 1976). For neuroticism, a simple genetic model is again adequate (Eaves and Eysenck, 1976a), although there is evidence that genetic differences in neuroticism become more pronounced with age (Eaves and Eysenck, 1976b).

In general, the results suggest that genetical variation in personality is mainly additive. The extensive data of Floderus-Myrhed *et al.* (1980), however, question the validity of an additive model for extraversion. Eaves and Young (1981) reanalyzed their data from 12,898 same-sex Swedish twin pairs and found that dominant gene action affects the expression of extraversion. Despite the difficulty in detecting dominance in twin studies (Martin *et al.*, 1978), with the number of twins available in this present study we have an opportunity to replicate this important finding.

While individual differences in the personality traits of extraversion, psychoticism, neuroticism and lie undoubtedly have a substantial genetic basis, the data on the genetics of the neurotic symptoms of anxiety and depression are much less clear. The dominant theories of causation have been overwhelmingly in the experiential domain, although Freud (1937) made it clear that to him the aetiology lay in the interaction of constitutional and experiential factors. A recent study of 587 pairs of twins found evidence for a substantial genetic component in both these symptoms (Eaves and Young, 1981). However, Torgersen (1983) in a study of 229 same-sex twins found evidence for a genetic component in neurosis only for male twins and for twins admitted to psychiatric hospitals. He has argued that different findings on the importance of genetic factors in the neuroses may be due to differences in sample selection. We hope to avoid some of the problems of sampling bias by conducting our study in a large sample free of the selection effects found in a treated population.

As with the neuroses, it is often assumed that individual differences in conservatism are due mainly to the socializing influence of the family (e.g., Feather, 1978). Indeed, Cavalli-Sforza *et al.* (1982) found in their analysis of the transmission of various traits that religious and political attitudes were mostly determined within the family. They discounted the suggestion that the transmission of these traits may have a genetic basis, despite the fact that it was not possible with their data to distinguish between cultural and biological inheritance. Certainly there is evidence from three independent twin studies (see Eaves *et al.*, 1978, for a summary) that genetic factors are a major source of variation in conservatism.

It is the aim of this present study to explore the extent to which different genetical and environmental sources of variation are important in determining variation in personality traits, neurotic symptoms and social attitudes. It is an opportunity to replicate and expand previous findings of personality traits and attitudes, as well as to clarify the role of genetic factors in the aetiology of neuroses.

## THE TWIN SAMPLE

A questionnaire which included instruments for measuring personality and attitudes was mailed to all twins aged eighteen years and over who were enrolled on the Australian NH&MRC Twin Registry. Between November 1980 and March 1982 questionnaires were mailed to 5967 adult twin pairs throughout Australia, and, after one or two reminders to non-respondents, completed questionnaires were returned by both members of 3810 pairs, a 64 per cent pairwise response rate. With this response rate from an enrolment which is already voluntary and unsystematic, there is ample scope for bias from population frequencies. We shall compare, where possible, the distribution of scores in this sample with those obtained in random samples in Australia.

Prior to mailing the questionnaire to the entire adult sample, a pilot questionnaire had been mailed to 100 pairs of adult twins in order to assess likely response rate and any problems in construction of the questionnaire. Completed responses were obtained from both members of sixty-five pairs, and thus the pilot predicted the total final response rate very accurately. Only minor changes were made to the final questionnaire as a result of problems observed in the pilot and perhaps because of this, only ninety-six responses from the original pilot sample of 200 were obtained when the final questionnaire was mailed some months later. However, we thus have ninety-six individuals who completed the entire questionnaire twice and whose duplicate responses have been used to assess the short-term repeatability of the various measures.

Diagnosis of the zygosity of same-sex pairs was based on their response to questions concerning their physical similarity and the frequency with which they were mistaken as children. If twins differed in their response to these items, they were asked to send recent photographs of themselves. This method of zygosity diagnosis has been found by other workers (Cederlöf *et al.*, 1961; Nichols and Bilbro, 1966; Martin and Martin, 1975; Kasriel and Eaves, 1976) to be about 95 per cent correct as judged against diagnosis based upon extensive typing, and this is approximately the same reliability as obtained by typing for the most common six or seven blood group polymorphisms. The sex, zygosity and age distribution of the twin sample is shown in Table 1.

**Table 1.** *Age, Sex and Zygosity Composition of the Sample*

|  | MZ Females | MZ Males | DZ Females | DZ Males | DZ Opposite-Sex |
|---|---|---|---|---|---|
| Number of pairs | 1233 | 567 | 751 | 352 | 907 |
| Mean age (years) | 35.66 | 34.36 | 35.35 | 32.26 | 32.90 |
| Standard deviation | 14.27 | 14.02 | 14.27 | 13.88 | 13.85 |
| Age range | 18–88 | 18–79 | 18–84 | 18–83 | 18–79 |

## TESTS

### 1 Delusions-Symptoms-States Inventory: Anxiety and Depression Scales (DSSI/sAD)

The DSSI/sAD (Bedford *et al.*, 1976) consists of seven state of anxiety and seven state of depression items. Each item is scored 0, 1, 2 or 3 according to the degree of distress claimed, e.g., none, a little, a lot or unbearably. The possible range of scores is 0–21 for both the anxiety and depression scales. This screening instrument was chosen because its reliability and validity have been established (Bedford and Foulds, 1977) and it is brief. Unlike other screening instruments, it provides separate scores for states of anxiety and depression. It had previously performed well in the course of an epidemiological study of neurosis and the social environment in Australia, proving itself to be a high-threshold instrument for the detection of states of anxiety and depression in a general population (Henderson *et al.*, 1981): only 3 per cent of men and 3.5 per cent of women had scores of 7 or more for depression, and only 1.0 per cent and 5.6 per cent for anxiety. It has been used here as an appropriate instrument for measuring symptoms by self-report in a large postal survey.

## 2 Eysenck Personality Questionnaire (EPQ)

The EPQ (Eysenck and Eysenck, 1975) attempts to summarize individual differences in personality by reference to three main constructs: extraversion (E), psychoticism (P) and neuroticism (N), along with a fourth factor, the lie scale (L), which is a measure of social desirability or the tendency to 'fake good'. The scale consists of ninety items of the Yes/No type. The reliability and validity of the EPQ scales, and the relationship between experimental definitions of E, P, N and L and the behavioural ones given by the EPQ are discussed in Eysenck and Eysenck (1975).

## 3 Conservatism Scale (C-Scale)

The C-Scale (Wilson and Patterson, 1968) was developed to measure the general personality dimension of conservatism with specific reference to 'resistance to change'. The scale, slightly abbreviated for Australian use by Feather (1975), consists of fifty items concerning attitudes to such topics as the death penalty, birth control, church authority and white superiority. The twins were asked to indicate whether or not they agreed with an item by circling 'Yes', '?' or 'No'. Conservative responses score 2, equivocal responses 1 and radical responses 0 so that total conservatism scores could range from 0 to 100 in the direction of increasing conservatism.

## METHODS FOR TESTING HYPOTHESES

The classical twin method is based upon the comparison of the degree of similarity of monozygotic (MZ) and dizygotic (DZ) twin pairs, and is the most common procedure for estimating the relative importance of genetic and environmental contributions to human individual differences. Any excess similarity of MZ over DZ twins is usually taken to indicate the presence of genetical factors producing variation in the trait concerned, and there have been numerous formulae suggested for estimating the proportion of variance due to genetical factors, the heritability. The inadequacies of such conventional analyses of twin data have been discussed in detail elsewhere (Jinks and Fulker, 1970). It suffices to say here that in the past ten years the advantages of a hypothesis testing approach to the investigation of the causes of individual differences over traditional formula estimates of heritability based upon untested assumptions have become apparent.

Several hypothesis testing approaches have been espoused, including path analysis of familial correlations (Rao *et al.*,1974), variance components analysis by maximum likelihood or weighted least squares, or pedigree analysis of raw scores from regular or irregular family structures (Eaves *et al.*, 1978). Each method has its strengths and weaknesses, but one thing they all have in common is a superiority over classical methods which make no attempt to test basic assumptions, obtain maximum likelihood estimates, or compare objectively one model of trait variation against another. Here we use the procedure of variance components analysis.

This procedure has been described extensively in the literature (Eaves and Eysenck, 1975; Martin, 1975; Clark *et al.*, 1980), so only a brief account will be given. The starting point for an analysis of twin data is an analysis of variance which is used to compute the variation, measured as the meansquares, between and within twin pairs. These are calculated for each sex and zygosity group or five in all, including DZ opposite sex pairs.

From standard statistical and genetical theory we can then write expectations for these meansquares in terms of the following parameters or unknowns (Jinks and Fulker, 1970). $E_1$ is environmental variance within families, specific to the individual and shared with no-one else, not even members of the same family. It also includes measurement error. $E_2$ is environmental variation shared by cotwins but differing between twin pairs and will include cultural and parental treatment effects. $V_A$ is the genetic variance due to the additive effects of genes in the absence of assortative mating (the tendency of like to marry like). Where there is assortative mating, the additive genetic variance between families is increased by an amount $V_A(A/1 - A)$, where $A$ (Fisher's assortative mating parameter) is the correlation between the additive deviations of spouses and is related to the marital correlation $\mu$ (the correlation between husbands and their wives) by $h^2\mu$ ($h^2$ is the heritability). $V_D$ is the genetic variance due to dominant gene action.

Collectively these expectations form a set of simultaneous equations known as a 'model' of variation and, for the parameters described above, this model is shown in Table 2. A standard procedure known as iterative weighted least squares is now used to estimate the parameters of the model. Providing that the observed meansquares are normally distributed (which they should be given the very large degrees of freedom in our sample), the parameter estimates are approximately maximum likelihood, and the fit of a given model can be tested by calculating the residual chisquare with $k - p$ degrees of freedom, where there are $k$ observed meansquares and $p$ parameter estimates.

**Table 2.** *Model for Meansquares of Twins Reared Together*

|    |         | $E_1$ | $E_2$ | $V_A$ | $V_D$ |
|----|---------|-------|-------|-------|-------|
| MZ | Between | 1 | 2 | $2 + 2A/1 - A$ | 2 |
|    | Within  | 1 | 0 | 0 | 0 |
| DZ | Between | 1 | 2 | $3/2 + 2A/1 - A$ | 5/4 |
|    | Within  | 1 | 0 | 1/2 | 3/4 |

In choosing the parameters we wish to estimate, we want to provide the most parsimonious description compatible with the data. Therefore a sensible hierarchy of models is as follows. First fit $E_1$ alone. Failure of this most simple model will indicate that there is significant between-families variation to be explained. A model including both $E_1$ and $E_2$ will test whether the between-families variation is entirely environmental in origin, while the $E_1V_A$ model will test whether the between-families variation is entirely genetic. If both two-parameter models fail, then models including all three sources of variation, either $E_1E_2V_A$ or $E_1V_AV_D$ may be tested. As the model matrix (Table 2) is not of full rank, a maximum of three parameters can be estimated, and all such three-parameter models will yield the same chisquare, the fourth degree of freedom simply testing the equality of MZ and DZ total variances.

The restriction to three parameter estimates means that we cannot test directly the relative importance of $E_2$ and $V_D$. Also, it should be noted that the coefficients of the extra additive variance due to assortative mating are the same as for $E_2$ and so they will be completely confounded. It is thus more appropriate to rename $E_2$ as $B$ (for 'between-families variation') where

$\quad B = E_2 + V_A(A/(1 - A)).$

Only if we have an estimate of the phenotypic marital correlation can we estimate $A$, and make some inference about the relative contributions of $E_2$ and the genetic variance due to assortative mating, to $B$.

The twin design is a poor one for the detection of dominance, but with the number of twin pairs available in the present study there was some chance that we would be able to detect its presence. Martin *et al.* (1978) showed that in the case of a trait with 90 per cent heritability, complete dominance and no assortative mating or $E_2$ (i.e., $B = 0$), 3330 twin pairs would be sufficient to detect dominance at the 5 per cent level with 95 per cent probability, and our sample size is somewhat larger than this. However, the number of twin pairs required rises to over 30,000 when there is only intermediate dominance. Even when significant estimates of $V_D$ are obtained, it should be noted that the expectations for $H_R$ and for additive $x$ additive epistasis ($I_R$) are identical in MZ and DZ twins (Mather, 1974) and so are completely confounded. Thus when significant estimates of $V_D$ are obtained, it should be remembered that these will include contributions from both sources of non-additive genetic variance.

As there is no necessary reason why the components of variation will be the same in both sexes, models are first fitted to the meansquares for males and females separately and then to all eight statistics combined. We can then calculate a heterogeneity chisquare for $k$ *df* by adding the male and female chisquares, each for $4 - k$ *df*, and subtracting from the chisquare ($8 - k$ *df*) for the corresponding model fitted to all eight statistics. The heterogeneity chisquare for $k$ *df* will indicate whether the same parameters are appropriate for both sexes. If it is not significant, then the DZ opposite-sex data may be added and the same model fitted to all ten statistics.


## RESULTS


### Scaling

In a genetic analysis it is most appropriate to choose a scale where there is no genotype-environment interaction so that genetic and environmental effects are additive. Jinks and Fulker (1970) have shown that in MZ twins the regression of absolute within-pair differences on pair sums provides a test for any systematic $G \times E_1$ interaction. Table 3 shows these regressions for MZ male and female twins for the raw scores and various transformations.

**Table 3.** *Proportions of Variance in Absolute Within-Pair Differences Accounted for by Regression on Pair Sums for the Raw Personality and Attitude Scores and Various Transformations*

|  |  | MZF | | MZM | |
|---|---|---|---|---|---|
|  |  | L | Q | L | Q |
| Anxiety | raw | .32*** | .03*** | .44*** | .04*** |
|  | angle | .14*** | .02*** | .23*** | .04*** |
|  | $\sqrt{x+1}$ | .11*** | .05*** | .21*** | .06*** |
|  | $\log_{10}(x+1)$ | .00* | .11*** | .05*** | .15*** |
| Depression | raw | .47*** | .05*** | .64*** | .03*** |
|  | angle | .33*** | .05*** | .49*** | .05*** |
|  | $\sqrt{x+1}$ | .30*** | .09*** | .46*** | .08*** |
|  | $\log_{10}(x+1)$ | .15*** | .21*** | .30*** | .21*** |
| Extraversion | raw | .02*** | .08*** | .01** | .10*** |
|  | angle | .01* | .01*** | .00 | .02*** |
|  | $\sqrt{x+1}$ | .11*** | .04*** | .09*** | .05*** |
|  | $\log_{10}(x+1)$ | .28*** | .01*** | .25*** | .01* |
| Psychoticism | raw | .15*** | .00* | .14*** | .00 |
|  | angle | .01** | .01** | .01* | .00 |
|  | $\sqrt{x+1}$ | .01*** | .01** | .01* | .00 |
|  | $\log_{10}(x+1)$ | .04*** | .02*** | .06*** | .00 |
| Neuroticism | raw | .00 | .05*** | .01** | .09*** |
|  | angle | .00 | .00 | .00 | .02** |
|  | $\sqrt{x+1}$ | .04*** | .03*** | .02*** | .06*** |
|  | $\log_{10}(x+1)$ | .20*** | .02*** | .17*** | .04*** |
| Lie | raw | .00* | .03*** | .00 | .03*** |
|  | angle | .01** | .00 | .00 | .00 |
|  | $\sqrt{x+1}$ | .09*** | .01*** | .05*** | .01** |
|  | $\log_{10}(x+1)$ | .30*** | .00 | .26*** | .00 |
| Conservatism | raw | .00 | .00 | .01* | .00 |
|  | angle | .00** | .00 | .02*** | .00 |
|  | $\sqrt{x+1}$ | .05*** | .00 | .09*** | .00 |
|  | $\log_{10}(x+1)$ | .15*** | .00 | .24*** | .02*** |

*.01 $<$ p $<$ .05     **.001 $<$ p $<$ .01     ***p $<$ .001

Notes:    Linear (L) and quadratic components after the linear regression has been removed (Q) are shown. These significance conventions apply in all subsequent tables.

The anxiety and depression scales both show significant and substantial linear regressions. These are best reduced by logarithmic transformation and although this results in an increase in the quadratic components, more extreme transformation (e.g., $\log_{10}(\log_{10}(x+1)+1)$) produces no greater improvement so we regard $\log_{10}(x+1)$ as most appropriate for both scales. The quadratic regressions of the extraversion, neuroticism and lie scales, and the linear regression of the psychoticism scale, are best reduced by angular transformation (arcsin $\sqrt{p}$) (Snedecor and Cochran, 1980). For conservatism, only the linear regression in males is significant, and even then it only accounts for a trivial proportion of the variance. Thus it is not necessary to transform conservatism scores, the almost perfect normality of the distribution of C-Scores indicating that the scale has uniform discriminating properties across the range, at least to the level of second-order effects.

Although in most cases transformations to minimize $G \times E$ interaction have a negligible effect on the results of fitting models to variance components, when there are extreme deviations from normality, as for the anxiety, depression and psychoticism scales, the results may differ markedly (Martin and Eysenck, 1976).

**Table 4.** *Means and Variances of the Twin Sample for Raw and Transformed Personality and Attitude Variables*

| | | MZF | | MZM | | DZF | | DZM | | DZO | |
|---|---|---|---|---|---|---|---|---|---|---|---|
| | | Mean | Variance | Mean | Variance | Mean | Variance | Mean | Variance | Mean | Variance |
| Anxiety | raw | 2.37 | 6.90 | 1.76 | 5.04 | 2.37 | 6.99 | 1.75 | 4.05 | 2.15 | 6.09 |
| | log(x + 1) | 0.42 | 0.10 | 0.33 | 0.09 | 0.41 | 0.10 | 0.34 | 0.09 | 0.39 | 0.10 |
| Depression | raw | 1.46 | 5.90* | 1.05 | 4.33 | 1.54 | 6.99 | 1.03 | 2.92 | 1.41 | 6.23 |
| | log(x + 1) | 0.26 | 0.09 | 0.19 | 0.08 | 0.27 | 0.10 | 0.21 | 0.08 | 0.25 | 0.10 |
| Extraversion | raw | 12.52 | 24.45 | 12.79 | 23.97 | 12.22 | 24.72 | 13.11 | 25.55 | 12.74 | 24.87 |
| | angle | 51.22 | 240.21 | 52.19 | 233.70 | 50.34 | 239.10 | 53.27 | 258.34 | 52.02 | 243.96 |
| Psychoticism | raw | 2.73* | 3.89* | 3.93*** | 6.45** | 2.91 | 4.43 | 4.19 | 6.74 | 3.61 | 6.89 |
| | angle | 18.19* | 53.07 | 22.26*** | 68.31 | 18.83 | 56.34 | 23.08 | 69.33 | 21.06 | 74.80 |
| Neuroticism | raw | 11.23 | 27.57 | 8.81* | 26.42 | 11.38 | 27.03 | 9.12 | 27.42 | 10.48 | 26.55 |
| | angle | 44.24 | 218.10 | 37.39** | 215.15 | 44.69 | 211.21 | 38.26 | 223.50 | 42.19 | 208.57 |
| Lie | raw | 10.26* | 19.50 | 8.97 | 19.20 | 10.05 | 20.11 | 8.72 | 18.58 | 9.22 | 18.61 |
| | angle | 44.28* | 178.44 | 40.40 | 181.19 | 43.70 | 182.31 | 39.73 | 172.67 | 41.20 | 169.49 |
| Conservatism | raw | 49.53** | 148.61 | 45.32 | 175.27 | 49.23 | 151.45 | 45.08 | 192.22 | 46.17 | 158.85 |

Note: Asterisks denote significant differences between MZ and DZ means and/or variances.

**Distribution of Scores and Sex Differences**

Before fitting models to explain trait variation it is important to test whether the individuals in the MZ and DZ groups have been drawn at random from the same population by testing whether the subgroup means and variances are equal. Table 4 lists the means and variances of the raw and appropriately transformed scores for the twin sample. Two-tailed t-tests and variance ratio tests were performed between MZ and DZ means and total variances, separately for males and females (Table 4). In the raw scores, five of the sixteen t-tests and four of the sixteen F-tests were significant at least at the 5 per cent level. However, there was no consistent pattern in these differences, and they tended to be trivial and significant only because of the very large numbers available. Transformation left differences in means unchanged whilst differences in variances were totally removed.

It is sometimes argued that the twin method is invalid because DZ twins may have less similar environments than MZ pairs. If this inequality were real and influenced the traits under study, then we would expect to find that the total variance of DZ twins was greater than that of MZs. Even granted that the variance ratio test for inequality is not very powerful in detecting such differences, the total variances of the transformed scores for MZ and DZ pairs are so similar that any such differential environmental effects must be of minor importance. Since the groups appear to be comparable, the MZ and DZ classes were combined in the examination of sex differences.

Table 5 presents the means and variances for the sample broken down by sex. Two-tailed t-tests and variance ratio tests were performed between male and female means and variances for the raw and transformed scores. Females have significantly higher anxiety, depression, neuroticism and lie scores and lower extraversion, psychoticism and conservatism scores than males. The distributions of scores in the twin sample are similar to those obtained in previous studies using the C-Scale

**Table 5.** *Means and Variances for Raw and Transformed Personality and Attitude Variables Separately for Males and Females*

|  |  | Females | | Males | |
|---|---|---|---|---|---|
|  |  | Mean | Variance | Mean | Variance |
| Anxiety | raw | 2.37*** | 6.92*** | 1.82 | 4.88 |
|  | log(x + 1) | 0.42*** | 0.10* | 0.34 | 0.09 |
| Depression | raw | 1.50*** | 6.40*** | 1.12 | 4.41 |
|  | log(x + 1) | 0.26*** | 0.10*** | 0.21 | 0.08 |
| Extraversion | raw | 12.45*** | 24.60 | 12.89 | 24.70 |
|  | angle | 51.03*** | 240.56 | 52.53 | 243.67 |
| Psychoticism | raw | 2.79*** | 4.08*** | 4.15 | 7.24 |
|  | angle | 18.43*** | 54.61*** | 22.94 | 72.76 |
| Neuroticism | raw | 11.32*** | 27.04 | 9.12 | 26.42 |
|  | angle | 44.50*** | 212.58 | 38.29 | 213.74 |
| Lie | raw | 10.12*** | 19.45 | 8.77 | 18.75 |
|  | angle | 43.89*** | 176.89 | 39.86 | 175.03 |
| Conservatism | raw | 49.00*** | 151.36*** | 45.21 | 174.77 |

Note:    Asterisks denote significant differences between female and male means and/or variances.

(Feather, 1977, 1978), DSSI/sAD (Henderson *et al.*, 1981) and EPQ (Eysenck *et al.*, 1980) in Australian samples. Although Eysenck *et al.* (1980) found in their Australian sample of approximately 600 males and females that females had higher extraversion scores than males, in their larger English standardization sample the pattern of differences was the same as we found. While it could be argued that there is less potential for bias in the sample of Eysenck *et al.* (1980), in view of our much larger sample one could question which is more representative of the Australian population. We also found that females have a greater variance than males in both the anxiety and depression scales, and are less variable in their psychoticism and conservatism scores. These results are identical for both the raw and transformed scores.

From the standardization data that exist, then, there is no evidence that our twin sample is atypical of the population from which it is drawn in the characteristics under study.

**Repeatability**

Table 6 shows the distribution of age, and the raw and transformed personality and attitude scores for the ninety-six individuals who completed both the pilot and the main questionnaire. They were typical of the total sample in age and distribution of scores except that the males tended to have lower conservatism and neuroticism scores, and higher extraversion scores than those of the total sample.

Estimates of repeatability (Table 6) were obtained by examining consistency of scores from the pilot and main questionnaire. Separate analyses of variance were performed to obtain meansquares between ($MS_{bi}$) and within ($MS_{wi}$) individuals and repeatabilities (intraclass correlations) were calculated as $R_i = (MS_{bi} - MS_{wi})/(MS_{bi} + MS_{wi})$. Where there were significant differences between scores on the two occasions, corrected correlations were calculated by removing the between-occasions effects from the within-individuals meansquare. The within-individual variance components ($S_w^2$) are also shown in Table 6. These are estimates of the portion of the total variance which is unrepeatable, or measurement error.

The repeatabilities for the three EPQ scales are all high, ranging from 0.70 to 0.92, and are similar in males and females. This is consistent with previous results (Eysenck and Eysenck, 1975). As the interval between the completion of the pilot and the main questionnaire ranged from one to ten months (mean three months), it is unlikely that memory would be an important factor in these results.

The reliabilities of conservatism in males and females are similarly high. This is consistent with an earlier finding (Eaves *et al.*, 1978) of a correlation of 0.60 between the conservatism score from Eysenck's Public Opinion Inventory and the conservatism score from a modified version of the C-Scale used here, administered three years apart to nearly 400 pairs of twins.

The reliabilities of the anxiety and depression scales range from 0.55 to 0.67 and are no lower than one would expect of symptoms which fluctuate in their severity. In a longitudinal study of a general population sample (N = 230) Henderson *et al.* (1981) administered the DSSI/sAD on two occasions three months apart. The anxiety scores correlated 0.62 and the depression 0.54. This sensitivity to change has also been reported by Bedford *et al.* (1976)

**Table 6.** *Distribution of Age, and Raw and Transformed Personality and Attitude Scores for Individuals Who Completed Both the Pilot and the Main Questionnaire*

| | | Females (n = 64) | | | | Males (n = 32) | | | |
|---|---|---|---|---|---|---|---|---|---|
| | | Mean | Variance | Repeatability | $S_w^2$ | Mean | Variance | Repeatability | $S_w^2$ |
| Age | | 35.98 | 195.16 | — | — | 32.59 | 177.42 | — | — |
| Anxiety | raw | 2.55 | 6.85 | 0.67 | 2.29 | 1.67 | 5.30 | 0.61 | 2.15 |
| | log(x + 1) | 0.44 | 0.10 | 0.63 | 0.04 | 0.30 | 0.10 | 0.62 | 0.04 |
| Depression | raw | 1.75 | 9.17 | 0.55 | 4.09 | 0.94 | 3.23 | 0.58 | 1.35 |
| | log(x + 1) | 0.29 | 0.10 | 0.66 | 0.03 | 0.18 | 0.07 | 0.58 | 0.03 |
| Extraversion | raw | 11.98 | 24.98 | 0.82 | 4.56 | 14.30 | 25.74 | 0.90 | 2.67 |
| | angle | 49.43 | 242.78 | 0.81 | 46.09 | 57.06 | 277.11 | 0.89 | 29.66 |
| Psychoticism | raw | 2.93 | 3.86 | 0.74 | 0.99 | 4.20 | 7.21 | 0.75 | 1.81 |
| | angle | 19.04 | 48.77 | 0.73 | 13.23 | 23.08 | 73.15 | 0.70 | 21.73 |
| Neuroticism | raw | 11.53 | 22.61 | 0.84 | 3.73 | 7.56 | 26.85 | 0.83 | 4.53 |
| | angle | 45.21 | 174.72 | 0.85 | 27.04 | 33.92 | 231.39 | 0.83 | 38.46 |
| Lie | raw | 10.53 | 20.57 | 0.83 | 3.52 | 7.80 | 12.77 | 0.78 | 2.80 |
| | angle | 45.24 | 187.61 | 0.84 | 31.78 | 37.08 | 116.87 | 0.79 | 25.19 |
| Conservatism | raw | 49.27 | 153.87 | 0.86 | 21.14 | 36.61 | 169.48 | 0.92 | 13.52 |

## Correction for Sex Differences and Regression on Age

A sex difference in means will inflate the within-pairs meansquare (WMS) of DZ opposite-sex pairs (DZOS). Since significant sex differences in means were found for all variables (Table 5) the variance terms due to these differences (and the degree of freedom associated with them) were removed from the WMS of DZOS pairs (Clark *et al.*, 1980).

If a variable is strongly age-dependent, this accentuates the differences between twin pairs and inflates the between-pairs meansquare (BMS). Linear correlations of age with the appropriately transformed variables are shown in Table 7. The correlations are significant in every case, but only for the lie and conservatism scales are they substantial. We corrected for age dependence in these two variables by regressing within-pair sums on age and replacing the BMS with one-half of the residual meansquare (with $n - 2$ d.f.). Meansquares and their degrees of freedom, corrected for sex differences and regression on age where appropriate, are shown in Table 8.

**Table 7.** *Two-Tailed Linear Correlations of the Personality and Attitude Scores with Age, Transformed Where Necessary*

|  |  | Females | Males |
|---|---|---|---|
| Anxiety | $\log(x + 1)$ | −.06** | −.09*** |
| Depression | $\log(x + 1)$ | −.14*** | −.17*** |
| Extraversion | angle | −.16*** | −.14*** |
| Psychoticism | angle | −.20*** | −.28*** |
| Neuroticism | angle | −.13*** | −.14*** |
| Lie | angle | .36*** | .38*** |
| Conservatism | raw | .44*** | .37*** |

We may also examine whether twins become more or less similar with age by correlating absolute within-pair differences with age; these are shown in Table 9. The correlations are small and non-significant for anxiety and extraversion, and for psychoticism only the DZ opposite-sex correlation is significant, with opposite-sex pairs becoming more similar with increasing age. For neuroticism and the lie scale the correlations are only significant for DZ females. This indicates that for females genetic differences in neuroticism and lie become more pronounced with age, but no such effect is apparent in males. Eaves and Eysenck (1976b) also found that genetic differences in neuroticism increase with age. Their sample was too small to subdivide by sex, but it was comprised mainly of females and we can therefore consider this a replication of their interesting finding. For conservatism the reverse is true: in males genetic differences become more pronounced with age, but not in females. In the case of depression, both MZ and DZ males become more similar with advancing age, but not females. While this latter finding is open to a number of interpretations, it is clear that if environmental circumstances of cotwins become more different as they get older, these do not appear to produce any greater differences in any of the personality and attitude variables we have measured here.

**Table 8.** *Observed Meansquares for the Appropriately Transformed Personality and Attitudes Variables, and their Degrees of Freedom*

| | | Anxiety[a] | | Depression[a] | | Extraversion[a] | | Psychoticism[a] | | Neuroticism[a] | | Lie[a, b] | | Conservatism[a, b] | |
|---|---|---|---|---|---|---|---|---|---|---|---|---|---|---|---|
| | | df | Mean-square | df | Mean-square | df | Mean-square | df | Mean-square | df | Mean-square | df | Mean-square | df | Mean-square |
| MZF | Between | 1229 | 0.134 | 1229 | 0.128 | 1232 | 368.00 | 1232 | 71.92 | 1232 | 330.85 | 1231 | 238.15 | 1231 | 200.39 |
| | Within | 1230 | 0.060 | 1230 | 0.061 | 1233 | 112.46 | 1233 | 34.18 | 1233 | 105.38 | 1233 | 77.54 | 1233 | 43.66 |
| MZM | Between | 566 | 0.122 | 566 | 0.103 | 565 | 347.84 | 565 | 98.61 | 565 | 315.18 | 564 | 220.57 | 564 | 250.49 |
| | Within | 567 | 0.057 | 567 | 0.054 | 566 | 116.46 | 566 | 37.98 | 566 | 115.65 | 566 | 98.59 | 566 | 62.44 |
| DZF | Between | 749 | 0.117 | 749 | 0.118 | 750 | 283.65 | 750 | 69.11 | 750 | 265.12 | 749 | 195.57 | 749 | 175.62 |
| | Within | 750 | 0.081 | 750 | 0.081 | 751 | 194.62 | 751 | 43.59 | 751 | 157.38 | 751 | 112.61 | 751 | 64.25 |
| DZM | Between | 351 | 0.097 | 351 | 0.091 | 350 | 292.18 | 350 | 86.66 | 350 | 263.16 | 349 | 186.59 | 350 | 238.67 |
| | Within | 352 | 0.076 | 352 | 0.059 | 351 | 224.60 | 351 | 52.05 | 351 | 183.94 | 351 | 105.36 | 352 | 85.06 |
| DZO | Between | 901 | 0.106 | 901 | 0.108 | 904 | 295.30 | 904 | 84.61 | 904 | 227.82 | 903 | 167.93 | 904 | 179.92 |
| | Within | 901 | 0.083 | 901 | 0.082 | 904 | 192.98 | 904 | 51.55 | 904 | 174.64 | 904 | 114.34 | 905 | 76.05 |

Notes:   [a]Corrected for sex differences.
         [b]Corrected for regression on age.

**Table 9.** *Two-Tailed Correlations of Absolute Within-Pair Differences in the Transformed Personality and Attitude Scores with Age*

|  |  | MZF | MZM | DZF | DZM | DZO |
|---|---|---|---|---|---|---|
| Anxiety | $\log(x + 1)$ | .02 | −.03 | −.01 | −.06 | −.01 |
| Depression | $\log(x + 1)$ | −.04 | −.18*** | −.01 | −.13* | −.14** |
| Extraversion | angle | .03 | .03 | .07 | −.04 | .01 |
| Psychoticism | angle | −.02 | −.04 | −.03 | −.01 | −.07* |
| Neuroticism | angle | .02 | .01 | .12** | .02 | .01 |
| Lie | angle | −.03 | −.01 | .09* | .03 | .05 |
| Conservatism | raw | .05 | .00 | .04 | .20*** | .12*** |

## Genetical Analysis of Trait Variation

We shall discuss the results of the model, fitting separately for each factor. In every case a model $(E_1)$ postulating that all variation was due to individual environmental experiences and error and that there were no greater differences between pairs than between members of the same pair failed badly and is omitted from summary tables. Our first conclusion then is that there are greater differences in personality and attitudes between twin pairs than between cotwins. We shall now see whether this familiacity is due to shared environment, shared genes, or both.

### Anxiety

The results of fitting models to log transformed anxiety scores are shown in Table 10. A purely environmental model $(E_1 E_2)$ fails adequately to describe the data in either males or females, while a simple genetic model $(E_1 V_A)$ gives a good fit in both sexes. No further reductions in chisquare were seen with addition of extra parameters. When the $E_1 V_A$ model is fitted to the combined male and female data, the chisquare for the heterogeneity of fit over sexes (obtained by adding the chisquare values for males and females and subtracting from the chisquare of the combined male and female data) is non-significant ($\chi_2^2 = 5.18$, P > 0.05). Although we are thus entitled to fit the same model to the joint data, we notice that, while the estimates for $E_1$ are similar, there is a larger $V_A$ component for females than males.

A full model incorporating different-sized $E_1$, $E_2$ and $V_A$ effects for males and females has been developed by Eaves (1977), illustrated in Eaves *et al.* (1978), and is shown in Table 11. $V_{Amf}$ is the covariance between the genetical effects acting in males and those acting in females. If the genes affecting a trait in males are quite different from those affecting the trait in females, then we expect $\hat{V}_{Amf}$ to be zero. If the genes acting in males and females are exactly the same but produce scalar differences in the two sexes, then we expect the correlation between the effects

$$r_{VAmf} = \hat{V}_{Amf} / \sqrt{\hat{V}_{Am} \cdot \hat{V}_{Af}}$$

to be one. A similar argument applies to $E_{2mf}$, the covariation between $E_2$ effects acting in males and females.

The results of fitting a model which specifies a common $E_1$ parameter but different-sized $V_A$ effects in males and females are shown in Table 12.

**Table 10.** *Summary of Model-Fitting to Log Transformed Anxiety Scores*

| | $\hat{E}_1$ | $\hat{E}_2$ | $\hat{V}_A$ | $\hat{V}_D$ | df | $\chi^2$ | $h^2$ |
|---|---|---|---|---|---|---|---|
| **Female** | | | | | | | |
| $E_1E_2$ | .068*** | .030*** | — | — | 2 | 25.47*** | |
| $E_1V_A$ | .061*** | — | .037*** | — | 2 | 0.23 | .38 ± .02 |
| $E_1E_2V_A$ | .060*** | −.002 | .039*** | — | 1 | 0.16 | |
| $E_1V_AV_D$ | .060*** | — | .033** | .004 | 1 | 0.16 | |
| **Male** | | | | | | | |
| $E_1E_2$ | .064*** | .024*** | — | — | 2 | 15.06** | |
| $E_1V_A$ | .058*** | — | .031*** | — | 2 | 1.29 | .35 ± .03 |
| $E_1E_2V_A$ | .056*** | −.010 | .042*** | — | 1 | 0.26 | |
| $E_1V_AV_D$ | .056*** | — | .012 | .020 | 1 | 0.26 | |
| **Female and Male** | | | | | | | |
| $E_1E_2$ | .067*** | .028*** | — | — | 6 | 45.37*** | |
| $E_1V_A$ | .060*** | — | .035*** | — | 6 | 6.70 | .37 ± 0.2 |
| $E_1E_2V_A$ | .059*** | −.004 | .040*** | — | 5 | 6.23 | |
| $E_1V_AV_D$ | .059*** | — | .027** | .009 | 5 | 6.23 | |
| **Female and Male and Opposite-Sex** | | | | | | | |
| $E_1E_2$ | .071*** | .024*** | — | — | 8 | 67.68*** | |
| $E_1V_A$ | .060 *** | — | .034*** | — | 8 | 10.36 | .36 ± 0.2 |
| $E_1E_2V_A$ | .059*** | −.008 | .043*** | — | 7 | 7.33 | |
| $E_1V_AV_D$ | .059*** | — | .020* | .016* | 7 | 7.33 | |

**Table 11.** *Model for Twin Meansquares Incorporating Different Genetic and Environmental Components of Variation for Males and Females*

| | | $E_{1M}$ | $E_{1F}$ | $E_{2M}$ | $E_{2F}$ | $E_{2MF}$ | $V_{AM}$ | $V_{AF}$ | $V_{AMF}$ |
|---|---|---|---|---|---|---|---|---|---|
| MZF | Between | 0 | 1 | 0 | 2 | 0 | 0 | 2 | 0 |
| | Within | 0 | 1 | 0 | 0 | 0 | 0 | 0 | 0 |
| MZM | Between | 1 | 0 | 2 | 0 | 0 | 2 | 0 | 0 |
| | Within | 1 | 0 | 0 | 0 | 0 | 0 | 0 | 0 |
| DZF | Between | 0 | 1 | 0 | 2 | 0 | 0 | 3/2 | 0 |
| | Within | 0 | 1 | 0 | 0 | 0 | 0 | 1/2 | 0 |
| DZM | Between | 1 | 0 | 2 | 0 | 0 | 3/2 | 0 | 0 |
| | Within | 1 | 0 | 0 | 0 | 0 | 1/2 | 0 | 0 |
| DZO | Between | 1/2 | 1/2 | 1/2 | 1/2 | 1 | 1/2 | 1/2 | 1/2 |
| | Within | 1/2 | 1/2 | 1/2 | 1/2 | −1 | 1/2 | 1/2 | −1/2 |

**Table 12.** *Estimates ( ± s.e.) Obtained after Fitting a Model Allowing Different Genetic Components of Variation in Males and Females for Log Transformed Anxiety Scores*

| | $\hat{E}_1$ | $\hat{V}_{A_M}$ | $\hat{V}_{A_F}$ | $\hat{V}_{A_{MF}}$ |
|---|---|---|---|---|
| | 0.060*** | 0.030*** | 0.038*** | 0.023*** |
| ± | 0.002 | 0.003 | 0.002 | 0.006 |

$$\chi^2_6 = 2.15 \, (p = .91)$$

$h^2_{males} = 0.33 ± .03$        $h^2_{females} = 0.39 ± .02$

**Table 13.** *Sources of Variance (percentages) for Log Transformed Anxiety Scores*

|  | Females | Males |
|---|---|---|
| $E_1$ — error | 38 | 45 |
| — individual environment | 61, 23 | 67, 22 |
| $V_A$ | 39 | 33 |

Fitting separate $V_A$ parameters for males and females causes a significant reduction in chisquare ($\chi^2_2 = 8.21$, $P < 0.05$). The correlation $r_{V_A mf} = 0.67$ is not significantly different from unity and indicates that the same $V_A$ effects which also act in females act in males, but with a smaller effect on the variance. Thus, in males approximately 33 per cent of the variation in anxiety is genetic in origin while in females this rises to approximately 39 per cent, with the remaining variance due to individual environmental differences and error. We may subtract the values of the residual meansquare (Table 6), obtained from the repeatability data, from the estimates of $E_1$ and so estimate the proportion of variance due to non-repeatable individual environmental differences (Table 13).

*Depression*

As in the case of anxiety, in both males and females, the $E_1 V_A$ model best describes the data, although in males there is some evidence that $E_2$ effects are also important (Table 14). The chisquare for the heterogeneity of fit over sexes is highly significant ($\chi^2_2 = 27.26$, $P < 0.001$), and inspection of the parameter estimates shows that there are larger $\hat{E}_1$ and $\hat{V}_A$ components for males than females.

Fitting separate $E_1$ and $V_A$ parameters for males and females (Table 15) causes a significant improvement ($\chi^2_3 = 24.97$, $P < 0.001$). The correlation $r_{V_A mf} = 0.73$ is not significantly different from unity which indicates that, as in the case of anxiety, the same $V_A$ effects which act in females also act in males but with smaller effect. Addition of an $E_2$ parameter in males results in a non-significant reduction of chisquare ($\chi^2_1 = 1.40$, $P > 0.05$), indicating that this effect is not necessary to describe variation. While the heritabilities are similar to those for anxiety, true within-family environment accounts for a greater proportion of the variance in depression than anxiety (Table 16).

*Extraversion*

The $E_1 V_A$ model is able to account for variation in female extraversion, but addition of the parameter $V_D$ results in an even better fit ($\chi^2_1 = 5.20$, $P > 0.05$). The latter model also provides the best description of the data in males, although the estimate of $V_A$ is negative. There is no heterogeneity of fit of the $E_1 V_A V_D$ model over the sexes ($\chi^2_3 = 1.92$, $P > 0.05$), so we may fit it to the joint male, female and opposite-sex data (Table 17). All three sources of variation are significantly greater than zero; their contributions to the total are shown in Table 18.

**Table 14.** *Summary of Model-Fitting to Log Transformed Depression Scores*

| | $\hat{E}_1$ | $\hat{E}_2$ | $\hat{V}_A$ | $\hat{V}_D$ | df | $\chi^2$ | $h^2$ |
|---|---|---|---|---|---|---|---|
| **Female** | | | | | | | |
| $E_1E_2$ | .069*** | .028*** | — | — | 2 | 22.04*** | |
| $E_1V_A$ | .062*** | — | .035*** | — | 2 | 1.20 | .36 ± .02 |
| $E_1E_2V_A$ | .062*** | −.000 | .035*** | — | 1 | 1.20 | |
| $E_1V_AV_D$ | .062*** | — | .034** | .001 | 1 | 1.20 | |
| **Male** | | | | | | | |
| $E_1E_2$ | .056*** | .021*** | — | — | 2 | 2.46 | |
| $E_1V_A$ | .052*** | — | .025*** | — | 2 | 1.85 | .32 ± .04 |
| $E_1E_2V_A$ | .053*** | −.010 | .013 | — | 1 | 0.46 | |
| $E_1V_AV_D$ | .053*** | — | .044** | −.021 | 1 | 0.46 | |
| **Female and Male** | | | | | | | |
| $E_1E_2$ | .065*** | .026*** | — | — | 6 | 54.72*** | |
| $E_1V_A$ | .059*** | — | .032*** | — | 6 | 30.31*** | |
| $E_1E_2V_A$ | .059*** | .003 | .028*** | — | 5 | 30.22*** | |
| $E_1V_AV_D$ | .059*** | — | .037*** | −.006 | 5 | 30.22*** | |
| **Female and Male and Opposite-Sex** | | | | | | | |
| $E_1E_2$ | .069*** | .023*** | — | — | 8 | 76.11*** | |
| $E_1V_A$ | .060*** | — | .032*** | — | 8 | 33.70*** | |
| $E_1E_2V_A$ | .059*** | −.002 | .034*** | — | 7 | 33.21*** | |
| $E_1V_AV_D$ | .059*** | — | .028*** | .005 | 7 | 33.21*** | |

**Table 15.** *Estimates ( ± s.e.) Obtained after Fitting a Model Allowing Different Genetic and Environmental Components of Variation in Males and Females for Log Transformed Depression Scores*

| | $\hat{E}_{1_M}$ | $\hat{E}_{1_F}$ | $\hat{V}_{A_M}$ | $\hat{V}_{A_F}$ | $\hat{V}_{A_{MF}}$ |
|---|---|---|---|---|---|
| | 0.053*** | 0.062*** | 0.026*** | 0.036*** | 0.022*** |
| ± | 0.003 | 0.002 | 0.003 | 0.003 | 0.006 |

$$\chi^2_5 = 8.73 \, (p = .12)$$

$h^2_{\text{males}} = 0.33 \pm .03$        $h^2_{\text{females}} = 0.37 \pm .02$

**Table 16.** *Sources of Variance (percentages) for Log Transformed Depression Scores*

| | | Females | Males |
|---|---|---|---|
| $E_1$ | error | 33 | 29 |
| | | 63 | 67 |
| | individual environment | 30 | 38 |
| $V_A$ | | 37 | 33 |

According to Fisher's fundamental theorem of natural selection (Fisher, 1931), the pattern of variation demonstrated, where the additive genetic variance is small relative to the non-additive genetic variance, indicates that extraversion is a character which has undergone selection in the course of human evolution. We speculate that selection has been favouring individuals with intermediate extraversion

**Table 17.** *Summary of Model-Fitting to Angle Transformed Extraversion Scores*

| | $\hat{E}_1$ | $\hat{E}_2$ | $\hat{V}_A$ | $\hat{V}_D$ | df | $\chi^2$ | $h^2_{narrow}$ | $h^2_{broad}$ |
|---|---|---|---|---|---|---|---|---|
| **Female** | | | | | | | | |
| $E_1 E_2$ | 143.5*** | 96.3*** | — | — | 2 | 91.18*** | | |
| $E_1 V_A$ | 115.2*** | — | 125.3*** | — | 2 | 5.26 | | |
| $E_1 E_2 V_A$ | 112.4*** | -37.9 | 165.3*** | — | 1 | 0.01 | .52 ± .02 | |
| $E_1 V_A V_D$ | 112.4*** | — | 51.6 | 75.8* | 1 | 0.01 | | |
| **Male** | | | | | | | | |
| $E_1 E_2$ | 157.9*** | 84.4*** | — | — | 2 | 53.99*** | | |
| $E_1 V_A$ | 124.7*** | — | 119.7*** | — | 2 | 10.35*** | | |
| $E_1 E_2 V_A$ | 118.6*** | -64.7 | 189.6*** | — | 1 | 2.26 | | |
| $E_1 V_A V_D$ | 118.6*** | — | -4.4 | 129.3** | 1 | 2.26 | | |
| **Female and Male** | | | | | | | | |
| $E_1 E_2$ | 148.1*** | 92.5*** | — | — | 6 | 150.84*** | | |
| $E_1 V_A$ | 118.1*** | — | 123.7*** | — | 6 | 17.33** | | |
| $E_1 E_2 V_A$ | 114.3*** | -47.3 | 173.9*** | — | 5 | 4.19 | | |
| $E_1 V_A V_D$ | 114.3*** | — | 32.2 | 94.5** | 5 | 4.19 | | |
| **Female and Male and Opposite-Sex** | | | | | | | | |
| $E_1 E_2$ | 158.7*** | 82.7*** | — | — | 8 | 166.92*** | | |
| $E_1 V_A$ | 119.7*** | — | 122.9*** | — | 8 | 19.59* | | |
| $E_1 E_2 V_A$ | 114.4*** | -38.2 | 165.6*** | — | 7 | 5.42 | | |
| $E_1 V_A V_D$ | 114.4*** | — | 50.9** | 76.4*** | 7 | 5.42 | .21 ± .09 | .53 ± .02 |

**Table 18.**   *Sources of Variance (percentages) for Angle Trans-formed Extraversion Scores*

| | |
|---|---|
| $E_1$ ⟨ error / individual environment | 47 ⟨ 17 / 30 |
| $V_A$ | 21 |
| $V_D$ | 32 |

scores. However, data other than those on twins are needed to clarify this issue (Martin *et al.*, 1978; Eaves *et al.*, 1977a, 1978).

### Psychoticism

Once again the environmental model fails badly, while the $E_1 V_A$ model gives a good fit in both men and women (Table 19). However, there is highly significant heterogeneity of fit over ($\chi_2^2 = 33.26$, P < 0.001) and inspection of the parameter estimates shows that there is a larger $V_A$ component in males than females. Allowing for different genetic components in males and females (Table 20) causes a great improvement ($\chi_3^2 = 36.31$, P < 0.001), but the correlation $r_{VAmf} = 1.09$ indicates that the same genes act in both sexes but produce twice as much variance in males. Thus in females approximately 35 per cent of the variation in psychoticism is due to additive genetic effects, while in males it accounts for 50 per cent. Eaves and Eysenck (1977) found that 49 per cent of the variation in psychoticism is genetic in origin but did not look for differences in gene expression between the sexes.

**Table 19.**   *Summary of Model-Fitting to Angle Transformed Psychoticism Scores*

| | $\hat{E}_1$ | $\hat{E}_2$ | $\hat{V}_A$ | $\hat{V}_D$ | df | $\chi^2$ | $h^2$ |
|---|---|---|---|---|---|---|---|
| **Female** | | | | | | | |
| $E_1 E_2$ | 37.74*** | 16.56*** | — | — | 2 | 14.87*** | |
| $E_1 V_A$ | 34.20*** | — | 20.14*** | — | 2 | 2.81 | .37 ± .02 |
| $E_1 E_2 V_A$ | 34.65*** | 4.15 | 15.56*** | — | 1 | 1.59 | |
| $E_1 V_A V_D$ | 34.65*** | — | 28.00*** | −8.29 | 1 | 1.59 | |
| **Male** | | | | | | | |
| $E_1 E_2$ | 43.36*** | 25.34*** | — | — | 2 | 13.16** | |
| $E_1 V_A$ | 37.78*** | — | 30.91*** | — | 2 | 0.28 | .45 ± .03 |
| $E_1 E_2 V_A$ | 38.09*** | 3.38 | 27.26*** | — | 1 | 0.05 | |
| $E_1 V_A V_D$ | 38.09*** | — | 37.41** | −6.77 | 1 | 0.05 | |
| **Female and Male** | | | | | | | |
| $E_1 E_2$ | 39.52*** | 19.33*** | — | — | 6 | 63.69*** | |
| $E_1 V_A$ | 35.32*** | — | 23.56*** | — | 6 | 36.35*** | |
| $E_1 E_2 V_A$ | 35.71*** | 3.84 | 19.35*** | — | 5 | 35.12*** | |
| $E_1 V_A V_D$ | 35.71*** | — | 30.86*** | −7.67 | 5 | 35.12*** | |
| **Female and Male and Opposite-Sex** | | | | | | | |
| $E_1 E_2$ | 42.37*** | 18.67*** | — | — | 8 | 88.22*** | |
| $E_1 V_A$ | 35.80*** | — | 25.37*** | — | 8 | 48.39*** | |
| $E_1 E_2 V_A$ | 36.39*** | 3.34 | 21.46*** | — | 7 | 46.94*** | |
| $E_1 V_A V_D$ | 36.39*** | — | 31.47*** | −6.67 | 7 | 46.94*** | |

**Table 20.** *Estimates ($\pm$ s.e.) Obtained after Fitting a Model Allowing Different Genetic Components of Variation in Males and Females for Angle Transformed Psychoticism Scores*

| | $\hat{E}_1$ | $\hat{V}_{A_M}$ | $\hat{V}_{A_F}$ | $\hat{V}_{A_{MF}}$ |
|---|---|---|---|---|
| | 35.70*** | 35.40*** | 19.92*** | 28.96*** |
| $\pm$ | 1.09 | 2.35 | 1.40 | 4.03 |
| | | $\chi_6^2 = 12.08 \, (\text{p} = .06)$ | | |
| | $h^2_{\text{males}} = 0.50 \pm .02$ | | $h^2_{\text{females}} = 0.36 \pm .02$ | |

**Table 21.** *Sources of Variance (percentages) for Angle Transformed Psychoticism Scores*

| | | Females | Males |
|---|---|---|---|
| $E_1$ | error | 24 | 30 |
| | | 64 | 50 |
| | individual environment | 40 | 20 |
| $V_A$ | | 36 | 50 |

In females, true individual environment accounts for a greater proportion of $E_1$ than error, while in males the reverse is true (Table 21). However, in both males and females, the contribution of true individual environment to variation in psychoticism is greater than has previously been reported (Eaves and Eysenck, 1977).

*Neuroticism*

In both males and females the simple genetic model provides the best fit to the data. Although the chisquare for the heterogeneity of fit over sexes is non-significant ($\chi_2^2 = 3.17$, P $> 0.05$), we notice that there are smaller $\hat{E}_1$ and larger $\hat{V}_A$ components in females than males (Table 22).

Fitting a model allowing different $E_1$ and $V_A$ components in males and females (Table 23) results in a significant reduction in chisquare ($\chi_3^2 = 12.64$, P $< 0.01$), the correlation $r_{VAmf} = 0.58$ indicating that there are differences in gene action in males and females. In both sexes approximately one-half the variation in neuroticism is genetic in origin, with individual environment accounting for just over a third of the total variation (Table 24). The correlation of age with absolute within-pair differences in DZ females discussed earlier also indicates that genetic differences become more pronounced as females get older.

*Lie*

The genetic model describes the lie data adequately, although there is some evidence that $E_2$ effects are also important in males. There is significant heterogeneity of fit of the $E_1 V_A$ model over sexes ($\chi_2^2 = 12.73$, P $< 0.005$), and we notice that there are larger

**Table 22.** *Summary of Model-Fitting to Angle Transformed Neuroticism Scores*

| | $\hat{E}_1$ | $\hat{E}_2$ | $\hat{V}_A$ | $\hat{V}_D$ | df | $\chi^2$ | $h^2$ |
|---|---|---|---|---|---|---|---|
| **Female** | | | | | | | |
| $E_1 E_2$ | 125.1*** | 90.5*** | — | — | 2 | 51.12*** | |
| $E_1 V_A$ | 104.7*** | — | 110.5*** | — | 2 | 0.42 | |
| $E_1 E_2 V_A$ | 104.8*** | 1.2 | 109.2*** | — | 1 | 0.42 | .51 ± .02 |
| $E_1 V_A V_D$ | 104.8*** | — | 112.8*** | −2.4 | 1 | 0.42 | |
| **Male** | | | | | | | |
| $E_1 E_2$ | 141.8*** | 76.8*** | — | — | 2 | 28.48*** | |
| $E_1 V_A$ | 118.9*** | — | 100.3*** | — | 2 | 1.72 | .46 ± .03 |
| $E_1 E_2 V_A$ | 116.5*** | −26.4 | 128.8*** | — | 1 | 0.27 | |
| $E_1 V_A V_D$ | 116.5*** | — | 49.7 | 52.7 | 1 | 0.27 | |
| **Female and Male** | | | | | | | |
| $E_1 E_2$ | 130.3*** | 86.1*** | — | — | 6 | 86.65*** | |
| $E_1 V_A$ | 109.1*** | — | 107.4*** | — | 6 | 5.85 | .50 ± .02 |
| $E_1 E_2 V_A$ | 108.4*** | −8.2 | 116.2*** | — | 5 | 5.30 | |
| $E_1 V_A V_D$ | 108.4*** | — | 91.5*** | 16.5 | 5 | 5.30 | |
| **Female and Male and Opposite-Sex** | | | | | | | |
| $E_1 E_2$ | 140.9*** | 72.0*** | — | — | 8 | 136.90*** | |
| $E_1 V_A$ | 110.9*** | — | 102.1*** | — | 8 | 18.42* | |
| $E_1 E_2 V_A$ | 107.6*** | −24.1 | 128.9*** | — | 7 | 12.16 | |
| $E_1 V_A V_D$ | 107.6*** | — | 56.7** | 48.1** | 7 | 12.26 | .27 ± .09 |

**Table 23.** *Estimates ( ± s.e.) Obtained after Fitting a Model Allowing Different Genetic and Environmental Components of Variation in Males and Females for Angle Transformed Neuroticism Scores*

| | $\hat{E}_{1M}$ | $\hat{E}_{1F}$ | $\hat{V}_{AM}$ | $\hat{V}_{AF}$ | $\hat{V}_{AMF}$ |
|---|---|---|---|---|---|
| | 117.4*** | 104.2*** | 95.4*** | 108.0*** | 59.4*** |
| ± | 6.4 | 3.9 | 8.0 | 5.6 | 13.9 |
| | | | $\chi_5^2 = 5.78\,(p = .33)$ | | |
| | $h^2_{males} = 0.45 ± .03$ | | | $h^2_{females} = 0.51 ± .02$ | |

**Table 24.** *Sources of Variance (percentages) for Angle Transformed Neuroticism Scores*

| | | Females | | Males | |
|---|---|---|---|---|---|
| | error | | 13 | | 18 |
| $E_1$ | | 49 | | 55 | |
| | individual environment | | 36 | | 37 |
| $V_A$ | | 51 | | 45 | |

$\hat{E}_1$ and smaller $\hat{V}_A$ components for males than females (Table 25). Fitting separate $E_1$ and $V_A$ parameters for the males and females (Table 26) results in a significant reduction in chisquare ($\chi_3^2 = 13.77$, P < 0.01), the correlation $r_{VAmf} = 0.93$ indicating that the same $V_A$ effects which act in females act in males but with smaller effect. Addition of an $E_2$ parameter in males does not improve the fit ($\chi_1^2 = 3.46$, P > 0.05).

The breakdown of total variation (Table 27) is similar to that obtained in previous studies of lie (Martin and Eysenck, 1976; Eaves *et al.*, 1978).

**Table 25.** *Summary of Model-Fitting to Angle Transformed and Age Corrected Lie Scores*

| | $\hat{E}_1$ | $\hat{E}_2$ | $\hat{V}_A$ | $\hat{V}_D$ | df | $\chi^2$ | $h^2$ |
|---|---|---|---|---|---|---|---|
| **Female** | | | | | | | |
| $E_1E_2$ | 90.8*** | 65.8*** | — | — | 2 | 42.96*** | |
| $E_1V_A$ | 76.8*** | — | 79.6*** | — | 2 | 0.55 | .51 ± .02 |
| $E_1E_2V_A$ | 77.3*** | 6.7 | 72.5*** | — | 1 | 0.18 | |
| $E_1V_AV_D$ | 77.3*** | — | 92.6** | −13.4 | 1 | 0.18 | |
| **Male** | | | | | | | |
| $E_1E_2$ | 101.2*** | 53.2*** | — | — | 2 | 3.37 | |
| $E_1V_A$ | 93.8*** | — | 60.0*** | — | 2 | 4.95 | .39 ± .03 |
| $E_1E_2V_A$ | 96.7*** | 32.7* | 24.8 | — | 1 | 1.52 | |
| $E_1V_AV_D$ | 96.7*** | — | 122.8*** | −65.3 | 1 | 1.52 | |
| **Female and Male** | | | | | | | |
| $E_1E_2$ | 94.1*** | 61.8*** | — | — | 6 | 49.39*** | |
| $E_1V_A$ | 82.3*** | — | 73.2*** | — | 6 | 18.23** | |
| $E_1E_2V_A$ | 83.5*** | 14.9* | 57.3*** | — | 5 | 15.34** | |
| $E_1V_AV_D$ | 83.5*** | — | 102.1*** | −29.9 | 5 | 15.34** | |
| **Female and Male and Opposite-Sex** | | | | | | | |
| $E_1E_2$ | 98.9*** | 53.5*** | — | — | 8 | 82.00*** | |
| $E_1V_A$ | 81.9 *** | — | 70.0*** | — | 8 | 24.90** | |
| $E_1E_2V_A$ | 82.6*** | 5.0 | 64.4*** | — | 7 | 24.09** | |
| $E_1V_AV_D$ | 82.6*** | — | 79.4*** | −10.0 | 7 | 24.09** | |

**Table 26.** *Estimates ( ± s.e.) Obtained after Fitting a Model Allowing Different Genetic and Environmental Components of Variation in Males and Females for Angle Transformed and Age Corrected Lie Scores*

| | $\hat{E}_{1_M}$ | $\hat{E}_{1_F}$ | $\hat{V}_{A_M}$ | $\hat{V}_{A_F}$ | $\hat{V}_{A_{MF}}$ |
|---|---|---|---|---|---|
| | 92.04*** | 76.26*** | 56.68*** | 77.44*** | 61.47*** |
| ± | 4.98 | 2.88 | 5.69 | 4.03 | 9.69 |
| | | | $\chi^2_5 = 11.13\,(p = .05)$ | | |
| | $h^2_{\text{males}} = 0.38 \pm .03$ | | | $h^2_{\text{females}} = 0.50 \pm .02$ | |

**Table 27.** *Sources of Variance (percentages) for Angle Transformed and Age Corrected Lie Scores*

| | Females | Males |
|---|---|---|
| $E_1$ — error | 50 ⟨ 21 | 62 ⟨ 17 |
| $E_1$ — individual environment | 29 | 45 |
| $V_A$ | 50 | 38 |

*Conservatism*

In contrast to the personality variables, not only the $E_1 E_2$ model but also the $E_1 V_A$ model gives a bad fit to the conservatism data in both sexes. However, a model which includes all three sources of variation ($E_1 E_2 V_A$) gives an excellent fit in both males and females (Table 28). But when this model is applied to the combined male and female data it fails badly, apparently because of heterogeneity of fit over sexes ($\chi_3^2 = 60.66$, P < 0.001). Inspection of the parameter estimates reveals that there are larger $E_1$ and $E_2$ components for males than females but a similar estimate of $V_A$ in both sexes.

**Table 28.**   *Summary of Model-Fitting to Age Corrected Conservatism Scores*

|  | $\hat{E}_1$ | $\hat{E}_2$ | $\hat{V}_A$ | $\hat{V}_D$ | df | $\chi^2$ | $h^2$ |
|---|---|---|---|---|---|---|---|
| **Female** | | | | | | | |
| $E_1 E_2$ | 51.45*** | 69.79*** | — | — | 2 | 41.31*** | |
| $E_1 V_A$ | 41.82*** | — | 77.82*** | — | 2 | 21.31*** | |
| $E_1 E_2 V_A$ | 43.58*** | 35.67*** | 41.92*** | — | 1 | 0.11 | .35 ± .06 |
| $E_1 V_A V_D$ | 43.58*** | — | 148.92*** | −71.33 | 1 | 0.11 | |
| **Male** | | | | | | | |
| $E_1 E_2$ | 71.11*** | 87.43*** | — | — | 2 | 11.24** | |
| $E_1 V_A$ | 59.59*** | — | 97.28*** | — | 2 | 13.32** | |
| $E_1 E_2 V_A$ | 62.69*** | 52.71*** | 43.28** | — | 1 | 0.20 | .27 ± .09 |
| $E_1 V_A V_D$ | 62.69*** | — | 201.41*** | −105.42 | 1 | 0.20 | |
| **Female and Male** | | | | | | | |
| $E_1 E_2$ | 57.67*** | 75.35*** | — | — | 6 | 108.31*** | |
| $E_1 V_A$ | 47.42*** | — | 83.99*** | — | 6 | 97.73*** | |
| $E_1 E_2 V_A$ | 49.58*** | 40.95*** | 42.50** | — | 5 | 60.97*** | |
| $E_1 V_A V_D$ | 49.58*** | — | 165.35*** | −81.90 | 5 | 60.97*** | |
| **Female and Male and Opposite-Sex** | | | | | | | |
| $E_1 E_2$ | 62.04*** | 69.78*** | — | — | 8 | 135.90*** | |
| $E_1 V_A$ | 46.43*** | — | 83.51*** | — | 8 | 110.94*** | |
| $E_1 E_2 V_A$ | 49.45*** | 34.33*** | 47.97*** | — | 7 | 64.41*** | |
| $E_1 V_A V_D$ | 49.45*** | — | 150.95*** | −68.66 | 7 | 64.41*** | |

**Table 29.**   *Estimates ( ± s.e.) Obtained after Fitting a Model Allowing Different Environmental Components of Variation in Males and Females for Age Corrected Conservatism Scores*

|  | $\hat{V}_A$ | $\hat{E}_{1M}$ | $\hat{E}_{1F}$ | $\hat{E}_{2M}$ | $\hat{E}_{2F}$ | $\hat{E}_{2MF}$ |
|---|---|---|---|---|---|---|
|  | 41.54*** | 62.05*** | 43.41*** | 49.41*** | 34.57*** | 37.13*** |
| ± | 6.34 | 3.26 | 1.69 | 7.49 | 6.12 | 4.96 |
|  | | | $\chi_4^2 = 4.40$ (p = .35) | | | |
|  | $h_{males}^2 = 0.27 ± 0.4$ | | | | $h_{females}^2 = 0.35 ± 0.5$ | |

Fitting separate $E_1$ and $E_2$ parameters for males and females (Table 29) causes a great improvement in fit ($\chi_3^2 = 60.01$, P < 0.001) and excellent agreement with the joint data. The correlation $r_{E2mf} = 0.90$ is not significantly different from unity and indicates that the same $E_2$ effects which act in males act in females but with a smaller effect on the variance. The significant correlation of absolute within-pair differences with age in DZ males and opposite-sex pairs (Table 9) indicates that in males genetic differences for conservatism become more pronounced with age.

As discussed above, our estimate of $E_2$ can be better described as a parameter $B$ which may be attributable to cultural variation ($E_2$) or additional genetic variation due to assortative mating (AM) or both. In fact $B = E_2 + V_A(A/(1 - A))$ where $A = h^2\mu$, $A$ is the marital correlation between additive deviations of spouses, $h^2$ the heritability and $\mu$ the observed marital correlation (Eaves, 1977). If an estimate of $\mu$ is available we can solve the quadratic equation

$$A = h^2\mu$$
$$= \mu(V_A(1 + (A/(1 - A))))/V_T$$

in $A$, where ($V_T = E_1 + B + V_A$), obtain $AM = V_A(A/(1 - A))$ (the extra additive genetic variation due to assortative mating) and by subtraction of this term from $B$ we can obtain an estimate of 'true $E_2$'.

We do not have an estimate of the phenotypic marital correlation for conservatism in the parents of twins in this study, but Feather (1978) in his use of the C-Scale in an Australian sample obtained a marital correlation of 0.675 from 103 husband-wife pairs. Using this value as our estimate of $\mu$ and the mean of $V_T$ for males and females as $V_T$, we obtain the breakdown of $B$ into $E_2$ and $AM$ as shown in Table 30. Thus, approximately 38 per cent of the variation in conservatism in males is genetic in origin and in females this rises to approximately 49 per cent. Cultural influences and parental transmission account for about 21 and 14 per cent of the variation in males and females respectively, the remaining variation being due to individual environmental experiences and error.

**Table 30.** *Sources of Variance (percentages) for Age Corrected Conservatism Scores*

| | Females | Males |
|---|---|---|
| $E_1$ — error | 36 ⟨ 18 | 41 ⟨ 9 |
| $E_1$ — individual environment | 36 ⟨ 18 | 41 ⟨ 32 |
| $V_A$ — total genetic | 35 ⟩ 49 | 27 ⟩ 38 |
| $E_2$ — assortative mating | 29 ⟨ 14 | 32 ⟨ 11 |
| $E_2$ — family environment | 29 ⟨ 15 | 32 ⟨ 21 |

## Correlations between Personality and Attitude Scores

Partial correlations, controlling for age, between the transformed personality and attitude variables are shown in Table 31. The correlations are similar for both sexes. Individuals who are more anxious and depressed tend to be introverted, more psychotic and neurotic, and have lower lie scores. Although the EPQ scales were designed to measure independent personality attributes, they do depart slightly from orthogonality, a result found previously (Eysenck and Eysenck, 1975). Extraverts tend to be more psychotic, less neurotic and lie less. More psychotic individuals tend to be more neurotic and, like neurotics, have lower lie scores. Less conservative individuals tend to be more psychotic while more conservative individuals score higher on the lie or social desirability scale. Similar correlations have been found with the Eysenck Radicalism scale elsewhere (Martin and Eysenck, 1976). An interesting sex difference is found with extraversion where introverted females appear to be more conservative but no such relationship is found in men. There is also a slight tendency for more liberal men to be more anxious and depressed. While many of these correlations are statistically significant, with the exception of those between anxiety, depression and neuroticism they are quite low. We are led to speculate whether it is environmental or genetic factors which are responsible for the covariation of the symptom states of anxiety and depression and the personality trait of neuroticism.

### Causes of Covariation between Anxiety, Depression and Neuroticism

We know from the univariate analyses that for anxiety, depression and neuroticism, within-family environment ($E_1$) and additive gene effects ($V_A$) are important causes of variation, although there are differences in the importance of these effects in males and females. We now investigate the extent to which these two sources of variation are responsible for trait covariation by using the technique of genetical analysis of covariance structures developed by Martin and Eaves (1977). This method tests simultaneously hypotheses about both the sources and the structure of covariation. Just as univariate models were fitted to meansquares, multivariate models are fitted to the between-and within-pairs meanproducts matrices. Detailed explanation and applications of this maximum likelihood technique can be found in Eaves *et al.* (1977b), Fulker (1978), Martin *et al.*(1979), Martin *et al.* (1981) and Clifford *et al.* (1981).

The simplest $E_1 V_A$ model includes a single general factor causing covariation between anxiety, depression and neuroticism plus a variance component specific to each variable for both the $E_1$ and $V_A$ causes of variation. For each source, then, we estimate three factor loadings and three specific variance components, or twelve parameters in all. Each meanproducts matrix contributes three meansquares from the diagonal and three off-diagonal meanproducts, making twenty-four unique statistics from the four between- and within-pairs matrices of MZ and DZ twins of the same sex. We are thus left with twelve degrees of freedom to test the goodness of fit.

Maximum likelihood estimates of factor loadings and specific variance components from each source are then obtained. The proportions of variance in each measure accounted for by these estimates are shown in Table 32. In both sexes this model gives an excellent fit to the data and all parameter estimates are significantly greater than zero (P < 0.01).

The results suggest that genetic variation in the symptoms of anxiety and depression is largely dependent on the effects of the same genes which determine variation in the trait of neuroticism. This follows from the finding that the specific genetic components of variation are small, nearly all of their genetic variance being due to the common factor. However, it is interesting that there is still substantial specific genetical variance for neuroticism, and it is possible that this may be manifested relatively independently of the two symptoms we have considered.

A factor of individual environmental effects also appears to influence all three variables, although specific $E_1$ variation is equally or more important in most cases.

**Table 31.** Partial Correlations, Controlling for Age, between the Transformed Personality and Attitude Variables Separately for Females, Upper Triangle, and Males, Lower Triangle

| | Anxiety log(x + 1) | Depression log(x + 1) | Extraversion angle | Psychoticism angle | Neuroticism angle | Lie angle | Conservatism raw |
|---|---|---|---|---|---|---|---|
| Anxiety log(x + 1) | — | .66*** | -.08*** | .15*** | .61*** | -.12*** | -.01 |
| Depression log(x + 1) | .60*** | — | -.10*** | .18*** | .57*** | -.09*** | -.03* |
| Extraversion angle | -.12*** | -.16*** | — | .08*** | -.17*** | -.09*** | -.11*** |
| Psychoticism angle | .12*** | .16*** | .04* | — | .12*** | -.31*** | -.21*** |
| Neuroticism angle | .60*** | .55*** | -.19*** | .10*** | — | -.15*** | .03* |
| Lie angle | -.11*** | -.08*** | -.08*** | -.31*** | -.16*** | — | .26*** |
| Conservatism raw | -.05* | -.05** | -.03 | -.17*** | -.02 | .23*** | — |

**Table 32.** *Results of Fitting a Multivariate* $E_1V_A$ *Model to Transformed Anxiety, Depression and Neuroticism Scores*

| | | $E_1$ | | $V_A$ | |
| --- | --- | --- | --- | --- | --- |
| | | factor | specific | factor | specific |
| **Females** | | | | | |
| Neuroticism | angle | .20*** | .29*** | .35*** | .16*** |
| Anxiety | $\log(x + 1)$ | .35*** | .27*** | .35*** | .03*** |
| Depression | $\log(x + 1)$ | .33*** | .31*** | .30*** | .06*** |
| | | $\chi^2_{12} = 6.90$ (p = .86) | | | |
| **Males** | | | | | |
| Neuroticism | angle | .22*** | .32*** | .34*** | .12*** |
| Anxiety | $\log(x + 1)$ | .31*** | .35*** | .30*** | .04** |
| Depression | $\log(x + 1)$ | .33*** | .35*** | .23*** | .09*** |
| | | $\chi^2_{12} = 12.52$ (p = .40) | | | |

Note:  Results are in terms of the proportion of variance accounted for by each source.

The proportion of variance due to error or fluctuating environment in anxiety and depression (Tables 13 and 16) is equal to or slightly greater than the specific environmental variance, which suggests that some of this fluctuating environment may contribute to $E_1$ factor variance. The specific variance component for neuroticism, on the other hand, is somewhat greater than the unrepeatable variance, so that there may be systematic environmental experiences influencing the trait of neuroticism which do not influence the symptoms we measure.

Genetic and environmental correlations of the variables are shown in Table 33. In both sexes, genetic correlations are much higher (around 0.8) than the corresponding environmental correlations (around 0.4), and are similar for the three variables. While the distinction has been made between personality traits and states (Foulds, 1965, 1974,), for the neurotic symptoms measured here, there is good evidence for a common genetic and within-family environmental basis.

**Table 33.** *Genetic and Environmental Correlations between Transformed Anxiety, Depression and Neuroticism Scores for Females, Upper Triangle, and Males, Lower Triangle*

**ENVIRONMENTAL**

| | | Neuroticism angle | Anxiety $\log(x + 1)$ | Depression $\log(x + 1)$ |
| --- | --- | --- | --- | --- |
| Neuroticism | angle | — | 0.47 | 0.45 |
| Anxiety | $\log(x + 1)$ | 0.44 | — | 0.54 |
| Depression | $\log(x + 1)$ | 0.45 | 0.48 | — |

**GENETIC**

| | | Neuroticism angle | Anxiety $\log(x + 1)$ | Depression $\log(x + 1)$ |
| --- | --- | --- | --- | --- |
| Neuroticism | angle | — | 0.80 | 0.76 |
| Anxiety | $\log(x + 1)$ | 0.81 | — | 0.88 |
| Depression | $\log(x + 1)$ | 0.73 | 0.79 | — |

## DISCUSSION

The results of this very large twin study vindicate in the strongest possible way many of the hypotheses proposed and supported by Eysenck during his career. It is possible to measure dimensions of personality and attitudes which are consistent in their pattern from study to study and culture to culture. These are highly repeatable, at least in the medium term. Work by others has shown them to have high validity in their ability to discriminate between important external criterion groups. A considerable proportion of variation in all these dimensions is due to genetic factors.

The single most astonishing finding from this very powerful study is the complete lack of evidence for the effect of shared environmental factors in shaping variation in personality, and their relatively minor contribution to variation in social attitudes. This replicates earlier studies based on smaller numbers in which it was possible that lack of power was responsible for the lack of evidence. The conclusion is now so strong that we must suspect those who continue to espouse theories of individual differences in personality which centre on family environment and cultural influences, of motives other than scientific.

While previous studies on the aetiology of neuroses and minor depression have yielded conflicting results (Young *et al.*,1971; Torgersen, 1983), our large twin study has provided a clear answer to the causes of individual differences in the symptoms of anxiety and depression. The data suggest that population variance in these measures is due only to additive genetic effects and the influence of environmental factors which are unique to the individual. Both symptoms appear to be influenced largely by the same genes in both sexes, but have greater effect in females than males. Environmental variance for depression is also greater in females, a result found previously by Eaves and Young (1981). We found no evidence for the importance of environmental influences shared by members of the same family, effects such as social class and parental treatment. Workers who postulate that early environmental experiences are a major influence on anxiety and depression in adulthood (Parker, 1979, 1981a, 1981b) must recognize that such experiences are not necessarily shared by cotwins; experience from parents is more likely to be a function of the child's genotype than of the family environment (Eaves, 1976; Eaves *et al.*, 1978).

Cultural theories of determination are also strongly rejected as an explanation for the development of the personality traits we have measured. Individual differences in psychoticism, neuroticism and lie can be explained simply by the additive effects of genes and individual environmental experiences. For extraversion there is also evidence that dominance is important. It may be difficult for the outsider to the field to appreciate how strikingly good are the fits of our simple models when consideration is given to the power with which they are tested and the many opportunities for them to fail should the assumptions on which they are based be false.

It is not necessarily true, however, that the same genetic effects are acting in males and females for all traits, or if they are that they will produce deviations on the same scale in both sexes. In psychoticism and lie there are scalar differences between the sexes: genetic differences are more pronounced in males than females for psychoticism, while for lie the reverse is true. Environmental variance for lie is also greater in males than females. A simple genetic model has previously been found to be most appropriate for explaining variation in psychoticism (Eaves and Eysenck, 1977) and lie (Martin and Eysenck, 1976), although no significant differences between the sexes in environmental and genetic contributions to variance were found in these smaller studies.

Neither is it true that gene effects must stay constant with age. The correlation of age with absolute within-pair differences in DZ females indicates that genetic differences in neuroticism become more pronounced as females get older, confirming a similar result in a smaller sample by Eaves and Eysenck (1976b). This sex difference is reflected in the striking evidence we found for the action of different genes on neuroticism in males rather than females, although their heritabilities are very similar. Our results for neuroticism are similar to those of Eaves and Young (1981), who found that both age and sex affected the expression of additive genetic and environmental differences in the extensive Swedish twin data of Floderus-Myrhed *et al.* (1980).

By contrast with the other variables, the results for extraversion are consistent over sexes and age. The fascinating finding for this variable which sets it apart from the others is the significant and substantial variation due to genetic dominance (Mather, 1966). This would indicate that extraversion is a character which has been subject to an evolutionary history of strong natural selection. Eaves and Young (1981), reanalyzing the data of Floderus-Myrhed *et al.* (1980), found similarly that dominant gene action affects the expression of extraversion, although there was also evidence that both age and sex affected the expression of genetic and environmental differences in extraversion.

The detection of considerable genetical non-additivity for extraversion contrasts well with the lack of evidence for dominance variance affecting neuroticism, and reinforces the view that these two traits are not only statistically independent but also quite independent in fundamental biological aspects. This finding may have important implications for the continuing controversy about the physiological basis of Eysenck's personality dimensions. Gray (1970) has argued that a 45 degree rotation of Eysenck's extraversion and neuroticism dimensions is justified on several biological grounds. Our genetical analysis ascribes quite different origins to the genetic variation for E and N. Since rotation would obscure this distinction, our results may favour Eysenck's position.

It has been asserted that cultural transmission from parents to offspring is the most important cause of familial aggregation in conservatism scores (Feather, 1978) and related attitudes (Cavalli-Sforza *et al.*, 1982). Our analysis shows, however, that a model which includes only individual and family environmental effects is totally inadequate as an explanation of variation in conservatism. In contrast to Eaves and Eysenck (1974), we also found that a model incorporating only individual environmental differences and additive genetic effects is inappropriate, although these authors acknowledge that a larger study, such as ours, might identify common environmental influences that are important to variation.

Our results are similar to those of three independent twin studies (Eaves *et al.*, 1978) which measured conservatism by three different instruments. The three studies showed remarkable consistency in assigning approximately equal proportions of variance to additive genetic effects, within-family environment and a between-families component of variation. When corrected for the effects of assortative mating, the heritabilities were around 50 per cent, while cultural effects accounted for less than 20 per cent of the total variation, and this is similar to our result.

In contrast to these studies, however, we find evidence for environmental ($E_1$ and

$E_2$) effects of different size in males and females. It seems that there is greater environmental variation in males than females, and although the cultural effects are qualitatively the same, they have less influence on female variation. While the genetic component is estimated to be the same in samples of both sexes, genetic effects apparently become more pronounced as males get older but not females. Conservatism scores are also apparently more stable over time in males, but genuine individual environmental influences are considerably more important than in females.

The high marital correlation reported for conservatism by Feather (1978) considerably inflates the genetic variance between families and appears to be as important a cause of familial aggregation of attitudes as cultural differences between families. The correlation of 0.675 is amongst the highest marital correlations for any character, physical or behavioural (Spuhler, 1968; Vandenberg, 1972), and the role of attitude concordance in mate selection and marital success needs further investigation. It might be objected that such a high marital correlation arises from convergence of attitudes after marriage rather than being an initial correlation at the time of mate selection. We know of no direct evidence to support or contradict this view. However, in an earlier study Martin (1978) found no correlation between the absolute difference in radicalism scores of husband and wife pairs and the number of years they had been married. The apparent lack of divergence between conservatism scores of MZ cotwins with age (Table 9) is not what one would expect if attitudes tended to converge towards those of spouses, although a high correlation between spouses might vitiate this test.

The final test of the validity of making generalizations from twin data about the sources of variance in the general population must be the ability to make predictions about the sources of covariation between other non-twin relatives. Such a study of conservatism was carried out by Eaves *et al.* (1978) on 445 individuals from pedigrees including parents, natural and adopted children. Fitting models to these irregular pedigrees yielded parameter estimates very similar to those from the present study, except that the most parsimonious model included only $E_1$, $V_A$ and the assortative mating parameter $A$. Inclusion of a family environment parameter in the model did not improve the likelihood and the estimate of $E_2$ was small and non-significant. Competing models which included effects of cultural transmission were less parsimonious, gave no improvement in likelihood and yielded estimates of cultural transmission parameters which were small and not significantly different from zero.

In view of the current interest in cultural transmission (e.g., Cavalli-Sforza and Feldman, 1973; Cavalli-Sforza *et al.*, 1982), it would be interesting to see which items are more culture- or sex-dependent and thus stimulate the development of new scales which could be used to illustrate the mechanisms of non-hereditary transmission between generations. Our results show that conservatism, as it is currently measured, is much more dependent on genetic and within-family environmental differences than between-family cultural differences. Eaves and Eysenck (1974) have suggested that this may be due to society promoting individuality and mobility, which in turn gives greater importance to genetic and individual environmental experiences, irrespective of family environment.

The fact that attitudes are, at least in part, sensitive to cultural differences may make them a useful paradigm for the exploration of models in which gene expression and cultural effects are not independent. This is in contrast to the personality traits and symptoms studied, where the environmental differences which determine differences are not organized on a cultural basis. The contrast between the causes of variation for social attitudes and personality supports the distinction previously made between the two and implies that attitudes do not simply result from the projection of personality variables onto the level of social attitudes.

The significant and substantial correlations between anxiety, depression and neuroticism replicate a previous finding that neuroticism is a trait which is closely associated with vulnerability to neurotic symptoms (Henderson *et al.*, 1981). Our analysis of the causes of genetical and environmental covariation of these measures shows that additive genetic effects are equally if not more important in their covariation than individual environmental factors and that genetic correlations are much higher (0.8) than environmental correlations (0.4). While the distinction between personality traits and symptoms may be justified because symptoms are transitory and take different forms (Foulds, 1965, 1974), the fact that correlations between neuroticism and the two symptoms are as high as between the symptoms themselves provides little evidence for this distinction.

Nevertheless, there are also substantial genetic effects on neuroticism (16 per cent of the total in females, 12 per cent in males) which are independent of the two symptoms we have measured. Although specific genetic variance is a small proportion of the total for depression (6 per cent in females, 9 per cent in males), it is possible that this fraction estimates the contribution made in this sample by the major gene polymorphisms which are alleged to predispose to major depression (Comings, 1979; Weitkamp *et al.*, 1981). On the other hand, the genetic factor variance (30 per cent in females, 23 per cent in males) may be regarded as the fraction contributing to neurotic or minor depression.

One hallmark of a good theory is its ability to stimulate new work. By this criterion, Eysenck's theories have certainly been successful over the past thirty years. His hypotheses concerning the nature and origin of individual differences in personality and attitudes have been subjected to increasingly stringent tests, of which the present study is one of the most exacting, and have passed them well. But where do we go from here? Numerous 'wrinkles' in the basic findings have come to light in our powerful study. What is the basis of sex and age differences in gene expression and environmental influences? If it is individual environmental influences rather than shared environment which are important in the differentiation of personality, what is the nature of these influences? Why do we detect no assortative mating for the personality dimensions when we do for most biologically important traits? Are there genes for major depression which are independent of those for minor depression? Is the genetical non-additivity detected for extraversion ambidirectional, indicating an evolutionary history of stabilizing selection towards intermediate values on this dimension? And many more questions could be asked. There is much to be done!

**ACKNOWLEDGMENTS**

The Australian NH&MRC Twin Registry is supported by the National Health and Medical Research Council of Australia, as was the work described in this chapter. Rosemary Jardine is supported by an Australian Commonwealth Postgraduate Award.

## REFERENCES

Beadle, G. W. and Ephrussi, B. (1937) 'Development of eye colours in *Drosophila*: Diffusable substances and their interrelations', *Genetics*, **22**, pp. 76–86.

Beadle, G. W., and Tatum, E. L. (1941) 'Genetic control of biochemical reactions in *Neurospora*', *Proc. Nat. Acad. Sci.*, **48**, pp. 499–506.

Bedford, A., and Foulds, G. A. (1977) 'Validation of the delusions-states inventory', *Brit. J. Med. Psychol.* **50**, pp. 163–71.

Bedford, A., Foulds, G. A. and Sheffield, B. F. (1976) 'A new personal disturbance scale (DSSI/sAD)', *Brit. J. Soc. Clin. Psychol.*, **15**, pp. 387–94.

Cavalli-Sforza, L. L. and Feldman, M. W. (1973) 'Cultural versus biological inheritance: Phenotypic transmission from parents to children (a theory of the effect of parental phenotypes on children's phenotypes)', *Am. J. Hum. Genet.*, **25**, pp. 618–37.

Cavalli-Sforza, L. L., Feldman, M. W., Chen, K. H. and Dornbusch, S. M. (1982) 'Theory and observation in cultural transmission', *Science*, **218**, pp. 19–27.

Cederlöf, R., Friberg, L., Jonsson. E. and Kaij, L. (1961) 'Studies on similarity diagnosis in twins with the aid of mailed questionnaires', *Acta Genet. Stat. Med.*, **11**, pp. 338–62.

Clark, P., Jardine, R., Martin, N. G., Stark, A. E. and Walsh, R. J. (1980) 'Sex differences in the inheritance of some anthropometric characters in twins', *Acta Genet. Med. Gemellol.*, **29**, pp. 171–92.

Clifford, C. A., Fulker, D. W. and Murray, R.M. (1981) 'A genetic and environmental analysis of obsessionality in normal twins', *Twin Research 3: Intelligence, Personality, and Development*, New York, Alan R. Liss, pp. 163–8.

Comings, D. E. (1979) 'Pc 1 Duarte, a common polymorphism of a human brain protein, and its relationship to depressive disease and multiple sclerosis', *Nature*, **277**, pp. 28–32.

Eaves, L. J. (1976) 'A model for sibling effects in man', *Heredity*, **36**, pp. 205–14.

Eaves, L. J. (1977) 'Inferring the causes of human variation'. *J. Roy. Statist. Soc.*, A, **140**, pp. 324–55.

Eaves, L. J. and Eysenck, H. J. (1974) 'Genetics and the development of social attitudes', *Nature*, **249**, pp. 288–9.

Eaves, L. J. and Eysenck, H. J. (1975) 'The nature of extraversion: A genetical analysis', *J. Person. Soc. Psych.*, **32**, pp. 102–12.

Eaves, L. J. and Eysenck, H. J. (1976a) 'Genetical and environmental components and unrepeatability in twin's responses to a neuroticism questionnaire', *Behav. Genet.*, **6**, pp. 145–60.

Eaves, L. J. and Eysenck, H. J. (1976b) 'Genotype x age interaction for neuroticism', *Behav. Genet.*, **6**, pp. 359–62.

Eaves, L. J. and Eysenck, H. J. (1977) 'A genotype-environmental model for psychoticism', *Adv. Behav. Res. Therapy*, **1**, pp. 5–26.

Eaves, L. J. and Young, P. A. (1981) 'Genetical theory and personality differences', in Lynn, R. (Ed.), *Dimensions of Personality*, Oxford, Pergamon Press, pp. 129–79.

Eaves, L. J. Last, K., Martin, N. G. and Jinks, J. L. (1977a) 'A progressive approach to non-additivity and genotype-environmental covariance in the analysis of human differences', *Br. J. Math. Statist. Psychol.*, **30**, pp. 1–42.

Eaves, L. J. Martin, N.G. and Eysenck, S. B. G. (1977b) 'An application of the analysis of covariance structures to the psychogenetical study of impulsiveness', *Br. J. Math. Statist. Psychol.*, **30**, pp. 185–97.

Eaves, L. J., Last, K., Young, P. A. and Martin, N. G. (1978) 'Model-fitting approaches to the analysis of human behaviour', *Heredity*, **41**, pp. 249–320.

Eysenck, H. J. and Eysenck, S. B. G. (1975) *Personality Questionnaire* (Junior and Adult), Hodder and Stoughton Educational, Buckhurst Hill, Essex, Chigwell Press.

Eysenck, H. J. and Prell, D. B. (1951) 'The inheritance of neuroticism', *J. Ment. Sci.*, **97**, pp. 441–65.

Eysenck, H. J. and Prell, D. B. (1956) 'The inheritance of introversion-extraversion', *Acta Psychologica*, **12**, pp. 95–110.

Eysenck, S. B. G., Humphery, N. and Eysenck, H. J. (1980) 'The structure of personality in Australian as compared with English subjects', *J. Social Psych.*, **112**, pp. 167–73.

Feather, N. T. (1975) 'Factor structure of the conservatism scale', *Australian Psychologist*, **10**, pp. 179-84.

Feather, N. T. (1977) 'Generational and sex differences in conservatism', *Australian Psychologist*, **12**, pp. 76–82.

Feather, N. T. (1978) 'Family resemblances in conservatism: Are daughters more similar to parents than sons are?' *J. Personality*, **46**, pp. 260–78.

Fisher, R. A. (1931) *The Genetical Theory of Natural Selection*, London, Oxford University Press.

Floderus-Myrhed, B., Pederson, N. and Rasmuson, I. (1980) 'Assessment of heritability for personality, based on a short-form of the Eysenck Personality Inventory. A study of 12898 pairs', *Behav. Genet.*, **10**, pp. 153–62.

Foulds, G. A. (1965) *Personality and Personal Illness*, London, Tavistock Publications.

Foulds, G. A. (1974) *The Hierarchical Nature of Personal Illness*, London, Academic Press.

Freud, S. (1937) *Analysis Terminable and Interminable*, London, Collected Papers, No. 5, Hogarth, pp. 316–57.

Fulker, D. W. (1978) 'Multivariate extensions of a biometrical model of twin data', *Twin Research: Psychology and Methodology*, New York, Alan R. Liss, pp. 217–36.

Fulker, D. W. (1981) 'The genetic and environmental architecture of psychoticism, extraversion and neuroticism', in Eysenck, H. J. (Ed.), *A Model for Personality*, Berlin, Springer-Verlag, pp. 89–122.

Gray, J. (1970) 'The psychophysiological basis of introversion-extraversion', *Behav. Res. Therapy*, **8**, pp. 249–66.

Henderson, A. S., Byrne, D. G. and Duncan-Jones, P. (1981) *Neurosis and the Social Environment*, Sydney, Academic Press.

Jinks, J. L. and Fulker, D. W. (1970) 'Comparison of the biometrical genetical, MAVA, and classical approaches to the analysis of human behaviour', *Psychol. Bull.*, **73**, pp. 311–48.

Kasriel, J. and Eaves, L. J. (1976) 'A comparison of the accuracy of written questionnaires with blood-typing for diagnosing zygosity in twins', *J. Biosoc. Sci.*, **8**, pp. 263–6.

Martin, N. G. (1975) 'The inheritance of scholastic abilities in a sample of twins', *Ann. Hum. Genet.*, **39**, pp. 219–29.

Martin, N. G. (1978) 'Genetics of sexual and social attitudes in twins', *Twin Research: Psychology and Methodology*, New York, Alan R. Liss, pp. 13–23.

Martin, N. G. and Eaves, L. J. (1977) 'The genetical analysis of covariance structure', *Heredity*, **38**, pp. 219–29.

Martin, N. G. and Eysenck, H. J. (1976) 'Genetic factors in sexual behaviour', in Eysenck, H. J. *Sex and Personality*, London, Basic Books, pp. 192–219.

Martin, N. G. and Martin, P. G. (1975) 'The inheritance of scholastic abilities in a sample of twins. I. Ascertainment of the sample and diagnosis of zygosity', *Ann. Hum. Genet.*, **39**, pp. 213–18.

Martin, N. G., Eaves, L. J., Kearsey, M. J. and Davies, P. (1978) 'The power of the classical twin study', *Heredity*, **40**, pp. 97–116.

Martin, N. G., Eaves, L. J. and Fulker, D. W. (1979) 'The genetical relationship of impulsiveness and sensation seeking to Eysenck's personality dimensions', *Acta Genet. Med. Gemellol.*, **28**, pp. 197–210.

Martin, N. G., Gibson, J. B., Oakeshott, J. G., Wilks, A. V., Starmer, G. A., Craig, J. and Perl, H. (1981) 'A twin study of psychomotor performance during alcohol intoxication: Early results', *Twin Research 3: Epidemiological and Clinical Studies*, New York, Alan R. Liss, pp. 89–96.

Mather, K. (1966) 'Variability and selection', *Proc. Roy. Soc. Lond. B*, **164**, pp. 328–40.

Mather, K. (1974) 'Non-allelic interactions in continuous variation of randomly breeding populations', *Heredity*, **32**, pp. 414–19.

Newman, H. H., Freeman, F. N. and Holzinger, K. J. (1937) *Twins: A Study of Heredity and Environment*, Chicago, University of Chicago Press.

Nichols, R. C. and Bilbro, W. C. (1966) 'The diagnosis of twin zygosity', *Acta Genet. Stat. Med.*, **16**, pp. 265–75.

Parker, G. (1979) 'Parental characteristics in relation to depressive disorders', *Brit. J. Psychiat.*, **134**, pp. 138–47.

Parker, G. (1981a) 'Parental reports of depressives: An investigation of several explanations', *J. Affect. Dis.*, **3**, pp.131–40.

Parker, G. (1981b) 'Parental representations of patients with anxiety neurosis', *Acta Psychiat. Scand.*, **63**, pp. 33–6.

Rao, D. C., Morton, N. E. and Yee, S. (1974) 'Analysis of family resemblance II', *Am. J. Hum. Genet.*, **26**, pp.331–59.

Shields, J. (1962) *Monozygotic Twins*, Oxford, Oxford University Press.

Snedecor, G. W. and Cochran, W. G. (1980) *Statistical Methods*, 7th ed., Iowa State University Press.

Spuhler, J. N. (1968) 'Assortative mating with respect to physical characteristics', *Eugen. Quart.*, **15**, pp. 128–40.

Torgersen, S. (1983) 'Genetics of neurosis: The effects of sampling variation upon the twin concordance ratio', *Brit. J. Psychiat.*, **142**, pp. 126–32.

Vandenberg, S. G. (1972) 'Assortative mating, or who marries whom?' *Behav. Genet.*, **2,** pp. 127–57.

Weitkamp, L. R., Stanger, H. C., Persad, E., Flood, C. and Guttormsen, S. (1981) 'Depressive disorders and HLA: A gene on chromosome 6 that can affect behavior', *New Engl. J. Med.*, **305,** pp. 1301–6.

Wilson, G. D. and Patterson, J. R. (1968) 'A new measure of conservatism,' *Brit. J. Soc. Clin. Psychol.*, **7,** pp. 264–9.

Young, J. P. R., Fenton, G. W. and Lader, M. H. (1971) 'The inheritance of neurotic traits: A twin study of the Middlesex Hospital Questionnaire', *Brit. J. Psychiat.*, **119,** pp. 393–8.

# 4. H. J. Eysenck and Behaviour Genetics: A Critical View

JOHN C. LOEHLIN

History will surely judge that Eysenck's multifarious contributions to psychology centre on the description, elaboration and interpretation of the key personality dimensions of extraversion, neuroticism and psychoticism, which along with intelligence form the major axes of his theory of individual differences. For Eysenck, an important aspect of the interpretation of these behavioural dimensions has always been an inquiry into their biological bases. One form this biological inquiry has taken is the assessment of the roles of genetic and environmental factors in accounting for individual variation in these traits. These efforts of Eysenck and his collaborators have drawn on the data and methods of behaviour genetics, and in turn have themselves made a substantial contribution to that discipline.

Eysenck's work in behaviour genetics has spanned a considerable range. First, there were the early twin studies in extraversion-introversion and neuroticism in the 1950s, with Prell, Blewett and MacLeod. Second, there are the later twin and family studies in the 1970s and 1980s of neuroticism, psychoticism and extraversion, done in collaboration with Eaves, Martin, Young and others. Third, there are the miscellaneous twin studies on various other topics, for example, sexual behaviour, social attitudes and smoking. Fourth, there are the animal studies, mostly connected with the development by Broadhurst in Eysenck's laboratory of the Maudsley reactive and non-reactive strains of rats. And fifth, there are Eysenck's writings on intelligence, in which he has often addressed behaviour genetic issues, although he has not, so as far as I know, himself actually carried out behaviour genetic studies in this area.

Eysenck's publications on these various topics have been numerous. A bibliography of his writings in the area of behaviour genetics, kindly provided to me by Professor Eysenck, lists no less than thirty articles and book chapters—and this does not include a number of books with extensive behaviour genetic material, such as *Sex and Personality* (1976), *The Structure and Measurement of Intelligence* (1979b) and *The Causes and Effects of Smoking* (1980).

**49**

The space available here will obviously not permit a detailed review of all Eysenck's empirical and theoretical contributions in the five areas mentioned above. Further, my role as critic requires that at least some of my examination be more than cursory. I will therefore focus on a single theme: Eysenck's tendency to overstate the case with respect to the genetic determination of the cardinal dimensions of his theory. I will not so much be faulting his conclusions—though I will do some of that—as arguing that Eysenck greatly exaggerates the security with which they can be reached from the evidence at hand.

## AN EARLY EXAMPLE: NEUROTICISM

My first example derives, appropriately enough, from Eysenck's first published behaviour genetic study, a twin study of neuroticism (Eysenck and Prell, 1951). In this study twenty-five pairs of monozygotic (MZ) twins and twenty-five pairs of dizygotic (DZ) twins were tested with a battery of seventeen measures. These included cognitive, motor and perceptual tasks, as well as a couple of questionnaire scales. The same test battery was given to twenty-one children who had been psychiatrically diagnosed as neurotic. The test intercorrelations based on the 100 children in the twin sample were factor analyzed, and the first factor rotated so as to make it a 'neuroticism' factor; i.e., a factor to which the tests contributed in approximately the same manner as they discriminated between the (presumptively normal) twins and the neurotic children. The highest loadings on 'neuroticism' were on two measures of body sway taken while the subject stood with closed eyes.

The intraclass correlation for identical twins on this neuroticism factor was .851; that for fraternal twins was .217. From this Eysenck and Prell obtained a heritability estimate of .810 for neuroticism, *via* a Holzinger formula. They express some reservations about the formula, and would 'lay more stress on the directly observed intraclass correlations' (p. 461n). Most modern behaviour geneticists would share their misgivings about the Holzinger coefficient. However, a more appropriate heritability estimate from the intraclass correlations under the same assumptions (additive genetic variance, random mating, no gene-environment correlation or interaction, and equal resemblance of identical and fraternal twin environments) would be obtained by taking twice the difference between the MZ and DZ correlations, that is, the estimate would be 1.286. We can thus suppose that (a) 128.6 per cent of the variance of neuroticism is due to the genes; or (b) some of the above-stated assumptions are wrong; or (c) sampling or other error has led to an exaggerated discrepancy between the MZ and DZ twin correlations. Alternative (a) is not too plausible. Alternative (b) is somewhat more credible, since a greater resemblance of identical than fraternal twin environments or the presence of a large amount of non-additive genetic variance could lead to disproportionately high MZ twin correlation. Alternative (c) is very plausible, since an intraclass correlation based on twenty-five pairs has a rather large sampling error (approaching .20 for a low correlation) and twice the difference between two such correlations has a very large sampling error indeed.

I do not intend by this any special criticism of Eysenck and Prell; they were using the technology of the day, and such matters are much clearer now than at the time they wrote. I merely want to establish that their quantitative finding might be less than completely secure. One should perhaps note that their results might be tenuous in another respect as well; namely, in the definition of the dimension whose heritability is being estimated. The use of only twenty-one individuals to establish differential weights for neuroticism on seventeen tests virtually guarantees that chance will play an appreciable role in the process, even if one were to assume no error at all in the definition of normality by the group of 100 twins.

Eysenck and Prell's paper was sharply criticized by Karon and Saunders (1958), and defended by Eysenck (1959). It is a curious interchange. One criticism, concerning sample selection, was cleared up by Eysenck without difficulty. In response to a second, that the variances on the neuroticism factor differ for the identical and fraternal twins at the .05 level of significance, Eysenck mumbles about the arbitrariness of the .05 level and the counter-intuitive direction of the difference. What he *should* have pointed out is that if Karon and Saunders had done the proper two-tailed $F$ test instead of the one-tailed test that they appear to have used, the difference would not have been statistically significant at all.

There is further discussion concerning which of two versions of Holzinger's $h^2$ statistic to use: the one Eysenck and Prell employed gave a heritability of .810, the alternative version, which Karon and Saunders believed to be more appropriate, would have given a lower figure of .580. Since, as mentioned earlier, the Holzinger statistic in either form is not much in favour these days, there seems little point in pursuing this matter further, except perhaps to fault Eysenck and Prell a little for not considering, computing and reporting both values.

Karon and Saunders go on to address other issues: the possible failure of the equal environments assumption, the question of whether the test battery selection might have been biased toward high heritability, and so on. Eysenck had something to say in reply to each of these points; the details need not concern us further here.

I would like, however, to call attention to the final paragraph of Eysenck's paper. In this he endorses Karon and Saunders' call for study of the mechanisms underlying the hereditary determination of neuroticism, and mentions ongoing work (presumably Broadhurst's) directed toward this end. Then Eysenck goes on to say: 'Until these studies are completed it would seem useful to repeat the Eysenck-Prell study with suitable technical improvements, in order to throw some further light on the relative importance of the factors in question' (p. 79). He believes that 'such studies would support the result of the original paper.' What he does not even hint at is that such a study had already been attempted in his laboratory, and that it had failed to yield such results.

Writing in the *Eugenics Review*, James Shields (1954) gives a brief account of that study. It was part of Blewett's dissertation research on the inheritance of neuroticism and intelligence; only the work on intelligence was published (Blewett, 1954). Shields reports:

> Blewett was also interested in 'neuroticism'. He hoped, with a different series of tests purporting to measure emotional instability, to repeat the experiment of Eysenck and Prell described above. However, Blewett's tests did not all intercorrelate with one another in the directions expected and he could not identify any of the factors obtained in his analysis as being 'neuroticism'. A factor, defined by tests such as body-sway, self-rating in neuroticism and certain scores on the Rorschach test, did not give evidence of hereditary determination and showed only a random relationship to our own rating of severity of maladjustment (p. 244).

In hindsight, given the small sample sizes (Blewett used twenty-six of each kind of twin pair) such an inconsistency between studies is only too understandable. And there may well have been other problems. Nevertheless, the existence of this study and its result would seem germane to Eysenck's stated belief that 'such studies would support the result of the original paper.' The chief result of the original paper was, of course, the finding of an extremely high heritability for neuroticism.


## A MODERN INSTANCE: EXTRAVERSION, NEUROTICISM, PSYCHOTICISM

The preceding is, to be sure, ancient history. Can we find modern instances of potentially misleading statements by Eysenck about the degree of heritability of his personality dimensions? Consider a relatively recent summary (Eysenck, 1979a, p. 525): 'Using the a-theoretical, purely psychometric devices constructed by the traditional producers of questionnaires and inventories, we find that approximately half of the variance is accounted for by genetic factors when MZ and DZ twins are studied, and when traditional indices of heritability are used.' Eysenck then goes on to contrast favourably his own methods: 'Using measures of the major personality dimensions P, E and N, and calculating heritabilities along the lines of modern biometrical genetical analysis, we get figures more in the band from 60% to 80% when test unreliability has been allowed for.'

Curiously, none of the four sources for this generalization that Eysenck cites gives heritability figures that actually lie between .60 and .80. That given for extraversion is .57 (Eaves and Eysenck, 1975, p. 108), those for neuroticism under two different assumptions are .57 and .59 (Eaves and Eysenck, 1976, p. 155), and that for psychoticism is .81 (Eaves and Eysenck, 1977, p. 22). Presumably, however, the central tendency of these values could be taken as falling in the stated range—provided one doesn't use the median or the mode as the measure of central tendency.

What is the reader of the above passage to conclude are the reasons for the higher heritability figures that Eysenck obtains? I venture that he or she will suppose that they chiefly reflect the first two factors mentioned: that the major Eysenckian dimensions are being studied, not just any old personality scales, and that modern biometrical genetical methods of analysis are being employed, not just traditional indices of heritability. But in fact it is the third factor which Eysenck slips in as an apparent afterthought, the allowance for test unreliability, that *entirely* accounts for the increase above the 'traditional' values. For convenience, I take figures from the paper by Young, Eaves and Eysenck (1980), a study which covers all three dimensions and provides heritability estimates for both children and adults. The respective non-error-corrected heritability values for E, N and P for adults are .51, .41 and .48, and for children, .54, .44 and .42. The average of these figures is .47. Contrary to what a casual reader might suppose, confining oneself to the major Eysenckian dimensions and using modern biometrical genetical methods yields results very much like the traditional 'approximately half of the variance'. Correction for unreliability of measurement makes all the difference.

What about such corrections? I personally believe that it is appropriate in principle to make them, although often tricky in practice. In the original sources *considerable* caution is expressed: 'If our response model is appropriate, we may wish to regard such unreliability as inherent in the trait we are measuring and thus prefer for most predictive purposes to work with the uncorrected figure of 49%' (Eaves and

Eysenck, 1977, p. 22). 'We may correct our heritability estimate for unreliability provided we can assume the Subjects × Items interactions estimate experimental error only . . . . If subjects and items interact, the contribution of experimental error to $E_1$ will be overestimated' (Eaves and Eysenck, 1975, p. 108). 'Misleadingly high heritability estimates could result from inappropriate corrections for unreliability' (Eaves and Eysenck, 1976, p. 159). In the summary statement all these cautions are forgotten, and the '60% to 80%' figure becomes the basis for suggesting 'a strong genetic component for variation along the major dimensions of personality, a component not noticeably weaker than that found in connection with intelligence' (Eysenck, 1979a, p. 525).

Now, taking raw heritability figures averaging .47 and error-correcting them up to the middle of the .60 to .80 range implies reliabilities for the Eysenck Personality Questionnaire scales in the neighbourhood of .67. When Eysenck is discussing these scales in other contexts, he thinks better of them than that. For normal samples, one-month test-retest reliabilities with a median of .85 are quoted, and internal consistency reliabilities with a median of .84 (Eysenck and Eysenck, 1976, p. 75f). Use of reliabilities like these would give corrected values more in the neighbourhood of .55 than .70. Dropping the reliabilities to around .80 to allow for some effects of scale transformation and sample restriction still leaves corrected values below .6 (where indeed most of the reported values actually fall).

But are even heritabilities at this level beyond cavil? While one doesn't dispute the right of Eysenck and his colleagues to apply particular biometrical genetic models and procedures to their data, and while I, for one, have always been impressed by their statistical and methodological sophistication, it may still be instructive to look informally at the data at the level of simple familial correlations—if only to get some sense of what the effects might be of making or not making various assumptions. I should emphasize that I am not inherently hostile to fitting formal behaviour genetic models to data, having done a certain amount of this sort of thing myself (Loehlin, 1978, 1979). But informality also has its merits. I might add that I am encouraged in this by a comment made by S. B. G. Eysenck and H. J. Eysenck in another context (1969, p. 76): 'with rough data of this kind, selected without the possibility of planned sampling, it may be a task of supererogation to use complex statistical methods for teasing out trends which are quite apparent to casual inspection.'

The paper by Young, Eaves and Eysenck provides two to four parent-child correlations in each of seven different subsamples (ranging from thirty-six to ninety-six pairs) for each of the three personality scales E, N and P—a total of ninety-six different correlations of a parent with a child on a personality dimension. The median of these ninety-six correlations is .13. The same paper presents eighteen correlations on these scales for DZ twin pairs. Their median is .17. Twelve correlations are presented for MZ twin pairs. Their median is .46. Numbers like these do not suggest, to casual inspection, heritabilities in the neighbourhood of .70.

Under the model that the authors generally find to fit personality data—additive genes, random mating and no common family environment—one can arrive from these correlations at four different estimates of heritability. One can double the parent-child correlation and get .26. One can double the DZ correlation and get .34. One can take the MZ correlation itself and get .46. Or one can take twice the MZ-DZ difference and get .58. If one supposes, as Young and his colleagues do, that the genes affecting a trait in childhood and adulthood might be somewhat different, one might wish to discount the first heritability estimate of .26 from the parent-child correlations as being too low. But the .34 from the DZ correlations should still be appropriate. It might even be a little on the high side, if there should be some undetected effect of common environment ($E_2$). Eaves and Eysenck (1975, p. 108) allow for the statistical possibility of such an undetected effect in similar data, at the level of 10–15 per cent of the phenotypic variance. On the stated assumptions, the MZ twin correlation ought not to exceed twice the DZ twin correlation. If it did not, all three of the twin-based heritability estimates would agree at .34. Error-corrected, using a reliability of .80, we are discussing something like .42 as a typical value of personality scale heritability, not .60 to .80. Or, if we allow for an effect of common environment at the level suggested as possible by Eaves and Eysenck, we could have estimates as low as .27.

Is there any basis on which the observed MZ twin correlations might be expected to be somewhat out of line on the high side? Failures of two assumptions might particularly be considered. First, it is possible that shared environment might be of special importance for MZ twins, that is, for this group $E_2$ might not be negligible. Second, non-additive forms of genetic variance, i.e., genetic dominance and epistasis, might play a significant role in personality. MZ twins share all their genetic variance, non-additive as well as additive. DZ twins share one-half of their additive genetic variance (when mating is random), but only one-quarter of the variation due to dominance, and a smaller fraction of epistatic variation.

On the first of these assumptions, that the difference is due to $E_2$, the heritability estimates of .27 to .42 given above would be appropriate. In this case the difference between the .13 of parent and child and the .17 of DZ twins could represent a greater degree of shared environment for the latter. However, the leap to an MZ twin correlation of .46 seems rather extreme, unless one assigns a rather large role to (say) the responses elicited from others by an individual's physical appearance. And what direct evidence there is does not point very strongly toward an effectively greater similarity of MZ twin environments, so far as personality is concerned. For example, identical twins who look more alike are not more similar in behaviour and personality than those who are less alike in appearance (Matheny, Wilson and Dolan, 1976; Plomin, Willerman and Loehlin, 1976). Identical twins whose parents try to treat them alike, who played together more as children, or who spend more time together as adolescents are only trivially more similar in personality than identical twins with less overlap of experience (Loehlin and Nichols, 1976, p. 52f). Nevertheless, further exploration of this issue is reasonable—MZ twins clearly share environmental similarities that *might* make them more alike, even though it is hard to demonstrate that much of this in fact takes place.

The other alternative is non-additivity of the genetic variance, i.e., the effects of genetic dominance and epistasis. As mentioned, these could have a considerably greater influence on the resemblance of MZ than of DZ twins, since the former share gene configurations completely and the latter only to a limited degree. Lykken (1982) has argued for the importance of non-additive genetic variation—he proposes the term 'emergenesis'—in accounting for excess MZ twin correlations in areas as diverse as personality traits and electroencephalographic (EEG) frequency spectra. For both EEG spectra and personality, MZ twins reared apart are not notably less similar than MZ twins reared together, suggesting that a failure of the genetic additivity assumption may be a more plausible explanation of the excess MZ twin correlation than is a failure of the assumption of equal environments.

If this is the case, Eysenck can retain the notion of a fairly substantial heritability of personality traits, but at the expense of the purely additive genetic models he and his colleagues have repeatedly claimed to represent good fits to their data. Even here, the heritabilities will not be spectacularly high: if there is no effect at all of common environment on MZ twins, the broad heritability will be equal to the MZ correlation itself, i.e., in the neighbourhood of .46; corrected for measurement error, perhaps .58. If shared environment is operative, in the range of 10 to 15 per cent suggested as a possibility by Eaves and Eysenck, the corrected heritability could be around .42.

Now I would not argue very strongly for any particular number in the range .27 to .58 as a typical value for personality scale heritability, but I do maintain that it is misleading to claim that the heritabilities of the major personality dimensions lie in the range 60 to 80 per cent, when most actual estimates fall below that range, and when on various more or less plausible assumptions the heritabilities could very easily be at half that level.

I apologize again for the simplemindedness of the preceding analysis. A sophisticated biometrician will object, for example, that in using correlations instead of covariances I am ignoring possible differences in the variances in the various groups. I would simply reply that at least in the Young *et al.* study such differences are not conspicuous, and that in their absence correlations are equivalent and easier to follow.

The biometrician may also object that I have insufficiently adjusted reliability estimates based on the original scales in the general population to deal with transformed scales in the twin sample. This is possible. It is also possible that I may have overadjusted, since the 'general population' in question turns out sometimes to be groups of students (Eysenck and Eysenck, 1976, p. 75) who may well be comparably restricted in range. In any case, if the twin sample is not reasonably representative of the general population, there are some problems for Eysenck in using anyone's analysis of these data to talk about the traits in general.

On the matter of error correction, let me merely add here my opinion that it does less violence to assume that a reliability coefficient will pretty will survive a non-linear but monotonic transformation of the scale than it does to base error corrections on assumptions as implausible as the one used in the case of P (Eaves and Eysenck, 1977). The procedure they used assumes, if I do not misread it, that all the items on the P scale will be equally often endorsed by respondents. This is demonstrably false for N items (Eaves and Eysenck, 1976), and seems equally unlikely for P. Do the investigators really wish to claim that people will as often agree to 'Would you take drugs which may have strange or dangerous effects?' as to 'When you catch a train do you often arrive at the last minute?' By the way, it may be recalled that this particular error correction yielded the one slender reed of .81 on which Eysenck's claim of an average heritability in the .60 to .80 band could rest.


## INTELLIGENCE


Eysenck's apparent willingness to weigh preconceptions favourably in their contest with evidence can be illustrated in another domain as well, the heritability of IQ. Consider his summary statement in his recent book on *The Structure and Measurement of Intelligence*: 'Intelligence as measured by IQ tests has a strong genetic basis; genetic factors account for an estimated 80% of the total variance, although this estimate has a standard error of some 5% to 10% attached to it' (Eysenck, 1979b), p. 227).

In Chapter 5 of that book, written by D. W. Fulker and H. J. Eysenck, the authors consider the heritability of IQ in some detail, providing, by my count, nineteen different estimates of the heritability of IQ derived from various sources of evidence: twin correlations, adoption studies, parent-child and sibling correlations, identical twins reared apart, and so on. I list the nineteen heritability estimates in order from smallest to largest: .47, .50, .52, .52, .59, .62, .64, .68, .68, .68, .69, .69, .69, .71, .74, .77, .79, .79, .80. The highest figure, .80, and the *only* one reaching Eysenck's summary estimate, is simply quoted from an earlier book by Eysenck. It derives from the variance shrinkage in an orphanage study, and is immediately qualified: 'The numbers in the study were too small to attribute much importance to the precise values of the shrinkage ...' (p. 117). One of the two instances of the next highest figure, .79, is given as an *upper limit* for the effects of reliability correction. It is what would occur if none of the environmental influences on the IQs of different children in a family were unique to individual children—hardly a very attractive assumption. The figure most emphasized by the authors in the chapter itself is .69, their estimate from the median IQs in a compilation of IQ studies by Erlenmeyer-Kimling and Jarvik, and they give the standard error of this estimate as ±.02, not '5% to 10%'.

Thus Eysenck's summary figure of .80 is hardly justified even by his own review of the evidence. How does it compare to others' assessments? Here are two recent summary statements about IQ heritability by behaviour geneticists. N. D. Henderson, writing in the 1982 *Annual Review of Psychology*, says, 'between .3 and .6, with broad heritability between .4 and .7' (p. 413); S. Scarr and L. Carter-Saltzman (1983), in a review chapter on 'Genetics and Intelligence', cite two ranges: .5 ± .1 (p. 217), and .4 to .7 (p. 297). A confident claim of .8 ± .1 is, under the circumstances, indeed remarkable.


**IN CONCLUSION**


Having discharged my obligation to be a critic, I would like to comment again on the very great positive contribution that Eysenck and his collaborators have made to the study of the inheritance of personality. Much relevant research has been carried out, and the raw variances and covariances are published in the original articles, so that anyone who prefers other interpretations can test them against the data. For this, we are all in Eysenck's debt.

Not the least significant aspect of Eysenck's role in this area has been as a facilitator of behaviour genetic research by others. A list of behaviour geneticists who have worked with Eysenck or his students would certainly include the vast majority of the major British names in this field, and quite an impressive number elsewhere around the world. The development of the twin register at the Institute of Psychiatry has directly contributed to the majority of the human behaviour genetic studies of normal traits done in Britain in the last decade—and not just narrowly Eysenckian studies: a case in point is the behaviour genetic analysis of Zuckerman's Sensation Seeking Scale (Fulker, S. B. G. Eysenck and Zuckerman, 1980). Perhaps if Eysenck did not believe so firmly in the high heritability of his personality dimensions, all this would not have come to pass. If so, we who are interested in behaviour genetics would indeed have been much the poorer. In that sense, I applaud his sturdy convictions. Long may they lead him forward!

# REFERENCES

Blewett, D. B. (1954) 'An experimental study of the inheritance of intelligence', *Journal of Mental Science*, **100**, pp. 922–33.

Eaves, L. and Eysenck, H. (1975) 'The nature of extraversion: A genetical analysis', *Journal of Personality and Social Psychology*, **32**, pp. 102–12.

Eaves, L. and Eysenck, H. (1976) 'Genetic and environmental components of inconsistency and unrepeatability in twins' responses to a neuroticism questionnaire', *Behavior Genetics*, **6**, pp. 145–60.

Eaves, L. J. and Eysenck, H. J. (1977) 'A genotype-environmental model for psychoticism', *Advances in Behavior Research and Therapy*, **1**, pp. 5–26.

Eysenck, H. J. (1959) 'The inheritance of neuroticism: A reply', *Journal of Mental Science*, **105**, pp. 76–80.

Eysenck, H. J. (1976) *Sex and Personality*, London, Open Books.

Eysenck, H. J. (1979a) 'Genetic models, theory of personality and the unification of psychology', in Royce, J. R. and Mos, L. P. (Eds.), *Theoretical Advances in Behavior Genetics*, Alphen aan den Rijn, The Netherlands, Sijthoff and Noordhoff, pp. 517–40.

Eysenck, H. J. (1979b) *The Structure and Measurement of Intelligence*, Berlin, Springer-Verlag.

Eysenck, H. J. (1980) *The Causes and Effects of Smoking*, Beverly Hills, Calif., Sage.

Eysenck, H. J. and Eysenck, S. B. G. (1976) *Psychoticism as a Dimension of Personality*, London, Hodder and Stoughton.

Eysenck, H. J. and Prell, D. B. (1951) 'The inheritance of neuroticism: An experimental study', *Journal of Mental Science*, **97**, pp. 441–65.

Eysenck, S. B. G. and Eysenck, H. J. (1969) 'Scores on three personality variables as a function of age, sex, and social class', *British Journal of Social and Clinical Psychology*, **8**, pp. 69–76.

Fulker, D. W., Eysenck, S. B. G. and Zuckerman, M. (1980) 'A genetic and environmental analysis of sensation seeking', *Journal of Research in Personality*, **14**, pp. 261–81.

Henderson, N. D. (1982) 'Human behavior genetics', *Annual Review of Psychology*, **33**, pp. 403–40.

Karon, B. P. and Saunders, D. R. (1958) 'Some implications of the Eysenck-Prell study of "The inheritance of neuroticism": A critique', *Journal of Mental Science*, **104**, pp. 350–8.

Loehlin, J. C. (1978) 'Heredity-environment analyses of Jencks's IQ correlations', *Behavior Genetics*, **8**, pp. 415–36.

Loehlin, J. C. (1979) 'Combining data from different groups in human behavior genetics', in Royce, J. R. and Mos, L. P. (Eds.), *Theoretical Advances in Behavior Genetics*, Alphen aan den Rijn, The Netherlands, Sijthoff and Noordhoff, pp. 303–34.

Loehlin, J. C. and Nichols, R. C. (1976) *Heredity, Environment, and Personality*, Austin, Tex., University of Texas Press.

Lykken, D. T. (1982) 'Research with twins: The concept of emergenesis', *Psychophysiology*, **19**, pp. 361–73.

Matheny, A. P., Jr., Wilson, R. S. and Dolan, A. B. (1976) 'Relations between twins' similarity of appearance and behavioral similarity: Testing an assumption', *Behavior Genetics*, **6**, pp. 343–51.

Plomin, R., Willerman, L. and Loehlin, J. C. (1976) 'Resemblance in appearance and the equal environments assumption in twin studies of personality traits', *Behavior Genetics*, **6**, pp. 43–52.

Scarr, S. and Carter-Saltzman, L. (1983) 'Genetics and intelligence', in Fuller, J. L. and Simmel, E. C. (Eds.), *Behavior Genetics: Principles and Applications*, Hillsdale, N. J., Lawrence Erlbaum, pp. 217–335.

Shields, J. (1954) 'Personality differences and neurotic traits in normal twin schoolchildren', *Eugenics Review*, **45**, pp. 213–46.

Young, P. A., Eaves, L. J. and Eysenck, H. J. (1980) 'Intergenerational stability and change in the causes of variation in personality', *Personality and Individual Differences*, **1**, pp. 35–55.

# Interchange

## EAVES REPLIES TO LOEHLIN

*Since many of Loehlin's critical remarks are directed against papers for which I must take prime responsibility, Professor Martin has kindly offered me the space allotted to him in which to reply to the more important points.*

The substance of Loehlin's first criticism rests not upon the primary sources of data and analysis but on secondary summaries attributed to Eysenck. Loehlin's critique may be crystallized thus:

1    Eysenck has stated that the heritability of personality dimensions is around 0.7.
2    The publications by Eaves and his colleagues in collaboration with Eysenck make no such claim.
3    The claim can only be made if a correction for unreliability is made.
4    The publications by Eaves and his colleagues in collaboration with Eysenck show that usual corrections for unreliability make demonstrably false assumptions in that the 'unreliable' variance itself can be shown to have a genetic component.
5    Therefore, the data cannot be used to support a heritability of 0.7.

It is depressing that so much of the discussion has focused on the precise value of the 'heritability'. The purpose of the extensive analyses fostered by Eysenck over the last decade has been the simultaneous estimation of *all* significant sources of variation: genetic, social and accidental; additive and non-additive. To focus on the estimates of heritability which, by and large, are often hard to find in the primary papers, is to obscure the fact that the main conclusion of the work is not that the heritability of personality has some particular value but that:

1    the family environment, as distinct from the unique experiences of the individual, makes a trivial contribution to personality differences;
2    mating is essentially random for personality differences;
3    for some measured aspects of personality there is striking evidence that quite different genes operate at different stages of development;
4    there is some evidence of sibling interactions between juveniles for certain aspects of behaviour;
5    genetic factors make a highly significant contribution to personality differences;
6    genetic effects on personality are highly specific, even to the level of individual item responses, and not just confined to the major dimensions of personality;

7   even what many psychometricians would dismiss as 'unreliability' may have a
    genetic component;

8   in large samples there is significant interaction between sex differences and
    genetic effects of personality;

9   such 'genotype x environment interaction' as might be claimed for person-
    ality on the basis of Eysenck's raw dimensions may be explained almost
    entirely by the properties of the scale of measurement and removed by a
    transformation which assumes equality of item difficulties and local
    independence.

The research encouraged by Eysenck has made significant headway in a field
which was a muddle only fifteen years ago. We do not believe, by any stretch of
imagination, that the genetics of personality is fully understood. For example, recent
data on very large samples (e.g., Eaves and Young, 1981; Martin and Jardine, this
volume) shed doubt on the assumption of genetic additivity for extraversion. There is
still much that needs to be done to relate the findings of the genetic studies to those
emerging from the studies of the physiological basis of personality and its relationship
to learning. We have done as much as anyone to discourage an obsession with
heritability which obscures the strength and subtlety of the findings.

The principal results of the primary publications have been replicated in
extremely large studies in Europe, the US and now, in this volume, Australia. They
establish Eysenck's dimensions of personality as paradigms of behavioural traits
whose mode of familial transmission is comparatively simple in contrast to that of
educational and sociological variables. They cast significant doubt on social learning
theories as vehicles for understanding family resemblance for personality. Those who
seek measurements which support the cultural transmission of individual differences
should look elsewhere. The 'modern methods of biometrical genetics' as Loehlin and
Eysenck describe them, are not biased towards a genetic model of inheritance, as
anyone who reads our publications will discover. These methods are as powerful for
an understanding of cultural as they are of genetic inheritance. If there is no genetic
component, there is no better way of finding out than by a properly constructed
family study. If we wish to analyze the effects of family interaction on behaviour, then
there is no better way than the properly constructed family study. It is, perhaps, a sad
reflection on social psychology and allied disciplines that some of the major recent
advances in modelling of the environment have been made by those whose primary
training and research has been in genetics.

# LOEHLIN REPLIES TO MARTIN AND JARDINE

Martin shares my high regard for the important empirical contributions made by
Eysenck and his colleagues to human behaviour genetics. In the present chapter he
and Jardine provide another substantial contribution in this tradition.

I was pleased to see that the new data from an Australian sample agree very well
with the British work cited in my chapter. After converting the meansquares of
Table 8 to correlations, as I did for those of the Young *et al.* study, the median MZ
and DZ correlations on the three major Eysenck scales are .48 and .21, as compared
to .46 and .17 in the British study. The differences between the MZ and DZ

correlations, from which estimates of heritability flow, are quite similar, suggesting that the (uncorrected) heritability estimates of slightly under .50 for the British data would be replicated in the Australian data. And indeed the median of the nine heritability estimates reported in Martin and Jardine's Tables 17, 19 and 22 is .46, as compared to a mean of .47 in the British data.

The reliability estimates for the EPQ scales from the small re-tested sample in the Australian study are also quite similar to those reported by Eysenck for Great Britain. The median of the raw score reliabilities for E, P and N in Table 6 is .82; the comparable British figure I cited in my chapter was .84, which I dropped to .80 to allow for the effects of scale transformation and restriction of range in a volunteer sample. I speculated that the effect of scale transformation on the reliabilities would be slight, but I allowed a little for it—Martin and Jardine's Table 6 suggests that I need not have worried about this: the raw score and transformed scale reliabilities on the EPQ scales are virtually identical.

In brief, the Australian, like the British, twin data suggest typical heritabilities after error-correction of around .55 for Eysenck's personality dimensions, well short of the '60% to 80%' range claimed as representative by Eysenck. And for the reasons mentioned in discussing the British data, the true figure could well be even a bit lower.

Now these have been summary figures, ignoring some possibly interesting differences among the individual scales. For readers who may find Martin and Jardine's maximum likelihood fitting of biometrical models a bit abstruse, let me try to tell a simpler story in terms of correlations. In each of the 'summary of model-fitting' tables in their chapter, four different models are considered. The models are fit first to males and females separately, then together, then with opposite-sex pairs thrown in.

The first of the four models, designated $E_1 E_2$, is essentially a test of whether the MZ correlations are higher than the DZ correlations. They always are, as shown by the large chisquares. (This account is a bit oversimplified—for example, it neglects possible variance differences; still, it should provide a reasonable sense of what goes on.)

The second model, $E_1 V_A$, will fit if the DZ correlation is approximately half the MZ correlation. This is the case, more or less, for the four scales reflective of maladjustment (depression, anxiety, neuroticism and psychoticism). It is what would be expected if the resemblance between twins is purely genetic in origin, with half as many genes shared, on the average, by DZs as by MZs.

If the DZ correlation is more than half the MZ correlation, as would be expected if shared environment is contributing similarly to the correlation of both kinds of twin pairs, the third model, $E_1 E_2 V_A$, can always be fit to the data (aside from variance differences). This pattern is shown by the conservatism scale, and to some extent by the lie scale (which could perhaps be considered a social conformity scale in this sort of volunteer sample). In both cases some effect of shared family environment on attitudes and values is not implausible.

Finally, if the DZ correlation is less than half the MZ correlation, the fourth model, $E_1 V_A V_D$, will always fit (again, neglecting variance differences). The extraversion scale shows this pattern. The MZ correlations (as calculated from the Table 8 meansquares) are .53 and .50 for females and males respectively, and the DZ correlations are .19, .13 and .21 for the female, male and opposite-sex pairs.

Now one of the hazards of the model-fitting approach is the risk of believing that a model that can be fit is therefore true. Essentially, what the data and statistical tests have shown is that the DZ resemblance for extraversion in this population is less than half the MZ resemblance. The presence of genetic dominance could be responsible for this, as the $E_1 V_A V_D$ designation suggests. But so could lots of other things that have at one time or another been proposed in the twin literature, such as exceptional environmental similarity of MZs, genetic epistasis, contrast effects, competition among DZ pairs, and so on. It is, to say the least, rather a leap from DZ correlations less than half of MZ correlations to conclusions about natural selection in man's evolutionary history. I could wish that Martin and Jardine had described the effect of dominant genes on extraversion as a 'possibility' rather than as a 'finding'. Nevertheless, further exploration of this interesting hypothesis is clearly appropriate.

# Part IV: Personality

# 5. Major Contributions to the Psychology of Personality

PAUL T. COSTA, JR AND ROBERT R. McCRAE

As this volume clearly shows, Hans Eysenck is, in the fullest sense of the term, a general psychologist. In the United States, however, he is most widely known as a personality psychologist, the creator (with his wife Sybil) of the MPI, EPI and EPQ. The task of defining his major accomplishments in the field of personality is therefore easy for Americans: quite simply, Eysenck will be remembered as the psychologist who brought order to the bewildering array of conflicting and overlapping traits by identifying neuroticism and extraversion as fundamental dimensions of personality.

To appreciate this accomplishment, it is necessary to recall the wild proliferation of personality constructs and measures over the past sixty years (Kelly, 1975). Allport had been willing to introduce the entire English language lexicon of trait names into the province of trait psychology (Allport and Odbert, 1936). Hathaway and McKinley (1940) adopted the then-current diagnostic categories as bases for their multiphasic personality inventory. Block (1961) and his colleagues required 100 different statements to characterize an individual. Even the factor analysts, who explicitly aimed at the identification of basic dimensions (Guilford and Zimmerman, 1949; Cattell, Eber and Tatsuoka, 1970), produced complicated systems that required the organization provided by second-order factors.

Each of these systems—and many more schemes and single constructs—has its merits; certainly each has its partisans. It is in the nature of personality that it can be usefully conceptualized in a variety of ways, and at various levels of specificity. But in the recent history of personality research, the result has been close to chaos. Scales bearing the same name measured different constructs; scales with quite different labels duplicated each other in content. Scientific communication was impossible. Vigorous intellectual competition between models of personality can lead to real progress, as differences and similarities are discovered; but when there are so many competing models, careful comparison between them becomes difficult or impossible, and researchers have often found it easier to start from scratch and propose entirely new systems—a solution that merely compounds the problem.

The correct solution is to develop a common language, a core of shared constructs that can form the basis for communication, a standard against which the contributions of new constructs can be measured. That fact is widely recognized, and most researchers hope, implicitly or explicitly, to provide the structure that will be adopted by all their colleagues. The most deliberate attempt in this direction was by Cattell (1957), who instituted a series of Universal Index Numbers for the factors he identified.

Cattell's scheme has not been widely adopted; Eysenck's has. As Wiggins (1968) notes, 'If consensus exists within the realm of temperament structure, it does so with respect to the importance of . . . extraversion and anxiety (neuroticism). The most systematic recognition of the primacy of these two dimensions may be found in . . . Eysenck' (pp. 309–10). More recently, Maddi (1980) concurred that 'there is broad consensus on the two most important second order factors . . . *introversion v. extraversion* . . . and *emotional health v. neuroticism*' (p. 463).

The importance of this contribution to a field as fragmented as personality psychology can hardly be overestimated, and bears comparison with the work of another English scientist, Newton. The concepts of force, motion, energy, momentum, acceleration were in general currency among Newton's contemporaries, but were used inconsistently. By providing unambiguous definitions of terms and mathematical specifications of their relations, Newton laid the foundation for the entire subsequent development of physics. Similarly, Eysenck's identification of E and N is increasingly recognized as the foundation of trait psychology.

**The Choice of E and N**

As historians of science, we may well ask what it was that made Eysenck successful when so many of his colleagues failed. There seem to be two closely related answers. First, he kept his system simple; and second, he made it as comprehensive as possible, a feat made possible only by identifying the broadest themes in the psychological literature.

Eysenck's decision to focus on two major dimensions of personality was a bold piece of scientific strategy. Eysenck was well aware that these two dimensions did not exhaust the domain of personality—the charge often levelled against him by critics. In fact, for years he has conducted research on a variety of other personality and attitudinal traits, ranging from social tough-mindedness (Eysenck, 1954) to aesthetic preference (Götz, Borisy, Lynn and Eysenck, 1979). But he chose to concentrate his attention on N and E, and he directed the attention of others to those dimensions by the publication of instruments measuring them.

The effect was to make his system the most easily assimilable, the one to which researchers familiar with one approach and ready to consider another could most easily turn. The dimensions of E and N could have been robbed of their heuristic value if Eysenck had simultaneously introduced several other scales. Although he first proposed the dimension of psychoticism much earlier, he did not incorporate it into his published inventories until 1975 (Eysenck and Eysenck, 1975). Its appearance at an early stage may well have diluted appreciation for the other dimensions, and made his simply one more personality system.

Of course, simplicity itself is not sufficient to account for the success of Eysenck's model. Based on insightful reviews of the literature and his own empirical work,

Eysenck (1947) went to the heart of trait psychology by recognizing the pervasive commonalities within measures of psychopathology on the one hand, and social interaction on the other. These two areas—representing personality psychology's ties to clinical and social psychology, respectively—had dominated the search for individual difference variables, and the identification of a single unifying dimension in each was destined to be a major discovery. Those who worked most closely in these areas tended to emphasize fine distinctions: differential diagnoses between anxiety and depression, or variations in leadership style. Eysenck saw the forests composed of these trees, with extraordinary effect. Because E and N do in fact saturate most questionnaires and adjective checklists, significant and often substantial relations are almost always found when these scales are correlated with others. As they used the MPI, EPI or EPQ, researchers quickly became convinced of their utility.

## Research and Applications

It is one thing to devise an elegant and valuable model; it is another to bring it to the attention of the entire field of personality research. Eysenck accomplished both.

Eysenck's publications are an essential element. Only with British understatement could we call him 'prolific', as a bibliography of over 600 books and articles attests. He has written both popular and formidably scholarly articles, and he has rarely hesitated to take strong and controversial stands. All this writing would be useless, however, unless he had something to say; his extensive research has amply provided this.

One line of research has been directed to validation of the two-dimensional model itself and its relation to other systems. An example is a factor analysis of Guilford, Cattell and Eysenck scales (Soueif, Eysenck and White, 1969), which clearly shows the importance of E and N factors in all three inventories.

Research on the relations between personality traits and basic psychological processes has been particularly important to Eysenck, who sees these studies as a technique for discovering the biological basis of personality. Thus, he has conducted research on the relations between personality and pain perception (Lynn and Eysenck, 1961), figural aftereffect (Eysenck, 1955), motor movements (Eysenck, 1964), and paired-associates learning (McLaughlin and Eysenck, 1967). Although much of this work is controversial, the strategy of combining trait research with experimental studies was pioneering.

Research on the genetic basis of personality has been in and out of favour, though it has generally fared better in Europe than in America, where a strong environmentalist bias has prevailed. Eysenck's sustained work in this area (e.g., Eaves and Eysenck, 1975) has contributed to a renewed interest in the inheritance of temperament, and his early conclusions on the substantial heritability of extraversion (Eysenck, 1956) seem to have been supported by later research.

Finally, hundreds of studies have been done showing the behavioural correlates of E and N and their practical applications (see Eysenck, 1971, for examples of the latter). From one point of view, these concrete findings are the ultimate fruit of personality research; from a more theoretical standpoint, they provide essential evidence for the utility of trait models. Over the past decade, when traits were often regarded as mere cognitive fictions (Shweder, 1975), repeated findings such as these bolstered the spirits of personality researchers and reminded us that individual differences are in fact a significant determinant of human conduct (Eysenck and Eysenck, 1980).

### Measuring Personality

Beyond doubt, the introduction of the MPI and its successors was a great boon to psychology. In these instruments, Eysenck presented tools that were both convenient and psychometrically sophisticated operationalizations of his model of personality; he thus enabled many researchers to extend his work in directions of interest to them.

Eysenck has always been properly concerned with basic issues in psychometrics, and has conducted extensive research on the reliability and validity of his published scales. Despite some ambiguity about whether E has a 'unitary' (Eysenck and Eysenck, 1967) or 'dual' (Eysenck and Eysenck, 1963) nature, the basic two-dimensional model has repeatedly been recovered in item factor analyses, and the reliability of the scales is excellent. Validity of the scales, as measured by their correlations with other standard measures of the same constructs or with peer nominations (Eysenck, 1969), is unsurpassed. For many researchers, the EPI scales are the 'gold standard' for the measurement of E and N.

The Eysenck scales have many other merits as well. They are short and easily administered and scored; the language has been carefully tailored for wide ranges of education and ability (though some modification for American subjects is often needed). Extensive normative information, based on national samples in Britain, provides a solid basis for interpreting scores. From a psychometric standpoint it is perhaps unfortunate that the N scale is not balanced for acquiescence, but it is unlikely that this detracts significantly from the validity of the scale. The items themselves are straightforward and easily understood by both test-taker and test-interpreter; the ambiguities introduced by so-called subtle items are avoided (Wrobel and Lachar, 1982). In short, the test is as simple and direct as the model it represents.

Because the basic phenomena—extraversion and neuroticism as dimensions of human personality—are so robust, the exact form of the instrument used to assess them is somewhat arbitrary. It is possible and reasonable in these circumstances to revise the test regularly, making minor improvements and keeping the wording current, and Eysenck has done just that. Contrast the almost superstitious reverence with which the MMPI is regarded, and the awkward interpretation and scoring needed now to make it applicable to current concepts of personality and psychopathology!

One of the most important applications of the EPQ has been in cross-cultural research (Eysenck and Eysenck, 1982). The EPQ has been translated into Greek, Hungarian, Chinese and many other languages, and the basic structure has been recovered in many cross-cultural contexts. Few other bodies of data provide such strong evidence that human nature is really universal as do these studies. Recall again the formidable problems that cross-cultural research using the Rorschach faced, and we can appreciate the value of Eysenck's models and measures.

## BUILDING ON EYSENCK'S FOUNDATIONS

All of this is not to say that E and N are the last words in trait psychology. Perhaps they are better regarded as the first. One of the chief merits of Eysenck's system is that it lends itself to improvement; it is easy to supplement, refine and build upon. And it is testimony to the value of Eysenck's system that other scientists have chosen it as the starting point for their own work. In the remainder of this chapter we will discuss some ways in which our work has attempted to extend Eysenck's and some prospects for future work.

## Specifying Facets of the Global Domains

In our initial work with trait systems, particularly those of Cattell (Cattell, Eber and Tatsuoka, 1970), Buss and Plomin (1975) and Eysenck, we quickly encountered one of the fundamental problems in trait psychology: on the level of first-order traits, there is little agreement among different theorists. Indeed, the term 'first-order trait' is itself misleading, since it suggests that all first-order traits are in some sense equal in level and scope. In practice, that is not the case at all. What Guilford calls 'general activity', for example, is broken into 'tempo' and 'vigour' by Buss and Plomin—yet each of these can be seen as first-order traits contributing to the second-order trait of extraversion.

To avoid the confusions and spurious exactitude of these 'orders', we have adopted a different set of terms. The largest groupings of traits we call 'domains', and we refer to all component traits, regardless of breadth or specificity, as 'facets'. In the language of mathematics, domains are sets whereas facets are proper subsets. Since a set with only five elements can have thirty distinct, non-null proper subsets (and a set of ten elements can have 1022), it is easy to see why, from the vast array of human thoughts, feelings and behaviours, different theorists have chosen somewhat different facets of each domain to represent basic traits.

Eysenck's solution to this problem was to ignore the many possible subsets and concentrate on the full sets themselves—the 'second-order' dimensions of E and N. This approach had the salutary effect of emphasizing the points of agreement between different systems and thus making progress possible for the field as a whole. Partisans of one school or another might dispute the merits of their favourite scheme, but, from the vantage point of a domain conception, the disinterested observer could begin to perceive what was replicable across instruments, and what was not.

The shift from a facet to a domain approach was, therefore, an extraordinarily fruitful one when Eysenck first proposed it in the 1940s and 1950s. However, there have always been good reasons for wanting more specific information than domain scales provide, and we believe the time has come to return to a more multifaceted approach to personality measurement. For the past several years we have been working on an instrument, the NEO (for Neuroticism-Extraversion-Openness to Experience) Inventory, that attempts to do just that.

Whereas the early factor analysts began by identifying facets and factoring them to find the higher-order structure, we reversed this process. We are far more confident about the global domains of E and N than we are about any specific traits, and we created facets by attempting to identify important distinctions within domains. Ideally, the facets would be mutually exclusive, would jointly exhaust the full domain, and would be at the same level of generality—neither too broad nor too narrow in scope. They would also correspond, if not to the natural divisions of the domain, at least to familiar and proven constructs which could be readily understood by others.

Six facets per domain seemed like a useful level of generality to us, and we were guided by previous literature in looking for familiar concepts to embody in scales. Perhaps most difficult was the criterion of exhaustiveness. We attempted to include all the major traits previously identified as elements of the domain, and added a few — like positive emotions—that seemed to be missing from most. A list of facets in the NEO model is given in Table 1.

What are the advantages of measuring specific facets? First, some theorists, notably Cattell (Cattell, Eber and Tatsuoka, 1970), believe that facets may be more psychologically meaningful than domain scores are. Allport (1961), who thought of traits as personal dispositions only approximated by common traits, would also probably object that global scores are far removed from the reality of the individual's personality. By accumulating evidence on the development and manifestations of both facets and domains, we may eventually be in a better position to determine which, if either, is the better level on which to study personality.

As applied to individuals, the facets give more detailed information on the forms in which the basic dimension is expressed. There are important differences between those who experience neuroticism chiefly as depression and those who experience it as anger. Likewise, it may be useful to know that, of two individuals both average in total extraversion, one is assertive but not warm, another warm but not assertive.

Measuring a variety of facets allows for internal replication of findings: if a criterion is related to all six facets of neuroticism, we can be confident that the observed correlations are not due to chance. Conversely, differential correlation of facets within a domain clarifies the nature of the association. We have reported that happiness and life satisfaction are related to extraversion (Costa and McCrae, 1980a; Costa, McCrae and Norris, 1980), but a more recent analysis (Costa and McCrae, 1984) suggests that this association is due primarily to the facets of warmth, assertiveness and positive emotions, and not to excitement seeking or gregariousness.

If we correlate EPI E and N scales with NEO facets in our longitudinal sample (see McCrae and Costa, 1983, for details of sample and procedure) we can identify the most salient aspects of Eysenck's scales. Table 1 gives the results for a group of 586 normal adult men and women. Agreement on the domain level is clearly indicated by the large convergent and relatively small divergent correlations. We can also see, however, that Eysenck's N reflects more anxiety and depression than it does hostility or impulsiveness; that Eysenck's E is more weighted by gregariousness than by activity.

Incidentally, it might be useful to clarify a confusion of terminology that may occur here. Eysenck (Eysenck and Eysenck, 1963) identifies 'impulsiveness' as one of the two 'natures' of extraversion. By that term, he means quick reactions and the willingness to take risks and dares. We prefer to use the terms 'activity' and 'excitement seeking' to indicate these facets of extraversion. We reserve the term 'impulsiveness' to refer to an aspect of neuroticism that consists of the inability to resist urges and cravings and leads to poor self-control. The similarity between excitement seeking and impulsiveness is more semantic than substantive: the correlation between the NEO scales measuring these traits is only .25, and they load on different factors. The impulsive person reacts to internal drives that, when frustrated, cause distress. The excitement seeker actively seeks out occasions of stimulation, and at worst suffers boredom if no exciting setting can be found. The prototypical instances of excitement seeking, such as race-car driving or mountain climbing, often require a good deal of the self-control that the impulsive person lacks.

**Table 1.**   *Correlations of EPI Scales with NEO Facets*

| NEO Inventory | Eysenck Personality Inventory | | |
|---|---|---|---|
| | N | E | Lie |
| **Neuroticism:** | | | |
| Anxiety | 70 | −08 | −23 |
| Hostility | 44 | 09 | −25 |
| Depression | 64 | −09 | −25 |
| Self-Consciousness | 59 | −21 | −18 |
| Impulsiveness | 44 | 24 | −41 |
| Vulnerability | 52 | −18 | −12 |
| **Extraversion:** | | | |
| Warmth | −16 | 43 | 06 |
| Gregariousness | −11 | 54 | −04 |
| Assertiveness | −30 | 42 | 03 |
| Activity | 02 | 35 | −07 |
| Excitement Seeking | 00 | 45 | −19 |
| Positive Emotions | −15 | 46 | −10 |
| **Openness:** | | | |
| Fantasy | 21 | 07 | −29 |
| Aesthetics | −02 | 07 | −06 |
| Feelings | 20 | 21 | −22 |
| Actions | −17 | 27 | −06 |
| Ideas | −17 | 00 | 03 |
| Values | 00 | 01 | −16 |

Note:   $N = 586$.   For all correlations greater than $\pm.11$, $p < .01$. Decimal points omitted.

Here we agree with Eysenck in substance, but believe our terminology is more communicative.

**Adding New Domains**

An examination of Table 1 also shows another respect in which our model differs from that of Eysenck: we include a dimension of Openness to Experience. Originally identified in the 16PF (Costa and McCrae, 1976), this third domain subsumes many constructs not related to either N or E, including dogmatism (Rokeach, 1960), mood variability (Wessman and Ricks, 1966), artistic interests (Holland, 1966) and hypnotic susceptibility (Tellegen and Atkinson, 1974). Although there are some small correlations with the EPI Lie scale, it is clear that openness is distinct from this factor.

In proposing openness (O) as a new domain of personality we join hundreds of other investigators who have offered new constructs to the field of personality. Why should ours be accorded any more attention than theirs? We believe the answer is that we offer O not simply as another construct, but as an extension of Eysenck's N and E domains. By putting our construct in a model which embraces those primary domains, we are in a much better position to demonstrate its utility. Every candidate for status as a domain of personality must past two tests: does it bring together a variety of facets (that is, is it a sufficiently broad construct), and is it independent of other, established domains—namely, E and N?

A model including facets of all three can easily be tested by factor analysis. The facets of openness in the NEO inventory certainly represent a broad scope of thoughts, feelings and behaviours: imagination, artistic interests, openness to inner feelings, the need for variety in actions, intellectual curiosity, non-dogmatic values. And a series of factor analyses (e.g., Costa and McCrae, 1980b; McCrae and Costa, 1983) has shown that openness facets do form a distinct third factor alongside N and E factors in both self-reports and ratings.

Eysenck has also proposed a third domain, psychoticism, and has suggested (personal communication, November 1982) that openness may be the opposite pole of psychoticism. Although such an identification would provide an elegant matching of the two models, it is unlikely to be accurate. As we have argued elsewhere, P as a domain seems to have to do with the bond between individual and society; O has to do with styles of regulating experience. These are quite different content areas, and a correlation between them would not really be expected. In some preliminary analyses of a new version of the P scale in our sample, we find virtually no correlation with O (McCrae and Costa, 1985).

On the other hand, we have found some exciting correspondences with another model of personality traits. Following Tupes and Christal (1961) and Norman (1963), Goldberg (1981) has recently revived interest in a five-factor model based on an analysis of English language trait terms. In a recent study using self-reports on an adjective checklist (McCrae and Costa, in press b) we recovered the five-factor structure labelled by Goldberg (1981) as surgency, agreeableness, conscientiousness, emotional stability and culture. Correlating scores on these factors with self-reports and spouse ratings on the NEO Inventory, however, leaves no doubt that surgency is really extraversion, and that emotional stability is the reverse of neuroticism. These correspondences have been acknowledged for some time (Norman, 1963), though rarely demonstrated empirically. More informative was the striking correspondence between the fifth factor and our openness measures. Together with a reanalysis of the literature on adjective factors themselves, these findings lead us to conclude that the fifth factor in English language trait names is in fact openness to experience.

One urgent empirical question that arises is the relation between psychoticism and the five-factor model, particularly the remaining factors of conscientiousness and agreeableness. It might be hypothesized that psychoticism is some combination of low conscientiousness and disagreeableness, and research is in progress to test this hypothesis.

## CONCLUSIONS

In comparison with the elaborate taxonomic system of Cattell or the extensive linguistic studies of Norman and Goldberg, or with his own enormous efforts in such areas as intelligence, learning theory, behaviour therapy and health, it might seem that Eysenck has only dabbled in personality taxonomy. But nothing could be further from the truth. One might as well conclude that, in relation to his contributions to mathematics, kinetics and optics, Newton only dabbled in astronomy.

The identification of E and N as fundamental dimensions of personality has provided a sure basis for progress in trait psychology over the past thirty years. Of course, Eysenck did not rest content with that achievement. But much of his work in other areas, for example, in cortical theories of learning, or in critiques of psychiatric diagnostic schemes, is based on his model of personality; like other researchers, he found it a useful basis for wide-ranging research. It seems clear that it will continue to be a cornerstone of personality psychology for years to come.

## REFERENCES

Allport, G. W. (1961) *Pattern and Growth in Personality*, New York, Holt, Rinehart and Winston.

Allport, G. W. and Odbert, H. S. (1936) 'Trait names: A psycho-lexical study', *Psychological Monographs*, **47**, pp. 1–171.

Block, J. (1961) *The Q-Sort Method in Personality Assessment and Psychiatric Research*, Springfield, Ill., Charles C. Thomas.

Buss, A. H. and Plomin, R. (1975) *A Temperament Theory of Personality Development*, New York, Wiley.

Cattell, R. B. (1957) 'A universal index for psychological factors', *Pychologia*, **1**, pp. 74–85.

Cattell, R. B., Eber, H. W. and Tatsuoka, M. M. (1970) *The Handbook for the Sixteen Personality Factor Questionnaire*, Champaign, Ill., Institute for Personality and Ability Testing.

Costa, P. T., Jr. and McCrae, R. R. (1976) 'Age differences in personality structure: A cluster analytic approach', *Journal of Gerontology*, **31**, pp. 564–70.

Costa, P. T., Jr. and McCrae, R. R. (1980a) 'Influence of E and N on subjective well-being: Happy and unhappy people', *Journal of Personality and Social Psychology*, **38**, pp. 668–78.

Costa, P. T., Jr. and McCrae, R. R. (1980b) 'Still stable after all these years: Personality as a key to some issues in adulthood and old age', in Baltes, P. B. and Brim, O. G., Jr. (Eds.), *Life-span Development and Behavior*, Vol. 3, New York, Academic Press.

Costa, P. T., Jr. and McCrae, R. R. (1984) 'Personality as a lifelong determinant of well-being', in Malatesta, C. and Izard, C. (Eds.), *Affective Processes in Adult Development and Aging*, Beverly Hills, Calif., Sage.

Costa, P. T., Jr., McCrae, R. R. and Norris, A. H. (1980) 'Personal adjustment to aging: Longitudinal prediction from neuroticism and extraversion', *Journal of Gerontology*, **36**, pp. 78–85.

Eaves, L. J. and Eysenck, H. J. (1975) 'The nature of extraversion: a genetical analysis', *Journal of Personality and Social Psychology.*, **32**, pp. 102–12.

Eysenck, H. J. (1947) *Dimensions of Personality*, London, Routledge and Kegan Paul.

Eysenck, H. J. (1954) *Psychology of Politics*, London, Routledge and Kegan Paul.

Eysenck, H. J. (1955) 'Cortical inhibition, figural aftereffect and theory of personality', *Journal of Abnormal and Social Psychology*, **51**, pp. 94–106.

Eysenck, H. J. (1964) 'Involuntary rest pauses in tapping as a function of drive and personality', *Perceptual and Motor Skills*, **18**, pp. 173–4.

Eysenck, H. J. (1969) 'The validity of the M. P. I.—Positive validity', in Eysenck, H. J. and Eysenck, S. B. G. (Eds.), *Personality Structure and Measurement*, San Diego, Calif., Robert R. Knapp.

Eysenck, H. J. (Ed.) (1971) *Readings in Extraversion-Introversion, 2: Fields of Application*, New York, Wiley.

Eysenck, H. J. and Eysenck, S. B. G. (1967) 'On the unitary nature of extraversion', *Acta Psychologica*, **26**, pp. 383–90.

Eysenck, H. J. and Eysenck, S. B. G. (1975) *Manual of the Eysenck Personality Questionnaire*, San Diego, Calif., EdITS.

Eysenck, H. J. and Eysenck, S. B. G. (1982) 'Recent advances in the cross-cultural study of personality', in Butcher, J. N. and Spielberger, C. D. (Eds.), *Advances in Personality Assessment*, Vol. 2, Hillsdale, N.J., Lawrence Erlbaum.

Eysenck, M. W. and Eysenck, H. J. (1980) 'Mischel and the concept of personality', *British Journal of Psychology*, **71**, pp. 191–204.

Eysenck, S. B. G. and Eysenck, H. J. (1963) 'On the dual nature of extraversion', *British Journal of Social and Clinical Psychology*, **2**, pp. 46–55.

Götz, K. O., Borisy, A. R., Lynn, R. and Eysenck, H. J. (1979) 'A new visual aesthetic sensitivity test: 1. Construction and psychometric properties', *Perceptual and Motor Skills*, **49**, 795–802.

Goldberg, L. R. (1981) 'Language and individual differences: The search for universals in personality lexicons', in Wheeler, L. (Ed.), *Review of Personality and Social Psychology*, Vol. 2, Beverly Hills, Calif., Sage.

Guilford, J. P. and Zimmerman, W. S. (1949) *The Guilford-Zimmerman Temperament Survey: Manual of Instructions and Interpretations*, Beverly Hills, Calif., Sheridan Supply.

Hathaway, S. R. and McKinley, J. C. (1940) 'A multiphasic personality schedule (Minnesota): I. Construction of the schedule', *Journal of Psychology*, **10**, pp. 249–54.

Holland, J. L. (1966) *The Psychology of Vocational Choice: A Theory of Personality Types and Model Environments*, Waltham, Mass., Blaisdell.

Kelly, E. L. (1975) 'Foreword', in Chun, K. T. *et al.* (Eds.), *Measures for Psychological Assessment: A Guide to 3,000 Original Sources and Their Applications*, Ann Arbor, Mich., Institute for Social Research.

Lynn, R. and Eysenck, H. J. (1961) 'Tolerance for pain, extraversion, and neuroticism', *Perceptual and Motor Skills*, **12**, pp. 161–2.

McCrae, R. R. and Costa, P. T., Jr. (1983) 'Joint factors in self-reports and ratings: Neuroticism, extraversion, and openness to experience', *Personality and Individual Differences*, **4**, pp. 245–55.

McCrae, R. R. and Costa, P. T., Jr (1985) 'Openness to experience', in Hogan, R. and Jones, W. H. (Eds.), *Perspectives in Personality: Theory, Measurement and Interpersonal Dynamics*, Greenwich, Conn., JAI Press.

McCrae, R. R. and Costa, P. T., Jr. (in press) 'Updating Norman's "adequate taxonomy": Intelligence and personality dimensions in natural language and in questionnaires', *Journal of Personality and Social Psychology*.

McLaughlin, R. J. and Eysenck, H. J. (1967) 'Extraversion, neuroticism and paired-associates learning', *Journal of Experimental Research in Personality*, **2**, pp. 128–32.

Maddi, S. R. (1980) *Personality Theories: A Comparative Analysis*, 4th ed., Homewood, Ill., Dorsey Press.

Norman, W. T. (1963) 'Toward an adequate taxonomy of personality attributes: Replicated factor structure in peer nomination personality ratings', *Journal of Abnormal and Social Psychology*, **66**, pp. 574–83.

Rokeach, M. (1960) *The Open and Closed Mind*, New York, Basic Books.

Souief, M. I., Eysenck, H. J. and White, P. O. (1969) 'A joint factorial study of the Guilford, Cattell and Eysenck scales', in Eysenck, H. J. and Eysenck, S. B. G. (Eds.), *Personality Structure and Measurement*, San Diego, Calif., Robert R. Knapp.

Shweder, R. A. (1975) 'How relevant is an individual difference theory of personality?', *Journal of Personality*, **43**, pp. 455–84.

Tellegen, A. and Atkinson, G. (1974) 'Openness to absorbing and self-altering experiences ("absorption"), a trait related to hypnotic susceptibility', *Journal of Abnormal Psychology*, **83**, pp. 268–77.

Tupes, E. C. and Christal, R. E. (1961) 'Recurrent personality factors based on trait ratings', *USAF ASD Technical Report*, pp. 61–97.

Wessman, A. E. and Ricks, D. F. (1966) *Mood and Personality*, New York, Holt, Rinehart and Winston.

Wiggins, J. S. (1968) 'Personality structure', *Annual Review of Psychology*, Vol. 19, Palo Alto, Calif. Annual Reviews.

Wrobel, T. A. and Lachar, D. (1982) 'Validity of the Wiener subtle and obvious scales for the MMPI: Another example of the importance of inventory item content', *Journal of Consulting and Clinical Psychology*, **50**, pp. 469–70.

# 6. Eysenck's Contribution to the Psychology of Personality

GORDON CLARIDGE

I have to say right at the beginning that it was with some diffidence that I agreed to present the 'predominantly negative' view of Eysenck's work in this debate about his contribution to personality theory. The reason is that I have always considered myself as veering more towards the sympathetic than towards the antipathetic pole of the love-hate-Eysenck dimension; and, as I shall try to show in this paper, my criticisms of Eysenck often reduce to differences of detail, emphasis, intepretation, experimental strategy and opinion about future directions, rather than amounting to fundamental disagreement with the broad style of his approach to personality. But perhaps I delude myself. Some years ago, at a symposium where Eysenck and I shared the floor as discussants, we were both asked to respond to a question about some point or other relating personality to drug effects. We disagreed and I recall that Eysenck, in his reply, commented with his usual dry humour that 'Dr Claridge has made something of a profession out of criticizing my theory.' So it is at the risk of reinforcing this image as an Eysenck 'hit man' (at least in the eyes of the recipient) that I offer this critical evaluation of his work.

Costa and McCrae, in their 'predominantly positive' essay which is the mirror twin to this paper, have made the task at one and the same time easier and yet more difficult. The forum they have chosen for debating Eysenck's contribution to personality theory is not one, I must confess, that I would have selected had our roles been reversed. Consequently, there is little among their early general points that one can find to disagree with: Eysenck must certainly rate among the most influential psychologists this century; without doubt he has brought order into the chaos of personality description; and his choice of theme was a brilliant insight. However, awkwardly for the format of this book, when Costa and McCrae turn to mild criticism of Eysenck—or, as they put it, 'adding new domains' to his theory—they persuade me to drop my own cudgels and rush to the defence of my old patron! For I cannot agree with them that adding what they call 'openness to experience' to the

73

existing dimensions of extraversion and neuroticism is the most convincing way to build upon Eysenck's ideas; to me—and I feel sure Eysenck himself would not demur—the suggestion seems arbitrary, plucked out of the air, idiosyncratic, and lacking the very logic of discovery which they appear to admire when praising Eysenck. This is not to say that the concept of 'openness to experience' is not, in its own right, a valid one. On the contrary, it could be said to offer an interesting perspective on facets of personality largely untouched by Eysenck's theory and, some would say, lacking in it: to quote from Costa and McCrae '... a broad scope of thoughts, feelings and behaviours: imagination, artistic interests, openness to inner feelings, the need for variety in actions, intellectual curiosity, non-dogmatic values.' Eysenckian theory has always sat awkwardly with such inward-looking concerns and while that might be a good reason for now pushing it to embrace them, the fact is that the theory in its present form is probably not very capable of doing so; or, if it is, only with revision of a different kind from that envisaged by Costa and McCrae—a point to which I shall return towards the end of this essay.

The problem with Costa and McCrae is that they misjudge where Eysenck's most novel contribution to our understanding of personality has really lain and therefore misplace their emphasis in offering a forward view of his theoretical approach. It is as though they stopped reading Eysenck after about 1957! For it was then, with the publication of his book, *Dynamics of Anxiety and Hysteria*—actually slightly before that, in his 1955 paper in the *Journal of Mental Science*—that Eysenck took the step which most drastically altered contemporary Western thought about personality. I am referring, of course, to his attempt to ground individual differences in their biological roots, to his search for the nervous system origins of the descriptive personality dimensions which he had earlier identified. The importance of that development can be judged by many criteria: the massive amount of research it has generated since then; the extent to which it has caught the imagination of others, whether to praise it, condemn it, or revise it; the ability of his biological theory to encompass a great deal of empirical data originally collected without reference to it; the convergence of his ideas with those of other workers, notably in Eastern Europe, where similar research, although having common origins, evolved quite separately until relatively recently; and, not least, the projected future place of Eysenck's contribution among the great schools of psychology. To take this last point further, I feel confident that, when Eysenck's work is ultimately evaluated from a truly historical perspective, it will be judged to have been significant because it represented a distinct surge forward in a long tradition of enquiry into the biology of temperament, a stream of thought stretching back to antiquity, emerging and re-emerging in several forms since then, and given a modern appearance by Eysenck's brilliant application of twentieth century psychological technology to an ancient question. An important part of the endeavour involved his use of factor analysis to identify major descriptive dimensions of personality whose biological correlates could then be sought; but in comparison with Eysenck's later work that exercise has, and I suspect will continue to have, the appearance of a tidying-up job, undertaken in preparation for the main task heralded by the 1950s extension to his theory.

By the same token as the above remarks, I cannot but feel that the search for future growing-points in Eysenck's theory—and hence for possible deficiencies in it—is most profitably directed towards its stance on the biology of personality and towards the ability of his *kind* of theory to answer, not just the particular questions posed by Eysenck himself, but also other, more searching, questions which will continue to be asked about the brain and the nature of Man. Missing this point, Costa and McCrae offer a superficial suggestion for elaborating Eysenck's schema of personality at its descriptive level, without reference to the sort of biological constructs that have given his theory such unique qualities.

Costa and McCrae also, incidentally, miss another point about Eysenck's work, namely its inextricable link with abnormal psychology. This has had several important consequences for the development of his theory, moulding it in very particular ways. Two of these are especially relevant here. One is that in identifying his descriptive dimensions Eysenck has always tried to anchor them firmly in the psychiatric sphere, defining their extremes by their aberrant or abnormal forms, a tactic having sound logistics in the continuity model of mental illness and in the idea that personality characteristics are, looked at from another point of view, the same things as predispositions to disorder. Another, related, consequence is that in seeking the biological bases of these dimensions (or predispositions) Eysenck has been able to strengthen his overall theory by drawing in data about their abnormal forms. We can therefore perceive in his approach a set of interdependent strategies for describing personality: look for the major ways in which people differ, as represented in the psychiatric disorders; find the normal personality counterparts of these 'types' and isolate their dimensional characteristics by factor analysis; then, keeping an eye on a wide range of evidence in the fields of normal and abnormal psychology, try to establish biological mechanisms that account both for normal individual variations and for the disorders to which these are aetiologically related. Eysenck's success in using this approach should surely caution us against departing drastically from it in seeking ways to improve upon his first approximation to personality description.

The fact that Costa and McCrae chose to conduct their own appraisal of Eysenck in a different universe of discourse from that intended here does, as mentioned earlier, make my own task of evaluation both easy and difficult. Easy because it eliminates repetitiveness in our respective contributions and allows me (as a not entirely uncommitted Eysenckian) to evade the responsibility of being artificially negative about Eysenck's work. Difficult because when earlier going through in my mind the possible format of this debate I anticipated that it would follow certain familiar ground rules, reflecting some topical concerns about Eysenck's theory as a biological theory of individual differences. As it is, I find myself both proponent and critic, in danger of becoming a straw man trying to beat himself to death!

More seriously, planning the structure of this discussion has faced two difficulties. One concerns the level of detail or generality at which it should be conducted. The other is finding a suitable point of entry into Eysenck's very extensive research on personality. Regarding the first problem, I have chosen what I feel is likely to be the most appropriate arrangement for this book, namely to try to draw out some of the broad areas of controversy that surround Eysenck's work, along the way pointing out where, as I see it, his theory might be modified and his general approach to individual differences usefully adapted to solve new problems in personality research. As for where to begin, it is probably most logical to start at the centre of Eysenck's theory, namely his proposal for a biological basis of introversion-extraversion (I-E) and neuroticism (N).

Currently the subject of some disagreement between Gray and Eysenck, the controversy surrounding that question is not new. Ever since the beginning of the 'biological' phase of Eysenck's theory, there has been a continuing attempt to try to construct the optimal conceptual nervous system that can account for those individual differences enclosed by the I-E and N dimensions of personality. Eysenck's first efforts, in the mid-1950s, led him to make use of the Pavlovian concept of cortical excitatory-inhibitory balance and to confine himself to the explanation of introversion-extraversion; neuroticism was given little causal status. Looked at in historical context both of these features of his early theorizing were understandable: reliance on a Pavlovian perspective on the nervous system because it was from there (in Pavlov's theory of 'nervous types') that the most explicit statements about temperament and brain organization had already come; concentration on introversion-extraversion because of the priority given by Eysenck to that dimension as a discriminator of the major forms of neurotic disorder.

The limitations of the original theory were quickly exposed, however, and two things soon became evident. First, although as statisically derived descriptive factors I-E and N were independent, at a causal level they were somehow interactive; this was revealed especially clearly in experimental studies which included neurotic patients (as extreme cases of both dimensions), where differences between individuals could not be explained by reference to introversion-extraversion alone (Claridge, 1960). Secondly, the Pavlovian concepts contained in the model seemed, perhaps because of unfamiliarity, difficult to relate to the real nervous system and hence appeared to defy further elaboration.

As is now well-known, the 1960s saw a flurry of activity in the Eysenck school which, in one way or another, attempted to deal with these two problems. Gray (1964) published some of the later Russian work on nervous typology, and wrestled with the twin problems of translating its constructs into Western terminology and trying to align them with Eysenck's I-E and N dimensions (Gray, 1967). I myself, in my 1967 book *Personality and Arousal*, proposed an alternative biological model, based mainly on studies of psychiatric patients, which I felt might correct some of the weaknesses in Eysenck's earlier theory. And Eysenck (1967), responding to criticism of his earlier formulation, completely revised it, arriving at a new conceptual nervous system model for introversion-extraversion and neuroticism.

This new model warrants some further scrutiny here since, as far as I can tell, it still essentially represents Eysenck's final statement on the biological basis of the two dimensions in question. With typical panache Eysenck was not content, as most of us had been, to refer merely to 'arousal' as a source of central nervous variation possibly related to personality differences; he also brought into play the closely related term, 'activation'. These two processes were, and I suppose still are, considered to relate, respectively, to introversion-extraversion and to neuroticism. Referred to the 'real' nervous system, arousal—stemming from the ascending reticular formation—is said to steer introverted and extraverted behaviour; while neuroticism reflects activation arising from the limbic system, 'emotional brain', or Papez circuit.

On the face of it, this revision does seem to handle quite well most of the difficulties inherent in the earlier model. It certainly incorporates reference to actual central nervous structures which a mass of evidence (Eysenckian and otherwise) suggests do underlie some important behavioural differences between individuals. Given that the two processes of arousal and activation are assigned equal status, it also allows for the infinite permutations of them demanded by the orthogonality of I-E and N as descriptive dimensions. This is true in two senses: first, if we are comparing *across* people, assigning them to a position in the two-dimensional space according to their characteristic 'setting-points' for arousal and activation; and, secondly, if we are using the model to describe *within-individual* behaviours that will always represent the interactive influence of the two processes.

But therein lies one of the snags of the theory. For in practice its very flexibility makes it difficult to arrive at predictions either about 'static' personality differences or about the underlying dynamics of the behavioural variations to which these give rise. To illustrate the point, let me take a typical experimental test of the model of the kind often quoted in the Eysenckian literature. Suppose we are comparing, say, reaction times to stimuli of varying intensity in subjects categorized according to their questionnaire scores of extraversion and neuroticism. Performance will presumably be influenced by the relative degrees to which the arousal (I-E) and activation (N) circuits are excited. If the situation is very anxiety-provoking for the subject then the latter will certainly be brought into play; if not he may be merely 'aroused'. And, of course, the extent to which all of this occurs will depend on the more permanent individual differences associated with the person's position on the I-E and N dimensions. A further complication in the hypothetical experiment I just quoted is that reaction times may not, even if other things are equal, be linearly related to stimulus strength; with very strong stimuli responses may become paradoxically slower—an example of the many inverted-U effects that litter the field. The likelihood of this happening will also show individual variation since, in order to account for such phenomena (assigned in Pavlovian theory to transmarginal inhibition), Eysenck built into his 1967 model the additional idea of inhibitory feedback mechanisms that are triggered off at very high levels of arousal and/or activation.

Given a system of such interactive complexity, the potential outcomes are clearly numerous, and disentangling the reasons for any one of them presents a daunting prospect. Of course, it could be argued, with justification, that the relationships between brain and personality—like those between brain and behaviour in general— *are* complex, and teasing them out will eventually be possible, with patience and ingenuity. However, my impression is that efforts in that direction, using Eysenck's 1967 model as a guideline, have faded out somewhat in recent years and that many of the questions raised originally by his theory remain unanswered. If we ask why, then I think we can discover many reasons. Some are a consequence of later developments in Eysenck's own work, to which I shall return. But there are two other more immediate reasons that have to do with the 1967 model itself.

One concerns the conceptually rather naive manner in which Eysenck has attempted to map personality differences onto the nervous system. I can perhaps best explain my disquiet on that score by borrowing the terminology of a different literature, that of neuropsychology, and the distinction made there between 'fixed structure' and 'dynamic process' views of brain activity (Cohen, 1982). It seems to me that it is in the former sense in which Eysenck has visualized the connection between his personality dimensions and the brain; that he sees introversion-extraversion as somehow 'localized' in the ascending reticular formation and neuroticism in the limbic system, analogous to the hemispheric localization of psychological functions like language and spatial ability. Yet his personality constructs are formally quite different from the latter and, furthermore, the physiological constructs he utilizes have more the properties of dynamic processes than of fixed structures. To put the argument another way, it seems more likely that the brain circuitry to which he refers is *actually* inextricably interconnected and that it is physiologically (and anatomically) unreal to partition it, as Eysenck does, into two components which somehow map, separately, onto what after all are merely statistically derived composites of behaviour. A further consequence of Eysenck's perspective here is that it encourages a simplistic 'additive' view of the biology of personality: that individual make-ups consist of a little bit of arousal and a great deal of activation, or moderate amounts of both, or not much of each, and so on. While to conceptualize the personality in that way might be just about acceptable at the descriptive level—though even there dubious— to do so at the biological level seems implausible.

Let me turn now to what I think is the second deficiency in Eysenck's 1967 model. Here we need to consider a somewhat different aspect of the purported relationship between the descriptive dimensions and the two causal processes allegedly underlying them. It is self-evident that both processes—arousal and activation—refer, at their high end, to states of increased central nervous excitability and, within the restraining limits of inhibitory feedback, to increased behavioural vigour. The most extreme example of CNS excitability should therefore be where both processes are operating in unison at their upper limits—in individual difference terms among neurotic introverts or, in psychiatric populations, dysthymic patients. This indeed seems to be the case. But what about other combinations of I-E and N? Especially, what about neurotic *extraverts* and their psychiatric counterparts, hysterics and psychopaths? Logically, they should have *low* arousal and *high* activation, one counteracting the other and giving them some intermediate biological status. But that certainly is not true; on the contrary, there is ample evidence that such individuals actually display the *lowest* arousal/activation of all of the individuals encompassed by Eysenck's I-E and N dimensions (Claridge, 1967). How do we explain this rather serious failure of the theory?

The difficulty, I suspect, lies in the interpretation of 'neuroticism'. Traditionally the term has been used rather loosely as a synonym for 'anxiety'; which of course it is—in introverts. But as developed by Eysenck—and especially with his increasing success in defining it independently of introversion-extraversion—it has, I would suggest, taken on a quite different meaning. For example, in the item content of the N-scale from the Eysenck Personality Questionnaire (Eysenck and Eysenck, 1975), neuroticism now seems to refer more to a general state of distress, unstable mood, or mental pain which, while reflecting dysthymic anxiety in the introvert, could have quite different origins in the extravert; one possibility is that the low arousal state ascribed by Eysenck to extraversion becomes uncomfortably so in some extreme individuals, leading to abnormal mood. There is no *a priori* reason why the existence of N as an orthogonal *descriptive* factor implies that it should have a unitary biological basis. Indeed, it may be that the price Eysenck has paid for achieving statistical independence of the factor is to sacrifice the possibility of finding such a basis.

Those who have followed the debate between Gray and Eysenck about the biological basis of introversion-extraversion and neuroticism will appreciate the significance of some of the points I have just made. For, although not always articulating them in quite the same way, Gray also seems to have recognized similar problems with Eysenck's 1967 model. He has neatly side-stepped them by collapsing N and I-E (at its introverted end) into a single continuum of anxiety, arguing that this allows one to find a better fit between the underlying biology and at least some of the personality variation described by Eysenck's dimensions; superimposed on the latter, Gray's scheme looks visually like a 45 degree rotation of I-E and N, 'anxiety' running diagonally from neurotic introversion to stable extraversion (Gray, 1970). On the face of it, this modified arrangement has much to recommend it, especially as Gray has also been able to offer a convincing biological explanation of the dimension based on thorough neurophysiological analysis of real brain (albeit real rat brain) structures that mediate anxiety (Gray, 1982). In this respect it is interesting to note that Gray's alternative formulation also avoids the awkward difficulty in Eysenck's model, remarked upon earlier, of regarding 'arousal' and 'activation' as somehow separable; for the neural circuitry emphasized by Gray includes, in a single dynamic mechanism, the limbic and midbrain structures mediating both of these allegedly different influences.

Although Gray's revision has certain obvious advantages it, too, has certain weaknesses, when looked at from the point of view of Eysenck's original aims. One, of course, is its almost complete reliance on data from animal research where the benefits of taking explanation closer to the nervous system are largely offset by the inability to deal with some questions of the kind raised, for example, by models that take human psychophysiology as their starting point; certainly some bridging of the gap between these two approaches is urgently needed.

A further limitation of Gray's model, as a *complete* alternative to Eysenck's, is that it begins to look rather ragged—and starts to lose its biological firmness—once Gray moves away from the explanation of anxiety and tries to account for personality variations in the other quadrants of the two-dimensional space enclosed by I-E and N. His bisection of the latter in order to define 'anxiety' led him to suppose that there might be another dimension, orthogonal to it; this, plausibly, Gray identified as 'impulsivity' (Gray, 1981). But the possible biological basis of *this* dimension raises problems, as Gray himself admits (Gray *et al.*, 1983). Without going into the detailed arguments, there seem to be at least two possibilities. One is that impulsive individuals are those whose physiological status is diametrically opposite to that of the highly anxious; in which case they are located in the wrong place, judged with reference to either the Eysenck dimensions or Gray's rotation of them, i.e., they fall in the stable extravert quadrant, rather than in the *neurotic* extravert quadrant where impulsivity originates.[1] The other possibility, which theoretically could allow for an explanation nicely independent of the neurophysiology of anxiety, is that impulsivity is due to increased sensitivity to reward; but, according to Gray, the neural basis of this is very uncertain.

There is actually a third possibility considered by Gray, one which exposes some further difficulties in current Eysenckian and neo-Eysenckian theories of personality, as well as introducing the next part of our discussion here. It concerns 'psychoticism' (P), the most recent of the personality dimensions developed by Eysenck. I shall consider psychoticism more fully in a moment, but first let me comment on its relevance to Gray's revision of the two-dimensional model. Quite apart from whether the new dimension measures what it sets out to measure (a point I shall return to) its existence in descriptive personality data has clearly caused considerable embarrassment to students of Eysenck, especially those seeking alternative biological explanations of his other two dimensions. As Gray *et al.* (1983) note, psychoticism correlates with impulsivity, making its status as an *independent* dimension difficult to maintain; yet it does seem to be a 'strong' concept (Eysenck and Eysenck, 1976). Faced with this dilemma, Gray resorts to what can only be considered a pathetic solution, namely to place P at some (unspecified) oblique angle to his major anxiety and impulsivity dimensions. Another worker who has been led into the same alley is Zuckerman (1984) who has tried to fit his concept of 'sensation-seeking'—which correlates with *both* impulsivity *and* psychoticism—into the Eysenck/Gray scheme of things; again with the difficulty of collapsing three dimensions into two—or perhaps two and a half!

The conclusion we are forced to, I think, is that as work on Eysenck's theory has progressed the picture regarding the biology of even those aspects of personality it encompasses has, inevitably, become more complicated. To the outsider it must seem like a hopeless mess; even to those inside it, trying to re-discover an elegant symmetry comparable to that of Eysenck's original model is proving a difficult task. My own feeling is that we are at some painful intermediate stage in which a great deal of data on the biology of I-E, N, P and various derivatives is accumulating and where several different alternatives to Eysenck's own model are, quite rightly, being tried for fit. None—to reverse the analogy—is the prince's shoe, but they all allow the occupant to walk, after a fashion. In the meantime, perhaps there is much to be said for not tampering too much with Eysenck's original conception of three independent dimensions of introversion-extraversion, neuroticism and psychoticism. While these may not map directly onto the nervous system in quite the way Eysenck believes, they nevertheless provide a firmly established *descriptive* framework within which to work; if only in offering a set of well-defined criteria by which to select individuals for study. To introduce a practical note here, we know very little, for example, about the relative biological status of people chosen according to the various possible combinations of scores on the I-E, N and P dimensions.

As mentioned a moment ago, the introduction of psychoticism, or rather its revival (for such it was), immensely complicated Eysenck's theory, at the same time, in my view, giving it a fresh lease of life. Despite the importance of this 'new' dimension, I feel it would be excessively repetitive to discuss it in detail again, since I have done so previously on two occasions (Claridge, 1981, 1983) and, even more recently, updated some of my thoughts on it (Claridge, 1985). Here I shall confine myself to a few general comments, using the discussion as a vehicle for moving towards my overall conclusions about Eysenck's theory and the possible future directions of biological personality research.

Probably the most controversial issue surrounding Eysenck's psychoticism dimension, and certainly the most relevant here, is whether his questionnaire measure of it—the P-scale (Eysenck and Eysenck, 1975)—actually measures psychotic traits, that is, traits that relate in some way to the psychoses, in a manner comparable to that which links the N-scale to the neuroses. My impression is that the prevailing opinion is that it does not; that, because of the heavy weighting in the scale towards items concerned with aggressiveness, impulsiveness, cruelty and emotional indifference, the general feeling is that P has more to do with psychopathy or anti-social behaviour. This certainly shows through in the handling of the dimension by Gray and Zuckerman, referred to above. Indeed, they go to great pains to emphasize its overlap with impulsivity and/or sensation-seeking, hence enabling them to assign it to the non-psychotic domain of personality description and hence, too, allowing them to avoid the awkwardness of having to incorporate a third dimension into their thinking; even Gray's attempt to tackle the latter problem is, as we have seen, half-hearted and indecisive. Influenced by their views and by those of others of a similar opinion, 'psychoticism' has almost passed into the linguistic currency of the Eysenck school as a synonym for 'psychopathy'. Eysenck himself has not helped in this regard because he has tended to discuss P very much within the context of its relevance to criminality, passing rather too easily from that to its status as a dimension of psychotic disposition. (This further example of his 'sleight of Hans' in debate is reminiscent of the habit he had, in his earlier writings, of using the terms 'hysteria' and 'extraversion' interchangeably.)

The fact that the P-scale may partly tap anti-social traits does *not*, however, entirely argue against it as a measure of truly psychotic characteristics. Quite the reverse, for there is considerable evidence, reviewed in my previous evaluations of the scale—and quoted by Eysenck himself—that such traits may be frequently observed in individuals who, on genetic or other grounds, would be expected to load highly on psychoticism (in its proper etymological sense). This does not mean to say that all is well with the P-scale. In its latest, published, form it is perhaps too weak, likely to capture individuals who are anti-social for many other reasons; it also lacks the discriminatory 'bite' imparted by the more manifestly psychotic items found in earlier versions.

There is also another, quite different, problem which again I have mentioned in my previous discussions of the P-scale but which I would like to re-emphasize here because I think it strikes at the heart of the questionnaire measurement of psychoticism. This concerns the general difficulty of measuring psychotic character-istics in normal people, especially if, like Eysenck, one chooses to do so by trying to identify relevant personality, or temperamental, traits. Here I am not referring to psychometric problems, like endorsement rates, response bias, or defensiveness; but rather to the peculiar quality of the psychotic personality: its contradictory nature, ambivalence, disharmony and the appearance, side by side, of opposing traits which may be difficult to capture in a single, unitary scale. I have elaborated that view of psychoticism elsewhere (Claridge, 1985) and even as I write this I notice that, in the slightly different context of trying to answer the question 'What is Schizophrenia', Manfred Bleuler (1984) has recently made a similar point; he refers to the 'ambitendencies' in the schizophrenic personality, '. . . the inner shambles and disunity: "I want what I don't want". "Being alone is horrible; I want to be alone".'

It is possible, of course, that high scores on Eysenck's P-scale do in some indirect way reflect the disharmony of traits which Bleuler believes (and I agree with him) is the crux of the psychotic personality. On the other hand, perhaps we need a new perspective on the question, to develop new ways of assessing the structure of 'psychoticism', by examining it not with reference to a *single* personality scale but as an unusual configuration of traits that belong to more than one of the Eysenckian dimensions, or their equivalents. Pursuing this last point, and returning briefly to Gray's revision of Eysenck, we could ask, for example, what kind of personality might be represented in people who show *both* high anxiety *and* high impulsivity—a logically possible, though apparently disharmonious, combination in Gray's scheme. Perhaps this *is* 'psychoticism'—or part of it—and perhaps herein lies the solution to Gray's dilemma over the location of Eysenck's third dimension.

It would help, of course, if we had a viable biological model for psychoticism. Eysenck himself (Eysenck and Eysenck, 1976), following Gray (Gray, 1973), has emphasized aggressiveness as the crucial feature, but personally I think this is incomplete, not least for the reasons just given with regard to the complexity of psychotic personality structure when considered even at the descriptive level. As an alternative I personally believe there may still be some mileage in the 'dissociation' model which I suggested some years ago (Claridge, 1967). This was based on the observation that psychotic patients show evidence of what appears to be an unusual 'uncoupling' of central nervous response, as judged by their patterns of psychophysi-ological activity; the same seems to be true of normal subjects with high scores on the

Eysenck P-scale (Claridge and Birchall, 1978) and may provide the basis for a general statement about the biological basis of psychoticism (Claridge, 1983; Claridge *et al.*, 1983). More speculatively, the notion of central nervous uncoupling suggests an intriguing biological match to the psychotic disharmony of personality traits referred to earlier.

The fact is, however, that none of the conceptual nervous systems currently on offer in the Eysenckian school offers a very satisfactory account of the biological basis of psychoticism. For that reason my colleagues and I have very recently started to pursue a different line of enquiry into the question (Claridge and Broks, 1985). It is one which, I believe, and for reasons I will come to, is not a drastic departure from Eysenck's own, but merely a development of it, though involving—to descend into the jargon of our times—something of a 'paradigm shift'. The approach I am referring to has entailed conjoining two themes that have previously lain somewhat outside the Eysenckian literature, but which may help to answer some of the questions it has asked, as well as others it could be criticized for not addressing.

One theme concerns the measurement of 'psychoticism'. Eysenck's approach to this has been to look for characteristics firmly embedded in the *personality* domain. An alternative is to seek to map across psychotic *symptomatology* into the general population; in practical terms to devise questionnaires with an item content that reflects the quality of cognitive and other disturbances found, in a more extreme form, among psychotics themselves. Work by others on such questionnaires (e.g., Chapman *et al.*, 1980) attests to their value and, persuaded by this, some years ago we started developing our own questionnaire which, in its latest version, has a two-scale format, including a scale of 'schizotypy'. Details of the questionnaire and its rationale can be found elsewhere (Claridge and Broks, 1985). Suffice it to say here that its style and content were very much influenced by recent thinking on the 'borderline states' (Spitzer *et al.*, 1979); the argument was that the clinical features of these conditions provide an ideal template for designing scales of psychotic characteristics, for use in normal populations.

The second theme that guided our thinking concerns our search for a point of entry into the possible biological basis of schizotypy, the latter aspect of 'psychoticism' being the one on which we have so far concentrated our efforts. There, as the most promising route, we chose to try to map across from recent findings, especially from neuropsychology, that schizophrenics show marked anomalies of hemisphere organization (Flor-Henry, 1983). Apart from the weight of evidence obtained on schizophrenics themselves, there was another, more fundamental theoretical reason for our choice. It can be argued that the disturbances in schizophrenia lie crucially in the higher nervous system, in perception, language, thought, social cognition and so on —indeed, as Frith (1979) has suggested, in all aspects of conscious awareness. And, of course, the study of the horizontal organization of the nervous system has become one powerful way of trying to expose the mechanisms underlying such processes. Transferring these ideas into the domain of personality research, we have recently been able to demonstrate that normal schizotypal individuals show patterns of hemisphere asymmetry consistent with those observed in schizophrenic patients, suggesting that here indeed may be a possible biological basis for at least certain features of 'psychoticism' (Broks, 1984; Rawlings and Claridge, 1984; Broks *et al.*, 1984).

The work to which I have just referred has, I believe, implications for Eysenck's theory of greater generality than its narrow relevance to our understanding of 'psychoticism'. For I would suggest that it articulates a deeper criticism of the perspective on personality taken by Eysenck and by others (including myself!) who have adopted a similar viewpoint. A manifest gap in the Eysenckian school of thought and one which has sometimes made it distasteful to others is its lack of concern with those aspects of the psychology of Man—feelings, ideas, motives and other experiential data—which many believe to be the essence of 'personality'. Eysenck's neglect of these features stems from his justifiable dislike of the alternative psychologies that have dominated their exploration. In seeking to bring experimental psychology to bear on the study of personality he has, with his preference for biological explanations, turned to conceptual nervous system models formulated within a behaviourist framework. Traditionally these models, even if originating in human psychophysiology, have referred their constructs to relatively low-level brain structures and, relying heavily on animal data, have been poorly fitted to explain those features of personality that implicate the higher mental processes. Attempts to relate the latter to the higher *nervous* processes that underlie them must surely be an important next step in the search for more complete biological models of personality. The example I have quoted here—examining individual differences in interhemispheric organization—is one way in which this might be achieved; as it happens, it could prove to be a particularly fruitful route to take, given that the differential functioning of the cerebral hemispheres plays such a crucial role in shaping human psychological activity.

Contemplating such an elaboration of Eysenck's basic ideas about brain and personality, one is led to ask a further question. How might future biological models hope to incorporate both these new ideas and the original constructs of Eysenckian theory? I would like to make a suggestion. My proposal is that Eysenck's personality dimensions (and derivatives of them) ought properly to be considered dimensions of *temperament*, that is, sources of variation finding physiological representation fairly low down in the nervous system, in limbic, reticular and related circuitry that has been the focus of much research by Gray and much speculation by Eysenck, Zuckerman, myself and others. An exact template of how that circuitry maps onto temperamental differences remains to be discovered, but it undoubtedly exists. Superimposed on it in Man (or, more correctly, interactive with it) is a further massive source of variation due to differences in the organization of the higher nervous system which, through language, thought, memory (both conscious and unconscious) and other cognitive processes shapes the expression of the underlying temperamental dispositions.

It is, of course, at the interface between these two levels of neural function that some of the most difficult conceptual problems for future personality theories lie. However, to return very briefly to schizophrenia research, it is instructive (and slightly encouraging) to realize that not dissimilar questions are being asked there. Thus, in a recent penetrating review of hemisphere research on schizophrenia Gruzelier (1983) considers the several possible alternative mechanisms that could account for schizophrenic behaviour: abnormal organization of higher nervous processes like language; deviant functioning in lower-level structures, such as hippocampus, mediating arousal and selective attention; or, more likely, an interplay between the two. The comparison, incidentally, is not mere analogy. For one of the important things Eysenck has surely taught us is to look towards the abnormal for our explanations of the normal and, in this respect, my guess is that with an understanding of the psychotic states will come a greater insight into many aspects of personality, including some that are presently referred to other 'dimensions'.

To conclude, if my evaluation of Eysenck in this paper has sometimes been harsher than I appeared to promise at the outset, this will be taken, I hope, as constructively complimentary rather than destructively critical. No one, least of all Eysenck, would wish to argue that scientific theories are immutable. However, the good ones are basically correct, though capable of change: the great ones are those that take a significant leap forward in our understanding of accumulated knowledge. I believe that Eysenck's theory is both good and great. If he himself has stayed with certain ideas, or been blind to others, longer than he should, then that is his prerogative. More important is the fact that the overall direction of his thinking about personality has the ineffable quality of having come from somewhere in the history of psychology and of going on into its future, not unchanged but still recognizable. Those who remain unconvinced have usually been obsessively preoccupied with the details of his theory, impatient with its failures of prediction, or angered by the uncompromising statements of a man committed to his viewpoint. But then that, too, is their prerogative—and a sure sign of individual psychological differences!

## NOTE

1   Gray's suggested solution to this difficulty is to align the low end of his anxiety dimension with 'venturesomeness', one of the two components into which the Eysencks have recently subdivided 'impulsivity' (Eysenck, S. B. G. and Eysenck, H. J., 1978). This does not, of course, solve the problem since it still leaves open the question of what is the biological basis of the other component, namely 'true' impulsivity—which is actually the stronger concept in personality theory and psychopathology.

## REFERENCES

Bleuler, M. (1984) 'What is schizophrenia?', *Schizophrenia Bulletin*, **10**, pp. 8–9.
Broks, P. (1984) 'Schizotypy and hemisphere function. II. Performance asymmetry on a verbal divided visual field task', *Personality and Individual Differences*, **6**, pp. 649–56.
Broks, P., Claridge, G., Matheson, J. and Hargeaves, J. (1984) 'Schizotypy and hemisphere function. IV. Story comprehension under binaural and monaural listening conditions,' *Personality and Individual Differences*, **5**, pp. 665–70.
Chapman, L. J., Edell, W. S. and Chapman, J. P. (1980) 'Physical anhedonia, perceptual aberration, and psychosis proneness', *Schizophrenia Bulletin*, **6**, pp. 639–53.
Claridge, G. (1960) 'The excitation-inhibition balance in neurotics', in Eysenck, H. J. (Ed.), *Experiments in Personality*, Vol. 2, London, Routledge and Kegan Paul.
Claridge, G. (1967) *Personality and Arousal*, Oxford, Pergamon Press.
Claridge, G. (1981) 'Psychoticism', in Lynn, R. (Ed.), *Dimensions of Personality. Papers in Honour of H. J. Eysenck*, Oxford, Pergamon Press.
Claridge, G. (1983) 'The Eysenck Psychoticism Scale', in Butcher, J. N. and Spielberger, C. D. (Eds.), *Advances in Personality Assessment*, Vol. 2, Hillsdale, Lawrence Erlbaum.
Claridge, G. (1985) *Origins of Mental Illness*, Oxford, Blackwell.
Claridge, G. and Birchall, P. M. A. (1978) 'Bishop, Eysenck, Block, and psychoticism', *Journal of Abnormal Psychology*, **87**, pp. 664–68.
Claridge, G. and Broks, P. (1985) 'Schizotypy and hemisphere function. I. Theoretical considerations and the measurement of schizotypy', *Personality and Individual Differences*, **5**, pp. 633–48.
Claridge, G., Robinson, D. L. and Birchall, P. M. A. (1983) 'Characteristics of schizophrenics' and neurotics' relatives', *Personality and Individual Differences*, **4**, pp. 651–64.
Cohen, G. (1982) 'Theoretical interpretations of lateral asymmetries', in Beaumont, J. (Ed.), *Divided Visual Field Studies of Cerebral Organisation*, London, Academic Press.

Eysenck, H. J. (1955) 'A dynamic theory of anxiety and hysteria', *Journal of Mental Science*, **101**, pp. 28–51.

Eysenck, H. J. (1957) *Dynamics of Anxiety and Hysteria*, London, Routledge and Kegan Paul.

Eysenck, H. J. (1967) *The Biological Basis of Personality*, Springfield, Charles C. Thomas.

Eysenck, H. J. and Eysenck, S. B. G. (1975) *Manual of the Eysenck Personality Questionnaire*, London, Hodder and Stoughton.

Eysenck, H. J. and Eysenck, S. B. G. (1976) *Psychoticism as a Dimension of Personality*, London, Hodder and Stoughton.

Eysenck, S. B. G. and Eysenck, H. J. (1978) 'Impulsiveness and venturesomeness: Their position in a dimensional system of personality description', *Psychological Reports*, **43**, pp. 1247–55.

Flor-Henry, P. (1983) *Cerebral Basis of Psychopathology*, Boston, John Wright/PSG.

Frith, C. D. (1979) 'Consciousness, information processing and schizophrenia', *British Journal of Psychiatry*, **134**, pp. 225–35.

Gray, J. A. (1964) *Pavlov's Typology*, Oxford, Pergamon Press.

Gray, J. A. (1967) 'Strength of the nervous system, introversion-extraversion, conditionability, and arousal', *Behaviour Research and Therapy*, **5**, pp. 151–69.

Gray, J. A. (1970) 'The psychophysiological basis of introversion-extraversion', *Behaviour Research and Therapy*, **8**, pp. 249–66.

Gray, J. A. (1973) 'Causal theories of personality and how to test them', in Royce, F. R. (Ed.), *Multivariate Analysis and Psychological Theory*, New York, Academic Press.

Gray, J. A. (1981) 'A critique of Eysenck's theory of personality', in Eysenck, H. J. (Ed.), *A Model for Personality*, Berlin, Springer-Verlag.

Gray, J. A. (1982) *The Neuropsychology of Anxiety*, Oxford, Clarendon Press.

Gray, J. A., Owen, S., Davis, N. and Tsaltas, E. (1983) 'Psychological and physiological relations between anxiety and impulsivity', in Zuckerman, M. (Ed.), *Biological Bases of Sensation Seeking, Impulsivity, and Anxiety*, Hillsdale, Lawrence Erlbaum.

Gruzelier, J. H. (1983) 'A critical assessment and integration of lateral asymmetries in schizophrenia', in Myslobodsky, M. (Ed.), *Hemisyndromes: Psychobiology, Neurology, and Psychiatry*, New York, Academic Press.

Rawlings, D. and Claridge, G. (1984) 'Schizotypy and hemisphere function. III. Performance asymmetries on tasks of letter recognition and local-global processing', *Personality and Individual Differences*, **5**, pp. 657–63.

Spitzer, R. L., Endicott, J. and Gibbon, M. (1979) 'Crossing the border into borderline personality and borderline schizophrenia: The development of criteria', *Archives of General Psychiatry*, **36**, pp. 17–24.

Zuckerman, M. (1984) 'Sensation seeking: A comparative approach to a human trait', *The Behavioural and Brain Sciences*, **7**, pp. 413–71.

# Interchange

## COSTA AND McCRAE REPLY TO CLARIDGE

Given the differences in our respective research interests, it is not surprising that we differ from Claridge in what we perceive as Eysenck's major contribution to personality psychology. It is also worth pointing out that perceptions of Eysenck's work differ geographically: few American psychologists would concur in Claridge's opinion that Eysenck's biological theories constitute the 'step which most drastically altered contemporary Western thought about personality.' Americans, noting all the perplexities in biological theory that Claridge points out, are more impressed with Eysenck's manifest success in describing and measuring personality. In the end, it is a tribute to his wide-ranging thought that Eysenck can be seen either as a brilliant taxonomist of individual differences, or as a pioneer in the study of the biological basis of personality.

Which aspect of Eysenck's work one chooses to emphasize is, therefore, somewhat arbitrary. It becomes important, however, when considering directions for future research. We have suggested that it is entirely in the spirit and tradition of Eysenck to extend the description of personality to new dimensions beyond E, N and P, provided that the new dimensions are independent, comparably broad, and well-grounded in empirical research. We have offered the concept of openness to experience as a candidate. Claridge thinks this approach is somehow illegitimate, a claim we would dispute.

Indeed, Claridge seems to have a peculiar view of Eysenck as a biological purist, even suggesting that his model of personality shows a 'lack of concern with . . . feelings, ideas, motives and other experiential data.' True enough, Eysenck considers these phenomena as phenotypic rather than genotypic aspects of personality, but he has hardly ignored them. As the manuals for his inventories show, personality is assessed, and scores interpreted, in precisely these terms. His research on such issues as political ideology and aesthetic sensitivity shows a far-reaching concern for individual differences in many domains not directly grounded in biology. Thus, Claridge's view that the proposal of an openness dimension is 'arbitrary' and 'idiosyncratic' because it is derived neither from biological theory nor by extrapolation from psychopathology seems unwarranted.

The first of these criticisms is anachronistic, for Eysenck himself proposed the basic dimensions of personality years before he formulated his biological theories. Indeed, the theories were created in order to explain observable differences in human beings. If individuals also differ along a dimension of openness to experience, a comprehensive theory of personality must also provide an explanation for those differences. It is probably fair to say that Eysenck would consider a theory of openness incomplete unless a plausible biological basis were proposed; this is a problem that we would be delighted to see Claridge and his colleagues tackle.

It is true that Eysenck has been strongly influenced in his choice of personality dimensions by abnormal psychology. Psychiatric disorders provide one of the most striking and significant instances of individual differences, and, particularly in the case of N, indisputably point to a major dimension of normal temperament. Eysenck has also shown the influence of E on the specific form of neurosis—dysthymic vs. hysteric—that individuals excessively high in N are likely to suffer. But it would be an overstatement to suggest that Eysenck's conceptualization of E is based solely on psychopathology. His postulation of an E dimension was also based on widespread observation of normal individual differences in sociability and liveliness. In the case of extraversion, it would appear more accurate to say that Eysenck applied a normal dimension to illuminate psychopathology than *vice versa*. Similarly, we would hope that researchers would investigate the influence of openness (as well as conscientiousness and agreeableness) on the manifestations of psychopathology; but even if no relations are found, we would hardly consider that grounds for disqualifying them as important dimensions of personality.

In view of Claridge's objections, it was heartening to us to hear recently from Eysenck himself that he now acknowledges the independence of openness from his three dimensions, and is willing to entertain the notion that P may be related to agreeableness or conscientiousness. 'If we could really demonstrate such fundamental agreement, then perhaps we would have the beginnings of a generally acceptable set of dimensions of personality' (Eysenck, personal communication, 24 February 1984).


## CLARIDGE REPLIES TO COSTA AND McCRAE

[Claridge incorporates his reply to Costa and McCrae in his chapter.]

# Part V: Intelligence

# 7. The Theory of Intelligence

ARTHUR R. JENSEN

## Background

Eysenck's vision has helped to restore the study of human intelligence from its formerly fallen status as merely a branch of applied psychometric technology to the status of a major phenomenon warranting the full force of empirical investigation and theoretical development in its own right, in the tradition of the natural sciences.

Four words characterize Eysenck's approach to the study of intelligence: objective, quantitative, analytical, biological. These adjectives would seem inevitable for one who has followed closely in the footsteps of Galton (1822–1911), Spearman (1863–1945), and Burt (1883–1971)—the principal founders of the British school of differential psychology, of which Eysenck has become the leading modern exponent. Indeed, Eysenck's academic pedigree is quite directly linked with these three historically influential figures. When I first met Eysenck, on 11 July 1956, I recall having noticed that his roomy office in the old Maudsley Hospital was adorned with a number of large portraits—a pantheon of his personal heroes in psychology, presumably. There were portraits of Galton and Spearman, along with those of Hull, Kraepelin, Pavlov, Thorndike and Thurstone. Only Sir Cyril Burt's image, surprisingly, was absent. Some years later, I asked Eysenck about this conspicuous omission. He remarked, 'I'd probably have a picture of Burt there, too, if he weren't such a neurotic character.' Burt had been Eysenck's major professor, but they had parted company, under somewhat less than amicable conditions, not long after Eysenck received his PhD (Eysenck, 1983a).

In his youth, Burt had known Sir Francis Galton personally. Burt's father had been Galton's physician, and Burt himself had been greatly influenced by Galton in his choice of a career in psychology as well as in his general outlook concerning the central position of individual differences. Perhaps more than any other scholar of his time, Cyril Burt understood and appreciated Galton's unique contributions to psychology and genetics. This legacy of Galtonian thought was undoubtedly conveyed to Eysenck during his student years under Burt. Galton had had a hand in the founding of the Psychology Department (as well as the Genetics Department), and had even donated equipment to the Psychological Laboratory at University College, London, where Eysenck did all of his undergraduate and graduate study in psychology. In addition, Eysenck has himself proved an avid reader of the writings of Galton and of books about Galton. (Many years ago Sybil Eysenck gave her husband Karl Pearson's monumental three-volume biography, *Life, Letters, and Labours of Sir Francis Galton*, as a birthday present. This biography remains one of Hans Eysenck's most treasured possessions.)

Then there was Charles E. Spearman, Burt's predecessor as Professor of Psychology at University College, and one of the most creative minds in the history of psychology. Spearman, too, had been greatly influenced by Galton's thinking about the nature of human mental ability, although Spearman himself never showed the kind of active research interest demonstrated by Burt in the inheritance of mental ability. Quite early in his academic career, however, Spearman invented the mathematical method known as factor analysis, which made it possible to substantiate objectively one part of what was originally Galton's theory of human ability, namely, that

1  the observed individual differences in mental abilities are largely attributable to differences in a *general* ability, and
2  individual differences in general ability are largely innate.

Spearman's efforts focused on the first hypothesis.

Spearman's applications of factor analysis to a great variety of psychometric tests showed that the all-positive intercorrelations among them could be explained in terms of a *general factor*, or *g*, which entered into people's performance on every test. Because those tests that most required reasoning, relation eduction and abstraction evinced the largest *g* loadings when factor analyzed, Spearman identified *g* with the concept of intelligence. Spearman's 'two-factor theory' of intelligence, as it came to be known, held that each test measured *g*, a *general* factor common to all tests, along with *s*, a *specific* source of variance peculiar to each test (Spearman, 1927). But this theory finally proved to be too simple to account for all the complex patterns of intercorrelations that were later found among various collections of tests.

Sir Cyril Burt, even before he succeeded Spearman in the Chair of Psychology in London University, had already contributed to the development of factor analysis in ways that allowed the extraction of other factors besides *g*. These other factors were termed 'group factors', because they reflect sources of variance which are not shared by all of the tests that enter into the factor analysis, but only by certain groups of tests. Thus arose Burt's now familiar 'hierarchical model' of human abilities, with the individual tests at the lowest level of the hierarchy, the group factors (also termed 'primary' or 'first order' factors) at the next level, and the *g* factor at the apex. The convariances among the individual test items form the total reliable variance of each test; the covariances among the tests form the variance in the group factors; and the covariances among the group factors form the variance in *g*. At each ascending level of the hierarchy, some of the specific sources of variance associated with each test item are 'sifted out', so to speak, such that the *g* factor cannot be described in terms of the 'face' characteristics of any single test or group of tests. The *g* factor is neither verbal, nor numerical, nor spatial, nor mnemonic, nor mechanical, etc. The sources of variance specifically associated with what can be properly described by terms such as these are ascribable to the group factors, leaving to g only that source of variance shared in common by *all* such abilities, as evinced by the positive correlation among them.

In addition to the concept of *general* ability, or *g*, the one other essential Galtonian hypothesis was also made explicit in Burt's formulation of intelligence as '*innate* general cognitive ability'.

These were the views of the factorial structure of mental abilities and of the main cause of individual differences that prevailed in the Psychology Department at London University when Eysenck was a student. This basic paradigm for intelligence has served throughout Eysenck's career as the essential springboard of all his thinking and research on this topic. Besides his empirical contributions (and those of his students and associates) to the development of this paradigm, Eysenck has distinguished himself as the foremost expositor of the Galtonian tradition in all its facets in the field of differential psychology. This role was fittingly recognized by his recently being chosen to deliver the Galton Lecture of the Eugenics Society (founded by Galton in 1904) in its 1983 Symposium on the Biology of Human Intelligence.

**Philosophy of Science**

One prominent feature in all of Eysenck's expository writing is the strong case he makes for his position by appealing to the philosophy of science, a subject upon which Eysenck is widely read and exceptionally sophisticated. Readers of Eysenck's books and articles on intelligence can hardly fail to be educated concerning the role of scientific definitions, constructs and paradigms, the interdependence of theory and measurement, and the ways in which these elements, in conjunction with empirical data, are involved in the advancement of scientific knowledge. The influence of science philosophers Karl Popper and Thomas Kuhn is strongly apparent in Eysenck's thinking. In addition, Eysenck frequently draws upon his lifelong interest in the history of the more advanced physical sciences for enlightening and reassuring parallels to the problems of theory and research in the less advanced behavioural sciences. Eysenck's writing in this vein is often provoked by the obvious need to counter the amazing accretion of naive misconceptions and obscurant notions about the nature and measurement of intelligence, a topic which has befuddled not only the general public, but many students and professional psychologists as well. Various psychological and ideological prejudices have tended to frustrate the advancement of proper scientific research in this field.

Eysenck likens the concept of intelligence to the concepts of physical science, such as mass, heat, magnetism, gravitation, etc., pointing out that none of these exists as a 'thing', or as a denotative noun. To argue about their actual existence, therefore, is quite meaningless. They 'exist' only as concepts, or hypothetical constructs, and derive their meaning solely from the theory of which they are part and parcel. Because they are inventions of the scientist's imagination, such concepts are to be evaluated in terms of their usefulness in the effort to understand certain objectively observed phenomena. Concepts, constructs and models are useful only to the extent that they give rise to empirically testable deductions, and to the extent that they can embrace seemingly diverse phenomena. In the case of intelligence, certain objectively observed phenomena are well established: (1) the existence of reliable individual differences in cognitive or intellectual performance; (2) the positive intercorrelations among a great many diverse tests of cognitive ability; (3) the orderly growth of abilities from infancy to maturity; (4) the highly distinctive pattern of the correlations of intelligence-test scores between different kinships, paralleling their degree of genetic relatedness; (5) the correlation between IQ and social mobility; and (6) the correlation of psycho-metric intelligence with anatomical and physiological variables, such as brain size and evoked electrical potentials in the cerebral cortex. A theory of intelligence must ultimately be able to comprehend all these phenomena and a good many more. Eysenck's interest in intelligence has consistently aimed toward this goal.

### Overview of Eysenck's Contributions

Although Eysenck's very first publication (1939)* dealt with intelligence, his writing on this topic was quite sporadic prior to 1970; out of hundreds of publications during this period, only about a dozen directly concerned intelligence or the measurement of abilities. Until about 1970 Eysenck's research programme was devoted almost entirely to personality and abnormal psychology. Studies reported in his first book, *Dimensions of Personality* (1947a), did make use of intelligence tests, however, demonstrating that the trait of neuroticism interacts with mental test scores, neurotics performing relatively better on a test of fluid intelligence or non-verbal reasoning (matrices) than on a test of crystallized intelligence (vocabulary). Eysenck's first popular book, *Uses and Abuses of Psychology* (1953a), also included chapters on abilities, their measurement and educational and occupational correlates. This book was also the first of Eysenck's writings to introduce the idea that individual differences in mental speed may be the essential basis of variance in psychometric *g*, a hypothesis then under investigation by Desmond Furneaux, one of Eysenck's most creative colleagues.

But it was not until after 1970 that the theory and measurement of intelligence emerged as a major interest to Eysenck. Since then, of course, he has proved amazingly prolific on this topic, writing five books, editing two and contributing some fifteen or more journal articles and book chapters (see References). The most definitive single source for Eysenck's views on intelligence is his textbook, *The Structure and Measurement of Intelligence* (1979a), but his lengthy commentaries and his own chapters in the two books he has edited (1973a, 1982a) also afford a quite comprehensive account of his position. In addition, two of Eysenck's pre-1970 publications warrant special comment because of their general theoretical significance.

The first of these publications (1939) is Eysenck's earliest, a review of L. L. Thurstone's famous monograph, *Primary Mental Abilities*, done while Eysenck was still a student under Burt. Thurstone (1887–1955) was then the leading American figure in psychometrics and factor analysis. Although it was originally agreed that Eysenck's name was to appear second, with Burt as first author, in a rather surprising turn of events (due to Burt's eccentricity, as later related by Eysenck, 1983a), the

---

*Works by Eysenck are cited in the text only by date; his name is omitted.

review was published with Eysenck's name listed as sole author. As Burt's research assistant, Eysenck's task had been to factor analyze the 1596 correlations upon which the critique of Thurstone's work was based—a Herculean task in the days of hand-cranked mechanical calculators. Thurstone himself had factor analyzed a collection of fifty-seven homogeneous tests representing a rather wide variety of cognitive abilities, such as verbal ability, abstraction, spatial visualization, numerical reasoning, rote learning, etc. Having factor analyzed the entire battery by his own methods (centroid analysis followed by rotation of the factor axes to 'simple structure'), Thurstone had arrived at the remarkable conclusion that nothing like Spearman's g was evident in this comprehensive collection of tests. His own method of factor analysis had yielded only a number of so-called primary factors closely corresponding to the categories of abilities the tests were originally selected to represent. However, when Eysenck factor analyzed the same matrix, this time using Burt's group factor method, it was found, as predicted by the Spearman-Burt model, that a large general factor emerged. In addition, there also emerged approximately the same group factors (or 'primaries') as those identified by Thurstone. The important point, however, was that the general factor, which accounted for 31 per cent of the total variance among all fifty-seven tests, accounted for five times more variance than any of the remaining factors. Thus it was shown that Thurstone's highly homogeneous tests of the 'primary mental abilities' were often more highly saturated with g than with the particular group factors (or 'primary factors' in Thurstone's terminology) which they were specially devised to measure. The diversity of tests in this analysis suggests that it is probably impossible to devise any kind of test having at least a moderate degree of cognitive complexity which is not significantly loaded on the g factor when factor analyzed among a large collection of diverse tests. Hence Eysenck's analysis of Thurstone's correlations is one of the more striking examples of the ubiquity of g in the cognitive domain, a fact which Thurstone (1947) was later to acknowledge in his use of oblique rotations of factor axes (a hierarchical type of analysis which permits the extraction of higher-order factors from the correlations among the obliquely rotated [i.e., correlated] primary factors, and thus allows the emergence of g as the single highest-order factor in the hierarchy). It should also be noted that the g extracted by this hierarchical method, provided the collection of tests entering into the analysis is large and highly varied, is essentially the same g as emerges from the factor analytic methods of Spearman and Burt. Other, mathematically more complex, methods, which have become widely used since the advent of high-speed computers, yield highly similar results.

The second of Eysenck's (1967) earlier articles with special significance for the later developments it presaged was his first real theoretical manifesto in this field. It is a key reference for students of Eysenck, and is still well worth reading today. Although this seminal article ranges over a number of topics, I will briefly mention three themes which have figured prominently in Eysenck's later work and which seem the most important for future developments in the theory of intelligence.

## *1 The Limitations of Factor Analysis*

Eysenck was among the first to voice the now generally agreed verdict that further progress in research on the nature of intelligence could not be made within the confines of factor analysis of psychometric tests. Factor analysis serves an indispensable function in identifying a limited number of independent dimensions of variance, or factors, in the whole domain of cognitive performance. But the factors themselves can only be objectively named and described in terms of the most salient observable characteristics of the particular tests that have gone into the factor analysis in the first place. One simply describes the types of tests that show the largest loadings on a given factor. This problem is of particular concern for the psychological description of the largest factor, *g*, as highly diverse tests often show highly similar *g* loadings. Once *g* has been extracted, along with any group factors, from a collection of tests, the technique of factor analysis, by its very nature, is itself incapable of further elucidating the psychological or biological nature or causes of the factors it reveals. Hence factor analysis must be supplemented by experimental and genetic methods in the investigation of individual differences in cognitive abilities. Unaided by these other methods, which appeal to data from outside the sphere of traditional psychometric tests themselves, psychometry and factor analysis, by 1960, had already gone about as far in advancing the science of human abilities as was logically possible within this framework. Factor analysis provided *g* as a good working definition of intelligence, but the nature of *g* was still a mystery.

2    *The Fractionation of g*

Working in Eysenck's Department, Desmond Furneaux had been investigating the hypothesis that *g* actually reflects three distinct aspects of problem-solving ability, an idea which Furneaux (1960) attributed to his study of E. L. Thorndike's *The Measurement of Intelligence* (1926), in which the tripartite nature of general intelligence was first systematically proposed. Following Thorndike (1974–1949), but with important modifications, Furneaux identified the three main parameters of mental test performance as follows: (1) *Mental Speed*, (2) *Continuance*, or persistence of effort to solve a problem when the solution is not readily apparent, and (3) *Error Checking*, i.e., the disposition to check the solution before writing it down. With a grant from the Nuffield Foundation, Furneaux developed a special test (which he dubbed the Nufferno Test), in which each item is individually timed, to measure each of these three aspects of an individual's problem-solving.

Strictly speaking, of course, only the first of these aspects, mental speed, is a cognitive variable. The other two aspects, persistence and carefulness in error checking, are really non-cognitive factors that belong more in the personality domain. Because all three factors could be shown to influence an individual's score on a highly *g*-loaded test of intelligence, however, the once unidimensional *g* may now be better understood as including conative elements as well. Still, as Eysenck was careful to point out, the most important consequence of Furneaux's empirical analysis for the theory of intelligence was the reinstatement of the mental speed factor to 'its theoretical pre-eminence as the main cognitive determinant of mental test solving ability' (Eysenck, 1967, p. 84). Specifically, Furneaux hypothesized a neural scanning mechanism in the cortex, the *speed* of which is the basic source of individual differences in intelligence.

After writing an elaborate technical paper (Furneaux, 1960) on this promising line of research, for Eysenck's *Handbook of Abnormal Psychology*, Furneaux himself did not develop this theme any further in his subsequent publications. Interest in the topic has since been perpetuated mainly through the writings of Eysenck, under whose instigation Furneaux's original ideas have been advanced and tested as a formal statistical model by another of Eysenck's co-workers, Owen White (1973, 1982), a specialist in statistical and mathematical psychology. One closely related discovery stemming from Furneaux's work, which now would be lost were it not for Eysenck's exposition of it in several publications (for example, 1979a, Ch. 8), concerns the relationship between the average difficulty level of highly *g*-loaded test items (as indicated by the percentage of subjects who 'fail' the item) and a subject's response latency or solution time (i.e., the time interval between presentation of the item and the subject's giving the 'correct' response). As shown in Figure 1, when the logarithm of response latency is plotted as a function of item difficulty, the relationship is linear. All subjects show the same slope; only the intercepts differ from one subject to another. This finding demonstrates that individual differences in the level of item difficulty attainable are associated with the single factor of mental speed.

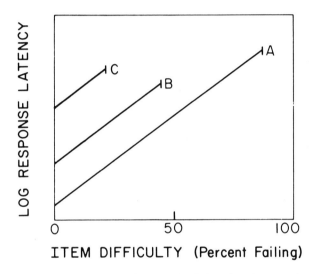

**Figure 1.** The relationship between item difficulty and solution time (response latency) for correctly answered items when the latter is plotted on a logarithmic scale. Hypothetical individuals A, B and C differ in ability (as indicated by the level of the most difficult items solved) and in mental speed. The slopes of the function are the same for all individuals; only the intercepts differ, and they are highly correlated with the highest level of item difficulty attained by each individual.

Although reported in several of Eysenck's publications from 1953 to 1979, this finding seems not to have been further substantiated or developed beyond its status in the initial report. If the phenomenon could be shown to hold up with some generality for a variety of homogeneous tests, it would constitute one of the most important discoveries to date in mental measurement theory. Over the years Eysenck has recognized the importance of this line of research and has sought to encourage more thorough investigation along these lines. In his own words, 'the scientific study of intelligence would gain much by following up the important leads given by Furneaux in this extremely original and path-breaking work' (1967, p. 85).

*3   Reaction Time and Intelligence*

Galton had originally suggested that individual differences in general ability, or intelligence, might be reflected in measurements of reaction time and other elementary capacities, such as sensory discrimination and perceptual speed. However, Galton's own efforts, as well as those of his American disciple James McKeen Cattell, failed to substantiate this expectation. As a result, the basic idea of measuring mental ability by means of 'brass instrument' laboratory techniques was cast into the limbo of discredited theories. And so it remained for at least half a century, awaiting the development of a better theoretical rationale and better instrumentation. These emerged in the form of information theory and advanced electronic technology. Information theory, as applied to cognitive psychology, provided an appropriate rationale, while technological advances in electronics provided the reliable and efficient measurement of reaction time. Improved statistical methods and computer techniques for the analysis of massive and complex data have also proved invaluable in this area of research.

   Eysenck's 1967 article presaged the application of these developments to the study of intelligence by reaction time techniques—a return to Galton's original notion, but with some important innovations. Eysenck had come across an obscure article (Roth, 1964) in a German journal, describing an experimental paradigm in which simple reaction time ($RT_0$) and choice reaction times ($RT_1$, $RT_2$, $RT_3$) to varying amounts of information (measured in bits, indicated in the subscripts of RT), as conveyed by the reaction stimulus, which consisted of a single light going on at random among sets of either 1, 2, 4 or 8 lights (corresponding to 0, 1, 2 or 3 bits of information, where bit $= \log_2$ of the number of alternatives in the set). Roth's experiment showed that the slope of RT on bits of information was negatively correlated with IQ, a finding which makes a great deal of sense if intelligence is viewed as information processing capacity. Bright and dull subjects differed negligibly in *simple* RT, but dull subjects showed a greater rate of increase in *choice* RT as the amount of information in the reaction stimulus (i.e., number of light/button alternatives) increased. The essential result, which has since withstood many replications (Jensen, 1982), was clearly consistent with a theory of intelligence based on the speed of mental processing of information. This conception, which had great appeal for Eysenck, stands in marked contrast to the prevailing view, originating with the work of Binet, in which intelligence is conceived as being merely the average level of a person's performance on some rather arbitrary collection of knowledge and skills items which only happens to correlate with some practical criterion such as scholastic achievement. Eysenck dismissed this Binetian conception of intelligence and hearkened back to Galton's original ideas as a more promising path for research on the nature of psychometric *g*.

## The Physiological Basis of Intelligence

A key motivation in all of Eysenck's theorizing and research has always been to advance psychology as one of the natural sciences. To this end, he has continually sought explanations of psychological phenomena in terms of their physical substrate. Hence, for Eysenck, scientific psychology divorced from biology is a contradiction.

One might even say that the ultimate 'psychologist's fallacy' is the psychological explanation of psychological phenomena. Eysenck would instead strive to find a physical explanation.

Eysenck has written extensively on the genetic inheritance of intelligence (1971a, 1973b, 1973c, 1975, 1978, 1979a, 1979b, 1979c, 1980a, 1980b, 1981b; Eysenck and Kamin, 1980), amassing evidence that some 70 to 80 per cent of the true variance (i.e., individual differences) in intelligence is attributable to genetic factors. Given this strong support from genetic research for the biological basis of intelligence, Eysenck was quick to see the logical 'next step' as being the direct measurement of some physical aspect of intelligence and the formulation of a theory of the neurophysiological processes underlying individual differences. The idea that speed of information processing is the primary variable which is manifested as psychometric *g*, and the fact that choice reaction time was found to be correlated with IQ, as theoretically expected, were important leads. But to secure an even more direct connection between psychometric *g* and its neurophysiological underpinnings, a further step still was needed.

The then recent developments in electroencephalography provided the means. A Canadian expert in this field, John P. Ertl (1966, 1968), and his co-workers (Chalke and Ertl, 1965; Ertl and Schafer, 1969) are credited with discovering the first essential link between intelligence and brain physiology, by measuring the electrical activity of the cerebral cortex, recorded as the average evoked potential, or AEP. The latency and amplitude of the brain's electrochemical reaction to a simple visual or auditory stimulus, such as a flash of light or a sharp 'click', were found to be significantly correlated with IQ. Probably as a result of variations in procedures and subject samples, observed correlations in the early studies were unduly erratic. As studies accumulated, however, these correlations tended to centre between 0.3 and 0.4. Gradually, the AEP came to be recognized as the first really promising link between a psychological trait and normal brain physiology.

In about 1970 Eysenck propitiously encouraged one of his doctoral students, Donna Elaine Hendrickson (1972), to choose as her thesis topic the relationship between auditory evoked potential and individual differences in verbal and spatial abilities. Hendrickson's results revealed that simple latencies of the AEP were correlated significantly (values ranging between 0.30 and 0.50) with the composite psychometric scores. These results become even more impressive, as Eysenck (1973a, p. 428) has noted, once certain appropriate statistical corrections have been made, in order to suppress the effects of cognitively irrelevant personality variables (neuroticism and extraversion are also correlated with AEP latencies) and in order to correct for attenuation due to measurement error. After correction, the correlations between the AEP and the psychometric test scores increase to about 0.7. A correlation of this magnitude is nearly as large as the *g* loadings of the psychometric tests themselves, and even approximates their genetic heritability. In his interpretation of Hendrickson's findings, Eysenck (1973a) wrote '. . . there can be no doubt that at long last a serious step has been taken in the direction of identifying the physiological basis of intelligence' (p. 429).

This was just the beginning of the investigations in this vein to be carried out in Eysenck's laboratory. Elaine Hendrickson subsequently collaborated with her husband, Alan E. Hendrickson, another of Eysenck's most brilliant students, in improving the measurement of individual differences in the AEP and in developing a highly complex and detailed neurophysiological theory to explain the nature of these differences, by hypothesizing a precise causal chain of events linking the AEP with psychometric *g*. The Hendricksons' theory and empirical findings first appeared as the lead article in the initial issue of Eysenck's then newly founded journal, *Personality and Individual Differences* (Hendrickson and Hendrickson, 1980). The Hendricksons later presented a more elaborate treatment of their theory and empirical studies in Eysenck's *A Model for Intelligence* (1982a). Recently, Eysenck and Barrett (1984) have more broadly explicated the general methodology of AEP for the study of intelligence.

The highly technical aspects of the Hendricksons' theoretical contribution, involving fine details in the physiology and chemistry of synaptic transmission, are well beyond the scope of this chapter. However, those aspects which are of central importance in the present context can be described briefly.

The Hendricksons' method of measuring the AEP is not in terms of latency or amplitude *per se*, but in terms of the overall complexity of the multiple-wave reaction following the evoking stimulus (as determined by 'computer-integrating' the total set of waves within a given time-locked epoch). This measurement of the AEP apparently yields larger correlations (in the range of 0.7 to 0.8) with IQ than do other measurements. When the AEP is measured in this way, moreover, its correlation with a given subtest of the Wechsler scale is directly related to that subtest's *g* loading, indicating that the AEP primarily reflects the physiological basis of psychometric *g*. Indeed, the size of these reported correlations even suggests the possibility that virtually all of the true variance in *g* might be measurable by the AEP, a finding which, if it should stand up under repeated replications in various laboratories, would be of momentous theoretical and practical importance. For one thing, this would mean that Spearman's characterization of *g* as a capacity for 'abstraction' and for 'the eduction of relations and correlates' is needlessly restrictive. Relation eduction would not be an essential condition for the measurement of *g*, as the stimuli used to trigger the evoked potentials are far too simple to evince any such 'higher' mental processes as those figuring in Spearman's description of *g*.

The theory of the essential nature of *g* arising out of the Hendricksons' work finally prompted Eysenck to relegate mental speed to a position of lesser importance in his theory of *g*. In his more recent thinking about intelligence, Eysenck has come to view speed as merely secondary, a derivative phenomenon which reflects some still more fundamental process. According to this more recent theory, the essential hypothetical construct in the study of intelligence is, instead, mental error rate (i.e., the rate of 'errors' in the transmission of neural impulses through the cerebral cortex). This theory proposes that individuals differ in the amount of 'noise' or error tendency in the transmission of information within the cortical system. The level of an individual's intelligence depends upon the probability that messages, neurally encoded as 'pulse trains', will be transmitted to their destinations in their identical form, without being degraded or distorted by random 'noise' in the nervous system. The lower the average fidelity of transmission, the longer the duration through which pulse trains must persist in order to produce the redundancy required to convey an error-free message. Hence the speed of information processing, as measured by choice reaction time, is seen as merely a derivative effect. More importantly, this pulse train theory also explains the reliable individual differences observed in the trial-to-trial variability of RT and evoked potential latencies, as well as the fact that intraindividual variability is correlated with psychometric *g*, perhaps to an even greater degree than the RT itself. Errors in neural transmission would, of course, exact a greater toll, in terms of speed and accuracy of processing, for more complex messages, as more complex messages would presumably involve longer pulse trains than simple messages. Thus, an explanation is provided for the fact that the correlation between RT and *g* increases as a direct function of the amount of information conveyed by the reaction stimulus. This theory is also consistent with the more general finding that degree of task complexity is closely related to a task's *g* loading (Marshalek, Lohman and Snow, 1983). Viewed in these terms, therefore, the theory is entirely compatible with Spearman's own characterization of *g*, at least at the gross level of psychometric tests.

Eysenck has repeatedly pointed out that much of the controversy regarding the theory of intelligence results from our failing to distinguish properly between the various classes of phenomena and levels of conceptualization to which the label 'intelligence' is often indiscriminately attached. Figure 2 has been used by Eysenck to

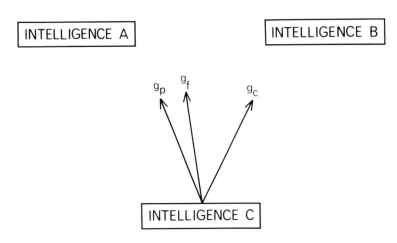

**Figure 2.** Intelligences A, B and C, with arrows indicating the types of measurements reflecting A and B to varying degrees suggested by the direction of the arrows: *g* = general factor of a battery of measurements, *p* = physiological indices, *f* = tests of fluid intelligence (e.g., Raven's Matrices, Block Designs), *c* = tests of crystallized intelligence (e.g., general information, vocabulary).

clarify this important point. Intelligence A denotes biological or innate intelligence, and thus reflects the influence of the individual's genotype as well as any non-genetic factors, pre-natal or post-natal, which may affect cerebral neurophysiology. It is Intelligence A with which Eysenck's definition and theory of intelligence are concerned. Intelligence B denotes the rather ill-defined, multifaceted collection of notions about intelligence as the term is popularly used, and includes the many common manifestations of intellectual ability which are evident in people's daily activities, at school, on the job, etc. Intelligence B reflects Intelligence A as modified by the great variety of experiences and diverse environmental influences to which persons are inevitably subjected throughout the course of their development from birth to later maturity and beyond. The conceptual boundaries of Intelligence B are so vague that they tend to encompass values, interests and personality factors, as well as a host of complexly determined achievements, in addition to cognitive abilities, as strictly defined. As such, Intelligence B is hardly an amenable datum for scientific study. Finally, Intelligence C denotes some objective measurement of certain abilities (or achievements) which are commonly associated with some aspect of Intelligence B. Intelligence C can be a quite suitable phenotype for scientific analysis. Tests can be devised to show substantial correlations with such varied aspects of Intelligence B as scholastic performance, occupational status, 'success' in life and other popularly perceived manifestations of mental ability.

As indicated by the arrows in Figure 2, tests vary in their degree of correlation with Intelligence A and Intelligence B. Tests of what R. B. Cattell (1971) has termed crystallized intelligence ($g_c$), i.e., tests drawing upon general information, vocabulary, reading comprehension, mathematical knowledge and the like, are more indicative of Intelligence B. Tests of fluid intelligence ($g_f$), i.e., tests involving matrices, figure analogies, block designs and the like, all of which include relatively little cultural and educational content, tend to reflect slightly more of Intelligence A. Choice reaction time or other measures of speed of information processing come still closer to Intelligence A, while purely non-behavioural physiological techniques, such as the average evoked potential measurements, provide an even more direct reflection of Intelligence A.

In what is probably his most comprehensive paper in this field, a veritable masterpiece of theoretical integration, Eysenck (1984) argues that the recent theorizing about Intelligence A represents a true scientific revolution in the conceptualization and measurement of intelligence. It is a revolution in Thomas Kuhn's (1970) sense, as a shift in the conceptual and methodological paradigm for a given realm of phenomena. Innumerable problems, of course, remain to be worked through in the process of 'normal science'. If ultimately successful, however, this research programme will essentially represent the scientific fruition of the Galtonian paradigm. In its modern development, this paradigm owes much to the renewed scientific impetus inspired by Eysenck and to the research endeavours of all those who, over the years, have been influenced by Eysenck's thinking.

## REFERENCES*

Cattell, R. B. (1971) *Abilities: Their Structure, Growth, and Action*, Boston, Houghton-Mifflin.

Chalke, F. C. R. and Ertl, J. P. (1965) 'Evoked potentials and intelligence', *Life Sciences*, **4**, pp. 1319–22.

Ertl, J. P. (1966) 'Evoked potentials and intelligence', *Revue de l'Université d'Ottawa*, **36**, pp. 599–607.

Ertl, J. P. (1968) 'Evoked potentials, neural efficiency and IQ', Paper presented at the International Symposium for Biocybernetics, Washington, D. C.

Ertl, J. P. and Schafer, E. W. P. (1969) 'Brain response correlates of psychometric intelligence', *Nature*, **223**, pp. 421–2.

Eysenck, H. J. (1939) Review of *Primary Mental Abilities* by L. L. Thurstone, *British Journal of Educational Psychology*, **9**, pp. 270–5.

Eysenck, H. J. (1943) 'Neurosis and intelligence', *The Lancet*, **18**, pp. 362–3.

Eysenck, H. J. (1944) 'The effect of incentives on neurotics, and the variability of neurotics as compared with normals', *British Journal of Medical Psychology*, **20**, pp. 100–3.

Eysenck, H. J. (1947a) *Dimensions of Personality*, London, Routledge and Kegan Paul.

Eysenck, H. J. (1947b) 'Student selection by means of psychological tests: A critical survey', *British Journal of Educational Psychology*, **17**, pp. 20–39.

Eysenck, H. J. (1948) 'Some recent studies of intelligence', *Eugenics Review*, **40**, pp. 21–8.

*Virtually all of Eysenck's publications on intelligence are listed here, although not all of them are referred to in the text.

Eysenck, H. J. (1953a) *Uses and Abuses of Psychology*, Harmondsworth, Penguin Books.

Eysenck, H. J. (1953b) 'The logical basis of factor analysis', *American Psychologist*, **8**, pp. 105–14.

Eysenck, H. J. (1959) 'Personality and problem solving', *Psychological Reports*, **5**, p. 592.

Eysenck, H. J. (1967) 'Intelligence assessment: A theoretical and experimental approach', *British Journal of Educational Psychology*, **37**, pp. 81–98.

Eysenck, H. J. (1969) 'Environmentalism—the new arrogance', *The Times Educational Supplement*, 12 December.

Eysenck, H. J. (1970) 'More on "Testing Negro Intelligence"', *The Humanist* (USA), March/April, p. 34.

Eysenck, H. J. (1971a) *Race, Intelligence, and Education*, London, Temple Smith.

Eysenck, H. J. (1971b) 'Relation between intelligence and personality', *Perceptual and Motor Skills*, **32**, pp. 637–8.

Eysenck, H. J. (1971c) 'Race, intelligence and education', *New Society*, 17 June, pp. 1045–7.

Eysenck, H. J. (Ed.) (1973a) *The Measurement of Intelligence*, Lancaster, Medical and Technical Publishers.

Eysenck, H. J. (1973b) *The Inequality of Man*, London, Temple Smith.

Eysenck, H. J. (1973c) 'IQ, social class and educational policy', *Change*, **5**, pp. 38–42.

Eysenck, H. J. (1973d) 'A better understanding of IQ and the myths surrounding it', *The Times Educational Supplement*, 18 May.

Eysenck, H. J. (1975) 'Equality and education: Fact and fiction', *Oxford Review of Education*, **1**, pp. 51–8.

Eysenck, H. J. (1976) 'Intelligence', in Eysenck H. J. and Wilson, G. D. (Eds.), *A Textbook of Human Psychology*, Lancaster, Medical and Technical Publishers.

Eysenck, H. J. (1977) 'When is discrimination?', in Cox C. B. and Boyson, R. (Eds.), *Black Paper*, London, Maurice Temple Smith.

Eysenck, H. J. (1978) 'Sir Cyril Burt and the inheritance of the I.Q.,' *New Zealand Psychologist*, **9**, p. 17.

Eysenck, H. J. (1979a) *The Structure and Measurement of Intelligence*, Heidelberg, Springer-Verlag.

Eysenck, H. J. (1979b) 'Race, intelligence and education', *New Scientist*, 15 March, pp. 849–52.

Eysenck, H. J. (1979c) 'Genetics and the future of education', *New Education*, **1, 2**, pp. 1–13.

Eysenck, H. J. (1980a) 'Intelligence, education, and the genetic model', in van der Kamp, L. J. Th., Langerakg, W. F. and de Gruijter D. N. M. (Eds.), *Psychometrics for Educational Debates*, New York, Wiley.

Eysenck, H. J. (1980b) 'Professor Sir Cyril Burt and the inheritance of intelligence: Evaluation of a controversy', *Zeitschrift für Differentielle und Diagnostische Psychologie*, 1, pp. 183–99.

Eysenck, H. J. (1980c) 'The family's influence on intelligence', *International Journal of Family Psychiatry*, **1**, pp. 21–9.

Eysenck, H. J. (1981a) 'The nature of intelligence', in Friedman, M. P., Das, J. P. and O'Connor, N. (Eds.), *Intelligence and Learning*, New York, Plenum.

Eysenck, H. J. (1981b) 'The structure and measurement of intelligence', *Die Naturwissenschaften*, **68**, pp. 491–7.

Eysenck, H. J. (Ed.) (1982a) *A Model for Intelligence*, Heidelberg, Springer-Verlag.

Eysenck, H. J. (1982b) 'The psychophysiology of intelligence', in Spielberger, C. D. and Butcher, J. N. (Eds.), *Advances in Personality Assessment*, Vol.1, Hillsdale, N. J., Erlbaum.

Eysenck, H. J. (1982c) 'Intelligence: New wine in old bottles', *New Horizons*, **23**, pp. 11–18.

Eysenck, H. J. (1982d) 'The sociology of psychological knowledge, the genetic interpretation of the IQ, and Marxist-Leninist ideology', *Bulletin of the British Psychological Society*, **35**, pp. 449–51.

Eysenck, H. J. (1982e) ' Main point missed' [Letter to Editor], *APA Monitor*, **13**, pp. 4–5.

Eysenck, H. J. (1983a) 'Sir Cyril Burt: Polymath and psychopath', *Association of Educational Psychologists Journal*, **6**, pp. 57–63.

Eysenck, H. J. (1983b) 'New light on the nature of intelligence', *New Horizons*, **24**, pp. 20–30.

Eysenck, H. J. (1984) *Revolution in the Theory and Measurement of Intelligence*, Unpublished manuscript.

Eysenck, H. J. and Barrett, P. (1984) 'Psychophysiology and the measurement of intelligence', in Reynolds, C. R. and Willson V. (Eds.), *Methodological and Statistical Advances in the Study of Individual Differences*, New York, Plenum.

Eysenck, H. J. and Cookson, D. (1969) 'Personality in primary school children, I. Ability and achievement', *British Journal of Educational Psychology*, **39**, pp. 109–30.

Eysenck, H. J. and Kamin, L. J. (1980) *The Great Intelligence Debate*, New York, Lifecycle Publications.

Eysenck, H. J. and White, P. O. (1964) 'Personality and the measurement of intelligence', *British Journal of Educational Psychology*, **34**, pp. 197–202.

Furneaux, W. D. (1960) ' Intellectual abilities and problem solving behavior', in Eysenck, H. J. (Ed.), *Handbook of Abnormal Psychology*, New York, Basic Books.

Hendrickson, D. E. (1972) *An Examination of Individual Differences in Cortical Evoked Response*, Unpublished PhD thesis, University of London.

Hendrickson, D. E. and Hendrickson, A. E. (1980) 'The biological basis of individual differences,' *Personality and Individual Differences*, **1,** pp. 3–33.

Jensen, A. R. (1982) 'Reaction time and psychometric g,' in Eysenck H. J. (Ed.), *A Model for Intelligence*, Heidelberg, Springer-Verlag.

Kuhn, T. S. (1970) *The Structure of Scientific Revolutions*, Chicago, University of Chicago Press.

Marshalek, B., Lohman, D. F. and Snow, R. E. (1983) 'The complexity continuum in the radex and hierarchical models of intelligence', *Intelligence*, **7,** pp. 107–27.

Roth, E. (1964) 'Die Geschwindigkeit der Verarbeitung von Information und ihr Zusammenhang mit Intelligence', *Zeitschrift für Experimentelle und Angewandte Psychologie*, **11,** pp. 616–22.

Spearman, C. E. (1927) *The Abilities of Man*, New York, Macmillan.

Thorndike, E. L. (1926) *The Measurement of Intelligence*, New York, Bureau of Publication, Teachers College, Columbia University.

Thurstone, L. L. (1947) *Multiple Factor Analysis*, Chicago, University of Chicago Press.

White, P. O. (1973) 'Individual differences in speed, accuracy, and persistence: A mathematical model for problem solving', in Eysenck, H. J. (Ed.), *The Measurement of Intelligence*, Lancaster, Medical and Technical Publishers.

White, P. O. (1982) 'Some major components of general intelligence', in Eysenck, H. J. (Ed.), *A Model for Intelligence*, Heidelberg, Springer-Verlag.

# 8. Eysenck on Intelligence: A Critical Perspective

JERRY S. CARLSON AND KEITH F. WIDAMAN

Hans J. Eysenck has made substantial contributions to the science of psychology and to its politics as well. Throughout his career Eysenck has dealt with issues of great importance and controversy, and has often taken stands on these issues that were unpopular and contrary to the *Zeitgeist*. To his credit Eysenck's opponents on these issues could count on an adversary who was at least equal to the task, who was ever ready to undertake debate in the scholarly arena. Our charge in the present chapter is to examine critically the views on intelligence propounded by Eysenck, a task that is somewhat unenviable, given Eysenck's contributions to psychology. Still, we trust that the synthesis arising out of our efforts and the accompanying chapter by Arthur Jensen will allow a more balanced and accurate portrayal of Eysenck's views on intelligence than would either effort alone.

In order to evaluate Eysenck's position on intelligence, one must acknowledge the dual role Eysenck has assumed regarding research on intelligence. On the one hand, in a series of books Eysenck (1953, 1973, 1979) has been reviewer of and arbiter on research on intelligence, attempting to summarize and shape this field of inquiry in the process. On the other hand, Eysenck and his colleagues (e.g., Eysenck, 1973, 1982; Hendrickson and Hendrickson, 1980; A. E. Hendrickson, 1982; D. E. Hendrickson, 1982; White, 1973, 1982) have made original contributions to theoretical and empirical issues in the study of intelligence. As a result, we have ordered this chapter in the following way. The first section deals with six approaches to the study of intelligence: ethological, psychometric, Binetian, Piagetian, information processing, and physiological. When discussing a given approach we briefly present our view of the state-of-the-science as well as Eysenck's position on the issues involved, noting especially points of disagreement between our and Eysenck's views. In the second section we consider three major issues: genetic versus environmental effects on intelligence, intelligence as competence versus intelligence as performance, and Galtonian measures of intelligence. These are perhaps the areas in which Eysenck has

**103**

made his most original contributions to research on intelligence. Our views on Eysenck's position on intelligence and what, in our view, are shortcomings and omissions thereof are noted throughout. The chapter concludes with a summary and review.

## APPROACHES TO THE STUDY OF INTELLIGENCE

### Ethological

The ethological approach in the study of intelligence and development requires a naturalistic framework placing primary importance on global relationships between the individual and the environment. The study of limited relationships through the laboratory approach is potentially misleading, providing little information on how individuals behave in and interact with their environment (Berry, 1980). In a recent paper Charlesworth (1979) presented a forceful argument in favour of an ethological approach to the description and study of intelligent behaviour. Charlesworth characterized the traditional study of intelligence, concentrating primarily on the psychometric, as dealing with only half of intelligence. Investigations within the traditional approach to intelligence tend to assume that intelligence is a trait, assessing the ability of persons to solve more or less esoteric problems in laboratory-like situations, carefully controlling the testing situation so that no intruding factors, which might easily affect such performance in real-world settings, may have effects on the behaviour assessed. Charlesworth urged the study of the complementary, other half of intelligence, the study of intelligent behaviour as it is exhibited in everyday situations, behaviours that adapt the person to the environment. The focus of research should be the interactions between the organism and the environment. Charlesworth argued for a return to naturalistic observational study, as Darwin and other naturalists did with various species during the nineteenth century and as a small number of researchers (e.g., Barker and Wright, 1954, 1966) have done with human subjects in the twentieth century.

We feel that the Charlesworth (1979) critique of the one-sided nature of traditional research on intelligence is itself rather one-sided. For example, much impetus for studying intelligence stems from the work of Galton, a cousin of Darwin, who was convinced of the veracity of the evolutionary position, which was based on data from naturalistic observation. Regardless of current opinion concerning its scientific merit, Galton's (1869) *Hereditary Genius*, a quasi-observational/historical study of English nobility, is a classic study of the evolutionary bases of intelligence. A second major line of work on intelligence follows the research of Binet whose efforts were spurred by the everyday problems surrounding education of the subnormal. This concern has been continued to the present day by the developer of the currently most widely used intelligence scales, David Wechsler. Throughout his writings, Wechsler (e.g., 1939, 1975) has continually stressed that intelligence is 'the aggregate or global capacity of the individual to act purposefully, to think rationally and to deal effectively with his environment' (1939, p. 3). In recent statements Wechsler (1975) reiterated that the abstract problem-solving, intellective aspects of intelligence were only a part, perhaps a rather small part, of intelligence. While the test batteries Wechsler assembled may not successfully reflect the full scope of the intelligence construct he described, the notion of intelligence as a global and adaptive quality of behaviour still provides the framework within which the Wechsler scales are utilized.

A third example is research on adaptive behaviour (AB) scales for the mentally retarded (e.g., Nihara, 1976; Nihara, Foster, Shellhaas and Leland, 1974). As the term 'adaptive behaviour' suggests, AB scales take as their starting point the behaviours shown by retarded persons in their everyday lives. As argued by Nihara *et al.* (1974), the IQ resulting from traditional intelligence tests is not diagnostic of the level of functioning exhibited by a retarded person on tasks in everyday life like eating, dressing, etc. After careful observation and classification of the types of behaviours shown by retarded persons, AB scales were developed to supplant IQ scores as descriptions of retarded persons' abilities.

These three lines of research, all part of the general paradigm of ability testing, have one common element: behaviours exhibited by persons in representative life situations helped delineate the domains of content included in the ability measures. Although many ability tests may now appear to fit Charlesworth's (1979) description, the descent of ability tests shows clear lines of applied interest regarding the adaptive behaviours of persons to their environs.

In his recent survey of research on intelligence Eysenck (1979) mentioned the adaptive, evolutionary significance of intelligence, citing the research by Galton and writings of Herbert Spencer. But Eysenck soon moved to a position potentially rather more susceptible to Charlesworth's (1979) criticism. After reviewing the factor analytic models of Spearman and others, Eysenck (1979) decried Binet's influence on the field of intelligence, echoing views voiced by Spearman (1927) that Binet was using a 'hotch potch' of tests measuring an ever-changing set of complex abilities, resulting in a single measure of intelligence that was an unequally weighted average of many unspecified processes. Eysenck, as Spearman (1927) before him, opted for the study of tests each having homogeneous content in laboratory-like contexts, feeling that only in this way could basic science advance in its description of intelligence and its physiological bases. However, by turning his back on more applied research on intelligence, Eysenck (1979) runs the risk of losing sight of the source of motivation for research on intelligence. Research on intelligence has always had both basic and applied aspects, and rightfully so. Applied matters have continually supplied impetus for the study of intelligence, suggesting new areas that need attention or new ways of studying old areas. We feel that basic research on intelligence is an essential pursuit, but feel just as strongly that researchers should not lose sight of the fact that intelligence is an attribute of adaptive behaviour for which any intelligence test provides only an imperfect indicator.

## Psychometric

It is difficult to date precisely the advent of psychometric research on intelligence, although a commonly cited figure is Galton, who gathered a set of anthropometric measures on persons attending the International Health Exhibition in 1884 (Boring, 1950). In time the psychometric tradition became identified with the factor analytic theories developed by Spearman (1904, 1927), Burt (1949), Thomson (1951), Vernon (1962, 1965, 1969), Thurstone (1938; Thurstone and Thurstone, 1941), and more recently by Guilford (1967; Guilford and Hoepfner, 1971) and by Cattell (1963, 1971) and Horn (1968, 1970; Horn and Cattell, 1967a, 1967b). Although there were bitter debates among proponents of different factor theories as late as the 1930s, during the next decade it became clear that Spearman (Spearman and Jones, 1941) accepted the existence of group, or primary, factors, and that Thurstone (Thurstone and Thurstone, 1941) accepted the existence of the general factor.

In an attempt at integration Eysenck (1979, pp. 33–48) considered what he termed a generalized Spearman-Thurstone model, the hierarchical factor model developed by Vernon (1962, 1969). In Vernon's model, depicted in Figure 1, the general factor resides at the apex of a hierarchy of ability factors, directly above two broad subgeneral factors labelled verbal:educational (v:ed) and spatial:mechanical (k:m). Below the subgeneral factors is a wide array of primary factors similar to those Thurstone had described, factors such as verbal comprehension, numerical facility and word fluency. Given the hierarchical factor model, Eysenck (1979) claimed that all major factor theories except 'The Structure of Intellect' proposed by Guilford could be accommodated within the Vernon model. Thus, one could infer that Spearman (1923, 1927) concentrated his theoretical and research efforts at the topmost, or general factor, level, while other British theorists, such as Burt, Thomson, and Vernon, pursued research primarily at the general and subgeneral levels, and rather less often at the primary factor level. In contrast, while acknowledging the existence of the general factor, Thurstone (1938; Thurstone and Thurstone, 1941) dealt almost exclusively in his theorizing with primary factors, or primary mental abilities. Of the later theories, the Cattell-Horn constructs of fluid and crystallized intelligence were equated by Eysenck (1979, p. 24) with the k:m and v:ed subgeneral factors, respectively. Only the orthodox version of the Guilford (1967; Guilford and Hoepfner, 1971) theory, which admits no general factors (but see Guilford, 1981, for a recent recanting of his hard-line position), is not easily represented within the Vernon model.

The attempt by Eysenck (1979) to bring virtually all factor analytic theories under the conceptual umbrella of Vernon's hierarchy was a laudable attempt at integration, but there are several points of contention that appear to cast doubt on the enterprise. The first of these pertains to differing interpretations of the general factor, and illustrates the problems incurred in research when one justifies one's position with arguments that affirm the consequent. Spearman (1923, 1927) posited three noegenetic laws (see Eysenck, 1979, pp. 25–7) that governed the appearance of novel content in the mind. Spearman thought that all tests of intelligence required the use of one or more of the three noegenetic laws, and that the efficiency and power with which a person exercised the laws was governed by the amount of mental energy at one's disposal. From this theoretical position Spearman predicted the emergence of a general factor, $g$, from the intercorrelations of mental tests, and felt that $g$ represented, essentially, mental energy. In contrast, Thomson (1951) began with a theory that the mind was made up of innumerable independent bonds. Responding to a question of a given type would require the action of a sample of these bonds, and the more similar another question was the more similar the sample of bonds required to arrive at an answer. Thomson (1951) showed, and his demonstration was supported in an elegant presentation by Maxwell (1972), that this sampling theory of bonds leads to the prediction that a general factor would emerge from correlations among ability tests, even though there was no common element among any set of three or more tests. Thus, on the basis of their contradictory theoretical positions, both Spearman and Thomson predicted the emergence of a general factor. When such a factor was found in each of a large number of studies (for reviews, see Spearman, 1927; Thomson, 1951; and Vernon, 1962), the results supported both the Spearman

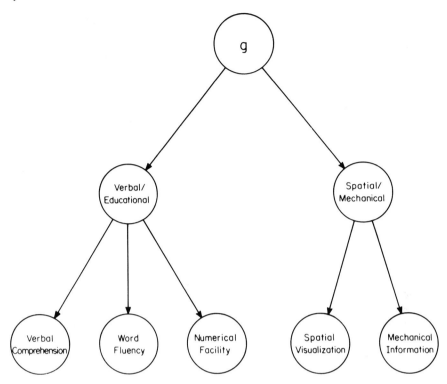

Figure 1.   The Vernon Hierarchical Model of Intellectual Abilities.
Source:   Vernon (1965)

and Thomson positions, but neither position uniquely. To claim that the Vernon (1965, 1969) hierarchy provides a summary agreeable to both Spearman and Thomson appears in important respects correct, at the level of factor patterns. But to imply, as Eysenck (1979) did, that the Vernon hierarchy represents a model that resolves differences between theorists such as Spearman and Thomson is incorrect: Spearman posited a single entity in common among all ability tests, while Thomson held that there is no one common element but simply overlapping samplings of elemental bonds. There is a theoretical chasm between these positions that is not easily bridged; one that cannot be narrowed by citing the similarity in the factor patterns predicted by each.

The second problem with the Eysenck integration concerns the Cattell-Horn theory of fluid and crystallized intelligences. In a number of places Eysenck (1979, p. 24; 1982, pp. 35–7) suggested that crystallized intelligence corresponds to the v:ed factor in the Vernon hierarchy and fluid intelligence to k:m, thereby bringing the theory of fluid and crystallized intelligence into agreement with the Vernon hierarchy. But both Cattell (1963, 1971) and Horn (1968, 1970, 1978) have often drawn sharp distinctions between fluid-crystallized theory and the British hierarchical view, especially Vernon's. One need go no further than to note that crystallized intelligence is marked by verbal-educational tests and by mechanical tests, since the knowledge assessed by mechanical tests is obtained through specific educational opportunities that are not equally available to all persons. This switching of the loading of tests of mechanical knowledge from the k:m (or fluid-like) factor onto the crystallized factor, which is indeed otherwise much more similar to v:ed, has been replicated in at least ten studies (e.g., Horn and Cattell, 1967a; Horn and Bramble, 1967; Cattell and Horn, 1978; Hakstian and Cattell, 1978), and calls into question the nature of the subgeneral factors postulated by the British hierarchical theorists. Additionally, in further elaborations of fluid-crystallized theory, although Cattell (1971) and Horn (1976, 1978, 1980) have diverged somewhat, they agree that there are more than two second-stratum abilities at the level of fluid and crystallized intelligences, citing the existence of such higher-order factors as spatial and fluency factors (Hakstian and Cattell, 1978; Horn, 1976). By failing to note crucial distinctions made regarding the nature of fluid and crystallized intelligences and the recent developments in the Cattell-Horn theory, Eysenck (1979) has again provided an impression of agreement among factor theories that does not fit the facts.

This leads to a third and final problem with Eysenck's views on factor theories: his insistence that the general factor from ability tests is both intellective and unitary in nature. While freely using analogies to biological and physical sciences to support his positions on intelligence, Eysenck (1979) criticized American researchers of conceiving of general intelligence as a 'gigantic molecule' built from the 'numerous atoms' that are the primary ability factors. One must, however, ask two questions. First, what evidence is presented that general intelligence is in fact unitary? Second, is it possible to construct a theory that would predict correlated ability factors yet no unitary general factor? In reply to the first question Eysenck (1979) provided little evidence that there is a unitary core to the general factor representing ability tests, aside from asserting Spearman's (1927) position regarding the three noegenetic laws. In a recent publication Eysenck (1983), citing the study by D. E. Hendrickson (1982), claimed that it appeared that Spearman's first noegenetic law, the apprehension of experience, was more central to the nature of the general factor than were either of the remaining two laws. This is a position similar to that of Galton, who sought to find relations between simple perceptual acuity and measures of intelligence, but in some contrast to that of Spearman (1927), who felt that the remaining two laws, governing the eduction of relations and eduction of correlates, were more central to intellective activity. The Galtonian cast of the current Eysenck position, emphasizing the importance of relatively low-level perceptual processing, and the reliance on a single unreplicated study that reported fairly astounding results (D. E. Hendrickson, 1982) is a rather weak basis supporting claims as to the unitary nature of *g*.

In answer to the second question one could cite the theory developed by Thomson (1951) in which there was no element in common among all types of intellective activity, yet the existence of a general factor was predicted. Taking a different tack, Horn (1968, 1970, 1976, 1978) has discussed a variety of bases for the general factor, none of which is intellective in nature. Such bases include *anlage* functions, which are largely low-level perceptual mechanisms that must function effectively for information to reach higher-order, intellective mechanisms. Other potential candidates include the general state of the physiological and functional brain, which receives a variety of insults during normal aging that may impair functioning in general, and the effects of constructs like motivation and attention.

Perhaps more important evidence that there may be no unitary nature to general intelligence are the life-span trends for different abilities reported by a number of researchers, most notably Horn and his associates (1970, 1978; Horn and Cattell, 1976; Horn and McArdle, 1980) and Schaie and his associates (Schaie and Strother, 1968; Schaie, Labouvie and Buech, 1973). These empirical studies have shown that performance on rather highly speeded and rather novel tasks tends to increase until the mid-20s or early 30s and then fall off rather rapidly with increases in age. On the other hand, performance on unspeeded, or power, tasks, and those measuring highly overlearned content, show small but continued increases throughout the period of adulthood until the age of approximately 60 to 70 years, after which performance on these measures also shows declines. Although factor analysis of such abilities may lead to the determination of an apparently unitary general factor, the nature of this general factor may be more illusory than real, with the general factor representing the 'gigantic molecule' built out of the 'atomic', more primary abilities that have different developmental precursors, different physiological bases and different life courses.

## Binetian

In his major theoretical writings Binet (Binet and Simon, 1916a, 1916b) claimed that intelligence was a broad construct that encompassed a variety of higher mental processes, such as reasoning, judgment and comprehension of complex relations. Eysenck (1979, p. 61) claimed that Binet's views 'incorporate a clear paradox', in that Binet was convinced that intelligence was comprised of several separable faculties yet his measure of intelligence yielded only a single score. As Eysenck noted, Tuddenham (1962) opined that Binet did not attempt to measure a single construct corresponding to general intelligence, or $g$, but rather provided an index of average intelligence or intelligence in general, a view on the nature of general intelligence shared by a number of theorists (e.g., Humphreys, 1962, 1976, 1979). Eysenck (1979, p. 61) went on to criticize the latter view of general intelligence on the grounds that it does not explain the tendency for tests of separable faculties or abilities to correlate in a fashion suggesting a single general factor; in contrast, theories, such as Spearman's and Eysenck's, that postulate a general ability common to all mental tests, provide explicitly for such findings.

As discussed in the preceding section, it is possible to derive a reasonable theory of primary and second-stratum factors, as Horn (1968, 1976, 1978) has done, that provides rationales for the appearance of correlated primary factors and, factoring these, correlated second-stratum factors, yet does not include provision for a single, unitary, general intellective ability. By overlooking different life-span trends for various abilities and alternative interpretations which Horn presents, we feel that Eysenck takes a narrower perspective on intelligence than the evidence seems to support.

## Piagetian

The voluminous theoretical and research effort undertaken during a lifetime of investigation by Piaget and a multitude of co-workers is much too great in magnitude to be dealt with here in any detail. However, one thing is clear: Piagetian research and theory deserve more attention in a review of research on intelligence than given by Eysenck (1979). While frequently decrying further factor analytic research and urging instead careful laboratory experimentation that seeks to examine the bases of individual differences on ability dimensions, Eysenck (1979, pp. 199–214) quickly dispensed with Piagetian research, suggesting that it 'supports, rather than confounds, the traditional paradigm.' Eysenck claimed that Piagetian tasks assess little more than general intelligence, relying primarily on the results of two factor analytic studies that revealed rather high loadings of Piagetian tasks on a general ability factor (Vernon, 1965; Tuddenham, 1970). To be sure, these studies and several others (e.g., Humphreys and Parsons, 1979; Carlson and Wiedl, 1976) have found that Piagetian items do covary highly with standard paper-and-pencil tests of mental abilities, but it is difficult to know how to interpret these findings. Although Piagetian items covary highly with other types of mental tests displaying individual differences, alternative patterns of results are possible that would be consistent with Piagetian theory but not with psychometric conceptions. For example, it is conceivable that no 6-year-old child would pass any presentation of a particular type of Piagetian task and that all 8-year-old children would pass every presentation. Both the lack of individual differences within age groups and the developmental differences across age levels could be easily incorporated into Piagetian theory. But the lack of interindividual differences within age groups would be anathema to the traditional paradigm, which counts on individual differences to provide grist for its theoretical and statistical mill.

Water retains an essential, chemical identity as it is raised from $-50°C$ to $+150°C$, even though the substance changes in its perceptible form from a solid into a liquid, and then into a gas. In a loosely analogical fashion, the essential identity of intellectual adaptation is preserved while the forms of intellective activity change greatly as children pass from the sensorimotor stage through the preoperational and concrete operational stages and arrive at the formal operational level. By showing this, Piaget has added greatly to our conceptions of the nature and functions of intelligence. This points up a contrast with the Eysenckian position on intelligence. If there is one thing in common, such as mental energy or the noegenetic laws, to all intellective activities, then individual differences and differences occurring as a function of age must be the result of quantitative differences in the common elements, e.g., differences in amount of mental energy or differences in efficiency in exercising the noegenetic laws. But Piaget stressed that ontogenetic changes are the result of qualitative differences, or differences in kind, rather than simply of quantity or degree. By failing to stress clearly this distinction, Eysenck apparently does not realize the ways in which Piagetian research complements, rather than either supports or confounds, the traditional paradigmatic approach to intelligence.

**Information Processing**

We feel that the field of human information processing, or cognitive psychology, may provide the most fruitful avenue in the foreseeable future for research on mental abilities and the ways in which persons solve intellective problems. This view is shared by many others, e.g., Estes (1981), Sternberg (1977a; Sternberg and Powell, 1983). Given the successes to date and the promise for the future, it is surprising that Eysenck (1979, 1982, 1983) should give so little attention to this type of research. In the present section two lines of research employing information processing paradigms will be briefly reviewed to illustrate the utility of this approach.

An important study, the first to investigate individual differences using currently accepted information processing paradigms, by Hunt, Frost and Lunneborg (1973), attempted to demonstrate the relationships between verbal and quantitative abilities and performance on a series of cognitive processing tasks. Two findings related to verbal ability were of note. The first related to rate of scanning in short-term memory using the Saul Sternberg (1969) paradigm. In the Sternberg paradigm a subject is shown, for a short period of time, a set of items to remember, usually consisting of from one to five letters or numbers. These items are termed the memory set. Shortly after studying the elements in the memory set, a probe item is displayed, and the subject must indicate, by pressing the appropriate button, whether the probe item was or was not in the memory set. Typical results have shown response time to be a linear function of the size of the memory set, suggesting that persons compare the probe item successively to each item in the memory set and that each such comparison takes a measureable amount of time, e.g., 40 milliseconds (ms.). Hunt and his colleagues found that high verbal subjects appeared able to scan items in short-term memory at a faster rate than low verbal subjects.

A second finding related to the Posner task, which involves speed of accessing name codes for letters from long-term memory. To use the Posner task, one must employ two conditions, the physical identity condition and the name identity condition. In the physical identity condition two letters are displayed, and a subject must indicate whether the two letters are physically and semantically the same or semantically the same and physically different. For example, AA is semantically and physically identical, but Aa, is semantically the same but physically different. In the name identity condition the subject must determine whether the two displayed letters have the same name regardless of their physical similarity. The latter, name identity determination, takes a somewhat longer amount of time than does determination of physical identity, presumably because the letter names must be retrieved from long-term memory. Hunt, Frost and Lunneborg (1973) found that high verbal subjects retrieved letter names from long-term memory more quickly than did low verbal subjects.

These findings by Hunt *et al.* (1973) were replicated and extended in a later study by Hunt, Lunneborg and Lewis (1975). Based on these investigations, Hunt (1976, 1978) developed a general model for representing individual differences in verbal ability. Although the framework proposed by Hunt is far from complete, our conceptions of mechanisms underlying verbal ability have been greatly enriched by the work of Hunt and his associates.

The second line of research is that initiated by Robert Sternberg (1977a, 1977b) on the cognitive processing components underlying analogical reasoning. Sternberg, whose approach was briefly described by Eysenck (1979), presented verbal, figural and geometric analogies of the form A:B::C:D to subjects and obtained reaction times to select the correct answer for each subject on each problem. By systematically varying the problems presented to subjects, Sternberg was able to obtain estimates of the amount of time a subject took to engage in each of the following cognitive components: *encoding*, the processing of a single fundament like A; *inference*, educing the relation between fundaments A and B; *mapping*, educing the relation between fundaments A and C; and *application*, educing the correlate D given fundament C and the relation educed from A and B. In this way Sternberg (1977a, 1977b) was able to obtain estimates of processes Spearman (1923, 1927) had considered central to the nature of general intelligence. By applying well-formulated regression models to the reaction time data, Sternberg was able to explain impressive proportions of reaction time variance at both the group and individual levels.

The Sternberg (1977a, 1977b) results pose both a promise and a problem for the Spearman-Eysenck view of general intelligence. Sternberg was able to obtain individual estimates of three cognitive components—inference, mapping and application—that are central to analogical reasoning. But split-half reliabilities of component scores were disappointingly low, averaging around .50. Further, the cross-task correlations of corresponding component scores, across verbal, figural and geometric content, were disturbingly low, generally less than .20 in magnitude. Finally, when component scores were correlated with paper-and-pencil tests of reasoning ability, the strongest correlations were typically found for the encoding component and the response constant, an unanalyzable combination of everything constant across problems aside from the explicit reasoning components. The reasoning components of inference, mapping and application showed very small and non-significant correlations. Although focusing attention only on the two original Sternberg reports (1977a, 1977b) does not do justice to his more recent extensive array of research studies, the results present problems of interpretation for the Spearman-Eysenck position.

The most recent published study we know of expressing the relationship of the Posner, Sternberg and Hick paradigms (the Hick paradigm will be discussed under 'Galtonian measures') to each other and to psychometric measures of intelligence was carried out by Vernon (1983). The Sternberg and Posner measures did correlate highly among themselves. Multiple regression analyses revealed that the reaction time measures correlated fairly highly with psychometric $g$, accounting for around 25 to 36 per cent of the variance if corrections for restriction of range were made. Similarly, the variance of the RT measures showed about the same level of association with IQ as did their reaction times. These results led Vernon (p. 69) to conclude that 'a moderately large part of the variance in $g$ is attributable to variance in speed and efficiency of execution of a small number of basic cognitive processes.' He pointed out further that the theoretical explanation for his results has not yet been developed, indicating that attentional processes may be implicated, as suggested by Carlson and Jensen (1982), or that individual differences in frequency of oscillation of synaptic potential might be involved, as theorized by Jensen (1979). In our view these are not, however, mutually exclusive theoretical perspectives.

We have been able only to allude to the scope and elegance of existing applications of information processing to intellective tasks. One conclusion seems clear: information processing models, by providing estimates of cognitive processes underlying more molar behaviours, appear to occupy an explanatory niche some-where between typical intelligence test scores, which are fairly gross products of complex intellective processes, and the rather molecular neurophysiological events that most assume are the substrate of such intellective processes. By attempting to relate directly typical test scores and measures of physiological activity, Eysenck (1983) seems to ignore the complexities involved in cognitive processes as well as in neurological response.

**Physiological**

The study of physiological substrates of intellective processes is still virtually in its infancy, but is an approach that promises to become increasingly important in the years to come. Although it is possible to trace interest and speculations about physiological bases in intelligence much farther, both Thorndike (1926) and Thurstone (1921, 1938) stated that reductions to the physiological level would perhaps provide the ultimate explanations and characterizations of mental abilities. Physiologically-based theorizing has influenced ideas and research on mental abilities in a number of ways. The early work by Penfield on electrical stimulation of cortical areas that led to vivid re-experiencing of previous events by patients demonstrated the physiological bases of memory. Clinical work by Luria (1961, 1966, 1980) with patients who had received brain injuries provided evidence of localization of functions in specific areas of the cortex, e.g., the importance of Broca's area for verbal comprehension and production. The work by Luria has also encouraged a great deal of research on neuropsychological test batteries, such as the Halstead-Reitan (see, e.g., Reitan, 1975) and the Luria-Nebraska batteries (Christensen, 1975; Golden, Hammeke and Purisch, 1980) which have been developed to aid clinicians in diagnosing the type and extent of brain damage incurred by patients. The research by Luria also led to the reconceptualization of human abilities by Das and his colleagues (see Das, Kirby and Jarman, 1975, 1979, for reviews) into simultaneous and successive processing abilities. Whether because of the applied, clinical nature of much of this research, because the evidence of localization of function does not fit into his theoretical scheme, or for other reasons, Eysenck (1979, 1982) largely overlooked these lines of research, regardless of the insights the research results provide into the physiological underpinnings of mental abilities.

## THREE MAJOR ISSUES

### Genetic versus Environmental Effects on Intelligence

Controversy concerning the contribution of hereditary factors to the development of human characteristics and capabilities is not new. It can be traced back to the early Greeks. The debate surrounding nature-nurture questions was particularly lively in Victorian England, and has continued to the present. Although in Victorian times the research base informing opinion on both sides of the nature-nurture debate was weak by today's standards, the controversy lacked neither intensity nor conviction. One of the most articulate spokesmen for the environmentalist side was John Stuart Mill. In his *Principles of Political Economy*, Mill (1864) made the following observation: 'Of all vulgar modes of escaping from the consideration of the effect of social and moral influences on the human mind, the most vulgar is that of attributing the diversities of conduct and character to inherent natural differences.' This view is shared by many today. It is consistent with the school of anthropology which has grown in the tradition of Franz Boas and Margaret Mead, as well as with much of contemporary sociology and psychology.

One of the most influential advocates of the significant contribution of hereditary factors to the development of human capabilities and characteristics was Sir Francis Galton. Galton pioneered the scientific study of individual differences and developed basic psychometric and correlational approaches for this purpose. He argued that intelligence as well as personal and moral qualities are largely inherited. The flavour of Galton's views is represented in an article he wrote for *Macmillan's Magazine* in 1865. He wrote (p. 318): 'intellectual capacity is so largely transmitted by descent that, out of every hundred sons of men distinguished in the open professions, no less than eight are found to have rivalled their father in eminence. It must be recollected that success of this kind implies the simultaneous inheritance of many points of character, in addition to mere intellectual capacity.'

Galton went on to state that 'eight per cent is as large a proportion as could have been expected on the most stringent hypothesis of hereditary transmission. No one, I think, can doubt, from the facts and analogies I have brought forward, that, if talented men were mated with talented women, of the same mental and physical characteristics as themselves, generation after generation, we might produce a highly-bred human race, with no more tendency to revert to meaner ancestral types than is shown by our long-established breeds of race-horses and fox-hounds.' We have here a call for eugenics. Galton, citing the relatively high fertility level of the less intelligent, felt that such an approach is ultimately responsible, being necessary for the preservation and development of society. Anything less would potentially guarantee that lesser endowed individuals would become so numerous that society would be threatened. Galton's firm belief in his observations and findings in specific and the laws and facts of science in general lay at the heart of these social and political convictions. In what only may be expressed as extreme reductionism, he stated in the same *Macmillan's* article that 'wherever else we turn our eyes, we see nothing but law and order, and effect following cause.'

Examination of Eysenck's writings makes clear the influence which Galtonian thought had on him. As an experimentalist, Eysenck has faith in the ultimate reducability of observed behaviour to fundamental laws and relationships; similar to and parallel with the laws of physics and biology. Eysenck is convinced that psychology can offer causal theories in a manner similar to the so-called 'hard' sciences. The treatment and elimination of the variables involved are different to be sure, but the promise remains the same. For Eysenck the search is for causal relationships, preferably through direct physical measurement. Concerning this point as it relates to intelligence, Eysenck (1982, p. 6) wrote the following in the introduction of his recent book, *A Model for Intelligence*: 'It always seemed likely that agreement on the "existence" of intelligence would not be reached as long as the concept was based on essentially phenomenological evidence, however elaborate the statistical treatment; what was clearly needed was the demonstration of a physical basis for what before had been treated as a mentalistic phenomenon.' As anticipated by Galton, Eysenck noted that 'the existence of such a physical basis was already implicit in the strong genetic determination of IQ measures.'

The evidence which Eysenck used to support his notions concerning the heritability of intelligence can be found in four main sources: *Uses and Abuses of Psychology* (Eysenck, 1953); *The IQ Argument* (published in the UK under the title, *Race, Intelligence and Education*) (Eysenck, 1971); *The Structure and Measurement of Intelligence* (Eysenck, 1979); and *The Intelligence Controversy* (published in the UK as *Intelligence: The Battle for the Mind*) (Eysenck and Kamin, 1981).

In his 1953 book Eysenck argued that *g*, or general mental ability, involves primarily speed of mental functioning. This view, again consistent with Galton, was based on work by Furneaux and anticipated that reaction time and average evoked potentials are the best measures of intellectual functioning (see Furneaux, 1960; Eysenck, 1967). In a chapter entitled 'Is Our National Intelligence Declining?', Eysenck expressed perspectives similar to those of Galton almost 100 years earlier: intelligence is largely inherited, and persons of high intelligence tend to have fewer offspring than less intelligent individuals. Although Eysenck was careful to suggest further research and point out the fact that group statistics say almost nothing about an individual's behaviour or test score, the reader is left with the notion that some sort of selective breeding would be of positive social value.

As early as 1953 Eysenck argued that 80 per cent of the variability in intelligence tests was due to genetic factors. The research that Eysenck reviewed to bolster his conclusion was generally presented and derived from five main lines of evidence: monozygotic-dizygotic twin data; orphanage data, where genetically very different children are raised in a virtually identical environment; the phenomenon of regression to the mean; the study of the relationship between IQs of real versus foster parents and children's IQs; and maze-bright, maze-dull work on rats done by Tyron.

*The IQ Argument* was a book written for popular consumption that addressed the issue of ethnic and race differences in intelligence being attributable to genetic factors. After admitting his hesitation and 'not a little aversion' to write the book, Eysenck proceeded to the following conclusions: (a) that intelligence is largely (approximately 80 per cent) heritable; (b) that substantial differences in measured IQ have been demonstrated for North American Caucasian and Negro samples; and (c) that it is probable that genetic differences account for the Caucasian-Negro differences. In addition, Eysenck argued that the American Negro population is genetically inferior to their African ancestors as the slavers tended to capture the less aggressive, duller types and the brighter individuals were more likely to escape. He wrote (Eysenck, 1971, p. 42): 'Thus there is every reason to expect that the particular sub-sample of the Negro race which is constituted of American Negroes is not an unselected sample of Negroes, but has been selected throughout history according to criteria which would put the highly intelligent at a disadvantage. The inevitable outcome of such selection would of course be the creation of a gene pool lacking some of the genes making for high intelligence.' Although Eysenck offered qualifiers that all the scientific evidence was not yet in and within-group variation cannot explain between-group differences, the picture remained fairly clear: genetic endowment seems to be largely responsible for the IQ differences between North American Negroes and Caucasians. On the more optimistic side, Eysenck conceded that phenotypic improvements can be made, but these would require massive efforts at environmental modification.

*The Structure and Measurement of Intelligence* (Eysenck, 1979) is a broadly conceived book dealing with models of intelligence and issues of measurement. It also contains three chapters, coauthored with D. W. Fulker, that deal directly with the nature-nurture question. In a chapter entitled 'Nature and Nurture: Heredity', Fulker and Eysenck outlined the general formulations involved in heritability estimates. Summaries and reanalyses of data were presented representing several lines of evidence: data on monozygotic-dizygotic twins reared together and apart; correlations between IQs of unrelated children living in the same home; correlations between foster parents and adopted children; correlations between natural parents and their children who were given up for adoption at birth; and inbreeding studies. The conclusion that Fulker and Eysenck (p. 127) reached was that 'the evidence relating to a strong heritable component in IQ is overwhelming with several lines of evidence converging on a strikingly consistent picture.' They concluded that 'as a result there can be little doubt that there is a strong biological basis to individual differences in intelligence as measured in modern industrial societies.' Not unexpectedly, the estimated contribution of genetic factors to variability in IQ is about 80 per cent for corrected estimates, and a more conservative 69 per cent for uncorrected estimates.

The other two chapters in *The Structure of Measurement of Intelligence* that bear on the nature-nurture issue concern environmental factors such as socio-economic status and schooling. As one would anticipate from the high heritability estimates of intelligence, Fulker and Eysenck were not very optimistic. The flavour of the general conclusion they reached has been stated by Eysenck (1981, p. 74) elsewhere, that 'the possibility of profound changes must be demonstrated in reality before their reality can be admitted. Simply to press for greater equality in education, in salaries, and in similar matters would not greatly alter the observed differences in IQ .... Those who believe in the possibility of manipulating intelligence by manipulating environmental variables bear the onus of proof, and so far that proof has not been forthcoming.'

*The Intelligence Controversy* consists of two divergent and antagonistic essays, one by Eysenck, although updated, essentially restating the views set forth in *The IQ Argument*; the other by Leon Kamin who set out to refute the assumptive and empirical base of Eysenck's arguments and conclusions. What becomes clear from reading the book is that Kamin and Eysenck differ almost completely in the paradigms that dominate their thinking, the former being critical of the Galtonian tradition, seeing scientific bankruptcy in the approach and social and political dangers in the conclusions which Eysenck reaches. Our purpose is not to do a comparative analysis of the Eysenck-Kamin debate. The record is available for the interested reader.

In our view there seems to be little doubt that genetic factors do play a significant role in variability in intellectual ability *within* groups of individuals. The preponderance of evidence, drawn from various approaches, allows no other conclusion. The question of *how much* of the variability in IQ measures can be attributed to hereditary factors is less clear. Eysenck suggests heritability estimates of around .80, apparently assuming that this figure is more or less a constant, across age and independent of social circumstance. But, summarizing a series of studies employing differing methodologies, Scarr (1981a) suggested that the best evidence for heritability of intellectual abilities in white populations ranges from .40 to .70, with age and environmental factors playing significant roles in the estimate. Analyzing more recent data, Plomin and DeFries (1980) indicated that heritability is around .50.

The 'true' heritability figure appears to be somewhat lower than Eysenck suggests, but one wonders how significant a heritability of even .50 might be. If, indeed, for white populations roughly half of the variance in IQ measures can be attributed to genetic factors, environmental factors, both within and between families, are still quite significant factors. It seems one-sided to avoid this and largely ignore or down-play the fact that environmental modification allows different phenotypes to develop from a common genotype.

Differences in phenotype can result from a common genotype interacting with different environmental conditions. This is called the range of reaction. As depicted in Figure 2, reaction ranges (RR) are related to both genetic potential and qualitative aspects of the environment. For example, a favourable genotype (B) may have a wider potential range of phenotypic expression than a less favourable genotype (A).

The reaction range model is clear in placing limitations on the modifiability of phenotypes; nonetheless significant changes are possible with appropriate, though often radical, environmental interventions. Gottesman (1963) has suggested that for average genotypes, environmental factors could account for $\pm$ 12 IQ points, a not insignificant figure if one considers the Gaussian curve and the difference in percentile ranking which a change of approximately one and one-half standard deviations (20–24 points) magnitude makes.

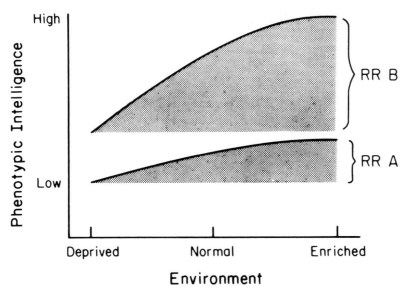

**Figure 2.** *Reaction Ranges (RR) for Two Different Genotypes (Greatest variability in phenotype related to environment is for the more favourable genotype B.)*

We know that the environmental conditions necessary to bring about changes in IQ which go to the limits of the reaction range are very rare, almost non-existent. We also know that social deprivation and lack of intellectual stimulation can lower measured IQ while stimulation and enriched environment can increase it. This does not suggest that heritability is unimportant. It is incorrect to assume a strong environmental hypothesis simply because phenotypic development is differentially affected by environmental circumstance. Similarly, it is incorrect to disregard environmental factors that would potentially allow individuals to develop to their potential. Our sense is that Eysenck does just that.

Eysenck's view that genetic factors are largely responsible for Caucasian-Negro differences in measured IQ is neither demonstrable nor refutable. As far as we know, there is no convincing evidence concerning heritability in non-Caucasian populations. Beyond this, observed differences *between* populations cannot be adequately explained by variability *within* a population. In order to test the hypothesis that genetic factors are responsible for between-group differences, the environments of the groups concerned would have to be equated. Otherwise, one must make the assumption that the environments for the groups in question are comparable. At best this assumption seems highly questionable when one considers the magnitude of social and cultural differences which exist between North American Negro and Caucasian populations.

In our view Eysenck's perspectives on the genetic determination of intelligence are both partially correct and partially incorrect. We agree with him that variability in IQ is related to genotype. But what is the strength of this relation? How important is it? The exact figure which should be used for heritability estimates is not clear. In fact, there may be several figures depending on age and environmental circumstance. For example, note the range of phenotypic expression for different genotypes in Figure 2. Eysenck's primary focus on genetic causes of interindividual variability in measured IQ is not so much wrong as one-sided. It overstates the case and directs attention away from efforts to understand the complex interactions between genotypic potential and environmental circumstance.


### The Competence-Performance Distinction

Eysenck views intelligence as a concept not unlike mass, heat, velocity or other concepts in the physical sciences. Through theory and the instruments to measure it, intelligence gains its definition. The often expressed idea that intelligence is what intelligence tests measure is neither tautological nor silly for Eysenck. For him operational definitions are as important to psychology as to physics. Eysenck (1979, p. 10) wrote that 'concepts are invented, not discovered; this is true not only of intelligence, but of all scientific concepts.'

The operational definitions of intelligence with which Eysenck seems most comfortable are : (a) culture fair tests which have high loadings on a general factor or *g*, one such test being the Raven Progressive Matrices; and (b) 'biological' measures, such as reaction time, inspection time and average evoked potential. Correlation of the latter measures with the former serves the function of validating each.

The distinctions made in Donald Hebb's (1949) theory of intelligence are important for Eysenck. Hebb suggested two different but related constructs: Intelligence A and Intelligence B. Intelligence A is theoretical, describing the general potential an individual has to learn from and adapt to an environment. It is largely determined by neurological factors of genetic origin. Intelligence B is the behaviour an individual exhibits and is a product of the interaction between genetic potential and environmental stimulation. Intelligence B is estimated through what Vernon (1962) called Intelligence C, actual performance on a culture fair test of *g*. For Eysenck appropriate measurement of Intelligence C will give fair representation of Intelligence B which in turn allows for reasonably accurate prediction of Intelligence A. He wrote (Eysenck, 1981, p. 22): 'Intelligence C—that is, IQ—is pretty closely related to Intelligence B, and the evidence suggests that Intelligence A is pretty closely related to Intelligence B in our society.' Accordingly, performance on tests such as the Raven will give fairly good indication of Intelligence A. Or conversely, individual differences in Intelligence A will be reflected by differences in performance on the Raven. If differences between individuals and/or groups on measures of Intelligence C can be shown, a *prima facie* case can be made that genetic factors, or Intelligence A, are implicated as responsible for these differences.

Although competence is often inferred from performance on intellective measures, the relationship is far from perfect. Eysenck is aware of this (see Eysenck, 1979, pp. 153–4), but does not seem to include this consideration in his generalizations concerning reasons for differences in performance on *g* loaded measures (Carlson, 1983b). As Scarr (1981b, p. 1161) suggested, 'Whenever one measures a child's cognitive functioning, one is also measuring cooperation, attention, persistence, ability to sit still, and social responsiveness to an assessment situation.' In addition to these factors work done by one of us strongly suggests that impulsivity, anxiety and ability to plan are significant variables affecting performance on tests such as the Raven Matrices and the Cattell Culture Fair Test.

A series of studies (see Carlson and Wiedl, 1980, for a summary) was designed to ascertain the effects of dynamic assessment approaches on performance on the Raven Matrices. First, several rather commonly used approaches to dynamic assessment were employed and compared to the standard manner of test administration (Carlson and Wiedl, 1979). These included simple feedback, elaborated feedback and verbalization. The condition which consistently led to improvements in performance on the Raven Matrices was verbalization, in which the child overtly described the task and how he approached it. The populations tested involved mildly retarded, normal and deaf children (for whom 'verbalizaton' was carried out with sign language) of varying ages. The significant improvements in performance on the Raven resulted from higher scores on the cognitively complex, conceptual items of the test (see Carlson and Jensen, 1980). It was concluded that the higher levels of performance more accurately reflected the cognitive competence of the subjects than the performance obtained using the standard procedure.

A second series of studies was carried out in an attempt to ascertain *why* verbalization results in higher levels of performance. The approach was to estimate the amount of variability in performance on the Raven due to what we called 'non-target' variables to see if verbalization would reduce that effect. 'Non-target' variables are those which can affect cognitive performance but are non-cognitive themselves. The 'non-target' variables of interest were impulsivity, anxiety, motivation and ability to plan (Das, 1983). Stating the results in summary form, we (Bethge, Carlson and Wiedl, 1982) found that the negative effects of impulsivity were reduced through the verbalization procedure. Verbalization led impulsive children to use strategies, as implied through changes in eye movement patterns, similar to those used by non-impulsive children. Similarly, it was found that verbalization reduces the negative effects of anxiety and lack of motivation and allowed children who were good at planning to perform at maximal levels (Carlson, 1983a).

A major conclusion from studies of dynamic testing procedures is that such procedures result in modifications in assessments of Intelligence C, allowing for more accurate inference of a child's level of Intelligence B and, perhaps, even Intelligence A. To the extent that performance reducing, 'non-target' variables differentially affect scores of some individuals and/or groups, observed differences in performance should not be taken at face value. Rather, exploration of *why* these differences occur should be undertaken.

Studies applying dynamic assessment procedures to children of different ethnic/racial groups are informative. Feuerstein *et al.* (1979) demonstrated that the application of their training techniques can lead to improvement in strategies for solving complex cognitive tasks and reduce differences between culturally advantaged and culturally disadvantaged groups in Israel. In other research, applying verbalization procedures designed to overcome potential deficiencies for children who do not verbalize spontaneously, Bridgeman and Buttram (1975) found that Negro children could perform on par with Caucasian children on the non-verbal analogy test of the Cognitive Abilities Test, a revision of the Lorge-Thorndike Intelligence test. The improvements noted for the Negro children were in the verbalization condition, while the standard administration of the test led to large Negro-Caucasian differences.

Similar results were obtained by Dillon and Carlson (1978) in a study in which Piaget-derived Matrices and Order of Appearance tasks (Winkelmann, 1975) were administered to 189 children representing three North American ethnic/racial groups: Caucasian, Negro and Mexican-American. It has been established that Piaget tasks are good measures of *g* (Humphreys and Parsons, 1979). The subjects ranged from 5 to 10 years of age and were divided into three age levels: 5–6, 7–8 and 9–10 years, with seven subjects in each cell. Several dynamic assessment procedures were employed, with verbalization and elaborated feedback proving to be more salient, improving performance over that assessed by traditional procedures ($C_1$). The verbalization procedure ($C_2$) simply involved the child overtly describing the task and his procedures as he solved it. The elaborated feedback procedure ($C_6$) involved the experimenter telling a child whether or not he was correct on an item and why. The child then went on to the next item, his performance being scored, of course, before any feedback was given. The results for the Matrices and Order of Appearance tasks were essentially the same. The Matrices results are summarized in Table 1 (after Carlson and Wiedl, 1980).

**Table 1.** *Means and Standard Deviations of Matrices for Three Age Groups, Ethnic Groups and Testing Conditions (C).*

| | Age: 5–6 | | | Age: 7–8 | | | Age: 9–10 | | |
|---|---|---|---|---|---|---|---|---|---|
| | $C_1$ | $C_2$ | $C_6$ | $C_1$ | $C_2$ | $C_6$ | $C_1$ | $C_2$ | $C_6$ |
| Anglo | ←————————→ | | | ←————————→ | | | ←————————→ | | |
| Mean | 1.29 ←−−→ .71 | | ←——→ 2.43 | 3.43 ←−−→ 2.43 | | ←——→ 4.29 | 4.14 ←——→ 6.00 | | ←−−→ 6.29 |
| SD | .95 | 1.11 | 2.23 | 2.37 | 1.51 | .95 | 2.80 | 1.73 | 1.60 |
| Mex-Am | ←————————→ | | | ←————————→ | | | ←————————→ | | |
| Mean | .57 ←−−→ 1.71 | | ←——→ 2.43 | 2.14 ←−−→ 2.71 | | ←——→ 4.00 | 4.29 ←——→ 5.71 | | ←−−→ 6.14 |
| SD | .98 | 1.70 | 2.23 | .90 | 1.50 | 1.41 | 2.29 | 1.38 | 1.07 |
| Black | ←————————→ | | | ←————————→ | | | ←————————→ | | |
| Mean | .57 ←−−→ .86 | | ←——→ 2.00 | 1.43 ←−−→ 2.71 | | ←——→ 4.14 | 2.71 ←——→ 5.72 | | ←−−→ 6.00 |
| SD | .79 | .85 | 1.83 | 1.40 | 1.60 | .90 | 1.38 | 1.25 | 1.00 |

−−− difference not significant.

——— difference significant.

As would be expected from verbal mediation theory, verbalization did not lead to increased levels of performance for the younger groups; it was, however, efficacious for the 9- to 10-year-old subjects. Elaborated feedback, on the other hand, resulted in higher performance for all groups. Interactions between the Caucasian, Mexican-American and Negro groups just failed to reach statistical significance, although inspection of the means and standard deviations will show a marked decline in the differences between the ethnic groups in the $C_2$ and $C_6$ conditions. Although the sample size was small and statistical significance was not reached, the study offered some supportive evidence that between-group differences on cognitive tasks may be reduced through use of dynamic assessment procedures.

Our research as well as that of others (see Guthke, 1980; Franzen and Merz, 1976) leads to the conclusion that performance on cognitive measures can be affected through dynamic approaches to assessment, yielding more accurate estimates of cognitive competence. The issue of whether or not such procedures can yield reliable compensations, i.e., reductions of the gap between ethnic/racial groups, is not resolved. Accordingly, pronunciations that such gaps in Intelligence C 'really' exist, allowing the inference that they represent differences in Intelligence B and therefore Intelligence A, seem premature. Caution in pronouncing differences, genetically-based at that, between groups of individuals would seem well advised.

## Galtonian Measures of Intelligence

As discussed earlier in the chapter, Eysenck's views concerning the nature and measurement of intelligence follow strongly in the Galtonian tradition. As Galton before him, the search is for the physical basis of intelligence. The assumption that a physical basis exists is predicated from the view that genetic factors primarily control the development of intelligence, necessitating a biological approach for its study. For Eysenck the major challenge in understanding intelligence is the development of direct, physical measurements of the construct. Along this line Eysenck (1979, p. 75) posed the following question: 'Can we formulate a physiological theory which can account for the major psychological and genetic facts, and which can produce measuring instruments, on the biological side, of reproducing the results which IQ tests can produce on the psychological side?' Eysenck's answer to this question is, not surprisingly, affirmative, although he realized that work in this area was just beginning. This affirmative response was based largely on a theoretical model of neuronal transmission developed by two of his co-workers, A. E. and D. E. Hendrickson, and results of studies involving three types of 'biological' (we use the term 'Galtonian') measures: average evoked potential, inspection time and reaction time. We will first take up the general aspects of the Hendrickson theory and then discuss each of the 'Galtonian' measures in turn.

## The Hendrickson Model and Average Evoked Potential

The model developed by the Hendricksons was first presented in 1972. Since then we have been able to locate four empirical and/or theoretical contributions they have made to the literature (Hendrickson and Hendrickson, 1980; Blinkhorn and D. E. Hendrickson, 1982; A. E. Hendrickson, 1982; and D. E. Hendrickson, 1982) that further explicate their views. The most extensive theoretical formulation was set forth in a chapter by A. E. Hendrickson in Eysenck's (1982) edited book, *A Model for Intelligence*. The basic metaphor that Hendrickson used to describe the mind was the computer. He noted (p. 152) that behavioural responses can be seen as computer programs. These programs may differ in a number of ways as (a) some programs have higher probability of success than others in leading to a desirable goal; (b) the amount of elapsed time for attainment of a goal varies between programs; (c) some programs require less 'cost' or energy or utilization of resources than less efficient programs; and (d) some programs involve more risk than others. Extending the metaphor and including these elements (probability, time, resource and risk criteria), Hendrickson developed an elaborate theory which focused on (a) the explanation of individual differences in genetically-based fluid intelligence, and (b) unbiased, 'biological' approaches to the assessment of fluid intelligence. The details of Hendrickson's theory are complex and best left to trained biologists and physiological psychologists for critical analysis. The general aspects of the theory are as follows.

For Hendrickson the computer's information input capacity and its reliability ('average amount of elapsed time between breakdowns or failures') have direct analogues in the human mind. The former is represented as redundancy and seen as the number of replicated components in the structural organization of the brain. Hendrickson suggested that redundancy is largely a product of the environment since learning is probably involved in the number of structural replications that develop.

Redundancy is represented by measures of crystallized intelligence. Reliability, on the other hand, is viewed as a characteristic of biological processes, representing the consistency and rapidity with which information is processed in the central nervous system. The mode of neuronal transmission is through the firing of individual neurons to form what are called 'pulse trains'. The capacity for error-free transmission is reflected by a parameter $R$ which is the probability that synaptic transmission will succeed. Individual differences in $R$ result in differences in the mean time to failure of a 'pulse train'. The higher the value of $R$, the greater amount of time of error-free transmission and the greater the intellectual capacity of the individual.

Hendrickson posited that the index which most accurately assesses $R$ capacity is average evoked potential (AEP). After describing work by Ertl and Schafer (1969) which showed AEP latencies (AEP latency-WISC IQ correlations ranged from $-.18$ to $-.35$) and wave complexity to be associated with psychometric intelligence, A. E. Hendrickson, (1982, p. 192) concluded that 'we can interpret the EEG AEP waveform as a kind of picture of the individual pulse trains that were set off by the primary stimulus. What follows then is the possibility of fairly direct measurement of the amount of error in the pulse train transmission, which might in turn have a monotonic relationship to the $R$ parameter.' Eysenck (1982, p. 8) went a step further, suggesting that 'the theory of $R$ as basic to intelligence also throws much light on the close relation observed between reaction time measurement (RT) and intelligence, and between inspection time (IT) measurement and intelligence.' We will attempt to examine that claim.

Evoked potentials which address information processing and memory are often called 'event-related potentials' (ERP). They can be elicited by sensory, cognitive or motor events and detected by means of bipolar scalp contact electrodes. The focus of most ERP research has been in the area of cognitive psychology, attempting to identify specific aspects of information processing 'stages' such as encoding, selecting, memorizing, decision-making, etc. (Hillyard and Kutas, 1983). The waveform evoked after stimulus onset is complex, representing exogenous or stimulus related activity as well as endogenous or cognitive processing activity. Most of the activity occurring before approximately 300 ms. relates to brain-stem activity and various exogenous factors. The task-related endogenous components of the wave are represented by the negative $N_d$ wave and positive $P_{300}$ wave. The $P_{300}$ wave is so named because of its occurrence approximately 300 ms. after stimulus presentation. The $P_{300}$ is of special interest in the study of cognitive processes and has been used in conjunction with Posner and Sternberg reaction time measures. For example, Kutas, McCarthy and Donchin (1977) found that while reaction time encompasses all the processes leading to decision and response, $P_{300}$ assesses stimulus evaluation processes (encoding, recognition, classification) independent of selection and execution.

The research informing the conclusions of A. E. Hendrickson and Eysenck was based on the assumption that AEP averaged over a number of trials is a good measure of $R$. The AEP measures involve wave latencies, variability in wave patterns across trials, and length of wave (i.e., complexity of trace). The stimulus used was an 85 decibel sound. Eysenck (1983) indicated that a sound of more than or less than 85 decibels did not stimulate the type of wave patterns which allow for correlations with IQ measures. The part of the wave considered significant is that which begins at the onset of the stimulus and ends at 256 ms., although Blinkhorn and Hendrickson (1982) analyzed episodes of 512 ms. The reasoning behind using 256 ms. episodes is that the average pulse train length is assumed to be about 230 ms.

The general finding of Blinkhorn and Hendrickson (1982) was that the complexity of trace, measured simply by the length of the trace line, correlated significantly with Raven's Advanced Progressive Matrices (APM) for a sample of thirty-three university students. The uncorrected correlation for the 256 ms. string with the APM was .54. The variability in wave patterns across trials did not correlate significantly with the APM.

The D. E. Hendrickson (1982) study was designed to replicate and extend the Blinkhorn and Hendrickson work. A primary sample of 219 school-age subjects was given the Wechsler Adult Intelligence Scale (WAIS). EEG data were collected on all subjects. The results showed strong correlations between WAIS IQ and AEP variance at 256 ms. (r = .72) and between WAIS IQ and 256 ms. strings (r = .72).

Although questions may arise concerning the robustness and meaning of these most impressive findings, Eysenck's (1983, p. 15) conclusion concerning their meaning was clear and straightforward: 'the EEG measure comes close to being a perfect measure of genotypic intelligence.' Concerning their robustness Eysenck (1983, p. 16) was somewhat more cautious: 'replication of the work here reported should be undertaken, to indicate whether or not it is essentially sound and reliable.' We certainly agree with the last statement while withholding judgment concerning the former.

The central reason for questioning the veracity of the AEP measure as an accurate measure of intelligence comes from the lack of clarity of interpretation of evoked potentials. Evoked potential waves are complicated phenomena and are related to many different events. Early evoked potentials indicate anatomic development of the cortex and the fact that pathways to the cortex are functioning. They do not indicate the degree to which the stimulus is processed by the peripheral receptors, more central nuclei, or the cortex (Parmellee and Sigman, 1983). It seems as though exogenous factors are primarily involved in the 256 ms. epochs reported by the Hendricksons and others, but so is selective auditory attention (Näätänen, 1982; Vanderhaeghen, 1982). Evidence implicating a specific exogenous factor comes from the apparent fact that stimuli of *only* 85 decibels will elicit the pattern of waves which will yield correlations with psychometric *g*. Accordingly, the relationship could be artifactual. As far as we could determine, no convincing reason has been offered as to why 85 decibel stimuli 'work' while other levels do not.

In summary, the meanings of specific waves of evoked potentials differ and are not agreed upon by physiological psychologists. Although the strong correlations between AEPs and psychometric intelligence which Eysenck and others report may be accurate, and that is an empirical question, two related questions remain. What is at the heart of these correlations? What are the functional relationships between early (< 256 ms.) evoked potential and intelligence? Perhaps the Hendrickson theory offers a beginning to understand these questions. At present the evidence is not in and an agnostic position concerning Eysenck's claims seems appropriate.

## Inspection Time

Inspection time (IT) is another paradigm that involves basically non-cognitive responses that appear to correlate fairly highly with IQ measures. The approach involves discrimination between two lines of obviously different length that are presented to the subject side-by-side on a tachistoscope. The task for the subject is to choose the longer line. The time of presentation of the lines is shortened to the point of the shortest exposure at which the subject can make the discrimination with an accuracy of 85 per cent. (Eysenck (1983) indicates that the accuracy rate is 97.5 per cent, but 85 per cent is the criterion used in most investigations.) Although not necessarily assumed by IT researchers (cf. Nettelbeck and Brewer, 1981), Eysenck (1983) suggested that the IT task is a valid measure of intellectual speed and a good index of *R*. He noted, however, that the highest correlations between IT and IQ were found for mentally subnormal subjects. Typical ITs for non-retarded subjects range from 100 to 150 ms.; for mildly retarded individuals the range is about double these figures. There is evidence (Lally and Nettelbeck, 1977) that differences in IT are not attributable to mental age as ITs for non-retarded 7- through 10-year-old children are very similar. Nettelbeck (1982) also indicated that the large IT differences between retarded and non-retarded persons can be related to differences in as yet unidentified cognitive strategies. A recent review by Brewer and Smith (1983) supported this perspective as it appears that retarded subjects employ different strategies in making speed-accuracy tradeoffs.

A recent publication by Nettelbeck and Kirby (1983) provided interesting reanalyzed results from a previous study as well as a new investigation relating IT, RT and intelligence. The reaction time assessment involved the Hick paradigm which will be discussed shortly. Inspection time was measured in the manner described above. In the reanalyzed study (Lally and Nettelbeck, 1977) the results showed that IT was the most consistent correlate of IQ, with the variance within bits of information in the reaction time task also correlating significantly with IQ. Nettelbeck and Kirby concluded that the magnitude of these correlations was largely due to the marked differences in performance between retarded and non-retarded subjects, inflating the IQ, IT and RT relationships. In the follow-up study by Nettelbeck and Kirby (1983) this problem was eliminated as analyses were carried out for a normally distributed sample as well as for samples excluding IQs greater than 85 and less than 115 respectively. The analyses included reaction time and movement time indices as well as visual and tactual inspection time. As far as inspection time is concerned, significant and consistent relationships were found between IQ and IT regardless of subject IQ classification. This led to the conclusion that IT is a promising measure, accounting for perhaps 25 per cent of the variance in IQ. This estimate is rather lower than Eysenck's (1983) pronouncement that for mildly retarded individuals IT-IQ correlations are between .8 and .9. Nettelbeck and Kirby indicated that caution should be employed in drawing generalizations from the results as several methodological issues still need to be worked out before inspection time can confidently be considered to be a reliable culture-fair measure of intelligence. Caution is further advised as not all studies employing the IT paradigm have yielded results showing that IT correlates with other RT measures or with psychometric intelligence. For example, Vernon (1983) found essentially no correlation between inspection time and measures of various reaction time paradigms (Hick, Posner, S. Sternberg) or WAIS and Raven measures of intelligence.

**Reaction Time**

The last Galtonian measure with which we shall briefly deal is reaction time. The most commonly employed reaction time paradigms are the Hick, S. Sternberg and Posner paradigms. The latter two paradigms were described early in this chapter under 'information processing'. Our discussion here will focus on the Hick paradigm. This paradigm involves the measurement of simple and choice reaction time. Simple reaction time is assessed as the time it takes the subject to lift his finger from a 'home' button after the onset of a single light. Choice reaction time involves the same measurement except the subject does not know which one of several lights will go on. The potential number of lights which may go on translates into bits of information. For the no redundancy condition in which only one light will go on, no bit of information is involved. Where the number increases to two, four or eight light combinations, one, two and three bits of information are assessed respectively. The apparatus consists of a panel which has eight light-button combinations plus a 'home' button. The subject presses the 'home' button. Between two and three seconds after a warning signal is given, a light will go on. The task of the subject is to lift his finger as quickly as possible from the 'home' button (RT) and move his finger to a button just in front of the light. Pressing the button in front of the light will turn off the light and record the movement time (MT), the time it takes to make the hand movement from the home button to the light button. Usually fifteen to twenty trials are given at each bit of information.

Our purpose is not to present a detailed review of the history of reaction time studies or empirical studies involving the Hick approach. A chapter at least as long as this one would be necessary for that; the interested reader is referred to two excellent review chapters by A. R. Jensen (1982, 1983). The approach we will take is to summarize as succinctly as possible the general findings of reaction time research as they relate to intelligence and to discuss how these findings correspond to Eysenck's perspectives on the relationship between intelligence and reaction time. (Note that although inspection time is a reaction time measure, we chose to present it separately from the paradigm outlined in this section.)

Most of the studies employing the Hick paradigm which relate RT to psychometric measures of *g* show similar results. All have confirmed what is known as Hick's law: RTs increase linearly as a function of bits of information (no, one , two and three bits assessed by one, two, four and eight lights respectively). The strongest and most consistent correlate of *g* with RT indices is for variability in reaction time. Jensen and Munro (1979) and Carlson and Jensen (1982), for example, found correlations between Raven Matrices performance and the standard deviation of reaction time to be .48 (N = 39) and .83 (N = 20), respectively. Interestingly, in both investigations movement time (MT) correlated significantly with Raven performance (rs = − .43 in both studies). In the Carlson and Jensen study the standard deviation of movement time also correlated significantly with the Raven (r = − .64).

Although correlations between *g* and RT are expected to increase across bits of information, most investigations do not show a clear trend in this direction. Both the Jensen and Munro and Carlson and Jensen studies showed fairly consistent and significant correlations between RT and *g* across bits of information. Neither study, however, found significant relationships between RT slope and Raven Matrices performance. A similar negative result was found in a subsequent investigation by Carlson, Jensen and Widaman (1983) where the RT slope-Raven correlation was only .09 (N = 105).

In short, certain reaction time parameters (RT intercept, RT medians and standard deviations) do correlate consistently with psychometric intelligence. The strengths of the relationships vary but tend to be rather smaller than the optimistic pronouncement by Eysenck (1983) that the correlation between RT and *g* at no bit of information is .45 but increases to around .76 at three bits of information. Although we are encouraged by the general results of the reaction time research, further work in the area should be aimed at uncovering the reasons for the correlations with IQ measures. This includes examination of variables such as attention in reaction time performance and the search for correlates of reaction time through the study of evoked potentials and event related potentials.

The role which voluntary, sustained attention might play in reaction time results and the relationships between certain RT parameters and psychometric intelligence were recently investigated by Carlson, Jensen and Widaman (1983). The hypothesis that attention may be a significant factor was guided by several lines of evidence. For example, Lansing, Schwartz and Lindsley (1959) found that if the warning signal preceded the stimulus by less than 100 ms., alpha blocking does not occur, and reaction times are high. If, on the other hand, durations of up to 400 ms. are used between the warning signal and the RT stimulus, almost full alpha blocking occurs and reaction times decrease. This suggests that higher levels of arousal and increased cortical efficiency are related to improved RT performance. Sanders (1977) found that time uncertainty between the warning signal and the stimulus increases RT and that increased stimulus intensity can decrease RT. Bertelson and Tisseyre (1968) found that a warning signal preceding the test stimulus by 200 ms. reduces RT. They reported some reduction in RT even if the warning signal is presented simultaneously with the RT stimulus. Support for the role which vigilance plays in RT results comes from the work of Krupski and Boyle (1978). They reported poor RT performance correlates with off-task glancing behaviour. Krupski (1975) found that lower magnitude of heart-rate deceleration (a physiological measure of attention), both at the warning signal and stimulus presentations, is related to increased RTs.

The results of the Carlson, Jensen and Widaman (1983) investigation supported the general hypothesis of their study. Significant correlations were found between total RT and total MT (r = .35), between standard deviations of RT and MT (r = .43), and between total RT and standard deviation of RT (r = .73). The correlations between movement time and reaction time seem to be related to attentional factors inasmuch as attention deployment is involved in both movement time and variability in movement time (Posner and Keele, 1969). Similarly, attention appears to play a significant role in the standard deviation of RT as the attention measure used in the study (random number generation task) did correlate significantly (r = .23) with that parameter.

A structural modelling approach was used to define RT, MT, *g* and attention latent variables and assess their relationships. This analysis showed that the attention latent variable does correlate significantly with the RT latent variable and the latent variable used to define *g* correlated with the RT latent variable.

The relationship among RT/MT parameters and the latent variables defined provides evidence that attentional factors are related to both RT and IQ, mediating, to a certain extent, the relationship between *g* and RT. More research must be done before firm conclusions are reached, but the general assumption which Eysenck makes that RT measures are *direct* indices of *g* may need revision and elaboration.

## SUMMARY AND CONCLUSIONS

In this chapter we have attempted to describe and evaluate critically the theoretical perspectives and empirical support underlying Eysenck's views on intelligence. Since our charge was to present a critical analysis, our efforts tended to emphasize points where we felt Eysenck's position to be weak or not fully substantiated. In some ways this emphasis may have resulted in a biased and/or incomplete overview and analysis of Eysenck's contributions and perspectives on intelligence. Since, however, a primarily positive view is represented in an accompanying chapter by Arthur Jensen, we trust that the reader will be given a broad base from which to inform himself and make judgments.

In evaluating Eysenck's contributions to and positions on intelligence research and theory, we have tried to place his views in the context of the field. First, the major approaches taken (ethological, psychometric, Binetian, Piagetian, information processing, and physiological) were described and our analysis of Eysenck's positions made. Second, areas which we consider to be of particular significance for Eysenck's perspectives were delineated and evaluated. These included genetic versus environmental effects on intelligence, the competence-performance distinction, and Galtonian measures of intelligence. Critical discussions of Eysenck's perspectives were incorporated in each section of the chapter, and will not be repeated here. We do feel that Eysenck has made significant contributions to the study of intelligence. His insistence to 'get to the heart' of the matter by examining the physiological bases of intelligence is praiseworthy and moves research on intelligence in new and exciting directions. Certain caveats concerning his views and the assumptions which guide them should, however, be made.

It appears to us that Eysenck does not sufficiently appreciate the value of the information processing approach and the promise which research using this paradigm has for uncovering and detailing the cognitive processes underlying intellective activity. The study of physiological correlates of intellectual abilities through analysis of cognitive event-related potentials seems to us to be a most promising avenue of research. At present, however, work in this area is only beginning. Accordingly, we feel that it is premature to state as unequivocally as Eysenck does that intelligence can be assessed with physiological indices, especially when those physiological indices assess the early evoked waveforms that do not reflect elements of cognitive processing. Intelligence A remains a theoretical construct and cannot yet be operationalized. It is misleading to suggest that it can.

We feel that Eysenck overestimates the contribution of genetic endowment when attempting to explain differences between ethnic/racial groups' performance on IQ tests. There is little doubt that genetic factors are significant for the development of mental abilities. At present, however, we do not have unequivocal measures of the abstract construct Intelligence A, which can only be estimated through what Vernon has called Intelligence C. In our view, performance differences on measures of Intelligence C, consistent as they may be, cannot be construed, *ipso facto*, as proof of differences in Intelligence A. We know, for example, that significant changes in measured IQ can be brought about by environmental stimulation. Questions concerning the generality and durability of such changes arise, and currently available evidence is not particularly encouraging. However, the reasons for ethnic differences in IQ, as well as achievement, most likely reflect deep-seated cultural and social factors that render intervention attempts only 'tip of the iceberg' remediations. We also know that performance on tests of general intellectual ability can be affected by a number of personality variables and the form of the assessment situation itself. To the extent that these variables differentially affect the performance of persons from different ethnic or racial groups, a source of bias of unmeasured proportions enters into the estimation of Intelligence C, hopelessly contaminating consideration of differences in the less tangible Intelligences B and A.

Eysenck has made significant contributions to theory and research in the field of intelligence. As is the case with pioneering efforts in any field, statements are made and perspectives advanced which need reformulation and further empirical support before they can be readily accepted. We hope that this chapter will aid in advancing our understanding of intelligence by suggesting areas to the reader where Eysenck's views are incomplete or even misleading and where further work needs to be done.

## REFERENCES

Barker, R. G. and Wright, H. F. (1954) *Midwest and Its Children: The Psychological Ecology of an American Town*, Evanston, Ill., Row, Peterson.

Barker, R. G. and Wright, H. F. (1966) *One Boy's Day: A Specimen Record of Behavior*, Hamden, Conn., Archon.

Berry, J. W. (1980) 'Ecological analyses for cross-cultural psychology', in Warren, N. (Ed.), *Studies in Cross-Cultural Psychology*, Vol. 2, New York, Academic Press.

Bertelson, P. and Tisseyre, F. (1968) 'The time-course of preparation with regular and irregular foreperiods', *Quarterly Journal of Experimental Psychology*, **20**, pp. 297–300.

Bethge, H.-J., Carlson, J. S. and Wiedl, K. H. (1982) 'The effects of dynamic assessment procedures on Raven Matrices performance, visual search behavior, test anxiety and test orientation', *Intelligence*, **6**, pp. 89–97.

Binet, A. and Simon, T. (1916a) 'The development of intelligence in the child', in Kite, E. S. (Ed. and Trans.), *The Development of Intelligence in Children*, Baltimore; Md., Williams and Wilkins. (Reprinted from *Année Psychologique*, 1908, **14**, pp. 1–90.)

Binet, A. and Simon, T. (1916b) 'New investigations upon the measure of the intellectual level among school children', in Kite, E. S. (Ed. and Trans), *The Development of Intelligence in Children*, Baltimore, Md., Williams and Wilkins. (Reprinted from *Année Psychologique*, 1911, **17**, pp. 145–201.)

Blinkhorn, S. and Hendrickson, D. (1982) 'Averaged evoked responses and psychometric intelligence', *Nature*, **295**, pp. 596–7.

Boring, E. G. (1950) *A History of Experimental Psychology*, 2nd ed., New York; Appleton-Century-Crofts.

Brewer, N. and Smith, G. A. (1985) 'Cognitive processes for monitoring and regulating speed and accuracy of responding in mental retardation: A methodology', *American Journal of Mental Deficiency*, in press.

Bridgeman, B. and Buttram, J. (1975) 'Race differences on nonverbal analogy test performance as a function of verbal strategy training', *Journal of Educational Psychology*, **67**, pp. 586–90.

Burt, C. (1949) 'The structure of the mind: A review of the results of factor analysis', *British Journal of Educational Psychology*, **19**, pp. 100–11, 176–99.

Carlson, J. S. (1983a) 'Dynamic Assessment in Relation to Learning Characteristics and Teaching Strategies for Children with Specific Learning Disability', Final Report for the US Department of Education, Grant #6068100426:89,027E.

Carlson, J. S. (1983b) 'Quelques alternatives à la théorie de l'intelligence d'Eysenck', *La Revue Canadienne de Psycho-Education*, **12**, pp. 138–41.

Carlson, J. S. and Jensen, C. M. (1980) 'The factorial structure of the Raven Coloured Progressive Matrices test: A reanalysis', *Educational and Psychological Measurement*, **40**, pp. 1111–16.

Carlson, J. S. and Jensen, C. M. (1982) 'Reaction time, movement time, and intelligence: A replication and extension', *Intelligence*, **6**, pp. 265–74.

Carlson, J. S., Jensen, C. M. and Widaman, K. F. (1983) 'Reaction time, intelligence, and attention', *Intelligence*, **7**, pp. 329–44.

Carlson, J. S. and Wiedl, K. H. (1976) 'The factorial analysis of perceptual and abstract reasoning abilities in tests of concrete operational thought', *Educational and Psychological Measurement*, **36**, pp. 1015–19.

Carlson, J. S. and Wiedl, K. H. (1979) 'Towards a differential testing approach: Testing-the-limits employing the Raven Matrices', *Intelligence*, **3**, pp. 323–44.

Carlson, J. S. and Wiedl, K. H. (1980) 'Applications of a dynamic testing approach in intelligence assessment: Empirical results and theoretical formulations', *Zeitschrift für Differentielle Psychologie*, **1**, pp. 303–18.

Cattell, R. B. (1963) 'Theory of fluid and crystallized intelligence: A critical experiment', *Journal of Educational Psychology*, **54**, pp. 1–22.

Cattell, R. B. (1971) *Abilities: Their Structure, Growth, and Action*, Boston, Mass., Houghton Mifflin.

Cattell, R. B. and Horn, J. L. (1978) 'A check on the theory of fluid and crystallized intelligence with descriptions of new subtest designs', *Journal of Educational Measurement*, **15**, pp. 139–64.

Charlesworth, W. R. (1979) 'Ethology: Understanding the other half of intelligence', in von Cranach, M., Foppa, K., Lepenies, W. and Ploog, D. (Eds.), *Human Ethology: Claims and Limits of a New Discipline*, Cambridge, Cambridge University Press.

Christensen, A. L. (1975) *Luria's Neuropsychological Investigation*, New York; Spectrum.

Das, J. P. (1983) 'Aspects of planning', in Kirby, J. (Ed.), *Cognitive Strategies and Educational Performance*, New York, Academic Press.

Das, J. P., Kirby, J. and Jarman, R. F. (1975) 'Simultaneous and successive syntheses: An alternative model for cognitive abilities', *Psychological Bulletin*, **82**, pp. 87–103.

Das, J. P., Kirby, J. R. and Jarman, R. F. (1979) *Simultaneous and Successive Cognitive Processes*, New York, Academic.

Dillon, R. and Carlson, J. S. (1978) 'The use of activation variables in the assessment of cognitive abilities of three ethnic groups: A testing-the-limits approach', *Educational and Psychological Measurement*, **38**, pp. 437–43.

Ertl, H. and Schafer, E. (1969) 'Brain response correlates of psychometric intelligence', *Nature*, **223**, pp. 421–2.

Estes, W. K. (1981) 'Intelligence and learning', in Friedman, M. P., Das, J. P. and O'Connor, N. (Eds.), *Intelligence and Learning*, New York, Plenum.

Evans, F. (1978) 'Monitoring attention deployment by random number generation: An index to measure subjective randomness', *Bulletin of the Psychonomic Society*, **12**, pp. 35–8.

Eysenck, H. J. (1953) *Uses and Abuses of Psychology*, Harmondsworth, Penguin.

Eysenck, H. J. (1967) 'Intelligence assessment: A theoretical and experimental approach', *British Journal of Educational Psychology*, **37**, pp. 81–98.

Eysenck, H. J. (1971) *The IQ Argument*, New York, The Liberty Press.

Eysenck, H. J. (Ed.) (1973) *The Measurement of Intelligence*, Baltimore, Md., Williams and Wilkins.

Eysenck, H. J. (1979) *The Structure and Measurement of Intelligence*, New York, Springer Verlag.

Eysenck, H. J. (1981) 'The nature of intelligence', in Friedman, M., Das, J. P. and O'Connor, N. (Eds), *Intelligence and Learning*, New York, Plenum.

Eysenck, H. J. (Ed.) (1982) *A Model for Intelligence*, New York, Springer Verlag.

Eysenck, H. J. (1983) 'Revolution dans la théorie et la mesure de l'intelligence', *La Revue Canadienne de Psycho-Education*, **12**, pp. 3–17.

Eysenck, H. J. and Kamin, L. (1981) *The Intelligence Controversy*, New York, John Wiley and Sons.

Feuerstein, R. *et al.* (1979) *The Dynamic Assessment of Retarded Performers*, Baltimore, Md., University Park Press.

Franzen, U. and Merz, F. (1976) 'Einfluss des Verbalisierens auf die Leistung bei Intelligenzprüfungen: Neue Untersuchungen', *Zeitschrift für Entwicklungpsychologie und Pädagogische Psychologie*, **8**, pp. 117–34.

Furneaux, D. (1960) 'Intellectual abilities and problem-solving behaviour', in Eysenck, H. J. (Ed.), *Handbook of Abnormal Psychology*, London, Pitman.

Galton, F. (1869) *Hereditary Genius: An Inquiry into Its Laws and Consequences*, New York, Appleton.

Golden, C. J., Hammeke, T. A. and Purisch, A. D. (1980) *The Luria-Nebraska Neuropsychological Battery*, Los Angeles, Calif., Western Psychological Services.

Gottesman, I. I. (1963) 'Genetic aspects of intelligent behavior', in Ellis, N. (ed.), *Handbook of Mental Deficiency*, New York, McGraw-Hill.

Guilford, J. P. (1967) *The Nature of Human Intelligence*, New York, McGraw-Hill.

Guilford, J. P. (1981) 'Higher-order structure-of-intellect abilities, *Multivariate Behavioral Research*, **16**, pp. 411–35.

Guilford, J. P. and Hoepfner, R. (1971) *The Analysis of Intelligence*, New York, McGraw-Hill.

Guthke, J. (1980) *Ist Intelligenz Messbar?* Berlin, VEB Deutscher Verlag der Wissenschaften.

Hakstian, A. R. and Cattell, R. B. (1978) 'Higher-stratum ability structures on a basis of twenty primary abilities', *Journal of Educational Psychology*, **70**, pp. 657–69.

Hebb, D. O. (1949) *Organization of Behavior*, New York, Wiley.

Hendrickson, A. E. (1982) 'The biological basis of intelligence. Part I: Theory', in Eysenck, H. J. (Ed.), *A Model for Intelligence*, New York, Springer-Verlag.

Hendrickson, D. E. (1982) 'The biological basis of intelligence. Part II: Measurement', in Eysenck, H. J. (Ed.), *The Structure of Intelligence*, New York, Springer-Verlag.

Hendrickson, D. E. and Hendrickson, A. E. (1980) 'The biological basis of individual differences', *Personality and Individual Differences*, **1**, pp. 3–33.

Hillyard, S. and Kutas, M. (1983) 'Electrophysiology of cognitive processing', *Annual Revue of Psychology*, **34**, pp.33–61.

Horn, J. L. (1968) 'Organization of abilities and the development of intelligence', *Psychological Review*, **75**, pp. 242–59.

Horn, J. L. (1970) 'Organization of data on life-span development of human abilities', in Goulet, L. R. and Baltes, P. B. (Eds.), *Life-Span Developmental Psychology: Research and Theory*, New York, Academic Press.

Horn, J. L. (1976) 'Human abilities: A review of research and theory in the early 1970's', *Annual Review of Psychology*, **27**, pp. 437–85.

Horn, J. L. (1978) 'Human ability systems', in Baltes, P. B. (Ed.), *Life-Span Development and Behavior*, Vol. 1, New York, Academic.

Horn, J. L. (1980) 'Concepts of intellect in relation to learning and adult development', *Intelligence*, **4**, pp. 285–317.

Horn, J. L. and Bramble, W. J. (1967) 'Second order ability structure revealed in rights and wrongs scores', *Journal of Educational Psychology*, **58**, pp. 115–22.

Horn, J. L. and Cattell, R. B. (1967a) 'Refinement and test of the theory of fluid and crystallized intelligence', *Journal of Educational Psychology*, **57**, pp. 253–70.

Horn, J. L. and Cattell, R. B. (1967b) 'Age differences in fluid and crystallized inteligence', *Acta Psychologica*, **26**, pp. 107–29.

Horn, J. L. and McArdle, J. J. (1980) 'Perspectives on mathematical/statistical model building (MASMOB) in research on aging', in Poon, L. W. (Ed.), *Aging in the 1980's: Psychological Issues*, Washington, D.C., American Psychological Association.

Humphreys, L. G. (1962) 'The organization of human abilities', *American Psychologist*, **17**, pp. 478–83.

Humphreys, L. G. (1976) 'A factor model for research on intelligence and problem solving', in Resnick, L. B. (Ed.), *The Nature of Intelligence*, Hillsdale, N. J., Lawrence Erlbaum.

Humphreys, L. G. (1979) 'The construct of general intelligence', *Intelligence*, **3**, pp. 105–20.

Humphreys, L. G., and Parsons, C. A. (1979) 'A simplex model to describe differences between cross-lagged correlations', *Psychological Bulletin*, **86**, pp. 325–34.

Hunt, E. (1976) 'Varieties of cognitive power', in Resnick, L. B. (Ed.), *The Nature of Intelligence*, Hillsdale, N.J., Lawrence Erlbaum.

Hunt, E. (1978) 'Mechanics of verbal ability', *Psychological Review*, **85**, pp. 109–30.

Hunt, E., Frost, N. and Lunneborg, C. (1973) 'Individual differences in cognition: A new approach to intelligence', in Bower, G. H. (Ed.), *Psychology of Learning and Motivation*, Vol. 7, New York, Academic Press.

Hunt, E., Lunneborg, C. and Lewis, J. (1975) 'What does it mean to be high verbal?', *Cognitive Psychology*, **7**, pp. 194–227.

Jensen, A. R. (1979) '*g:* Outmodel theory or unconquered frontier?', *Creative Science and Technology*, **2**, pp. 16–29.

Jensen, A. R. (1982) 'Reaction time and psychometric *g*', in Eysenck, H. (Ed.), *A Model for Intelligence*, New York, Springer Verlag.

Jensen, A. R. (1983) 'Methodological and statistical techniques for the chronometric study of mental abilities', in Reynolds, C. and Willson, V. L. (Eds.), *Methodological and Statistical Advances in the Study on Individual Differences*, New York, Plenum.

Jensen, A. R. and Munro, E. (1979) 'Reaction time, movement time, and intelligence', *Intelligence*, **3**, pp. 121–6.

Krupski, A. (1975) 'Heart rate changes during a fixed reaction time task in normal and retarded adult males', *Psychophysiology*, **12**, pp. 262–7, (67).

Krupski, A. (1980) 'Attention processes: Research, theory and implications for special education', in Keogh, B. (Ed.), *Advances in Special Education I*, Greenwich, Conn., JAI Press.

Krupski, A. and Boyle, P. (1978) 'An observational analysis of children's behavior during a simple reaction-time task: The role of attention', *Child Development*, **49**, pp. 340–7, (47).

Kutas, M., McCarthy, G. and Donchin, E. (1977) 'Augmenting mental chronometry: The P300 as a measure of stimulus evaluation time', *Science*, **197**, pp. 792–5, (95).

Lally, M. and Nettelbeck, T. (1977) 'Intelligence, reaction time, and inspection time', *American Journal of Mental Deficiency*, **82**, pp. 273–81.

Lansing, R., Schwartz, E. and Lindsley, D. (1959) 'Reaction time and EEG activation under alerted and nonalerted conditions', *Journal of Experimental Psychology*, **58**, pp. 1–7.

Luria, A. R. (1961) *The Role of Speech in the Regulation of Normal and Abnormal Behavior*, New York, Liveright.

Luria, A. R. (1966) *Human Brain and Psychological Processes*, New York, Harper and Row.

Luria, A. R. (1980) *Higher Cortical Functions in Man*, 2nd ed., New York, Basic Books.

Maxwell, A. E. (1972) 'Factor analysis: Thomson's sampling theory recalled', *British Journal of Mathematical and Statistical Psychology*, **25**, pp.1–21.

Mill, J. S. (1864) *Principles of Political Economy*, New York, D. Appleton.

Näätänen, R. (1982) 'Processing negativity: An evoked-potential inflection of selective attention', *Psychological Bulletin*, **92**, pp. 605–40.

Nettelbeck, T. (1982) 'Inspection time: An index for intelligence?', *Quarterly Journal of Experimental Psychology*, **34**, 299–312.

Nettelbeck, T. and Brewer, N. A. (1981) 'Studies of mild mental retardation and timed performance', *International Review of Research in Mental Retardation*, **10**, pp. 61–106.

Nettelbeck, T. and Kirby, J. (1983) 'Measures of timed performance and intelligence', *Intelligence*, **7**, pp. 39–52.

Nihara, K. (1976) 'Dimensions of adaptive behavior in institutionalized mentally retarded children and adults: Developmental perspective', *American Journal of Mental Deficiency*, **81**, pp. 215–26.

Nihara, K., Foster, R., Shellhaas, M. and Leland, H. (1974) *AAMD Adaptive Behavior Scale*, Washington, D.C., American Association of Mental Deficiency.

Parmellee, A. and Sigman, M. (1983) 'Perinatal brain development and behavior', in Haith, M. M. and Campos, J. J. (Eds.), *Handbook of Child Psychology, Vol. 2. Infancy and Developmental Psychobiology*, New York, Wiley.

Plomin, R. and DeFries, J. C. (1980) 'Genetics and intelligence: Recent data', *Intelligence*, **4**, pp. 15–24.

Posner, M. and Keele, S. (1969) 'Attention demands of movements', *Proceedings of the Seventeenth Congress of Applied Psychology*, Amsterdam, Zeittinger.

Reitan, R. M. (1975) 'Assessment of brain-behavior relationships', in McReynolds, P. (Ed.), *Advances in Psychological Assessment*, Vol. 3, San Francisco; Calif., Jossey-Bass.

Sanders, A. (1977) 'Structural and functional aspects of the reaction process', in Dornic, S. (Ed.), *Attention and Performance VI*, Hillsdale, N. J., Erlbaum.

Scarr, S. (1981a) 'Genetic differences in "g" and real life', in Friedman, M., Das, J. P. and O'Conner, N. (Eds.), *Intelligence and Learning*, New York, Plenum.

Scarr, S. (1981b) 'Testing *for* children: Assessment and many determinants of intellectual competence', *American Psychologist*, **36**, p.1159–66.

Schaie, K. W. and Strother, C. R. (1968) 'A cross-sequential study of age changes in cognitive behavior', *Psychological Bulletin*, **70**, pp. 671–80.

Schaie, K. W., Labouvie, G. V. and Buech, B. U. (1973) 'Generational and cohort-specific differences in adult cognitive functioning: A fourteen-year study of independent samples', *Developmental Psychology*, **9**, pp. 151–66.

Spearman, C. (1904) '"General intelligence" objectively determined and measured', *American Journal of Pyschology*, **15**, pp. 201–93.

Spearman, C. (1923) *The Nature of 'Intelligence' and the Principles of Cognition*, London, Macmillan.

Spearman, C. (1927) *The Abilities of Man*, New York, Macmillan.

Spearman, C. and Wynn Jones, L. L. (1941) *Human Ability*, London, Macmillan.

Sternberg, R. J. (1977a) *Intelligence, Information Processing, and Analogical Reasoning: The Componential Analysis of Human Abilities*, Hillsdale N. J., Lawrence Erlbaum.

Sternberg, R. J. (1977b) 'Component processes in analogical reasoning', *Psychological Review*, **84**, pp. 353–78.

Sternberg, R. J. and Powell, J. S. (1983) 'The development of intelligence', in Flavell, J. H. and Markman, E. M. (Eds.), *Cognitive Development*, in Mussen, P. H. (Ed.), *Handbook of Child Psychology*, Vol. 3, New York, Wiley.

Sternberg, S. (1969) 'The discovery of processing stages: Extension of Donders' method', in Koster, W. G. (Ed.), *Attention and Performance II. Acta Psychologica*, **30**, pp. 276–315.

Thomson, G. H. (1951) *The Factorial Analysis of Human Ability*, 5th ed., Boston, Mass., Houghton Mifflin.

Thorndike, E. L. (1926) *Measurement of Intelligence*. New York: Teachers College Press.

Thorndike, E. L., Bregman, E. O., Cobb, M. V. and Woodyard, E. (1926) *The Measurement of Intelligence*,

New York, Columbia University, Teachers College.

Thurstone, L. L. (1921) 'Intelligence and its measurement: A symposium', *Journal of Educational Psychology*, **12,** pp. 201–7, (07).

Thurstone, L. L. (1938) 'Primary mental abilities', *Psychometric Monographs*, No. 1.

Thurstone, L. L. and Thurstone, T. G. (1941) 'Factorial studies of intelligence', *Psychometric Monographs*, No. 2.

Tuddenham, R. D. (1962) 'The nature and measurement of intelligence', in Postman L. (Ed.), *Psychology in the Making: Histories of Selected Research Problems*, New York, Alfred A. Knopf.

Tuddenham, R. D. (1970) 'A "Piagetian" test of cognitive development', in Dockrell W. B. (Ed.), *On Intelligence: The Toronto Symposium on Intelligence, 1969*, London, Methuen.

Vanderhaeghen, C. N. (1982) 'Psychobiologie de l'attention temps de reaction et potentiels evoqués', *L'Année Psychologie*, **82,** pp. 473–95.

Vernon, P. E. (1962) *The Structure of Human Abilities*, 2nd ed., London, Methuen.

Vernon, P. E. (1965) 'Ability factors and environmental influences', *American Psychologist*, **20,** pp. 723–33.

Vernon, P. E. (1969) *Intelligence and Cultural Environment*, London, Methuen.

Vernon, P. E. (1983) 'Speed of information processing and general intelligence', *Intelligence*, **7,** pp. 53–70.

Wechsler, D. (1939) *The Measurement of Adult Intelligence*, Baltimore, Md., Williams and Wilkins.

Wechsler, D. (1975) 'Intelligence defined and undefined: A relativistic appraisal', *American Psychologist*, **30,** pp. 135–9.

White, P. O. (1973) 'Individual differences in speed, accuracy, and persistence: A mathematical model for problem solving', in Eysenck, H. J. (Ed.), *The Measurement of Intelligence*, Baltimore, Md., Williams and Wilkins.

White, P. O. (1982) 'Some major components in general intelligence', in Eysenck, H. J. (Ed.), *A Model for Intelligence*, New York, Springer-Verlag.

Winkelmann, W. (1975) *Test Zur Erfassung kognitiver Operationen*, Braunschweig, Westerman.

# Interchange

## JENSEN REPLIES TO CARLSON AND WIDAMAN

Carlson and Widaman by no means come across as antagonists of Eysenck. Their few criticisms and the many questions they raise seem to me to be a highly judicious and thoughtful selection of the issues that would arise from a critical discussion of Eysenck's work on intelligence by any group of technically qualified and scientifically motivated scholars. It is good commentary in that it provokes thoughtful reaction and appreciation of the need for further clarification or theoretical and empirical development of Eysenck's ideas about intelligence and its many manifestations. In this respect, some of the points made by Carlson and Widaman seem to me much more central than others. I will here try to indicate briefly what seem to me to be the least crucial issues and the most important issues they raise.

First, I would argue that a researcher who strives to do something more than to produce a theoretically neutral, or eclectic, and comprehensive textbook on a given subject, but rather hopes to advance the scientific frontier of the subject, must be quite selective in the phenomena, problems, hypotheses and methods on which he focuses his efforts. Research talent consists, in large part, of having a 'sixth sense' in this selectivity—of intuitively making the scientifically fruitful bets. Eysenck possesses this knack, I think, in greater degree than most other research psychologists. In the realm of intelligence Eysenck has remarkably focused on what seem to me to be the most crucial questions. Therefore, it seems to me a trivial point that Eysenck's writings on intelligence are not as comprehensive of every school of thought or of every facet of empirical research on intelligence as would be possible if that were his primary aim. Better to dig vertically into a few crucial problems than to spread horizontally over many phenomena, if the aim is scientific advancement.

It could be argued, for example, that Eysenck has not dealt extensively with Piaget because he has seen that Piaget's conception of intelligence really concerns the different phenomenal manifestations of $g$. The different performances of children of varying ages which are elicited by the various developmental tasks of Piaget's *méthode clinique* can be viewed as different manifestations of $g$ interacting with tasks of increasing complexity. Once it has been shown that these Piagetian tasks measure Spearman's $g$ to about the same degree as many standard tests of intelligence, it is apparent that Piaget presents no unique source of variance for study under the heading of intelligence. It is much more likely that the age discontinuities in performance on Piaget's tasks will have to be explained in terms of the information-processing demands of the specific tasks than in terms of discontinuity in the development of the neurophysiological substrate of $g$. An ability which develops in a smoothly gradual fashion can be manifested across the period of development as

133

stepwise stages or qualitative differences in performance, if the task demands of the measuring instruments increase in informational complexity in a stepwise fashion. This kind of discrete or stepwise increase in information-processing demands appears to characterize the classical Piagetian tests. But Piagetian tasks, viewed as single 'items', are not at all unique, as Carlson and Widaman suggest, in showing little or no individual differences *within* certain age groups while showing large individual differences *between* certain age groups. The same characteristics are true of any single age-scaled *item* (scored as 'passed' or 'failed') in standard psychometric tests such as the Stanford-Binet and Wechsler scales.

Another wise selective choice by Eysenck was to become thoroughly familiar with, but to avoid theoretical involvement with, the research and discussion on what he (following Hebb) terms Intelligence B, i.e., the highly varied phenomenal manifestation of intelligence in human behaviour as observed in its natural habitat. His essentially Galtonian focus on Intelligence A and its relationship to Intelligence C will, I think, prove more rewarding, scientifically, than will attempts to systematize Intelligence B. The discovery of the process of combustion did not come about through the observation of fire, as fascinating as that might be in its own right, but through precise measurements of chemical reactions in the laboratory which bore no superficial resemblance to fire *per se*. Similarly, I see more promise in Eysenck's 'Galtonian' analytic approach to the phenomenon of intelligence than in the more global, ethological and psychological approaches.

Carlson and Widaman take issue with Eysenck's position on the probable causes of the observed racial differences in IQ, particularly the black-white difference. If there is a scientifically more defensible position than Eysenck's, I have not found it cogently argued. Eysenck acknowledges the fact that a genetic component in racial differences in mental abilities has not been empirically proved. But neither has a genetic hypothesis been disproved. Entirely environmental explanations, on the other hand, have fared badly indeed; those which have been susceptible to the test of objective evidence have already been disproved. The challenge of accounting for the approximately one standard deviation difference between black and white Americans has not been met by those who eschew even open agnosticism regarding the involvement of genetic factors. The *ad hoc* assumption of test bias to explain racial differences, when no such bias can be demonstrated by any objective psychometric or statistical analyses for the majority of standardized tests in current use, can be scarcely more than preference for the popular, although empirically unsupported, answer to a perplexing and disturbing question. Eysenck has acknowledged the perplexity and explicated the difficult facts. He does not shun the truly open question which has proved to be the one academic taboo of this era.

By far the most important question raised by Carlson and Widaman, scientifically, is whether $g$ is the result of a single process or of a number of processes. This is the central question in this field today. That it cannot be resolved by the factor analysis of psychometric tests is now recognized by virtually all the experts. The correlation of the average evoked potential (AEP) with psychometric $g$ seems consistent with the hypothesis of $g$ as a unitary process. But this conclusion will depend largely upon how much of the $g$ variance remains explained by the AEP after there have been sufficient replications of the promising results from Eysenck's laboratory. If the final outcome is highly consistent with the present picture painted by Eysenck, it is hard to see how one could escape a decisive refutation of Sir Godfrey Thomson's sampling theory of $g$ and all its close relatives in cognitive psychology, which argue that cognitive tasks are correlated because two or more independent, elementary information-processing components are involved in every task or because all complex *g*-loaded tasks invoke the operation of certain metaprocesses which coordinate the deployment of the elementary processes in problem-solving. The character of future theories of intelligence will depend essentially on whether multiple-process theories of *g* are decisively refuted or are clearly upheld.

A theory of mental ability must also explain the non-*g* variance (i.e., the various group factors and specificity) that consistently emerges in factor analyses of psychometric tests. Eysenck's theory is still undeveloped in this respect. If certain group factors (e.g., verbal, numerical, spatial) show significant heritability independent of *g*, we should expect to find distinct brain processes underlying the group factors, differing somehow from the process (or multiple processes) underlying *g*. Eysenck's order of priority in researching these questions, however, seems to me strategically correct, with *g*, the single largest component of variance in psychometric tests, being given top priority for theoretical development and empirical exploration.

# CARLSON AND WIDAMAN REPLY TO JENSEN

In his chapter, 'The Theory of Intelligence', Jensen has provided an informative perspective on Eysenck and his contributions to research and theorizing on intelligence. Eysenck's Galtonian orientation is outlined and the fundamental elements of his recent theorizing concerning the biological bases of intelligence are given. Jensen aptly characterized Eysenck's approach to the study of intelligence with four words: objective, quantitative, analytical, biological. We agree with Jensen that these descriptors summarize the essence of Eysenck's approach. The question of the extent to which Eysenck has been successful in developing theory and research on intelligence which meets the criteria implicit in the terms has not been settled. In this very brief response we will attempt to summarize our views concerning this question.

The quantitative aspects of Eysenck's work on intelligence are obvious; in his writings on intelligence, as in other domains of interest, Eysenck has posed theoretically intriguing questions and supplied highly quantitative answers to them. The question is not with the quantitative nature of Eysenck's work, which has been buttressed with results from an impressive array of statistical methods. We simply wonder about the reliability of some of the quantitative answers Eysenck has supplied. One example is estimates of heritability. Eysenck has clung to his position that genetic endowment explains 80 per cent of the variance of IQ scores, even though recent work, reviewed in our chapter, suggests both lower estimates and the influence on these estimates of various subject characteristics, such as socio-economic level, ethnic group identity, and family characteristics. A second example is the magnitude of the correlation between certain physiological measures and IQ. As Jensen noted in his chapter, Eysenck (1973) admitted that corrections for attenuation and other manipulations were required to raise .30 to .50 correlations between evoked potential indices and IQ up to .70. However, in his recent work Eysenck (1983a) called for a revolution in intelligence testing given recent results showing a .84 correlation between evoked potential measures and IQ, and staunchly denied (1983b) that any sort of correction was applied. The simple fact is that the .84 correlation between physiological indices and IQ is so high as to challenge credibility. We would prefer to consider Eysenck's results as highly tentative until they are well replicated in other laboratories.

The analytical nature of Eysenck's efforts on intelligence is perhaps most impressively shown in the model which splits intelligence into the three components: mental speed, persistence, and error checking. Since the first presentation of this model in the 1950s, the tripartite model has been an interesting and potentially useful alternative to models that treat performance on intelligence tests as indicative of a global, unanalyzable entity or as only one index in an overwhelmingly complicated and empirically poorly supported multi-factorial model. The major question at this time is, given the extensive and impressive mathematical bases derived by Furneaux and White, why so little empirical research has been generated by the model. If the tripartite model could change drastically our thinking about intelligence, why have Furneaux and White each pursued apparently a single empirical investigation to test predictions derived from the model and published their results in somewhat obscure journals? The elegance of the highly analytical tripartite model of intelligence is unquestioned; the empirical status of the model is unclear.

Eysenck's attempts to understand intelligence from the biological perspective and his views that individual differences in intelligence stem largely from genetic factors represent the essence of Galtonian thinking. Research and theory concerning the biological bases of intelligence and its development are without question of enormous scientific interest. It seems to us, however, that environmental and ecological factors do play significant roles in the development of intelligence and its manifestation throughout life. Accordingly, environmental and ecological factors should not be disregarded as disregard can threaten the overall objectivity of intelligence theorizing. Eysenck's almost exclusive focus on biological factors does not allow as rich a theory or differentiated view of intelligence as would a more catholic approach. Environmental and ecological analyses would not imply that biological and genetic factors are insignificant; rather, consideration of such factors would provide a larger picture of intelligence than Eysenck presently does. Recent work by Wilson and Matheney (1983) is informative on this point. Their research has shown clear relationships between developing IQ and the adequacy of specific home environmental variables and characteristics of the mother. Wilson and Matheney suggest that while inheritance is perhaps the primary datum related to parental behaviours and characteristics and offspring's mental growth, family environment does make significant contribution to children's cognitive functioning. Analyses of this type plus more largely conceived ecological analyses of how intelligence is manifested in daily life are critical for a fully developed, objective theory of intelligence.

## REFERENCES

Eysenck, H. J. (1973) *The Measurement of Intelligence*, Baltimore, Md., Williams and Wilkins.

Eysenck, H. J. (1983a) 'Révolution dans la théorie et la mesure de l'intelligence', *La Revue Canadienne de Psycho-Éducation*, **12**, pp. 3–17.

Eysenck, H. J. (1938b) 'Révolution dans la théorie et la mesure de l'intelligence: Réponse à quelques critiques', *La Revue Canadienne de Psycho-Éducation*, **12**, pp. 144–7.

Wilson, R. S. and Matheney, A. P. (1983) 'Mental development: Family environment and genetic influences', *Intelligence*, **7**, pp. 195–215.

# Part VI: Social Attitudes

# 9. The Psychological Bases of Political Attitudes and Interests

CHRISTOPHER BRAND

It was axiomatic to the philosophers of ancient Greece that there would be some relation between the character of a people and its political institutions and policies. Moreover, since this relationship was held to involve causal influences going in both directions, the nature of the State would be of moral importance both as an expression of and as an encouragement to the virtues of its people.

Twentieth century experience of the provision to new nation-states of constitutions that enshrine Western traditions of justice and democracy may inspire little confidence as to the straightforwardly causal influence of the State itself upon its people; but the century's passion for politics—a passion that has, however temporarily, replaced previous interests in religion amongst the talking classes—suggests that political ideas are certainly seen today as expressing and even instantiating personal virtues and vices. It is not just that references to the 'liberalism' or 'conservatism' of a person's views are a commonplace of journalistic writing and of everyday working life amongst those employed in humanitarian endeavours. The dimension of *Right versus Liberal/Left*—with its gradations of 'far-', 'ultra-', Centre- and so forth—is already a more acceptable way of describing daily human variability than are many of those 'personality traits' that emerge from professional personological research; yet this dimension itself has increasingly been rivalled by writers' references to another dimension for which Eysenck, following William James, had used Shakespeare's nomenclature (in *King Lear*) of 'tough-' *versus* 'tender-mindedness'. Whether there is truly some broad but essentially unitary dimension that runs through references to 'extremism', 'totalitarianism', 'fanaticism', 'statism' and relentless ideological preoccupation as opposed to 'moderation', 'pragmatism', 'social democracy' and (to use the popular term coined by the present British Prime Minister) 'wetness' must be the central concern of the present essay. But, whatever qualifications must attend the postulation of such broad dimensions as Eysenck's conservatism (C) and tough-mindedness (T), it deserves remark that, through the

1970s, the rise of despotic and lawless corporate states, and of corporatism and terror within those forty countries of the world that remained democracies within the rule of law, suggests Eysenck's far-sightedness when, first of all in the 1940s, he indicated some possible relations between psychology and extremist politics that deserved empirical attention.

## EYSENCK'S THEORY OF POLITICAL ATTITUDES

The most recent and adequate account both of Eysenck's theory and of the evidence that he takes to attest it can be found in *The Psychological Basis of Ideology* (Eysenck and Wilson, 1978). Lest it seem surprising that such concern with political ideology should be shown by two colleagues in the field of clinical psychology, it should be said at once that Eysenck has never attempted to impose any *a priori* distinctions between political, religious, social and moral attitudes, nor even between attitudes, personality, values, interests, occupational preferences and psychopathology. Indeed, over the years it has very much been Eysenck's role to operate as a unifying theoretician across all areas of psychology. He has repeatedly pointed to general empirical regularities and explanatory principles, and not least to those that might unify correlational and experimental psychology and allow developmentalists and personologists and cognitivists and psychometricians—if not perhaps behaviourists and psychoanalysts—to talk peace to each other if they could begin to share his breadth of vision.

Of course, all distinctly scientific activity requires the posing of questions within certain initial constraints—especially that of achieving some kind of quantification and measurement of the phenomena that require explanation. At its most modest, science at least requires the observation of regularities in nature that—precisely because they are not isolated and unique events—can be submitted to repeated enquiry. Insofar as most psychologists would wish to concern themselves ultimately with the understanding of at least some unique individuals and extraordinary events, such scientific constraints may seem too restrictive; but the psychologist who would like to understand the unique stance of Prime Minister Thatcher or General Secretary Gorbachev will hardly deny that such understanding would make at least some reference to law-like generalizations; and Eysenck, for his part, would allow that such scientific explanation would be unlikely to tell the whole of any individual human story. There need be no contest here except with the theorist who strangely wants to call his theory psychological while ruling out the scientific method altogether and substituting notions that would not earn a living for even a third-rate historian or novelist.

Eysenck's insistence upon looking at regularities yields immediately another distinctive feature of his theory of attitudes. For, with the help of factor analysis, it is possible (again within various methodological constraints) to pose the question, 'What are the major regularities to be found amongst people's attitudes?' It is true that such a question can only be properly answered with reference to a particular population and with reference to a particular collection of items; and some psychologists may allege disappointment at having the question answered chiefly with regard to literate Western populations as surveyed by questionnaire and allied techniques. Still, it is quite open to the critic to expand the range of such studies if he genuinely suspects parochialism; and, meanwhile, Eysenck would point to the robustness of his major dimensions of attitudes across many different countries—not all of them English-speaking (see, *e.g.*, Sidanius and Ekehammer, 1982)—and across the various techniques that different researchers have already used. At least across such populations as have been sampled, Eysenck's most general empirical claims would be: (1) that there are linear relations between stated attitudes which allow meaningful talk of 'dimensions' rather than 'types' of opinionation; (2) that some 30 per cent of covariation between attitudes can be statistically accounted for by a two-dimensional space, the independent axes of which might be named as *conservatism versus liberalism* and *tough-mindedness* (or, as Wilson prefers, *realism*) *versus tender-mindedness* (or *idealism*)—see Figure 1.

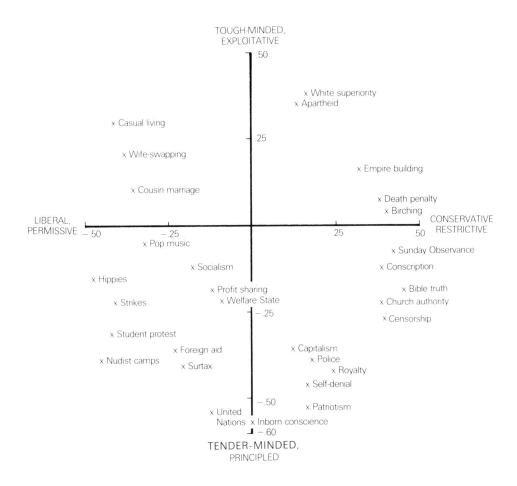

**Figure 1.** indicates the causes that are favoured by people who differ around Eysenck's two-dimensional space for social attitudes. A suggested positioning of Eysenck's two dimensions (as he has historically conceived them) is indicated. The loadings of items on these dimensions have been estimated from Eysenck's (1976) data for 1442 quota-sampled British adults. It can be observed that high-'T' subjects dislike most conventional forms of political endeavour and that the major political parties make no conspicuous effort to represent their views.

The essential modesty of such claims should not be neglected by the critic who is eager to accuse Eysenck of being unduly dogmatic and simplistic.

Names and definitions are, however, mere pegs on which to hang ideas and correlational findings until scientific inquiry has progressed; and Eysenck would acknowledge two important questions that need to be posed about his two-dimensional scheme.

The first is that of whether two dimensions are really sufficient to describe the ways in which people's attitudes are organized. For example, a person might conceivably approve of a strong military posture for his country (perhaps in righteous reaction to supposedly unenlightened and hostile neighbours) while abjuring racism, anti-Semitism, sexism, traditional Christianity and yet other beliefs that more normally tend to correlate with militarism and thus to define *tough-minded conservatism*. To the extent that such a combination of attitudes occurred with any frequency Eysenck's scheme would come under straightforward pressure to de-emphasize the importance of general *conservatism* and to allow a third dimension of, say, 'progressive nationalism'. But, even at a lower frequency, the occurrence of such opinionation would still tend to make for a statistically distinguishable factor of 'militarism' for all that such a factor would still have some positive correlation with other broadly conservative attitudes. In fact, Eysenck's and Wilson's findings typically allow just such an option—just as they have sometimes yielded factors concerned with 'economic conservatism' (support for capitalism and private property as opposed to nationalization and trade unionism) that have appeared almost independent of the omnipresent broad dimension of 'social conservatism'. Eysenck's scheme is not, then, some kind of attempt to deny that there might be other ways in which opinions might meaningfully covary; his empirical finding is simply that, in studies conducted over the past fifty years, his two-dimensional space has time and again proved adequate to accommodate the outstanding features of attitudinal co-variation in the general population. (One reason for this has doubtless been that, especially in Britain since the 1960s, so few respondents outside the universities support such causes as nationalization and trade union power that such items can yield little covariation with other statements of attitude.)

The second problem is that of whether, even accepting Eysenck's two dimensional space as empirically adequate, the particular dimensions of C and T provide the best way of characterizing that variation. Other workers (see Brand, 1981) have sometimes preferred to talk of two dimensions of *authoritarianism versus humanitarianism* and of *hedonism versus moralism* (or *religionism*)—such dimensions running at approximately 45 degrees to Eysenck's C and T, as indicated in Figure 2. On this question Eysenck is seen at his most radical in comparison with other social-scientific students of attitudes. Rather than relying on refinements of factor analysis, he has preferred to move straight to the questions of what are the psychological and developmental bases of attitudinal differences.

At the psychological level of explanation, Eysenck's inclination has been to consider C as reflecting differences in personal interests and involvements: some people, for example, the elderly and the middle-class, have more of an interest in property rights in particular and in the *status quo* in general. By contrast, Eysenck has viewed T as an expression of limitations in the ability to acquire civilized restrictions on primitive urges to sex, violence and exploitativeness: at the outset of his theorizing Eysenck attributed tough-mindedness to the unconditionability that he associated with extraversion, but today he considers T to represent the projection of his

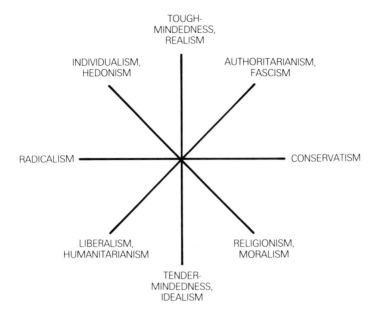

**Figure 2.** shows rotations of Eysenck's dimensions of C and T that have sometimes seemed psychometrically more adequate as ways of representing the major differences between people in social attitudes (see Brand, 1981). For example, Sinclair (1979) found two distinguishable types of conservatism: one involved approval of 'medals', 'official secrets', 'defence spending', 'school prizes' and 'prosecuting trespassers'; the other involved approval of 'strict morality' and disapproval of 'legalizing marijuana', 'enthanasia', 'abortion' and 'protest marches'.

dimension of psychoticism (P) on to the plane of attitudes. (Empirical correlations between T and P are about .30: see Powell and Stewart, 1978; Sinclair, 1979.) Since P itself has a strong link to well-known gender differences—correlating substantially with sexual predatoriness and perversion, criminality and drug-abuse—Eysenck's hope is clearly that this dimension (which he has sometimes, reflecting proper uncertainty as to its true nature, called *psychopathy* and, inversely, *superego*) will prove capable of scientific precisification—perhaps, as has sometimes been suggested by Eysenckians (see Lynn, 1981), as a dimension of unconditioned responsiveness to threat or as reflecting differences in how the brain modulates arousal levels. Whatever the exact bases in psychological mechanisms, Eysenck's claims to scientific status for T also invoke intriguing observations to the effect that T is substantially heritable as judged by twin studies at the Maudsley Hospital; indeed, C too has proved heritable in this work as in other studies of broadly conservative preferences (e.g. Grotevant *et al.*, 1977). Expressing his faith that T can to some notable extent be reduced to P, Eysenck and his wife have in recent years suggested that high-P scorers should be referred to straightforwardly as tough-minded even when no special attempt has been made to survey their social attitudes; and Eysenck has sought further confirmation of the real, biological basis of P in its links with physiological variables such as HLA-B27 and 5-HIAA. Although he has been less expressly reductionist about C, both he and Wilson would probably acknowledge that its positive correlation (amongst adults) with age and with the conscientiousness (or, alternatively, hypocrisy) of the high scorer on the less-than-happily named lie (L) scale would perhaps hold out prospects of finding some partial biological basis for C in line with its heritability.

Such a summary account of the main features of Eysenck's theory cannot begin to do justice to the enormous empirical input that has informed and sometimes changed it over some thirty years—an input that is still only partially covered by Eysenck and Wilson's book. But no presentation of the theory would be complete without remarking, at least at a very general level, its historical plausibility: the C dimension is, at least as *Right versus Liberal/Left*, a commonplace of journalistic and historical description of political differences from the French Revolution onwards; and the idea that such anti-Semitic, power-crazy, law-hating, mass-murdering figures as Hitler and Stalin shared a perverted genius that distinguished them quite radically from more moderate champions of 'Right-' and 'Left-wing' ideologies is also broadly acceptable. Although Eysenck himself would acknowledge that his past attempts to link C to social class and T to extraversion were not conspicuously successful, his present linking of C with age and of T with disagreeable masculine qualities looks a plausible way of finding biologically-based explanations of opinionation; as such it deserves the dignity of sustained attempts to falsify it.


## OBJECTIONS—ANCIENT AND MODERN


Strong objections to Eysenck's claims are naturally to be expected from professional political extremists. It is bad enough for it to be suggested to Communists and neo-Nazis that they have anything at all in common; but to suggest that what they share is 'psychoticism' is almost calculated to make them see red—or black. Neo-Nazis are, admittedly, better able to shrug off Eysenck's claims, partly because they are not in the main very interested in reading psychology books, and partly because they do typically admit to a frank hostility to other social groups that would barely stop short at their deportation. (By contrast, while Communists classically deplore religion they normally opt for the changing of people's beliefs rather than the elimination of believers as the summit of their ambitions when answering questionnaires in the West.)

Even if neo-Nazis have been dilatory in excoriating Eysenck, it should be recognized that there are other broadly Right-wing objections to Eysenck's analysis. The first of these is that Eysenck's scheme allows insufficient distinction between favouring beliefs and regimes that are 'merely' authoritarian rather than fully totalitarian: whereas many Western democracies are themselves the descendants of nation-states that were by modern standards extremely authoritarian (to the extent, in Britain, of disembowelling political and religious opponents as recently as 400 years ago), such states never dreamed of the total control of every aspect of society that is the ambition of the modern totalitarian—often with initial benevolent intent in the name of some kind of socialism. Henry VIII, in short, was no Pol Pot. Such an attempt to rehabilitate quaint old authoritarianism, as practised by ex-President Galtieri, may even be accompanied by attempts to suggest that authoritarians exhibit traits once prized by social scientists such as 'achievement motivation' and the Protestant ethic. While the burden of such an objection is that some forms of despotism and jingoism are markedly less unacceptable than others, the second objection is more radical and insists that liberal capitalism has simply nothing to do with either totalitarianism or authoritarianism: rather it will be said that the ethos of capitalism is that of freedom (including economic freedom) within the law, and that its individualism has no room for treating people according to their 'type' (whether of race, creed, sex, sexual orientation, etc.)—and thus that it offers nothing to the insensitive, unempathic, unbusinesslike, authoritarian personality, let alone to the megalomaniacal corporatist with his grand designs of social engineering.

All such objections have essentially one tendency in common: they aim to assert the primacy of the rotated dimension of *authoritarianism versus humanitarianism* and to establish the believer's position at his favoured end of that dimension. Thus Western socialists would wish it believed that they are primarily opposed to all prejudice and dogmatism and are essentially tolerant and compassionate in their attitudes. Libertarian supporters of capitalism often seem to settle for that position as well—differing from socialists merely on the rather technical economic questions of how such a Good Society might best be brought about; while traditional Right-wingers would stress their antipathy to all delusional mollycoddling of the weak or otherwise less desirable members of their society and assert the need for a new order. As to any second dimension of *hedonism versus moralism*, it might be allowed that Communists and Conservatives were particularly opposed to each other historically (and are still so opposed in the more backward and priest-ridden parts of the world); but it could be claimed that, with the widespread abandonment of Christianity and the adoption of unprecedented permissiveness in sexual and marital matters, this dimension was no longer politically relevant in the late twentieth century West—and certainly not a dimension on which either the mass or the minority parties of the Left and Right take any conspicuous stand.

Of course, if Eysenck could deliver the goods—if he could demonstrate some biological similarity between extremists of Left and Right—it would perhaps be a different matter. As things stand, however, he has largely failed to provide any uniquely distinguishing features of the tough-minded person unless it be that of being male by gender; his early attempts to show high levels of extraversion in Communists and Fascists did not get very far; and, even if it were one day shown that active Communists and neo-Nazis were high scorers on his P-scale—which has quite marked negative correlations with educational aspirations and attainments—this might reflect no more than the low social status and poor education of people who have not found it possible to channel their political ambitions in more conventional ways.

Such criticisms, it should be noted, still allow of a personological influence on political attitudes. But it is not one that will be to Eysenck's liking, for it is merely the dimension of *authoritarianism* which, as developed by members of the Frankfurt School (Adorno *et al.*, 1950), is presumed to be under the control of harsh socialization procedures (including, Freudians may still say, harsh potty-training). Moreover, it will be said, even this influence of personality on attitudes is arguably much overrated. Although a person's upbringing may dispose him to racism, sexism, punitiveness and militarism, his appreciation of his own interests—an appreciation that is assisted by the political education that is daily offered him by politicians and journalists—must surely be expected to influence his final opinions and voting preferences in ways that Eysenck himself envisaged more sensibly before he became so enamoured of biological forces. How, after all, in Britain, does the 50 per cent of the population that is 'authoritarian' actually vote? Is it not more commonly for the Labour Party in protection of its manual, State-sector jobs and council houses?

Politics, it will be said, is chiefly about interest groups and not about poorly-thought-out personal prejudices that no sane man would discuss at the average bar. Empirically it is well known that many people maintain lasting loyalty to political parties with which they (and their parents) once identified for all that those parties notoriously change their views on tariff barriers, Keynesian economics, the value of nuclear defence and so forth: many voters will no sooner desert their party than they would desert their local football team after a bad season.

## THE ACCEPTABLE FACE OF PSYCHOTICISM

The scholarly psychologist may well remark at this stage the trouble that Eysenck has heaped upon his head by shifting the concept of *tough-mindedness* so far from the usage that was given to it by William James. At least one source of the argument is fairly clearly that, in the sense in which Eysenck has used the term, few people—at least, few readers of psychology—are very eager to appear tough-minded. By contrast, James' view was that, even within Christianity, there was a place for tough-mindedness—for the recognition of evil in the world and for a resolute determination to combat it; there was room for the knight-errant as well as for the saint.

Of course, Eysenck is quite in line with the general drift of twentieth century psychology in his appreciation that 'seeing evil' in others is as often an illusion (even if he would not say a 'projection') as it is a genuine achievement. Again, so long as the highest scores achieved on Wilson's 'realism' are those of members of the Dutch Reformed Church and the John Birch Society, it is easy to see why Eysenck should long have tended to regard T as an index of deviance from civilized values—a process that culminated naturally in seeing its origins in psychoticism. Nevertheless, while Communists, socialists and liberal capitalists strive to dissociate their thinking from any connection with tough-mindedness, psychoticism and authoritarianism, it is worth asking whether Eysenck might not have tempered the wind a little to the shorn lamb.

At least in the terms that the English language makes available for describing personal virtues, it is not difficult to find 'positive' qualities that are, in human experience, somewhat hard to combine with the affectionate, trusting, accepting, sensitive, tolerant, cooperative ways of the low-P scorer. These are, for want of a better word, the qualities of the will: initiative, resolution, analyticity, persistence, courage, determination, self-sufficiency, competitiveness and so on. For all that we might each hope to be endowed with a fair sprinkling of qualities from both these packages, we sense a difficulty as much as when we contemplate how we might be at once energetic and conscientious, both exuberant and careful.

It is easy to see how, if a psychometrician devises a test for 'trust', even if he does not start from the negative pole of 'suspicion', he is likely to end up with a measure of 'trust *versus* suspicion' rather than of 'trust *versus* self-sufficiency'. The influence of the dimensions of general neuroticism ($N$) and intelligence ($g$) will militate in favour of such an outcome: for relatively neurotic (emotional) people tend to feel apprehensive about many things, and people of lower intelligence (given their normal, partly self-created circumstances) will have positively good reason to feel so. Rather than ask a person, 'Do you trust your spouse?', it is clearly necessary for the psychometrician who would capture the tension between the virtues of the will and the virtues of affection to invite the testee to choose whether the statement 'I trust my spouse' or, alternatively, 'I am determined to make my spouse happy' best represents his or her feelings. It is easy to recognize that such difficult choices are unpopular both with testees and testers; but, when such forced-choice procedures of testing are used they do yield a somewhat more positive characterization of the person whose strong point is not his affection for others. One such procedure, deriving from the psychoanalytic reflections of Adler (Crandall, 1975) contrasts altruistic qualities of social interest with individualistic, efficient, competitive qualities; another, originating as an attempt to measure 'needs' (Edwards, 1963; Maddi, 1972, p. 451) yields empirically a contrast between the needs to 'affiliate' and to 'nurture' on the one hand as against the needs to be 'autonomous' and 'aggressive' (or competitive) on the other; a third technique using forced choices, from an author who was once very critical of the validity of Eysenck's T (Christie, 1956), contrasts trusting and kindly attitudes with 'Machiavellian' cynicism and manipulativeness that tend empirically to be associated with clinically effective interpersonal skills in the tasks of the social psychology laboratory. As it turns out, Machiavellianism has in fact shown a correlation of .44 with T (Stone and Russ, 1976); similarly, one study of Edinburgh students (McAllister, 1981) found correlations with T of $-.35$ for 'nurturance' and $+.70$ for 'autonomy'.

The contrast that appears on forced-choice measures between stereotypically masculine and stereotypically feminine virtues is of course unreal insofar as the technique has denied respondents the opportunity to assert that they may be blessed with both types of quality in large measure. This situation has a simple and familiar parallel in the measurement of the 'masculinity' or 'femininity' of a person's interests and occupational preferences: here too the tester has to choose whether to force subjects to decide between liking wrestling and liking ballet or whether to allow them to declare for (or against) both interests. Allowing unconstrained indications of interest will reliably produce two independent dimensions of 'masculine interests' and 'feminine interests' (e.g., Grygier, 1976); and this will tempt the psychologist to believe that typical sex differences require to be explained by reference to two separate, gender-related types of causal input. But the fact is that a major determinant of developed interests of all kinds is intelligence itself (e.g., Heim *et al.*, 1977); and, once that factor is allowed its proper causal status the only other dimension will involve the contrast of *masculinity versus femininity*.

The argument is thus that the Eysencks' efforts to measure affectionate qualities have resulted in a scale that does not allow registration—at its opposite, high-P end— of the more positive masculine qualities. The P scale, insofar as it reflects departures from benevolence, does so partly by including departures that result from low intelligence, low education and high neuroticism; the P scale, indeed, correlates negatively with intelligence (sometimes as highly as $-.44$: see Davis, 1974) and positively with neuroticism. It thus bears comparison with those attempts to measure positive masculine qualities of the will that have similarly not tried to avoid picking up variance from $g$ and $N$. The most notable of such attempts was that of Witkin, whose measures of field-independence tap the analyticity, non-conformism and scientific hard-headedness of the male while also correlating positively with general intelligence and negatively with psychopathology (e.g. Blackburn, 1972). In the questionnaire realm Cattell's dimension of independence (which he used to call Promethean Will) functions similarly: the dimension involves components of competitiveness (Cattell's E), rejection of tradition (Q1), self-sufficiency (Q2) and individualism (M), but tends to carry positive loadings for intelligence and negative loadings for broadly neurotic tendencies (e.g., Turner *et al.*, 1976).

What is being suggested, very simply, is that variables such as P, 'need for autonomy', Machiavellianism, independence and so forth would in fact turn out to correlate positively amongst themselves and negatively with such variables as altruism, social interest and Cattell's Pathemia if only they were all freed from their present associations with *g* and *N*. They would present a broad contrast between qualities of will and affection and presumably represent a major general sex difference. (In a similar way it might be claimed—in line with Eysenck's intuitions about extraversion over the years—that there is a broad dimension that contrasts energy and conscience once the present influences of *g* and *N* on such variables as creative fluency and behavioural impulsivity and simple hypocrisy are extracted—see Brand, 1984.)

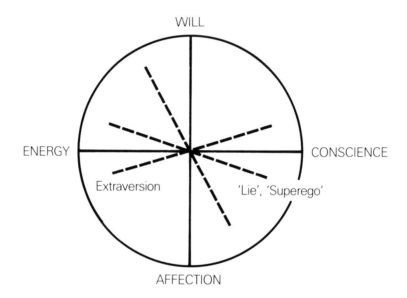

**Figure 3.** *A Hypothesis as to How Eysenck's Dimensions of Personality Might Relate to Broadly Contrasted Personal Strengths if the Influence of g and N Were Partialled Out*

Not the least of the advantages of recognizing two broad dimensions (see Figure 3) that liberate Eysenck's measures of P, E and L from their tendencies to pick up variance from *g* and *N* is that it becomes easier to envisage personological bases for attitudes that might seem reasonably agreeable to ideological enthusiasts themselves. For example, to envisage that Left-wing activists might be high in independence, 'autonomy' and Machiavellianism would not seem too wide of the mark; indeed, such people have sometimes seemed to have a marked interest in argument and analysis, being markedly more aggressive than Fascists in such respects (Eysenck and Coulter, 1972); and it is surely central to their ideology that they have a simplifying analysis of society's evils which they intend to champion to its predetermined historical conclusion regardless of all ties of affection that might otherwise bind them to the middle-class people from whose ranks they often come. Again, people of broadly conservative views who could not be described as socially withdrawn can plausibly be characterized as approving of restraint, conscientiousness and respect for traditional inhibitions in social intercourse, as their scores on Eysenck's lie scale unfailingly indicate; by contrast, people of liberal views often seem to champion exuberance, spontaneity, creativity and the discharge of energy in general—partly, one may presume, because such behaviour comes naturally to them. As Sir Isaiah Berlin has put it (see Parekh, 1982): 'We choose values because we find that we are unprepared to live in any other way.'

It would be wrong, of course, to presume too intimate a connection between a person's own personal strengths and the values—let alone the voting habits—that he or she will come to adopt. People may—perhaps especially if they are to some degree neurotic—come to admire attributes and life-styles that are different from their own. But it is surely worth considering possibilities that are plausible both as modifications of Eysenck's own ideas and as ways of capturing some of our commonplace expectations as to how personality is related to values. If a less Eysenckian way of considering such possibilities is desired, the familiar personality dimensions of *anality* (Kline and Cooper, 1983) and *sensation-seeking* (Zuckerman, 1982) might quite easily be projected on to the above two-dimensional scheme (see Figure 4); these personality

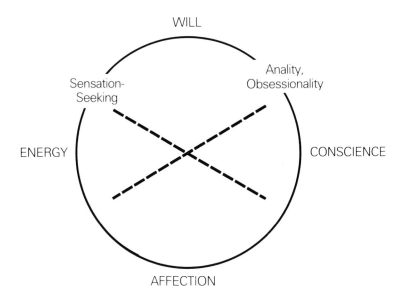

**Figure 4.** *A Suggestion as to How Kline's 'Anality' and Zuckerman's 'Sensation-Seeking' Would Relate to Personal Strengths in the Absence of Influence from g and N*

dimensions, it may be observed, are typically assessed by asking people in the same questionnaire about both their behaviour and their attitudes. Alternatively, if it were desired to hypothesize as quite independent entities the distinctive values that might be most keenly appreciated by people of different personal qualities around the two-dimensional space, Figure 5 might serve as a point of departure; for it seems reasonable to suppose that the authoritarian, with his notorious black-and-white ways of boxing up the world, values order and systematization more than mercy and tolerance; and reasonable to hypothesize that the hedonistic sensation-seeker will prefer freedom and anarchic self-determination to any particular respect for the historic rights of other people. Few people would relish having to make such stark choices, and most would certainly hope that their abilities and experience would enable them to reconcile such conflicting moral demands; but, when it is a feature of the human condition that such moral choices do sometimes have to be made, it is likely—especially in days when codes of conduct do not reign supreme—that those choices will be guided to some extent by more basic features of our own personalities. (One example of such contrasts emerging in the activities of intelligent people in the real world is Robertson's (1982) study of judges: here two separate dimensions distinguished the judges, one being their degree of sympathy for the State in civil cases and the other being their sympathy for the prosecution in criminal cases.)

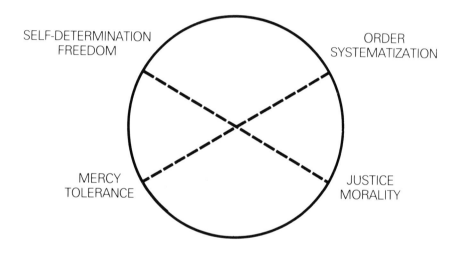

SELF-DETERMINATION FREEDOM

ORDER SYSTEMATIZATION

MERCY TOLERANCE

JUSTICE MORALITY

**Figure 5.** *Values That Might Naturally (Disregarding the Influences of g and N) Be Related to the Distinctions between Personal Strengths That Have Been Suggested in Figures 3 and 4*

Such, at least, is one way of removing Eysenck's conceptualization of social attitudes from the more obvious objections without taking it too far into the realm of unfalsifiability. Of course, one weak feature is that it may seem to some to leave conservatives in general and authoritarians in particular as far too normal variants on the social scene; in particular, those who wish to claim a monopoly of compassion may be indignant at their political opponents being offered a monopoly of concern for order and even the conventional forms of conscientiousness. This type of problem will be addressed in the next section of this chapter, but it is important to admit here that there is no way of getting round the liberal's wish to cast the authoritarian into outer darkness unless he will also allow the fact of the matter that *conservatism* has, at least within that slice of the past that is known to social science, been associated with rather modest levels of general intelligence. Quite simply, the keen Left-winger's objection to being at all approximated to the Fascist chiefly reflects an appreciation of that intellectual difference, for all that eager radicals may wish to deny that intellectual differences are of any importance to them. If the above modification of Eysenck's scheme should appear to make authoritarianism respectable, it is only because the critic has failed to see the way in which intelligence has been allowed to draw all its proper variance to itself—variance which certainly includes some 30 per cent of the reliable variance between people in C. Indeed, it is right to say that some of the heritable variance on Eysenck's scales of C and T might simply be put down to *g* and its social expression.

## THE DYNAMICS OF 'LEGITIMIST' AND 'UTOPIAN' POLITICS

Although it may be possible to preserve many of the largest features of Eysenck's vision by means of the above manoeuvres, a stubborn question remains that of whether such a scheme can provide any explanatory purchase on attitudes that are more distinctively party-political. Undoubtedly the major problem is that modern political thought is so greatly concerned with economic matters—rather than with such traditional topics as religion and the defence of the realm against enemies and criminals. To make matters worse, in their economic beliefs the parties of today's Left and Right tend to espouse theories that are strangely at odds with what Eysenck's personologizing might seem to decree.

For the Left, two key economic beliefs have an unequivocally 'authoritarian' character—once authoritarianism is stripped of its usual connotation of illiteracy. One of these is a classical '-ism', quite equivalent to nationalism and racism: it is Marxist class-ism, according to which the interests of different social classes must be seen as radically opposed, and according to which the disinheritance of the property-owning bourgeoisie is both desirable and inevitable. The second is an example of classical statism, for the twentieth century socialist supposes that expansion of the State—once into the ownership of the means of production, latterly into a provision of services that is still thought to be incomplete when modern Welfare States spend some 40 per cent of Gross National Product. On the other hand, enthusiasts on the political Right in the West favour the economic freedom of people to retain or invest their capital as they will, regardless of moralistic restrictions such as obligations to provide minimum wages, redundancy payments or a faithful surrender of profits to taxation; in such 'libertarianism' (see Lepage, 1982) they may proudly appear as anarchically hedonistic as any classical supporter of 'free love' or 'a woman's right to choose'.

This problem—of the existence of 'authoritarianism of the Left' and of 'anarcho-individualism of the Right'—is paralleled by another that is extremely mundane. As mentioned above, the votes for socialist parties come just as much from people with classically authoritarian views as from those who abhor all *-isms* (except class-ism); and the complementary paradox is that, perhaps because of their incomes, many entrepreneurs who cast their votes for the Right enjoy life-styles that are far more hedonistic (including multiple divorces, abortions, call-girls, heavy drinking and so forth) than the classical subscriber to atheism and free love could ever have dreamed of. In short, dockers are not known for their piety towards immigrants, women and homosexuals; and casino-owners are not known for their high rates of prayer and Bible study.

One way out of such paradoxes might clearly be to acknowledge some third, independent dimension of *capitalism versus socialism*. But, although Eysenck has sometimes toyed with this possibility, the data from surveys have not normally demanded it; and, in any case, such a move would be sadly premature if it threw away the possibility, indicated above, of using 'authoritarianism' and 'hedonism' as helpful descriptions of the tendencies that are involved in distinctively modern forms of Left- and Right-wing ideology.

The alternative solution is that the ideologies of the modern Left and Right should be seen primarily as *spanning* the dimensions of *authoritarianism versus humanitarianism* and *hedonism versus moralism* respectively (see Brand, 1981). There are three quite attractive features to such a hypothesis. The first is that a constant if unspoken preoccupation of an ideological opponent of, say, a present ruling elite and its authoritarian ways must be with how society will be ordered, and by whom, after the hoped-for revolution; conversely, though authoritarians commonly appear to lack sympathy for quite a wide variety of minority groups, they nevertheless possess quite an idyllic conception of how pleasing (and even how equal) society would be if it were composed only of people of their own type. Again, the outspoken advocate of freedom will quickly find on reflection that most of the modern freedoms that he treasures—whether they be sexual, intellectual or economic—can exist only within some (even if it is not the present) kind of framework of law and just dealing between people; and those who devoutly wish that their compatriots were more religious or morally concerned will invariably have to admit that some types of human activity are not to be governed by their moral code. In the past the Christian churches tended to leave their followers free in economic matters (at least after the Reformation); whereas lately many Western church leaders have seemed to link their Christianity with some version of socialism, while wishing to allow their flocks a larger freedom in matters of sex and procreation. In fact the Christian churches have arguably been rather upstaged in the twentieth century because they have lacked any very certain code about economic matters and have never seized their opportunities to condemn the great dishonesty of inflation; but they may resume a more central role as Western societies become increasingly concerned with what response they should make to man's increasing capacity for both military and criminal destructiveness and for sexual depravity and disease, birth control and genetic engineering.

A second attraction of the idea that, at their broadest, the major organized political parties achieve a dynamic compromise along the full range of the dimensions of *humanitarianism* and *moralism* is that it would seem to capture something of the notable variety of people who vote for them. Modern Conservative and traditional Liberal parties, on the one hand, attract support from both middle-aged, religious, rural dwellers and financially successful, pleasure loving urbanites; on the other hand, parties of the Left attract both the twentieth century higher educated elite and the relatively authoritarian voters of the urban working class. Admittedly these groups that link hands politically owe some of their differences in opinionation to differences in intelligence; and it might further be pointed out that these strangely allied groups share important economic interests in common insofar as the first two work in the free enterprise sector of the economy while the last two have tended to find remuneration in the public sector. But if such alliances form across intellectual and educational levels, this of itself reinforces the idea that political parties involve large dynamic compromises between extremes; and the tendency (at least in Britain—see Dunleavy, 1982) for private sector workers to vote Conservative and for public sector workers to vote Labour is open to various interpretations—including the possibility that both occupational and political preferences are influenced by personality.

A third attractive feature is simply that there is a general moral distinction between the dynamic compromises that are arguably made by the Left and the Right. However many matters may be disputed between authoritarians and humanitarians, these very different figures commonly strive to justify their favoured policies by reference to the future good that will demonstrably follow from their adoption; though expelling immigrants or discriminating 'positively' in favour of employing them may be literally unfair, these means are held by their protagonists to be justified by the fine Utopian ends that will thereby be achieved. By contrast, the champions of both freedom and morality typically want their favoured arrangements not because they will demonstrably advance the sum total of social happiness but because they are simply held to be right; here the moral reasoning that is invoked is essentially retrospective—whether it invokes some kind of scriptural authority or whether it sees people as the possessors of inalienable rights by virtue of their national inheritance or their human nature. These tendencies, with their differing appreciation of the importance of ends in relation to means, might be termed Utopian and Legitimist respectively; and they would seem naturally suited to the arguing of cases for change, reform and even violent revolution on the one hand, and continuity, tradition and even fastidious legalism on the other.

If modern socialist supporters can thus be characterized as Utopian, one clear prediction is that they would have a particularly wide range of scores on measures of *authoritarianism versus humanitarianism* that managed to tap such a dimension at a personological level; conversely, if modern conservatives are broadly Legitimistic, the prediction would be that they would vary widely on such personality traits as project on to the dimension of *hedonism versus moralism*. There are, however, two substantial obstacles that impede the route to any strongly reductionist thesis. The first is that political parties have to plan to deal with a country's international position as well as with its internal affairs. The problem here is that Utopian plans to change one's own country may require a strongly legitimistic posture to the effect that other countries are morally bound not to interfere with one's own internal experiments; on the other hand, a Legitimist party that felt pride in its country's internal arrangements might be sorely tempted to bring those same human rights and dignities to other lands by means of the sword. In short there can be little relation between domestic and foreign policies unless it consists in Utopian ideas that all countries can grow economically without doing so at each other's temporary expense, or in the Legitimist idea of letting countries make their own choices and mistakes so long as they do not attempt to coerce other sovereign nations. The second problem is that political parties may change considerably over time. In the modern West parties of the Right have lately donned many of the clothes that were once worn by nineteenth century Liberals: in particular they champion free enterprise and (on the 'moralistic' side) a sound currency. In the past, however, under Disraeli, the British Conservative Party rejoiced in a 'One Nation' mixture of imperialistic enthusiasm and sympathy for the worst-off; and, mixed with Keynesian economics, strands of 'wet' Utopian thinking are still in evidence in that Party even after ten years of leadership by Mrs Thatcher. On the other hand, the British Labour Party, which was once in favour of free trade and respect for the rights of Catholics and others to educate their children equally at State expense gradually shifted through the 1970s to the Utopianism of protectionist tariffs and positive discrimination in favour of particular minority groups. It is probably more natural for socialism to be associated with a mixture of humanitarian and authoritarian policies—for the history of the twentieth century suggests that grand designs of social engineering can seldom be undertaken without the eventual mass-murder of political opponents, and that even the more modest versions of socialism seem to require large standing armies—whether of soldiers, police, bureaucrats or social workers. But it has to be allowed that socialism and capitalism are not the only ideologies to have influenced from time to time the present parties of the Left and Right. Clearly the parties of the Left once provided a home for free thinkers and for anti-establishment views of all kinds; whereas today they often seem to stand four-square behind elderly trade unionists as they fight defensive campaigns to secure their tenure in the monopoly use of outmoded technologies.

Necessarily, the present chapter has focused on whether Eysenck's simple and novel theory, a light and elegant vessel when it was constructed around 1950, is able to negotiate the choppy waters of the real world of political opinionation and activity. Some of his early claims and findings—as to the essential two-dimensionality of the realm of social attitudes and as to the possibility of there being biological influences upon our most cherished convictions—have really survived astonishingly well, and have indeed gained support with the passing years. Other claims—as to the distinctive involvement of Extraversion and Psychoticism, and as to the final predictability of actual voting habits from personality—have proved more controversial. Perhaps Eysenck's strangest disservice to his own cause was to try to contrive a psychology of politics without making much reference to intellectual differences and their expression in personality and values. At the same time his recognition of a T dimension linked to sex differences was really quite visionary at a time when sex differences were little considered by psychologists. The Eysencks' own measurement of this dimension has perhaps taken too little trouble to reflect the more 'positive' aspects of masculinity; but, in a century that has seen more reason than did Nietzsche to be profoundly mistrustful of the work of the (masculine) will, this is understandable.

Eysenck, admittedly, put less stress than William James upon the way in which people make moral choices—choices which they would rather avoid, no doubt—as to whether to be 'tough' or 'tender'; but his scheme still lends itself to registering important similarities between political views and personages of the Left and Right that committed ideologues would prefer us to ignore. In an important sense Eysenck was too kind to the Left when he accepted the limitations of the scientific method and confined his personology of Communism to Communists of the West in the 1950s: for there is not much that is libertarian or merrily anarcho-hedonistic about the world's Communist countries today. Nevertheless, it was right that a psychologist should have tried to understand the more organized, articulate and civilized expressions of political thought as well as those that are little more than grunts or reflexes or hypocritical ratiocinations of lawless power: for, if the Greeks were right, we must master the association between private and public virtues, whichever way the direction of causation flows.

## REFERENCES

Adorno, T. W., Frenkel-Brunswick, E., Levinson, D. J. and Sanford, R. N. (1950). *The Authoritarian Personality*, New York, Harper.

Blackburn, R. (1972) 'Field dependence and personality structure in abnormal offenders', *British Journal of Social and Clinical Psychology*, **11, 2**, pp. 175–7.

Brand, C. R. (1981) 'Personality and political attitudes', in Lynn, R. (Ed.), *Dimensions of Personality*, Oxford, Pergamon Press.

Brand, C. R. (1984) 'Personality dimensions', in Nicholson, J. and Beloff, H. (Eds.), *Psychology Survey* V, London, Methuen.

Christie, R. (1956) 'Eysenck's treatment of the personalities of Communists', *Psychological Bulletin*, **53**, pp. 439–51.

Crandall, J. E. (1975) 'A scale for social interest', *Journal of Individual Psychology*, **31**, pp. 187–95.

Davis, H. (1974) 'What does the P scale measure?', *British Journal of Psychiatry*, **125**, pp. 161–7.

Dunleavy, P. (1982) 'Voting and the electorate', in Drucker, H. M. (Ed.), *Developments in British Politics*, London, Macmillan.

Edwards, A. L. (1963) *Edwards Personal Preference Schedule*, New York, Psychological Corporation.

Eysenck, H. J. (1976) 'The structure of social attitudes', *Psychological Reports*, **39**, pp. 463–6.

Eysenck, H. J. and Coulter, T. (1972) 'The personality and attitudes of working-class British communists and fascists', *Journal of Social Psychology*, **87**, pp. 59–73.

Eysenck, H. J. and Wilson, G. D. (Eds.) (1978) *The Psychological Bases of Ideology*, Lancaster, MTP Press.

Grotevant, H. D., Scarr, S. and Weinberg, R. A. (1977) 'Patterns of interest similarity in adoptive and biological families', *Journal of Personality and Social Psychology*, **35, 9**, pp. 667–76.

Grygier, T. J. (1976) *The Dynamic Personality Inventory: Manual*, Windsor, National Foundation for Educational Research.

Heim, A. W., Unwin, S. M. and Watts, K. P. (1977) 'An investigation into disordered adolescents by means of the Brook Reaction Test', *British Journal of Social and Clinical Psychology*, **16, 3**, pp. 253–68.

Kline, P. and Cooper, C. (1983) 'A factor-analytic study of measures of Machiavellianism', *Personality and Individual Differences* **4, 5**, pp. 569–71.

Lepage, H. (1982) *Tomorrow Capitalism*, London, Open Court.

Lynn, R. (Ed.) (1981) *Dimensions of Personality*, Oxford, Pergamon Press.

McAllister, N. M. A. (1981) 'Power-hungry students?—A comparison of elected and non-elected students', Edinburgh University Final Honours Thesis, Department of Psychology.

Maddi, S. R. (1972) *Personality Theories*, Illinois, Dorsey.

Parekh, B. (1982) 'The political thought of Sir Isaiah Berlin', *British Journal of Political Science*, **12,** pp. 201–26.

Powell, G. E. and Stewart, R. A. (1978) 'The relationship of age, sex and personality to social attitudes in children aged 8–15 years', *British Journal of Social and Clinical Psychology*, **17, 4**, pp. 307–18.

Robertson, D. (1982) 'Judicial ideology in the House of Lords: A jurimetric analysis', *British Journal of Political Science*, **12**, pp. 1–25.

Sidanius, J. and Ekehammer, B. (1982) 'Test, of a biological model for explaining sex differences in sociopolitical ideology, *Journal of Psychology*, **110**, pp. 191–5.

Sinclair, F. (1979) 'The personality and social attitudes of depressives', University of Edinburgh Final Honours Thesis, Department of Psychology.

Stone, W. F. and Russ, R. C. (1976) 'Machiavellianism as tough-mindedness', *Journal of Social Psychology*, **98**, pp. 213–20.

Turner, R. G., Willerman, L. and Horn, J. M. (1976) 'Personality correlates of WAIS performance', *Journal of Clinical Psychology*, **32**, pp. 349–54.

Zuckerman, M. (Ed.) (1982) *Biological Bases of Sensation-Seeking, Impulsivity and Anxiety*, Hillsdale, N. J., Lawrence Erlbaum.

# 10. Eysenck on Social Attitudes: An Historical Critique

JOHN RAY

Although it is probably a common impression that Eysenck's work on social attitudes is limited to a single foray, in the form of his 1954 book, *The Psychology of Politics*, social attitudes in fact constituted one of his very earliest interests—an interest which continues to this day. To my knowledge his earliest paper on the topic was published *during* the Second World War (Eysenck, 1944) and he continued to defend his position as recently as 1981 (Eysenck, 1981/82). Nonetheless, it is clear that *The Psychology of Politics* is his major statement in the area. A collection of his later work, together with some minor updating of his position is, however, available in a recent book (Eysenck and Wilson, 1978), also ambitiously entitled *The Psychological Basis of Ideology*.

Reading Eysenck's earliest writings is an experience surprising for the discovery that what Eysenck is saying now has changed so little in his lifetime. Whatever else he may be, he is extraordinarily consistent about his basic themes. In one of his very earliest papers (Eysenck, 1940) we see perhaps the first sign of what was to become a besetting habit of thought for Eysenck—the tendency to describe almost anything in terms of two dimensions. In this paper, presumably written before the war, we find Eysenck explaining the appreciation of poetry in terms of the two dimensions of extraversion and neuroticism. He still uses these variables as major personality descriptors—though quite recently supplemented by a third dimension: 'P' or 'psychoticism' (Eysenck and Eysenck, 1976).

In his 1944 paper (written in 1942) Eysenck pooled the work of several previous attitude researchers and factor analysts in an endeavour to find what their various results had in common. He concluded that two dimensions of social attitudes could be detected: radicalism-conservatism and 'practical-theoretical'. The latter concept he also identified with the 'tough-mindedness' versus 'tender-mindedness' of William James. He then proceeded to his own factor analysis of some data which he obtained from Flugel and Pryns. These data consisted of responses to a series of contentious

155

issues by members of a number of rather eccentric-sounding special-interest groups in pre-war England. The most amusing of the issues was 'Gymnosophy'—which turns out to be nudism. Eysenck found three factors but was able (surprise) to give confident interpretations to only two of them. He concluded that these two factors were very similar to those he had just identified in the work of previous authors. If we look at the high-loading items on his second factor as given by Eysenck himself, however, we find that for his largest and apparently least eccentric group of subjects there were only three items that loaded really highly. They were all negative loadings—indicating that they were 'theoretical' or 'tender-minded' in Eysenck's terms. They were: 'Abstemiousness', 'Vegetarianism' and 'Non-smoking'. I in my naivety when I first looked at these items failed to note the negative sign and thought that Eysenck was proposing 'Abstemiousness', 'Vegetarianism' and 'Non-smoking' as signs of *tough*-mindedness. Given the strength of will required to give up smoking and the delights of the carnivore, I could see some glimmer of sense in the proposal. It turns out, however, that Eysenck is asserting the opposite. It is apparently 'tender-minded' to be abstemious. The two highest *positive* loadings were 'Birth-control' and 'Abortion'. Perhaps it is true to say that practising birth control and allowing abortions is tough-minded but surely that is a very incidental judgment rather than being what the factor is about. Australians might have called it the 'wowser' factor. (In Australia 'wowsers' are Methodists, morals campaigners, teetotalers, etc. The best translation into standard English might be 'killjoy'. It is a very dismissive term.) 'Old-fashioned asceticism' or 'Puritanism' might be other reasonable names for what it measures. I cannot to this day see why it is infinitely less tough-minded to be a non-smoker or a vegetarian than it is to practise contraception (the loadings indicate that non-smoking and contraception are *opposites* on whatever it is that the factor measures) but I can see that it is more Puritan. Already in this 1944 paper, then, we have the first sign of one of Eysenck's traits that is to figure largely later on: an ability to see in factor-analytic results much more than others would be likely to see.

It must be pointed out at this early stage, however, that there has always been a peculiar leniency shown in the psychological literature towards factor analysts. I have already set out at length elsewhere (Ray, 1973c) an example of just how arbitrary factor-naming can be in the psychological literature generally, so I will not repeat it here. The gist of it, however, is that a factor which was initially said to measure 'authoritarianism' in a preliminary version of a paper became a measure of 'Australian chauvinism' in the final version. Although there is no doubt something in common between the two concepts, I would submit that there is also a lot of difference. We have, then, a rather good example of how little rigour there commonly is in interpreting the results of factor analysis. Factors are taken as measuring what the analyst says they do and any questioning of his interpretation is extremely rare. *Proof* that a factor measures anything at all is even rarer. There has somehow developed a tradition that exempts factor analysts from the rigours of proof (validity demonstrations) that are expected of those who construct scales by other means. Almost anyone who has ever done a factor analysis must know what an odd assortment of items one often finds, all loading high on one factor. Identifying the common thread in these items is almost always a task requiring considerable imagination and creativity; so much so that it is not uncommon for new words to be invented for the purpose. Although he may have other justifications for doing so, Cattell's use of such words as 'surgency' and 'rhathymia' to describe his factors seems a good instance of this. When, therefore, the poor, benighted factor analyst has finally managed to 'identify' his factors, no-one usually has the heart to ask him for proof that his items really do measure what he says they do. The fact that some common thread can be perceived in a purely conceptual way between many disparate items (face validity) is generally counted a sufficient achievement. The analyst is normally not even expected to show that the measure provided by his factor is reliable—despite the fact that scales derived from factor analysis can easily turn out to be anything but reliable (e.g., Ray, 1971a). Eysenck, therefore, was probably somewhat shielded by this tradition. To have questioned the interpretation of his second factor would have breached one of psychology's guild-rules. Even so, as we shall later see, such questions were finally raised.

As it happened, Eysenck's 'discovery' of two main factors in social attitudes was fortuitous. It formed the basis for what was to become an attractive solution to a considerable puzzle of twentieth century politics: that the further out on the Right or the Left one moved, the more one began to notice that those on the Right and on the Left had a lot in common. Right- and Left-wing extremists, instead of being utterly different from one another, in fact seemed remarkably similar. To go from the extreme Left to the extreme Right was like travelling in a circle. You ended up somewhere remarkably like where you started. This was perhaps more evident before 1945 than it is now. Although there was a certain sense in which one was Right-wing and the other was Left-wing, Hitler's Germany and Stalin's Russia had striking similarities. This 'same but different' phenomenon was something that anyone with any political consciousness would have had to cope with in the 1930s and 1940s.

Eysenck's habits of thought led to what still is a very clever solution to this puzzle. He maintained that political allegiances should be conceived not on one dimension but on two—with an addition to the traditional radical-conservative dimension of tough-tender mindedness. Thus Fascists and Communists were the same in that both were high on tough-mindedness but different in that one was radical and the other was conservative. The two major parties traditional in Anglo-Saxon countries, on the other hand, were unified in being much more tender-minded than the totalitarian parties of Europe. Eysenck's diagram reproduced in Figure 1 illustrates this proposition.

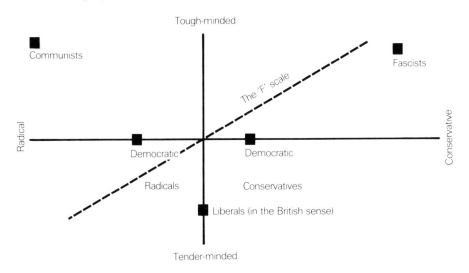

**Figure 1.** *Eysenck's Two-Dimensional Schema for Describing Political Attitudes and Parties*

As well as making this powerful proposal for the description of existing political reality, Eysenck took the much bolder step of trying to show that such dimensions existed in the minds of men. His two dimensions were to be not mere political abstractions but factors of social attitudes—products of the empirical procedures of factor analysis when such were applied to a large body of expressions of social attitudes made by ordinary people. His was a purported *discovery* about people. His dimensions did not exist just in the mind of some ivory-tower sophist. He proposed, in other words, a congruence between political and psychological reality. There were tough-minded radical governments because there were tough-minded radical people. I, as it happens, concur with Eysenck in believing that Communists tend to be (among other things) tough-minded radicals. I do not, however, believe—as we shall see— that Eysenck has *succeeded in showing* in his own empirical work that Communists are in fact tough-minded radicals.

Although Eysenck's theory was something of an intellectual breakthrough, he was unfortunate that the *Zeitgeist* had changed by the time that he got his 'discovery' into print. The theory was first published as such in 1954 in *The Psychology of Politics*. By that time the great Nazi monster had fallen and the political scenario no longer mirrored the psychological scenario that Eysenck was putting forward. Indeed, the euphoria of war-time cooperation with Russia made even the Bolshevist monster seem not so bad after all. For some reason this euphoria lasted much longer among intellectuals than it did among the general public. While the Berlin airlift of 1949 probably marked fairly well the end of optimism about Russia as far as the general public was concerned, intellectuals continued for much longer to accept the idealism of Communism at face value. They seemed to see the Russian Communists as simply Leftists who had been particularly successful at implementing their programme. This view was largely shared by the Left generally. I can remember how even into the 1960s Australian Leftists would dismiss accounts of the 30 million who died under Stalin as fabrications of 'the capitalist press'. When it gradually became known through Communist sources that in his 1956 secret speech to the twentieth Communist Party Congress the chairman of the Communist Party of the Soviet Union himself (Nikita Khrushchev) had confirmed the truth of these 'lies', that particular perceptual defence crumbled but others seemed to replace it fairly readily. 'The pressure of external military threat' seems to be a popular excuse for the brutalities of the Soviet system among Marxist intellectuals nowadays, but since it was during war-time that Hitler did away with the Jews, I cannot see why Hitler could not similarly be excused! Before the Second World War many intellectuals found much to admire in Hitler's 'New Germany', so it might be a reasonable hypothesis that intellectuals are just susceptible to idealism of any kind regardless of its real outcomes. In the post-war era, however, the demise of Hitler meant that only Communism remained to draw the loyalties of Western intellectuals. In this climate the need was to distance ourselves from Hitler and to find out how Fascism came about, so that any resurgence of it could be prevented. Military defeat of the Fascists had made their own explanations for themselves dismissible, and explanations of Fascism had to be found which would be so damning that no-one could ever seriously entertain it again. Eysenck's work did little to fill this need.

A work that splendidly filled this need, however, was ironically largely a re-hash of an old Nazi theory—*The Authoritarian Personality* by Adorno, Frenkel-Brunswik, Levinson and Sanford (1950). Working mainly in California, this group of American and expatriate German Jews took the Nazi typological theory of Jaensch (1938), reversed its value judgments, added Freudian elements to its originally largely perceptual emphasis and showed that it applied in America as well as in Germany. Eysenck (in Eysenck and Wilson, 1978) records that one of the authors of the 'California' study (Else Frenkel-Brunswik) freely acknowledged to him the role of Jaensch's theory in forming her own thinking even though Jaensch was not listed in the references of *The Authoritarian Personality*.

The changed world political scene of the 1950s and 1960s made a one-dimensional account of politics plausible and even desirable. *The Authoritarian Personality* was nothing if not one-dimensional. According to this book, Fascists were simply extreme conservatives and almost all ills, mental and social, could be traced to or associated with a Rightist ideology. Both Fascism and Conservatism were presented as more or less extreme manifestations of an underlying 'authoritarian' personality (measured by the famous 'F' (for 'Fascism') scale), and such a personality was a 'disease'. One must add that given the role of Marxist intellectuals (such as Adorno) in the composition of this book, the thrust of its conclusions cannot be regarded as entirely surprising. This strange book, then, effectively denied any possibility of such a thing as Left-wing authoritarians and ignored such prominent facts as the struggle against Hitler being led by a Right-wing conservative British leader, Winston Churchill. There could be no-one who throughout all his life opposed more violently all that Hitler had stood for, yet Adorno *et al.* were saying that the two were really the same. As his pact over the partition of Poland showed, Joseph Stalin had been quite happy to cooperate with Hitler. It was the *conservatives*, fighting against great odds, who brought about the destruction of Fascism, not the Leftists. Yet from Adorno *et al.* we would expect Hitler and Churchill to be brothers! Sibling rivalry might have been invoked, but Adorno *et al.* did not even seem to see that there was anything there to explain. To them psychoanalytic speculation was far more real than the world of everyday politics.

If *The Authoritarian Personality* was very poor at providing an explanation for the characteristic contempt that pre-war conservatives and Fascists had for one another, Eysenck's *The Psychology of Politics* made it crystal clear. Fascists were tough-minded and conservatives were tender-minded. Fascists saw conservatives as weak and ineffectual. Conservatives saw Fascists as brutal and aggressive. The opposition between the two arose because they were in fact opposites in important respects. In the circumstances one might be forgiven if one assumed that *The Psychology of Politics* must have soon eclipsed *The Authoritarian Personality* in the influence it had upon psychological researchers. Eysenck's work was elegant, clear, careful, objective and in general very 'scientific' by the standards of the day. *The Authoritarian Personality*, by contrast, was a nightmare of subjectivity, intellectual dishonesty and almost complete lack of scientific caution (Christie and Jahoda, 1954; McKinney, 1973). The fact is, of course, that *The Authoritarian Personality* had infinitely greater impact on psychologists than Eysenck's work did. In the immediate post-war era intellectuals generally wanted to believe the best of Stalin and the Russian experiment. To accept Eysenck's account would have meant accepting that Communism was in many important ways similar to the now universally decried Nazism. No wonder Eysenck was unpopular! When the world had just suffered so grievously at the hands of a Right-wing tyrant, who wanted to believe that similar perils from a Left-wing tyranny might be in the offing? Social scientists might be able to accept that Leftists can be 'dogmatic' (a surely minor charge—is not Mother Teresa of Calcutta dogmatic about God's love for the poor?) in Rokeach's (1960) terms, but anything more threatening was rejected.

The scientific means that enabled Eysenck's work to be substantially ignored was a remarkable series of articles in a prestigious American journal (the 1956 *Psychological Bulletin*) which appears to have caused even Eysenck to abandon the field for many years. Four papers by Rokeach, Hanley and Christie appeared in this volume which mounted most scathing attacks on Eysenck and his work in social attitude and political research. It may be noted that although Rokeach is the author of what might be seen as a 'rival' theory to Eysenck's, Christie at least was even-handed in that he is also a severe critic of *The Authoritarian Personality* (Christie and Jahoda, 1954; Christie, Havel and Seidenberg, 1956).

The criticisms made of Eysenck all seem to have been well-supported: Eysenck's sampling *was* rudimentary; he *did* use an old-fashioned (pre-computer) 'counting' system to score his items which distorts the meaning of non-responses; he *did* make a number of minor mistakes in the citation details of references he used; he *did* assign identities to his factors which require considerable imagination to be seen as justified. The point about these criticisms, however, is that similar criticisms could be levelled against almost any other study in the field at that time. A level of rigour and care was demanded of Eysenck that was far in excess of what was demanded of others. Perhaps the clearest indication of how nit-picking the criticism was is that Christie took Eysenck to task in round terms (Christie, 1956b, p. 446) for referring to the California F scale as a measure of 'authoritarianism'! If Christie were to tear out just one hair for every time that someone has referred to the F scale as such a measure, he would have been a bald man twenty years ago!

In particular, the criticisms of Eysenck's sampling were extraordinary. To this day at least 95 per cent of social psychological research that is published in the journals makes no attempt at sampling whatsoever. Psychology as a discipline seems to be characterized by the absurd belief that what is true of an unselected group of American college students will be true of humanity in general (Ray, 1981). In this context Eysenck should be something of a scientific hero. He did at least make a rough attempt to find out what was the case among the general public. Yet he was singled out for a criticism that is politely left unmentioned in almost all other psychological research. I, as it happens, agree fully with Christie that Eysenck's sampling inadequacies totally vitiate the major conclusions he wished to draw from his data, but I would reject most of the literature on authoritarianism as totally worthless for the same reason. Would Christie do the same? His own continued use of student 'samples' would suggest not. It seems clear that Eysenck was taken to task not because his work was particularly bad but because his conclusions were politically unacceptable. Eysenck's biographer also gives very strong support to this conclusion (Gibson, 1981).

Perhaps the most damaging criticism of Eysenck was made by Rokeach and Hanley (1956)—that Eysenck in some way 'fudged' his data by presenting false mean scores for the various political groups he studied. This was an almost unprecedented direct attack on a scientist's honesty. The way this terminally grave accusation was supported was to attempt a speculative reconstruction of scale means for the various groups from item mean data presented by Eysenck in an earlier publication. They give little weight to the possibilities of rounding error, and they do admit that they have no way of allowing for non-responses. They obtain total score means that differ from

Eysenck's and claim as a result that Eysenck's own data reveal him as some sort of crook. Eysenck treats this extravagant inference with the contempt it deserves by simply pointing out that he and his critics scored the same data in different ways so of course the results must differ. He might have been better served in American eyes to stand less on his dignity and become as litigious over the matter as Americans would surely be in similar circumstances. What might seem a properly reserved and dignified response in British eyes could well be seen as an admission of guilt in American eyes.

The major difference between Eysenck and his critics would seem to have been over the content of Eysenck's 'T' scale. Neither side of the argument seemed to be listening to the other at all. There is no doubt that the factor-analytic manoeuvres adopted by Eysenck for the derivation and construction of his T scale were unusual. That is not to say, however, that they were unjustified. Eysenck, like everyone else before and after him, was confronted by the dilemma that although the form of government they practise when in power is terminally authoritarian, Communists will never admit to anything but the most liberal, tolerant and humanistic ideology. Although political practice may quite evidently vary in two dimensions, political ideology seems to vary only in one dimension. The only people who normally have a kind word of any sort for authority are the conservatives and, as both the Second World War and the subsequent Cold War show, it is precisely conservatives who are the most unrelenting opponents of authority when it gets carried away with itself. To me the gap between Communist beliefs and Communist practice is simply the most vivid possible proof of what a vast and dangerous pathology wishful thinking really is. Eysenck shared with the authors of *The Authoritarian Personality* the strangely naive view that if people behaved in a certain way, then there must somewhere be, in those people, an attitude of some sort which directly corresponded to that behaviour and justified it. The possibility that large slices of humanity could be so misled by wishful thinking as to deny even to themselves their own real motives (even to the bitter end) could somehow just not be allowed. Freud would certainly have had no such difficulty. Perhaps it was really a sort of arrogance. Both the California authors and Eysenck thought that if people really did have evil but hidden motives, the psychologist with his bag of tricks must surely be able to penetrate the disguise. Perhaps in general there are some grounds for such confidence, but when the people upon whom the bag of tricks are to be used (in this instance Marxists and Communist sympathizers) are taken from among one's own colleagues and students, the tricks cannot be expected to fool anyone very much.

At any event, if there is a finding that all the tough-minded, pro-authority statements are assented to by conservatives, there are two possible interpretations of that finding: (1) one can conclude, as Adorno *et al.* (1950) did, that this proves that only conservatives are authoritarian, or (2) one can conclude, as Eysenck does, that there is something wrong with the analysis that produced such an absurd conclusion. Both Christie and Eysenck appear to agree that the conclusion is absurd, but they disagree over what to do about it. Christie thinks that if we just look harder we *will* find attitude statements that *will* show Communists as tough-minded. Eysenck, who has already looked very hard, knows that that will not work and proposes instead that what we will have to look hard at are not our data but our methods of analyzing them. He therefore quite explicitly describes and justifies at great length an arbitrary rotation of his factors which in his view makes greater sense than some mechanical rotation. He then refers to one of his arbitrarily rotated factors as reflecting 'tough-mindedness'. The 'arbitrary' rotation was, however, supported by a very plausible theory. Eysenck said that it was unreasonable to expect that political attitudes could ever be 'just' tough-minded. They had to be either Right-tough or Left-tough. One cannot be tough-minded without some opinion to be tough about. This eminently reasonable proposition, however, seems to have gone in one ear and out the other as far as Eysenck's critics were concerned. They observed that there were no items which loaded on Eysenck's T factor alone (a terrible sin in factor analysis), and seemed in consequence to have thought that they had caught Eysenck in yet another deception. Following orthodox factor-analytic thinking, they concluded that there could not in the circumstances be said to be any T factor there at all. They seemed oblivious to the fact that it was precisely the adequacy of orthodox factor-analytic procedures that Eysenck was calling into question. No-one could have put his proposals with greater energy, clarity and persuasiveness than Eysenck, but they seem to have gone straight over the head of his critics. Orthodox thinking evidently had too strong a grip on their imaginations. Rokeach and Hanley (1956), in other words, presented it as a *discovery* that Communists scored high on only some of Eysenck's 'tough-minded' items. They seemed to think that in so doing they had caught Eysenck out in some way. Yet Eysenck himself had already demonstrated at great length that this was precisely what his theory required. Their discovery was one that Eysenck had already been shouting from the rooftops.

Where Eysenck *was* vulnerable was in the content of his T ('tough-mindedness') items. He had not yet shown that *any* of his items measured tough-mindedness. Had his critics simply hammered this point they might have made a more genuine contribution. The extensive retabulation of results they undertook which had only the effect of showing what Eysenck had shown already were superfluous. To extract new generalities from the items loading high on Eysenck's factors, they needed to overcome the traditional indulgence shown over factor-naming (alluded to at the beginning of this paper). As a factor analyst, Eysenck had a certain protective mantle. Faults other than his factor-naming had therefore to be found by his critics.

Amid all their other criticisms Eysenck's critics did manage to make some fairly telling criticisms about factor-naming. They are points that Eysenck has never answered. Had his critics focused their criticisms, instead of criticizing so many things, Eysenck might have been forced to defend his factor-naming.

An abiding criticism of Eysenck's 1954 book, then, is the same as could be made of Eysenck's 1944 work: Eysenck sees depths and meanings in attitude items which run far beyond what it is reasonable to see. This can perhaps best be seen in Eysenck's very latest version of his R and T factors. In Eysenck (1976) the high-loading items on his T ('tough-mindedness') factors are as follows: 'wife-swapping', 'patriotism', 'self-denial', 'moral-training', 'chastity', 'royalty' and 'casual living'. These were the only items with loadings above .40. 'Tradition' and 'divine law' loaded .39 with 'censorship', 'inborn conscience' and 'Bible truth' loading .38. Eysenck is certainly correct in seeing continuities between this factor and his earlier results from 1944 onwards, but how to identify what underlies the items concerned is not nearly as obvious as Eysenck implicitly claims. The very obvious theme in such items is not tough-mindedness but old-fashioned morality or religious morality. Religion and morality have always been closely intertwined, and restrictive morality is now increasingly old-fashioned. I would submit that each of the items listed above describes something religious, moral (in the sense of sexual morality) or old-fashioned. *That* is what the factor is all about. To say it concerns 'tough-mindedness' is a farce.

I am not saying that certain types of religious or anti-religious sentiment cannot be tough- or tender-minded. If political sentiments can be tough- or tender-minded so surely can religious sentiments be tough- or tender-minded. The point is that we have no evidence that any of the sentiments identified by Eysenck as tough-minded are in fact tough-minded. All we have is Eysenck's word for it. To him the factor exists, can be replicated and therefore must measure something, and he as the factor analyst is the one who must have the decisive word on what that something is. Eysenck writes as if it is obvious what the factor measures, but the emperor in this case has long ago been declared to have no clothes. To put the matter another way: we could say that the items of Eysenck's T factor are either definitionally tough-minded (which is what Eysenck appears to say) or that they are empirically tough-minded. In the latter case we have an empirical hypothesis that can be tested by correlating the T factor with some independently validated measure of tough-mindedness. No-one has attempted this. In the former case we simply have to argue over what the words of the items loading highly on the factor actually say. Do they of themselves embody tough-mindedness of some (or any) sort as a consistent and obvious underlying theme, or is some other theme (or themes) apparent? If I believe in casual living and wife-swapping, does that clearly and explicitly make me tough-minded? Might it not be rather more likely to make me other things—such as uninhibited or decadent? If the items that loaded highly on Eysenck's T factor said such things as 'power', 'authority', 'strength', 'honour', 'aggression', 'destruction', then we might be quite strongly inclined to believe that we were dealing with a tough-mindedness factor, but even then this would be only a preliminary hypothesis. (They might, for instance, measure 'hostility' rather than tough-mindedness.) If we wished to use such a factor to show something about any group in the population, we would then have to produce the sort of validating evidence that is normally expected of any psychological scale—peer ratings showing that people who assent to such items are in fact seen by others as tough-minded, etc. All this, however, is very far from the situation prevailing with Eysenck's T scale.

The way that Rokeach and Hanley (1956) made much the same point was to show that people are classified by Eysenck as tough-minded Leftists if they oppose Sunday observance, religion and compulsory religious education on the one hand, and on the other hand support abortion, divorce and trial marriage. To call what such a group of opinions have in common *anything but* religion and morality is fairly inconceivable but, nonetheless, to Eysenck they measure 'tough-mindedness'.

It seems inevitable that we must ask *why* Eysenck adopts such a peculiar view. Why is it a view that he never even tries to justify? One might say that there are, after all, some items on the T scale which are not directly concerned with religion and morality. These tend to be the low-loading items (i.e., items not very central to the factor) and in any case merely demonstrate that religious people do have *some* characteristic opinions on non-religious issues. They tend, for instance, to be traditionalists or to be ascetic. Even in such cases, however, the religious element is seldom far away. To be ascetic, for instance, is a very great tradition in many religions and is a quite conventional sign of holiness for many people. To be in favour of royalty is in England not at all irrelevant to religion. Most English people are at least nominal members of the Church of England, and guess who is the Head of the Church of England?

Another possibility is that Eysenck is really laughing up his sleeve. His biographer (Gibson, 1981) believes that Eysenck sometimes writes books (e.g., his first book on race and IQ) with the deliberate expectation that this will bring down opprobrium on his head. If one believes that there is no such thing as bad publicity, this could be a reasonable thing to do. Eysenck is one of the world's most cited authors by his fellow psychologists (Gibson, 1981), and it is my impression that it is the loose and subjective writings in psychology that attract attention. Really rigorous work tends not to attract much interest from one's colleagues. Who, for instance, could imagine a more hilarious proposition than that we should turn to a group of Jewish Marxists for a dispassionate and rigorous account of the sources of Nazism? Would one be tempted to treat Ulster's Rev. Ian Paisley as an authority on the Pope? Yet psychologists to this day still seem to take much of their thinking on Fascism (and hence conservatism) from *The Authoritarian Personality*—a book written by authors who were entirely Jewish and at least some of whom were Marxists! I infer that 'attackability' is almost a precondition for relevance in psychology. Oscar Wilde once made an exhortation that ran something along the lines of: 'Remain, as I do, incomprehensible; to be great is to be misunderstood.' Maybe Eysenck has taken that advice to heart.

On the whole, however, the foregoing explanation seems just too Machiavellian. A simpler explanation is that for all his stress on objectivity and scientific rigour Eysenck is human after all and sometimes gets carried away by his passions. Religion and politics have long been notorious for their tendency to expose people as seeing only what they want to see and believing only what they want to believe. Gibson (1981) believes that Eysenck is very political, and I see no reason to disagree. It must be recollected that Prof. Dr. Eysenck is not an Englishman but a Weimar German (perhaps even the last of the great, speculative, German-speaking psychologists). He was born and bred among the very liberal (even libertine) high culture of Weimar Germany. He grew up observing with extreme distaste the roving political street gangs (Right and Left) of pre-war Germany and detests equally their modern-day equivalents. He must find it hard to tell the difference between modern-day anti-Apartheid or anti-Nazi (or even anti-Eysenck) demonstrators and the KPD (*Kommunistische Partei Deutschlands*) or NSDAP (*National Sozialistische Deutsche Arbeiter Partei*) street gangs of his youth (see also Ray, 1971b). He has therefore become almost more English than the English. He has embraced almost as a religion the traditionally tolerant, pluralistic, restrained values of English political thought (though the Irish might have a different view of traditional English political *practice*; many Irish find Adolf Hitler and Oliver Cromwell rather hard to tell apart) and deplores the recurrent brutalities of European political practice with a fervency that would do any Englishman proud. One sign of this extreme Anglophilia is that his post-war letters to his father were written in English—a language his father hardly understood (Gibson, 1981). I also have a copy of a publication by Eysenck and Levey (1967) in an East German journal which was printed in German bearing the footnote '*Übersetzung aus dem Englischen von Jürgen Mehl*'. In other words, even when he wished to publish in a German journal (had he tried to have it published elsewhere but without success?) he still would not write in German but wrote in English and had someone else translate it for him—and this from someone who in his youth and teenage years was proud of his literary ability in German! In such circumstances we can see that no-one could be more convinced than Eysenck about how evil political brutality is and how uncompromisingly it must be opposed. His extreme rudeness to Konrad Lorenz when he learned that Lorenz in his day had made his peace with his Nazi overlords (Lorenz was really only interested in ducks and the like; to him a few obeisances to the authorities must have seemed a small price to pay for the peace he needed for his studies of his feathered friends) is an instance of this (Gibson, 1981).

I infer that Eysenck's political passions to this day blind him to the obvious fact that he has *failed* in his search for psychological evidence of Left-wing authoritarianism. He *knows* it exists and he knows that he must oppose it. Therefore he concludes that he has in fact found evidence of it and that he has exposed it. He claimed to be able to show that Leftists were 'tough-minded' (a term to him largely synonymous with authoritarianism) but all he managed to show is that they were disrespectful of conventional religion and its concomitant morality. He identifies it as authoritarian to reject religion! Given the way in which men have been (and in some parts of the world still are) enslaved by religious authority for almost all of recorded history, I would have thought quite the opposite—that to reject religion is normally the first step along the way to a healthy questioning of all authority. With their dogmas, potentates and keys to the kingdom of heaven, it seems to me that conventional Western religions are nothing if not authoritarian. If 'Do as we say or you will go to Hell' is not authoritarian, what is?

Perhaps the tragedy of Eysenck's work in the psychology of politics is that although he was not alone in failing to find evidence of psychological authoritarianism among Leftists, he came very close to making the discovery he so earnestly desired. To see this we must first see why such evidence was not found. Generally, the reasons are threefold: psychologists have assumed that what is true of their students will be pretty similar to what is true of the world as a whole (Ray, 1981); they have assumed that ideology and vote will closely correspond; they have assumed that attitude and personality will go fairly closely together. All these assumptions are suspect when stated so baldly, so let us see what happens when we reject each one of them.

Ray (1972, 1974) records a study wherein fresh conscripts into the Australian Army were given what was initially intended as a balanced F scale. Australian Army conscripts were at the time selected by a random birth-date ballot procedure from the entire Australian population of 18-year-old males. 'Dodging' seems to have been very difficult in comparison with the US experience. This sample, then, was vastly more representative in socio-economic and educational terms than the usual student sample (or, more properly, 'non-sample'). The findings of the study were that the especially-written 'Leftist' items which were supposed to 'balance' the items of the original F ('Fascism') scale correlated highly positively with the original F scale items. Anti-authoritarian items turned out to be highly pro-authoritarian! Using non-student subjects, I was able to show that sentiments such as 'Human beings are more important than efficiency', 'Dictatorships are totally wrong', 'All men are equal' and 'Individual freedom is a basic human right' were all authoritarian (assuming that we concede that the Adorno *et al.* (1950) F scale does measure authoritarianism). Non-students are obviously *very* unkind to the preconceptions of psychologists! (It might be noted in passing that analyses were also done to exclude acquiescent response bias as an explanation for these results.) There was certainly no difficulty in finding psychological authoritarianism of a Leftist kind with this sample.

Let us now question the relationship between vote and ideology. In 1973 I reported in the *European Journal of Social Psychology* a study in which I applied successfully balanced (i.e., acquiescence-free) versions of the California F and Rokeach D scales to a random population sample taken in Sydney, Australia, by door-to-door means. I also asked for intended vote from each respondent. I found that *neither* the F nor the D scale predicted vote. The inference from this is that *high F scorers were just as likely to vote Leftist as Rightist.* There were just as many authoritarians of the Left as there were of the Right! Again, there was no shortage of psychological authoritarianism among Leftists. Hanson (1975) also records that the F scale often fails to predict vote.

Let us now question the relationship between attitude and behaviour. So far I have accepted for the purposes of the argument the conventional view that the Adorno F scale does measure authoritarianism. This is, however, a highly dubious proposition. For a start the F scale will not seem to predict behaviour reasonably categorized as authoritarian (Titus, 1968; Ray, 1976). People who tend to boss others around are just as likely to get low F scale scores as high. When the F scale does seem to predict the things it ought, the correlations are usually just as well explained by saying that the F scale is measuring nothing more than conservatism (Ray, 1973d, 1983). In these circumstances I devised a new scale in behaviour inventory format— i.e., a *personality* scale—which *did* predict authoritarian behaviour highly significantly. I called it the 'Directiveness' scale. It is really a very simple-minded construction, containing items like 'Do you tend to boss people around?' and 'If anyone is going to be Top Dog would you rather it be you?' Studies have now shown that this scale does *not* have any overall relationship either to political ideology or to political party vote (Ray, 1979, 1982). In other words, both Leftists and Rightists are equally likely to be shown by this scale as highly authoritarian. Other findings of authoritarianism in Leftists are the well-known work of Rokeach (1960) and the extensive series of papers by Rothman and Lichter (see Lichter and Rothman, 1981/82).

I have listed briefly three types of finding to show that, although Eysenck's empirical work was badly flawed, his basic theory is sound. I take that theory to consist of the view that two rather than one dimensions are needed to describe political allegiance and behaviour, and that the two dimensions are radicalism-conservatism and authoritarianism of some sort.

Perhaps sadly, it seems that for most of the time Eysenck was dimly aware of the three conditions I have specified for turning theory into sound empirical findings. He generally made at least some effort to use community rather than student samples; he noted as early as 1951 that there was something funny about the relationship between vote and ideology; and he maintained all along that his second dimension was really a personality dimension rather than an attitude dimension *per se*. Some further comment about Eysenck's moves in this direction seems appropriate.

Perhaps because of Christie's abrasive criticisms or perhaps because of increasing command of economic resources, Eysenck's later work would appear to be noteworthy for its use of representative sampling. The samples he used in his 1971, 1975 and 1976 studies seem to have been much the sort used by commercial polls. Only in the case of the 1975 sample, does he give us any useful demographic background on the respondents. We find that a *quota* sample of London contained 215 females and 153 males. It is well-known that females tend to be overrepresented in the cities but this seems gross. If the polling organization had such problems getting the sex quota right, one can only imagine what might have happened to the other quotas. In all these studies, the chance of Left-wing authoritarianism emerging was limited by the simple fact that Eysenck used no measures of authoritarianism other than his peculiar T scale.

On the relationship between ideology and vote Eysenck deserves some kudos for anticipating the well-known essay by Lipset (1960) on 'working-class authoritarianism'. Lipset argues that vote is determined by economic self-interest rather than by ideology and that in consequence economic conservatism will separate out from other forms of conservatism—with the middle class high on economic conservatism and low on general conservatism, while the working class will be low on economic conservatism and high on general conservatism. Precisely this hypothesis was tested in Eysenck (1951) but was rejected. In the same paper, Eysenck concluded that *if vote is controlled* the workers are more conservative in general ideology. Later in Eysenck (1975) the basic Lipset thesis was accepted (though without making any reference to Lipset). Thus after many years Eysenck has ended up with three rather than two factors in both the attitude and personality domains. Just as he has added a P factor to E and N in the personality domain, he has added economic radicalism to R (general ideological radicalism) and T ('tough-mindedness') in the attitude domain. It does not yet seem to have dawned on him how largely irrelevant this makes all his previous studies of ideology.

Strictly speaking, it is inaccurate to refer to Eysenck now having three attitude factors. Eysenck has always maintained, that the T factor is not a fully fledged attitude factor in its own right. He describes it as a 'projection' onto (or the influence on) the attitude domain of a personality variable (extraversion). He long maintained, that there was only one true dimension in social attitudes—radicalism-conservatism. This is a position that Wilson and I have also maintained (Wilson, 1973). At any event, Eysenck's thinking here gives rise to a testable hypothesis. Authoritarians should be extraverted. Strangely, in spite of the interest that Eysenck's theories have provoked, no-one but Eysenck seems to have tested this until very recently. Eysenck's own tests used the dubious T scale so are not conclusive. I therefore (Ray, 1980) correlated both the California F scale (which Eysenck acknowledge as a measure of Rightist authoritarianism) and the directiveness scale with measures of Eysenck's E (extraversion) and found the reverse of what Eysenck had predicted. High F scorers were *intro*verted! The directiveness scale showed no significant correlation with E at all.

Eysenck had what I would claim was the correct insight—that the second variable in the psychology of politics is a personality rather than an attitude variable—but was limited by his straightjacketed notions of what constitute the variables of personality in pursuing the insight fully. It might be objected that since extraversion did correlate significantly with the F scale, Eysenck was not too far off— he just got the sign of the correlation wrong. Unfortunately, the correlation was a low one ($-.12$ and $-.18$ with Eysenck's two subfactors of extraversion), and even then it was probably due to the conservatism component of the F scale rather than anything else (Ray, 1980). In the same study introversion was also found to correlate (more highly) with general social conservatism (Ray, 1984).

In justice, it must be said that there may be some basis outside his own work for Eysenck's view that authoritarians are extraverted. In a study of modern-day neo-Nazis (Ray, 1973a), clear indications suggested that such people were quite extraverted. Modern-day neo-Nazis are however a far cry from the historical German article. Some are motivated as much by a love of uniforms and of shocking people as they are by anything else. Inferences from such deviant groups to the population as a whole would be quite untenable.

Eysenck himself has begun to waffle a bit about what the personality variable underlying T really is. In the concluding chapter of *The Psychological Basis of Ideology* he describes the psychological basis for political authoritarianism as 'the personality variable P (and possibly E)'. E (extraversion) is being edged out. Even the replacement of E by P, however, does not get Eysenck out of trouble with the evidence. In Ray and Bozek (1981) it was shown on a general population sample that Eysenck's P scale correlates negatively with the F scale (where Eysenck would predict a positive correlation).

It takes no theoretical innovation at all to find the elusive personality variable 'underlying' authoritarianism. Why not start with authoritarianism itself? Both Adorno *et al.* (1950) and Eysenck seem driven by the need to find hidden signs of authoritarianism in attitudes. They both try to *measure* authoritarianism by attitude scales. Why not just measure authoritarianism directly by a conventional personality scale that asks questions not about great social issues (attitudes) but rather about how the individual person himself feels and behaves (personality)? The directiveness scale is such a scale (Ray, 1976), and had Eysenck adopted such a straightforward approach instead of the devious, over-clever, indirect approach he did adopt he would have had his ideology-free measure of authoritarianism from the beginning. Surely no-one can question Eysenck's view that political decisions will reflect both the attitudes and the personalities of those involved, so where is the difficulty in saying that of the two key dimensions needed to explain political allegiances and actions, one should be measured by an attitude scale and the other by a personality scale?

That Eysenck did not move in this direction is probably due to the fact that probably all psychologists find it hard to live with the gap between attitudes and behaviour. This gap has been well-known at least since the time of La Piere (1934) and has repeatedly been confirmed (Ray, 1971b, 1976). Just because (for example) a person says, 'Hard work is a good thing', there is absolutely no warrant that the person so saying will himself tend to work hard. Psychologists never seem very happy with such a situation. They always seem to think (or even assume) that there should be at least *some* tendency for those who think hard work is a good thing to work hard themselves. Reality, unfortunately, seems uncooperative. For Adorno *et al.* (1950) attitude/behaviour congruity was a straight assumption. They assumed throughout that the people who evinced authoritarian attitudes would also be the ones who tended towards authoritarian behaviour. They were, of course, eventually shown to be quite wrong in this (Titus, 1968; Ray, 1976; Ray and Lovejoy, 1983). Eysenck was a better theorist and was more aware of the role of other factors, but even he seems to have been unable to accept that there was *no* reflection in attitudes of basic behaviour tendency.

In a sense, he was right. Attitudes and behaviour are not *totally* isolated from one another (Kelman, 1974). The relationship between them, however, is usually far from simple. It is *simple* or isomorphic relationships we have to question rather than *all* relationships. Finding the relationship, in other words, is simply another research task. We cannot assume it, and it need not leap out and grab us. It may be subtle rather than obvious. Even the relationship between personality and behaviour may be far from obvious. Because personality is usually measured by asking people how they characteristically behave in various situations, scores on personality scales usually predict actual behaviour rather well (insofar as the .3 or .4 correlation that is all psychologists can usually aspire to can be regarded as 'rather well'). Nonetheless, one finding that seemed unusually fascinating (and relevant) was that a scale of achievement orientation predicted authoritarian behaviour better than did a scale of authoritarian personality (Ray and Lovejoy, 1983). Both scales were orthodox personality scales yet the 'obvious' predictor of the two was not the stronger. In retrospect the finding seems easy enough to explain. One simply has to make the point that human behaviour is characteristically multi-causal (the same behaviour may be emitted to serve several different ends), and acting in a domineering way towards others may be done either because the person likes doing so as such or because he wishes to use his ability to influence the behaviour of others to achieve some other end. In other words, bossing others around may be just one of the many things the achievement-motivated person may have to do in his scramble towards the top. When we observe authoritarian behaviour happening we must be very careful what inference we make about the motives of the person so behaving. It is *possible* that he is doing it just because he likes it (the authoritarian), but it is more likely that he is doing it in order to achieve some quite separate materialistic goal that he values. If the relationship between personality and behaviour can be complex and not immediately obvious, how much more so must the relationship between attitude and behaviour be complex and non-obvious? Psychologists have always recognized this complexity at least in part. No-one, for instance, would dispute the importance of situational factors in modulating behaviour. The sort of complexity I am suggesting, however, is, I think, much greater than is normally envisaged. When we find that authoritarian behaviour is *not* associated with authoritarian attitudes but *is* associated with achievement motivation, I think it becomes clear how exceedingly simplistic almost all the research in the area has been so far. Unfortunately, even very recent work seems to be largely stuck in the same simplistic mould (e.g., Altemeyer, 1981).

In conclusion, we must say that Eysenck's basic theory was supported. Leftists *are* quite as likely to be authoritarians as are Rightists. Eysenck even had all the basic insights needed to turn this theory into decent empirical findings. In the end he fell short of the goal and resorted to strange stratagems to conceal his failure. When I was a guest in Eysenck's department in 1977 someone (probably Simon Hasleton) remarked to me that Eysenck was really an old-fashioned grand theorist and not an empiricist at all. I think there is some truth in that observation. I at least will always honour his creativity, even if I cannot accept the interpretation he places on his empirical work.

As some sort of epilogue to this chapter, I think it behoves me to point out that there is a well-developed alternative theory to Eysenck's which, perhaps because it has largely been developed by economists and perhaps because it does not put Leftists in a particularly good light, seems virtually unknown among psychologists. This is the libertarian theory as spelt out in a vast range of publications including von Hayek (1944), von Mises (1949) and Friedman (1962). As two of the authors mentioned gained Nobel prizes for work they did in connection with this theory, it seems very strange to me that psychologists know so little of it.

As background to the theory one needs to note that the normal human form of government is tyranny. For most of human history men have been ruled by kings, emperors, caesars, pharaohs, etc. The exceptions in the ancient world (Athenian democracy, the early Roman republic) were fleeting and, in historical terms, the modern-day alternatives are so recent as to be little more than an eyeblink in the total experience of the human race. Even today most of the human race is ruled by dictatorships of one sort or another. Hard though it may be for us to cope with, it is democracy which is the aberration, not tyranny. Libertarians have an explanation for that aberration and fear that it might be a short-lived one. Libertarians deal with Eysenck's problem of Communist/Nazi similarities by denying that there are any important differences between the two. They further fear that although the Fascists may have lost the war, they have won the peace and that we all one day will be Nazis or Communists.

Let us look again at Nazi/Communist similarities. Although both Hitler and Stalin were quite happy to call themselves Nazis and Communists respectively, both formally characterized their regimes as 'socialist'. Libertarians see no reason to reject that description. Both regimes did proclaim a supremacy of the community's needs over individual needs, and even democratic socialists do the same. If any individual (e.g., a businessman) happens to be standing in the way of what are perceived as community needs, he will get short shrift from democratic socialists, Communists and Fascists alike. The only difference is that, although the democratic socialists may imprison him, they are unlikely to kill him. Democratic socialists also, of course, involve more people in the decision over what community needs and interests are in the first place. There are other similarities: Communists claim to speak for 'the people'. Nazis spoke for 'das Volk', which translates roughly as 'the people'. Communism and Nazism might have different bogeymen ('capitalists' versus 'the Jews') but, at least in pre-war Germany, the same individuals would often be caught under either rubric. Hitler wanted to ban Einstein's physics because it was 'Jewish'. Stalin wanted to ban Einstein's physics because it was 'bourgeois' (Eysenck and Wilson, 1978).

In the libertarian view Nazism was simply a less full-blown and more simple-minded version of Communism. (The Israeli scholar, Unger (1965), also argues that Nazism was less totalitarian than Communism.) Both exerted extensive controls over the whole of society and ran the economy at State command. It could be argued that Nazism was in some ways a more successful form of socialism than Communism. Nazis had to rely less on repression within Germany precisely because their methods and rhetoric were more genuinely congenial to the German people than were the methods and rhetoric of Stalin to the Russian people. Even anti-Nazi pre-war writers such as Roberts (1938) acknowledge that Hitler was the most popular man in Germany at the time. The rivalry between Nazism and Communism was sibling rivalry: between national socialism and international (really Russian) socialism.

In a sense, both Hitler and Stalin have had the last laugh. Both stood for the replacement of individual decisions by government, party or bureaucratic decisions. Yet, at the hands of the democratic socialists, all countries of the world have since the Second World War been marching in precisely that direction. Even in the United States the extent to which the government has taken over the spending of the national income since the Second World War is staggering. In England all major industries are owned and run by the government, and government is the major provider of accommodation for the masses. The economy of Britain is now surprisingly similar to that of Eastern bloc countries such as Hungary. So entrenched is socialism in England that even the energetic Mrs Thatcher has been unable to budge it. Even freedom of speech is restricted in the UK for those who have uncongenial ideologies—as the National Front member found who put up a sign in his front yard saying: 'House for sale: Whites only'. He was imprisoned for his pains. Dislike of blacks is widespread in Britain (Britain is the only predominantly Anglo-Saxon country with an explicitly racist political party mounting major campaigns in national elections) but expression is officially repressed. No doubt all the things that democratic socialists have done were done with good intentions, but let us remember that Hitler and Stalin also claimed good intentions.

The great prophet of the twentieth century was probably Mussolini. His ideas of course preceded Hitler's, and most of the once-decried features of his corporatist State are now commonplace in advanced 'Western' countries. In a sense what Britain and other 'Western' countries are doing is returning to a historical norm at an only slightly slower pace than that adopted by Communists and Fascists. That norm is collectivism and the form of government that goes with it is, at best, paternalistic. The ancient civilizations of the Nile and the Euphrates were remarkably like ant colonies, and we may end up that way again. Human beings evolved as essentially social, cooperating, labour-sharing animals, and there has always been a perceived need for someone to direct the labour and share out the product. Kingship or aristocracy has been the usual way of legitimating individuals in that role. Nazism had more room in its ideology for quasi-divine leaders and privileged elites, and was more in harmony with historical human practice, but, despite all ideology, Communists have ended up with a similar system. The auguries for other political systems are not good. Collectivism has the sort of universal attraction of a return to the womb: others take the responsibility for one's basic physical needs and in return one forgoes most of one's abilities and opportunities for individualistic, independent, responsible endeavour.

It may seem that the foregoing account has placed far too much emphasis on the economic system as the touchstone of what a society is like. This leading role of the economic system is a basic libertarian thesis. Historically, a few peoples on the fringes of North-West Europe made the transition from a hunting society to civilization rather quickly (at various times in the last 2000 years), and in the process some of the independence of mind more appropriate to a life of hunting carried over into the new life. This independence was only a leaven as the civilizations these people founded did produce from time to time tyrants as powerful and as brutal as any (e.g., England's Henry VIII). Nonetheless, there was generally more decentralization of power (among the barony and others) than in an Oriental despotism, and the individualism this allowed transformed outside influences (particularly the rebirth of learning after the fall of the Byzantine Empire) into first the Protestant Reformation and then finally into the English Industrial Revolution. One of the central pillars of State power (State religion) was undermined and new sources of power (money in the hands of the bourgeoisie) independent of the State were created. Of these two great revolutions, however, only the latter brought about fundamental social changes. After the Reformation, Protestant princes simply took over from where Catholic princes had left off. The system of social hierarchy and patronage remained essentially unaltered. A seed had been sown in that revolution from the bottom up had been shown to be possible but there were to be long travails before the type of social organization actually changed. It is therefore to the economic revolution, the industrial revolution, that we must look for the beginnings of the modern world.

During the time that the power of princes was still weak from the conflicts of the Reformation, there was more opportunity for the individualism of the North-West European peoples to show through in other ways. People began to experiment with new ways and devices for making money. They improved their traditional machines and processes for spinning, weaving, mining and metal-working, and got away with it because the despot was too weak from other conflicts to jump on such apparently minor displays of individualism. The rest, as they say, is history. The process of innovation was enormously profitable and underwent exponential growth. Almost before anyone had realized it, a new phenomenon—capitalism—was born. Money and power always walk hand in hand, and all these new holders of substantial wealth (the capitalists) were a new, highly fractionated and quite subversive source of power and influence. They guarded jealously the independence that had made their wealth possible, and traditional society, weakened as it was by religious strife, could not meet such an unprecedented challenge. In the Victorian era *laissez-faire* capitalism came to open political power. If capitalism took traditional society by surprise, however, the effects of capitalism were also a surprise to most of the bourgeoisie. Not only was a new independent middle class created, but the affluence and its consequent independence after a while trickled down to the working class as well. Giving the worker the opportunity to change his job, his occupation, his employer completely destroyed the basis of feudal power, and it soon destroyed the power of the capitalists as well. Power was again fractionated and the bourgeoisie in turn lost its leading role. Politics became mass politics.

Thus we arrive at the modern era. The workers have no more grasp of the mechanisms of capitalism than did the old land-owning elites, and they hanker for a return to the womb. Twentieth century socialism in its various forms (Bolshevik, democratic and Fascist) is the response. The almost accidental flowering of capitalism transformed the world in a few short years but it was an unnatural flowering by human standards and the heat of disapproval is already withering it. Thus a highly collectivized but popularly accepted society that uses technology but is not dominated by it (such as Hitler's Germany) would seem to be what the future holds for the advanced nations of today.

In all the above little has been said of the role of conservatism. Socialism has been painted in fairly bleak terms. Is conservatism the great white hope? Far from it. Libertarians take a fairly orthodox view of conservatives as simply cautious, careful people whose values are of the past. But since the past contains both libertarian elements (in the economic sphere) and repressive elements (in the sphere of religion and morality), conservatives have no consistent theme and undo the good they do by giving occasional support to liberty in one sphere by trying to repress liberty in other spheres. Socialist repression has an air of inevitability about it. Conservative repression is a functionless shadow of a moral system that once had the important economic function of ensuring that all children were born with a father to provide for them. In time, then, conservatives too will come to accept collectivism as part of what was and therefore must be, and even the limited conservative opposition to collectivism will die.

Is there any hope for the individual in our future? Perhaps there is. Perhaps the egg once broken can never be completely put back together again. Human beings constantly do many unnatural things (such as wearing clothes), so the fact that tyranny is man's natural form of government need not mean that it is his inevitable future. Libertarians certainly do what they can to slow down the ever-advancing power of the bureaucratic State (e.g., Green, 1982).

If the Libertarians are right, not even Eysenck's theory can modify the traditional Right-Left view of politics into a workable description of reality. There is no static Right-Left divide or any other static political polarity. Instead all we have is a continuing dynamic progress towards restoring an equilibrium that was accidentally disturbed by a completely unforeseen and unprecedented historical event. When that restoration is accomplished, all politics will revert to what has always been their essential element—competition for power among individuals.

# REFERENCES

Adorno, T. W., Frenkel-Brunswik, E., Levinson, D. J. and Sanford, R. N. (1950) *The Authoritarian Personality*, New York, Harper.

Altemeyer, R. (1981) *Right-Wing Authoritarianism*, Winnipeg, University of Manitoba Press.

Christie, R. (1956a) 'Eysenck's treatment of the personality of Communists', *Psychological Bulletin*, **53**, pp. 411–30.

Christie, R. (1956b) 'Some abuses of psychology', *Psychology Bulletin*, **53**, pp. 439–51.

Christie, R. and Jahoda, M. (1954) *Studies in the Scope and Method of "The Authoritarian Personality"*, Glencoe, Ill., Free Press.

Christie, R., Havel, J. and Seidenberg, B. (1956) 'Is the F scale irreversible?', *J. Abnorm. Soc. Psychol*, **56**, pp. 141–58.

Eysenck, H. J. (1940) 'Some factors in the appreciation of poetry, and their relation to temperamental qualities', *Character and Personality*, **9**, pp. 160–7.

Eysenck, H. J. (1944) 'General social attitudes', *J. Social Psychol*, **19**, pp. 207–27.

Eysenck, H. J. (1951) 'Primary social attitudes as related to social class and political party', *Brit. J. Sociology*, **2**, pp. 198–209.

Eysenck, H. J. (1954) *The Psychology of Politics*, London, Routledge.

Eysenck, H. J. (1971) 'Social attitudes and social class', *Brit. J. Soc. Clin. Psychol.*, **10**, pp. 210–12.

Eysenck, H. J. (1975) 'The structure of social attitudes', *Brit. J. Soc. Clin. Psychol.*, **14**, pp. 323–31.

Eysenck, H. J. (1976) 'Structure of social attitudes', *Psychol. Reports*, **39**, pp. 463–6.

Eysenck, H. J. (1981/82) 'Left-wing authoritarianism: Myth or reality?', *Political Psychology*, **3, 1/2**, pp. 234–8.

Eysenck, H. J. and Eysenck, S. B. G. (1976) *Psychoticism as a Dimension of Personality*, London, Hodder and Stoughton.

Eysenck, H. J. and Levey, A. (1967) 'Konditionierung, Introversion-extroversion und die Stärke des Nervensystems', *Zeitschrift fur Psychologie*, **174**, pp. 96–106.

Eysenck, H. J. and Wilson, G. D. (1978) *The Psychological Basis of Ideology* Lancaster, MTP Press; Baltimore, Md., University Park Press.

Friedman, M. (1962) *Capitalism and Freedom*, Chicago, Ill., University of Chicago Press.

Gibson, H. B. (1981) *Hans Eysenck: The Man and His Work*, London, P. Owen.

Green, D. G. (1982) 'Arguments for liberty', *Political Quarterly*, **53**, pp. 418–32.

Hanson, D. J. (1975) 'Authoritarianism as a variable in political research', *Il Politico*, **40**, pp. 700–5.

Hayek, F. A. von (1944) *The Road to Serfdom*, London, Routledge.

Jaensch, E. R. (1938) *Der Gegentypus*, Leipzig, Barth.

Kelman, H. C. (1974) 'Attitudes are alive and well and gainfully employed in the sphere of action', *Amer. Psychologist*, **29**, pp. 310–24.

La Piere, R. (1934) 'Attitudes and actions', *Social Forces*, **13**, pp. 230–7.

Lichter, S. R. and Rothman, S. (1981/82) 'Jewish ethnicity and radical culture: A social psychological study of political activity', *Political Psychology*, **3**, pp. 116–57.

Lipset, S. M. (1960) *Political Man*, New York, Doubleday.

McKinney, D. W. (1973) *The Authoritarian Personality Studies*, The Hague, Mouton.

Mises, L. von (1949) *Human Action*, London, Hodge.

Ray, J. J. (1971a) 'Correspondence', *Bull. Brit. Psychol. Soc.*, **24**, p. 352.

Ray, J. J. (1971b) 'Ethnocentrism: Attitudes and behaviour', *Australian Quarterly*, **43**, pp. 89–97.

Ray, J. J. (1972) 'Militarism and psychopathology—Comments on Eckhardt and Newcombe's "Comments"', *J. Conflict Resolution*, **16**, pp. 319–40.

Ray, J. J. (1973a) 'Antisemitic types in Australia', *Patterns of Prejudice*, **7, 1**, pp. 6–16.

Ray, J. J. (1973b) 'Dogmatism and sub-types of conservatism', *European J. Social Psychol.*, **3**, pp. 221–32.

Ray, J. J. (1973c) 'Factor analysis and attitude scales', *Australian and New Zealand J. Sociology*, **9, 3**, pp. 11–13.

Ray, J. J. (1973d) 'Conservatism, authoritarianism and related variables: A review and an empirical study', in Wilson, G. D. (Ed.), *The Psychology of Conservatism*, London, Academic.

Ray, J. J. (1974) 'Authoritarian humanism', in Ray, J. J. (Ed.), *Conservatism as Heresy*, Sydney, ANZ Book.

Ray, J. J. (1976) 'Do authoritarians hold authoritarian attitudes?', *Human Relations*, **29**, pp. 307–25.

Ray, J. J. (1979) 'Does authoritarianism of personality go with conservatism?', *Australian J. Psychology*, **311**, pp. 9–14.

Ray, J. J. (1980) 'Are authoritarians extraverted?', *Brit. J. Soc. Clin. Psychol.*, **19**, pp. 147–8.

Ray, J. J. (1981) 'Is the ideal sample a non-sample?', *Bull. Brit. Psychol. Soc.*, **34**, pp. 128–9.

Ray, J. J. (1982) 'Climate and conservatism in Australia', *J. Social Psychol.*, **117**, pp. 297–8.

Ray, J. J. (1983) 'The workers are not authoritarian: Attitude and personality data from six countries', *Sociology and Social Research*, **67**, pp. 166–89.

Ray, J. J. (1984) 'Political radicals as sensation-seekers', *J. Social Psychol.*, **122**, pp. 293–4.

Ray, J. J. and Bozek, R. S. (1981) 'Authoritarianism and Eysenck's "P" scale', *J. Social Psychol.*, **113**, pp. 231–4.

Ray, J. J. and Lovejoy, F. H. (1983) 'The behavioral validity of some recent measures of authoritarianism', *J. Social Psychol,* **119**, pp. 173–9.

Roberts, S. H. (1938) *The House That Hitler Built*, New York, Harper.

Rokeach, M. (1960) *The Open and Closed Mind*, New York, Basic Books.

Rokeach, M. and Hanley, C. (1956) 'Eysenck's tender-mindedness dimension: A critique', *Psychological Bulletin*, **53**, pp. 169–76.

Titus, H. E. (1968) 'F scale validity considered against peer nomination criteria', *Psychol. Record*, **18**, pp. 395–403.

Unger, A. L. (1965) 'Party and State in Soviet Russia and Nazi Germany', *Political Quarterly*, **36**, pp. 441–59.

Wilson, G. D. (1973) *The Psychology of Politics*, London, Academic.

# Interchange

## BRAND REPLIES TO RAY

Ray, as the official 'critic' for the present symposium, has had fulsome fun with Eysenck's scheme. Clearly, he and I agree about a wide range of matters—especially as to the basic support that exists for Eysenck's theory, as to the need for a more convincing measure of T (or, indeed, P), and as to Eysenck's underestimation of the true authoritarianism of the Left. At the same time I doubt that he has a valid or integrated alternative to Eysenck's theory; and I am quite certain that the 'libertarian' perspective of fashionable economics does not strictly require a fundamental antithesis between entrepreneurial capitalism and all other (as Ray would have them, 'collectivist') ideologies—especially that of traditional Christianity with its respect for both law and love.

As riders to our agreements, the following matters deserve remark. (1) Ray's reminders of the apparent emptiness of T—of its failure to achieve high-loading items in many studies—sit ill alongside his incomprehension at its correlation with smoking: for smoking, like other historically male habits, correlates with psychoticism (e.g. Brand, 1981). Ray prefers his 'directiveness' scale as a measure of the broadly masculine tendencies that I have referred to as those of *will versus affection*, but in so doing he simply ignores Eysenck's findings as to the biological bases of both T and P. If he ever finds that quota-sampled supporters of wife-swapping and apartheid are not distinguished by being smokers I will take off my hat to him. (2) Ray's amusing account of Eysenck's (1976) latest full-scale study of attitudes shows a deference to Eysenck's own interpretation of his results that scrutiny of the published data would correct; the more traditional Eysenckian rotation of the axes is the one provided in my chapter (see Figure 1). (3) Ray's enthusiasm for seeing 'conservatives' as Hitler's chief opponents ignores the facts not only that Russia finally bore the brunt of the War and that Roosevelt was a Democrat but that Churchill—for many years a Liberal—ran (from May 1940) a National Government from which the Leader of the Conservative Party (together with other 'appeasers') had been forced out of the highest office with the important assistance of Labour Members of Parliament who subsequently were called to serve in the Cabinet. At a bottle of brandy a day, and with a penchant for perusing the titillating magazine *Blighty* while visiting British troops in France (see Gilbert, 1983), Churchill was no simple straight-laced moral conservative, for all that the venerable General Franco—likewise no totalitarian—might have been (see Johnson, 1983). (4) It does not disturb me one bit that the authors of *The Authoritarian Personality* were 'entirely Jewish': Jews are overrepresented amongst social scientists for some very good reasons, including their unique experience of the de-Christianized West, the genius of their people, and the special position of those who escaped the Holocaust as precocious migrants who had seen what was coming under the various forms of socialism (and especially Nazism) that were on offer in Europe of the 1930s. The Frankfurt School's acceptance of Freudianism and Marxism should not obscure its empirical achievements.

As to serious disagreements, I will await with interest any forthcoming demonstration that three dimensions—rather than Eysenck's two—are required to embrace the realm of social attitudes. Ray knows as well as I do that strictly Nobel-prize-winning libertarianism is a minority sport; acclaim for it is indeed confined to just as small an elite as ever favoured Communism in the West in the heyday of that ideology. To me it seems more natural to allow that real (as distinct from intellectual) libertarianism is a reasonably flourishing business that makes a dynamic common cause with the traditional Christian belief in the parable of the labourers in the vineyard: *viz.* that labourers agree the terms of their hire with their employers and are entitled to just that and—in economic terms—no more. Modern corporatism may try to disrupt this alliance and to issue wondrous rights to workers without any corresponding duties; but there it makes a mistake, as the 'black economies' of the Soviet Empire (and, very sadly, of modern Britain) testify. More futuristically, I suppose that those entrepreneurs who would like to enjoy the freedoms of polygamy, sperm banks, genetic engineering and so forth will have to deal with advocates of traditional Christian morality in some form of legitimistic compromise as to what can be allowed as right and proper. Of course, it would be folly to neglect the influence of intelligence and education in these matters—as I suspect that Ray has done when 'finding' that high-scorers on the F scale subscribe to simplistic (while apparently liberal) opinions.

It is possible, as Ray warns, that collectivism will take over. I rather sympathize with his view that the journalist Mussolini, whose activities were so applauded by Lenin in 1914, might prove to have been the man who first understood the sad fate that awaited the twentieth century. But our century has yet to enjoy its own religious revival; and I would be decently optimistic—'more English than the English', as Ray might have it—that such a revival would take (by way of a 'legitimistic compromise') a freedom-respecting rather than a corporatist form.

## REFERENCES

Brand, C. R. (1981) 'Personality and political attitudes', in Lynn, R. (Ed.), *Dimensions of Personality*, Oxford, Pergamon Press.
Eysenck, H. J. (1976) 'The structure of social attitudes', *Psychological Reports*.
Gilbert, M. (1983) *Finest Hour*, London, Heinemann.
Johnson, P. (1983) *A History of the Modern World*, London, Weidenfeld and Nicolson.

## RAY REPLIES TO BRAND

Brand puts forward a number of schemata for conceptualizing the dimensions underlying social attitudes which are broadly similar to those proposed by Eysenck. He puts forward arguments based on current political realities that offer some plausibility to his schemata. This type of evidence, however, has always favoured

Eysenck. No-one to my knowledge disputes the plausibility of the Eysenckian two-dimensional description of the political domain. The difficulty is in finding psychometric evidence which supports it. The plain and basic trouble is that Leftists in Western countries will never acknowledge support for those authoritarian and totalitarian practices that so characterize their brethren in the poorer countries of the world (including the Eastern bloc). In the West only Rightists have a kind word to say for authoritarianism in government. We thus have the paradox that while politics are clearly multidimensional, attitudes seem to be remarkably unidimensional. Brand offers nothing towards a solution of this problem. New schemata or revised schemata are all very well but what is needed is evidence to support them. Two of his unreferenced assertions are, however, very interesting. The first—that Adorno-type authoritarians are quite as likely to vote Leftist as Rightist—is one which I have been pointing out for some time (Ray, 1973, 1983) and readers should be aware that there is extensive evidence for it. The second—that Conservatives tend to be of much lower intelligence—is more contentious. The only evidence I know of for it is in the much-flawed work of McClosky (1958). McClosky's scale of conservatism was all one-way worded. People who agree with almost anything thus get high scores on it regardless of whether or not they are actually conservative. That unintelligent people should agree with almost anything seems to me a lively possibility. McClosky's correlations may, in other words, be simply an acquiescence artifact.

It seems to me that the important fact which both Brand and Eysenck have overlooked is that both Stalin and Hitler were socialists—by both self-ascription and practice. Hitler's political party (abbreviated as 'Nazis') was in fact the National Socialist German Worker's Party. Hitler was a considerable social welfare innovator (e.g., the *Kraft durch Freude* movement) and his success at curing German unemployment was through the thoroughly socialist expedient of increased public works. He identified the enemies of his people slightly differently ('Jews' rather than 'the bourgeoisie'), but his use of conspiracy theory for purposes of political explanation is rivalled only by modern-day Leftist conspiracy theory ('the military-industrial establishment' or that ever-serviceable explanation for almost anything untoward, 'the CIA'). Hitler's main difference seems to be that he liked his own people, his 'Volk'. Even pre-war anti-Nazi writers acknowledge that he was the most popular man in Germany (Roberts, 1938) and he did attain power by democratic means. He had a higher percentage of the popular vote in the last election he fought than most recent British governments have had. Stalin, by contrast, never faced a popular election and the paranoia behind the vast purges (mass-murder) he visited on his own people is only too evident.

It seems to me, then, that the multidimensionality of politics is more apparent than real. What we have is a single continuum stretching from respect for the individual and his rights at one end to socialism and love of State power at the other. People at both ends believe that they act in the name of maximizing human welfare but the means are very different. Extreme socialists (such as Stalin and Hitler) believe that mass-murder of the unworthy can maximize welfare. Less extreme socialists (as in Leftist governments of the Western world) find it sufficient to tax the unworthy into insignificance. If theft is having your property taken from you against your will, then taxation is simply legalized theft. Both theft and murder are crimes that can be committed by both governments and individuals. In all cases they reduce the rights and liberties of individuals. Socialists believe that such crimes by the State can be justified by the greater wisdom or the more compassionate objectives of the State.

Old-fashioned Liberals (now mostly to be found in 'conservative' parties) doubt the wisdom of the State and point to the costs of its compassion. Fortunately, in a true democracy neither extreme of policy is very likely. Individuals are generally left some rights and there is generally some minimum guarantee of care for all. Historically we had an excess of individualism in Victorian times followed by an excess of socialism in the early and mid-twentieth century (i.e., Hitler and Stalin). Perhaps we can be optimistic and now believe that some countries have settled on a balance between the two. Just exactly what balance is optimum, however, will probably always be a source of dispute.

The major problem for psychologists must be the paradox that the people who are least likely to voice support for authority or authoritarianism (i.e., Leftists) seem to be the most extreme practitioners of authoritarianism when in government. Labour Party governments expand the role and power of the State faster than Conservative Party governments. Stalin was more totalitarian than Hitler (Unger, 1965). Pol Pot murdered a greater proportion of his country's people than any Argentine junta would ever dream of. Communist tyrannies never give way to democracy but conservative tyrannies (e.g., Galtieri, Franco, Papadopoulos) always do. It must all lead surely to the conclusion that denial is the besetting psychopathology of the Left, but how and why this pathology arises must be a deeper enquiry.

**REFERENCES**

Brand, C. R. (1985) 'The psychological bases of political attitudes and interests', chapter in this volume.

McClosky, H. (1958) 'Conservatism and personality', *Amer. Pol. Sci. Rev.*, **52**, pp. 27–45.

Ray, J. J. (1973) 'Dogmatism and sub-types of conservatism', *Europ. J. Soc. Psychol.*, **3**, pp. 221–32.

Ray, J. J. (1983) 'Half of all authoritarians are Left-wing: A reply to Eysenck and Stone', *Political Psychology*, **4**, pp. 139–44.

Roberts, S. H. (1938) *The House That Hitler Built*, New York, Harper.

Unger, A. L. (1965) 'Party and State in Soviet Russia and Nazi Germany', *Political Quarterly*, **36**, pp. 441–59.

# 11. Psychotherapy and Freudian Psychology

EDWARD ERWIN

## STANDARD PSYCHOANALYTIC THERAPY

In some of his papers Eysenck has discussed standard psychoanalytic therapy and 'eclectic' psychotherapy. In this section I will discuss only the former.

Standard (or orthodox) psychoanalysis is a lengthier form of treatment than most other forms of psychotherapy, lasting two years or more on average. It involves systematic use of free association, interpretation and transference neurosis, and normally has as its goal the uncovering and resolution of the major emotional problems thought to originate in the patient's childhood (White, 1956, p. 322).

In his (1952) paper Eysenck concluded, on the basis of studies by Denker (1946) and Landis (1938), that roughly two-thirds of neurotic patients recover or improve to a marked extent within about two years of the onset of their disorder, whether they are treated by psychotherapy or not. This so-called 'spontaneous remission' rate was then compared to the improvement rate for psychoanalytic and eclectic treatment. Because neither type of therapy showed a greater than two-thirds improvement rate, Eysenck concluded that the data failed to prove that psychotherapy, Freudian or otherwise, facilitates the recovery of neurotic patients. He also pointed out that there were problems with the data and that they did not necessarily *disprove* the possibility of therapeutic effectiveness. In subsequent publications, especially in Eysenck (1966), he again stressed that his conclusion was (1) that firm evidence of psychoanalytic effectiveness was lacking, and *not* (2) that psychoanalysis is ineffective. Despite these warnings, many critics have raised objections that are telling only if Eysenck had been trying to demonstrate thesis (2). See, for example, Smith *et al.*'s discussion (1980, p. 14) and Farrell (1981, p. 178).

Pointing out that Eysenck has sometimes been misunderstood helps explain why certain critics believe incorrectly that they have provided a satisfactory rebuttal, but it hardly shows that no-one has refuted his position. In order to clarify the issues, it will

**179**

help to lay out Eysenck's original argument, as I have tried to do elsewhere (Erwin, 1980a).

1   If there is no adequate study of psychoanalytic therapy showing an improvement rate of at least two-thirds or better than that of a suitable no-treatment control group, then there is no firm evidence that the therapy is effective.
2   There is no adequate study of either kind.
3   Therefore, there is no firm evidence that the therapy is effective.

The premises of the above argument logically entail the conclusion; so, if both premises are true, then the conclusion is true. To attack the argument successfully, one must show that at least one premise is false or, more weakly, is unwarranted. Once this requirement is made clear, it becomes evident that some replies to Eysenck's argument are irrelevant, and others even lend additional support to his conclusion. For example, pointing out that Eysenck has never been psychoanalyzed presents no challenge to either premise; the contention is simply irrelevant to his argument. In contrast, if one could demonstrate that psychoanalytic outcomes cannot be studied scientifically, this result would not only be consistent with both premises, it would also lend further support to Eysenck's conclusion. Other irrelevant and self-defeating challenges are discussed in Erwin (1980a).

Two objections that *are* relevant concern Eysenck's interpretation of certain studies and his assumption of a two-thirds spontaneous remission rate. For example, Bergin (1971; Bergin and Lambert, 1978) questions Eysenck's counting of dropouts as clinical failures. After eliminating dropouts from the final tabulation and making other adjustments, Bergin found a 91 per cent improvement rate for one of the studies discussed by Eysenck. If Bergin's interpretation of the data could be shown to be correct, then this would refute Eysenck's second premise. However, Bergin makes no attempt to demonstrate the soundness of his interpretation; his point, which I believe has been misunderstood, was that the data admit of more than one reasonable interpretation. His conclusion (Bergin, 1971, p. 225), that there is no valid way to assess the effects of psychoanalysis from the information available, is consistent with both of Eysenck's premises; furthermore, if Bergin is right, then there is additional support for Eysenck's conclusion. The general point is that showing that existing studies of psychoanalysis are inherently ambiguous, and that Eysenck's interpretations are not the only defensible ones, is insufficient to refute Eysenck's argument.

The same kind of point can be made about spontaneous remission rates. Several critics (Luborsky, 1954; Rosenzweig, 1954) have challenged Eysenck's assumption of a two-thirds spontaneous remission rate, but have not established a lower rate. Bergin (1971) cites some studies which suggest a rate of approximately 30 per cent, but he does not establish that this rate is correct, nor does he claim to; in fact, he warns against accepting any general rate (Erwin, 1980a; see also Rachman, 1971). Farrell (1981) also does not try to establish a rate significantly lower than Eysenck's, but argues instead that spontaneous remission rates are too uncertain to be used to establish the effectiveness of psychoanalysis.

If Farrell is right, then Eysenck's original argument should be revised as follows:

1   If spontaneous remission rates are too uncertain (to be used to establish the effectiveness of psychoanalysis) and there is no adequate study with an improvement rate better than that of a suitable no-treatment control group, then there is no firm evidence of psychoanalytic effectiveness.

2   The spontaneous remission rates are too uncertain, and there is no adequate controlled study with the proper results.
3   So there is no firm evidence of psychoanalytic effectiveness.

Again, a general point emerges: undermining a two-thirds spontaneous remission rate without establishing a significantly lower rate is not an effective strategy for a Freudian. It does nothing towards demonstrating the effectiveness of psychoanalysis, and it permits an easy revision in Eysenck's original argument.

There is an additional, deeper reason why criticizing Eysenck's spontaneous remission rate is not likely to prove effective. Suppose that someone were to demonstrate a much lower general rate or, more feasibly, a much lower rate for a specific kind of clinical disorder, e.g., phobias. One might then point to case studies of psychoanalysis in which client improvement surpassed either the general or the more specific rate. Would this finding then establish the effectiveness of psychoanalytic therapy? It would not. One would still have to rule out alternative hypotheses which are not merely possibly true, but are quite plausible given the current evidence about causes of client improvement. For example, there have been studies in which clients have been given a credible pseudo-therapy, and improved significantly more than those in a wait list control (Lick, 1975; Rosenthal, 1980). A second example is suggested by Frank's (1983) report that many of his patients experienced a marked drop in symptomatic distress following the initial work-up and *before* they received a placebo therapy. The only way to rule out the possibility that client improvement resulted from the initial interview, placebo factors, the skill of the therapist in dealing with people, etc. is to do suitable controlled studies. Exceeding an established spontaneous remission rate *may* rule out one hypothesis—that improvement was due to factors that would have been effective even in the absence of formal treatment— but it is too weak to confirm that the *therapy* caused any beneficial therapeutic results. If this is right, then why bring in spontaneous remission rates at all? I think that it would be widely agreed today that they should not now figure prominently in discussions of therapeutic effectiveness. I suspect that Eysenck's motivation for discussing them in his original (1952) paper was that he wished to consider the best data available, and he knew that no controlled experiment had been done. Because some psychoanalysts believed that their clients' improvement showed that psychoanalysis is sometimes effective, it was relevant to point out that these results were insufficient. In the absence of controlled study, a necessary condition of using such data to confirm effectiveness is that one's improvement rate exceed a relevant, established base rate. Eysenck then tried to show that, for the studies he considered, this necessary condition had not been met. He did not claim that meeting this condition was also sufficient. On the contrary, he pointed out even in his (1952) paper that there are obvious shortcomings in any actuarial comparison and that definite proof would require a carefully planned and much more methodologically adequate study.

The fact that certain variables, such as the passage of time and client expectancy prior to treatment, require control before one can reasonably infer clinical effectiveness undermines another criticism of Eysenck's position. Some analysts and their patients claim to be able to *see* that psychoanalysis is sometimes successful. This was also Freud's view, but it is open to an obvious objection. One may sometimes see that a client has improved (although even here there are difficulties), but to establish a causal connection between that outcome and the psychoanalytic therapy, one must rule out plausible rival explanations, including those mentioned earlier. It is difficult to see how to do that for a treatment that takes as long as psychoanalysis, unless one does a controlled experiment. If the need for experiments is conceded, then the only satisfactory reply to Eysenck is to find adequately controlled studies of psychoanalysis with a favourable outcome. It is doubtful, however, that even one such study exists in the entire literature. Bergin's (1971) review cited seven studies of psychoanalysis, but he did not claim that any had a good design. These studies, and others cited by Bergin and Suinn (1975), are criticized in Erwin (1980a). Fisher and Greenberg (1977) cite six studies and then say (p. 322): 'While we cannot conclude that the studies offer unequivocal evidence that analysis is more effective than no-treatment, they do indicate with consistency that this seems probable with regard to a number of analysts and their nonpsychotic, chronic patients.' I am not sure what this conclusion means, but *if* Fisher and Greenberg are asserting that the studies they cite make it probable that analysis, when used by some analysts, is more effective than no treatment for non-psychotic, chronic patients, then I disagree. All of these studies have obvious methodological flaws, as Fisher and Greenberg concede (p. 321); these flaws are too serious to permit any of the studies, or all together, to provide any firm evidence of effectiveness. To cite just one problem, none of the six studies had a control group sufficient for ruling out a placebo explanation of the results. Other design flaws are revealed by Rachman and Wilson (1980) and Kline (1981). (Kline does make a favourable comment about the Duhrssen and Jorswiek (1965) study, but see Rachman and Wilson's discussion pp. 59–60.)

Rachman and Wilson (1980) and Erwin (1980a) reach the same conclusion: that acceptable evidence of psychoanalytic effectiveness does not exist. Similar conclusions have been reached by other reviewers, including some who are sympathetic to Freudian theory (e.g., Kline, 1981, p. 398). Gene Glass, who helped construct perhaps the most exhaustive survey ever made of the therapeutic outcome literature (Smith, Glass and Miller, 1980), points out that he believes that psychoanalysis is by far the best theory of human behaviour, but adds that there exists in the Smith *et al.* data base not a single experimental study that qualifies by even 'the shoddiest standards' as an outcome evaluation of orthodox psychoanalysis (Glass and Kliegl, 1983, p. 40).

Even if all recent reviewers agreed (and Fisher and Greenberg do not), that would still not be conclusive, but there *is* good reason to accept Eysenck's (1952) conclusion that firm evidence of psychoanalytic effectiveness is lacking. The reason is this: in more than thirty years of discussion, no-one has been able to cite supporting evidence from controlled studies, base rate comparisons, uncontrolled clinical reports or from any other source that has been able to withstand critical appraisal. That is good reason to believe that such evidence does not exist.

Some supporters of Freudian therapy will agree with the above conclusion, but are nevertheless likely to make certain replies.

1    It is sometimes complained that outcome studies focus almost exclusively on symptom remission and that this is a wholly inadequate criterion from a Freudian point of view. It is possible that psychoanalysis produces a different type of benefit for at least some patients, such as the development of insight, character change, or resolution of id-ego conflicts. My reply is this: I have not tried to rule out this possibility, but the same sorts of epistemological problems that confront claims about symptom remission arise for claims about these other therapeutic benefits. In the absence of controlled study, where is the evidence to support the claim that any of these other benefits typically result from pyschoanalytic treatment?

2   A Freudian might try to explain the lack of evidence by stressing that it is both impractical and unethical to do an adequately controlled study of psychoanalysis. I have not argued that this explanation is wrong; whether it is right or wrong, to offer it is to concede the main conclusion that I have tried to support; that evidence is lacking.

3   Some Freudians may point out that very few therapists today use orthodox psychoanalysis. I agree with this point, but, as Wolpe (1981) stresses, one should not underestimate the powerful influence that Freudian theory and therapy continue to exert, especially in the United States. Many so-called 'eclectic' therapists use psychoanalytically oriented therapy and are committed to the view that some of the ingredients of orthodox analysis, such as transference or free association, are therapeutically useful; such therapists, then, have a reason to be concerned about outcome studies of psychoanalysis. Of course, lack of evidence of (orthodox) psychoanalytic effectiveness does not guarantee lack of evidence for the effectiveness of psychoanalytically oriented psychotherapy. I turn next to this latter kind of therapy.

## PSYCHOANALYTICALLY ORIENTED PSYCHOTHERAPY

The term 'psychotherapy' is sometimes used to encompass all psychological therapies; it is then useful to distinguish some of the newer techniques from 'psychoanalytically oriented therapy'. This latter category is somewhat vague, but includes the various insight, verbal, or dynamic therapies (see Karasu, 1977) and excludes behaviour therapy and the cognitive therapies. In this section I will not consider evidence for the behavioural or cognitive therapies (see Erwin, 1978, Ch. 1; Kazdin and Wilson, 1978; Rachman and Wilson, 1980).

There have been several optimistic reports published recently about psychotherapy (e.g., Banta and Saxe, 1983), but they generally rely heavily on the work of Smith, Glass and Miller (1980). The latter investigators introduce a new statistical method called 'meta-analysis' and use it to demonstrate the effectiveness of various types of psychotherapy (including psychoanalytically oriented versions).

In using meta-analysis one calculates an 'effect size' for a study by subtracting the average score for the control group from the average score for the treatment group and dividing the result by the within-control group standard deviation. Smith *et al.* (1980) found 475 controlled studies of psychotherapy and calculated 1760 effect sizes for these studies. The reason that the effect sizes outnumber the studies is that many studies had more than one outcome measure.

Based on their calculations, Smith *et al.*, reached four major conclusions. The two that are most pertinent to the present discussion are these.

1   Psychotherapy is beneficial, consistently so and in many different ways. Its benefits are on a par with other expensive and beneficial interventions such as schooling and medicine.

2   Different types of psychotherapy (verbal or behavioural; psychoanalytic, client-centred or systematic desensitization) do not produce different types of or degrees of benefit (Smith *et al.*, 1980, pp. 183–4).

1 and 2 together imply that different types of psychotherapy are equally effective and produce substantial benefits.

Although Smith *et al.*'s work has been widely cited, several recent articles have exposed various difficulties in their argument. One of the most serious concerns their grouping together and weighting equally evidence from relatively good and bad studies. Smith *et al.*'s primary justification for doing so is that the results of good and bad studies, they claim, are roughly the same. In reply, I argue (Erwin, 1984c) that their argument for this latter conclusion depends on an indefensible assumption about what counts as a good study and that their justification fails for other reasons. Rachman and Wilson (1980) also argue in detail that Smith *et al.*'s treatment of the evidence seriously weakens their overall argument (see also Eysenck, 1983a; Wilson and Rachman, 1983).

Even if the above criticism is set aside, Eysenck (1983b) has raised another serious problem. In Smith *et al.*'s summary (1980, p. 89), most of the verbal psychotherapies have an effect size only marginally greater than the effect size for what they call a 'placebo treatment'. This raises the question: what would the results be if a meta-analysis were restricted to studies comparing verbal psychotherapy to a placebo control? Prioleau, Murdock and Brody (1983) attempt to answer this question. For outpatient neurotics they found a close to zero difference between the effect size of the verbal psychotherapy and placebo therapy.

A number of issues are raised by the work of Prioleau *et al.* (see the responses by Glass, Smith and Miller (1983) and others), but I want to concentrate on one. Prioleau *et al.* (1983) contend that there is not a single convincing demonstration anywhere that the benefits of (non-behavioural) psychotherapy exceed those of a placebo for real patients. One response is to say that if this is true, then there is no firm evidence of (non-behavioural) psychotherapeutic effectiveness in treating neuroses (Eysenck, 1983b). Frank (1983), however, suggests that a placebo *is* psychotherapy. Along the same lines Cordray and Bootzin (1983) argue that a placebo control condition is appropriate for answering questions about theoretical mechanisms but not for demonstrating effectiveness. They point out that credible placebo interventions are themselves often effective treatments. The suggestion, then, is that verbal psychotherapy may be effective even if it works no better, or only marginally better, than a placebo.

Are credible placebos generally effective? Before answering, it should be noted that many placebos used in psychotherapy research have not been credible, or at least not as credible as the treatment to which they were compared (Kazdin and Wilcoxin, 1976). As to placebos that are credible, I know of no evidence that they are generally *powerful* forms of treatment. Placebo procedures are generally selected on the basis of the following criterion: on current theory and the available empirical evidence, they are not likely to be effective except insofar as their *believability* itself produces beneficial change. Suppose, however, that a placebo is credible to the client, and consequently does generate favourable expectations of improvement, and that as a result the client improves. Should we say in such a case that the placebo was effective? Some researchers will say 'no', on the grounds that it was the client's expectations, and not the specific ingredients of the placebo procedure, that caused the change. I am not convinced, however, that this view is correct. In the case in question the specific ingredients of the placebo treatment cause a change in expectations, which in turn causes improvement. We should not conclude that a psychological therapy is ineffective merely because it works by affecting a client's psychological state, such as his expectations; such a view might condemn *all* psychological therapies as being ineffective. Perhaps, as some writers have suggested (Bandura, 1977), all or most effective psychological therapies work by affecting the client's expectations.

I agree, then, that a credible placebo may be an effective therapy. I will call such a placebo 'weakly effective' if and only if it tends to produce favourable therapeutic effects but does so only because of its credibility. Saying that a therapy is *weakly effective* does not imply that it may not occasionally have strong effects. Kazdin (1980) discusses a case where the use of Kreboizen appeared to have a powerful effect on cancer symptoms because of the patient's confidence in the treatment, even though Kreboizen has been judged to be a (chemically) worthless drug for treating cancer. The point of classifying a therapy as being only 'weakly effective' in this technical sense is to indicate that it is *replaceable* by any other procedure that is equally credible and has the capacity to create the same favourable expectations of improvement.

Suppose that the insight or verbal psychotherapies are, at best, equal in effectiveness to weakly effective placebos. The implications of this hypothesis for the psychotherapy enterprise are disastrous. In a sense, then, it does not matter whether we take equivalence to a credible placebo to be a sign of ineffectiveness or of weak effectiveness: the adverse consequences will follow on either alternative. For example, if the insight psychotherapies are at best weakly effective, then the standard psychotherapy theories—in particular Freudian theory—would not correctly explain why any of these therapies work. Equivalence would also raise serious questions about the typical training that psychotherapists receive. Finally, it would seem more cost-effective in many cases to use a sugar pill, which proved to be as effective as psychoanalytically oriented psychotherapy in the Brill *et al.* (1964) study, *or* some other minimal but credible placebo, in preference to more elaborate and more expensive psychotherapies. Other adverse consequences for the psychotherapy enterprise are discussed in Erwin (1984b).

Research that is now being conducted may provide the solid evidence that is now lacking, but the *current* evidence for the strong effectiveness of psychoanalytically oriented psychotherapy, although not non-existent, is fragmentary and very weak indeed, as shown by Rachman and Wilson (1980). One persistent problem, if we exclude research on the behavioural and cognitive therapies, is the rarity of well controlled studies in which the therapeutic effects of psychotherapy exceed those of a *credible* placebo. As noted earlier, Prioleau, Murdock and Brody (1983) claim that there is not even one study of this sort dealing with real patients; they also cite several reasonably designed studies in which a credible placebo control was used but the placebo patients did approximately as well as the psychotherapy patients (Brill *et al.*, 1964; Gillan and Rachman, 1974; McLean and Hakstian, 1979). Even if Prioleau *et al.* (1983) are wrong, and there are some studies of the right type with the right results, it is difficult to escape the following conclusion. Apart from studies of some behavioural and cognitive techniques, there is no solid body of scientifically acceptable research that will now justify our saying: for a wide range of clinical problems and patients, these are the psychotherapy techniques that have been shown to be more than weakly effective for *this* type of client having *this* type of problem. Conclusion: any brief discussion of such a complex and controversial issue as that of the effectiveness of psychotherapy is likely to omit important subtleties and qualific-ations. I would like to mention one. When some clients and therapists talk about psychotherapy, they are not referring to any particular technique other than listening to the patient's problem and giving comfort and advice. I have no doubt that for certain sorts of problems, say marital problems or difficulties in raising children, 'psychotherapy' of this sort is sometimes beneficial. I assume that Eysenck would also agree that giving advice and solace is sometimes useful—and sometimes is not. When he and other critics raise doubts about the evidence for psychotherapeutic effectiveness, they are talking about specific techniques (beyond giving advice) and specific clinical problems (primarily, the neuroses).

## PSYCHOANALYTIC THEORY

### The Clinical Evidence

Freudians have marshalled what looks like impressive evidence for Freudian theory. I do not think that today many philosophers would reject such 'evidence' *a priori*, on the grounds that Freudian theory is untestable in principle. (For arguments that at least parts of the theory are testable, see Grünbaum, 1979.) In any event I shall assume that Freudian evidential claims need to be carefully scrutinized before one can reasonably conclude that supporting evidence does not exist, or, more strongly, that it *cannot* exist.

In discussing the putative evidence, it is customary to distinguish between clinical and experimental data. Clinical evidence is usually gleaned from psychoanalytic therapy sessions, although data obtained through the use of other kinds of therapies might also be relevant. Experimental evidence is obtainable only when certain sorts of experimental controls are used, such as those discussed by Campbell and Stanley (1963).

Although it is convenient to use the aforementioned terminology, I do not want to suggest a contrast between the two types of evidence. Behaviour therapists have employed single subject experimental designs in therapy sessions (Hersen and Barlow, 1976). So some clinical evidence might also be experimental evidence, and conversely. In speaking of 'clinical evidence', then, I am not necessarily referring to *non-experimental* evidence.

Some psychoanalysts eschew non-clinical, experimental testing because they believe it unnecessary. As Freud commented, although such testing might do no harm, it is not needed given the wealth of clinical observations that support Freudian theory (Luborsky and Spence, 1971). Other analysts hold that more evidence is needed, but question the reliance on non-clinical, experimental studies because of methodological doubts. One of the main complaints is that in trying to devise strict controls, the experimenter is forced to test propositions that bear only a faint resemblance to Freudian hypotheses.

Whether or not a general scepticism about extra clinical testing is warranted, many analysts, perhaps most, have based their theoretical claims on clinical evidence. How credible is this evidence? Eysenck has expressed strong doubts about its worth: '... we can no more test Freudian hypotheses "on the couch" than we can adjudicate between the rival hypotheses of Newton and Einstein by going to sleep under an apple tree' (quoted in Grünbaum, 1983a).

Before commenting directly on the clinical evidence, it might be useful to circumscribe our subject. First, some Freudian hypotheses are either not theoretical or are not causal. An example which is neither is that most patients do not agree with the analyst's initial interpretation of their symptoms. I assume that few commentators would deny that this hypothesis might be confirmed by clinical evidence, but this is not the sort of hypothesis I want to discuss. In assessing the clinical evidence, I will talk only about Freud's theoretical hypotheses that make a causal claim. Second, I will concede from the outset that such hypotheses might be *disconfirmed* by clinical observations. An example might be the hypothesis that symptom substitution will invariably result if symptoms are eliminated without resolution of underlying id-ego conflicts. What I am asking is whether some such hypotheses are *confirmed* by the clinical evidence. Third, I also agree that it is logically possible that some clinical evidence might be confirmatory. For example, it *might* be possible to confirm to some extent some Freudian causal hypothesis in a clinical setting by using a single subject experimental design. I am not discussing testability in principle, however; I am asking if *existing* clinical evidence has confirmed any of the kinds of hypotheses in question.

Once the logical possibility of clinical confirmation is conceded, it becomes difficult to rule out such confirmation on *a priori* grounds. How, then, can one decide if there exists somewhere some clinical evidence that confirms some Freudian hypothesis? Are we to examine every case study that has ever been published, including those discussed by Freud himself? The task would be monumental, but it is unnecessary if we can develop empirical arguments of a general nature, similar to those used to discredit (uncontrolled) clinical confirmation of Freudian therapeutic claims. Such arguments have been developed by Adolf Grünbaum (1983a, 1983b, 1984).

One obvious difficulty with relying on psychoanalytic clinical evidence is that it is contaminated with suggestibility effects. As Horowitz (1963) and certain other Freudians have pointed out, the patient's behaviour in the analytic setting is often greatly influenced by the suggestions, both intended and unintended, of the analyst. These suggestions might be less worrisome if analysts accepted only patients who were sceptical of Freudian theory, but that is not what occurs. As Greenson (1959) points out, one test of suitability for analysis is the prospective patient's capacity to discern connections between his present problem and a portion of his prior history, presumably his early childhood. Another test is to see how the person responds to some tentative speculation by the analyst concerning his problem. Any patient who survives such tests and remains in analysis two years or more is likely to have some faith in Freudian theory or therapy. Furthermore, there is direct evidence that the analyst's suggestions do influence so-called 'free' associations (Marmor, 1970) and dream reports (Fisher, 1953).

Freud was also aware of the need to discount the influence of the analyst's suggestions and he did so by appealing to what Grünbaum (1983b p. 17) calls 'Freud's Master Proposition': a neurosis can be dependably eradicated *only* by the conscious mastery of the repressions that are causally required for its pathogenesis, and *only* the therapeutic techniques of psychoanalysis can generate this requisite insight into the specific pathogen. Freud also offered an interesting defence of this master proposition by using two allegedly necessary conditions for satisfactorily explaining an hysterical symptom in terms of a traumatic event (Grünbaum, 1983a). If the master proposition is warranted, and if Freud had evidence that his therapy was sometimes successful, then he had warrant for inferring that at least some of his psychoanalytic interpretations were correct. As Grünbaum (1983a, 1984) shows, however, Freud's argument breaks down at crucial points. The defence of the master thesis is defective, apparently because of a logical mistake; there is evidence from the success of some behaviour therapies and from spontaneous remission data that the master proposition is false; and there is no firm evidence that psychoanalysis brings about cures of neurosis. Grünbaum (1983a, 1984) also shows that without the use of Freud's device for decontaminating the clinical data, or some adequate substitute, the 'evidence' from clinical studies has even more serious weaknesses than Freud realized. Freudians might still try to show that, despite Grünbaum's powerful arguments, the clinical data are confirmatory, but as of now this has not been done. It should be stressed, furthermore, that the issue is not whether or not Freudian theory is scientific (Flax, 1981), unless one identifies being scientific with having evidential support; nor does the issue concern the logical possibility of clinical confirmation. What Grünbaum has tried to show is that the existing clinical evidence provides no firm warrant for any of Freud's causal hypotheses.

One could also object to Grünbaum's criticisms on the grounds that he does not consider more recent developments of Freudian theory (Flax, 1981). However, as Eagle (1983) argues, neo-Freudian theorists, such as Kohut and Kernberg, must face the same sorts of epistemological problems as Freud did, if they wish to appeal to clinical evidence for confirmation. It might also be objected that the epistemological problems arise because Freud's clinical theory is interpreted in causal terms. Some hermeneuticians suggest that this interpretation is a mistake, engendered in part by Freud's desire to make his theory conform to the standards of the natural sciences. It needs to be shown, however, that the hermeneutical, acausal reading of Freudian hypotheses avoids the epistemological problems without rendering the hypotheses trivial; there is reason to believe that this demand cannot be met (Grünbaum, 1983b; Moore, 1983; von Eckardt, 1984).

*Conclusion*

Grünbaum's work (1983a, 1983b, 1984) creates a strong presumption that existing clinical data provide little, if any, support for Freudian theory. If this presumption is to be overcome, an analyst must show how the epistemological difficulties are to be resolved. If that cannot be done, then the best bet is to look for support in (non-clinical) experimental studies.

**Experimental Evidence**

In recent years some commentators (Kline, 1972, 1981; Fisher and Greenberg, 1977; Farrell, 1981) have argued that experimental studies provide strong support for central parts of Freudian theory; other writers (Eysenck, 1972; Erwin, 1980b) have examined some of the same studies and concluded that the evidence they yield is at best very weak. This disagreement is predictable if one accepts a Kuhnian-type relativism that holds that standards for assessing evidence are relative to a paradigm and that, consequently, those in different paradigms inevitably have insoluble disagreements about the interpretation of data. However, there is no need to invoke a relativistic hypothesis here if, as I shall argue, the standards in question can be rationally defended or criticized without relying on assumptions peculiar to any particular paradigm. The standards I have in mind concern the warrant for accepting hypotheses and the identity of Freudian hypotheses.

*Warrant*

Some supporters of Freudian theory (e.g., Hall, 1963) write as if a hypothesis may be warranted simply by deriving from it, and suitable auxiliary assumptions, a prediction that is then discovered to be true. This standard, however, is too weak. Operant conditioning theory predicts that people will repeat behaviour that is contingent upon some rewarding environmental event, but finding that this sometimes occurs does not warrant our accepting an operant conditioning explanation of why it occurs; a cognitive or physiological theory might explain the behaviour just as well. Freud's theory of dreams, to take another example, predicts that people will dream, but so do non-Freudian rivals; that people dream hardly shows that Freud's account of why they dream, or what dreams mean, is correct. In general, if an hypothesis, *H*, predicts some observation, *O*, the finding of *O* does not warrant the acceptance of *H* if some other hypothesis, *H*, explains *O* and any other relevant data at least as well. This suggests a necessary condition for a hypothesis being warranted: data warrant the acceptance of an hypothesis only if rival hypotheses that are at least as credible are ruled out, or at least can be discounted (warrant condition). By 'accepting' an hypothesis, I do not mean merely using it as a guide for experimentation; I mean believing it to be true, or approximately true. I am also assuming that any relevant background data, and not merely the data from a single experiment, must be considered in assessing *H*. Finally, in asking how well two hypotheses explain the same data, several factors may have to be weighed, such as simplicity, comprehensiveness, and initial credibility or likelihood given the background data; there is no rule agreed upon by philosophers of science or scientists to determine exactly how these factors are to be weighted. Hence, two researchers might disagree about whether *H* is warranted even though they examine the same data, but such disagreements are not necessarily unresolvable.

Suppose that instead of talking about a hypothesis being warranted *simpliciter*, we talk about *degrees* of warrant or confirmation. Is it necessary to rule out competing hypotheses that are equal or superior in plausibility before *any* degree of evidential support is provided for a given hypothesis? In another paper (Erwin, 1980b) I suggested that this was so on the grounds that if two equally plausible hypotheses, $H_1$ and $H_2$, explain the data equally well, then the data do not tell us which of these hypotheses is true. At best, the data confirm a disjunction: $H_1$ or $H_2$. It might be objected, however, that even if the data do not tell us which hypothesis is true, they may provide at least some support for both rather than no support for either. This objection is strengthened if it can be shown that a sufficient condition of confirmation for *H* is any increase in the probability of its being true. If this probabilistic account can be relied on, one might then argue that if a series of experiments rules out four of six competing hypotheses, then this increases the chances of the remaining two being correct, thus providing some degree of support for each.

I do not think that the 'increase in probability' view of confirmation is correct (see Achinstein, 1983, for counter-examples), but I also doubt that any other view of confirmation can be proved at the present time. Given the disagreement among philosophers of science about theories of confirmation, it is probably unwise to rest anything substantial on any one account. For that reason, and because I have doubts about the standard used in Erwin (1980b), I shall not assume that data provide no support whatsoever for *H* merely because some equally plausible rival has not been ruled out. However, I do think it plausible to say that in such a situation, the data do not provide *strong* support for either *H* or its rival. If we have just as much (or more) reason to believe $H_2$ as $H_1$, and if $H_2$'s being warranted eliminates any reason for believing $H_1$, then we are not warranted in believing $H_1$.

*Freudian Hypotheses*

As noted earlier some analysts are sceptical about relying on non-clinical, experimental evidence because, they argue, to meet the stringent demands of controlled study, investigators inevitably transform Freud's theoretical hypotheses into something else. This is particularly likely to happen if an experimenter insists on providing an operational reformulation of Freudian concepts. For example, consider Ellis' (1956, p. 140) reformulation of the hypothesis of the existence of the id: 'Operational reformulation: Human beings have certain basic needs or desires, such as hunger, sex, and thirst needs, toward the expression of which they inherit tendencies, but which can be considerably modified by experiential reinforcement or social learning.' Ellis may not have been trying to give an exact translation of Freud's postulation of an id, but if he was, his attempt fails. Even if Freud were entirely wrong about the so-called 'mental apparatus', even if there were no unconscious mind, id, ego or superego, Ellis' translated statement might well be true. Indeed, even the most adamant anti-Freudian could concede that humans have the basic needs that Ellis mentions and that the expression of these needs can be modified by environmental events. Establishing that this is so would not confirm the existence of the id.

I do not agree that an experimenter *must* seriously distort Freudian hypotheses in trying to test them; to agree would be to concede that the experimental testing of Freudian theory is impossible. It is worth stressing, however, that we are discussing *Freudian* hypotheses and not non-Freudian analogues. It has become commonplace to find support for Freudian theory in evidence that at best confirms propositions that are clearly not identical with any of Freud's theoretical hypotheses. For example, some find it obvious that Freudian slips occur, but they do not mean slips that meet the criteria laid down by Freud in his *Psychopathology of Everyday Life* (1965). Instead, they mean any slip of the tongue or pen regardless of its causal genesis. Another example is the work of Dollard *et al.* (1939), which Kline says (1981, p. 237) demonstrates beyond all reasonable doubt the operation of the Freudian defence mechanism of displacement. In the Dollard *et al.*, book the term 'displacement' is used in a loose, non-Freudian sense. The authors apply it in any case where aggression directed at a given object is prevented and is then redirected toward another object (Dollard *et al.*, 1939, p. 40) regardless of why this redirection occurs. One example given is that of kicking a chair instead of one's enemy. In this and in other cases Dollard *et al.*, do not require, as Freud did, that the ego be protecting itself from instinctual demands of the id; the behaviour automatically qualifies as an instance of displacement even if it can be explained by operant conditioning theory, or is caused by some *conscious* cognitive event. Some of their other examples are discussed in Erwin (1984a).

We need, then, some way of excluding confirmation of pseudo-Freudian views. One might use, as Kline (1972, p. 350) does, the concept of a 'distinctively Freudian' hypothesis. I assume that he means by this phrase an hypothesis that is peculiar to Freudian theory (or, certain neo-Freudian reformulations). Whether or not we use the same concept as Kline, we do need to draw some sort of distinction between psychoanalytic propositions and those that form no part of Freudian theory but which are, especially in popular writings, often confused with Freudian hypotheses.

In sum, before an experiment can warrant our accepting one of Freud's theoretical hypotheses, it must be the case that: (1) the warrant condition mentioned earlier is met, and (2) the hypothesis that is warranted by the experiment be part of

Freudian theory. A third condition is implicit in the second, but might as well be explicitly stated: (3) that the hypothesis be theoretical. There are difficulties in drawing a single, general theoretical/observational distinction that will serve the same purposes that certain philosophers had in mind, but there are clear instances of propositions that are non-theoretical in that they describe only what is observable.

If the above conditions are acceptable, then there is reason to be sceptical about recent evaluations of the experimental evidence (Kline, 1972, 1981; Farrell, 1981; Fisher and Greenberg, 1977). Many of the studies cited fail to meet one or more of the three conditions. There is no room here to demonstrate this for every single study, but some important illustrations will be discussed.

## The Kline (1972, 1981) Reviews

Kline (1972) discusses most of the published experimental studies of psychoanalysis. His work is important because it is the first book to bring together so much of the scattered literature and because it contains valuable commentary on the evidence. Kline criticizes many of the experimental studies, but also argues that fifteen Freudian hypotheses have been verified. He writes: 'From these conclusions it seems clear that far too much that is distinctively Freudian has been verified for the rejection of the whole of psychoanalytic theory to be possible' (p. 350).

In my view the exemplar investigations that Kline cites as evidence (pp. 345–6) do not warrant the acceptance of any Freudian hypothesis. One problem with some of these studies is that the hypothesis they test is not Freudian. For example, the studies by Cattell (1957) and Cattell and Pawlik (1964) test the hypothesis that there are three major motivational factors in human behaviour, but the studies fail to show that these factors are identical to Freud's id, ego and superego. Another problem is that some of the studies violate the warrant condition: they fail to rule out plausible alternative explanations of their findings; in some cases, the failure results from reliance on a projective measure that would be acceptable if Freudian theory were confirmed but which lacks independent empirical support. For example, Friedman (1952) used unfinished castration fables to measure castration anxiety. In the fables a child finds his toy elephant broken, and the subject is asked what is wrong with it. Mention of loss of tails, for example, is assumed to be a sign of high castration anxiety. No attempt is made to establish this assumption; no evidence is offered that castration fables measure castration anxiety at all. Without such evidence, the results cannot be taken as confirming the hypothesis being tested.

Another important example of a violation of the warrant condition is work on perceptual defence *if* interpreted as establishing the existence of repression. In a typical perceptual defence experiment, stimulus words are presented to a subject by use of tachistoscope. A 'higher threshold' is usually defined as a greater number of tachistoscopic exposures prior to conscious recognition. For example, if a subject requires more exposures before recognizing a negative word, such as 'raped' or 'whore', that word is said to have a higher threshold. A perceptual defence result is said to occur when negatively or positively valued stimuli have higher thresholds for a subject than neutral stimuli. Contrary to what some commentators have said, occurrence of this effect is not by itself evidence for the existence of repression or the activation of any other Freudian defence mechanism. In his (1961) review of the literature, Brown discusses ten different explanations of results of perceptual defence experiments, and points out that many more than ten were available in the literature. The Freudian explanation, such as that offered by Blum (1955), was only one of many competing explanations, and it was not shown to be superior to the others.

In the 1960s N. F. Dixon and others tried to demonstrate that perceptual defence effects not only occur but are sensory in origin rather than being caused by response processes. No evidence was provided, however, for thinking that the negative stimuli in perceptual defence experiments were defended against by the subjects or were incorporated into an unconscious mind. Dixon himself (1971, p. 244) stresses that perceptual defence effects (and other subliminal perceptual phenomena) provide no warrant for postulating an unconscious. They do provide evidence of discrimination without awareness which affects recognition thresholds, but lack of awareness does not mean the operation of an unconscious mind. Indeed, if Dixon's own physiological explanation (1971) of subliminal effects is warranted, a Freudian explanation is unnecessary.

I stress both the theoretical neutrality of perceptual defence effects and Dixon's interpretation of his own studies because Kline (1972, 1981) and Farrell (1981) rely heavily on Dixon's work to establish the occurrence of repression. Kline (1981, p. 226) claims that it follows from his (Kline's) definition of 'repression' that perceptual defence effects are examples of repression; so, proving that perceptual defence effects occur proves that Freudian repression occurs. In defining 'repression', he (p. 195) quotes Freud as saying that 'the essence of repression lies simply in the function of rejecting and keeping something out of consciousness.' However, this does not capture what Freud meant by 'repression'. Freud makes clear that the concept of repression and of the other defences is linked to that of the unconscious. Repression occurs only when unconscious (not merely preconscious) processes occur that primarily have the purpose of protecting the ego against instinctual demands of the id (Erwin, 1984b). If there is no id or ego and no unconscious, then there is no repression in Freud's sense. As already argued, the mere fact that there is discrimination without awareness and that this discrimination affects recognition thresholds does not establish that any subject has defended against threatening material by incorporating it into the unconscious. Repression could be the cause of perceptual defence effects, but there is no firm evidence so far that it is.

Kline's remaining exemplar studies (1972, pp. 345–6) are criticized either in Eysenck and Wilson (1973) or Erwin (1980b). Kline (1981) updates his previous work, taking into consideration studies published after 1972, including ones discussed in Fisher and Greenberg (1977). However, the summary of verified concepts remains essentially the same as Kline (1972). The main additions are: the work of Kragh and his associates on percept genetics, cited in support of repression and other defences, and one additional hypothesis supported by the work of Silverman.

Kragh (1960) points out that there are similarities but also important differences between his work and studies of perceptual defence. In a typical study he and his associates use a tachistoscope to present what are called 'DMT' and 'MCT' pictures to groups of subjects at increasingly greater exposure times. One picture shows a boy with a violin, the head and shoulders of a threatening and ugly male having been inserted at the right of the boy. A parallel picture shows a young man centrally placed and an old ugly man above him. The subjects are instructed to make a drawing of what they have seen without paying any attention to whether their impression is correct or not. If they feel unable to make any kind of drawing, they are allowed to make markings instead. Kragh (1960) uses the term 'hero' to denote the person who is seen (drawn, marked) by a subject at the place of the main person in the picture. A 'secondary' figure is the person seen at the place of the secondary person in the picture. Results are scored using Freudian defence categories. For example, a drawing is classified as 'repression' if the hero or/and the secondary figure have the quality of stiffness, rigidity, lifelessness, or of being 'disguised', or is (are) seen as an animal. What evidence does Kragh (1960) provide to show that repression is the cause of the subject's drawing the figures in this way? None at all. He simply stipulates that 'repression' and the other Freudian categories will be applied if certain kinds of drawings are made. Without such evidence the studies of Kragh and his associates, whatever their value in distinguishing between psychiatric groups, provide no warrant for accepting the existence of any Freudian defence mechanism.

Kline (1981, p. 234) makes the following comment about this lack of evidence: 'Regrettably the only evidence for the validity of the DMT and MCT defense mechanism variables is effective face-validity. That is, if one examines what behavior is actually entailed in obtaining a score for a given mechanism, one makes a value judgment that the behavior resembles closely what Freud described as the appropriate mechanism.' One may make such a judgment (I am not sure why it should count as a *value* judgment), but without supporting evidence it would be unwarranted; it is not self-evident or obviously true that such drawings are caused by the operation of Freudian defence mechanisms.

The additional hypothesis that Kline (1981) says is verified concerns libidinal wishes and psychopathology: that the activation of an unconscious wish increases psychopathology and that the wish is as specific as is hypothesized in psychoanalytic theory (p. 383). The evidence is taken from the work of Silverman and his colleagues.

Silverman's approach involves the use of subliminal stimulation to stir up unconscious oedipal fantasies. A tachistoscope is used to present subliminal negative stimuli, such as pictures of a lion charging or a man snarling, or messages such as 'Fuck Mommy'. Controls are shown neutral stimuli such as a picture of a man reading a paper or a message such as 'People Walking'. In some experiments Silverman and his associates claim to have increased or decreased pathology in their subjects. One of the difficulties in interpreting these experiments is that questionable tests were used to measure psychopathology. This problem was avoided in another experiment (Silverman, Ross, Adler and Lustig, 1978) that used a simple dependent variable, 'competitive performance', as measured by scores in a dart tournament. Heilbrun (1980) reports on three attempted replications of this work; all three failed. These failures of replication by an independent investigator are important, especially because most of the studies using the Silverman technique were done by him or his colleagues or were reported in unpublished doctoral dissertations. In his reply to Heilbrun, Silverman (1982) mentions six other attempted replications, with four having positive results and two negative results. At best the evidence is mixed, but it should be noted that all four of the positive studies are also unpublished doctoral dissertations, studies that Kline (1981, p. 44) tends to discount.

In another study (Silverman, Frank and Dachinger, 1974) the effectiveness of systematic desensitization was said to have been enhanced by activating unconscious fantasies. However, it is possible that what Silverman compared was simply a relevant stimulus (for the treatment group) and an irrelevant stimulus (in the control). To test this possibility, Emmelkamp and Straatman (1976) tried to replicate the Silverman *et al.* (1974) study, using a relevant stimulus in the control sessions. They failed to replicate; Condor and Allen (1980) also tried to replicate and failed. (See Silverman's reply, 1982, and their comments, Allen and Condor, 1982.)

The utility of Silverman's work for decreasing psychopathology or enhancing therapeutic effects of other treatments is not likely to be decided until further research is published by independent investigators. Whatever results are found, however, a problem remains: Silverman relies on psychoanalytic theory to justify the assumption that his subliminal stimuli stir up unconscious fantasies; no firm independent evidence is provided that this is so. Without such evidence, what is, at most, demonstrated is that certain kinds of subliminal stimuli produce certain sorts of interesting effects. Whether this would have any bearing on psychoanalytic theory is unclear. (For additional comments on Silverman's work, see the following section.)

### *The Fisher and Greenberg (1977) Review*

Fisher and Greenberg review many of the same studies as Kline (1981), but they also rely partly on unpublished doctoral dissertations. Kline (1981, p. 44) omits the latter group of studies from his discussion on the grounds that almost all competent research of this sort appears later in published papers. Because I want to focus on the stronger studies, I will follow Kline's practice and discuss only those that have been published.

Fisher and Greenberg (1977, p. 414) sum up their work by first explaining their major reservations about Freud's ideas and then listing those items they affirm to be basically sound. There are seven items in the latter category: I will discuss each in turn.

### 1    *The oral and anal character concepts as meaningful dimensions for understanding important aspects of behaviour*

I will not discuss the studies Fisher and Greenberg cite in support of the above because the relevant hypotheses are not theoretical. Consider, for example, what the authors say about the anal character (p. 393). They do not assert that anyone with one 'anal' characteristic will display the rest; the claim is merely that some people are parsimonious, compulsive and stubbornly resistant, and that this fact is of some psychological significance. (Fisher and Greenberg, p. 393, also say that the anal character does display a significant pattern of the three traits and that this seems to follow from Freud's account; however, this is tautological given what is meant by 'anal character'.) The relevant theoretical propositions about the etiology of either 'anal' or 'oral' traits, Fisher and Greenberg concede (p. 393), have not been empirically confirmed.

### 2    *The Oedipal and castration factors in male personality development*

Fisher and Greenberg discuss at least nine hypotheses in this category, but what we really know, they say (1977, p. 219), can be reduced to three propositions.

The first proposition, despite the use of the term 'pre-Oedipal', is not theoretical and is relatively trivial: that both males and females are closer to mother than father in the pre-Oedipal period (i.e., before the age of 3 or 4). It would not be surprising if this proposition were true of most children given the child rearing practices of our culture.

The second proposition, that at some later point each sex identifies more with the same than the opposite-sex parent, is also non-theoretical. It should also be noted that not all of the studies cited by Fisher and Greenberg support this hypothesis. For example, Krieger and Worchel (1959) found no consistent pattern of opposite-sex parent identification in their subjects.

The third proposition is that there are defensive attitudes detectable in persons beyond the Oedipal phase which suggest that they have had to cope with erotic feelings toward the opposite-sex parent and hostility toward the same-sex parent. One might object that even this proposition is not distinctively Freudian: it might be true for non-Freudian reasons of some females who have had an incestuous sexual relationship with their father. However, Fisher and Greenberg make clear (p. 200) that they are postulating a Freudian variable, castration anxiety, as at least a partial cause of the pattern of erotic-hostile involvements. Castration anxiety, they claim, is a common occurrence in men and has been shown to be intensified by exposure to heterosexual stimuli. The one supporting study they cite (on p. 220), apart from three unpublished doctoral dissertations, is by Sarnoff and Corwin (1959). This study assumes without any argument that certain responses to the so-called 'castration anxiety' card of the Blacky cartoons is evidence of castration anxiety. The card shows a cartoon depicting two dogs; one dog is standing blindfolded, and a large knife appears about to descend on his outstretched tail. The second dog is an onlooker to this event. It was assumed that subjects had a high degree of castration anxiety if, for example, they accepted the following statement as best describing the emotions of the onlooking dog: 'The sight of the approaching amputation is a deeply upsetting experience for the Black dog who is looking on; the possibility of losing his own tail and the thought of the pain involved overwhelm him with anxiety.' No evidence was provided that subjects accepting this statement had any degree of castration anxiety whatsoever. Without such evidence, the study cannot be taken as establishing that anyone has an unconscious fear of being castrated. Other methodological difficulties are discussed in Eysenck and Wilson (1973). Another study (Blum, 1949) also relied on the use of the Blacky cartoons. The remaining published studies of castration anxiety cited by Fisher and Greenberg (Friedman, 1952; Hall and Van de Castle, 1965; Schwartz, 1956) have been criticized elsewhere (Erwin, 1980b; Eysenck and Wilson, 1973). The basic difficulty with these studies is their reliance on an unwarranted assumption about what measures castration anxiety.

## 3   The relative importance of concern about loss of love in the woman's as compared to the man's personality economy

That all or most women in our society have been more concerned about loss of love than men is not a theoretical proposition; if it is true, that would not be surprising given the greater pressures on women to be married. Whether it is true or not, however, cannot to decided on the basis of the evidence cited by Fisher and Greenberg. Apart from two unpublished doctoral dissertations, they rely on exactly two studies. One study (Gleser, Gottschalk and Springer, 1961) found for eleven males and thirteen females significantly higher scores for separation anxiety for the females. Given that these clients were all psychiatric patients, however, it would be rash to generalize from this small sample to groups of normal clients. For a much larger sample ($N = 90$) of subjects who were not psychiatric patients, the difference between males and females in separation anxiety was not statistically significant. The second study (Manosevitz and Lanyon, 1965) did not directly study fear of loss of love. Forty-nine college females and sixty-four college males were asked to complete the Fear Survey Schedule. Although females reported more fears than men, the authors point out that it is possible that the former were simply more honest in reporting their fears. The women on the average did score higher than men on 'Feeling rejected by others', but it is not clear that this reflects a fear of loss of love. On another item, which arguably better reflects such a fear ('Being rejected by a potential spouse'), the men scored slightly higher than the women. In sum, neither study provides unequivocal evidence for hypothesis 3; each could be interpreted as providing counter-evidence *if* the validity of the measures could be assumed.

### 4   The aetiology of homosexuality

Fisher and Greenberg (1977, p. 247) point out that Freud's ideas about male homosexuality have been only partially tested. They contend, however, that the available empirical data support his core concept about the kind of parents who are likely to shape a homosexual son. They are more cautious about the aetiology of female homosexuality; they conclude (p. 253) only that the empirical findings are more supportive of, than opposed to, Freud's formulation.

The studies that Fisher and Greenberg rely on are, in my view, too weak to warrant acceptance of Freud's view about the aetiology of either male or female homosexuality. There is no need to review these studies here; they are effectively criticized by Kline (1981, pp. 342–53). Kline concludes (1981, p. 353) that there is no sound evidence in support of the psychoanalytic theory of the aetiology of homosexuality, except perhaps for evidence provided by Silverman *et al.* (1973). As with Silverman's other work, it is important that replications of this study be made by independent investigators. There is also reason to question the validity of his dependent measures: the sexual feelings assessment and a Rorschach assessment. Suppose, however, that such objections are waived and it is agreed that one of his groups of homosexual subjects did experience an intensification of homosexual orientation and that the other group did feel less threatened; assume, further, that these results were caused by the presentation of the subliminal stimuli. There still remains the same sort of problem discussed earlier in connection with Silverman's experiments. He assumes that: (a) homosexuals generally have castration anxiety; (b) the subliminal presentation of the words 'Fuck Mommy' accompanied by a picture of a nude man and woman in a sexually suggestive pose triggers unconscious incestuous wishes; (c) the triggering of such wishes causes an increase in castration anxiety; and (d) that, in turn, causes an intensification of homosexual orientation. Other assumptions are made about the reduction of castration anxiety and the diminishment of homosexual orientation. No evidence is presented for any of these assumptions; consequently, his conclusions about the aetiology of homosexuality are not warranted by his results.

### 5   The influence of anxiety about homosexual impulses upon paranoid delusion formation

Fisher and Greenberg (1977, pp. 257–8) derive two testable propositions from Freud's theory of the aetiology of paranoid delusions.

a   The paranoid delusion represents a defensive attempt to control and repress unacceptable homosexual wishes by projecting them.

b   The persecutor in the paranoid's delusion would (in terms of its homosexual equation) be of the same sex as the paranoid.

Fisher and Greenberg contend (p. 269) that the second hypothesis has been disconfirmed, but that the first has received 'rather good experimental verification'. They interpret the first hypothesis, however, as *not* implying that repressed homosexuality is the major cause of paranoia; they take the evidence to show merely that paranoids are repressed homosexuals.

Attempts to confirm hypothesis (a) generate a tricky epistemological problem. As Fisher and Greenberg stress (p. 259), according to Freudian theory, unconscious impulses that are disturbing are presumably repressed and contained so as to prevent their overt expression. So the authors take the position (p. 259), I think correctly, that the appearance of either overt displays of homosexuality or of homosexual imagery by a paranoid would contradict rather than confirm Freud's theory of paranoia. The epistemological dilemma, then, is this: if the paranoid overtly evidences his homosexuality, Freud's theory is contradicted; if he does not, then the assumption that the paranoid is homosexual will be unwarranted. Those who have tried to confirm hypothesis (a) have generally tried to circumvent this dilemma by finding *indirect* evidence of repressed homosexuality in paranoids. A major issue, then, is the quality of such evidence.

In three of the studies cited by Fisher and Greenberg a Rorschach test was used to establish the presence of homosexuality. Aronson (1952) and Meketon *et al.* (1962) found supporting data for hypothesis (a); Grauer (1954) had negative results. A fourth study (Zeichner, 1955) used both the Rorschach and Thematic Apperception Tests and found mixed but generally supporting data. However, none of these four studies qualifies as providing strong evidence either for or against hypothesis (a) without solid evidence for the assumption that the projective tests that were used did detect the presence of homosexuality. In another study Daston (1956) studied recognition times for words judged to have homosexual, heterosexual and non-sexual meaning; the words were presented tachistoscopically. He assumed that faster recognition times for the homosexual words indicated homosexuality. However, as Fisher and Greenberg point out (p. 265), one could just as reasonably assume that if the paranoids were anxious about their homosexuality, they would have slower recognition times for homosexual words; in that case, Daston's findings disconfirm hypothesis (a). However, in the absence of evidence either for Daston's crucial assumption or for its negation, the results are neither confirmatory nor disconfirmatory. In another study Wolowitz (1965) tested for the presence of homosexuality in thirty-five paranoid and twenty-four non-paranoid male schizophrenics by asking each subject to move a sequence of photographs along a tunnel toward himself until he found the place where it looked best. It was assumed that placing the male photos closer to one's self was evidence of homosexuality. Because the paranoids did not do this, Wolowitz took his findings to disconfirm Freud's hypothesis. Fisher and Greenberg point out (p. 264) that the paranoids might have acted defensively; so their fear of having their homosexuality detected might have caused them to place the photos of males farther from themselves than those of neutral objects. Fisher and Greenberg add that what is impressive is that the paranoids and non-paranoids reacted *differently*. However, unless we have evidence that reacting differently in this situation, or placing the photos of males closer to one's self or farther from one's self, is evidence of homosexuality, Wolowitz's study yields evidence neither for nor against hypothesis (a).

Watson (1965) used three tests to measure homosexuality. First, he assumed that repressed homosexuals would have a higher mean score than a control on the MMPI Masculinity-Femininity Scale. Because the paranoids in the study did just the opposite compared to non-paranoid schizophrenics, Watson took this result to run counter to Freud's paranoia-repressed homosexuality hypothesis. A second assumption was that repressed homosexuals would obtain a lower mean score than controls on the Homosexuality Awareness Scale. The paranoids did score lower than the controls. One might conjecture than this occurred because the paranoids were homosexual but were repressing their homosexuality and thus acting defensively; however, this is only a conjecture. No evidence was provided for the second assumption: that those scoring lower on the scale were repressing their homosexuality. A third assumption was that repressed homosexuals would respond less quickly than controls to a TAT-like picture having a high level of homosexual content compared to a neutral picture. Again, no evidence was provided for that assumption. In addition, the only evidence that the 'homosexual card' had a high level of homosexual content and that the 'neutral card' did not was that five student nurses believed that this was so; they were not asked for evidence to support this belief.

One final published study cited by Fisher and Greenberg is that by Zamansky (1958). He tested five hypotheses that he claimed to be reasonable if one initially assumes that paranoids are characterized by strong homosexual needs. The hypotheses were tested by presenting in a tachistoscope-like viewing apparatus pairs of pictures (e.g., of males and females, and of scenes with and without 'homosexually threatening' items). Two of the five hypotheses were not supported, which could be taken as evidence against the initial assumption if Zamansky's other assumptions are all warranted; if the conjunction of his five hypotheses is reasonable given the initial assumption that paranoids are characterized by strong homosexual needs, then the falsification of even one conjunct would falsify the assumption. However, not all of Zamansky's other assumptions are warranted. One crucial assumption, for which he provides no evidence, is that if the subjects look longer at pictures of males than females when the subject's task is disguised (they were told to determine which picture in each pair was larger), that is because the subjects are repressed homosexuals. Another unwarranted assumption is that when the question of preference for male or female pictures is made explicit, and so more conscious, unconscious defensive forces are set into motion and this causes the preferences of the paranoids to approximate those of non-paranoid persons. The failure to provide evidence for either assumption renders Zamansky's results neither confirmatory nor disconfirmatory for the hypothesis that all or most paranoids are repressed homosexuals.

Why did Zamansky's paranoid subjects look longer at the male photos? One cannot be sure, but one plausible explanation, suggested by Eysenck and Wilson (1973), is that being generally suspicious and finding males more of a possible threat, paranoid subjects are likely to pay more attention to pictures of males. Why, however, did the paranoids state a greater preference for pictures of women than men? Eysenck and Wilson suggest that the subjects, after being shown pictures of homosexual encounters, were worried about being labelled 'homosexuals'. However, even this relatively straightforward explanation is not necessary; perhaps the paranoids truly *preferred* the pictures of females. Kline (1981, p. 335) refers to Eysenck and Wilson's explanation as *ad hoc* speculation and says: 'These comments seem worthless to us, although if readers prefer this explanation to the psychoanalytic hypothesis they are of course free to adopt it.' I agree that the Eysenck-Wilson explanation is speculative and *ad hoc* in the sense of being offered after the experiment was done, but why is it worthless? If there is clear and compelling independent evidence that the Freudian account of paranoia is correct, then Zamansky's explanation of his findings might be more plausible. In the absence of such evidence, however, which is more plausible to believe: that subjects showing no overt signs of homosexuality really are homosexuals but are repressing their feelings and because of this look longer at pictures of males, and because of an unconscious defensive reaction state a preference for pictures of females; or that the paranoids acted as they did because they were suspicious (and perhaps had a genuine preference for pictures of females)? I see no evidential basis for saying that the first account is more likely to be true than the second.

I conclude that, despite much ingenuity, the investigators in the experiments discussed by Fisher and Greenberg have uniformly failed to solve the epistemological problem mentioned at the beginning of this discussion: that of warranting the assumption that paranoid individuals are homosexual even when they never provide overt manifestations of homosexuality.

## 6   The soundness of the train of interlocking ideas about the anal character, homosexuality and paranoid delusion formation

Fisher and Greenberg provide no independent support for hypothesis 6; they rely on arguments they give for their hypotheses 1, 4 and 5. Because I have already criticized the arguments for these other three hypotheses, hypothesis 6 requires no separate discussion.

## 7   The possible venting function of the dream

The authors' chapter on Freudian dream theory is, in my judgment, one of the most interesting sections of their book. They argue for certain revisions of the theory, but they also hold to one key assumption: that the dream is a vehicle for expressing (or venting) drives and impulses from the unconscious sector of the 'psychic apparatus' (p. 47). Concerning this hypothesis, they argue that the evidence shows that: (a) when people are deprived of dream time they show signs of psychological disturbance; and (b) conditions that produce psychological disequilibrium result in increased signs of tension and concern about specific themes in subsequent dreams (p. 63). They do *not* claim, however, that these findings confirm Freud's idea that dreams serve to vent either wishes or drives from the unconscious: 'One can say these findings are *congruent* with Freud's venting model. But it should be added that they do not specifically document the model' (p. 63; Fisher and Greenberg's italics). The key difficulty in establishing that the venting model applies to *any* dreams is this: even if it can be shown that a dream expresses a certain impulse, how do we know that the impulse originates in the unconscious? Fisher and Greenberg take the position (p. 47) that presently there is no reliable scientific way of answering this question.

*Farrell's Review*

Farrell (1981) is concerned more than Kline, or Fisher and Greenberg, with philosophical issues concerning Freud's views. Where he does discuss the experimental evidence, he makes rather cautious claims, but he does argue for some positive conclusions. I have discussed all of his arguments elsewhere (Erwin, 1984a) and concluded that they do not provide strong support for any part of Freudian theory.

## CONCLUSION

The foregoing discussion clearly requires certain qualifications, including the following:

1  In addition to the lack of positive evidence, there may be disconfirming evidence for certain parts of Freudian theory (see Fisher and Greenberg, 1977, for some examples). However, I have been concerned only with the positive evidence; I have not argued that any psychoanalytic proposition is false.

2  A deeper criticism of certain studies could be made by demonstrating that a comprehensive rival theory provides a better explanation of the results than does Freudian theory. Eysenck would probably wish to do this in some cases by appealing to his own conditioning theory of neurosis (Eysenck, 1982). I have not made such attempts in order to avoid controversies about the evidential status of psychological theories other than Freud's.

3  I have tried to examine the most important studies of Kline (1972, 1981) and Fisher and Greenberg (1977): most of the exemplar studies of the former (Kline, 1981, pp. 432–3) and the published positive studies of the latter. However, it is still possible for a Freudian to argue that the unexamined studies provide strong support for parts of Freudian theory.

4  My main purpose has been to highlight the main weaknesses in the experimental literature, but in some cases my discussion has necessarily been superficial. The work of Kline, and Fisher and Greenberg, is important and deserves a much fuller reply than I have given. Such a reply, in my view, should consider such topics as: the weight accorded to simplicity and systematicity; the need for alternative theory; the trade-off between initial likelihood (or unlikelihood) and other explanatory virtues; and the heuristic value of Freudian theory.

5  As indicated earlier, I disagree with those who argue that it is logically impossible to test Freudian theory. However, it *might* be true that it is impossible in practice to devise and carry out adequate tests at least for some Freudian hypotheses; *if* that were true, that might explain some of the failed attempts at confirmation.

In conclusion, the experimental studies I have discussed have serious weaknesses; I doubt, for reasons I have given, that they provide strong support for any part of Freudian theory. This suggests a more general doubt. I began by pointing out that some critics have argued recently that: (1) Eysenck's criticisms of psychoanalytic therapy have now been satisfactorily answered (Farrell, 1981; Brown and Herrnstein,

1975); (2) psychoanalytically oriented psychotherapy has now been shown to produce substantial benefits (Smith, Glass and Miller, 1980); and (3) a substantial part of Freudian theory has now received strong empirical support (Kline, 1972, 1981; Fisher and Greenberg, 1977). I have tried to raise serious doubts about each of these claims.

## REFERENCES

Achinstein, P. (1983) *The Concept of Evidence*, New York, Oxford University Press.

Allen, J. and Condor, T. (1982) 'Whither subliminal psychodynamic activation? A reply to Silverman', *Journal of Abnormal Psychology*, **9**, pp. 131–3.

Aronson, M. (1952) 'A study of the Freudian theory of paranoia', *Journal of Projective Techniques*, **16**, pp. 397–411.

Bandura, A. (1977) 'Self-efficacy: Toward a unifying theory of behavioral change', *Psychological Review*, **84**, pp. 191–215.

Banta, H. D. and Saxe, L. (1983) 'Reimbursement for psychotherapy: Linking efficacy research and public policymaking', *American Psychol.*, **38**, pp. 918–23.

Bergin, A. (1971) 'The evaluation of therapeutic outcomes', in Bergin, A. and Garfield, S. (Eds.), *Handbook of Psychotherapy and Behavior Change*, New York, Wiley.

Bergin, A. and Lambert, M. (1978) 'The evaluation of therapeutic outcomes', in Garfield, S. and Bergin, A. (Eds.), *Handbook of Psychotherapy and Behavior Change*, New York, Wiley.

Bergin, A. and Suinn, R. (1975) 'Individual psychotherapy and behavior therapy', *Annual Review of Psychology*, **26**, pp. 509–56.

Blum, G. (1949) 'A study of the psychoanalytic theory of psychosexual development', *Genet. Psychol. Monographs*, **39**, pp. 3–9.

Blum, G. (1955) 'Perceptual defense revisited', *Journal of Abnormal Social Psychology*, **51**, pp. 24–9.

Brill, N., Koegler, R., Epstein, L. and Fogey, E. (1964) 'Controlled study of psychiatric outpatient treatment', *Archives of General Psychiatry*, **10**, pp. 581–95.

Brown, R. and Herrnstein, R. (1975) *Psychology*, Boston, Mass., Little, Brown.

Brown, W. (1961) 'Conceptions of perceptual defense', *Brit. Journal Psychol. Monogr. Suppl*, No. 35.

Cattell, R. (1957) *Personality and Motivation Structure and Measurement*, Yonkers, New York Book Co.

Cattell, R. and Pawlik, K. (1964) 'Third-order factors in objective personality tests', *Brit. J. Psychol.*, **55**, pp. 1–18.

Condor, T. and Allen, G. (1980) 'Role of psychoanalytic merging fantasies in systematic desensitization: A rigorous methodological examination', *Journal of Abnormal Psychology*, **89**, pp. 437–43.

Cordray, D. and Bootzin, R. (1983) 'Placebo control conditions: Tests of theory or of effectiveness?', *Behavioral and Brain Sciences*, **6**, pp. 286–7.

Daston, P. (1956) 'Perception of homosexual words in paranoid schizophrenia', *Perceptual and Motor Skills*, **6**, pp. 45–55.

Denker, P. (1946) 'Results of treatment of psychoneuroses by the G.P.', *New York State Journal of Medicine*, **46**, pp. 2164–6.

Dixon, N. (1971) *Subliminal Perception: The Nature of a Controversy*, New York, McGraw-Hill.

Dollard, J., Doob, L., Miller, N., Mowrer, O. and Sears, R. (1939) *Frustration and Aggression*, New Haven, Conn., Yale University Press.

Duhrssen, A. and Jorswiek, E. (1965) 'An empirical statistical investigation into the efficacy of psychoanalytic therapy', *Nervenarzt.*, **36**, pp. 166–9.

Eagle, M. (1983) 'The epistemological status of recent developments in psychoanalytic theory', in Cohen, R. and Laudan, L. (Eds.), *Essays in Honor of Adolf Grunbaum*, Boston, Mass., D. Reidel.

Ellis, A. (1956) 'An operational reformulation of some of the basic principles of psychoanalysis', in Feigl, H. and Sciven, M. (Eds.), *Minnesota Studies in the Philosophy of Science*, Vol. 1, Minneapolis, Minn., University of Minnesota Press.

Emmelkamp, P. and Straatman, H. (1976) 'A psychoanalytic reinterpretation of the effectiveness of systematic desensitization: Fact or fiction?', *Behav. Res. & Therapy*, **14**, pp. 245–9.

Erwin, E. (1978) *Behavior Therapy: Scientific, Philosophical and Moral Foundations*, New York, Cambridge University Press.

Erwin, E. (1980a) 'Psychoanalytic therapy: The Eysenck argument', *Amer. Psychol.*, **35**, pp. 435–43.

Erwin, E. (1980b) 'Psychoanalysis: How firm is the evidence?', *Nous*, **14**, pp. 443–56.

Erwin, E. (1984a) 'The standing of psychoanalysis', *Brit. J. Philosophy Science*, in press.

Erwin, E. (1984b) 'Is psychotherapy more effective than a placebo?', Unpublished manuscript.

Erwin, E. (1984c) 'Establishing causal connections: Meta-analysis and psychotherapy', *Midwest Studies in Philosophy*, IX, pp. 421–36.

Eysenck, H. J. (1952) 'The effects of psychotherapy: An evaluation', *Journal of Consulting Psychology*, **16**, pp. 319–24.

Eysenck, H. J. (1966) *The Effects of Psychotherapy*, New York, Inter-Science Press.

Eysenck, H. J. (1972) 'The experimental study of Freudian concepts', *Bull. Brit. Psychol. Soc.*, **25**, pp. 261–8.

Eysenck, H. J. (1982) 'Neobehavioristic (S-R) theory', in Wilson, G. T. and Franks, C. M. (Eds.), *Contemporary Behavior Therapy: Conceptual and Empirical Foundations*, New York, Guilford.

Eysenck, H. J. (1983a) 'Special review: The benefits of psychotherapy. A battlefield revisited', *Behav. Res. & Therapy*, **21**, pp. 315–20.

Eysenck, H. J. (1983b) 'The effectiveness of psychotherapy: The specter at the feast', *Behavioral and Brain Sciences*, **6**, p. 290.

Eysenck, H. J. and Wilson, G. (1973) *The Experimental Study of Freudian Theories*, London, Methuen and Company.

Farrell, B. A. (1981) *The Standing of Psychoanalysis*, New York, Oxford University Press.

Fisher, C. (1953) 'Part I: Studies on the nature of suggestion, Part II: The transferrence meaning of giving suggestions', *J. of Amer. Psychoanalytic Assoc.*, **1**, pp. 222–55 and 406–37.

Fisher, S and Greenberg, R. (1977) *The Scientific Credibility of Freud's Theories and Therapy*, New York, Basic Books.

Flax, J. (1981) 'Psychoanalysis and the philosophy of science: Critique or resistance?', *J. of Philosophy*, **78**, pp. 561–9.

Frank, H. (1983) 'The placebo is psychotherapy', *Behavioral and Brain Sciences*, **6**, pp. 291–2.

Freud, S. (1965) *The Psychopathology of Everyday Life*, New York, W. W. Norton.

Friedman, S. (1952) 'An empirical study of the castration and Oedipus complexes', *Genet. Psychol. Monogr.*, **46**, pp. 61–130.

Gillan, P. and Rachman, S. (1974) 'An experimental investigation of desensitization and phobic patients', *Brit. J. of Psychiat.*, **124**, pp. 392–401.

Glass, G. and Kliegl, E. (1983) 'An apology for research integration in the study of psychotherapy', *J. of Consulting and Clinical Psychol.*, **51**, pp. 28–41.

Gleser, G., Gottschalk, L. and Springer, K. (1961) 'An anxiety scale applicable to verbal samples', *Archives of General Psychiat.*, **5**, pp. 593–605.

Grauer, D. (1954) 'Homosexuality in paranoid schizophrenia as revealed by the Rorschach test', *Journal of Consulting Psychology*, **18**, pp. 459–62.

Greenson, R. (1959) 'The classic psychoanalytic approach', in Arieti, S. (Ed.), *American Handbook of Psychiatry*, Vol. 2, New York, Basic Books.

Grünbaum, A. (1979) 'Is Freudian psychoanalytic theory pseudo-scientific by Karl Popper's criterion of demarcation?', *American Philosophical Quarterly*, **16**, pp. 131–41.

Grünbaum, A. (1983a) 'The foundations of psychoanalysis', in Laudan, L. (Ed.), *Mind and Medicine*, Berkeley, Calif., University of California Press.

Grünbaum, A. (1983b) 'Freud's theory: The perspective of a philosopher of science', *Proceedings and Addresses of the American Philosophical Association*.

Grünbaum, A. (1984) *The Foundations of Psychoanalysis: A Philosophical Critique*, Berkeley, Calif., University of California Press.

Hall, C. (1963) 'Strangers in dreams: An experimental confirmation of the Oedipus complex', *J. of Pers.*, **31**, pp. 336–45.

Hall, C. and Van de Castle, R. (1965) 'An empirical investigation of the castration complex in dreams', *J. of Pers.*, **33**, pp. 20–7.

Heilbrun, K. (1980) 'Silverman's subliminal psychodynamic activation: A failure to replicate', *Journal of Abnormal Psychology*, **89**, pp. 560–6.

Hersen, M. and Barlow, D. (1976) *Single Case Experimental Designs: Strategies for Studying Behavior Change*, New York, Pergamon Press.

Horowitz, L. (1963) 'Theory construction and validation in psychoanalysis', in Marx, M. (Ed.), *Theories in Contemporary Psychology*, New York, Macmillan.

Karasu, T. (1977) 'Psychotherapies: An overview', *Amer. Journal. of Psychiat.*, **134**, pp. 851–63.

Kazdin, A. (1980) *Research Design in Clinical Psychology*, New York, Harper and Row.

Kazdin, A. and Wilcoxin, L. (1976) 'Systematic desensitization and non-specific treatment effects: A methodological evaluation', *Psychol. Bull.*, **83**, pp. 729–58.

Kazdin, A. and Wilson, G. T. (1978) *Evaluation of Behavior Therapy: Issues, Evidence and Research Strategies*, Cambridge, Mass., Ballinger.

Kline, P. (1972, 1981) *Fact and Fantasy in Freudian Theory*, London, Methuen.

Kragh, V. (1960) 'The defense mechanism test: A new method for diagnosis and personnel selection', *Journal of Applied Psychology*, **44**, pp. 303–9.

Krieger, M. and Worchel, P. (1959) 'A quantitative study of the psychoanalytic hypotheses of identification', *Psychol. Reports*, **5**, p. 448.

Landis, C. (1938) 'Statistical evaluation of psychotherapeutic methods', in Himie, S. (Ed.), *Concepts and Problems of Psychotherapy*, London, Heinemann.

Lick, J. (1975) 'Expectancy, false galvanic skin response, feedback and systematic desensitization in the modification of phobic behavior', *Journal of Consulting and Clinical Psychology*, **43**, pp. 557–67.

Luborsky, L. (1954) 'A note on Eysenck's article "The effects of psychotherapy: An evaluation" ', *Brit. J. of Psychol.*, **45**, pp. 129–31.

McLean, P. and Hakstian, A. (1979) 'Clinical depression: Comparative efficacy of outpatient treatments', *Journal of Consulting and Clinical Psychol.*, **47**, pp. 818–36.

Manosevitz, M. and Lanyon, R. (1965) 'Fear survey schedule: A normative study', *Psychol. Reports*, **17**, pp. 699–703.

Marmor, J. (1970) 'Limitations of free association', *Archives of General Psychiat.*, **22**, pp. 160–5.

Meketon, B., Griffith, R., Taylor, V. and Wiedeman, J. (1962) 'Rorschach homosexual signs in paranoid schizophrenics', *Journal of Abnormal & Social Psychol.*, **65**, pp. 280–4.

Moore, M. (1983) 'The nature of psychoanalytic explanation', in Laudan, L. (Ed.), *Mind and Medicine*, Berkeley, Calif., University of California Press.

Prioleau, L., Murdock, M. and Brody, N. (1983) 'An analysis of psychotherapy versus placebo studies', *Behavioral and Brain Sciences*, **6**, pp. 275–85.

Rachman, S. (1971) *The Effects of Psychotherapy*, New York, Pergamon Press.

Rachman, S. and Wilson, G. T. (1980) *The Effects of Psychological Therapy*, New York, Pergamon Press.

Rosenthal, T. (1980) 'Social cueing processes', in Hersen, M., Eisler, R. and Miller, P. M. (Eds.), *Progress in Behavior Modification*, Vol. 10, New York, Academic Press.

Rosenzweig, S. (1954) 'A transvaluation of psychotherapy—A reply to Hans Eysenck', *J. of Abnormal and Social Psychol.*, **127**, pp. 330–43.

Sarnoff, I. and Corwin, S. (1959) 'Castration anxiety and the fear of death', *J. of Pers.*, **27**, pp. 374–85.

Schwartz, B. (1956) 'An experimental test of two Freudian hypotheses concerning castration anxiety', *J. of Pers.*, **24**, pp. 318–27.

Silverman, L. (1982) 'A comment on two subliminal psychodynamic activation studies', *J. of Abnormal Psychol.*, **91**, pp. 126–30.

Silverman, L., Frank, S. and Dachinger, P. (1974) 'Psychoanalytic reinterpretation of the effectiveness of systematic desensitization: Experimental data bearing on the role of merging fantasies', *J. of Abnormal Psychol.*, **83**, pp. 313–18.

Silverman, L., Kwawer, H., Wolitzky, C. and Coron, M. (1973) 'An experimental study of aspects of the psychoanalytic theory of male homosexuality', *J. of Abnormal Psychol.*, **82**, pp. 178–88.

Silverman, L., Ross, D., Adler, J. and Lustig, D. (1978) 'Simple research paradigm for demonstrating psychodynamic activation: Effects of Oedipal stimuli on dart-throwing accuracy in college males', *J. of Abnormal Psychol.*, **87**, pp. 341–57.

Smith, M., Glass, G. and Miller, T. (1980) *The Benefits of Psychotherapy*, Baltimore, Md., Johns Hopkins University Press.

von Eckardt, B. (1984) 'Adolf Grünbaum and psychoanalytic epistemology', in Repper, J. (Ed.), *Beyond Freud*, forthcoming.

Watson, C. (1965) 'A test of the relationship between repressed homosexuality and paranoid mechanisms', *J. Clin. Psychol.*, **21**, pp. 380–4.

White, R. (1956) *The Abnormal Personality*, New York, Ronald Press.

Wolowitz, H. (1965) 'Attraction and aversion to power: A psychoanalytic conflict theory of homosexuality in male paranoids', *J. of Abnormal Psychol.*, **70**, pp. 360–70.

Wolpe, J. (1981) 'Behavior therapy versus psychoanalysis: Therapeutic and social implications', *Amer. Psychol.*, **36**, pp. 159–64.

Zamansky, H. (1958) 'An investigation of the psychoanalytic theory of paranoid delusions', *J. of Pers.*, **26**, pp. 410–25.

Zeichner, A. (1955) 'Psychosexual identification in paranoid schizophrenia', *J. of Projective Techniques*, **19**, pp. 67–77.

# 12. Psychotherapy and Freudian Psychology: The Negative View

PAUL KLINE

In 1952 Eysenck launched his first savage attack against the effectiveness of psychoanalytic therapy. His message was stark and clear and over the last thirty years Eysenck has not really changed his position. Psychoanalysis as a therapy does not work. Indeed, it is worse than useless: it can even be deleterious to patients' recovery. Furthermore, and this was perhaps the most important issue, all this stems from the fact that psychoanalytic therapy is quite unscientific, being untestable, unquantified and rampantly speculative.

In academic psychology, certainly in Great Britain, based upon a study of the courses for honours degrees, this view still obtains. Freud is relegated to the historical portions of courses. His influence is admitted *mais ce n'est pas le science*.

In this chapter I want to scrutinize this position, because, in my view, it contains a number of highly confused arguments, and set it against the context of empirical evidence that has been collected and in some cases minutely examined since Eysenck's first (1952) claim. Indeed almost 2000 references were cited by Fisher and Greenberg (1977) in their study of Freudian theory, while Kline (1972, 1981) dealt with only slightly fewer, in his case excluding certain research on methodological grounds.

## EFFECTIVENESS OF THERAPY AND THEORY

The main confusion that demands clarification concerns the relation of the effectiveness of psychotherapy and its underlying theory. This is an argument which is quite general, applying to all parts of psychotherapy, not simply psychoanalysis. There is a simple logical point, stressed by Cheshire (1975), that the correctness or falsity of a theory cannot be judged by the effectiveness or otherwise of a therapy that claims to be based upon it. Thus, for example, it could be the case that all the therapists

**205**

following a particular theory were hopeless practitioners, lazy, misunderstanding the theory, hating their patients. Similarly since it does appear that the personality of the therapist affects therapeutic outcome (e.g., Truax, 1963)—a wondrous finding—if the practitioners of a given theory are 'good therapists', then this alone can account for success. Thus studies of the outcome of therapy are not strictly relevant to the underlying theory. Freudian theory must stand or fall by different criteria. Even if it is true that psychoanalytic therapy is ineffective, it could be the case that psychoanalytic theory is correct.


## THE VALUE OF PSYCHOANALYTIC THEORY


At this point an objection might be raised by acute readers: if psychoanalysis is an ineffective therapy, what is the use of psychoanalytic theory? Such an argument misunderstands the nature of psychoanalytic theory and of scientific theory in general.

It is clear that Freud (e.g., 1933) regarded psychoanalysis as a science. It was primarily intended as an account of the psychology of man. Freud (1940), for example, argued that the discovery of the Oedipus complex was one of the great discoveries of mankind: free association was a tool (like the X-ray) for discovering normally hidden, unconscious, mental processes. It was little more than coincidental that the theory was developed from the psychotherapy of patients except that, in patients, exaggerations of normal processes are held to occur and these make observations easier than among normal individuals.

Thus the importance and value of psychoanalytic theory at least to its founder was that it was a comprehensive account of human nature. That it was therapeutically valuable was of course an advantage. Certainly, in my view, the value of Freudian theory lies exactly in this point. With a few simple concepts, the unconscious, the Oedipus complex, repression, the whole gamut of human behaviour can be embraced. What other psychological theory, other than offshoots of psychoanalysis, is at home with totemism, nightmares, paranoia, capitalist greed, vegetarianism, the arts, . . . there is no end to the list. As Conant (1947) has argued, psychoanalytic theory has persisted despite the fact that data are at hand which do not fit well with it, because there is simply no alternative.

Thus even if it is not a sound basis for psychotherapy the theory is not made worthless. This same point can apply to any theory of human behaviour. A genetic theory of behaviour is hardly diminished because its application to psychotherapy is not promising. Similarly on the basis of psychoanalytic theory none should have great hopes for psychotherapy. This is why, of course, analysts are careful in choosing patients. From this it is clear that there is no demand that a scientific theory of human behaviour, or that psychoanalytic theory, be effective in psychotherapy.

However, I would like to make a final point concerning the relation of psychotherapy to psychological theory. When finally an adequate theory of human behaviour is developed, it must form the basis of psychotherapy. This is not contrary to my initial arguments that the effectiveness of therapy was not a measure of a theory. It is simply the case that a good theory of human behaviour by definition will inform us how to proceed in psychotherapy, how and why the patient-therapist interactions are important, what the determinants of the problem are. It will still be possible to apply these insights wrongly or to ignore them in psychotherapy. Hence the original argument stands.

From this discussion, however, it should be obvious that the study of Freudian psychology and psychotherapy must concentrate on the underlying theory, not on the effectiveness of its related psychotherapy. Only when there is a clear theory of behaviour (psychoanalytic or otherwise) does it make sense to investigate the effectiveness of the therapy.

In this chapter, therefore, I intend to examine psychoanalytic theory, to scrutinize the claims of Eysenck that psychoanalytic theory is unscientific and false. Eysenck (Eysenck and Wilson, 1973) has spoken clearly about his view of the theory: what's true isn't new, what's new isn't true. This discussion cannot be complete. I have argued the case in detail previously (Kline, 1972, 1981) and it would be impossible to summarize this work in a chapter of this length, without producing merely dogmatic assertions. Instead I shall illustrate the critical points with recent and in some cases unpublished research. It must be remembered, however, that what is discussed here is but a selection from a large corpus of evidence which can be seen in Kline (1981) and Fisher and Greenberg (1977).

## SCIENTIFIC METHOD AND PSYCHOANALYTIC THEORY

Eysenck (e.g., 1965) and Eysenck and Wilson (1973), together with many other writers, for example, Medawar (1969), have made strong claims concerning the hopelessly unscientific nature of Freudian theory. Ricoeur (1970) and other philosophers have different objections, namely that psychoanalytic theory is essentially concerned not with the environment but with the phenomenology of the environment and hence cannot be the subject of scientific enquiry.

Before I begin to examine the empirical evidence it is clear that these objections must first be met. As a start, I shall discuss the objections raised by Eysenck and by most academic psychologists.

1   *The data of the theory.* The data on which psychoanalytic theory was based were the free associations of patients both direct and to their dreams. It is also clear that Freud's self-analysis considerably influenced his theorizing. There is no disagreement here with Eysenck or other writers of Freudian theory. Such are not the data of an adequate scientific theory.
2   *The lack of quantification.* Without quantification it is difficult to test a scientific theory. Psychoanalysis has no quantification. Again this is an important point.
3   *Poor sampling.* In the main Freud's patients were neurotic Viennese, often Jewish women. Other analysts tended to deal with similar patients. These hardly contribute a good sample of homo sapiens, yet Freudian theory makes universal assertions. Later in the development of psychoanalysis attempts were made to extend this sampling base, for example, by Malinowski (1927) and Roheim (e.g., 1952). However, this objection is certainly well made, although it is ironical that such an objection comes from experimental psychology which would appear to have been overly dependent on the hooded, laboratory-bred rat, helped out by pigeons and American undergraduate students.

4 *Unclear reporting.* Although by general agreement Freud was a fine writer his case reports almost never reveal any data as such. They combine data and interpretation in such a way as to make checking and replication impossible. This, too, cannot be argued with.

5 *Methods of recording data.* Freud did not record what patients said. At the end of the day, after five or six one-hour sessions, sometimes emotionally fraught, he would make notes. Thus the accuracy of the recollections must constitute a source of bias. Of course Eysenck and critics, who do not hold with psychoanalytic theory, cannot use the further argument that by repression we would expect Freud to forget conveniently what failed to fit psychoanalysis, remembering only confirmatory material. Such points again are hard to refute.

6 It is argued by Eysenck that Freudian theory is so confused that it cannot be refuted, refutability being the essence of the scientific method, as conceived by Popper (1959). For example, the assertion that man is dominated by two drives, Eros and Thanatos, the life and death instincts, certainly fully extends the skills of experimental design. *Prima facie* there is a sound case here.

7 Added to this is Eysenck's argument that Freudian theory is so loosely framed that it can explain anything (*post hoc*) but predict nothing. This, too, is in part true.

8 Medawar (1969) has objected to psychoanalytic theory because all opposition to it is regarded in the theory as resistance, i.e., it stems not from logical grounds (thus the objections can be ignored) but has emotional causes. This objection is, of course, sound, but I shall ignore it. Indeed, the whole notion of examining the evidence for the theory and scrutinizing its truth or falsity to observed data is *ipso facto* a denial of this particular point. This aspect of psychonalaytic theory can simply be ignored.

Such are the basic arguments of those objecting to Freudian theory. As has been seen, except for perhaps two points, they are well taken. How can they be answered?

## Replies to the Objections

Apologists for Freudian theory, such as the present writer, who do not believe it should be abandoned as unscientific, accept the objections but advance another set of arguments. As has been mentioned previously, psychoanalytic theory other than in academic psychology persists because it can embrace so much of human behaviour. It is, in its scope and power, the kind of theory needed in psychology. Our argument is that Freud had rare insight into human nature such that despite objections to his methods he was able to arrive at important truths about human behaviour. Furthermore, he dealt with data (free associations) that are usually ignored in most psychologies. Thus what is needed is to try to restate the theory, collect relevant data, and sift them through so that what does accord with observations can be incorporated into a solid data-based theory. What are the implications of this argument?

Farrell (e.g. 1964, 1982) has dealt with just these points, from the viewpoint of philosophy, and his theoretical position is that underpinning the research discussed in this chapter. In essence he has argued that psychoanalysis should be considered to be not one theory but a collection of theories, and that each of these should be scrutinized for its truth or falsity. Some parts will assuredly turn out to be incorrect, others may stand the empirical test. This approach, it will be noted, makes two assumptions. First, it takes the Popperian (1959) view that the critical need for a scientific theory is that it be refutable. The second assumption, which has been challenged (e.g., Martin, 1964), is that Freudian theory can be reformulated so that it may be tested without changing it. On logical grounds Martin (1964) is probably sound. For two statements differently worded are not *per se* identical. However, if carefully formulated there seems no *prima facie* reason why Freudian theories stated in a logically testable way should be different from their previous forms. Indeed, careful scrutiny of the twenty-four volumes can often reveal just the necessary statements. Thus the research to be discussed in this chapter is concerned with hypotheses derived from psychoanalytic theory, which is regarded as a collection of theories. It is the logical-positivist approach.

To break up Freudian theory thus, of course, destroys one of its most attractive features—its coherence and wide explanatory power. However, if many of the concepts prove to be sound then it can be reconstituted. In any case this is the purpose of the exercise, to see in the light of the evidence what parts are true. This is not an essay in attempting to prove psychoanalysis, on the contrary it is an attempt to incorporate into a scientific theory of behaviour those insights of psychoanalysis that do fit the data. If none do, the whole theory can be abandoned. It should further be noted that this approach effectively answers Ricoeur's (1970) argument that psychoanalysis is concerned with psychic reality, individual phenomenology. If this is correct, testing hypotheses in the manner which we have described will fail: they will all be rejected.

One final point remains to be made concerning this method of studying the validity of Freudian theory. When the hypotheses have been reformulated, it goes without saying that rigorous standards of experimental design are necessary. A poor experiment is poor, no matter how elegant the hypotheses. Thus in my survey of the evidence pertaining to Freudian theory (Kline, 1972, 1981), I insisted that sampling was good both in respect of numbers and as a reflection of a population: that tests were valid so that little use was made of Rorschach results unless the particular variables were validated: that the statistical analysis was appropriate and finally that the interpretations were such as could be drawn from the results.

Eysenck and Wilson (1973) tried to argue in counter to my first survey that I had failed to take into account, if Freudian theory appeared to be supported, alternative hypotheses. In my later account this problem was dealt with more explicitly. In the study of psychoanalytic theory this is in fact a difficult issue. Thus if we have twenty experiments, each apparently confirming different parts of psychoanalytic theory, is it more elegant, more in accord with Occam's razor to regard each as confirming the relevant aspect of psychoanalysis, or to produce, as do Eysenck and Wilson (1973), twenty *ad hoc* hypotheses (more strictly *post hoc*) tied to no theory of any kind other than to reject any confirmation of psychoanalysis? From this I would argue that despite the clear objections to the scientific nature of psychoanalysis, rejection, in the light of its power, and apparent insights, is arbitrary. The theory, regarded as a collection of theories, can be restated as a set of testable hypotheses and experiments relevant to them can be conducted. This is the basis of the research which I shall now discuss.

## PERCEPT GENETICS AND DEFENCE MECHANISMS

The first aspect of psychoanalytic theory which I shall consider is that concerned with defence mechanisms. There are several reasons for this. First, defences are key concepts in psychoanalytic theory. Freud (1923a) states that the neurotic conflict takes place between the ego and the id. Defences allow the ego to bar the entry into consciousness of id material. Indeed, the whole notion of defence, particularly repression, is critical to the dynamic aspects of psychoanalytic theory. Defences are also important in the understanding of psychotherapy, since neurotic symptoms are seen as defences while psychotic symptoms are regarded as the result of the failure of defences.

Freud (1923a) and Fenichel (1945) describe a number of separate defences of which the most important are sublimation, a successful defence because it allows expression of the id drive, repression, denial, projection (favoured by paranoid schizophrenics) reaction-formation, where conscious feeling is the opposite of the unconscious, and isolation. Clearly these defences, if shown to occur, would be important in underpinning psychotherapy theoretically. Thus from the viewpoint of this chapter, research bearing on their scientific validation is peculiarly pertinent.

Kline (1981) and Dixon (1982) have argued that perceptual defence, when using experimental methods where the subjects are never able to report (and apparently are never consciously aware of) the emotionally important stimuli, is an experimental analogue of repression. There seems little doubt about the findings. Cancer patients, for example, show raised thresholds to the subliminal stimulus 'cancer'. I do not want to discuss these further here; instead I shall examine the results achieved with percept-genetic methods (which have certain similarities with perceptual defence experiments), especially the Defence Mechanism Test (Kragh, 1969).

## PERCEPT-GENETIC THEORY AND METHOD

Percept-genetics, developed by Kragh and Smith (1970), investigates the development of perception, a normally instantaneous process, without awareness, and unavailable to introspection, by what they call fragmenting the stimulus. This is done by presenting the stimulus subliminally to subjects, who have to describe it, tachisto-scopically in a series of exposures each at gradually decreasing speeds until veridical or close to veridical perception is achieved.

The term 'percept genetics' reflects the concern of the theory with how perception is built up, perception being conceptualized in the Gestalt tradition as an ongoing process between the individual and his world. By presenting the stimulus in the percept-genetic series it is argued that this normally instantaneous process of perception can be observed (Westerlundh, 1976). In observing this process, important events and life experiences of emotional significance, as well as habitual ways of dealing with the world, i.e., defences, are claimed to reveal themselves (Kragh, 1955; Kragh and Smith, 1970). Obviously if such claims were verified, percept-genetics would become one of the most important experimental approaches in psychology.

**The Techniques**

The essence of the techniques developed over the years by Smith and Kragh and their colleagues in Scandinavia is the presentation of the same stimulus in series at gradually increasing levels of stimulus intensity. Two sets of stimuli have been widely used, those in the Defence Mechanism Test (Kragh, 1969) upon which I shall concentrate the discussion, for obvious reasons, and the Meta Contrast Technique (Kragh and Smith, 1970), although in principle a wide variety of stimuli might prove useful.

**The DMT**

There are two pictures. Each has three elements: the hero, placed centrally, the hero's attribute (gun, car or violin) and a threat figure, a man or woman with a threatening face. Parallel forms, with different sexes to aid identification, are used. As has been indicated, the response is the drawing and description of each exposure in the series. The scoring takes into account the type, intensity and frequency of the precognitive defensive organization. The place in the series is also important, as are the succession of phases in the series. All the scoring procedures are reliable with some experience. The main defences measured by the DMT with a brief indication of their signs are set out below, although for a full description of this test and its theory readers must be referred to Kragh (1969) or Kragh and Smith (1970).

> *Repression.* The figures are living but not human; or they are objects.
> *Isolation.* The hero and the secondary figure are separated. One of them may not even be seen.
> *Reaction-formation.* In this the threat is turned into the opposite. The threatening face is seen as sweet and beautiful.
> *Identification with the aggressor.* The hero becomes the aggressor.
> *Turning against self.* The hero or his attribute is seen as damaged or the attribute is regarded as worthless or dangerous to the hero.
> *Denial.* The threat is denied.

**The Validity of the DMT and Percept-Genetic Claims**

Obviously if the DMT were shown to be valid, this would be *ipso facto* confirmation of the defence mechanisms. Consequently the evidence for the validity of this technique is an important issue. In this discussion of the validity of the DMT I shall omit reference to the claims concerning the emergence of critical emotional experiences and the parallelism between development of personality and the percept, although some highly interesting case material can be found in Kragh and Smith (1970).

With respect to the measurement of defences a most important point should be noted. The argument is really about the identification of the defences. Thus Kragh and Smith essentially state that the protocols enable the defences to be observed. Thus when a subject says that the ugly threatening face is angelic, such a response *is* by definition a reaction-formation. In that sense further evidence is not required.

However, the difficulty here is that now all depends on the value judgment of the testers. Reliability studies are not helpful since the manual can allow high agreement that is quite arbitrary. Thus suppose the threatening face is described as 'delicate'. Is that a reaction-formation? Thus although the DMT does allow processes to be observed that in many cases resemble the processes described by Freud, there still seems a need for some kind of independent evidence pertaining to these judgments.

Kragh and Smith (1970) and later investigations such as that of Westerlundh (1976) show impressive discriminatory power between clinical groups. However, such groups differ in more than defences, and except in the case of paranoids (Freud, 1911) (projection and reaction-formation), it is not clear what defences should discriminate what groups. A further point needs to be mentioned. As Cooper (1982) makes clear, the DMT seems able to discriminate accident prone pilots in a number of air-forces. The rationale for this is that a defending pilot delays his reality-based responses and in modern jets this is fatal.

From all this three main points emerge. First, it is clear that the discriminatory power of the DMT in clinical and occupational groups suggests that it is concerned with variance important in personality. In addition the processes observable in the protocols to the DMT do, to this writer at least, impressively resemble Freudian defence mechanisms. However, clear evidence as to what the DMT variables are is necessary.

Recently Cooper and Kline have attempted to investigate the validity of the DMT and of percept-genetic methods to reveal defence mechanisms. First a pilot study (Kline and Cooper, 1977) was carried out using new stimuli. Since oral erotism (Freud, 1905) is regarded in Freudian theory as partially repressed in adults, it was argued that oral stimuli should produce defences. Thus the oral stimulus of the test PN (Corman, 1969) which shows a pig suckling its young and a neutral control picture of a pig used in a bacon advertisement were administered in percept-genetic series to eight subjects. The results were clear-cut. To the bacon pig there were no distortions or defences in the protocols. To the suckling pig there were protocols which showed clear defences. No external confirmation in this pilot study was sought. We were simply investigating the claim that other stimuli could yield defences. One example of denial illustrates the point. By exposure 5 the subject has correctly perceived that a piglet is being fed. At exposure 6 there is denial, 'Pig with spots and udders, little pig may not be feeding but talking.' At exposure 7 the subject admits feeding but there is denial again at 8, '. . . uncertain whether piglet is feeding or vocalizing.'

Of course, this all depends on the value judgment as to whether or not such a response is denial. Consequently Cooper (1982) and Cooper and Kline (1983) sought to gather external evidence concerning the validity of the DMT scores in an intensive study of thirty subjects. The relation of the DMT scores to perceptual defence measures of repression, to the 16PF personality test (Cattell *et al.*, 1970) purporting to measure the main dimensions of personality and to other measures of defence, was examined. It was a construct validity study attempting, *inter alia*, to locate the DMT scores in personality factor space. It is not possible to discuss all the findings here but the most important can be set out. The first question concerned the independence of the DMT variables. Scrutiny of the correlation matrix showed that the variables were separate: only opposite-sex identification and identification with the aggressor were significantly correlated (.43).

The correlations of the DMT with the 16PF test are of interest, because some moderate correlations can be hypothesized on theoretical grounds. For example, factor 2, suspiciousness, is held to involve projection. Similarly repression might be expected to correlate with high G, superego and Q4, tension. Such hypotheses are, however, difficult to draw and not too much should be made of the results. Few of the correlations were significant between the 16PF and the DMT, although the majority of the hypothesized correlations were in the right direction. Certain of the correlations were good fits to the psychoanalytic theory. For example, radicalism correlated .36 with projection which, in the light of Freudian views on leadership and the projection of unacceptable feelings onto opponents, is not without interest. Similarly it was noteworthy in our male sample that opposite-sex introjection was positively correlated with tender-mindedness (.43) and dependence (.44). The two large higher-order temperamental factors, N and E, anxiety and exvia or extraversion, did not correlate significantly with the DMT variables. This is good because generally personality measures tend to load mainly on N and E. This aspect of the study indicated that the DMT did not simply correlate with the 16PF test. Overall the intercorrelations made sense.

The DMT is, of course, a visual test. The correlation of the DMT variables with Witkin's (1962) field dependence (measured here by the group embedded figures test) is important in establishing that the DMT is not really tapping the perceptual factor loading the GEFT. Fortunately this was not the case.

The final part of the construct validity study concerned the correlations between the DMT scores and the measure of repression obtained from a perceptual defence score to the term VD. As we have argued previously (Kline, 1981), this latter seems to be a sound measure of repression. In fact the DMT repression score failed to correlate with it. Indeed, since this score had no significant correlation with any variable, it appears highly likely that it needs a new scoring scheme. It does not appear to be valid.

In summary, this construct validity study of the DMT is by no means unfavourable. I now want to discuss the second part of the study by Cooper (1982) where the DMT was related to an external criterion. In this part of the research Cooper scored the DMT objectively for the presence or absence of the signs indicating defences, and subjected the scores for the student sample and from a sample of trainee pilots (N = 70) to G analysis (Holley, 1973). G analysis consists of correlating *people* rather than variables, using the G index of correlation and subjecting the correlation matrix to factor analysis. This factor analysis is a Q analysis since the loadings are on subjects. Factors thus constitute groups. From the Q factors factor scores (for items) can be calculated, just as factor scores for subjects can be from the factors in R analysis of variables.

There were several noteworthy findings. First, the correlation between the first factor in the two groups was high (.7) demonstrating that the results were not due to capitalization on chance. In G analysis clear results are often found but there is poor replication of factors between samples (e.g., Hampson and Kline, 1977, among criminal offenders). Among the trainee pilots the factor scores (on the first factor) showed a correlation of .49 with success in training, well beyond the predictive power of standard psychometric tests for this group. As has been previously argued this fits in neatly with the claim that the DMT measures defences since reality-based decision would appear to be essential for pilots. Among the student sample the correlations of the other variables with this factor score were examined. The perceptual defence measure of repression correlated .50 and Cattell's N, shrewdness .33. The perceptual defence correlation is indeed support for the claims that the DMT measures defences.

In conclusion, this investigation generally supports the validity of the DMT although its repression measure would appear not to be valid. These findings, when taken together with the clinical data of Kragh and Smith (1970), Westerlundh (1976) and other Scandinavian workers, strongly support the validity of the DMT. In so doing they of course support the Freudian hypothesis concerning defence mechanisms.

What is certainly clear is that percept-genetic methods, although far more research into them is required, do enable us to investigate objectively Freudian defences. It is also interesting and heartening that the defences thus observed as reported in the clinical Scandinavian studies show not only the defences described by Freud but other distortions of reality which he missed. This is as it should be that psychoanalytic theory can be extended and improved by scientific and objective investigation.

An essential notion of psychoanalytic theory is unconscious conflict. Defences are seen as ways of coping with such conflict. However, empirical validation of the conflict itself would appear extremely difficult. That is why the work of Silverman and his colleagues in New York is so interesting. He claims to be able to manipulate such conflict experimentally and thus, of course, provide powerful evidence for the relevant parts of Freudian theory. I shall now scrutinize the research.

## THE WORK OF SILVERMAN: THE ACTIVATION OF UNCONSCIOUS CONFLICT

Silverman and his colleagues have published a considerable number of papers reporting results from the application of his techniques and his students have further contributed in dissertations. Silverman (1971, 1976) contains good accounts of the work while Silverman (1980) is a useful summary of all results published and unpublished up to that date.

### The Theoretical Basis

As we have indicated, the basis of this work is the Freudian proposition that psychopathology results from reaction to the pressure of unacceptable drives and their derivatives. These produce anxiety. If the subsequent defences are successful psychopathology does not occur. If the defences fail then anxiety and the drive derivatives emerge.

### The Method

The aim of the methods is to activate these drive-derivatives. However, this has to be done without allowing them to become conscious to the subjects because if they do so, they cease to be linked to the psychopathology. The point is, in Freudian theory, that they are unconscious conflicts.

Drive-related stimuli are presented to subjects subliminally through a tachistoscope, thus activating unconscious conflicts. Effectively Silverman has tailored perceptual defence experiments to the demands of testing psychoanalytic theory. It should be pointed out that the effectiveness of this method is attested to by a number of findings which will be discussed in more detail later in this section.

1   Drive-activating stimuli presented subliminally do increase psychopathology.
2   The same stimuli presented above threshold have no effect.
3   Neutral stimuli have no effect.
4   Drive-reducing stimuli presented subliminally decrease psychopathology.
5   Drive-reducing stimuli presented above threshold have no effect.

Such experimental control is normally considered to be good evidence for the hypotheses under investigation.

**Examples of Stimuli**

A growling tiger chasing a monkey; a roaring lion, charging; a snarling man with a dagger in his upraised hand; a man, teeth showing, attacking a woman. These stimuli, need it be said, activate oral aggression. Sometimes illustrated sentences are used as the subliminal activation. Examples are: beating dad is wrong: beating dad is OK (a drive-reducing stimulus); people are walking (neutral); mummy and I are one (reducing symbiotic conflicts); my girl and I are one and daddy and I are one.

Watson (1975) has criticized this work by Silverman on a variety of grounds. Some of his arguments are important, and before discussing the findings obtained from this work these points must be taken up. The most telling criticism concerns the measures of psychopathology used by Silverman. These consist of rating scales (e.g., for sexual arousal), word association tests and indices derived from the Rorschach test. For almost none of these is there clear evidence of validity. This is certainly true and for this reason alone it is necessary to be duly cautious about the findings. However, there are factors which suggest that although without evidence of validity (which is not the same as being invalid) these tests worked satisfactorily. In the first place there are numerous studies all showing the same trend of results. Secondly and more important, the experimental variable (conflict) was manipulated, as we have seen, such that changes and no changes were expected. These occurred. If the tests were not valid, alternative explanations are hard to find. Thus taken as a set of results this work still stands up, although there is no doubt that better measures of psychopathology are desirable.

Watson (1975) also argues far less convincingly that in his view there is an alternative explanation for the findings—in terms of information processing. I cannot accept this point. I fail to see how information processing theories can have anything to say concerning the differential properties of stimuli such as 'beating dad is OK' and 'beating dad is wrong'. Critical in these experiments was the selection of activating, reducing and neutral stimuli. Such selection was closely bound to psychoanalytic theory and it is misleading to argue that information processing ideas can account for the results.

Watson's final point concerns the identity of the unconscious as conceptualized in psychoanalytic theory and as defined by visual thresholds. This is an important issue, which in a chapter of this length cannot be dealt with, mainly because of the huge volume of evidence which it is necessary to sift before coming to a proper judgment. However, this has been done in Kline (1981). Thus it was pointed out that the results from perceptual defence studies and from percept genetics, which we have discussed in this chapter, all suggest that there is an identity, and that subliminal perception studies can bear on the psychoanalytic unconscious. For an exhaustive and scholarly treatment of this topic of subliminal perception and its implications for psychology, readers must be referred to Dixon (1982) who is in agreement with these conclusions.

## Some Findings

Silverman *et al.* (1978) showed that the subliminal presentation of 'beating dad is wrong' impaired performance in dart playing, while 'beating dad is OK' improved performance. The neutral stimulus of 'people are walking' had no effect. These findings are held by the authors to support the concept of the Oedipus complex. The argument is that anxiety provoked by arousal of Oedipal conflicts destroys the simple motor skill of dart-playing. The sexual symbolism of dart-playing is probably not highly important. Is there a more simple explanation of the findings? For example, if a really unpleasant dental incident had been shown (about which most people are anxious) presumably this would have had the same effect. There really does seem to be no likely alternative. Without Oedipal theory it is difficult to claim that beating dad is wrong should upset dart-players, or that the second stimulus should improve performance. This finding vindicates Silverman's method and provides modest support for the Oedipus complex.

Silverman *et al.* (1973) investigated the role of mother in the aetiology of male homosexuality, in a sample of thirty-six homosexuals and thirty-six heterosexual controls. There were three sessions in which measures were taken before and after stimulation (three Rorschach cards and ratings of sexual attractiveness for pictures of males and females). The three sessions were: incest: subliminal stimulus 'Fuck Mummy' plus picture; symbiosis: subliminal stimulus 'Mummy and I are one' plus picture; control: subliminal stimulus 'person thinking'. After the incest sessions, homosexuals increased their homosexual attraction score, which did not happen in the control session, or for the control heterosexuals. Thus this study indicates that incest conflicts when aroused can affect homosexual feelings. The study again supports the psychoanalytic claim that incestuous conflicts are implicated in homosexuality (Fenichel, 1945) and the efficacy of the Silverman technique. However, it also illustrates Watson's criticisms about the measures which are certainly of unknown validity and, in the case of the Rorschach test, probably not valid (which is why they have not been discussed here). However, if the rating scale were invalid and/or if the Freudian hypotheses were correct, the results are difficult to explain.

Silverman (1976) summarized the results from a large number of clinical studies. For example, in sixteen experiments with more than 400 schizophrenics, aggressive subliminal stimuli with oral overtones increased psychopathology while neutral stimuli had no effects. In three studies it was demonstrated that subliminal activation of aggressive wishes against the self increased scores on ratings of depression, in accord with Freudian theory. Again neutral stimuli had no effect. Silverman also shows in this paper that it is not merely the general negative effect of the stimuli producing the changes but the specific content.

I have commented previously (Kline, 1981) that this work seems good support for the psychoanalytic theory, on which alone the content of the stimuli depends and, of course, for the method itself, but that two reservations must be made. The first has been discussed—the validity of the measures of psychopathology. The second concerns the stimuli. While the activating stimuli are clearly powerful, compared with the controls, it would be interesting to compare the effect of similar but not theoretically activating stimuli, e.g., 'Fuck Daddy'. In other words it is still an assumption that the subliminal stimuli do activate unconscious conflicts.

Similar studies where the subliminal stimulus, activating the conflict over symbiotic gratification, was designed to reduce psychopathology are reported by Silverman (1976). With more than 200 schizophrenics the stimulus 'Mummy and I are one' and its picture reduced pathology. Subliminal presentation of the neutral stimulus had no effect. Kaye (1975) used three stimuli in a comparative study: 'Mummy and I are one'; 'My girl and I are one'; 'Daddy and I are one'. He found that among schizophrenics the second stimulus was more powerful than the first, while the third had no effect. Again, with the reservations already made, the experiments support the psychoanalytic claims concerning the importance of unconscious conflicts in psychopathology. As with the percept-genetic studies which were discussed earlier in this chapter, they also enable the theory to be modified, as exemplified by Kaye (1975) where the subliminal stimulus 'My girl and I are one' was more effective than the symbiotic original, probably because it reduces anxiety over incestuous wishes.

In conclusion, it seems reasonable to argue that Silverman's methods do enable empirical study of the unconscious dynamics of psychopathology to be carried out. With improved measurements and even tighter experimental manipulation it appears that this aspect of psychoanalytic theory could be put to a rigorous experimental sift.

So far in this chapter two experimental approaches to the verification of psychoanalytic hypotheses concerning unconscious mental processes have been described together with their results. These are important because they bear upon aspects of psychoanalytic theory that are central to the whole theoretical formulation and to mental disorders and their treatment. However, other research methods can be used and I want to describe these now more briefly.

## CROSS-CULTURAL METHODS

Many Freudian hypotheses are essentially environmental, for example, the theory of psychosexual development (Freud, 1905), involving fixation at anal, oral and phallic developmental phases, depending upon, in part, weaning and toilet-training practices. The Oedipus and castration complexes are also regarded as the outcome of family relationships, a relationship reflected in transference (Fenichel, 1945). All these important psychoanalytic concepts are, therefore, in part at least, environmentally (in the family) determined. The tentative genetic hypothesis concerning the Oedipus complex put forward in *Totem and Taboo* (Freud, 1913) may be ignored.

For hypotheses such as these, the cross-cultural setting constitutes a real-life experiment. Kline (1977) has examined this approach to testing Freudian theory in considerable detail but the main conclusions can be briefly set out. There are several advantages in the cross-cultural study of Freudian hypotheses.

1   In familial and environmental variables there is likely to be greater variance among different cultures than within any one culture. So if we are interested in the effects of age of weaning, it is possible to find societies showing great diversity. Furthermore, if such diversity could be found in, say, British society it would be associated with other abnormal variables. Thus the British mother who breastfeeds her children to the age of 5 years is likely to vary in other respects from the norm.

2   Such testing of Freudian hypotheses in other cultures investigates their universality. This is important, since their original basis was Viennese but their claims are universal.

Analysts have not been slow to see these points. Berkley-Hall (1921) attributed many of the characteristics of Hinduism to repressed anal eroticism and Devereux (e.g., 1951) linked the behaviour of the Mohave Indians to their child-training practices.

   With such a powerful rationale, it is surprising that cross-cultural psychology has not figured more extensively in the study of Freudian hypotheses. For this, however, there is a reason. There are severe practical research problems which must be listed. Since there are various distinct methods in cross-cultural psychology these will be dealt with separately.

### Cross-Cultural Testing

The basic problem here lies in establishing the validity of the tests. Clearly, in the case of personality questionnaires some items may be culture-bound (Cattell, 1957), e.g., items referring to something specific to a culture. Others may be relatively culture-free. However, this is difficult to tell from simply reading items and it is necessary to ensure before using tests that the items are working, through item and factor analyses in both cultures. However, there is a problem with tests, even more profound than the validity of individual items. This concerns the meaning of a variable in a culture, the emic-etic dilemma (Berry and Dasen, 1974). Cross-cultural comparison of a variable implies that it is an emic construct, i.e., that it has meaning in the cultures concerned. The emic view (which is held by most cross-cultural psychologists) is that only variables significant for a particular culture should be studied. Essentially this rules out cross-cultural testing. This seems best dealt with by establishing that tests are functioning properly both at item and scale level by item and factor analysis. If they are, it is difficult to argue that they are not culturally equivalent.

   With personality questionnaires there is the added problem of sampling. If it is necessary to test in societies with a low literacy level, the difficulties are obvious. Further problems are involved in translation. This also ignores the fact that attitudes to testing, in a culture not familiar with tests, may be different from those in the West. Response sets especially of acquiescence may become intrusive. Kline (1977) has documented these points in full.

   Nevertheless, it can be said, in conclusion, that if it is first demonstrated that the personality questionnaire is working and valid in the cultures concerned, cross-cultural comparisons can be made and are meaningful. Rasch scaling (Rasch, 1960) is a possibility here, but Rasch analysis of personality questionnaires has its own problems (Barrett and Kline, 1983).

   For all these reasons many cross-cultural researchers have turned to projective tests. Spain (1972) has an excellent review of their cross-cultural use which is extensive. Nevertheless, I agree largely with Eysenck (1959) that projective tests, as normally scored, for reasons of poor reliability with poor evidence of validity and clearly influenced by factors such as testers' attitudes, subjects' beliefs about the tests and other superficial factors (Vernon, 1964), are not suitable for scientific study in the West, let alone when further cross-cultural problems are added.

These problems are severe. As Lee (1953) found, the TAT pictures are highly culture-bound to middle-class pre-war America, and his attempts to produce an African version were only successful with certain tribes. In any case as Deregowski (e.g., 1966) has shown, cultural factors influence the recognition of pictures, and Wober (1967) has suggested that some cultures are not visually oriented but are more responsive in other perceptual modes, a hypothesis with important implications for cross-cultural testing.

With such difficulties, why bother with projective tests? Two arguments answer this point. First, in the hands of sensitive and skilled investigators, insightful findings can be made. An outstanding example of this is Carstairs' (1957) study of the Rajputs of Central India. However, this is not science, for all depends on the judgment of the researcher. Holley (1973) proposed an objective scoring scheme for the Rorschach which followed by G analysis and factor analysis, as described earlier in this chapter in the study by Cooper (1982), seemed to yield objective, replicable findings. This scheme, which can be applied to any projective test, which involves essentially making a content analysis of the test protocols, has been tried with some success by Hampson and Kline (1977) with the TAT and the House, Person, Tree test (Buck, 1948) and cross-culturally in Thailand by Kline and Svaste-Xuto (1981). From this it would appear that projective tests could be used cross-culturally in the scientific study of Freudian theory.

## Hologeistic Methods

The hologeistic method (as used by Whiting and Child (1953) in their studies of child training and personality), involves rating ethnographic and anthropological reports of societies for child-rearing procedures and for, say, personality traits and correlating the scales. Thus theories of personality development (not only psychoanalytic) can be put to a quantitative test. It thus maximizes the two great advantages of the cross-cultural validation of Freudian theory—the heterogeneity of variance and the access to examining the universality of the hypotheses. It is, therefore, in my view a most powerful method for the scientific study of Freudian theory.

Needless to say, there have been numerous objections raised against this method. Campbell and Naroll (1972) discuss eleven problems; those that are important in respect of psychoanalytic theory I shall now examine. One of their objections concerns sampling. They argue that the societies described in anthropology are only a small fraction of the total number of societies, thus hologeistic studies must be affected by sampling bias. From the viewpoint of testing psychoanalytic theory this is not important. Provided that the societies which have been described are heterogeneous for the relevant variables, then the theory can be investigated. Furthermore, 500 societies are better than one. Strictly with this limitation, universality cannot be tested, and this is accepted.

There is the related uncertainty of what constitutes a tribe or society. This is a complex problem about which anthropologists fail to agree. Nevertheless, a worthwhile cross-cultural sample of societies such that each member is different can be drawn, and such a sample should be used or portions of it in hologeistic studies, as is done by most of the workers in this field.

Without doubt the most important issue raised by Campbell and Naroll (1972) concerns the accuracy of the data in the anthropological reports. Since random error lowers correlations, the fact that significant correlations can be obtained means either that this source of error is negligible or that there is some kind of systematic bias. When hologeistic studies use large number of societies based upon the reports of many different anthropologists, systematic bias is unlikely. However, it is possible, if, for example, they were all Freudians, they would put emphasis on variables such as weaning and pot-training in accord with theory.

Campbell and Naroll suggest that quality controls should be used in the evaluation of anthropological reports. Such factors as length of stay in the culture, familiarity with the language, degree of participation in the culture, whether the behaviours were observed or merely recounted, and how many subjects showed the behaviour must all influence the quality of the report. In addition, reliability between observers and baseline rates for behaviours in society to assess normality are all necessary.

These implied criticisms of anthropological data can be well-founded. For example, a psychoanalytic anthropological study of the Chinese passion for gambling (which I shall not use as scientific evidence for the theory) was based on a sample of fewer than twenty Chinese waiters from San Francisco. Given that there are one billion Chinese, this sampling is bizarre. However, it must be noted that all these faults are sources of error. Error reduces correlations so that any correlations obtained, provided that many anthropologists have contributed the data thus eliminating systematic bias, are likely to be reduced in size.

A number of other difficulties are raised by these authors. Thus they criticize the interpretation of correlations as demonstrating causal links. This is a fair criticism but it can be overcome by factoring the correlations. As Cattell (e.g., 1973) and Cattell and Kline (1977) have argued, simple structure factors can have causal status. Similarly their objection that in large matrices some correlations will be significant by chance can be nullified by splitting the sample. Truly significant correlations will reveal themselves in both. Care must be taken in this approach not to mask genuine regional differences.

These are the main objections to the hologeistic method raised by Campbell and Naroll (1972). As can be seen, most of them can be answered and it still appears that this method offers powerful opportunities to put certain aspects of psychoanalytic theory to the test.

In this chapter I do not want to detail all the results which have been obtained from the hologeistic method. This has already been done in Kline (1977, 1981). Interpretation of findings is complex and could not be properly dealt with in a chapter of this length. One study I should like to describe briefly since it illustrates well the power of this method. This is a study of the Oedipus complex (Stephens, 1962).

As part of that research, Stephens (1961) investigated by means of the hologeistic method menstrual taboo. The rationale for the work came from *Totem and Taboo* (Freud, 1913) from which it can be deduced that the extensiveness of menstrual taboos in any society reflects the intensity of castration anxiety felt by the men in that society. Since the anthropological literature contains no measure of castration anxiety, its antecedents and consequences, as hypothesized in Freudian theory, were rated across seventy-two societies together with a measure of menstrual taboo. Typical antecedents were: *post partum* sex taboo; severity of masturbation punishment; strictness of father's obedience commands. In all there were ten such measures plus a total score. The results were impressive. Each of the ten antecedents was related to the menstrual taboo scale in the expected direction, the majority significantly. The total score was related at a significance level of .0000001. The most pertinent variables were the *post partum* sex taboo and severity of masturbation punishment; the least, severity of punishment for disagreement. This study is impressive support for the Freudian claim that castration anxiety originating in the Oedipal situation is a widespread phenomenon. Non-Freudian hypotheses to explain these findings would have to be very much *post hoc*.

With this example I shall leave the hologeistic method. It is in principle a powerful approach to validating psychoanalytic theory. At the beginning of this section on cross-cultural methods I mentioned the psychometric approach—using tests cross-culturally. Unfortunately, although it would appear to be an effective method, despite its problems, little has been done. Many investigations have simply used projective tests, as they stand, results which cannot be used as scientific evidence. Psychometric tests (questionnaires and objective tests) have been little used mainly because there are few validated questionnaires measuring variables relevant to Freudian theory. The present writer has carried out small pilot studies with his own measures of oral personality (Kline, 1980b) and anal personality (Kline, 1971), but no substantive findings were made either in India or Africa. Similarly objectively scored projective tests have not been used. For this reason it has to be argued that the power of cross-cultural testing in the elucidation of Freudian theory remains to be actualized. However, the potential is there.

This leads on to the final method which I want to examine in this chapter, *the psychometric method*. By psychometric method is meant the use of tests followed by factor analysis, the methodology which has yielded much in the field of abilities and, although there is less agreement, in the field of personality.

Kline (1980a) has argued that from the factors revealed by psychological tests a psychometric model of man may be constructed, a model which is a special version of a trait model. In this psychometric model the factors emerging from factor analyses are used in a linear multiple regression to predict behaviours. The better the prediction, the better the model. The task of psychometrics is to reveal the critical factors. It is in this context that the psychometric method can be used in the elucidation of psychoanalytic theory. Psychosexual developmental theory is essentially a trait theory. In this part of Freudian theory it is claimed (Freud, 1905) that certain personality constellations are derived from fixation at different phases of psychosexual development. Oral, anal and phallic characters are described. If these personality constellations truly occur then they should be measurable using personality questionnaires. If they can be measured, furthermore, then the relationship of these variables to their child-rearing antecedents can be examined. In summary, it is clear that psychometric methods are ideally suited to the investigation of psychoanalytic psychosexual theory. It must be pointed out that this involves more than the study of personality syndromes and their childhood determinants, for psychosexual fixation is involved in Freudian theory in a wide variety of abnormal behaviour. For example (see Fenichel, 1945), fixation at the oral phase is related to anorexia, alcoholism and depression, while stuttering and obsessionality are held to involve anal fixation.

Because this psychosexual theory, at least as it relates to the occurrence of personality syndromes, is amenable to objective testing there has been a considerable body of research into it. This has been fully examined in Kline (1981) and I do not intend to summarize it here, other than to state that there is good evidence for the syndromes of oral (optimistic and pessimistic) and anal personality, as described in the literature but that there is as yet no clear evidence for the relation of these syndromes to either child-rearing procedures or pre-genital erotism. Indeed, anal character is clearly a factorial dimension—of obsessional personality (Kline and Storey, 1978).

I want to describe one piece of research into the determinants of oral personality because (a) it highlights the problems in adequately testing psychoanalytic theory and (b) it reports negative findings, which Eysenck and Wilson (1973) claim is never done. Kline (1980b) developed by factor and item analysis two tests of oral personality which were shown to be reliable and valid—OOQ and OPQ measures of oral optimistic personality and oral pessimistic personality (Kline and Storey, 1977). The validation of these tests, of course, supported the Freudian claims concerning the existence of these two personality syndromes. To study the aetiology of these constellations a number of hypotheses were derived from psychosexual theory and put to the test. This had to be done because the direct method of asking adults how they were weaned and fed is unlikely to be accurate, the great difficulty with retrospective investigations. The hypotheses were:

1  Dentists are more oral sadistic than doctors.
2  Oral optimists will like warm, milky foods; pessimists raw, crisp foods.
3  Vegetarians will differ from non-vegetarians on oral traits.
4  Members of the Dracula Society will show high scores on oral traits.
5  High scorers on oral traits will show greater perceptual defence to oral stimuli than others.
6  Wind-instrument players will show more oral traits than string players.
7  Pen-chewers will be higher on OPQ than non-chewers.
8  Smokers will show more oral traits than non-smokers.

To investigate these hypotheses, different samples were used totalling 570 subjects. Although various reasons for failure can be adduced (see Kline and Storey, 1980, for the details) seven of these hypotheses were not supported. Thus the Freudian theory is not confirmed unequivocally. The three hypotheses that were confirmed are interesting because these were the ones concerned with mouth activity. Thus pen-chewers (although a small sample) did score significantly higher on OPQ than non-chewers. Since, and this is very important, neither OPQ nor OOQ contains any items referring to eating, smoking or anything to do with the mouth, explanation of this finding, other than by psychoanalytic theory, is difficult. In two studies smoking was related to scores on OPQ. In one the point biserial correlation between OPQ and smoking was .38. In the second heavy smokers scored significantly higher than light smokers on OPQ (the criterion for heavy smoking being twenty or more cigarettes a day). Since extraversion and neuroticism could well be implicated in smoking, it was shown that this effect was not due to either or both of these variables. Finally, food preference was related to scores on OPQ and OOQ but not, as a control, to scores on E and N. High OPQ scores liked asparagus, bananas and cream, nuts, honey, tapioca, baked fish and (their favourite) fruit fools. This last, a sweet mix of cream and fruit, is a very satisfactory finding from the viewpoint of Freudian theory.

Thus although more hypotheses failed than did not, these results do confirm, to a surprising degree, a link between personality traits and oral behaviours, as claimed in psychoanalytic theory. Clearly there is a need for more follow-up work with bigger samples and observation rather than report of food preferences. One point is clear. Psychosexual theory can be put to the scientific test.

## CONCLUSIONS

Several clear conclusions may be drawn from the discussion in this chapter.

1   First, it is certainly incorrect to argue that psychoanalytic theory is not falsifiable and impossible to put to the scientific test. If psychoanalytic theory is broken down into separate hypotheses, these can be tested, as has been amply illustrated.
2   Secondly, it cannot be argued that only relatively trivial aspects of the theory can be tested. Four distinct methods have been examined which enable a wide variety of psychoanalytic hypotheses to be put to the test. Contrary to what might be expected by those inexperienced in the scientific study of psychoanalysis and reared on what has become a modern myth that psychoanalysis is untestable, even those aspects that deal with unconscious processes have become amenable to study using percept-genetic techniques and the method of conflict activation. Cross-cultural studies are well able to investigate those Freudian hypotheses concerned with the environmental determinants of behaviour, while psychometric methods can deal with the temperamental, trait-like components.
3   From the results which have been discussed, it is clear that some Freudian hypotheses have been refuted, while others have stood the objective empirical test. Two points need to be emphasized here. First, this is by no means a complete list of all the Freudian concepts which have been verified. Secondly, it is not expected that all Freudian concepts would stand the scientific test. On the contrary, one of the hopes of the scientific study of Freud is that his great insights can be modified in the light of evidence, and incorporated into a scientific account of behaviour.

These are the direct conclusions that may be drawn from this chapter. Some further arguments can also be developed. Even from the rather sparse findings reported, it is clear that some Freudian concepts have been supported. To proceed further it is now necessary to list other verified concepts. This list must inevitably appear dogmatic. However, it is fully supported by evidence examined in Kline (1981) and Fisher and Greenberg (1977). From these surveys it is reasonable to state that the following concepts have some experimental support. Syndromes resembling the anal and oral characters (but links to child-training unconfirmed not refuted); Oedipus and castration complexes; repression and other defences; psychological meaning and dreams; sexual symbolism of dreams; libidinal wishes and psychopathology; the link between paranoia and repressed homosexuality; and (one study) a link between appendicitis and birth fantasy.

This list contains some of the central concepts of psychoanalysis. It is, therefore, impossible to reject the theory *in toto*. What is necessary is to develop a theory of behaviour which embraces these verified concepts. One attempt to do this (which, however, used all the concepts of psychoanalysis) was that of Dollard and Miller (1950) in which Freudian theory and learning principles (classical and operant conditioning) were linked together. In fact, as was argued in Kline (1981), learning theory and psychoanalysis can be regarded as complementary rather than anti-thetical, psychoanalytic theory in this view explaining reinforcement, for as Juvenal knew 2000 years ago, although until recently apparently evading behavioural psychologists, bread and circuses are not enough for man. In any case, modern philosophies of science regard scientific theories not as pertaining to some truth in the real world but simply as describing phenomena more or less elegantly and accurately. Thus there is no difficulty in having more than one theory, although a unification is preferable on grounds of elegance.

Finally, it should now be obvious why detailed study of the effectiveness of psychoanalytic therapy is not appropriate. Apart from the earlier argument that the effectiveness or otherwise of a therapy does not necessarily reflect the quality of its underlying theory, psychoanalytic therapy would not be expected to be effective because it contains theoretical error, i.e., not all the psychoanalytic concepts have been verified. Thus even if effectively applied, it would not be necessarily efficient.

In summary, I hope that the objective study of Freudian theory will continue, for in reality little has been done relative to what is required. In this way the empirically sound concepts can be discovered, others modified in the light of the evidence and others rejected. Those that stand, concerned with fundamental aspects of the human mind, can then be utilized in a scientific account of human behaviour. Such an account can then be used to underpin psychotherapy. Whether such a theory be called psychoanalytic or Freudian is unimportant; what matters is that the psychoanalytic insights are not abandoned in the desperate desire of psychologists to attain to science.

## REFERENCES

Barrett, P. and Kline, P. (1983) 'A Rasch analysis of the EPQ', *J. Person. and Group Psychol.*, in press.
Berkley-Hall, O. (1921) 'The anal erotic factor in the religion, philosophy and character of the Hindus', *Internat. J. Psychoanal.*, **2,** p. 306.
Berry, J. W. and Dasen, P. R. (1974) *Culture and Cognition*, London, Methuen.
Buck, J. N. (1948) 'The HTP Test', *J. Clin. Psychol.*, **4,** pp. 151–9.
Campbell, O. T. and Naroll, R. (1972) in Hsu, F. L. K. (Ed.), *Psychological Anthropology*, Cambridge, Mass., Schenkman.
Carstairs, G. M. (1957) *The Twice-Born: A Study of a Community of High-Caste Hindus*, London, Hogarth.
Cattell, R. B. (1957) *Personality and Motivation Structure and Measurement*, Yonkers, New World.
Cattell, R. B. (1973) *Personality and Mood by Questionnaire*, New York, Jossey-Bass.
Cattell, R. B. and Kline, P. (1977) *The Scientific Analysis of Personality and Motivation*, London, Academic Press.
Cattell, R. B., Eber, H. W. and Tatsuoka, M. M. (1970) *Handbook for the Sixteen Personality Factor Questionnaire*, Champaign, Ill., IPAT.
Cheshire, N. M. (1975) *The Nature of Psychodynamic Interpretation*, Chichester, Wiley.
Conant, J. B. (1947) *On Understanding Science*, New Haven, Conn., Yale University Press.
Cooper, C. (1982) 'An experimental study of Freudian defence mechanisms', unpublished PhD thesis, University of Exeter.
Cooper, C. and Kline, P. (1983) 'The Defence Mechanism Test', *Brit. J. Psychol.*, in press.
Corman, L. (1969) *The Test PN*, Paris, Presses Universitaires de Paris.
Deregowski, J. B. (1966) 'Difficulties in pictorial perception in Africa', *Int. Soc. Res.*, University of Zambia.

Devereux, G. (1951) 'Cultural and characterological traits of the Mohave related to the anal stage of psychosexual development', *Psychoanal, Quart.*, **20**, pp. 398–422.

Dixon, N. F. (1982) *Preconscious Processing*, Chichter, Wiley.

Dollard, J. and Miller, N. E. (1950) *Personality and Psychotherapy*, New York, McGraw-Hill.

Eysenck, H. J. (1952) 'The effects of psychotherapy: An evaluation', *J. Consult. Psychol.*, **16**, pp. 319–24.

Eysenck, H. J. (1959) 'The Rorschach Test', in Buros, O. K. (1959) (Ed.), *The Vth Mental Measurement Year Book*, New Jersey, Gryphon Press.

Eysenck, H. J. (1965) 'The effects of psychotherapy', *International Journal of Psychiatry*, **1**, pp. 99–142.

Eysenck, H. J. and Wilson, G. D. (1973) *The Experimental Study of Freudian Theories*, London, Methuen.

Farrell, B. A. (1964) 'The status of psychoanalytic theory', *Inquiry*, **4**, pp. 16–36.

Farrell, B. A. (1982) *The Standing of Psychoanalysis* Oxford, Oxford University Press.

Fenichel, O. (1945) *The Psychoanalytic Theory of Neurosis*, New York, Norton.

Fisher, S. and Greenberg, P. R. (1977) *The Scientific Credibility of Freud's Theories and Therapy*, Hassocks, Harvester Press.

Freud, S. (1905) 'Three essays on sexuality', Vol. 7, pp. 135–243 of *The Standard Edition of the Complete Psychological Works of Sigmund Freud*, London, Hogarth Press and Institute of Psychoanalysis (1966).

Freud, S. (1911) 'Psychoanalytic notes on an autobiographical account of a case of paranoia (dementia paranoides)', Vol. 12, 3, of *The Standard Edition of the Complete Psychological Works of Sigmund Freud*, London, Hogarth Press and Institute of Psychoanalysis (1966).

Freud, S. (1913) 'Totem and taboo', Vol. 12, 1, of *The Standard Edition of the Complete Psychological Works of Sigmund Freud*, London, Hogarth Press and Institute of Psychoanalysis (1966).

Freud, S. (1923a) 'The ego and the id', Vol. 19, 3, of *The Standard Edition of the Complete Psychological Works of Sigmund Freud*, London, Hogarth Press and Institute of Psychoanalysis (1966).

Freud, S. (1923b) 'New introductory lectures in psychoanalysis', Vol. 22, of *The Standard Edition of the Complete Psychological Works of Sigmund Freud*, London, Hogarth Press and Institute of Psychoanalysis (1966).

Freud, S. (1933) *New Introductory Lectures on Psychoanalysis*, London, Hogarth Press.

Freud, S. (1940) 'An outline of psychoanalysis', Vol. 23, 141, of *The Standard Edition of the Complete Psychological Works of Sigmund Freud*, London, Hogarth Press and Institute of Psychoanalysis (1966).

Hampson, S. and Kline, P. (1977) 'Personality dimensions differentiating certain groups of abnormal offenders from non-offenders', *Brit. J. Criminol.*, **17**, pp. 310–31.

Holley, J. W. (1973) 'The Rorschach', in Kline, P. (Ed.), *New Approaches in Psychological Measurement*, Chichester, Wiley.

Kaye, M. (1975) 'The therapeutic value of three merging stimuli for male schizophrenics', PhD thesis, Yeshiva University.

Kline, P. (1971) *Ai3Q Personality Test*, Windsor, NFER.

Kline, P. (1972) *Fact and Fantasy in Freudian Theory*, London, Methuen.

Kline, P. (1977) 'Cross-cultural studies and Freudian theory', in Warren, N. (Ed.), *Studies in Cross-Cultural Psychology*, Vol. **1**, pp. 50–90, London, Academic Press.

Kline, P. (1980a) 'The psychometric model', in Chapman, A. and Jones D. (Eds.), *Models of Man*, Leicester, BPS.

Kline, P. (1980b) *OOQ and OPQ Personality Tests*, Exeter, Department of Psychology.

Kline, P. (1981) *Fact and Fantasy in Freudian Theory*, 2nd ed., London, Methuen.

Kline, P. and Cooper, C. (1977) 'A percept-genetic study of defence mechanisms', *Scand. J. Psychol.*, **18**, pp. 148–52.

Kline, P. and Storey, R. (1977) 'A factor-analytic study of the oral character', *Brit. J. Soc. Psychol.*, **16**, pp. 317–28.

Kline, P. and Storey, R. (1978) 'The Dynamic Personality Inventory: What does it measure?', *Brit. J. Psychol.*, **69**. pp. 375–83.

Kline, P. and Storey, R. (1980) 'The aetiology of the oral character', *J. Genetic Psychol.*, **1365**, pp. 85–94.

Kline, P. and Svasti-Xuto, B. (1981) 'The responses of Thai and British children to the CAT', *J. Soc. Psychol.*, **113**, pp. 137–8.

Kragh, U. (1955) *The Actual Genetic Model of Perception Personality*, Lund, Gleerups.

Kragh, U. (1969) *DMT Manual*, Stockholm, Scandinavska, Tesforlaget, AB.

Kragh, U. and Smith, G. (1970) *Percept-Genetic Analysis*, Lund, Gleerups.

Lee, S. G. (1953) *TAT for African Subjects*, Pietermaritzberg, University of Natal Press.

Malinowski, B. (1927) *Sex and Repression in Savage Society*, New York, Harcourt Brace.

Martin, M. (1964) 'Mr Farrell and the refutability of psychoanalysis', *Inquiry*, **7**, pp. 80–98.

Medawar, P. B. (1969) *Induction and Intuition in Scientific Thought*, London, Methuen.

Popper, K. (1959) *The Logic of Scientific Discovery*, New York, Basic Books.

Rasch, G. (1960) *Probabilistic Models for Some Intelligence and Attainment Tests*, Copenhagen, Denmark Institute of Education.

Ricoeur, P. (1970) *Freudian Philosophy: An Essay in Interpretation*, New Haven, Conn., Yale University Press.

Roheim, G. (1952) 'The anthropological evidence and the Oedipus complex', *Psychoanal Quart.*, **21**, pp. 537–42.

Silverman, L. H. (1971) 'An experimental technique for the study of unconscious conflict', *Brit. J. Med. Psychol.*, **44**, pp. 17–25.

Silverman, L. H. (1976) 'Psychoanalytic theory: The reports of my death are greatly exaggerated', *Amer. Psychol.*, **31**.

Silverman, L. H. (1980) *A Comprehensive Report of Studies Using the Subliminal Psychodynamic Activation Method*, New York, Research Center for Mental Health.

Silverman, L. H., Kwawer, J. S., Wolitzky, C. and Coron, M. (1973) 'An experimental study of aspects of the psychoanalytic theory of male homosexuality', *J. Abnorm Psychol.*, **82**, pp. 178–88.

Silverman, L. H., Ross, D. L., Adler, J. M. and Lustig, D. A. (1978) 'Simple research paradigm for demonstrating psychodynamic activation: Effects of oedipal stimuli on dart-throwing accuracy in college males', *J. Abnorm. Psychol.*, **87**, pp. 341–57.

Spain, D. H. (1972) in Hsu, F.L.K. (Ed.), *Psychological Anthropology*, Cambridge, Mass., Schenkman.

Stephens, W. N. (1961) 'A cross-cultural study of menstrual taboos', *Genet. Psychol. Monogr.*, **64**, pp. 385–416.

Stephens, W. N. (1962) *The Oedipus Complex Hypothesis: Cross-Cultural Evidence*, New York, Free Press of Glencoe.

Truax, C. B. (1963) 'Effective ingredients in psychotherapy: An approach to unraveling the patient-therapist interactions', *J. Consult. Psychol.*, **10**, pp. 256–63.

Vernon, P. E. (1964) *Personality Assessment*, London, Methuen.

Watson, J. P. (1975) 'An experimental method for the study of unconscious conflict', *Brit. J. Med. Psychol.*, **48**, pp. 301–2.

Westerlundh, B. (1976) *Aggression, Anxiety and Defence*, Lund, Gleerups.

Whiting, J. M. and Child, I. L. (1953) *Child Training and Personality*, New Haven, Conn., Yale University Press.

Witkin, H. A. (1962) *Psychological Differentiation: Studies of Development*, New York, Wiley.

Wober, M. (1967) 'Sensotypes', *J. Soc. Psychol.*, **70**, pp. 181–9.

# *Interchange*

## ERWIN REPLIES TO KLINE

Kline and I appear to agree about the following: (1) the effectiveness of psycho-analytic therapy has not been demonstrated; (2) establishing its *ineffectiveness* would not refute all of Freudian theory; (3) Freudian theory is testable in principle (and at least parts of it in practice); and (4) the non-experimental clinical evidence is inadequate. What we mainly disagree about is the interpretation of *some* of the experimental studies. (Kline, 1981, discusses hundreds of studies, but some had negative results and many others are criticized by him because of methodological defects.)

In his contribution to this volume Kline discusses the experimental work of Silverman, Kragh and their respective associates. Because I have already argued in my paper in this volume that this work fails to support Freudian theory, I will make only a few brief comments on it.

1    I agree that Silverman's work, summarized in Silverman (1976), is potentially of great interest, but some reservations are in order. Kline mentions two: the first concerns Silverman's measures of psychopathology; the second concerns the assumption that his subliminal stimuli activate unconscious conflicts. The second is more important to the assessment of psychoanalytic theory. If there is no evidence that Silverman is activating unconscious conflicts—if, as Kline says, this is still an assumption—then Silverman's work provides no support for any psychoanalytic hypothesis. A third reservation should be added to those mentioned by Kline: independent investigators have tried to replicate Silverman's work and have failed. For example, Haspel and Harris (1982) tried to replicate Silverman *et al.*'s (1978) study of the effects of subliminal stimuli on dart-throwing performances, but were unable to do so. Several other failed replications are discussed in my paper.

Incidentally, in discussing Silverman's work, Kline mentions Dixon (1981) as agreeing that subliminal perception studies can bear on hypotheses about the psychoanalytic unconscious. I doubt that Dixon and Kline agree on this point. When Dixon uses the expression 'unconscious perception', he means 'discrimination without awareness'; he is not talking about a Freudian unconscious. Referring to his own concept, he writes '. . . that this concept should have been rejected in the one context but accepted in the other is presumably because of an unwarranted confusion of physiological processes which do not give rise to awareness with Freud's concept of an unconscious. This confusion is unfortunate' (Dixon, 1981, p. 22). Dixon also describes (p.

183) the link that some people make between such concepts as *perceptual defence* and those of psychoanalytic theory as 'unwarranted'. (For arguments against interpreting perceptual defence studies as supporting psychoanalytic theory, see Erwin, 1984).

2   My objection to the work of Kragh (1960) and his associates is that they provide no evidence that their DMT (Defence Mechanism Test) measures the effects of Freudian defence mechanisms. Contrary to what Kline suggests, one cannot just stipulate that a subject's description of an ugly, threatening face as 'angelic' is an example of reaction-formation in the Freudian sense. The subject's response might be caused by something other than the attempt by the ego to deal with threatening material from the unconscious; if there is some other cause, then Freudian reaction-formation has not occurred. Kline, however, agrees that independent evidence is needed. He refers to two studies: one is an unpublished dissertation (Cooper, 1982); the other is a forthcoming paper by Cooper and Kline (1984).

It is in the first of these papers (Cooper, 1982) that an attempt is made to relate the DMT to external criteria.

First, Cooper found a correlation of .49 between success in aviation training and the operation of defence mechanisms in trainees, as measured by the DMT. Concerning this finding, Kline says, 'As has been previously argued this fits in neatly with the claim that the DMT measures defences since reality based decision would appear to be essential for pilots.' This argument is unconvincing. The ability to make 'reality based decisions' may be essential for completing successfully an aviation training course, but so are other characteristics, such as strong motivation, intelligence and good eyesight. Is there good evidence that most who fail such a course lack the ability to make reality-based decisions? Even if we had such evidence, how would we know that this lack of ability was generally caused by the operation of Freudian defence mechanisms? In brief, there is no firm evidence for the operation of Freudian defence mechanisms in failed trainee pilots; if there were, the appeal to studies of the DMT to establish the existence of such mechanisms would be superfluous.

The second external piece of evidence Kline mentions is a correlation of .50 between a general DMT score indicating defences and a perceptual defence measure of repression. As I argued in my paper in this volume and in Erwin (1984), perceptual defence effects do not provide evidence for the occurrence of repression or any other Freudian defence mechanism. If that is right, then correlating a DMT score with a perceptual defence score does not establish that the former is a measure of a Freudian defence effect.

3   The remainder of Kline's paper contains an interesting discussion of methods for testing Freudian hypotheses. His main contention is not that the use of these methods has confirmed Freudian theory, but that they can be used for that purpose in the future; however, he also mentions some existing studies that require comment.

As an illustration of the use of the hologeistic method, Kline mentions the Stephens' (1961) study of castration anxiety. Ten assumed antecedents of castration anxiety were related to a 'menstrual taboo scale'. The significance level for the total score was impressive: .0000001. What is less impressive is the absence of firm evidence that *any* of Stephens' variables, such as severity of sex training, are antecedents of castration anxiety. It is not sufficient to point out that Freudian theory *hypothesizes* that these are antecedents of castration anxiety: evidence is needed to warrant that part of Freudian theory. Without such evidence, the Stephens' (1961) study provides no evidence for the existence of castration anxiety.

To illustrate the use of another method, the psychometric method, Kline refers to a study by Kline and Storey (1980) on the aetiology of the oral character. Most of the findings were negative, but some were not. Kline's overall view of Freud's theory about the aetiology of both the oral and anal syndromes is that the weight of the evidence is negative, but because of methodological problems, this evidence does not refute the theory; nor does the positive evidence confirm it (Kline, 1981, p. 127).

4   In his closing comments, Kline says that modern philosophies of science regard scientific theories not as pertaining to some truth in the real world but simply as describing phenomena more or less elegantly and more or less accurately. I have two comments. First, not all philosophers of science accept this view; I doubt that most do, although it is difficult to tell in the absence of clear criteria for deciding who is a philosopher of science. Second, if Kline accepts this 'non-realist' view of theories, it is difficult to make sense of his treatment of Freudian theory. If he believes that it is not literally true that repression occurs or that Silverman's subjects experienced unconscious fantasies, then he should not attempt to explain perceptual defence effects in terms of repression, or Silverman's results in terms of unconscious fantasies. If it is not true that repression or unconscious fantasies exist, then it is not true that repression or unconscious fantasies *cause* any observable phenomena.

5   There is one other philosophical point on which Kline and I appear to disagree, and this may explain some of our disagreement about certain studies. He asks: if we have twenty experiments, each apparently confirming different parts of psychoanalytic theory, is it more elegant to regard each as confirming the relevant aspect of psychoanalysis or to produce twenty *ad hoc* rival hypotheses tied to no theory of any kind? My position, briefly argued in Erwin (1980, pp. 452–4), is that it may be necessary to rule out such atheoretical, rival hypotheses if our background evidence renders them sufficiently plausible, even though when taken together they are less elegant than Freudian theory. I would concede, however, as Kline says, that the issue is a difficult one.

**Conclusion**

Most of Kline's paper is designed to show that there are methods for testing Freudian theory. I have not disagreed with this conclusion, but I have tried to show that his paper provides no existing, firm evidence for any part of Freudian theory.

**REFERENCES**

Cooper, C. (1982) 'An experimental study of Freudian defense mechanisms', unpublished PhD thesis, University of Exeter.

Cooper C. and Kline, P. (1984) 'The defense mechanism test', *Brit. J. Psychol.*, in press.

Dixon, N. F. (1981) *Preconcious Processing*, New York, John Wiley.

Erwin, E. (1980) 'Psychoanalysis: How firm is the evidence?', *Nous*, **14**, pp. 443–55.

Erwin, E. (1984) 'The standing of psychoanalysis', *Brit. J. Philosophy of Science*, in press.

Haspel, K. and Harris, R. (1982) 'Effect of tachistoscopic stimulation of subconscious Oedipal wishes on competitive performance: A failure to replicate', *J. of Abnormal Psychol.*, **91**, pp. 437–43.

Kline, P. (1981) *Fact and Fantasy in Freudian Theory*, London, Methuen.

Kline, P. and Storey, R. (1980) 'The etiology of the oral character', *J. Genetic Psychol.*, **136**, pp. 85–94.

Kragh, V. (1960) 'The defense mechanism test: A new method for diagnosis and personnel selection', *Journal of Applied Psychol.*, **44**, pp. 303–9.

Silverman, L. H. (1976) 'Psychoanalytic theory: The reports of my death are greatly exaggerated', *Amer. Psychol.*, **31**, pp. 621–37.

Silverman, L. H., Ross, D., Adler, J. and Lustig, D. A. (1978) 'Simple research paradigm for demonstrating subliminal psychodynamic activation', *J. of Abnormal Psychol.*, **87**, pp. 341–57.

Stephens, W. (1961) 'A cross-cultural study of menstrual taboos', *Genet. Psychol. Monogr.*, pp. 385–416.

# KLINE REPLIES TO ERWIN

In this chapter Erwin essentially attempts to refute critics of Eysenck's objections to Freudian theory and the efficacy of its therapy. In respect of the efficacy of therapy I am largely in agreement with Erwin—the necessary type of controlled study has not been done. However, since most of my work has concentrated upon the theory, in a brief reply of this nature I shall concentrate on this aspect of Erwin's chapter.

Erwin makes a number of important points with considerable skill as befits a philosopher. However, they do not always withstand scrutiny. His chief objection is that if a study supports Freudian theory, I am inclined to cite it without regard to possible alternative explanations. Now this was a criticism of my first 1972 edition which I sought to correct. As an example of this defect he cites a study by Friedman (1952) in which I accept that loss of tails in a story about elephants is a sign of castration complex. Erwin complains that I have no evidence for this, implying that there must be some other alternative explanation. Erwin here can be easily refuted.

1   I agree that there is no direct evidence for the validity of this index.

2   The notion of castration complex is rich. Its description would include *inter alia* that children 'with it' would make such drawings. Thus, in this sense evidence for validity is not necessary. The test responses are a part of the complex itself.

3   If this is objected to, then there must be some alternative explanation of the correlation. This is Erwin's point.

4   However, what is this alternative? I am unable and was unable to provide one. Erwin, however, who arraigns me for not providing an alternative, fails to provide one himself. *Logically* an alternative explanation is always possible. In this case, a sensible or even plausible one is extremely hard. It is up to the opposition to provide it.

Another example of this putative error, cited by Erwin, is my reliance on the work of Dixon on repression. I claimed that perceptual defence was an example of repression. Now although I actually quote Freud to support this identification, Erwin argues that 'this does not capture what Freud meant by repression'. While this may be so it raises a more general issue. That is that in studies of Freudian theory there *is* an element of value judgment. My citation may be misleading, so may Erwin's. There is no absolute here, readers must judge in the light of their knowledge of the theory. However, it is misleading to assert dogmatically that *X* or *Y* is or is not an accurate representation.

Erwin makes a similar point concerning the percept-genetic work of Kragh which I regard as good evidence for psychoanalytic defences. He writes, 'what evidence is there that repression is the cause of the subject's drawing ...' Now my case is this, not that the drawing is 'caused' by repression (strange word for a philosopher) but is an 'example' of repression, and similarly for the other defences. I do not think that Erwin can ever have seen a percept-genetic series. When suddenly, independently of the stimulus, a subject draws the horrible face as a smiling pleasant angel, anyone at all familiar with the Freudian description of reaction-formation would be forced to say that this is an example of it. However, this is, as I said, a judgment. Judgments are necessary in this field.

There is a further point about the constant search for other hypotheses. First, in any science alternative explanations are not necessarily of the same status in disconfirming an experimental study. For example, parapsychological or astrological hypotheses could be used to explain many results. These are not usually taken seriously because (a) they are *a priori* unlikely, and (b) because a simple explanation is to be preferred—Occam's razor. Thus the constant search for *ad hoc* and *post hoc* explanations in objective studies of psychoanalysis leads to a plethora of hypotheses to explain the results, in contrast to the relative unity of Freudian theory. This search for alternative explanations is well exemplified in the studies of latent homosexuality in paranoid schizophrenia. I contrasted the psychoanalytic explanation with that given by Eysenck and Wilson (1973) which I described as worthless—worthless because it was *ad hoc*, embedded in no theory, and not even intuitively plausible. As summarized by Erwin it was not too bad perhaps. In its original form it was *a priori* unlikely (scientific research must choose hypotheses to study and ignore the unlikely ones; it is an activity not simple ratiocination). Suspicious paranoids, the argument runs, are more suspicious of men who pose a greater threat than do women, and hence look longer at pictures of males. Why the connection between suspicion and length of looking, between men and threat? In addition, paranoids are alert to the shrink's attempts to label them homosexual and this explains their caution in showing preference for male pictures. These connections are arbitrary. They cannot be regarded as serious counter-explanations to predicted findings. If the results had been different, Eysenck and Wilson could have argued that the paranoids alert to the shrink's attempts to label them homosexual double bluffed and admitted preference for male pictures. However, they looked longer at pictures of females because females are a threat in a world where male dominance is being challenged. This is not science, it is idle speculation.

In brief, I argue that Erwin's attempts to disconfirm the experimental evidence which I have cited, together with Fisher and Greenberg (1977), are not wholly satisfactory. What Erwin has demonstrated (and I am in full agreement with him here) is:

1 that alternative explanations are almost always possible;
2 that there can never be full agreement concerning the formulation of Freudian theory (even where I cite Freud, Erwin claims that it is misleading).

That is why, as I have always argued, value judgments as to the viability of alternatives and the salience of hypotheses must be made by researchers aided by their knowledge of research design and psychoanalytic theory. Logically these judgments may be wrong. The research scientist must live with some uncertainty. The philosopher alone may be certain. But it is wise to remember that now no longer is philosophy queen of the sciences.

## REFERENCES

Eysenck, H. J. and Wilson, G. (1973) *The Experimental Study of Freudian Theories*, London, Methuen.
Fisher, S. and Greenberg, R. (1977) *The Scientific Credibility of Freud's Theories and Therapy*, New York, Basic Books.
Friedman, S. (1952) 'An empirical study of the castration and Oedipus complexes', *Genet. Psychol. Monogr.*, **46**, pp. 61–130.

# Part VIII: Behaviour Therapy

# 13. Contemporary Behaviour Therapy and the Unique Contribution of H. J. Eysenck: Anachronistic or Visionary?

CHRISTOPHER R. BARBRACK AND CYRIL M. FRANKS

Hans Eysenck has been a prominent figure in psychology for at least three decades. His reputation as a gifted intellectual and scholar, dedicated scientist, prolific author and inspiring teacher is rarely disputed. It rests upon a tangible record of distinguished professional accomplishments. Whether he coined the term 'behaviour therapy' is a trivial issue and should not obscure the fact that tracing the roots of behaviour therapy inevitably leads to his pioneering work in learning theory, experimental psychology, psychopathology and psychologically-based therapy. Still, the question whether Eysenck has been influential in the development of behaviour therapy is a subject of disagreement. In this chapter we take up the question of Eysenck's contribution to contemporary behaviour therapy as it exists, and we speculate about his potential for contribution to future development in the field.

Behaviour therapy came into being when psychoanalysis was the predominant force in clinical psychology and psychiatry. The impetus to establish behaviour therapy came in part from scepticism over psychoanalysis' unsupported claims of effectiveness. The founders of behaviour therapy may have been influenced as much by aversion to psychoanalysis as by convictions about the therapeutic potential of modern learning theory. Rejection of psychoanalysis tended to generalize to ideas and methods used in psychoanalysis irrespective of any *necessary* connection between the two. This resulted in a wholesale discreditation of major conceptual tools and areas of knowledge. For example, theory was de-emphasized. Personality theory and traits were the primary targets of this purge, undoubtedly due in part to the prominent role they played in psychoanalysis. Biological factors fared no better.

Whereas most early behaviour therapists sought to develop ways of changing behaviour, Eysenck's first ambition was to understand behaviour and, in pursuing this goal, he developed a profound appreciation for the complexity of human

**233**

behaviour. The aversion for psychoanalysis he shared with other behaviour therapists may have been tempered by his desire to understand the complexities of human behaviour. Thus, he did not fall in line and dispute the value of personality theory and traits. Nor did he discount the importance of genetic and biological factors. In choosing this path Eysenck drove a wedge between himself and mainstream behaviour therapy. Years later many behaviour therapists began to question the importance and utility of conditioning, and the gap between Eysenck and mainstream behaviour therapists was widened. These historical developments have played a significant role in limiting Eysenck's influence in behaviour therapy.

Hence, at this time we concede that Eysenck's major influence is not in the form of particular clinical innovations or practical discoveries. This is not to say that he has not invented or made discoveries but rather that behaviour therapists have failed to take advantage of much that he has to offer. Rather, we believe that his major influence has been and is in the form of concepts, attitudes, values and work habits, and that the impact of these has been and continues to be mediated largely by prominent behaviour therapists who were once his students and junior colleagues. Focusing on Eysenck's more subtle and indirect contributions leaves the established connections between Eysenck and behaviour therapy wide open to dispute. Creating this vulnerability was never our intention, but we do not consider this state of affairs undesirable. Debates are common in scientific and professional circles and the effects often are salutary as long as the issues are expressed with reason and *ad hominem* attacks are eschewed.

Given the changing nature of behaviour therapy and because the interplay between Eysenck and behaviour therapy is ongoing, arguments about Eysenck's influence or lack of influence must be tentative. From the perspective of traditional historical analysis the question of his influence is premature and, as such, will remain an open issue and topic of debate for years to come. To argue otherwise would require either divine omniscience or an intellectual arrogance and intolerance for opposition—perhaps a combination of the two—rather than the kind of intellectual curiosity that leads to an unfinished but balanced and fair-minded appraisal of Eysenck's work.

From our vantage point recent developments in behaviour therapy increase the likelihood of a reconciliation between Eysenck and behaviour therapy. These developments include: (1) acknowledgment of the complexity of human behaviour and a corresponding emphasis on the need to take this complexity into account; (2) appreciation for the utility of traits, referred to in the behavioural literature as 'response clusters' and 'behavioural hierarchies' and (3) reappraisal of genetic and biological influences on behaviour. Until recently this third area has received the least attention but, in our opinion, interest in it is likely to eclipse most other new developments in the field. Behaviour therapists' high regard for empirical data suggests that it will be increasingly difficult for them to ignore or discount the burgeoning evidence of genetic, biochemical, physiological and neurological influences on behaviour. For reasons set forth later, personality theory's conspicuous absence from this list of new developments is regrettable.

## EXAMINING EYSENCK'S INFLUENCE: SOME PRELIMINARY CONSIDERATIONS

To gauge Eysenck's influence fairly, behaviour therapy must be defined. Otherwise, there is no clear standard against which to judge the merits of discrepant evaluations of his work and one opinion is as good as another. In 1960, Eysenck defined behaviour therapy as 'the attempt to alter human behaviour and emotion in a beneficial manner according to the laws of modern learning theory' (1960a, p. 1). By 1974 this deceptively simple notion had mushroomed into a compendium of sometimes disparate ideas and practices, culminating in the 'official' definition now commonly accepted by the Association for Advancement of Behaviour Therapy:

> Behaviour therapy involves primarily the application of principles derived from research and experimental and social psychology for the alleviation of human suffering and the enhancement of human functioning. Behaviour therapy emphasizes the systematic evaluation of the effectiveness of this application. Behaviour therapy involves environmental change in social interaction rather than the direct alteration of bodily processes by biological procedures. The aim is primarily educational. The techniques facilitate and improve self control. In the conduct of behaviour therapy, the contractual agreement is usually specified in which mutually agreeable goals and procedures are specified. Responsible practitioners using behavioural approaches are guided by generally accepted ethical principles (Franks and Wilson, 1975, p. 3).

This broad and general definition reflects the prevailing lack of consensus in the professional community.

Much of Eysenck's work is based upon extensions of Pavlovian-type conditioning. Therefore, estimates of his influence hinge, in part, on the status of classical conditioning in the definition of behaviour therapy. If classical conditioning were to be regarded as fundamental, then Eysenck's influence could be demonstrated without too much difficulty. Conversely, if such conditioning were relegated to a less than fundamental status or excluded altogether, then Eysenck's influence would be more difficult to establish. We believe that any credible analysis of Eysenck's work must specify some definition of behaviour therapy in which the status of classical conditioning is clearly set forth.

In this chapter Eysenck's contributions are examined in the light of a definition of behaviour therapy that accords fundamental status to classical conditioning. This is not to suggest that classical conditioning and behaviour therapy are one and the same or that classical conditioning necessarily leads to a unifying or comprehensive theory of behaviour. Moreover, the importance we attach to classical conditioning does not represent a departure from positions expressed elsewhere (Franks, 1982; Franks and Barbrack, 1983a). Our critical analysis of the nature and scope of conditioning's utility is not to deny its essential role in behaviour therapy, and our endorsement of the importance of classical conditioning in behaviour therapy is a matter of public record (Franks and Barbrack, 1985).

We see little value deriving from analyses of Eysenck's work based on the vague standards of 'clinical experience'. Clinical experience is inevitably subjective and based upon a very restricted sample. This sample may be representative of some larger population but insofar as practitioners rarely, if ever, establish the essential properties of clinical samples, it is not possible to identify the larger groups that are supposedly represented by the sample. Sweeping generalizations, based entirely on clinical experience must, at best, be viewed with extreme caution. The term 'clinical', or one of its various derivatives, is often used to create an aura of legitimacy for subjective bias and unfounded speculation.

Likewise, we fail to see merit in basing evaluations of Eysenck's work on broad speculations about what field-based behaviour therapists actually practise and find effective. The activities of behaviour therapists are not known at this time. It follows, therefore, that the only available standard by which to judge Eysenck's influence is what behaviour therapists espouse rather than guesswork about either how they perform or what they have come to value as the result of clinical experience.

To summarize thus far, it is our thesis that Eysenck's influence has been and is mediated largely by other prominent behaviour therapists and that his contribution to behaviour therapy is best viewed in these terms. In the absence of reasonable alternatives, Eysenck's work must be evaluated against an explicit standard which sets forth a position on the status of classical conditioning in behaviour therapy. We dispute the value of vague criteria based on clinical experience for drawing conclusions about Eysenck's contributions. Finally, we insist that, at this time, the question of Eysenck's influence on behaviour therapy warrants ongoing consideration rather than premature closure. This point is particularly important insofar as recent developments in behaviour therapy may pave the way for a reappraisal of the merits of Eysenck's work and a corresponding increase in his influence.

## EYSENCK'S INFLUENCE ON BEHAVIOUR THERAPY AS SCIENCE

Eysenck's scientific inclinations have not led to intellectual rigidity or narrow-mindedness. A man of diverse interests, he has explored a variety of areas including parapsychology and hypnosis (Eysenck, 1944; Gibson, 1981). Yet for the most part he has tended to avoid the fads that periodically capture the attention and ardour of many clinical psychologists. In that change and improvement are not synonymous, it is reassuring that many of his beliefs remain intact over the years. In particular, he has never wavered from the view of psychology as a science or from the value of psychologists performing research (Eysenck, 1972, 1979a). His work relentlessly reflects the high premium placed on the methodology of behavioural science as a tool for generating knowledge about behaviour and its aberrations. Clinical applications are of secondary importance but are by no means neglected. The predictions that guide his research stand or fall on the basis of empirical evidence rather than personal investment. Many have seized upon the notion of programme research, but few have succeeded in melding together the raw data of behavioural psychology into a cohesive whole. No-one has dedicated himself or herself to this formidable task more effectively than Eysenck. The conclusion that 'further investigation is needed to ...' appears frequently in the behaviour therapy literature and represents the great value attached to replication and refinement by behaviour therapists. However, by their subsequent research activities, many behaviour therapists indicate that this phrase is more cosmetic than predictive. Eysenck is one of a rare breed of behavioural researchers who is responsive to the incompleteness and ongoing nature of scientific inquiry. In contrast to the common practice of publishing isolated studies, devoted to questions of fleeting interest, Eysenck has committed years of work to series of studies, each building on its predecessors, each systematically designed to diminish the ambiguity and confusion that shroud some aspect of human behaviour. Theory and practice in behaviour therapy are intimately related and it is only by systematic research programmes, rather than a hodge-podge of unrelated, technique oriented studies, that advances are likely to occur.

Recent developments not only portend continued indifference toward programme research, but also a movement away from an emphasis on research altogether. For example, some have despairingly acknowledged that clinical practice is affected very little by research in behaviour therapy (e.g., Barlow, 1980; Wilson,

1982). Others argue that the interests and inclinations of clinicians are incompatible with the requirements of clinical research, making it unrealistic to expect practitioners to conduct research (e.g., Strupp, 1981). Advocates of professional school training contend that practitioners need only be trained as 'consumers' of research and that conducting research is not an essential function of professional psychologists (Peterson, 1976). These trends are antithetical to Eysenck's position. Admittedly, Eysenck is not a practitioner and therefore no model of how clinicians can function as behavioural scientists, but this does not automatically disqualify his contributions. Without formal argument, Eysenck consistently has shown by example the essential and possible relationships between research and practice in behaviour therapy. Recent trends in behaviour therapy suggest a growing disenchantment with science and, in this respect, may be a further indication of Eysenck's waning influence. If correct, these developments signal a trend that behaviour therapists may live to regret.

## THEORY IN BEHAVIOUR THERAPY: WHAT DOES EYSENCK HAVE TO OFFER?

At present there is no comprehensive, unified theory that takes account of all or most of human functioning. Eysenck (1982), Bandura (1977) and Staats (1981) have all attempted to develop a unified theory and, in their own fashion, each has fallen short of the mark. In this respect behaviour therapy fares no better than the main body of psychology from which it stems. Skinner's (1953, 1974) relentless opposition to theory has not helped matters, and behaviour therapy is still dominated, especially in operant circles, by those who hold that theory is of minimal relevance.

How are behaviour therapists able to function without a theory of personality? If a patient states a problem, what is to be selectively attended to and to be ignored? What information does the therapist elicit and how is this information understood? What rules govern these issues and what is the justification for these rules?

If it be assumed that behaviour therapists do ask questions and selectively attend to patient responses, it also seems reasonable to assume that some theory or theories guide their questioning, decision-making and contingent intervening. Unless shown otherwise, it is safe to assume that such theories are so implicit that they are insulated from critical awareness and possible modification. That these theories are poorly developed and ill-defined is an unavoidable conclusion. That interventions guided by these theories are haphazard, at best, is unconscionable.

In stark contrast are those conditions created by Eysenck's theoretical contributions. Eysenck's appreciation for theory is evident even in his earliest work (1947). Over the years he has developed and refined a theory of personality (1947, 1976a), and theories of neurosis (1976b; Eysenck and Rachman, 1965), hysteria (1957) and criminality (1977). He has used rigorous psychometric procedures to develop and refine the widely used *Eysenck Personality Inventory* (Eysenck and Eysenck, 1963). This scale, as well as other measurement devices created, is derived from theory. For Eysenck there is a reciprocal relationship between theory and data: theory is used to interpret data and data are used to test the accuracy of theory.

Over the years many of Eysenck's predictions have been disconfirmed by Eysenck himself and by others (e.g., *The Behavioral and Brain Sciences*, 1979). Errors and inconsistencies have been identified (e.g., Gray, 1972). As a result, critics such as

Lazarus seek to discredit the value of his work. Such attempts are legitimate but, by and large, what is often most evident is the critic's failure to appreciate one or more significant aspects of Eysenck's work.

Eysenck's dedication to precise formulation and operational definitions makes his statements readily amenable to rigorous investigation. This brings with it disadvantages as well as advantages. Clearly articulated theories lend themselves to investigation and the attendant risk of refutation. The vague generalities that characterize much of clinical psychology are less readily investigated, and risk of rejection is correspondingly less. Thus, that Eysenck can be shown clearly to be wrong is more a reason for tribute than a cause for scorn and derision.

Without a theoretical blueprint there is no basis for designing situations in which a prediction or clinical notion can be determined to be correct or incorrect, accurate or inaccurate. Without theory predictions are not made or are made but not justified, and do not fit into some larger context. Without theory clinical notions are not formulated in ways that permit crucial tests. To be sure, research is conducted and data are gathered, and clinical notions are espoused and tried out. But without theory data are confusing and difficult to interpret in a compelling, definitive way. Data are not churned out in neat little bundles that obviously mean this or that. On the contrary, data must be organized according to rules. Theory is a source for these rules and is a basis for interpreting data. If data can be organized any way and if interpretations are plucked out of thin air, then data will be organized and interpreted in ways that are most compatible with a particular point of view. Alternative organizations and rival interpretations can be blissfully ignored. However, when virtually any organization or interpretation will do, then all organizations and interpretations are arbitrary and meaningless. Fortunately, journal editorial processes contain these practices to some extent, but the notional dogma spewed forth by noted clinicians remains virtually unbridled.

In summary, theory development in behaviour therapy is needed. The absence of theory may contribute to the alarming tendency of clinical psychologists (Garfield and Kurtz, 1976) and behaviour therapists (Swan and MacDonald, 1978) to describe themselves as 'eclectic'. The flight to eclecticism obscures the detrimental effects of having no theory. Eclecticism provides no answer to the questions raised above (p. 237). It gives no clue about methods of assessment, it encourages treatment planning by intuition, it is silent on the need for predictions about treatment effectiveness, it does not indicate how therapy should be evaluated and, beyond *ad hoc*, commonsense explanations, it cannot shed much light on the meaning of evaluative data.

Eysenck has much to offer on this score in terms of the substance of his theories and related procedures, how such theories and procedures can be developed, and what form they might take. The practice of behaviour therapy should be irrevocably wedded to theory if we are to be guided by our founding principles. Unfortunately, much of current practice in behaviour therapy falls short of this ideal. It is to Eysenck's credit that he repeatedly and forcibly reminds us of the necessity for theory and practice to go hand in hand.

## TRAITS: EYSENCK'S ADVOCACY AND BEHAVIOUR THERAPISTS' RESISTANCE

Eysenck's desire to understand the nature of human behaviour surpasses the strength of his alliance with mainstream behaviour therapy. Consequently, at any given time certain of his positions have been at odds with those supported by most behaviour therapists. The necessity for theory and, more specifically, personality theory, is one example of this discordance. The issue of traits, fundamental to Eysenck's research (Eysenck, 1947, 1982), is another. From its inception behaviour therapy was founded on the supremacy accorded to observable behaviour, and the rejection of traits and all other hypothetical constructs. Traits were odious because of their association with psychoanalytic notions about underlying causes of overt 'symptomatic' behaviour. Traits were also held to be inevitably linked to tautological reasoning, and denigrated as 'explanatory fictions' that allowed confusion to masquerade as understanding. Behaviour therapists' antipathy for traits has endured over the years.

Sustained resistance to Eysenck's particular conception of traits is not surprising inasmuch as he defines traits in terms of genetics, underlying biological factors and behavioural causation (1963, 1976c). From a broader perspective the rejection of traits is puzzling in view of the manner in which early learning theorists (e.g., Hull) used unobservable constructs with impunity.

Traits can be defined and used in various ways. Regrettably, behaviour therapists seem to believe that acceptance of traits must imply that overt behaviour is caused by underlying biological factors and predispositions. This was and is one way to conceptualize traits (Edwards and Endler, 1983), but it is not the only way. Long ago many well-known theorists (e.g. Burt 1941) clarified the technical nature of trait construction and showed conclusively that traits do not necessarily imply underlying causes of behaviour (Anastasi, 1983). For some reason this argument did not assuage the concerns of the founders of behaviour therapy other than Eysenck. While this intransigence may have served an historical purpose, this position has not only outlived its usefulness but also represents a major barrier to new developments in contemporary behaviour therapy.

When Paul (1966) challenged behaviour therapists to develop specific interventions for individuals with specific problems, an important aspect of his mandate seems to have eluded most behaviour therapists. There seems to have been little recognition of the need for organizing principles and procedures to accomplish the task of describing complex individuals with complex problems in a coherent, integrated and useful fashion. Simple-minded ABC-type methods of assessment and narrow-minded, linear conceptions could not and probably never will be able to deal effectively with behavioural complexity. The few behaviour therapists who have recognized this dilemma have not made significant progress in modifying the ways in which their colleagues deal with complexity (Hersen, 1981). In the early sixties Staats (1981) began to work with traits (e.g., self-concept) which he defined as classes of learned, interrelated behaviours, and Wahler (1975) has utilized the concept of 'response clusters' for ten years. In 1980 the psychiatric manual, *DSM III*, sets forth correlated behaviours associated with various psychiatric conditions.

Levy (1983) points out that no form of therapy has devoted attention to establishing treatment (x) traits relationships, and he contends correctly that this failure is probably due to theoretical inadequacies in the various approaches to therapy. This is clearly the case in behaviour therapy and resolution of the treatment-patient match problem may require some basic theoretical developments.

Behaviour therapy's accommodation of trait-related ideas has progressed at a snail's pace, perhaps because recent developments in this area have created and will continue to create extraordinary predicaments for behaviour therapists. At the heart of this dilemma is the necessity of pitting one of behaviour therapy's fundamental assumptions against another. Some of this conflict is more apparent than real, but some may result in essential modifications of the nature of behaviour therapy.

Ultimate reliance on empirical evidence is a cornerstone of behaviour therapy. Of no lesser importance is the assumption that behaviour is largely a product of environmental influences and learning processes. A relatively minor conflict between these aspects of behaviour therapy is created by the growing evidentiary basis (Levy, 1983) for the proposition that clusters of behaviours vary together in systematic ways. The validity of this proposition cannot be discounted because of glaring flaws in design or psychometric procedures. A resolution of the conflict created by this evidence could be accomplished without doing damage to any fundamental assumption of behaviour therapy, if behaviour therapists accepted traits defined as correlated clusters of behaviour (Voeltz and Evans, 1982).

By adopting this position behaviour therapists would lose nothing and would reap many benefits. For example, conceptualizing behaviour in terms of hierarchical behaviour clusters is effective in accounting for what psychodynamic therapists refer to as 'symptom substitution' (Kazdin, 1982). Even greater utility could be derived if research efforts were devoted to determining what behaviours tend to covary predictably. Wahler argues, for example, that modification of certain types of behaviours, which he refers to as 'keystone' behaviours, is likely to lead to changes in many other related behaviours. There is no reason to assume that all of these correlated changes would be positive. Hence, assessing and evaluating in terms of response clusters would permit the determination of unintended positive changes and would also take account of unanticipated negative outcomes.

A problem of more far-reaching proportion is created by the burgeoning evidence supporting the proposition that traits are underpinned by genetic predispositions (Henderson, 1982) and biological influences (Depue, 1979; Flor-Henry, 1976; Sachar, 1982). Incorporating these ideas into the mainstream of behaviour therapy would require major changes, but ignoring this evidence would represent disregard of the fundamental importance behaviour therapists attach to empirical data. However this dilemma is resolved, sooner or later, behaviour therapists will endorse a position *vis-à-vis* traits that is similiar to what Eysenck has been espousing for years.

Current methods of behavioural assessment do not take sufficient account of response clusters because theory and research have not progressed far enough to conceptualize and define what is to be measured. If advances are made on the conceptual level, technical problems involved in behavioural assessment could be eradicated. In fact, promising advances are already underway (e.g., Haynes, 1983).

## EYSENCK'S APPLICATION OF THEORY AND TRAITS

Eysenck (1982) believes that his recent theoretical formulation of the origin and treatment of a large class of neuroses represents a unified theory. Admittedly, the 'unified' aspect of this claim has not inspired much support, but his ideas are good ones nonetheless. Simply stated, he argues that the origin of neuroses can be accounted for in terms of Pavlovian conditioning (his inclusion of the notion of preparedness and of two types of anxiety incubation enhances the heuristic value of his previous formulations without damaging them insofar as both of these additions can be subsumed by Pavlovian principles). Further, he argues that extinction should be the basis for treatment of all such neuroses. In formulating this position Eysenck interweaves Pavlovian (Type B) conditioning principles, the personality dimensions (that overarch specific traits) of psychoticism, extraversion and neuroticism, and propositions about conditionability to explain why different modes of treatment (e.g., flooding versus desensitization) should be used for different neurotic configurations.

The notion that Eysenck's work is of little practical value to clinicians is an astonishing prejudice that is without foundation. Actually, it is the practical aspect of Eysenck's work that may persuade behaviour therapists to reappraise him. To illustrate, Eysenck's theoretical work provides answers to the questions raised above (p. 237). Such answers are not only practical but essential to routine clinical functioning. Further, as illustrated above, Eysenck's theoretical work sheds light on the problem of treatment-patient match, and this problem also confronts behavioural practitioners on a daily basis. If for no other reason than behaviour therapists' lack of progress in this area, Eysenck's work deserves (re)consideration.

## EYSENCK'S CONTRIBUTIONS: AN OVERVIEW OF SELECTED TOPICS

Given its magnitude, it is impossible to cover Eysenck's work in a single chapter. Therefore, a few examples of his contributions to behaviour therapy are presented for illustrative purposes.

First, his theoretical work (Eysenck, 1982) has a very important bearing on the issue of negative outcomes in psychotherapy. The notion that in some cases behaviour therapy might not only be ineffective but that it might actually cause a patient to become worse is generally ignored by run-of-the-mill behaviour therapists. Eysenck may be the only well-known behaviour therapist to acknowledge negative outcomes. In fact, he goes several steps further and uses incubation theory to explain how negative outcome in behaviour therapy could be caused by the misapplication of a particular technique or by the interpersonal style of the therapist! The topic of negative outcomes in behaviour therapy should be given high priority by practitioners and scholars alike (Barbrack, 1985), and can no longer be dismissed by the perennial champions of behaviour therapy's innocence and virtue.

Second, Eysenck (1970) has developed interesting assessment procedures. These procedures specify what information he believes to be relevant for diagnostic purposes and, as indicated, this specification is vitally important to clinical practice. His assessment procedures elicit information about the aetiological factors of psychological disorders and, in turn, this information forms the basis for selecting appropriate treatments. The gap between assessment data and treatment selection has long been a topic of despair in clinical psychology. The substance or the form of Eysenck's approach to this problem may provide the basis for establishing the 'missing link'.

Finally, Eysenck's writing (Eysenck, 1963, 1971; Eysenck and Levey, 1971) reveals an abiding interest in neuropsychological and biophysiological topics. In the past clinical psychologists were so bent on disposing of the 'medical model' that they launched an indiscriminate boycott of the entire field of medicine. Maintaining this position now would be irresponsible in view of recent and relatively spectacular developments in psychopharmacology (Alford, 1983), neuroradiology (e.g., Caparulo, Cohen and Rothman, 1981) and neuropsychology (Golden, 1981). As the

popularity of these areas grows, clinical psychologists, including behaviour therapists, will 'discover' ideas that Eysenck has expressed over the last thirty years.


## EYSENCK'S ANALYSIS OF THERAPEUTIC EFFECTIVENESS


Eysenck's original critical appraisal (1952) of the putative effectiveness of psychotherapy sent shock waves through the clinical psychology establishment. Subsequent
publications (Eysenck, 1960b, 1965), while even more negative, have tended to cause
less of a stir, perhaps because of a general awareness that his criticisms will be
dissected, reanalyzed, rebutted and eventually dismissed. Garfield (1981) believes that
Eysenck's first critique had a salutary effect and speculates that an upswing in
research on therapeutic effectiveness may have been spurred by Eysenck's challenge.

Creating a climate in which clinicians must be less complacent and must perform
more competently is a worthy goal, but it is not clear that this was Eysenck's aim. If
this were his aim, then it is not clear that he considered the realistic cost/benefit
aspects of his attack (Barbrack, in press). In any case we believe that Eysenck's
sustained effort in this area has contributed to widespread scepticism about therapeutic effectiveness and to the development of stringent accountability measures that are
imminent in psychotherapy (Clairborn, Stricker and Bent, 1982).

Assuming that Eysenck has contributed to the development of external accountability in clinical psychology, is this a worthwhile contribution? We believe it is, but
because so little is known about the behaviours of field-based practitioners, it is
difficult to support this attitude with a conviction based on empirical data. For what
they are worth, the results of a recent survey (Norcross and Prochaska, 1983) of
private practitioners indicate that a significant portion of clinical work may be
conducted by middle-aged eclectics, who most often engage in marital therapy and
feel quite satisfied with themselves as therapists. These practitioners gave no
indication of dreading critical appraisals of their work, perhaps because the insidious,
dulling effects of eclecticism obstruct their views of the imminence of external review.

Because of the intimate nature of the therapeutic relationship, some may regard
accountability as an unnecessary intrusion and thereby resent Eysenck for whatever
role he may have played in bringing it about. For those who live in North America,
such unwarranted feelings can be eliminated by reconceptualizing psychotherapy in
terms of a business model. At least in the USA and Canada, private sector behaviour
therapists are in the business of selling a service. It is to their advantage that patients
feel the need for therapy, and believe that receiving it fulfils their expectations and
justifies the expense. Behaviour therapists must create and maintain these positive
attitudes or else go out of business. Likewise, behaviour therapists have a vested
interest in preventing, or at least discrediting, public pronouncements that behaviour
therapy is ineffective or potentially harmful. With so much at stake, should behaviour
therapists be allowed to be the only ones to evaluate their own effectiveness? The
answer is 'obvious', depending on one's point of view. In any case Eysenck's
advantage as an evaluator of therapy is that he is not a practitioner and has no
financial investment in the outcomes of such evaluations. The likelihood of his being
more objective in his evaluations is great but, surprisingly, this point is never made. If
mentioned at all, his status as a non-practitioner is often a basis for discounting his
work because 'he doesn't know what it's like to do therapy.'

Thus far behaviour therapists have had little cause for concern over Eysenck's penchant for critical investigation. In fact, behaviour therapy has fared well from his comments on the comparative effectiveness of various therapeutic approaches (Eysenck, 1978). As espoused, behaviour therapy is more clearly defined and demonstrably more effective than its rivals. However, this is no reason for complacency. Behaviour therapist 'drift' is a reality (Hersen, 1981). After drifting for some time it is probable that behaviour therapists are no longer practising behaviour therapy as espoused and supported in the literature. Data gathering, homework assignments and goal-based evaluations are often early casualties in this process (Barlow, 1981). Hence, external review may result in some surprises for some behaviour therapists. Perhaps it is unfortunate that behaviour therapy has not been the focus of an Eysenckian attack. If nothing else, this experience might have inoculated behaviour therapists against the stress of having their failures exposed in public.

## EYSENCK'S INFLUENCE ON BEHAVIOUR THERAPY: A 'FINAL' ANALYSIS

Whether one considers Eysenck a gadfly or guardian angel, it is unwise to dismiss him too casually. Still, when all is told, the conclusion that Eysenck's influence on behaviour therapy is a fraction of what it could be is unavoidable. The reason may be, in part, related to the following: (1) he writes so clearly and specifically that others understand his position and dismiss it for the sake of something they like better even if it is not understood nearly as well; (2) his manner of expression is dogmatic; (3) the material he presents is too technical and demands much effort to read; (4) his approach demands that treatment plans be formulated on the basis of psychological knowledge, that predictions be made about treatment effectiveness and that treatment be assessed against this standard—and it is much easier to 'fly by the seat of your pants' and 'shoot the breeze' in therapy sessions; (5) behaviour therapists may find data gathering and treatment evaluation tedious and even aversive; and (6) some behaviour therapists may not understand or appreciate the practical value of theory.

We believe that these and other barriers to Eysenck's influence will fall as the knowledge base of behaviour therapy expands. For influence already exerted in behaviour therapy, Eysenck has earned our gratitude. As behaviour therapy continues to evolve, one day Eysenck will receive the full measure of appreciation his unique contribution deserves.

## REFERENCES

Alford, G. S. (1983) 'Pharmocotherapy', in Hersen, M., Kazdin, A. E. and Bellack, A. S. (Eds.), *The Clinical Psychology Handbook*, New York, Pergamon Press.

American Psychiatric Association (1980) *Diagnostic and Statistical Manual of Mental Disorders*, 3rd ed., Washington, D. C., American Psychiatric Association.

Anastasi, A. (1983) 'Evolving trait concepts', *American Psychologist*, **38**, pp. 175–84.

Bandura, A. (1977) 'Self efficacy: Toward a unifying theory of behavior change', *Psychological Review*, **84**, pp. 191–215.

Barbrack, C. R. (1985) 'Negative outcomes in behavior therapy', in Mays D. T. and Franks C. M. (Eds.) *Negative Outcome in Psychotherapy and What to Do about It*, New York, Springer.

Barbrack, C. R. (in press) 'What's the meta? Meta-analysis data in search of an information audience (that's what)', *The Behavioral and Brain Sciences*.

Barlow, D. H. (1980) 'Behavior therapy: The next decade', *Behavior Therapy*, **11**, pp. 315–28.

Barlow, D. H. (1981) *Behavioral Assessment of Adult Disorders*, New York, Guilford.

*The Behavioral and Brain Sciences* (1979), **2**, pp. 155–99, special issue.

Burt, C. (1941) *The Factors of the Mind: An Introduction to Factor Analysis in Psychology*, New York, Macmillan.

Caparulo, B. K., Cohen, D. J. and Rothman, S. L. (1981) 'Computed tomographic brain scanning in children with developmental neuropsychiatric disorders', *Journal of the American Academy of Child Psychiatry*, **20**, pp. 1338–57.

Clairborn, W. L., Stricker., G. and Bent, R. J. (1982) 'Peer review and quality assurance', (Special issue), *Professional Psychology*, **13, 1**.

Depue, R. A. (1979) *The Psychobiology of the Depressive Disorders*, New York, Academic Press.

Edwards, J. M. and Endler, N. J. (1983) 'Personality research', in Hersen, M., Kazdin, A. E. and Bellack, A. S. (Eds.), *The Clinical Psychology Handbook*, New York, Pergamon Press.

Eysenck, H. J. (1944) 'States of high suggestability and the neuroses', *American Journal of Psychology*, **57**, pp. 406–11.

Eysenck, H. J. (1947) *Dimensions of Personality*, London, Routledge and Kegan Paul.

Eysenck, H. J. (1952) 'The effects of psychotherapy', *Journal of Consulting Psychology*, **16**, pp. 319–24.

Eysenck, H. J. (1957) *The Dynamics of Anxiety and Hysteria*, London, Routledge and Kegan Paul.

Eysenck, H. J. (1960a) 'The nature of behaviour therapy', in Eysenck, H. J. (Ed.), *Experiments in Behaviour Therapy*, New York, Macmillan.

Eysenck, H. J. (1960b) 'The effects of psychotherapy', in Eysenck, H. J. (Ed.), *Handbook of Abnormal Psychology*, London, Pitman.

Eysenck, H. J. (1963) 'Biological basis of personality', *Nature*, **199**, pp. 1031–4.

Eysenck, H. J. (1965) 'The effects of psychotherapy', *International Journal of Psychiatry*, **1**, pp. 99–142.

Eysenck, H. J. (1970) 'A dimensional system of psychodiagnostics', in Mahrer, A. R. (Ed.), *New Approaches to Personality Classification*, New York, Columbia University Press.

Eysenck, H. J. (1971) 'Human typology, higher nervous activity, and factor analysis', in Nebylitsyn, V. D. and Gray, J. A. (Eds.), *Biological Bases of Individual Behavior*, New York, Academic Press.

Eysenck, H. J. (1972) 'Behavior therapy as a scientific discipline', *Journal of Consulting and Clinical Psychology*, **36**, pp. 314–19.

Eysenck, H. J. (1976a) 'Genetic factors in personality development', in Kaplan, A. R. (Ed.), *Human Behavior Genetics*. Springfield, Ill., C. C. Thomas.

Eysenck, H. J. (1976b) 'The learning theory model of neurosis: A new approach', *Behavioural Research and Therapy*, **14**, pp. 251–68.

Eysenck, H. J. (1976c) *The Measurement of Personality*, Lancaster, Medical and Technical Publishers.

Eysenck, H. J. (1977) *Crime and Personality*, 3rd ed., London, Paladin.

Eysenck, H. J. (1978) 'An exercise in mega-silliness', *American Psychologist*, **33**, p. 517.

Eysenck, H. J. (1979a) 'The place of theory in the assessment of the effects of psychotherapy', *Behavioral Assessment*, **1**, pp. 77–84.

Eysenck, H. J. (1979b) 'The conditioning model of neurosis', *The Behavioral and Brain Sciences*, **2**, pp. 155–66.

Eysenck, H. J. (1982) 'Neobehavioristic (S-R) theory', in Wilson, G. T. and Franks, C. M. (Eds.), *Contemporary Behavior Therapy*, New York, Guilford Press.

Eysenck, H. J. and Eysenck, S. B. G. (1963) *The Eysenck Personality Inventory*, San Diego Education and Industrial Testing Service, London, University of London Press.

Eysenck, H. J. and Levey, A. (1971) 'Conditioning introversion-extraversion and the strength of the nervous system', in Nebylitsyn, V. D. and Gray, J. A. (Eds.), *Biological Bases of Individual Behavior*, New York, Academic Press.

Eysenck, H. J. and Rachman, S. (1965) *The Causes an Cures of Neurosis*, San Diego, Calif., Robert R. Knapp.

Flor-Henry, P. (1976) 'Lateralized temporal-limbic dysfunction and psychopathology', *Annals of the New York Academy of Science*, **280**, pp. 777–95.

Franks, C. M. (1982) 'Behavior therapy: An overview', in Franks, C. M., Wilson, C. T., Kendall, P. C. and Brownell K. D. (Eds.), *Annual Review of Behavior Therapy: Theory and Practice*, New York, Guilford.

Franks, C. M. and Barbrack, C. R. (1983a) 'Behavior therapy with adults: An integrative perspective', in

Hersen, M., Kazdin, A. E. and Bellack, A. S. (Eds.), *The Clinical Psychology Handbook*, New York, Pergamon Press.

Franks, C. M. and Barbrack, C. R. (1983b) 'New applications for old principles' [Review of *Behavior Modification: Principles, Issues and Applications*, 2nd ed.], *Contemporary Psychology*, **27.**

Franks, C. M. and Wilson, G. T. (1975) *Annual Review of Behavior Therapy*, Vol. 3, New York, Brunner/Mazel.

Garfield, S. L. (1981) 'Psychotherapy: A 40 year appraisal', *American Psychologist*, **36,** pp. 174–83.

Garfield, S. L. and Kurtz, R. M. (1976) 'Clinical psychologists in the 1970s', *American Psychologist*, **31,** pp. 1–9.

Gibson, H. B. (1981) *Hans Eysenck: The Man and His Work*, London, Peter Owen.

Golden, C. J. (1981) *Diagnosis and Rehabilitation in Clinical Neuropsychology*, Springfield, Ill., Charles C. Thomas.

Gray, J. A. (1972) 'The psychophysiological nature of introversion-extraversion: A modification of Eysenck's theory', in Nebylitsyn, V. D. and Gray, J. A. (Eds.), *Biological Bases of Individual Behavior*, New York, Academic Press.

Haynes, S. N. (1983) 'Behavioral assessment', in Hersen, M., Kazdin, A. E. and Bellack, A. S. (Eds.), *The Clinical Psychology Handbook*, New York, Pergamon Press.

Henderson, N. D. (1982) 'Human behavior genetics', in Rosensweig, M. R. and Porter, L. W. (Eds.), *Annual Review of Psychology*, Palo Alto, Calif., Annual Reviews.

Hersen, M. (1981) 'Complex problems require complex solutions', *Behavior Therapy*, **12,** pp. 15–29.

Kazdin, A. E. (1982) 'Symptom substitution, generalization, and response covariation: Implications for psychotherapy outcome', *Psychological Bulletin*, **91,** pp. 349–65.

Levy, L. H. (1983) 'Trait approaches', in Hersen, M., Kazdin, A. E. and Bellack, A. S. (Eds.), *The Clinical Psychology Handbook*, New York, Pergamon Press.

Norcross, J. C. and Prochaska, J. O. (1983) 'Psychotherapists in independent practice: Some findings and issues', *Professional Psychology: Research and Practice*, **14,** pp. 869–81.

Paul, G. L. (1966) *Insight versus Desensitization in Psychotherapy*, Springfield, Calif., Stanford University Press.

Peterson, D. R. (1976) 'Is psychology a profession?', *American Psychologist*, **31,** pp. 572–81.

Sachar, E. J. (1982) 'Endocrine abnormalities in depression', in Paykel, E. S. (ED.), *Handbook of Affective Disorders*, New York, Guilford.

Skinner, B. F. (1953) *Science and Human Behavior*, New York, Macmillan.

Skinner, B. F. (1974) *About Behaviorism*, New York, Knopf.

Staats, A. W. (1981) 'Pragmatic behaviorism, unified theory, unified theory construction methods and the Zeitgeist of separatism', *American Psychologist*, **36,** pp. 239–56.

Strupp, H. H. (1981) 'Clinical research and practice, and the crisis of confidence', *Journal of Consulting and Clinical Psychology*, **49,** p. 216.

Swan, G. E. and MacDonald, M. L. (1978) 'Behavior therapy is practice: A national survey of behavior therapists', *Behavior Therapy*, **9,** pp. 799–807.

Voeltz, L. M. and Evans, I. M. (1982) 'The assessment of behavioral interrelationships in child behavior therapy', *Behavior Assessment*, **4,** pp. 131–65.

Wahler, R. G. (1975) 'Some structural aspects of deviant child behavior', *Journal of Applied Behavior Analysis*, **8,** pp. 27–42.

Wilson, G. T. (1982) 'Psychotherapy process and procedure: The behavioral mandate', *Behavior Assessment*, **13,** pp. 291–312.

# 14. On Sterile Paradigms and the Realities of Clinical Practice: Critical Comments on Eysenck's Contribution to Behaviour Therapy

ARNOLD A. LAZARUS

> In taking stock of the situation I observe how many of us seem so stupefied by admiration of physical science that we believe psychology in order to succeed need only imitate the models, postulates, methods and language of physical science. (Gordon W. Allport)

Pragmatically-minded clinicians will gravitate to those theories and methods that have the greatest heuristic merit and are most relevant to the exigencies of patient care and responsibility. Scientist-practitioners will display limited tolerance for the contributions of academicians whose cogent comments are restricted to the intellectual icons contained in their ivory towers. In terms of a 'survival of the befitting', theories that fail to generate techniques which meet the needs of a wide spectrum of the clinical population will soon fall into disfavour—even if elegantly worded and supported by seemingly immaculate data. Thus, Eysenck's (1947, 1952a, 1953) books on the dimensional analysis of personality, as well as his treatise on Pavlovian theory and psychiatric practice (Eysenck, 1957), which were required readings during my graduate studies in the mid-1950s, have gathered dust in some forgotten corner of my library. On any bookshelf the volumes that are dog-eared from frequent reference by clinicians in search of pragmatic leads are not likely to bear the Eysenckian imprimatur. Consequently, I lost touch with Eysenck's offerings during the past two decades, but upon accepting the invitation to write this essay, I perused some of his current articles and chapters on behaviour theory and therapy.

Behaviour therapy has come a long way since Eysenck's (1959, 1960, 1964) first foray into the field, and I was curious to see what impact recent developments have had on his earlier thinking. The answer in two words is 'zero impact'. Eysenck (1982,

Acknowledgment: I am grateful to Dr Allen Fay and Dr Terry Wilson, whose incisive comments enhanced the accuracy and the organization of this critique.

247

1983) has clung to the outmoded and solipsistic view that 'all neurotic disorders are curable by means of Pavlovian extinction.' As I shall emphasize, the field has moved away from vague medical terms such as 'neurotic' and 'cure', toward operational and quantifiable descriptions (for example, avoidance behaviour, negative self-statements, rapid ejaculation, tachycardia), and the value of animal analogues for elucidating affective reactions in human beings has fallen into disrepute. In a curious *ex cathedra* statement Eysenck (1982) alleges that the decision by the American Psychiatric Association to delete the term 'neurosis' is 'based on political pressures and scholastic infighting' (p. 262). Actually, it is in keeping with the modern 'problem-oriented record approach' in medicine (Weed, 1968) and psychiatry (Hayes-Roth, Longabaugh and Ryback, 1972).

From a practitioner's perspective a most telling point is that Eysenck has been 'concerned with the *origin* of the neurosis, not so much with its maintenance' (Eysenck, 1982, p. 259). It is in fact the secondary gains, eliciting stimuli, and other precipitating and *maintaining factors* that are the primary concerns of behavioural clinicians. 'Most clinicians realize that presenting complaints are often tangentially related to the client's fundamental problems. How to ferret out the relevant antecedents, how to identify the significant problems, and how to discern those subtle and elusive but critical maintaining variables—these are the concerns that confront practitioners' (Woolfolk and Lazarus, 1979).

Eysenck (1982) argues that 'to have a proper theory of treatment, a proper theory of the origins of neurosis is required' (p. 216). This is highly debatable, but it does explain his preoccupation with the putative origins of psychological dysfunction. There are numerous maladies for which the understanding of origins has had no impact on eventual remedies. This is not to decry the ultimate value of seeking to understand the origins of maladaptive behaviour and emotional suffering (which still appears to be a long way off!). It must nevertheless be stressed that in many therapeutic areas effective remedies have existed, and diseases have been cured without any understanding of aetiological factors. Moreover, the origin of a condition may have little bearing on its appropriate treatment. For example, childhood autism does not stem from faulty learning *per se*, yet the application of classical and operant conditioning procedures can have salubrious effects (for example, Lovaas, 1977; Rimland, 1964; Steffen and Karoly, 1982). Does Eysenck believe that since techniques based on conditioning paradigms can overcome various types of maladaptive behaviours, these maladaptive behaviours must, in turn, have been acquired by conditioning? Lazarus (1971) termed this 'the effect-cause fallacy', and pointed to Davison's (1968) caveat that 'from evidence regarding efficacy in changing behavior, one cannot claim to have demonstrated that the problem evolved in an analogous fashion.' Indeed, even if psychiatric problems were shown to stem from repressed complexes, the treatments of choice for many conditions would still be desensitization, assertiveness training and other *behavioural* techniques, rather than free association or related psychoanalytic methods.

What is the cornerstone of Eysenck's theory of the origin of 'neurotic' behaviour? Classical conditioning! He eschews the contemporary point of view in which 'both classical and instrumental conditioning are regarded as cognitively determined phenomena' (Franks and Wilson, 1979, p. 17) and asserts that 'it is Pavlovian conditioning that speaks the language of the paleocortex' (Eysenck, 1982, p. 258). Yet Franks and Wilson (1979) refer to 'the tenuous foundations upon which conditioning, presumed to be one of the cornerstones of behavior therapy, is based

... and to the limitations of the various forms of conditioning as explanatory, descriptive, or predictive concepts in behavior therapy' (p. 16). Franks (1984) states: 'Conditioning and S-R learning theory principles and techniques were once supposed to represent the heart of behavior therapy. Unfortunately, while their past contributions to behavior therapy are impressive, there is little reason to suggest that either conditioning or S-R learning theory alone can serve as an adequate conceptual basis for the behavior therapy of today. The word "conditioning" is itself devoid of precise meaning.' According to Franks and Barbrack (1983), 'The precise relationships between classical and operant conditioning remain equivocal and some would doubt whether conditioning as a concept exists at all' (p. 511). Nevertheless, for Eysenck (1982), 'various subtraumatic UCSs (unconditioned stimuli) result in the final CR (neurotic breakdown)' (p. 216). While paying lip-service to the fact that 'peacetime neuroses' do not result from traumatic UCSs but have an insidious onset, Eysenck makes much of Watson and Rayner's (1920) well-known aversive training of Little Albert, and Campbell, Sanderson and Laverty's (1964) highly *traumatic* learning experiments wherein people were subjected to chemically induced respiratory paralysis (the so-called unconditioned response). The problem, of course, is that at the human level, sustained *conditioned emotional responses* (i.e., those not subject to rapid extinction) are almost impossible to obtain, even when subjects are carefully selected for their high levels of 'neuroticism', autonomic lability and 'introversion', and even when 'biologically prepared' stimuli are introduced (cf. Franks and Wilson, 1978). Consequently, Eysenck is forced to rely on *eyeblink conditioning*—hardly a prototype of 'neurotic learning' or a 'conditioned emotional reaction'!

Actually, Eysenck has provided a tenable theory to account for persistent maladaptive behaviours and emotional disturbances that stem from traumatic antecedents. Among my present patients are two rape victims, and a man whose pervasive anxiety and phobias were precipitated by a near-fatal car accident. Eysenck's theory of a particular stress impinging upon someone whose genetic constitution and learning history render him or her susceptible to 'anxiety' and/or 'hysteria' seems to fit these cases. His notion of incubation (Eysenck, 1979) can perhaps account for the unabated strength of the anxiety responses of these patients. But when applying such concepts to the remaining 90 per cent of my clients, I find them as much help as pre-Columbian maps would be to a modern-day navigator.

A pivotal issue that must be addressed is the extent to which those who have never practised therapy are likely to render useful judgments and insightful comments about the processes and methods of psychological treatment. This is not to gainsay their capacity to provide incisive criticisms of theories and outcome research. Unfortunately, Eysenck does not restrict himself to this level of discourse. In matters pertaining to basic assessment, technique selection and the nuances of client-therapist interaction, it may be argued that non-therapists who lack clinical skills and who have not experienced the 'battlefront conditions' of patient responsibility are likely to provide platitudes rather than pearls. By his own acknowledgment Eysenck (1965) never has been, and never could have been, a competent therapist.

> Individuals differ considerably in their ability to get on with other people, to have empathy with their troubles, to be sympathetic towards them, and to think of different ways of helping them....
> As one completely lacking in this ability, I have often felt that although my knowledge of learning theory is probably not much inferior to theirs, it would never, by itself, suffice to enable me to duplicate the splendid work that they are doing (p. 157).

His admirably frank disclosure of clinical inexperience has not deterred Eysenck from offering innumerable comments about treatment procedures and techniques. After editing two books on 'behaviour therapy' (Eysenck, 1960, 1964)—a potpourri of competent, pertinent and irrelevant papers—he has been regarded in some circles as an authority and spokesperson for behavioural treatments.

Since Eysenck is neither a clinical researcher nor a practising therapist, his role is essentially that of an influential armchair critic and commentator. Because of his prominence as a personality theorist and his eminence as an academician, Eysenck's pronouncements have seldom gone unnoticed. Thus, his initial inquiry into the effects of traditional psychotherapy (Eysenck, 1952b) had widespread reverberations. He had ventured into territory that was formerly sacrosanct, thereby arousing the ire of several high priests who worshipped at the altar of the psychoanalytic couch. Several years later, when first expounding the virtues of behaviour therapy, Eysenck (1959) played right into the hands of his critics. In bold italics he declared: *'Get rid of the symptom and you have eliminated the neurosis.'* As a beacon of clinical naïveté, the foregoing statement is probably unparalleled in the annals of therapeutics. Twenty-five years later behavioural researchers and practitioners alike are still struggling to live down a spate of pejorative labels. Behaviour therapy to this day is deemed to be narrow, superficial, mechanistic, symptom-centred and naïve by a majority of clinicians.

Of course, Eysenck was attempting to convey the idea that a *problem-focused approach* to therapy expedites clinical decision-making and sidesteps the Freudian quagmire of putative unconscious complexes and other untestable intrapsychic entities. But his lamentable emphasis on so-called 'symptoms' was not an isolated literary lapse or semantic *faux pas*. He has continued (Eysenck, 1982) to rely on medical or disease analogies, and he invokes underlying traits (for example, 'neuroticism') to account for various 'disorders' or 'neuroses' (why not maladaptive behaviours?), and he still advocates 'symptomatic treatment'. Webster's *Dictionary* defines *symptom* as follows: '1: subjective evidence of disease or physical disturbance 2: something that indicates the existence of something else.' Treating 'symptoms' is very much at variance with the basic behavioural precept—*identify and modify target behaviours.*

Eysenck's penchant for medical analogies is clearly exemplified in his discussion of the term 'relapse'. 'If a patient has brittle bones and breaks his leg skiing, the leg can be set and will heal in due course; if he goes skiing again and again breaks his leg, is that a relapse? Would it be a relapse if he broke his arm? A cured neurotic has as much risk of having a (second) neurotic attack as anyone else has of having a (first) attack' (Eysenck, 1970, p. 144). A term such as 'cured neurotic' stands in stark contrast to the descriptive, operational language used by behavioural practitioners. Successful behaviour therapy outcomes (individuals, couples, or families functioning more harmoniously as the result of diminished anxiety and augmented coping responses and social skills) have little bearing on recovery or relief from a disease, which is what 'cure' usually denotes. So-called ' neurotic attacks' and fractured bones might be apt descriptions of the 'combat neuroses' that some soldiers acquire under traumatic conditions, but as already emphasized, the clients we see in our daily practices usually suffer from insidious behavioural excesses and deficits that manifest themselves in chronic incapacities, often in the service of secondary gains and other functional rewards.

Lest it be thought that Eysenck has retracted his earlier viewpoint or modified his stance, the reader is referred to Eysenck, 1982, pp. 206–7, where he not only restates his 1959 position, but claims that it has 'stood the test of time remarkably well'. For Eysenck, behaviour therapy designates 'the use of classical conditioning techniques in connection with implementing changes in autonomic reactions of patients who regard their own behaviour as maladaptive.' Again, this narrow definition would exclude the vast majority of clients who seek our help. Eysenck maintains that behaviour therapy aims to 'cure' what he terms 'emotional disorders' by means of 'extinction'. He states that the management of 'behaviour disorders' through 'positive conditioning' falls outside the compass of behaviour therapy and belongs within the orbit of 'behaviour modification'. Yet his definition of behaviour therapy as 'the attempt to alter human *behaviour and emotion* in a beneficial manner according to the laws of modern learning theory' (Eysenck, 1964, p. 1) contradicts the foregoing dichotomy. In fairness, it must be said that Eysenck does recognize operant psychology but confines himself to the classical conditioning model to explain aetiology. Yet it remains unclear what place he accords behaviour modification in the therapist's arsenal.

Most theorists and therapists would agree that behaviour therapy can no longer be defined in terms of 'modern learning theory' and that it now transcends narrow stimulus-response formulations. Terms such as 'expectancies', 'encoding', 'plans', 'values' and 'self-regulatory systems', all operationally defined, have crept into the behaviour literature. Thus, Franks and Wilson (1978) designated 1976 'the Year of Cognition for both theoretician and practitioner' (p. vii), and stressed that the 'cognitive connection . . . is neither a passive fad nor indicative of a paradigm shift, and it is to be viewed neither as an independent third force nor as a putative link between the behavioral and psychodynamic enclaves' (p. 13). A year later, after thoroughly reviewing the behavioural literature, Franks and Wilson (1979) concluded that, among cognitive behaviour therapists, 'conditioning is gradually being deemphasized as a monolithic explanatory entity and, if the concept is used at all, it is given some minor role as an agent in certain circumscribed situations' (p. 7). Eysenck, however, has clung steadfastly to Pavlovian conditioning, and his only acknowledgment of the role of cognitive factors invokes Pavlov's second signalling system (Eysenck, 1976). Indeed, for him cognitive theories are anathema (see Eysenck, 1979). Thus, when introducing terms such as 'frustrative nonreward', 'conflict', 'uncertainty' and 'uncontrollability', he is quick to emphasize that 'these concepts can be defined operationally and their use does not render our theory "cognitive"' (Eysenck, 1982, p. 216).

It is important to illuminate the main drawbacks of Eysenck's proscriptive anti-cognitive position. Consider the following hypothetical experiment. We subject one group of children to Watson and Rayner's (1920) punishment paradigm (making a nocent noise contingent on contact with a white rat). Another group of children is simply but authoritatively told to avoid white rats because they carry deadly diseases.[1] Those children from each group with the strongest avoidance reactions to white rats are then subjected to a deconditioning experience. Following Jones (1924), the children are fed candy and ice cream while rats in cages are brought progressively nearer. The critical question is whether the children in the 'cognitive learning' versus 'sensory conditioning' group would become desensitized to (unafraid of) the rats. I would hypothesize that, without some verbal reassurance and/or modelling techniques, only those children who underwent the Watson type of sensory conditioning would respond to the Jones deconditioning procedure. In the cognitive learning group modelling may prove effective because, when seeing respected peers and responsible adults handling the supposedly noxious rats without harm, the children can *reason* that the animals do not carry deadly diseases. The point of this illustration is not to suggest that intellectual reasoning proceeds very far with phobic sufferers, but to underscore the fatuity of rigid stimulus-response behaviourism and to emphasize that the content of a phobia is no less important than its structure. The first group of children would be avoiding rats; the second group would be backing away from illness and death.[2]

Eysenck's omission of *cognitive content* appears to be the greatest lacuna in his thinking. Here is a prototypic example:

> Consider an imaginary experiment in which a male subject is instructed to imagine a certain type of explicit sexual situation. The investigator predicts (and finds, through the use of a penis plethysmograph) that after a given period of time an erection results. Thus a causal chain can be inferred from the instruction to the erection, involving an intervening variable that itself cannot be observed from the outside, but that has the same status as a drive or a habit. (Eysenck, 1982, p. 254)

Consonant with his S-R outlook, Eysenck delves no deeper into this image-in, erection-out connection. But suppose that the subject in this experiment begins with Eysenck's 'certain type of explicit sexual situation', and soon shifts to scenes of mutilation and carnage which happen to be idiosyncratically stimulating and sexually arousing. By ignoring the content of the so-called 'drive or habit', we lose the true clinical relevance of the experiment.

Eysenck has not retracted or revised his anachronistic view that behaviour therapy is best defined in terms of 'modern learning theory', despite trenchant criticisms from several quarters (for example, Locke, 1971; MacKenzie, 1977; Erwin, 1978). He (Eysenck, 1982) maintains that those 'who rely on the argument that no universally agreed theory of learning and conditioning exists, and that there are many anomalies that puzzle existing theories, are in error if they go on to argue that principles of behaviour therapy cannot be deduced from such theories as do exist' (p. 209). Moreover, he draws from the 'hard sciences' to underscore the point that two alternative theories often exist side by side in such areas as gravitation, heat and the theory of light. In his zeal to defend his position Eysenck misses an obvious but telling point. While physicists may espouse alternative views and embrace conflicting theories, there is nevertheless agreement regarding the parameters of the particular theories in question—Einstein's field theory may be at odds with the quantum theory of particle exchange, but physicists know the postulates that underlie these divergent theories. Psychologists, on the other hand, cannot agree on the axioms, postulates or principles that comprise so-called 'modern learning theory'. As Erwin (1978) has underscored, so-called laws of learning are either unconfirmed, tautologous or too restricting to have much relevance in the therapeutic arena.

According to Franks (1982): 'Gone are the days when behaviour therapy could readily be defined in terms of specific stimuli or something called modern learning theory. Gone are the days of reliance upon the clear-cut and unequivocal mechanisms of classical and operant conditioning' (p. 3). As Kazdin and Wilson (1978) underscore: 'The once simple definition of behaviour therapy as the application of "modern learning theory" (conditioning principles) to clinical disorders is now part of its short, successful, and often stormy history' (p. 1). The generally accepted definition advocated by the Association for Advancement of Behavior Therapy is: '. . . the primary application of principles derived from research in experimental and social psychology to alleviate human suffering and enhance human functioning.'

These differences in definition are fundamental. Eysenck's narrow outlook ignores the complexities that experimental and social psychologists have been dealing with explicitly. Thus, contemporary learning theorists have shown that 'thought' or 'cognition' must be included in any account of behaviour—especially human behaviour (Bower, 1978), and that humans (and animals) code inputs before they emit outputs. (Many years ago, Zener (1937) suggested the necessity of a cognitive theory to account for the Pavlovian conditioning of dogs.) Of course, Eysenck acknowledges that human beings *think*, but his S-R emphasis downplays the role of cognition, even in terms of the s-r mediational variety (cf. Davison, 1980). Thus, Eysenck (1982) stresses that 'it should not be assumed that vicarious experiences or informational instruction cannot be themselves viewed or explained in terms of conditioning' (p. 221), whereas I would be inclined to caution that it should not be assumed that conditioning is either a necessary or sufficient explanation of the impact of vicarious learning and informational instruction. As Meichenbaum and Butler (1980) have pointed out, 'psychologists have a penchant for finding one concept, one construct, and then pushing it to its limits across phenomena and across populations' (p. 32). We need not belabour the fact that the non-mediational model of conditioning provides an attenuated and truncated view of human functioning.

Nevertheless, Eysenck (1982) claims that his neo-behaviouristic position does not disregard cognitive factors, and includes considerations of language, imagery and symbolism. Yet he glosses over the complexities of semantic memory and symbolic generalization, and embraces Pavlov's (1927) contention that 'a word is as real a conditioned stimulus for man as all the other stimuli in common with animals. . . .' He also agrees with Wolpe (1968) that 'human neuroses are like those of animals *in all essential respects*' (p. 559). Many years ago Harlow (1953) underscored that 'the results from the investigation of simple behaviour may be very informative about even simpler behaviour, but very seldom are they informative about behaviour of greater complexity.' London (1964) inquired: 'May not men leap from cliffs for other reasons than those for which dogs salivate to bells?' (p. 38). (I am not dismissing the fact that human psychology has been enriched by laboratory experiments. Rather, my point is that their ultimate value for the practitioner is extremely limited. In terms of their therapeutic yield, it would seem that the operant conditioning model has proved most fertile.)

Eysenck unquestioningly and uncritically accepts certain dubious assumptions and draws conclusions that are, at best, polemical. As already mentioned, he constantly extrapolates from animal studies to human functioning, seemingly unaware that the complexity of human interaction renders infrahuman research a pale, if not sterile, paradigm of human learning. Allied to the foregoing is a syllogistic argument that goes something like this: 'Psychology in general, and behaviour therapy in particular, should adhere rigorously to the principles and procedures of well-established sciences such as genetics and biology. Since biochemical breakthroughs have resulted from infrahuman experiments, and since animal studies have shed light on the aetiology and treatment of certain human diseases, therefore psychology (behaviour therapy) should follow suit.' Thus, support for his 'theory of incubation', which purports to explain situations wherein seemingly unreinforced exposures to the CS result in increased fear responses rather than extinction (Eysenck, 1968, 1979), rests almost exclusively on data derived from dogs and rats.[3] Indeed, as the following paragraph illustrates, Eysenck seems to lose sight of the fact that rats are not part of the 'human field'.

The potency of 'threat' (CSs) as compared with UCS has also been demonstrated in the human field (Bridger & Mandel, 1964); the principle appears to have wide applicability (see also Cook & Harris, 1937). Maatsch (1959), like the authors mentioned, has reported a similar continued increase in an avoidance CR—in his case, in rats subjected to a single shock trial . . . . (Eysenck, 1982, p. 230)

Thus, after reviewing numerous studies on dogs, Eysenck finally addresses himself to humankind, only to revert to infrahumankind in the very next sentence! His 'neobehaviouristic (S-R) theory' overlooks a crucial metatheoretical point, namely that terms such as 'stimulus' and 'response' are *explanatory fictions*. 'They are words referring to concepts that we *make up* to explain what we call data' (Davison, 1980). Eysenck not only takes these terms seriously, but by wearing the blinders of bias, he is able to filter out the middle of the distribution, and ends up dividing things into two piles (for example, disorders of the first kind and disorders of the second kind; introversion and extraversion).

Let us briefly comment on his arbitrary distinction between what he terms 'disorders of the first kind' (anxieties, phobias, obsessive-compulsive states, reactive depressions) which he assumes arise out of classical conditioning, and 'disorders of the second kind' (psychopathic behaviour, alcoholism, hysteria, personality disorders, hypochondria, nocturnal enuresis) which purportedly stem from the failure of a conditioning process to occur. Distinctions of this kind have limited utility for practitioners since, in the real world, enuretic children, hypochondriacal patients and substance abusers often also suffer from anxieties and phobias, and Eysenck's putative differentiations become blurred. Similarly, his clear distinction between classical and instrumental or operant conditioning flies in the face of considerable evidence that has accrued with respect to their reciprocity. 'I believe that the two methods are sufficiently differentiated and can be shown to apply largely to different bodily systems, so that a clear distinction becomes desirable' (Eysenck, 1982, p. 208). The entire area of *biofeedback* has shown that autonomic reactions can be modified by direct input from an operant conditioning paradigm (for example, Birbaumer and Kimmel, 1979; Wickramasekera, 1975), and a 'clear distinction' is neither desirable nor theoretically valid.

Most of the criticisms directed at Eysenck seem to fall into two general clusters— he has not kept pace with the times, and he couches his terms in broad rather than specific categories. In addition to the many points already made in this chapter, an example of the former is that he still advocates 'extinction and neutralization of homosexual tendencies' (Eysenck, 1982, p. 260), and an example of the latter is his contention that 'behaviour therapy is significantly better in its effects than is either spontaneous remission, psychotherapy of the orthodox kind, or psychoanalysis' (Eysenck, 1982, p. 233). Having underscored his fixation on 'conditioning', 'neurosis' and so-called 'modern learning theory', there is no point in belabouring the fact that Eysenck's brand of iconoclasm is anything but topical or forward-looking. Let us 'end this essay by focusing once more on his sometimes meaning less (and often) inaccurate) generalizations.

To ask whether psychotherapy is effective (Eysenck, 1952b) is like posing the question, 'Is medicine effective?' In both instances one would at the very least ask for specific details about the particular methods (or medicines) employed, the maladies for which they had been prescribed and the context within which they were administered. Eysenck's (1982) statement that 'behaviour therapy is significantly better' (p. 233) is in contradiction to the specificity factor in psychotherapy (Lazarus, 1984), and is in marked contrast to Paul's (1967) admonition to ascertain '*what* treatment, by *whom*, is most effective for *this* individual, with *that* specific problem, and under *which* set of circumstances' (p. 111). For Eysenck, specificity implies the broad use of traits and types (introversion, neuroticism, dysthymia) rather than discrete problem areas. There is evidence that behaviour therapy is better than orthodox psychotherapy or psychoanalysis in the treatment of specific phobias, obsessive-compulsive disorders, assertion deficits, sexual inadequacy, some kinds of marital distress and various habits from tics to nocturnal enuresis (Rachman and Wilson, 1980). If Eysenck tended to speak at this level of specificity, meaningful dialogues might be possible. The degree of specificity now possible in our field of endeavour permits the addressing of issues such as dividing claustrophobic clients into predominantly 'behavioural reactors' and 'physiological reactors'. The former appear to respond better to exposure procedures than to relaxation, whereas the latter seem to be more suited to relaxation methods (Öst, Johansson and Jerrelmalm, 1982). Contrast the foregoing with Eysenck's attempt at specificity: '... differences in extraversion-introversion can be of crucial relevance for the appropriateness of such different therapies as Ellis's rational-emotive psychotherapy and C. Rogers's client-centered psychotherapy, with the former benefiting introverts, the latter extraverts' (Eysenck, 1982, p. 243). There are innumerable objections to the foregoing dichotomy, but suffice to say that rational-emotive therapy covers such a wide range of techniques (Ellis and Grieger, 1977) that Eysenck's claim is rendered meaningless.

In short, a practitioner who confined himself or herself to Eysenck's brand of 'behaviour therapy' would not only fail to make a living, but would also produce unstable outcomes, since virtually everyone who seeks therapy suffers both from various autonomic excesses as well as from behaviour or response deficits (Lazarus, 1976, 1981). As was emphasized some time ago (Lazarus, 1970), 'since Eysenck is not a therapist he can afford to think in dichotomous terms ... whereas most clinicians necessarily adopt multidimensional approaches to treatment.' My ultimate criticism is that a person of Eysenck's profound, even awesome, intellect who could have done so much to advance behaviour research and therapy has possibly undermined it.

## Notes

1   While Eysenck (1982) views informational instruction as a form of conditioning, this overinclusive definition stretches the term beyond its lexical boundaries and distorts its scientific meaning. English and English (1958) state that it is a form of 'theory begging' to use *conditioning* as a synonym for all kinds of learning, and argue that 'the term conditioning is best reserved for those forms of learning that bear a *close resemblance* to the experimental design of conditioning' (pp. 107–8).

2   By viewing all phobias as conditioned avoidance responses (or conditioned emotional reactions) Eysenck (1982) completely overlooks the fact that phobias can be used as manipulative ploys, as face-saving pretexts and as symbolic retreats. Moreover, his theory bypasses the critical role sometimes played by interpersonal factors in generating and maintaining phobic responses. As Lazarus (1966) underscored, crucial interpersonal conflicts and imitation (modelling) seem to be responsible for the genesis of several phobic disorders, and the patient's family system tends to maintain the character and extent of the identified patient's avoidance responses.

3   Eysenck has a penchant for finding an obscure reference that appears to support one of his contentions, whereupon he reifies the construct by making it seem like an established phenomenon. Such is the case with what Eysenck refers to as the 'Napalkov phenomenon', the mainstay of his incubation concept. The Napalkov (1963) study reported that following a single conditioning trial, repeated administration of the CS did not result in experimental extinction, but brought about increases in blood pressure of the dogs used in the investigation. Furthermore, Napalkov reported that in some cases this hypertensive state lasted over a year. To quote Levis and Malloy (1982): 'Given our current state of knowledge in this

area, such an effect is incredible to say the least as well as very difficult to reconcile with the existing literature. Furthermore, Napalkov only provided a one-paragraph summary of his work without citing a primary source of reference, making it impossible to determine exactly what experimental procedures were used.... Over (20) years have passed without replication, making it understandable why researchers in the area have ignored or are unfamiliar with his work' (p. 85).

# REFERENCES

Allport, G. W. (1947) 'Scientific models and human morals', *Psychological Review*, **54**, pp. 182–92.

Birbaumer, N. and Kimmel, H. D. (1979) *Biofeedback and Self-Regulation*, Hillsdale, N. J., Erlbaum.

Bower, G. H. (1978) 'Contacts of cognitive psychology with social learning theory', *Cognitive Therapy and Research*, **2**, pp. 123–47.

Campbell, D., Sanderson, R. and Laverty, S. G. (1964) 'Characteristics of a conditioned response in human subjects during extinction trials following a single traumatic conditioning trial', *Journal of Abnormal and Social Psychology*, **68**, pp. 627–39.

Davison, G. C. (1968) 'Systematic desensitization as a counter-conditioning process', *Journal of Abnormal Psychology*, **73**, pp. 91–9.

Davison, G. C. (1980) 'And now for something completely different: Cognition and little r', in Mahoney, M. J. (Ed.), *Psychotherapy Process*, New York, Plenum.

Ellis, A. and Grieger, R. (1977) *Handbook of Rational-Emotive Therapy*, New York, Springer.

English, H. B. and English, A. C. (1958) *A Comprehensive Dictionary of Psychological and Psychoanalytical Terms*, London, Longmans Green.

Erwin, E. (1978) *Behaviour Therapy; Scientific, Philosophical, and Moral Foundations*, Cambridge, Cambridge University Press.

Eysenck, H. J. (1947) *Dimensions of Personality*, London, Routledge and Kegan Paul.

Eysenck, H. J. (1952a) *The Scientific Study of Personality*, London, Routledge and Kegan Paul.

Eysenck, H. J. (1952b) 'The effects of pyschotherapy', *Journal of Consulting Psychology*, **16**, pp. 319–24.

Eysenck, H. J. (1953) *The Structure of Human Personality*, London, Methuen.

Eysenck, H. J. (1957) *The Dynamics of Anxiety and Hysteria*, London, Routledge and Kegan Paul.

Eysenck, H. J. (1959) 'Learning theory and behaviour therapy', *The Journal of Mental Science*, **105**, pp. 61–75.

Eysenck, H. J. (Ed.) (1960) *Behaviour Therapy and the Neuroses*, London, Pergamon Press.

Eysenck, H. J. (Ed.) (1964) *Experiments in Behaviour Therapy*, London, Pergamon Press.

Eysenck, H. J. (1965) *Fact and Fiction in Psychology*, Harmondsworth, Penguin Books.

Eysenck, H. J. (1968) 'A theory of incubation of anxiety fear responses', *Behaviour Research and Therapy*, **6**, pp. 309–22.

Eysenck, H. J. (1970) 'A mish-mash of theories', *International Journal of Psychiatry*, **9**, pp. 140–6.

Eysenck, H. J. (1976) 'Behaviour therapy—dogma or applied science?', in Feldman, P. and Broadhurst, A. (Eds.) *The Experimental Basis of Behaviour Therapy*, New York, Wiley.

Eysenck, H. J. (1979) 'The conditioning model of neurosis', *The Behavioural and Brain Sciences*, **2**, pp. 155–66.

Eysenck, H. J. (1982) 'Neobehavioristic (S-R) theory', in Wilson, G. T. and Franks, C. M. (Eds.) *Contemporary Behavior Therapy*, New York, Guilford Press, pp. 205–76.

Eysenck, H. J. (1983) Personal communication.

Franks, C. M. (1982) 'Behavior therapy: An overview', in Franks, C. M., Wilson, G. T., Kendall, P. C. and Brownell, K. D., *Annual Review of Behavior Therapy: Theory and Practice*, Vol. 8, pp. 1–38.

Franks, C. M. (Ed.) (1984) *New Developments in Behavior Therapy*, New York, Haworth Press.

Franks, C. M. and Barbrack, C. R. (1983) 'Behavior therapy with adults: An integrative perspective', in Hersen, M., Kazdin, A. E. and Bellack, A. S. (Eds.) *The Clinical Psychology Handbook*, New York, Pergamon Press.

Franks, C. M. and Wilson, G. T. (Eds.) (1978) *Annual Review of Behavior Therapy: Theory and Practice*, Vol. 6, New York, Brunner/Mazel.

Franks, C. M. and Wilson, G. T. (Eds.) (1979) *Annual Review of Behavior Therapy: Theory and Practice*, Vol. 7, New York, Brunner/Mazel.

Harlow, H. F. (1953) 'Mice, monkeys, men and motives', *Psychological Review*, **60**, pp. 23–32.

Hayes-Roth, F., Longabaugh, R. and Ryback, R. (1972) 'The problem oriented medical record and psychiatry', *British Journal of Psychiatry*, **121**, pp. 27–34.

Jones, M. C. (1924) 'The elimination of children's fears', *Journal of Experimental Psychology*, **7**, pp. 383–90.

Kazdin, A. E. and Wilson, G. T. (1978) *Evaluation of Behavior Therapy: Issues, Evidence, and Research Strategies*, Cambridge, Mass., Ballinger.

Lazarus, A. A. (1966) 'Broad spectrum behaviour therapy and the treatment of agoraphobia', *Behaviour Research and Therapy*, **4**, pp. 95–7.

Lazarus, A. A. (1970) 'Reply to discussants', *International Journal of Psychiatry*, **9**, pp. 162–4.

Lazarus, A. A. (1971) *Behavior Therapy and Beyond*, New York, McGraw-Hill.

Lazarus, A. A. (1976) *Multimodal Behavior Therapy*, New York, Springer.

Lazarus, A. A. (1981) *The Practice of Multimodal Therapy*, New York, McGraw-Hill.

Lazarus, A. A. (1984) 'The specificity factor in psychotherapy', *Psychotherapy in Private Practice*, **2**, pp. 43–8.

Levis, D. J. and Malloy, P. F. (1982) 'Research in infrahuman and human conditioning', in Wilson, G. T. and Franks, C. M. (Eds.), *Contemporary Behavior Therapy: Conceptual and Empirical Foundations*, New York, Guilford.

Locke, E. A. (1971) 'Is "behavior therapy" behavioristic?', *Psychological Bulletin*, **76**, pp. 318–27.

London, P. (1964) *The Modes and Morals of Psychotherapy*, New York, Holt, Rinehart and Winston.

Lovaas, O. I. (1977) *The Autistic Child: Language Development Through Behavior Modification*, New York, Irvington.

MacKenzie, B. D. (1977) *Behaviorism and the Limits of Scientific Method*, Atlantic Highlands, N. J., Humanities Press.

Meichenbaum, D. and Butler, L. (1980) 'Egocentrism and evidence: Making Piaget kosher', in Mahoney, M. J. (Ed.), *Psychotherapy Process*, New York, Plenum.

Napalkov, A. V. (1963) 'Information process of the brain', in Wiener, N. and Schade, J. P. (Eds.), *Progress in Brain Research*, Vol. 2, Amsterdam, Elservier.

Öst, L-G., Johansson, J. and Jerrelmalm, A. (1982) 'Individual response patterns and the effects of different behavioural methods in the treatment of claustrophobia', *Behaviour Research and Therapy*, **20**, pp. 445–60.

Paul, G. L. (1967) 'Strategy of outcome research in psychotherapy', *Journal of Consulting Psychology*, **31**, pp. 109–18.

Pavlov, I. P. (1927) *Lectures on Conditioned Reflexes*, New York, International Publishers.

Rachman, S. J. and Wilson, G. T. (1980) *The Effects of Psychological Therapy*, 2nd ed., New York, Pergamon Press.

Rimland, B. (1964) *Infantile Autism*, New York, Appleton-Century-Crofts.

Steffen, J. L. and Karoly, P. (Eds.) (1982) *Autism and Severe Psychopathology: Advances in Child Behavioral Analysis and Therapy*, Vol. 2, Lexington, Mass., Lexington Books.

Watson, J. B. and Rayner, R. (1920) 'Conditioned emotional reactions', *Journal of Experimental Psychology*, **3**, pp. 1–14.

Weed, L. L. (1968) 'Medical records that guide and teach', *New England Journal of Medicine*, **278**, pp. 593–600.

Wickramasekera, I. (Ed.) (1975) *Biofeedback, Behavior Therapy and Hypnosis*, Chicago, Ill., Nelson-Hall.

Wolpe, J. (1968) 'Learning therapies', in Howels, J. G. (Ed.), *Modern Perspectives in World Psychiatry*, Edinburgh, Oliver and Boyd.

Woolfolk, R. L. and Lazarus, A. A. (1979) 'Between laboratory and clinic: Paving the two-way street', *Cognitive Therapy and Research*, **3**, pp. 239–44.

Zener, K. (1937) 'The significance of behavior accompanying conditioned salivary secretion for theories of the conditioned reflex', *American Journal of Psychology*, **50**, pp. 384–403.

# Interchange

## BARBRACK AND FRANKS REPLY TO LAZARUS

We learn more from error than from confusion. (Francis Bacon)
No wind blows in favour of a ship that has no direction. (Montaigne)

Lazarus offers a scintillating display of verbal calisthenics, a demonstration *par excellence* of his consummate skill with words. There is even a grain of truth in some of Lazarus' contentions. But when all is said, if not done, there is little substance to the bulk of his accusations. It is not so much that he is wrong sometimes about specifics—one could forgive him this and in any event space does not permit more than a cursory examination of his errors and distortions—as that his presentation evidences a fundamental misunderstanding of behaviour therapy, its unique approach to intervention and what it is that we are trying to accomplish. Lazarus misinterprets the nature of theory in psychology and fails to recognize the focal role that theory plays in the development of behaviour therapy—a role which sharply differentiates it from all other therapeutic interventions, with the possible exception of psychoanalysis. How then can Lazarus possibly evaluate, let alone appreciate, the contributions of Eysenck to behaviour therapy? No wonder that, albeit unwittingly, he raises a strawman to attack and, whatever may be said about Eysenck, it cannot be said that he is a man of straw.

Perhaps because of a belief in the inevitable triumph of nurture over nature, perhaps because of the predominance of operant conditioning and its attendant situational stance, most behaviour therapists in the USA stress environmental determinants, behavioural specifics and grass-roots empiricism to the neglect of constitutional, more enduring modes of functioning and the importance of theory. This may account in part for the failure to appreciate Eysenck's contribution to behaviour therapy.

Eysenck's emphasis on biological determinants is never exclusive or at the expense of environmental and situational factors. Additionally, he takes pains to point out the limits of his theory and the occasions when his model is not appropriate. For example, in an invited address to the AABT and the Second World Congress of Behaviour Therapy in Washington in December 1983 Eysenck was careful to make clear that his theory of neurosis is not necessarily applicable to the existential variety.

To take another example, while espousing the biological underpinnings of autism, Eysenck would probably argue that this puzzling disorder is more usefully conceptualized and investigated in terms of both the biological components which impede learning and the imposition of an inadequate reinforcement repertoire. Thus, the Eysenck that Lazarus constructs for his verbal jousting is more than a man of straw; it is a creation of his personal predilections.

258

Some three decades ago a small group of then unknown psychologists, chiefly Eysenck's doctoral students, participated in an extensive series of weekly meetings at Eysenck's home. We list the names of as many of these individuals as one of us who was present can recall. All are now prominent figures in behaviour therapy throughout the world—Australia, the United States, Canada, Germany, Egypt, the United Kingdom and elsewhere. Here are the names: Yates, Poser, Brengelmann, Broadhurst, Jones, Soueif, Martin, Meyer, Beech, Payne, Franks. There were more.

Accepting the definition of psychology as 'the scientific study of behaviour' and the regrettable but indisputable fact that all attempts to understand and alleviate mental health problems stemmed at that time from medicine, psychiatry or social work, they set out to develop a viable system that satisfied two basic criteria: (1) that it arose out of the body of knowledge and methodology of psychology as defined above; and (2) that it could be articulated in sufficiently precise fashion to permit the generation of testable predictions. They chose a Hullian/Pavlovian-based conditioning model since it was the only one that met these two requirements at that time. But in so doing they stressed, then as now, that this was a starting point in the quest and not a sterile paradigm or endpoint in itself. A theory, like a therapy for that matter, is of use only until a more effective adaptation comes along. If bias is obligatory, bigotry is anathema.

What Lazarus apparently fails to recognize is that, as long as the process leads to appropriate modification, the potential for refutation of specific components is a measure of the strength of a theory rather than an indication of weakness. Thus, when Lazarus triumphantly quotes Franks and Barbrack's criticisms of conditioning, he is indeed scoring a point but the point is for, rather than against, Eysenck and all of us who are scientifically inclined.

Lazarus' notion of technical eclectic, use whatever 'works', is equally myopic. As detailed elsewhere (Franks, 1984), it glorifies a notional approach to behaviour therapy which relies on a myriad of dubiously validated techniques rather than a conceptual framework. This is the antithesis of everything for which behaviour therapy stands. Contrast this with the detailed, theory oriented programmes in behaviour research and theory generated by Eysenck and his students.

This brings us to our final, but far from inconsequential, point. Lazarus rejects the very *raison d'être* of behaviour therapy and, in so doing, is oblivious to the less tangible aspects of Eysenck's contribution to the field. If Eysenck remains among the most cited figures in the professional literature, this is due in no small measure to the legion of theses and research studies dedicated explicitly to the rigorous examination of predictions derived from Eysenck's theories. Eysenck's influence is thus more indirect than direct, but this does not eliminate its significance. There are now scores of erstwhile students with well-established enclaves of programme research in behaviour therapy throughout the world. Students rather than disciples, they have learned from Eysenck's example the power of critical evaluation. That is the only 'party line'. What greater legacy can a scientist leave to the world!

It is Lazarus' prerogative to reject behaviour therapy in favour of his clinical melange. What is less acceptable is his wholesale rejection of Eysenck and his theory predicated upon a lack of appreciation of behaviour therapy as outlined above, its origins and its unique position in the world of mental health. Lazarus is a fair-minded and gifted clinician, a master writer and a loyal friend. It is too bad that one whose influence on clinicians is great has such a small view of behaviour therapy and one of its more eminent founding fathers.

**REFERENCE**

Franks, C. M. (1984) 'On conceptual and technical integrity in psychoanalysis and behavior therapy, two fundamentally incompatible systems', in Arkowitz, H. and Messer, S. (Eds.), *Psychoanalysis and Behavior Therapy: Are They Compatible?*, New York , Plenum Press.

## LAZARUS REPLIES TO BARBRACK AND FRANKS

In his less biased moments the recondite Eysenck might wish that Barbrack and Franks had produced a dispassionate document instead of resorting at times to outright hagiolatry. Their exposition juxtaposes veneration and an inadvertent damning-by-faint-praise. It is as if Barbrack and Franks strained so hard to find substantive points in Eysenck's writings that they overreached their objectives and were forced to retract. For example, was it necessary for them to point out that Eysenck's brand of behaviour therapy finds favour only with some of his former 'students and junior colleagues'? Even I was more charitable in my assessment of his impact!

Barbrack and Franks' attempt to resurrect classical conditioning is a direct contradiction of their prior denouncement of this term. 'Conditioning itself is a word devoid of any precise meaning. . . . The evidence with respect to the utility of concepts of conditioning and their relationships to contemporary behaviour therapy is best summed up in terms of the ancient Scottish verdict, "not proven"' (Franks and Barbrack, 1983, pp. 511–12). Similarly, whereas they lauded the definition of behaviour therapy currently endorsed by the Association for Advancement of Behaviour Therapy—stating that it attempts to combine the best elements of doctrinal and epistemological definitions (Franks and Barbrack, 1983, p. 509)—they now derogate it in the service of Eysenckian simplicity as reflecting a compendium of disparate ideas, and highlighting the 'prevailing lack of consensus in the professional community'. Is it asking too much to expect consistency in such matters?

The chapter by Barbrack and Franks is riddled with inaccuracies and unsubstantiated pronouncements. For instance, they declare that behaviour therapists' rejection of psychoanalysis resulted *pari passu* in the de-emphasizing of theory; that there is a movement away from research altogether, and even a growing disenchantment with science. The facts are completely antithetical to the foregoing assertions. While there is a high degree of diversification among behaviour therapists, the literature reveals several central notions to which the vast majority subscribe. They place great value on meticulous observation, careful testing of hypotheses and continual self-correction on the basis of empirically derived data. Moreover, behaviour therapists display due regard for scientific objectivity, and extreme caution in the face of conjecture and speculation. They favour a rigorous process of deduction from testable theories and show a fitting indifference toward persuasion and hearsay (cf. Kazdin, 1983). Barbrack and Franks (and Eysenck) appear to misunderstand that it is possible to be *scientific* without being *scientistic* (that is, totally committed to the proposition that the methods of the natural sciences should be used in all areas of investigation). Experienced practitioners realize that there is an artistic dimension to the therapeutic enterprise that will probably always exist beyond the delimited frontiers of science. Nevertheless, contrary to Barbrack and Franks' declamatory remarks, this in no way negates the essential relationship between research and practice in behaviour therapy.

I am accused by Barbrack and Franks of seeking to discredit the value of Eysenck's contributions because of demonstrated errors and inconsistencies, while failing to appreciate one or more significant aspects of his work. (Barbrack and Franks had the advantage of reading my chapter before writing theirs!) I suppose that I am guilty as charged, for I regard Eysenck's writings on the theory and practice of therapy as retrogressive and atavistic. I am by no means alone in this regard. In a letter from an esteemed colleague and a former President of the Association for Advancement of Behaviour Therapy, the following sentiments were expressed: 'I assigned Eysenck's (1982) chapter in my Intervention course last fall, and told the class that it was like entering a time capsule back to 1963!' (Davison, 1984).

Barbrack and Franks revile near-sighted behaviour therapists who, according to their caricatures, appear to flounder under a cloud of atheoretical and random eclecticism. Who are these 'run-of-the-mill' behaviour therapists that are so erratic, misinformed and irresponsible? No documentation is provided.

Barbrack and Franks incorrectly assert that behaviour therapy has neglected biological considerations. Whereas early behaviourism leaned towards total environmentalism, behaviour therapy started from a neuropsychological base (for example, Wolpe's, 1958, 'reciprocal inhibition' hypothesis) and has not downplayed the genetic diathesis as Barbrack and Franks allege. Recent advances in 'behavioural medicine' and in biological psychiatry have been incorporated into the armamentarium of behaviour therapists—but, by definition, the direct alteration of bodily processes by biological procedures lies outside the purview of behaviour therapy. Developments in biophysiology and psychopharmacology will have as much bearing on 'ideas that Eysenck has expressed over the last thirty years' as the debt that modern-day neuroanatomy owes to Gall's system of phrenology.

Barbrack and Franks undertook the task of writing the pro-Eysenckian chapter *vis-à-vis* his 'contributions' to the field of behaviour therapy. I was charged with the responsibility of writing the *negative* critique. The discerning reader may discover that, shorn of its gratuitous and panegyrical analects, the Barbrack-Franks chapter is perhaps only slightly more supportive and positive than my own. As I read it, the 'case for the defence' has served to bolster my essential point—having failed to keep pace with the times, Eysenck exists far behind the mainstream of current thought and evidence in the burgeoning field of behaviour therapy.

## REFERENCES

Davison, G. C. (1984) Personal communication.

Eysenck, H. J. (1982) 'Neobehavioristic (S-R) theory', in Wilson, G. T. and Franks, C. M. (Eds.) *Contemporary Behavior Therapy*, New York, Guilford Press, pp. 205–76.

Franks, C. M. and Barbrack, C. R. (1983) 'Behavior therapy with adults: An integrative perspective', in Hersen, M., Kazdin, A. E. and Bellack, A. S. (Eds.), *The Clinical Psychology Handbook*, New York, Pergamon Press, pp. 507–23.

Kazdin, A. E. (1983) 'Treatment research: The investigation and evaluation of psychotherapy', in Hersen, M., Kazdin, A. E. and Bellack, A. S. (Eds.), *The Clinical Psychology Handbook*, New York, Pergamon Press, pp. 265–84.

Wolpe, J. (1958) *Psychotherapy by Reciprocal Inhibition*, Stanford, Calif., Stanford University Press.

# Part IX: Sexual and Marital Behaviour

## 15. Personality, Sexual Behaviour and Marital Satisfaction*

GLENN WILSON

Kinsey's surveys in the 1940s and 1950s were a monumental step forward in the scientific study of human sexuality. They provided US population norms for most forms of sexual behaviour, both conventional and 'perverted', giving the first genuine perspective on who does what, with whom and how often. Although attention was focused primarily on national averages for various activities (against which most Americans were interested to compare themselves), Kinsey was impressed with the enormous differences that appeared between social groups and between individuals. Analysis in terms of demographic variables such as age, gender and social class was provided in the Kinsey reports, but no information was gathered concerning the personality of respondents.

The same was true of the celebrated studies of Masters and Johnson of people's physiological responses during sexual activity. Again, interest was centred on the *typical* sexual response cycle, and the comparison between men and women. Considerable individual differences in responsiveness were observed but these were not investigated in connection with personality.

It was this gap in knowledge concerning the origin of individual differences in sexual attitudes and behaviour that led Eysenck to undertake the research reported in *Sex and Personality* (1976). This paper reviews these findings and extends them with accounts of more recent research by Eysenck and others that elaborates them in some way.

### EYSENCK'S HYPOTHESES

Eysenck began with hypotheses concerning the way in which his three major

---

* This chapter is an updated revision of the chapter called 'Personality and Sex' in Lynn, R. (Ed.) (1981) *Dimensions of Personality: Papers in Honour of H. J. Eysenck*, Oxford, Pergamon Press.

**263**

dimensions of personality, extraversion, neuroticism and psychoticism, would be expected, on the basis of his personality theory, to correlate with sexual attitudes and behaviour. Extraverts, he supposed, would attempt to compensate for their lack of cortical arousal by seeking stimulation within the sexual sphere, whereas introverts would 'shy away from more stimulating forms of sexual behaviour.' Thus extraverts should have intercourse earlier in life than introverts, more frequently, with more different partners and in more different positions. They should also indulge in longer pre-coital love-play and more varied types of sexual behaviour than introverts. These same predictions could be arrived at through another related line of argument. Introverts are more readily socialized because of their high cortical arousal and are therefore less likely to engage in forms of sexual behaviour that are socially deplored (promiscuity, extramarital affairs and 'perversions').

Some evidence was already available concerning these points. Schofield (1968) had described the characteristics of the most sexually active young people in Britain, and although their personality was not measured by questionnaire, the description of these people corresponded with that of the extravert—outgoing, active and sociable. One of the best single indicators of sexual experience, especially for girls, was cigarette smoking, which is known to go with extraversion.

Prior to Eysenck's work the only study of sexual behaviour that included a measure of extraversion was that of Giese and Schmidt (1968). Within a sample of over 6000 unmarried German students, they found that extraverts engaged more than introverts in most forms of sexual activity. High E students had more frequent intercourse, more often petted to orgasm, used more varied positions of intercourse and longer pre-coital love-play, and were more likely to have tried fellatio or cunnilingus. The only activity more frequent in introverts than extraverts was masturbation, which is a solitary activity. This tendency for introverts to masturbate more than extraverts has since been confirmed by Husted and Edwards (1976).

Giese and Schmidt found that the correlations between extraversion and sexual experience were greater for men than for women. This could be because men initiate more sexual activity than women, with the result that their personality is more clearly manifested through their sexual behaviour than is the case for women, who often just follow the lead of their male partners. It will be seen later, however, that a woman's permissiveness of attitude is more readily reflected in her level of premarital experience than is the case for men, since men are limited more by opportunity than their own sexual morality.

Other studies relevant to the extraversion hypothesis are those of Zuckerman and colleagues (1974, 1976), using the Sensation-Seeking Scale, which has some overlap with Eysenck's E scale (as well as with psychoticism). Zuckerman found that all kinds of sexual experience were more common in high sensation-seekers.

The second main hypothesis that Eysenck put forward with respect to sex and personality was that people scoring high on his N scale would be anxious and inhibited in sexual matters. Although they might have a high drive for sex, their fear of punishment, especially in relation to social contact, would place them in a conflict situation. Again, the only research that Eysenck could find that had directly tested this hypothesis was that of Giese and Schmidt in Germany. They had used a short, probably unreliable, measure of N, and did not find it very powerful as a predictor of sexual activity. Among men, high N scorers masturbated more frequently, had a greater desire for intercourse and claimed to have spontaneous erections more often than low N scorers. High N women had less frequent orgasms and complained more about menstrual discomfort. These findings accord with much clinical and survey data concerning the relationship between anxiety and sexual dysfunction.

Some writers, such as Halleck (1967), had maintained that permissiveness in society puts pressure on girls to engage in premarital sex against their inclination, thus causing emotional problems. Diamant (1970), however, found no relationship between 'adjustment' and experience of premarital sex; nor was there any relationship between adjustment and the number of sexual partners. Diamant did find that men with non-permissive attitudes, who were presumably out of step with their peers, showed more maladjustment. Unfortunately, it is not clear how adjustment was measured since it was based on impressionistic ratings of MMPI profiles, and was probably a mixture of neurotic and psychotic tendencies.

Eysenck's third major dimension of personality, psychoticism, is characterized by the tendency to be cold, impersonal, hostile and cruel towards other people. High P scorers may be solitary and isolated from other people, or belligerent and troublesome; either way, their behaviour is bizarre and they do not easily fit in with the rest of society. Generalizing from these characteristics, Eysenck hypothesized that high P individuals would tend to be anti-social and impersonal in their sex lives, also showing a predilection for sadism and other 'perversions', and a preference for physical sex without caring or involvement. Since men score higher on P than women, high P scorers might also be expected to show a more stereotypically masculine pattern of sexual attitudes and behaviour. With the exception of the Zuckerman studies already mentioned, research bearing directly on these hypotheses was not available before Eysenck's studies.

## EYSENCK'S SEX QUESTIONNAIRE

For assessing sexual attitudes and behaviour Eysenck assembled a questionnaire containing over 100 items. This was derived partly from existing questionnaires, such as that of Thorne, Haupt and Allen (1966), and covered most aspects of sex. Attitude items took the form of statements with which subjects could agree or disagree, for example, 'The opposite sex will respect you more if you are not too familiar with them'; 'Sex without love (impersonal sex) is highly unsatisfactory'; 'Conditions have to be just right to get me excited sexually'. Other items referred to sexual experience, the respondent being asked about activities he or she had participated in, from petting through to intercourse and oral sex, preferred frequency of intercourse, the extent of satisfaction obtained, and the incidence of problems such as impotence, premature ejaculation and orgasm difficulty.

The questionnaire was completed anonymously by 423 male and 379 female unmarried students aged 18 to 22, from various universities and colleges around Britain, who also completed the EPQ. Answers to the Sex Questionnaire were intercorrelated and subjected to principal component analysis with promax rotation. Fourteen primary factors were extracted that were fairly readily interpretable and which showed a high degree of factor similarity between men and women. These are listed together with examples of high loading items in Table 1. Since these fourteen factors were themselves intercorrelated, it was possible to refactor them to obtain two orthogonal higher-order factors. The first of these two 'superfactors' combined all types of dissatisfaction, deprivation and peculiarity, and was therefore called *sexual*

**Table 1**  *Sexual Attitude Areas Identified by Factor Analysis*

| Factors | Examples of items |
|---|---|
| 1 Satisfaction | I have not been deprived sexually |
| | My love life has not been disappointing |
| 2 Excitement | It doesn't take much to get me excited sexually |
| | I get very excited when touching a woman's breasts |
| 3 Nervousness | I don't have many friends of the opposite sex |
| | I feel nervous with the opposite sex |
| 4 Curiosity | Sex jokes don't disgust me |
| | I would agree to see a 'blue' film |
| 5 Premarital sex | Virginity is a girl's most valuable possession |
| | One should not experiment with sex before marriage |
| 6 Repression | Children should not be taught about sex |
| | I think only rarely about sex |
| 7 Prudishness | I don't enjoy petting |
| | The thought of a sex orgy is disgusting to me |
| 8 Experimentation | A person should learn about sex gradually by experimenting with it |
| | Young people should be allowed out at night without being too closely checked |
| 9 Homosexuality | I understand homosexuals |
| | People of my own sex frequently attract me |
| 10 Censorship | There are too many immoral plays on T.V. |
| | Prostitution should not be legally permitted |
| 11 Promiscuity | Sex without love ('impersonal sex') is not highly unsatisfactory |
| | I have been involved in more than one sex affair at the same time |
| 12 Hostility | I have felt like humiliating my sex partner |
| | I have felt hostile to my sex partner |
| 13 Guilt | At times I have been afraid of myself for what I might do sexually |
| | My conscience bothers me too much |
| 14 Inhibition | My parents' influence has inhibited me sexually |
| | Conditions have to be just right to get me excited sexually |

*Source:*      Eysenck (1976).

*pathology.* The second main factor dealt with permissiveness and active, intense sexuality and was therefore named *libido.* These two major factors showed a high degree of factor similarity between males and females and were virtually uncorrelated within each gender group.

## PERSONALITY, SEXUAL ATTITUDES AND BEHAVIOUR

When EPQ dimensions were projected onto these sex factors, the results in Table 2 were obtained. This shows the direction of the association between the personality and sexual attitude factor (+ or −) and its strength (one + or − indicating a weak relationship, two signs meaning a moderate relationship and three signs a strong relationship). Table 2 shows that people scoring high and low on the three personality dimensions have quite different patterns of sexual attitudes, differences which generally bear out the earlier predictions. Extravert students were high on Promiscuity and low on Nervousness and Prudishness, which, taken together with the behavioural results, paints a picture of extraverts as hedonists and happy philanderers. They appear to epitomize the permissive approach to sex, with frequent changes of sex

**Table 2**  *Sexual Attitudes Related to Personality*

| | Factors | E | N | P |
|---|---|---|---|---|
| 1 | Satisfaction | + | – – – | – |
| 2 | Excitement | + | + + | + |
| 3 | Nervousness | – – – | + + | 0 |
| 4 | Curiosity | 0 | + | + + |
| 5 | Premarital sex | + | 0 | + + |
| 6 | Repression | 0 | 0 | – |
| 7 | Prudishness | – – | + | + |
| 8 | Experimentation | + | 0 | 0 |
| 9 | Homosexuality | 0 | + | + |
| 10 | Censorship | – | 0 | – |
| 11 | Promiscuity | + + | 0 | + + + |
| 12 | Hostility | 0 | + + + | + + + |
| 13 | Guilt | 0 | + + + | 0 |
| 14 | Inhibition | 0 | + + + | + |
| | *Summary factors* | | | |
| A | Sexual pathology | – | + + + | + |
| B | Libido | + | + | + + + |

*Source*:  Eysenck (1976).

*Note*:   +, 0, and − signs indicate positive, zero and negative relationships respectively.

partner and an appetite for frequent sex contacts. Introverts tended to be more puritanical, valuing virginity and fidelity and playing down the importance of physical sex.

High N scorers were high on Excitement, Nervousness, Hostility, Guilt and Inhibition, and low on Satisfaction. High P scorers were high on Curiosity, Premarital sex, Promiscuity and Hostility. Neurotics and psychotics, then, both showed a 'pathological' or 'non-conforming' pattern of sexual reactions, and both showed strong sex drive, but whereas high P subjects tended to act out their libidinous, promiscuous and oral desires, neurotics did not. The inhibitions, worries and guilt feelings of high N scorers apparently prevented them from consummating their desires. So although neurotics and psychotics both reported dissatisfaction, they did so for different reasons—high Ns because they were repressed and high Ps because they were insatiable. Questions relating to the occurrence of sexual problems revealed that N was related to female orgasmic difficulty and male impotence, while neither E nor P was much implicated in dysfunction.

## MALE-FEMALE DIFFERENCES

Eysenck also analyzed his questionnaire to identify the items that discriminated most powerfully between men and women, constructing a twenty-seven item masculinity-feminity scale (Table 3). Males are revealed as more favourable toward pornography, orgies, promiscuity, voyeurism, prostitution, premarital and impersonal sex than are females. They also seem to be more easily excited sexually and masturbate more often. However, while men are less prudish than women and felt less guilt, women express greater contentment with their sex lives.

This pattern of findings may be explained by supposing that men have a stronger

**Table 3**   *Sexual Attitudes That Differentiate Men and Women* (percentage endorsements of men and women and the difference between them)

| | | M | F | Diff. |
|---|---|---|---|---|
| 1 | Sex without love ('impersonal sex') is highly unsatisfactory. | 43 | 60 | − 17 |
| 2 | Conditions have to be just right to get me excited sexually. | 15 | 42 | − 27 |
| 3 | Sometimes it has been a problem to control my sex feelings. | 50 | 38 | + 12 |
| 4 | I get pleasant feelings from touching my sexual parts. | 81 | 66 | + 15 |
| 5 | I do not need to respect a sex partner, or love him/her, in order to enjoy petting and/or intercourse with him/her. | 43 | 26 | + 17 |
| 6 | Sexual feelings are sometimes unpleasant to me. | 6 | 11 | − 5 |
| 7 | It doesn't take much to get me excited sexually. | 75 | 44 | + 31 |
| 8 | I think about sex almost every day. | 87 | 61 | + 26 |
| 9 | I get excited sexually very easily. | 68 | 40 | + 28 |
| 10 | The thought of a sex orgy is disgusting to me. | 15 | 40 | − 25 |
| 11 | I find the thought of a coloured sex partner particularly exciting. | 32 | 11 | + 21 |
| 12 | I like to look at sexy pictures. | 80 | 45 | + 35 |
| 13 | My conscience bothers me too much. | 13 | 20 | − 7 |
| 14 | I enjoy petting. | 95 | 88 | + 7 |
| 15 | Seeing a person nude doesn't interest me. | 6 | 28 | − 22 |
| 16 | Sometimes the woman should be sexually aggressive. | 95 | 88 | + 7 |
| 17 | I believe in taking my pleasures where I find them. | 34 | 19 | + 15 |
| 18 | Young people should be allowed out at night without being too closely checked. | 69 | 54 | + 15 |
| 19 | I would particularly protect my children from contact with sex. | 6 | 12 | − 6 |
| 20 | I like to look at pictures of nudes. | 84 | 44 | + 40 |
| 21 | If I had the chance to see people making love, without being seen, I would take it. | 67 | 37 | + 30 |
| 22 | Pornographic writings should be freely allowed to be published. | 74 | 55 | + 19 |
| 23 | Prostitution should be legally permitted. | 82 | 63 | + 19 |
| 24 | I had some had sex experiences when I was young. | 13 | 20 | − 7 |
| 25 | There should be no censorship, on sexual grounds, of plays and films. | 73 | 53 | + 20 |
| 26 | Sex is far and away away my greatest pleasure. | 35 | 26 | + 9 |
| 27 | Absolute faithfulness to one partner throughout life is nearly as silly as celibacy. | 41 | 28 | + 13 |
| 28 | The present preoccupation with sex in our society has been largely created by films, newspapers, television and advertising. | 45 | 54 | − 9 |
| 29 | I would enjoy watching my usual partner having intercourse with someone else. | 18 | 6 | + 12 |
| 30 | I would vote for a law that permitted polygamy. | 31 | 11 | + 20 |
| 31 | Even though one is having regular intercourse, masturbation is good for a change. | 55 | 39 | + 16 |
| 32 | I would prefer to have a new sex partner every night. | 7 | 2 | + 5 |
| 33 | Sex is more exciting with a stranger. | 21 | 7 | + 14 |
| 34 | To me few things are more important than sex. | 44 | 26 | + 18 |
| 35 | Sex is not all that important to me. | 11 | 19 | − 8 |
| 36 | Group sex appeals to me. | 33 | 10 | + 23 |
| 37 | The thought of an illicit relationship excites me. | 52 | 32 | + 20 |
| 38 | I prefer my partner to dictate the rules of the sexual game. | 9 | 37 | − 28 |
| 39 | The idea of 'wife swapping' is extremely distasteful to me. | 37 | 63 | − 26 |
| 40 | Some forms of love-making are disgusting to me. | 15 | 30 | − 15 |

*Source*:   Eysenck and Wilson (1979).

sex drive than women, particularly as regards desire for variety in partners and activities. Inevitably, men are more often frustrated than women who, relatively speaking, command a seller's market in the field of sex. This interpretation is supported by Wilson (1978), who found a greater discrepancy between sexual fantasy and reality in men than women and by Zuckerman, Tushup and Finner (1976), who found that sexual attitudes and activities were more highly correlated in women than men.

Some psychologists argue that social role learning is sufficient to account for the different sexual attitudes and inclinations of men and women, but there are good reasons to suppose that evolution has led to such a divergence. Females invest more in motherhood than males do in fatherhood, so it is more in the interests of females to select prime mates and induce them to help in child-rearing, while it is more in the interests of men to fertilize a variety of different women (Wilson, 1981). A biological interpretation is also supported by studies of the effects of male and female hormones on sexual inclinations (Eysenck and Wilson, 1979). Of course, the separation is not total; as with all other attributes on which there are established sex differences, there is a great deal of overlap between men and women.

Not unexpectedly, the male-female differences in attitude shown in Table 3 were similar to the differences between high and low P individuals within each sex separately. In other words, the psychoticism factor seems to parallel masculinity in terms of its effect on sexual inclinations. Correlations between P and M-F scores for men and women were respectively .54 and .74. There was also a significant, though much lower, association between extraversion and masculinity of attitudes.

Also consistent with the idea of a connection between P and masculinity of sexual tendencies was the finding that sex offenders have higher P scores than other prisoners. The mean P score for sex offenders (including those convicted of rape, indecent assault, and buggery) was 11.07 as compared with a prisoner mean of 6.25. Thus active sexuality seems to be correlated with both P and masculinity.

## CONSERVATISM AND SEXUAL BEHAVIOUR

The EPQ Lie Scale was also found to correlate with sexual behaviour. Generally, high L scorers were like low P scorers in sexual behaviour, being unadventurous and conventionally well-behaved. This could mean that high L scorers were 'faking good' on the Sex Questionnaire, but it could also mean they are conforming, 'respectable' people. L scores are correlated with conservatism (Wilson, 1973), and several researchers have shown conservatism to go with restricted sexual experience and a general dislike of sexual stimuli (Joe, Brown and Jones, 1976; Thomas, Shea and Rigby, 1971; Thomas, 1975; Schmidt; Sigusch and Meyberg, 1969).

Physiological responses to erotic stimuli measured by penile tumescence were found to correlate inversely with the L Scale by Farkas, Sine and Evans (1979). They supposed that this relationship was mediated by conservative attitudes, and suggested that a more direct measure of conservatism might relate more strongly to sexual arousal. Other EPQ variables failed to show any relationship with sexual arousal measured physiologically, except for a weak relationship between N and speed of reaching maximum tumescence.

## ADULT SAMPLES

The results using the Eysenck Sex Questionnaire so far described were obtained with student samples. Eysenck later went on to study a more general adult sample consisting of 427 males and 436 females. Results were very much in accord with those found for students. Factor analysis produced a similar set of primary factors which were summarized by higher order analysis into the two factors shown in Figure 1.

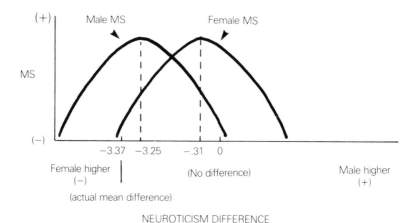

**Figure 1** *Two Major Dimensions of Sexual Attitudes and Behaviour*
*Source:* Eysenck (1976).

Personality correlates of sexual attitudes and behaviour were also much the same as those found for students and again similar for men and women. Extraversion was again associated with permissiveness, a liking for variety and a strong libido. Neuroticism was associated with sexual excitability and a wide range of difficulties and conflicts. Psychoticism went with a tough, adventurous and impersonal approach to love and sex and high 'Lie' scorers showed conservative attitudes and behaviour.

There was an interesting difference between men and women in the personality correlates of sexual behaviour. Participation in group sex was related to P in women, but E in men. This could be taken as meaning that a liking for group sex is relatively 'normal' for men, being merely a reflection of sociability, whereas women who engage in such behaviour are 'unfeminine' and therefore likely to be eccentric and non-conforming. Such an interpretation is compatible with the fact that men are generally more interested in group sex than women.

## SEXUAL ATTITUDES OF MALE PRISONERS

Eysenck (1976) applied his Sex Questionnaire to a sample of 186 male patients in Broadmoor Hospital for the criminally insane. Most of these patients had been committed for crimes of violence such as murder and assault, but there were also some sex offenders and arsonists. The most outstanding feature of the results was that patients were apparently more inhibited sexually than 'normal' controls. They claimed not to be easily excited, to think rarely about sex and look upon it as being for procreation rather than pleasure. This is consistent with the Wilson and Maclean (1974) finding that, compared with bus drivers, male prisoners were less favourable towards issues concerning sexual freedom and were less inclined to laugh at 'dirty' jokes. Similarly, Thorne, Haupt and Allen (1966) found felons and sex offenders in the US to be repressed and conservative in the area of sexual attitudes.

It is possible that prisoners fill out research questionnaires in a guarded way so as to give a good impression of themselves to facilitate release. Indeed, their EPQ Lie scores are elevated (8.03 for Broadmoor patients compared with 3.64 for a normal group), which raises doubt about the validity of these findings concerning prisoners' sexual attitudes. However, their account of their actual sexual experience also suggests a restrictive background. There were more things they would like to have done, and more things they have done that they did not enjoy. On their own report, they emerge overall as more inhibited and less satisfied.

Apart from the problem of 'faking good' on these questionnaires, there is the possibility that the fact of their incarceration was partly responsible for the lack of experience and satisfaction of these prisoners. Since the studies described above do not permit these effects to be untangled, the conclusions based on them are suspect.

## PERSONALITY AND MARITAL CHOICE

Since many of Eysenck's subjects were married couples it was possible to investigate the extent of similarity of marriage partners with respect to EPQ variables. As it turned out, there was only a slight tendency for couples to be similar with respect to personality (correlations being: P, .14; E, .06; N, .22; L, .17). Given the large numbers involved, these are all significant except for E, but they are by no means high. Taking these results together with others reported by Insel (1971), Nias (1977) and Eysenck and Wakefield (1981), low positive correlations on EPQ variables in married couples are indicated, those for P and N being higher than that for E (which approximates to zero).

Such similarity as has been observed seems to result from initial partner choice rather than a progressive merging of personalities through the course of the marriage. Eysenck and Wakefield (1981) actually found a slight tendency for the libidos of husband and wife to diverge as a function of length of marriage. Wives of high libido men showed a greater decrement in libido with age than wives of low libido men. However, caution should be exercised in the interpretation of this finding since the data were cross-sectional, not longitudinal.

Hirschberg (1979) reported that extraverted men prefer voluptuous, large-breasted women who themselves tend to be extraverted in personality, so we might expect this to make for some homogamy in personality. Also, Bentler and Newcomb (1979) found a higher divorce rate among couples who were initially dissimilar in personality, which should result in a tendency for couples in long-standing marriages to appear as more similar. Thus it is surprising that more personality homogamy was not observed.

Other attributes show much larger correlations between husband and wife. Eysenck and Wakefield found correlations of .73 for marital satisfaction, .41 for sexual satisfaction, .43 for libido, .51 for radicalism and .56 for tender-mindedness. Similar correlations among married couples have been reported for conservatism (.53), dogmatism (.51) and inflexibility (.41) by Kirton (1977). These levels of similarity are much like the degree of assortative mating typically observed for IQ (Eysenck, 1979), although many of these variables correlate with age and so the apparent homogamy may simply reflect the age similarity in married couples.

Couples who live together without legal marriage have been distinguished on the basis of personality. Catlin, Croake and Keller (1976) studied MMPI profiles of eighty-nine cohabiting student couples in the US and found slightly elevated scores on the Psychopathic Deviate and Hypomania Scales for both men and women, and the Masculinity and Schizophrenia Scales for men only. Such a pattern of non-conformity and high energy in cohabiting couples suggests high P on the EPQ. But with cohabitation becoming increasingly popular in Western societies this personality relationship may cease to apply. In Sweden, where about half of young couples are now cohabiting, Lewin and Trost (1979) found little difference between cohabitors and legally married people.


## MARITAL SATISFACTION


In their detailed and impressive monograph Eysenck and Wakefield (1981) studied the relationships between personality, attitudes, sexual behaviour and marital satisfaction in 566 couples recruited through newspaper and magazine advertisements. These couples had been married for varying lengths of time, ranging from 0 to 40 years and their compatibility was assessed with an extended form of the Locke-Wallace Marital Adjustment Test.

First to be considered was the role of the individuals' personality scores in predicting marital satisfaction in themselves and their partner. In line with previous research (e.g., Eysenck, 1980; Zaleski and Galkowska, 1978), high P and N were associated with marital unhappiness (in both self and spouse), while E was of little consequence. The Lie score showed a small but significant correlation with marital satisfaction for its owner only, not the spouse, which is interesting support for its validity as an indicator of social desirability responding. Combining the personality scores of husband and wife, a multiple correlation of .43 was obtained with total marital satisfaction (the sum of MS for husband and wife), with male and female scores contributing about equally to the predictive power of personality.

Also of interest was the *difference* between male and female personality scores in determining marital happiness, which bears on the old dispute between similarity and complementation theories of marital compatibility. Eysenck and Wakefield found that, beside the generally detrimental effect of P, it was better for the husband if his wife had a similar P score and better for the wife if the husband's P score was about 1.5 points higher than her own (this being approximately the average difference between men and women). In the case of N, satisfaction was optimized for the husband when his wife was 3.25 points higher than himself (again representing the average male-female difference), while for wives satisfaction was optimized when the husband was about the same on N (Figure 2).

These interactions between husband and wife personality in determining marital

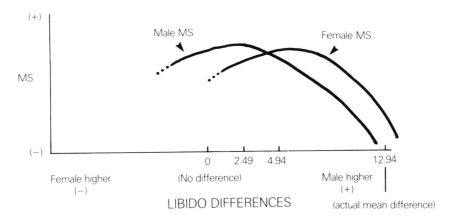

**Figure 2** *Relationship between Neuroticism Differences and Marital Satisfaction of Males and Females*
*Source*: Eysenck and Wakefield (1981).

happiness are more supportive of similarity theory than complementation, but they are more obviously consistent with a compromise position, the gender-asymmetry theory described by Eysenck and Wilson (1979). According to this theory, marital happiness is greatest when typical sex differences (whether due to biology or culture) are matched in the case of an individual couple, otherwise the similarity principle applies. The simplest example is height, where tall men marry women nearly as tall as themselves and short men marry women even shorter than themselves. The result is a high correlation but a predictable degree of difference. Gross deviations from this pattern are presumed to be unstable at all stages from first meeting through to the latter years of marriage. Since men are typically higher on P than women and women are typically higher on N, it follows that higher levels of P in husbands and higher levels of N in wives would be better tolerated than differences which run counter to this expectation.

When all the effects of personality were considered, both individual scores and interactions between partners, 20 per cent of the variance in marital satisfaction was accounted for. The L score contributed about 1 per cent of this and N and P nearly all the rest.

Eysenck and Wakefield used an inventory of social attitudes in their study, and found that radicalism was associated with dissatisfaction in both the self and the spouse, whereas tender-mindedness showed no connection. When differences between the two partners in social attitudes were considered as predictors of marital satisfaction, it was tender-mindedness rather than radicalism that came out as being important. Again, the differences that maximized satisfaction were in the direction of the traditional differences between men and women. Husbands were happiest with a wife who was 3.5 points more tender-minded than themselves, while wives were happiest with a husband 6 points tougher than themselves (this corresponding with the average sex difference on the scale). Thus results for tough-mindedness are similar to those for P, which is not surprising considering the two variables overlap conceptually and empirically.

The Sexual Attitudes Questionnaire was also included in the study and, not surprisingly, sexual satisfaction was found to correlate with overall marital satisfaction. More interesting was the finding that high libido in men was detrimental to marital satisfaction, whereas female libido was unrelated. In libido also there was a tendency for sex-typical differences to be associated with satisfaction. Men were happiest when they were 2.49 points higher on libido than their wives, and women were optimally satisfied by a husband who was 4.94 points higher in libido than themselves (Figure 3). Eysenck and Wakefield note that since the average difference between men and women on libido was 12.19 points, most men were too high on libido relative to their wives to allow maximum satisfaction (which would explain why low libido men were more satisfied in their marriage).

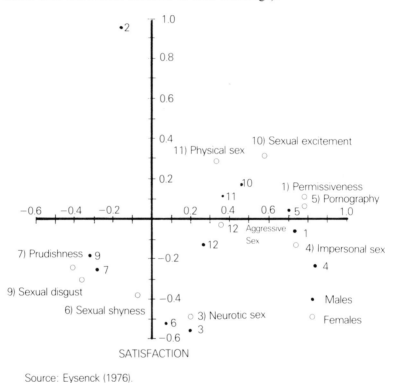

Source: Eysenck (1976).

**Figure 3** *Relationship between Libido Differences and MS of Males and Females*
*Source*: Eysenck and Wakefield (1981).

Another interesting sex difference concerned the role of sexual satisfaction as a contributor to overall marital satisfaction. Sexual satisfaction was more integral to the marital satisfaction of the wife than the husband. Men readily attained their optimal level of sexual satisfaction, but women very seldom did (a finding which may have relevance to understanding the process of many a marital breakdown).

Detailed examination of the relationship between particular sexual behaviours and marital satisfaction revealed some interesting facts. For example, a wife's report of impotence in her husband was associated with unhappiness in both spouses, but the husband's awareness of non-orgasm in his wife did not diminish his own satisfaction to any appreciable extent. Experience of premarital intercourse made no difference to the marital satisfaction of the husband, but the same in the wife was slightly detrimental.

Many other facts can be gleaned from the Eysenck and Wakefield data, but the most significant finding to emerge is that personality, attitudes and libido have effects upon marital happiness both in absolute terms and in combination. With respect to the ideal combinations of these attributes, similarity theory is generally upheld, but with two important qualifications. One is that having both partners high on an attribute like psychoticism which is individually detrimental to marital happiness is usually worse than having only one partner high on that attribute. The second is that complementation sometimes applies in the special sense that couples who match a gender-typical asymmetry on personality and other attributes are likely to be happier than those who do not.

Although the similarity effects observed by Eysenck and Wakefield might seem small in magnitude, it should be remembered that they appeared against a background of assortative mating that was sometimes quite strong. If partners were randomly mated, the similarity effect upon marital happiness would presumably be greatly magnified. Also noteworthy is the fact that an extremely large gender difference on a variable that has a similarity effect, such as libido, makes for almost inevitable compatibility problems within a marriage.

## GENETIC FACTORS IN SEXUAL BEHAVIOUR

Eysenck's (1976) book includes an analysis of the responses of twins to his Sex Questionnaire, conducted in collaboration with N. G. Martin of Birmingham University. The classical Holzinger formula for estimating heritabilities is criticized as not taking account of all relevant variables, such as trait dominance and assortative mating. A more sophisticated statistical procedure for partitioning variance in a trait into genetic and environmental components is then described. Each of the two major sources of variance is further subdivided into *within-family* variance, which includes all factors specific to the individual as well as errors of measurement, and *between-family* variance, which deals with effects common to one family and not shared by others.

Applying this form of analysis to their twin data on sex (using 153 pairs of male twins and 399 female twin pairs), Martin and Eysenck found that in the case of men, libido was about two-thirds determined by additive (dominance-free) genetic factors, whereas cultural influences were more important for women. There was also evidence of a between-family environmental effect in women, but not men, suggesting that daughters are more influenced by family standards than are sons. These findings confirm a widespread belief that the sexual attitudes and behaviour of women are more strongly influenced by environmental pressures than those of men.

With respect to sexual satisfaction the position was more complicated. There was some evidence for the involvement of genetic factors, but environmental influences seemed to be more important with both sexes. This makes sense when it is remembered that sexual fulfilment depends upon the cooperation of other people (lovers, spouses, etc.) whereas libido is relatively independent of the behaviour of other people. In the case of women, there was actually a tendency for DZ twins to be *more* alike in satisfaction than MZ twins. A possible interpretation of this is in terms of competition for scarce resources. MZ women attract the same kind of man and move in the same circle of friends, therefore they have to compete for attention more than DZ twins. Male twins go out and meet people away from the home more than women, and so do not compete to the same extent.

Martin, Eaves and Eysenck (1977) also demonstrated a genetic influence for age of first intercourse. Since early intercourse was correlated with libido, tough-mindedness and extraversion (in both men and women), the genetic effect on this aspect of sexual behaviour could have been mediated by these personality factors. As regards the environmental component, cultural influences (between-family variance) were found to be less important than individual experiences. Again, there was some indication of competition effects in the female data only.


## HORMONES AND PERSONALITY

Since sexual behaviour is to some extent genetic, and so is personality, it is reasonable to expect some connections between sex hormones and personality. In practice it has proved difficult to establish these for a variety of reasons. (1) Hormones exist in the blood in minute quantity and only recently has it become feasible to measure them with any degree of accuracy. (2) Their level fluctuates from time to time according to time of day, phase of the menstrual cycle, general health, recent experiences of success or failure, anticipation of sexual activity, etc. (3) Only a small proportion of the hormone is free to act; the rest is bonded to globulin in such a way as to be inactive. (4) Hormone levels themselves are not the only critical factor; variations in receptor sensitivity to these hormones, which are independently determined, have also to be considered. (5) Adult levels of sex hormone may be less important than those prevailing during pre-natal brain development. Given these complications, it is not surprising that studies of sex hormone effects in adults have produced complex and contradictory results.

Daitzman (1976) measured androgen and oestrogen secretion in student samples on two separate occasions and correlated the results with a variety of personality tests, including the EPQ. Since there were only seven women in his sample, discussion will be restricted to results for the seventy-six men. These were in many respects counter to expectation. Androgen secretion was significantly related to neuroticism, while correlations with psychoticism and extraversion were positive but insignificant. Surprisingly, heterosexual experience was negatively related to androgen, although a favourable parental attitude to sex was positively correlated. Oestrogen levels were also correlated with N, while correlations with P and E were again positive but small. Again, correlations with sexual experience were negative. Thus androgen and oestrogen seemed to have parallel effects on personality and behaviour, raising levels of P, E, and especially N, and lowering sexual experience. When the androgen/oestrogen balance was examined it was found that a high androgen ratio was negatively correlated with both masculinity and sexual experience.

In view of the difficulties discussed above, it is not surprising that these results are so difficult to interpret. The correlation between hormone levels and N could be spurious in that high N subjects might be more reactive to the anticipation of having a blood sample taken, this anxiety reflecting itself in a temporary increase in hormones.

Somewhat different results were obtained in a later study by Daitzman and Zuckerman (1980). Within a sample of forty unmarried male students, testosterone was significantly correlated with extraversion, dominance, heterosexual interest and experience, and an absence of neuroticism (a traditionally masculine pattern of characteristics). Oestradiol likewise correlated with heterosexual interest and experience, but was also correlated with homosexual experience and various psychopathic and psychotic traits. The authors do not attempt to explain why these results differ from those of Daitzman (1976).

Persson and Svanborg (1980) studied free (unbonded) hormone levels in a representative sample of 70-year-old men and women, arguing certain advantages in studying older people of restricted age range. Older men are less likely to be at a saturation level of androgen, so variations are more likely to have behavioural significance. A high level of androgen activity relative to oestrogen in men was found to be associated with dominance, confidence and energy. High androgen men were also less troubled with neurotic symptoms and had a higher frequency of sexual intercourse than men with a lower androgen/oestrogen balance. In the case of women, high oestrogen was associated with low neuroticism, a tendency towards affiliation (seeking friends and social contacts) and a high frequency of sexual intercourse. These results were summarized by the authors as suggesting that mental health and positive traits in general tend to go with a homotypic hormone balance, i.e., a high ratio of male hormones in a man and a high ratio of female hormones in a woman. There are several possible explanations of this. (1) Having atypical hormones may make adjustment more stressful, thus leading to psychiatric symptoms. (2) Psychiatric stress may lead to changes in the hormone balance. (3) Mental health, sexuality and hormone balance may be jointly affected by aging processes so as to produce these correlations.

Many clinical and laboratory studies show that androgen excess in men is associated with high energy levels, assertiveness, aggression and confidence, while androgen deficiency leads to anxiety and moodiness. The effect of oestrogen treatment on women is less clear, but there is some evidence that it leads to an increase in extraversion and a decrease in neuroticism (Rose, 1972; Herrmann and Beach, 1976; Herrmann and Beach, 1978). Oestrogen administered to adult men inhibits sex drive and aggression and has been used for this purpose with sex criminals.

Studies with rodents, primates and humans, show that androgens administered to a female foetus before birth masculinize the subsequent behaviour of that individual in various ways. Such females typically display higher levels of energy and aggression, independence and self-assurance, tomboyish behaviour and reduced levels of maternalism (Quadagno, Briscoe and Quadagno, 1977; Reinish, 1977). Also relevant is the finding of Wilson (1984) that lower-voiced opera singers are less emotional and more sexually active than their higher-voiced counterparts, associations that are presumably mediated by sex hormones during development.

These studies of the biochemical basis of sexuality and personality are quite new, and rapid development in the field can be expected. Indications are that androgens are involved in libido, masculinity and psychoticism, and perhaps also extraversion to some extent, while oestrogen is in some way connected with affiliation, empathy and sexual receptivity in women. Deficiencies in either seem to be connected with negative mood states, anxiety and failure to perform the appropriate sex role, especially when it is the homotypic hormone that is lacking. It will be some time before the relative contributions of pre-natal secretion, current circulation levels and receptor sensitivity are fully understood.

## PERSONALITY AND SEXUAL CONDITIONING

Since Eysenck had supposed that the connection between E and sexual behaviour is partly due to individual differences in conditionability, Kantorowitz (1978) studied the role of personality in the laboratory conditioning of sexual arousal—both *positive conditioning*, showing erotic slides during a phase of masturbation immediately preceding orgasm, and *deconditioning* to similar slides presented in the resolution phase just after orgasm were studied.

Despite a small sample (eight men aged 18–23), Kantorowitz found a significant positive correlation between E and the pre-orgasmic conditioning of arousal and a significant inverse correlation between E and post-orgasmic deconditioning. In other words, extroverts were positively conditioned to sexual arousal more easily than introverts, and introverts were more easily deconditioned. High N scores seemed to have an effect parallel to that of introversion, but this was not statistically significant.

Such findings might explain why extraverts are more sexually active and adventurous in real life, but they are difficult to reconcile with Eysenck's theory that introverts are generally more conditionable than extraverts. J. A. Gray's modification of the Eysenck theory which says that extraverts are reward oriented and therefore more conditionable in appetitive contexts, while introverts are more susceptible to fear of punishment and are therefore more conditionable in contexts involving anxiety and guilt seems to explain this result more easily. Kantorowitz suggests that introverts might have been more conditionable at both phases of the masturbation sequence (since this experimental procedure is bound to involve some degree of anxiety), but the high state of sexual arousal prior to ejaculation could have suppressed that anxiety, thus allowing extraverts to show greater conditioning. After orgasm, anxiety would predominate and there would be nothing to stop the introverts appearing as more conditionable.

Recent additions to Eysenck's theory (Eysenck and Levey, 1972) would suggest another explanation of the Kantorowitz finding. There is increasing evidence that introverts only condition better than extraverts under conditions of low arousal (e.g., when reinforcement is partial and weak). When the UCS is very strong extraverts show superior conditioning, and Eysenck has used the concept of protective (or 'transmarginal') inhibition to account for this. Apparently, introverts find strong stimulation so aversive that a neurological defence mechanism comes into play which drastically reduces input. Since it can be presumed that conditions of very high arousal prevail just prior to orgasm, transmarginal inhibition might reduce the conditionability of introverts to a level below that of extraverts, whereas introverts would show superior conditioning in the relative calm of the post-orgasmic phase.

Whichever interpretation is correct, personality does seem to be involved in processes of sexual arousal and conditioning. The Kantorowitz results also have clinical implications: pre-orgasmic conditioning may be of more use as a treatment technique with stable, extravert patients, while post-orgasmic deconditioning might produce better results with patients who are emotional introverts.


## DEVIANT SEXUALITY

The idea that high sexual arousal has power to suppress anxiety could help to explain the deviant behaviour of rapists. Barbaree, Marshall and Lanthier (1979) studied penile tumescence in ten convicted rapists and ten male students while they listened to verbal descriptions of mutually consenting sex, rape, and violent, non-sexual assault. While mutually consenting sex produced the greatest anatomical arousal in both groups, the non-rapists were 'turned-off' by rape sequences in direct proportion to the extent of force and brutality used in the description. Although not particularly aroused by assault *per se*, the rapists showed little diminution of sexual arousal when violence was applied in the furtherance of sex. Such a result implies that rapists are deviant, not so much because they are specifically aroused by non-consent and violence, but because these components fail to inhibit sexual arousal to the extent that they do in normal men. This in turn may be due to a failure of the social conditioning we call 'conscience', or desensitization to the emotional effects of violence because of the frequency of its occurrence within the subculture of the rapist.

The difficulty with impulse control that seems to characterize rapists ought to be reflected in high P and E scores on the EPQ, the effect of N being somewhat ambiguous. This prediction is consistent with such results as are available, although, as mentioned previously, prisoners are cagey about filling out questionnaires that might affect their future.

At the opposite extreme from the lack of inhibition displayed by rapists is the possibility that some men gravitate towards impersonal sex targets because they are made anxious by women. Wilson and Gosselin (1980) gave the EPQ to large samples of sexually variant men who were contacted through clubs catering to fetishists, transvestites and sadomasochists and the mailing lists of suppliers of special garments and equipment for such predilections. The results (Table 4) indicated that these men were generally more introverted and higher on neuroticism than age-matched controls, although no higher on N than normal women. P scores of variant men were not significantly elevated, but a group of women who specialized in meeting their requirements were notably high on P, as well as being relatively extraverted. All in all, this group of men appeared shy and timid, while their professional and amateur

**Table 4** *Mean Scores (and Standard Deviations) of Variant and Normal Groups on Personality Factors Measured by the Eysenck Personality Questionnaire.*

| | Number in group | Extraversion | Neuroticism | Psychoticism | Lie Scale |
|---|---|---|---|---|---|
| Sadomasochists | 133 | 10.68 (5.3) | 11.03 (5.9) | 3.50 (3.0) | 7.92 (4.2) |
| Rubberites | 87 | 10.87 (−) | 10.49 (−) | − (−) | 8.91 (−) |
| Leatherites | 38 | 12.55 (4.6) | 9.94 (5.9) | 3.29 (1.9) | 8.97 (4.6) |
| Transvestites | 269 | 9.96 (5.4) | 13.27 (5.8) | 3.27 (2.3) | 8.32 (4.2) |
| Transsexuals | 16 | 9.50 (5.2) | 13.06 (5.5) | 3.19 (2.3) | 11.12 (4.2) |
| Dominant women | 25 | 14.04 (5.5) | 12.68 (4.5) | 5.92 (3.8) | 7.00 (4.4) |
| Control males[1] | 50 | 12.38 (5.1) | 9.17 (5.1) | 3.09 (2.6) | 8.07 (4.1) |
| Control females (1)[2] | 416 | 12.24 (4.9) | 12.63 (5.4) | 2.35 (2.1) | 8.86 (3.9) |
| Control females (2)[3] | 27 | 11.97 (5.0) | 12.57 (5.3) | 2.28 (2.2) | 8.84 (4.1) |

*Source:* Wilson and Gosselin (1980).

*Notes:* 1 Control males are matched in age and social class with male variant groups.

2 This group of females is age-matched with the various male groups from EPQ standardization data.

3 These control females were collected specifically for our study and are age-matched for comparison specifically with the dominant women.

'mistresses' were the perfect foil to them, being dominant and extravert. A similar tendency for paedophile men to be introverted and shy has been reported by Wilson and Cox (1983).

Although a lack of social skill and inability to form relationships with women may be one predisposing factor in the development of variant sexual outlets, there are other factors to be considered. In Eysenck's theory, introversion would increase the likelihood of accidental conditioning of sexual arousal to inanimate materials such as rubber and leather and so help to explain the positive (enjoyable) aspects of such fixations. Once acquired, such variant interests may be self-reinforcing because they isolate the individual even further from social contacts. The transvestites may be an interesting exception in this respect, however. When cross-dressed and playing the female role they reported feeling more relaxed and sociable than when in the male mode, and this observation was supported by a shift in EPQ scores in the direction of lowered N and increased E (Gosselin and Eysenck, 1980).

Personality scores also distinguish one sexual predilection from another. When sadomasochists were divided into those who were primarily sadistic and those whose main interests were masochistic, the masochists appeared as more introverted than the sadists, and slightly lower on P. In fact, neither the sadists nor the leatherites were distinguishable from control males on E, while all the other variant men were significantly introverted.

Homosexual and bisexual men also tend towards the neurotic-introvert quadrant of Eysenck's E and N variables (Evans, 1970; Wilson and Fulford, 1979), as do lesbians (Eisinger *et al.*, 1972). However, the personality differences are not very striking. In fact, the tendency towards introversion is probably insignificant. Furthermore, it could be argued that the higher N scores observed in homosexual men and women could be due to the fact that subjects are often obtained through clinical channels, or to anxiety and conflict arising from their socially marginal status.

Bisexual men are distinguished from homosexual men primarily on the P dimension. Mean scores obtained by Wilson and Fulford were 4.25 for bisexuals and 2.10 for exclusive homosexuals. Heterosexual men scored in between these figures both in this study and in the test norms. This was one of several observations that led Wilson and Fulford to argue that bisexuals cannot be regarded as intermediate between exclusive homosexuals and exclusive heterosexuals, but in fact constitute a third independent sex orientation category exhibiting high levels of libido and masculinity, which leads to a greater generalization of sex targets.


## SEXUAL DYSFUNCTION


There is currently a great deal of interest in the question of female orgasmic difficulty. Despite considerable variability in the occurrence of female orgasm both within and between cultures (Eysenck and Wilson, 1979), it is widely presumed that women who do not regularly achieve orgasm are in some sense abnormal and in need of treatment. Eysenck's finding that women who complain of orgasm difficulties are higher in N than those who do not implies that there is an element of truth in this presumption. On the other hand, orgasm is by no means synonymous with sexual satisfaction in women (Hoon and Hoon, 1978), and a good case can be made for the theory that biologically the female orgasm is an artifact of the common neurology of men and women (Symons, 1979; Wilson, 1981). Since it never occurs with animals in the wild, female orgasm could hardly have evolved any survival function and is therefore best regarded as a capacity which, like piano playing, is not 'natural' but good if you can do it.

In any case, it is interesting to look at personality correlates of female orgasmic capacity. Eysenck (1976) found orgasm difficulty to be correlated with high N, but another study (Shope, 1968) found just the opposite—girls who had orgasms were apparently *less* stable than those who did not. However, since few details are available concerning the measure of 'emotional stability' used by Shope it was quite possibly more like a measure of 'expressiveness' than neuroticism, and this is more an extraverted characteristic. Fisher (1973) reported that orgasmic women are distinguished in terms of voice quality, high orgasm voices being judged as more natural and variable in tonal range, and with more use of emphatic and dramatizing sounds like sighs and deep breaths. These attributes also suggest expressiveness and would lend themselves well to the vocal sounds that often accompany women's orgasm.

High P should also be associated with orgasm, since high P women are more like men (who seldom have difficulty in this respect). Testosterone injections make women more responsive sexually (Kane, Lipton and Ewing, 1969), and persistence (a traditionally male characteristic) is also correlated with orgasmic ability (Fisher, 1973). It is surprising that Eysenck's research failed to show any significant association between P and orgasmic ability in women, although the slight difference that was found was in the expected direction (P scores of 3.06 and 2.77 for orgasmic and non-orgasmic women respectively).

Eysenck's finding of high N in men with potency disorders was complemented by a study by Munjack, Kanno and Oziel (1978) who reported high levels of anxiety, depression and general psychopathology in men with ejaculatory problems. Subjects were nineteen men who complained of premature ejaculation, and sixteen men with retarded ejaculation (inability to ejaculate in a state of normal desire and erection). Both groups were significantly higher than controls on the EPQ N scale as well as several other measures of anxiety and depression. Both premature and retarded ejaculators were also significantly higher than controls on the Schizophrenia and Social Introversion Scales of the MMPI, suggestive of high P and low E. The only variable to distinguish premature from retarded ejaculation was the Masculinity-Femininity scale of the MMPI, retarded ejaculation being significantly more 'masculine'.

The results of recent research on both women and men confirm Eysenck's finding that sexual dysfunction is most strongly associated with N. Insofar as P and E are implicated at all, they would seem to be favourable to sexual functioning, activity and potency. This is not the case with sexual deviation, where high P and E may be associated with a lack of impulse control of the kind that can lead to sexual assault.


## CONCLUSION


This paper has reviewed research by Eysenck and his associates concerning the way personality influences our sexual attitudes and behaviour and marital choice and satisfaction. These are important areas of life in which biologically-based personality factors can be seen to manifest themselves.

For the most part, the extrapolation of personality into sexuality follows predictable lines. Extraverts go for an active, pleasure oriented, variable and sociable sex life and tend to be permissive in their attitudes. Introverts are relatively quiet, controlled, private and discriminating in their sexual behaviour and tend towards puritanism. High N people show anxiety and conflict in sexual matters; they are not short on desire, but inhibited in performance, and so tend to develop dysfunctions such as orgasm difficulty, impotence and dissatisfaction. Low N people are the reverse, being unemotional, free of performance problems and contented with their love lives. High P scorers extend their unconventional and impersonal tendencies into their sex lives; they are sensation-seekers, enjoying group sex and variant activities and they rate physical sex above loving intimacy. Low P scorers (like high L scorers and conservatives) are conventional, considerate and loving. Differences between men and women parallel the differences between high and low P scorers, suggesting that androgens (whether pre-natal or contemporary) are involved with both masculinity and psychoticism.

Personality also appears to influence the kinds of deviant sexual behaviour that are adopted by some people, particularly men. Rapists seem to have high libido, but lack the social inhibitions that cause most men to ensure consent before undertaking sex with a woman. Thus, they tend to be high on P and E (impulsive and lacking in socialization). A high N score might be supposed to give rise to high sex drive, but this is likely to be offset by a tendency towards fear and anxiety. Sexual variations characterized by impersonal outlets such as fetishism, masochism and transvestism tend to be adopted by men who are afraid of social contact (thus usually introverted and high on N).

These deviant forms of sexual expression are largely male because females do not seem to have such a powerful targeting sex drive. Women's difficulties are more likely to be in forming satisfying long-term relationships (attractiveness and social skills) or in obtaining sufficient arousal and orgasm. Women who do not achieve satisfaction and those with orgasm difficulties are likely to be high on N, and perhaps also tending towards low E and P. The most common form of sexual dysfunction in men is premature or retarded ejaculation, which is also associated with high N and to a lesser extent introversion.

Clinicians who acquaint themselves with these findings concerning the relationship between constitutional personality and sexual inclination might better understand the sexual problems of their patients. The social lesson to be gained from these findings is that no rigid moral system can easily accommodate the striking individual differences that occur among human sexual needs and preferences. As Eysenck (1976) notes, puritanism may suit introverts, old people and a high proportion of women, but it is an impossible code for others to sustain. Permissiveness suits extraverts, high P individuals, young people and many men, but its public manifestation may become offensive to many others. There is also a danger of permissiveness becoming a paradoxically repressive orthodoxy, inducing naturally reserved people to engage in activities that they find distasteful.

Eysenck's work on personality in relation to marital satisfaction is a definite step forward in resolving the long-standing dispute between similarity and complementation theorists. It shows why correlational studies have consistently supported the similarity theory, yet at the same time explains why complementation theory is so persistent—it contains an element of truth in that gender asymmetry is usually best matched within an individual partnership. Against a general background of assortative mating and similarity effects upon satisfaction, there are some masculine and feminine qualities that complement each other. Eysenck's research is also valuable in reminding us that certain attributes brought to the partnership by each individual are predictive of marital unhappiness regardless of the chemistry of the relationship. Finally, the work is important for its demonstration that men and women have different motives and needs within marriage. The factors which make for a successful match to a man are not necessarily the same as those which make for satisfaction in a woman. Eysenck's work shows greater sophistication than most previous studies in viewing marital outcome from the perspective of husband and wife independently.

## REFERENCES

Barbaree, H. E., Marshall, W. L. and Lanthier, R. D. (1979) 'Deviant sexual arousal in rapists', *Behaviour Research and Therapy*, **17**, pp. 215–22.

Bentler, P. M. and Newcomb, M. D., (1979) 'Longitudinal study of marital success and failure', in Cook, M. and Wilson, G. D. (Eds.), *Love and Attraction*, Oxford, Pergamon Press.

Catlin, N., Croake, J. W. and Keller, J. F. (1976) 'MMPI profiles of cohabiting college couples', *Psychological Reports*, **38**, pp. 407–10.

Daitzman, R. J. (1976) 'Personality correlates of androgens and oestrogens'. PhD Thesis, University of Delaware.

Daitzman, R. J. and Zuckerman, M. (1980) 'Disinhibitory sensation-seeking, personality and gonadal hormones', *Personality and Individual Differences*, **1**, pp. 103–10.

Diamant, L. (1970) 'Premarital sexual behaviour, attitudes and emotional adjustment', *Journal of Social Psychology*, **82**, pp. 75–80.

Eisinger, A. J., Huntsman, R. G., Lord, J., Merry, J., Polani, P., Tanner, J. M., Whitehouse, H. and Griffiths, P. D. (1972) 'Female homosexuality', *Nature*, **238**, p. 106.

Evans, R. B. (1970) 'Sixteen Personality Factor Questionnaire scores of homosexual men', *Journal of Consulting and Clinical Psychology*, **34**, pp. 212–15.

Eysenck, H. J. (1976) *Sex and Personality*, London, Open Books.

Eysenck, H. J. (1979) *The Structure and Measurement of Intelligence*, Berlin, Springer.

Eysenck, H. J. (1980) 'Personality, marital satisfaction and divorce', *Psychological Reports*, **47**, pp. 1235–8.

Eysenck, H. J. and Levey, A. (1972) 'Conditioning introversion-extraversion and the strength of the nervous system', in Neblitzen, V. D. and Gray, J. A. (Eds.), *Biological Bases of Individual Behaviour*, New York, Academic Press.

Eysenck, H. J. and Wakefield, J. A. (1981) 'Psychological factors as predictors of marital satisfaction', *Advances in Behaviour Research and Therapy*, **3**, pp. 151–92.

Eysenck, H. J. and Wilson, G. D. (1979) *The Psychology of Sex*, London, Dent.

Farkas, G. M., Sine, L. F. and Evans, I. M. (1979) 'The effects of distraction, performance demand, stimulus explicitness and personality on objective and subjective measures of male sexual arousal', *Behaviour Research and Therapy*, **17**, pp. 25–32.

Fisher, S. (1973) *Understanding the Female Orgasm*, Harmondsworth, Penguin.

Giese, H. and Schmidt, A. (1968) *Studenten Sexualität*, Hamburg, Rowohlt.

Gosselin, C. C. and Eysenck, S. B. G. (1980) 'The transvestite "double-image": A preliminary report', *Personality and Individual Differences*, **1**, pp. 172–3.

Halleck, S. L. (1967) 'Sex and mental health on the campus', *Journal of the American Medical Association*, **200**, pp. 684–90.

Herrmann, W. M. and Beach, R. C., (1976) 'Psychotropic effects of androgens: A review of clinical observations and new human experimental findings', *Pharmacopsychiatry*, **9**, pp. 205–19.

Herrmann, W. M. and Beach, R. C. (1978) 'The psychotropic properties of oestrogens', *Pharmacopsychiatry*, **11**, pp. 164–76.

Hirschberg, N. (1979) 'Individual differences in social judgment: A multivariate approach', in Fishbein, M. (Ed.), *Progress in Social Psychology*, New Jersey, Erlbaum.

Hoon, E. F. and Hoon, P. W. (1978) 'Styles of sexual expression in women: Clinical implications of multivariate analyses', *Archives of Sexual Behaviour*, **7**, pp. 105–16.

Husted, J. R. and Edwards, A. E. (1976) 'Personality correlates of male sexual arousal and behaviour', *Archives of Sexual Behaviour*, **5**, pp. 149–56.

Insel, P. M. (1971) 'Family similarities in personality, intelligence and social attitudes', PhD thesis, University of London.

Joe, V. C., Brown, C. R. and Jones, R. (1976) 'Conservatism as a determinant of sexual experience', *Journal of Personality Assessment*, **40**, pp. 516–21.

Kane, F. J., Lipton, M. A. and Ewing, J. A. (1969) 'Hormonal influences in female sexual response', *Archives of General Psychiatry*, **20**, pp. 202–9.

Kantorowitz, D. A. (1978) 'Personality and conditioning of tumescence and detumescence', *Behaviour Research and Therapy*, **6**, pp. 117–23.

Kirton, M. (1977) 'Relatedness of married couples' scores on Adorno type tests', *Psychological Reports*, **40**, pp. 1013–14.

Lewin, B. and Trost, J. (1979) 'Unmarried cohabitation in Sweden', in Cook, M. and Wilson, G. D. (Eds.), *Love and Attraction*, Oxford, Pergamon Press.

Martin, N. G., Eaves, L. J. and Eysenck, H. J. (1977) 'Genetical, environmental and personality factors influencing the age of first intercourse in twins', *Journal of Biosocial Science*, **9**, pp. 91–7.

Munjack, D. J., Kanno, P. H. and Oziel, L. J. (1978) 'Ejaculatory disorders: Some psychometric data', *Psychological Reports*, **43**, pp. 783–9.

Nias, D. K. B. (1977) 'Husband-wife similarities', *Social Science*, **52**, pp. 206–11.

Persson, G. and Svanborg, A. (1980) 'Personality, mental symptoms and sexuality in relation to androgen and oestrogen activity in plasma in a 70-year-old population', Unpublished paper, Gothenberg, Sweden.

Quadagno, D. M., Briscoe, R. and Quadagno, J. S. (1977) 'Effect of perinatal gonadal hormones on selected non-sexual behaviour patterns: A critical assessment of the nonhuman and human literature', *Psychological Bulletin*, **84**, pp. 62–80.

Reinish, J. M. (1977) 'Prenatal exposure of human foetuses to synthetic progestin and oestrogen affects personality', *Nature*, **266**, pp. 561–2.

Rose, R. M. (1972) 'The psychological effects of androgens and oestrogens: A review', in Shader, R. I. (Ed.), *Psychiatric Complications of Medical Drugs*, New York, Raven Press.

Schmidt, G., Sigusch, V. and Meyberg, U. (1969) 'Psychosexual stimulation in men: Emotional reactions, changes of sex behaviour and measures of conservative attitudes', *Journal of Sex Research*, **5**, pp. 199–217.

Schofield, M. (1968) *The Sexual Behaviour of Young People*, Harmondsworth, Penguin.

Shope, D. F. (1968) 'The orgastic responsiveness of selected college females', *Journal of Sex Research*, **4**, pp. 204–19.

Symons, D. (1979) *The Evolution of Human Sexuality*, New York, Oxford University Press.

Thomas, D. R. (1975) 'Conservatism and premarital sexual experience', *British Journal of Social and Clinical Psychology*, **14**, pp. 195–6.

Thomas, D. R., Shea, J. D. and Rigby, R. G., (1971) 'Conservatism and response to sexual humour', *British Journal of Social and Clinical Psychology*, **10**, pp. 185–6.

Thorne, F. C., Haupt, T. D. and Allen, R. M. (1966) 'Objective studies of adult male sexuality utilizing the Sex Inventory', *Journal of Clinical Psychology Monograph Supplement*, No. 21, October.

Wilson, G. D. (1973) *The Psychology of Conservatism*, London, Academic Press.

Wilson, G. D. (1978) *The Secrets of Sexual Fantasy*, London, Dent.

Wilson, G. D. (1981) *Love and Instinct*, London, Temple Smith.

Wilson, G. D. (1984) 'The personality of opera singers', *Personality and Individual Differences*, **5**, pp. 195–201.

Wilson, G. D. and Cox, D. N. (1983) 'Personality of paedophile club members', *Personality and Individual Differences*, **4**, pp. 323–9.

Wilson, G. D. and Fulford, K. W. M. (1979) 'Sexual behaviour, personality and hormonal characteristics of heterosexual, homosexual and bisexual men', in Cook, M. and Wilson, G. D. (Eds.), *Love and Attraction*, Oxford, Pergamon, Press.

Wilson, G. D. Gosselin, C. C. (1980) 'Personality characteristics of fetishists, transvestites and sadomasochists', *Personality and Individual Differences*, **1**, pp. 289–95.

Wilson, G. D. and Maclean, A. (1974) 'Personality, attitudes and humour preferences of prisoners and controls', *Psychological Reports*, **34**, pp. 847–54.

Zaleski, Z. and Galkowska, M. (1978) ' Neuroticism and marital satisfaction', *Behaviour Research and*

*Therapy*, **16,** pp. 285–6.

Zuckerman, M. (1974) 'The sensation-seeking motive', in Maher, B. (Ed.), *Progress in Experimental Personality Research*, Vol. 7, New York, Academic Press.

Zuckerman, M., Tushup, R. and Finner, S. (1976) 'Sexual attitudes and experiences: Attitude and personality correlates and changes produced by a course in sexuality', *Journal of Consulting and Clinical Psychology*, **44,** pp. 7–19.

# 16. Marriage and Sex: Moving from Correlations to Dynamic Personality by Personality Interactions—Limits of Monocular Vision

DAVID G. GILBERT

The hope of understanding and predicting marital and sexual behaviour and attitudes in terms of individual differences in personality is an old and venerable goal. This chapter attempts to show that the models generally used to date to accomplish this goal are inadequate. Suggestions for more adequate research are provided.

## Introduction

Eysenck has attempted to explain the great variety of marital satisfaction and sexual behaviour and attitudes by means of his personality superfactors and genetics and thereby gain support for and insight into his model of personality. The initial focus of this chapter is upon his contributions to the marital literature. Then his contributions to the sexual literature will be considered. Criticisms are made of his work, as well as of the two fields in general.

## PERSONALITY AND MARITAL SATISFACTION

Eysenck's approach to the understanding of marital satisfaction is similar to that of researchers during the first half of the century, but contrary to the thinking of the vast majority of current ones. The inadequacy of both Eysenck's and current mainstream marital research is discussed and a model that seeks to integrate the two approaches is briefly outlined.

### Fifty Years of .25 Correlations

During the first half of the century there were several prospective studies that evaluated the relationship between premarital personality and background factors and marital success/satisfaction (MS). Marital satisfaction generally correlated from .20 to .30 with single personality traits related to neuroticism (N), and correlated around .50 with predictive scores formed by combining personality traits, background and demographics (Adams, 1946; Burgess and Wallin, 1953; Kelly and Conley, 1985; Kelly, 1939; Terman, 1951; Terman and Oden, 1947). The only predictive work in the past few decades was a small study by Bentler and Newcomb (1978). This study, like that of Terman, found personality variables taken prior to marriage to be much more predictive of MS than background and demographic variables. Cross-sectional correlational studies support the longitudinal findings. Large-scale studies by Burchinal *et al.* (1957), Burgess and Wallin (1953), Cole, Cole and Dean (1980), Dean (1966) and Terman (1938) have all found correlations (generally from .18 to .40) between neuroticism and MS.

Traits other than neuroticism have not been extensively evaluated. However, a very strong effect for personality is suggested by Robins' longitudinal study of conduct disordered (high psychoticism?) children. It was found that 78 per cent of the conduct disordered children grew up to become divorced, while this figure was only 21 per cent for matched controls (Robins, 1966, p. 104).

## Eysenck on Personality and Marital Satisfaction

Eysenck's major piece of research on the topic of marriage is a cross-sectional study of 566 couples done in cooperation with James Wakefield, Jr. (Eysenck and Wakefield, 1981). Given the numerous studies of a similar nature carried out prior to the study, it is their interpretation of the results, not the results themselves, that is surprising.

MS correlated with N and psychoticism (P) to the same degree ($-27$ and $-24$ respectively for males; and $-19$ and $-19$ for females). The extremely small positive association between extraversion (E) and MS was significant for males ($r = .09$), but not for females ($r = .04$). Multiple linear correlations, utilizing P, E, N and L to predict MS, were $R = .34$ for males, and $R = .35$ for females. In contrast to the small correlations with personality, the multiple correlations of MS with approximately thirty questions related to the marital sexual relationship were high, .65 for males, .72 for females.

These findings led Eysenck and Wakefield to report that '... an astonishingly high proportion of the total MS variance is accounted for by our questionnaires (67% of the total variance, or 74% of the "true" variance).' They conclude that their '... data suggest that much of the satisfaction (or otherwise) a person derives from ... marriage is contributed by his own personality', including individual sexual factors. They then state that '... there are many people whom it would not be wise for anyone to marry!'

Prospective studies have not addressed this issue of the relative contributions of who one is, whom one marries, and their interaction. However, evidence suggests that previously divorced married individuals are not significantly less happy than individuals without a history of divorce (Glenn and Weaver, 1977). Furthermore, findings by Eysenck and others show that the marital satisfaction and personality of one's spouse correlate almost as highly as one's own personality with one's MS. These findings are consistent with the view that whom one marries is a highly important determinant of one's MS. Why Eysenck downplays this possibility is not clear.

Furthermore, Eysenck's conclusion that sexual behaviour/satisfaction (possibly mediated by personality) determines MS must be questioned because over forty-five years ago Terman (1938, p. 260) persuasively argued that sexual satisfaction is a reflection of MS, not the other way around. Clinicians have noted that happy marriages can put up with significant sexual dysfunctions, while in distressed marriages there is little tolerance for deviations from sexual perfection (O'Leary and Arias, 1983). In accepting sexual processes as independent causal processes, rather than as reflections of or dimensions of MS, Eysenck makes the same mistake as do the systems and behavioural theorists who tend to view process as a cause, rather than a sample of the behaviour they seek to explain.

Not only should we interpret cautiously any causal inferences implied by correlations between MS and sexual satisfaction, but we must also question the strength and nature of these correlations. The marital satisfaction inventory used by Eysenck includes items pertaining to sexual behaviour, and the sexual inventories include items that are more directly related to the quality of the relationship than to specific sexual activities. Certainly future studies should control for common item overlap (Nicholls, Licht and Pearl, 1982).

## MATE PERSONALITY COMBINATIONS

### Spouse Similarity: The Chicken or the Egg?

A major question in the field of marital theory and therapy is that of the cause of spouse similarity, the tendency for spouses to be more similar on indices of psychopathology and MS than if they married at random. The two major competing hypotheses are premarital disposition (assortive mating) versus marital interaction-induced concordance.

Homogamy, the condition where like is married to like, has been found to occur generally for education, religion, age, race and social class, as well as for psychological factors (reviewed by Merikangas, 1982). Numerous studies have shown only a very slight tendency for spouse similarity for psychological factors with no pathological implications, but have shown moderate tendencies for more pathological variables such as primary affective disorder, schizophrenia, alcoholism, antisocial personality and neurosis.

Proponents of the interaction hypothesis have argued that those studies that have shown increasing concordance in couples with increasing length of marriage support the interactional view. However, Merikangas (1982) notes that these studies were not adequately controlled and suggests that the majority of studies do not support the theory that marital interaction produces concordance for psychopathology. She concludes her review by stating that prospective studies will be needed to determine the relative contributions of premarital disposition and marital interaction to the observed concordance of marital couples for psychopathology (Merikangas, 1982).

Unfortunately, Eysenck and Wakefield (1981) used a cross-sectional design. They evaluated the similarity of their husband-wife correlations and found no correlation for E, and very low ones for N (.13) and P (.14), moderate ones for sexual attitudes (.43, .41) and high ones for marital satisfaction (.73). There was no increase in similarity for these variables with increase in length of marriage. Therefore, they concluded that the interactional hypothesis was not supported, and that assortive mating, by the acceptance of the null hypothesis, was. Their conclusion was that 'marital satisfaction ... appears to be the most direct measure ... of what the spouses selected each other for'. This ready rejection of interactional explanations in favour of initial assortive mating is consistent with simplistic deductions from Eysenck's biological-genetic-trait orientation. However, there are reasons why the interactional hypothesis cannot so easily be discarded.

Eysenck's procedures, like those of researchers preceding him, tested only what might be called the very slow-induction model of interpersonally generated similarity. This model assumes that changes in spouse similarity take place slowly, over a large number of years. The methods used by Eysenck and by others look at linear trends for up to forty or more years of marriage and are totally inadequate to detect changes that might occur within the first year or two of marriage. This failure to use techniques sensitive to rapid initial changes has resulted in a number of still viable interactional alternatives to the assortive mating hypothesis.

The first of the three interactional alternatives is that of induced similarity by an individual with psychopathological traits upon a less pathological partner. In support of this alternative, there is strong experimental evidence that depressed individuals communicate to strangers, as well as their spouses, in a manner that induces immediate negative effect in the listener (Blumberg and Hokanson, 1983; Coyne, 1976; Howes and Hokanson, 1979).

A second form of rapidly-induced similarity would be one in which neither partner was characterized by pathological traits prior to marriage, yet one or both have an interpersonal skill deficit, such as a lack of conflict resolution skills. Such deficits are thought by many to be a primary cause of marital distress (Jacobson and Margolin, 1979).

The third possibility is that a mismatch of two personalities exists. This mismatch results in rapid increases in distress in both spouses. Unfortunately, there has been virtually no research evaluating marital satisfaction as a function of the match/mismatch of the multivariate personality profiles of the two spouses.

These three models offer highly plausible alternatives to Eysenck's conclusion that similarity of spouse MS and personality does not change over time and that the correlation between spouses must, therefore, be a result of assortive mating for MS, P and N. Only longitudinal studies with repeated frequent sampling prior to and during marriage will provide anything resembling a definitive answer to which model best fits reality.

## Similarity and Marital Satisfaction

A number of theorists have speculated as to what matches might be productive of marital distress or satisfaction (Burgess and Wallin, 1953; Gilbert, 1981; Terman, 1938; Winch, 1958). Findings generally suggest that there is a very slight tendency for individuals more similar in personality, socio-economic status and background to be better adjusted and happier with their marriage than those less similar (Nias, 1977). Consistent with this generalization, Terman (1938, p. 35) found that out of 545 items, marital distress was most highly associated with the item showing one spouse liking and the other disliking to argue.

The Eysenck and Wakefield (1981) study made a contribution in that it provided support for Eysenck's asymmetry hypothesis, the idea that sex-typical differences in personality are less detrimental to MS than sex-atypical differences. These findings, along with the calculations of the personality differences associated with maximal marital satisfaction, are a step towards greater sophistication in the analysis of spouse matches.

This step falls far short, however, of evaluating the multivariate personality profile of the husband with that of the wife. Eysenck and Wakefield evaluated only the two simplest types of interactions: (1) differences between spouses on a given variable; and (2) the interaction of one husband personality variable with a different wife variable. The fact that this univariate interactional analysis did not account for much of the variation in MS does not mean that a more sophisticated analysis of the multivariate pattern of one spouse with that of the other would be of equally little value.

## TOWARDS MORE ADEQUATE RESEARCH AND MODELS OF MARITAL BEHAVIOUR AND SATISFACTION

Eysenck's large correlational tables with small correlations may be of interest to some, but the rapid defection of marital researchers from correlational and trait research since the 1960s suggests that most psychologists desire models of interpersonal processes that are richer conceptually, more comprehensive and capable of causally accounting for a higher portion of the variance. This rechannelling of energies has led to valuable contributions by systems and behavioural psychologists (Gottman, 1979; Jacobson and Margolin, 1979; Watzlawick and Weakland, 1977).

Though the systems and behavioural research orientations have been of great value in pointing out the importance of what happens in marital relationships from the short-term process perspective, they have consistently ignored or denied the importance of the personality factors that predictive studies have shown to be of true explanatory value. Thus, there is a clear need for a model that integrates concepts and findings of personality theory with interpersonal process theory. A great deal of hard work will be needed if integrated, powerful and clinically useful models of sexual and marital behaviour are to be developed.

### DARING TO DO IT CORRECTLY

Table 1 is designed to promote high-quality integrated theoretical models and research. It allows one to compare the work of Eysenck with that of other cross-sectional trait, longitudinal trait, behavioural and systems research. The following paragraphs correspond in order to the nine items listed in Table 1.

1  The importance of taking steps to assure confidential and independent completion of questionnaires by spouses has been emphasized by many leaders in the field (Bowerman, 1964; Terman, 1938), yet the work of Eysenck and many others has not provided such assurance.

**Table 1** *A Framework for Progress in Marital Research*

|  | HJE | CROSS | PRED | BEH | SYS |
|---|---|---|---|---|---|
| 1 Independent completion | − | 0 | + | 0 | ? |
| 2 Representative sample | − | − | +/0 | ? | ? |
| 3 Correlation versus causation and sample versus cause | − | − | 0 | − | − |
| 4 Longitudinal-predictive versus cross-sectional | − | − | + | − | − |
| 5 Generalizability-specificity | 0 | 0 | 0 | 0 | − |
| 6 Multimethod | − | − | − | + | 0 |
| 7 Experimental | − | − | − | 0 | − |
| 8 Interaction/circular causation | − | − | − | + | + |
| 9 Personality profile by personality profile interactions | − | − | − | − | − |

Note:   HJE = Eysenck; CROSS = cross-sectional studies; PRED = predictive/longitudinal studies;
    BEH = behavioural research; SYS = systems research.
    '+' = issue addressed generally; 'O' = issue frequently not or minimally addressed;
    '−' = generally not addressed; '?' = status not clear.

2   A representative sample of the group of interest is important. For example,
    cross-sectional marital studies that do not include divorced couples limit the
    degree to which one can generalize to divorce-predisposed and highly
    distressed marriages. Longitudinal studies can largely circumvent this pro-
    blem of differential attrition.

3   The tendency to infer causation from correlational data associated with MS
    is a strong one in Eysenck's work, as well as in the field in general. This is
    especially true in the case of the strong association of MS with marital
    process variables such as sexual satisfaction and communication patterns.
    Behavioural and systems theorists generally assume that spouse communic-
    ation plays a dominant causal role in determining MS. There are two
    problems with these assumptions. First, even if there is some significant
    causal relationship between self-reported MS and these marital process
    variables, one must be aware that these processes are not independent of MS,
    but are better conceptualized as samples of or dimensions of MS, and thus
    not causal in any strong sense. Secondly, there is not strong evidence that
    marital satisfaction is caused by such process variables. White (1983) has
    interpreted his data as suggesting that spouse communications may be more a
    result than a cause of MS. Furthermore, the evidence is not strongly
    supportive of the view that communications training has a positive long-term
    effect on MS (Schindler, Hahlweg and Revenstorf, 1983).

4   Longitudinal predictive studies are clearly the only way to answer the causal
    questions asked by Eysenck. Leaders in the field have repeatedly noted this
    for the past forty-five years (Bowerman, 1964; Terman, 1938; Spanier and
    Lewis, 1980). Unfortunately, there has been practically no work in this area
    for the past three decades. Feldman and Feldman (1975) argue in favour of
    short-term longitudinal studies that follow individuals and couples through
    critical transitions.

5   The first step towards understanding the degree to which the negative
    communication patterns characteristic of distressed spouses are specific to
    their communications with each other, as opposed to a generalized trait, has

been taken (Birchler, Weiss and Vincent, 1975; Vincent, Weiss and Bitchler 1975). Why these results showed distressed couples to communicate in a negative manner with their spouses, but not with strangers, is not clear, Possibly classically conditioned negative emotional responses or habit patterns specifically related to the spouse in a manner suggested by Berkowitz's (1983) work on aggression play a role. Such conditioned emotional responses might lead to emotional-state-dependent associations, goals and communicational strategies.

6   Multimethod approaches have rarely been used by marital researchers outside the behavioural persuasion. Behaviourally oriented researchers and therapists frequently rely upon both self-report and behavioural measures (Jacobson and Margolin, 1979). In addition, several research groups have combined physiological, behavioural and self-report measures (Levenson and Gottman, 1983; Notarius and Johnson, 1982). However, only one group has looked at all three of these measures plus personality (Gilbert, Hermecz and Davis, 1982, 1983). These findings suggest that a great deal of information can be gained by combining physiological measures with behavioural and self-report measures during the study of MS and marital conflict resolution. Twin studies for the analysis of genetic contributions to MS may also be of value as a component of a multimethod approach (Taylor, 1971).

7   Experimental designs have rarely been used in marital research, but some recent experimental work by the present author and his colleagues has proved that such approaches can be highly rewarding (Gilbert, Hermecz and Davis, 1982, 1983). In a study that independently manipulated the content and affect of marital problem-related messages, males who listened to their spouse presenting messages with neutral affect and non-blaming contents experienced orienting-response-like cardiac deceleration, while wives experienced defensive-response-like cardiac acceleration. In contrast, males who listened to their spouse presenting messages with negative affect and blaming contents experienced defensive-response-like cardiac acceleration, while wives experienced orienting-response-like deceleration. These sex-by-message interactions were interpreted as being consistent with previous work showing that husbands want their wives to speak in a less emotional manner, while wives want their husbands to be more emotionally responsive (Burke, Weir and Harrison, 1976). Marital dissatisfaction, non-listening and emotional responses, neuroticism and a lack of subsequent problem resolution were all associated with large listener heart rate and electrodermal responses.

8   Circular causation has been emphasized by most systems and behavioural marital theorists. This is the view that any behaviour (communication) of the wife is a response to the behaviour of the husband, which in turn is a response to the wife, etc. The sequential analysis of patterns of communication, underlined by the concept of circular causation, has been an important step forward in the field (Gottman, 1979). Now the relationship of personality by personality interactions to such sequences needs to to be addressed.

9   The effects of the interaction of the personality profile of the husband with the personality profile of the wife have not been studied in terms of either marital process or satisfaction. Instead, most analyses are performed by linear uni- or multivariate correlational methods that cannot detect import-

ant interactions among variables. For example, Hall, Hesselbrock and Stabenau (1983) have noted that tall men and short women are relatively free in the choice of their spouse's height. On the other hand, tall women and short men rarely select each other. Interactions such as this sex-by-height effect or interactions of E and N would go undetected by analyses traditionally used in marital and sex research.

The joint analysis of husband and wife personality profiles creates a large number of couple types. In the simplest case sixteen couple types are derived from the interaction of the husband's and the wife's 2 × 2 personality matrices. Using two levels of E and two of N for both husband and wife, Gilbert (1981) was able to develop hypotheses for each of the sixteen possible couple types. The nature of the hypotheses was much more specific and clinically relevant than if E and N were considered independently .

## PERSONALITY AND SEXUAL BEHAVIOUR/ATTITUDES

Eysenck has published more research on the relationship of personality to sexual behaviour than any other author. Prior to his work there was surprisingly little scientific study of the relationship of personality to sexual behaviour and attitudes, most of the work having focused on female orgasmic dysfunction. Studies showed this dysfunction frequently to have small, marginally significant associations with neuroticism, but virtually no association with other personality measures or with background or marital variables (Fisher, 1973; Terman, 1938). Before Eysenck's investigations the only work on the relationship of the full range of sexual behaviour and attitudes studied only unmarried college students (Giese and Schmidt, 1968).

### Eysenck's Hypotheses

Eysenck's hypotheses (1972, 1976) followed directly from his three-factor theory of personality. His theory suggests that extraverts prefer higher levels of stimulation and have less well-developed consciences than do introverts. These sensation-seeking and socialization factors are seen as working together to predict that extraverts will experience more sexual activity sooner and with more variations and partners than introverts. The high emotional reactivity of individuals scoring high on neuroticism (N) is predicted to cause them to worry more about sex, to be more disgusted by certain sexual acts and to have more sexual inhibitions. The individual scoring high on Eysenck's third personality factor, psychoticism (P), is predicted to be characterized as having an impersonal, cold and aggressive orientation to both sex and life in general.

### Eysenck's and Related Questionnaire Studies

Most of these hypotheses have found marginally significant support by Eysenck and, in some cases, by other workers. The predicted correlations for E have most frequently been substantiated (Eysenck, 1976; Farley *et al.*, 1977; Giese and Schmidt,

1968; Schenk, Phrang and Rausche; 1983). The correlations are generally from .10 to .20. However, the instability of these small correlations is seen by the fact that efforts to replicate Eysenck's finding of a correlation between E and libido failed to obtain significance in a sample of 631 husbands and 631 wives (Schenk *et al.*, 1983).

The relationship of N to sexual attitudes and behaviour appears to be very weak and unreliable. Of the numerous comparisons made by Giese and Schmidt (1968), very few were found to be associated with N. Barton and Cattell (1972) found very small but significant positive correlations between emotional stability and sexual satisfaction. Arrindell (Arrindell, Boelens and Lambert, 1983; Arrindell, Emmelkamp and Bast, 1983) found significant negative correlations (r $= -.22$ and $-.36$) between sexual satisfaction and N in female, but not male spouses. In a group of 631 couples, Schenk, Phrang and Rausche (1983) found no correlations stronger than r $= -.10$ between N and sexual satisfaction. Cases of sexual dysfunction have average scores only very slightly higher on N than controls (Eysenck, 1976, pp. 66–7; Fisher, 1973). Furthermore, although the sexual problems of some individuals clearly do relate to underlying neurotic problems, highly neurotic individuals frequently enjoy excellent sexual functioning; it can no longer be assumed that sexual difficulties are a function of neuroticism (Kaplan, 1974, p. 482). As predicted, P has generally been found to correlate to a small degree in a negative direction with sexual satisfaction and in a positive direction with libido, and cold and impersonal sex (Eysenck, 1976). Like others, Eysenck has found a relatively large and consistent tendency for women, compared to men, to report more conservative, less 'perverse', and less active and aggressive desires and attitudes in virtually all sexual matters (Eysenck, 1976; Hagen, 1979; Iwawaki and Eysenck, 1978; Iwawaki and Wilson, 1983; Symons, 1980).

## Physiological and Genetic Studies

Physiological studies have not supported Eysenck's hypotheses. Two studies, Farkas, Sine and Evans (1979) and Griffith and Walker (1975), failed to find a relationship between personality factors (P, E, N) and penile and vaginal responses to erotic stimuli respectively. A third study (Kantorowitz, 1978) found E, but not N, to relate to conditioned penile responses.

Eysenck believes that genetic factors are very important determinants of sexual behaviour and attitudes and of male-female differences in sexual and non-sexual behaviour. He and his colleagues (Martin and Eysenck, 1976; Martin, Eaves and Eysenck, 1977) have interpreted their twin studies as suggesting that male libido is primarily determined by genetic factors and that age of first intercourse is partially genetically determined. However, he correctly notes that his results are open to other interpretations because of small sample size (see Haviland, McGuire and Rothbaum, 1983). Unfortunately, there do not appear to be any other studies in this area.

## Methodological Problems

With generally much less than 10 per cent of the variance explained by any given personality variable, one must be especially alert to the possibility that common method variance is accounting for the correlations that Eysenck sees as supporting his theory. This is of paramount importance because physiological studies (noted earlier) have not demonstrated differential sexual responsivity as a function of personality.

Poor reading ability and/or random marking produce high scores on both the P scale and rarely answered (deviate and 'perverted') Sex Questionnaire items. If only a small percentage of respondents randomly marked a portion of their questionnaires, spurious correlations would appear between P and indications of cold, impersonal and deviant sexual behaviour and attitudes independently of whether such behaviour is actually true of true high-P individuals. How possible this is, is seen by the fact that a very high percentage of the items in his sex questionnaires have highly skewed response distributions. For the Inventory of Attitudes to Sex (Eysenck, 1976, p. 80), 40 per cent of the items were answered 'yes' by fewer than 15 per cent or by more than 75 per cent of the males. Other forms of method variance could account for some or all of the correlations of personality with reported sexual attitudes and behaviour. All of the potential errors associated with purely correlational studies and dealing with data solely in the self-report domain must be considered. There is an obvious need for multimethod approaches designed to circumvent methods variance problems.

## Conclusions: Personality and Sex

Eysenck's research has been successful in showing that simple linear univariate correlations of his higher-order personality factors with higher- or lower-order sexual behaviour factors are not of much explanatory value. After controlling for common methods variance, it is unlikely that more than 5 per cent of the variance of sexual activity and attitudes are generally explained by univariate correlations with his personality variables. The field is in great need of multimethod, multitrait approaches that are more focused on the understanding of the patterns of variables and processes related to the behaviours of concern than with confirmation of theories of personality. On the other hand, Eysenck has stated that we should not be discouraged by the smallness of the correlations since they are generally significant and in the directions hypothesized by his theory of personality (1972).

## Directions for Future Research

The integration of personality models with exchange and other interactional models would appear to be a promising goal. The work of Schofield (1968) showed that young males who had experienced intercourse tended to be more attractive than average, while females tended to be less so than average. This suggests that attractive females do not need to exchange sex for dates; their looks attract males. Similarly, the social skills of some intelligent stable extraverts who are low on psychoticism may be especially valued characteristics that can be exchanged for sexual or other favours. The personality-social exchange model suggests the interesting possibility that some attractive individuals may become popular and thus more socially extraverted because of this popularity. Such popularity-induced social interaction might be more responsible than Eysenck's hypothesized physiological causes for the tendency for extraverts to engage in more sexual activity sooner.

A multidimensional exchange model that includes personality would have heuristic advantages in that it would suggest that we ask not only if or how often someone had sex, but with whom, and with how desirable a partner. In line with this call for greater specification and integration, future studies should not only aim at estimating the heritabilities of different sexual behaviours, but should also try to understand by what mechanisms the genes are having their effects. Attractiveness, intelligence and social personality may be genetically determined external variables that play a much more important role in influencing one's sex life than the less socially observable physiological factors postulated by Eysenck (1976).

## CONCLUSIONS: PERSONALITY, MARRIAGE AND SEX

There are a number of common denominators in Eysenck's marital and sexual work. Both are based on cross-sectional questionnaire studies of large numbers of subjects. Personality correlates both with marital satisfaction and with self-report sexual measures to small degrees in the directions hypothesized by Eysenck. In both areas there is a relative lack of interest in the relationship of personality to variables under investigation. This lack of interest may be due to the smallness of the correlations found by Eysenck and others, and to a recognition that these associations may be largely an artifact of methods variance.

This chapter suggests that multivariate, multimethod, interactive models that include a focus on process will prove much more powerful and attractive to potential researchers than the correlational approach used by Eysenck and others. It also suggests that much more effort must be made to use designs that are capable of identifying causal relationships. One well-designed prospective longitudinal design is usually worth more than dozens of cross-sectional studies.

The author, like Eysenck, believes that an understanding of human behaviour requires an understanding of genetics, biology and personality. Furthermore, it seems reasonable to assume that much of our genetic and biological programming was designed to deal with social interactions and contingencies. It is likely that the personality theorists of the future will focus more on interpersonal interactions as a function of the multivariate personality profiles of the interactants. Such an approach is certainly consistent with the currently popular behavioural, exchange and interactional approaches.

## REFERENCES

Adams, C. R. (1946) 'The prediction of adjustment in marriage', *Educational and Psychological Measurements*, **6**, pp. 185–93.

Arrindell, W. A., Boelens, W. and Lambert, H. (1983) 'On the psychometric propereties of the Maudsley Marital Questionnaire (MMQ): Evaluation of self-ratings in distressed and "normal" volunteer couples based on the Dutch version', *Personality and Individual Differences*, **4**, pp. 293–306.

Arrindell, W. A., Emmelkamp, P. M. G. and Bast, S. (1983) 'The Maudsley Marital Questionnaire (MMQ): A further step towards its validation', *Personality and Individual Differences*, **4**, pp. 457–64.

Barton, K. and Cattell, R. B. (1972) 'Marriage dimensions and personality', *Journal of Personality and Social Psychology*, **21**, pp. 369–75.

Bentler, P. M. and Newcomb, M. D. (1978) 'Longitudinal study of marital success and failure', *Journal of Consulting and Clinical Psychology*, **46**, pp. 1053–70.

Berkowitz, L. (1983) 'Aversively stimulated aggression', *American Psychologist*, **38**, pp. 1135–44.

Birchler, G. R., Weiss, R. L. and Vincent, J. P. (1975) 'Multimethod analysis of social reinforcement exchange between maritally distressed and nondistressed spouse and stranger dyads', *Journal of Personality and Social Psychology*, **31**, pp. 349–60.

Blumberg, S. R. and Hokanson, J. E. (1983) 'The effects of another person's response style on interpersonal behavior in depression', *Journal of Abnormal Psychology*, **92**, pp. 196–209.

Bowerman, C. E. (1964) 'Prediction studies', in Christensen, H. T. (Ed.), *Handbook of Marriage and the Family*, Chicago; Ill, Rand McNally.

Burchinal, L. G., Hawkes, G. R. and Gardner, B. (1957) 'Personality characteristics and marital satisfaction', *Social Forces*, **35**, pp. 218–22.

Burgess, E. W. and Wallin, P. (1953) *Engagement and Marriage*, Chicago, Ill, Lippincott.

Burke, R. J., Weir, T. and Harrison, D. (1976) 'Disclosure of problems and tensions experienced by marital partners', *Psychological Reports*, **38**, pp. 531–42.

Cole, C. L., Cole, A. L. and Dean, W. G. (1980) 'Emotional maturity and marital adjustment: A decade replication', *Journal of Marriage and the Family*, **42**, pp. 533–9.

Coyne, J. C. (1976) 'Depression and the response of others', *Journal of Abnormal Psychology*, **85**, pp. 186–93.

Dean, D. G. (1966) 'Emotional maturity and marital adjustment', *Journal of Marriage and the Family*, **28**, pp. 454–7.

Eysenck, H. J. (1972) 'Personality and sexual behaviour', *Journal of Psychosomatic Research*, **16**, pp. 141–52.

Eysenck, H. J. (1976) *Sex and Personality*, Austin, Tex., University of Texas Press.

Eysenck, H. J. (1983) *I Do: Your Guide to a Happy Marriage*, London, Century.

Eysenck, H. J. and Wakefield, J. A., Jr. (1981) 'Psychological factors as predictors of marital satisfaction', *Advances in Behaviour Research and Therapy*, **3**, pp. 151–92.

Eysenck, H. J. and Wilson, G. (1979) *The Psychology of Sex*, London, Dent.

Farkas, G. M., Sine, L. F. and Evans, I. M. (1979) 'The effects of distraction, performance demand, stimulus explicitness and personality on objective and subjective measures of male sexual arousal', *Behaviour Research and Therapy*, **17**, pp. 25–32.

Farley, F. H., Nelson J. G., Knight, W. C. and Garcia-Colberg, E. (1977) 'Sex, politics and personality': A multidimensional study of college students', *Archives of Sexual Behaviour*, **6**, pp. 105–19.

Feldman, H. and Feldman, M. (1975) 'The family life cycle: Some suggestions for recycling', *Journal of Marriage and the Family*, **37**, pp. 277–84.

Fisher, S. (1973) *The Female Orgasm*, New York, Basic Books.

Giese, H. and Schmidt, A. (1968) *Studenten Sexualitat*, Hamburg, Rowohlt.

Gilbert, D. G. (1981) 'A biopsychosocial systems theory of communication and conflict in marriage and family', Unpublished manuscript.

Gilbert, D. G., Hermecz, D. A. and Davis, H. C. (1982) 'Heart rate and skin conductance responses during marital communication as a function of message and personality', *Psychophysiology*, **19**, p. 562.

Gilbert, D. G., Hermecz, D. A. and Davis, H. C. (1983) *Heart Rate and Electrodermal Responses during Marital Communication as a Function of Message, Personality and Marital Satisfaction*, Manuscript to be submitted for publication.

Gottman, J. M. (1979) *Marital Interaction: Experimental Investigations*, New York, Academic Press.

Griffith, M. and Walker, E. C. (1975) 'Menstrual cycle phases and personality variables as related to response to erotic stimuli', *Archives of Sexual Behavior*, **4**, pp. 599–603.

Hagen, R. (1979) *The Bio-Sexual Factor*, Garden City, N. Y., Doubleday.

Hall, R. L., Hesselbrock, V. M. and Stabenau, J. R. (1983) 'Familial distribution of alcohol use: II. Assortative mating of alcoholic probands', *Behavior Genetics*, **13**, pp. 373–82.

Haviland, J. M., McGuire, T. R. and Rothbaum, P. A. (1983) 'A critique of Plomin and Foch's " A twin study of objectively assessed personality in childhood"', *Journal of Personality and Social Psychology*, **45**, pp. 633–40.

Hines, M. (1982) 'Prenatal gonadal hormones and sex differences in human behavior', *Psychological Bulletin*, **92**, pp. 56–80.

Howes, M. J., and Hokanson, J. E. (1979) 'Conversational and social responses to depressive interpersonal behavior', *Journal of Abnormal Psychology*, **88**, pp. 625–34.

Iwawaki, S. and Eysenck, H. J. (1978) 'Sexual attitudes among British and Japanese students', *The Journal of Psychology*, **98**, pp. 289–98.

Iwawaki, S. and Wilson, G. D. (1983) 'Sex fantasies in Japan', *Personality and Individual Differences*, **4**, pp. 543–5.

Jacobson, N. S. and Margolin, G. (1979) *Marital Therapy: Strategies Based on Learning and Behavior Exchange Principles*, New York, Brunner/Mazel.

Kantorowitz, D. A. (1978) 'Personality and conditioning of tumescence and detumescence', *Behaviour Research and Therapy*, **16**, pp. 117–23.

Kaplan, H. S. (1974) *The New Sex Therapy*, New York, Brunner/Mazel.

Kelly, E. L. (1939) 'Concerning the validity of Terman's weights for predicting marital happiness', *Psychological Bulletin*, **139**, pp. 202–3.

Kelly, E. L., and Conley, J. J. (1985) 'Personality and compatability: A prospective analysis of marital stability and marital satisfaction', *I. of Personality and Soc. Psych.* in press.

Levenson, R. W. and Gottman, J. M. (1983) 'Marital interaction: Physiological linkage and affective exchange', *Journal of Personality and Social Psychology*, **45**, pp. 587–97.

Martin, N. G. and Eysenck, H. J. (1976) 'Genetic factors in sexual behaviour', in *Sex and Personality*, Austin, Tex., University of Texas Press.

Martin, N. G., Eaves, L. J. and Eysenck, H. J. (1977) 'Genetical, environmental and personality factors influencing the age of first intercourse in twins', *Journal of Biosocial Science*, **9**, pp. 91–7.

Merikangas, K. R. (1982) 'Assortative mating for psychiatric disorders and psychological traits', *Archives of General Pyschiatry*, **39**, pp. 1173–81.

Nias, D. K. B. (1977) 'Husband-wife similarities', *Social Science*, **52**, pp. 206–11.

Nicholls, J. G., Licht, B. G., and Pearl, R. A. (1982) 'Some dangers of using personality questionnaires to study personality', *Psychological Bull.*, **92**, pp. 572–80.

Notarius, C. I. and Johnson, J. S. (1982) 'Emotional expressions in husbands and wives', *Journal of Marriage and the Family*, **44**, pp. 483–9.

O'Leary, K. D. and Arias, I. (1983) 'The influence of marital therapy on sexual satisfaction', *Journal of Sex and Marital Therapy*, **9**, 171–81.

Robins, L. N. (1966) *Deviant Children Grown Up*, Baltimore, Md, The Williams and Wilkins Company.

Schenk, J., Pfrang, H. and Rausche, A. (1983) 'Personality traits versus the quality of marital relationship as the determinant of marital sexuality', *Archives of Sexual Behavior*, **12**, pp. 31–42.

Schindler, L., Hahlweg, K. and Revenstorf, D. (1983) 'Short and long term effectiveness of two communication training modalities with distressed couples', *The American Journal of Family Therapy*, **11**, pp. 54–64.

Schofield, M. (1968) *The Sexual Behaviour of Young People*, Harmondsworth, Penguin Books.

Spanier, G. B. and Lewis, R. A. (1980) 'Marital quality: A review of the seventies', *Journal of Marriage and the Family*, **42**, pp. 825–39.

Symons, D. (1980) 'Precis of the evolution of human sexuality', *The Behavioral and Brain Sciences*, **3**, pp. 171–214.

Taylor, C. C. (1971) 'Marriages of twins to twins', *Acta Geneticae Medicae et Gemellologiae*, **20**, pp. 96–113.

Terman, L. M. (1938) *Psychological Factors in Marital Happiness*, New York, McGraw-Hill.

Terman, L. M. (1951) 'Predictive data: predicting marriage failure from test scores', *Marriage and Family Living*, **12**, pp. 51–54.

Terman, L. M. and Oden, M. H. (1947) *The Gifted Child Grows Up: Twenty-Five Years Followup of a Superior Group*, Palo Alto, Calif., Stanford University Press.

Vincent, J. P. Weiss, R. L. and Bitcheler, G. R. (1975) 'A behavioral analysis of problem solving in distressed and nondistressed married and stranger dyads', *Behavior Therapy*, **6**, pp. 475–87.

Watzlawick, P., and Weakland, J. H. (1977) *The Interactional-View* New York, Norton.

White, L. K. (1983) 'Determinants of spousal interaction: Marital structure or marital happiness', *Journal of Marriage and the Family*, **45**, pp. 511–19.

Winch, R. F. (1958) *Mate-Selection: A Study of Complimentary Needs*, New York, Harper and Row.

# Interchange

## WILSON REPLIES TO GILBERT

Gilbert is perfectly right to point out the limitations of Eysenck's work on sex and marriage, and I find little to argue with in his proposals for ideal research in the field. However, it is asking too much of any one researcher, even the energetic and redoubtable Hans Eysenck, to have single-handedly done everything that he recommends. Eysenck's entry into the field of sex and marriage is fairly recent, and in a short time he has made a very appreciable contribution.

One of Gilbert's main criticisms is that cause and effect often seems to be inferred on the basis of correlations. This is such a well-known trap that it is hard to imagine that Eysenck would not be aware of it. When Eysenck and Wakefield talk of sexual satisfaction 'accounting for' a certain proportion of variance in marital satisfaction, I would presume they mean this in a statistical rather than causal sense. They are really only describing degrees of common variance, but since the focus of the paper is on marital satisfaction, this is always treated as the response measure. On p. 188 they note that '10% of the variance in MS is simply measurement error'; this, at least, could not be misinterpreted as a causal statement. Anybody familiar with research of this kind understands 'accounts for' to mean 'statistically predicts', not 'causally determines'. Had the paper been about factors predicting sexual satisfaction, then presumably marital satisfaction would have been found to account for it to the same extent. Having said this, I must agree with Gilbert that in their penultimate paragraph Eysenck and Wakefield do seem to be slipping into the presumption that sexual dissatisfaction 'produces' marital dissatisfaction, a proposition that is indeed highly debatable.

In other cases it is possible to infer direction of cause and effect with a little more confidence. The role of the relative height of a couple is a good example; it is much easier to conceive of people's height influencing their marital compatibility than *vice versa*. Certain social background factors such as age and education, IQ and personality variables that are known to be genetically-based are also more reasonably viewed as causes of sexual and marital behaviour than *vice versa*. Although it is not possible to be certain, it seems much more logical to suppose that a discrepancy between the partners in emotionality, with the husband being more stable than the wife, has a beneficial effect upon marital satisfaction, than to argue that high levels of marital satisfaction lead to divergence between the partners on emotionality.

Gilbert is correct in saying that ideal marriage outcome research is longitudinal rather than cross-sectional. Particularly in answering questions about whether couples start out as similar on certain dimensions or whether they grow to be alike, the longitudinal strategy is superior. He is also right in saying that divorced couples should, if possible, be included in the studies since this is a much more decisive marital breakdown. Couples who express dissatisfaction with their union, but who still live together and cooperate at least to the extent of participating in the same research study, are not half so far gone. Of course, cross-sectional studies are more often done because they are quicker and easier to do, and divorced couples are frequently omitted because they are difficult to contact. Given agreement about what kind of study might be more ideal, the question is whether Eysenck's particular cross-sectional studies have added significantly to knowledge in the field.

Eysenck (1980) has reported a study of personality in divorced people, comparing them with couples still married. Unfortunately, this is one of the comparisons that suffers most from the cross-sectional design. Although higher N and P scores were found for the divorcees relative to married controls, the very small differences of a point or two on each scale could well have been an effect of the divorce rather than a cause. Eysenck interprets the study as suggesting that personality plays 'a definite though not overwhelmingly strong part in driving a couple to divorce'. Several times he mentions the need for replication but does not admit the ambiguity concerning cause and effect. With Gilbert, I find this surprising, considering how keenly Eysenck attacks the cause and effect issue with respect to smoking and lung cancer.

By contrast, I think the Eysenck and Wakefield study is an important contribution to the field. Gilbert concedes that it takes us a step forward in providing support for the gender asymmetry hypothesis—that sex—typical differences in personality sometimes optimize the chances of marital satisfaction. Another distinct contribution of this research is the demonstration that the degree of difference that is optimal depends upon whether satisfaction is being judged by the husband or by the wife. In other words, the kind of pairing that is best for a man is not necessarily the same as that which is best for a woman. Previous research has not been geared to investigate this issue. Gilbert's suggestion that we should be evaluating the compatibility of multivariate personality profiles of husband and wife is a worthy ideal which he is welcome to pursue, though I suspect that little predictive power will be gained and the results will be so complex as to be of little practical usefulness.

I do not think Gilbert is correct in saying that Eysenck 'downplays' the importance of whom one marries. The final sentence of Eysenck and Wakefield specifically draws attention to this factor. As I read it, Eysenck is just making the point that the individual personalities that are brought to the marriage are every bit as important as the blend between them, a statement that I would have thought was justified by Eysenck's evidence and that of others.

In conclusion, I think Gilbert's paper is a valuable contribution to the field and an excellent guide as to the direction that researchers might profitably go in the future. He is right to point out the dangers of inferring causation from correlations, and the possibility of illusory relationships arising out of item overlap and common methods variance. He is right about the need for longitudinal studies to test certain causal hypotheses and the advantage of including divorced people in the research design. Altogether it is an astute and penetrating critique of Eysenck's approach, though I do not see it as detracting much from the very considerable and original contribution that Eysenck has made to the understanding of the role of individual difference factors in sex and marriage.

## REFERENCE

Eysenck, H. J. (1980) 'Personality, marital satisfaction and divorce', *Psy. Rept.* **47**, pp. 1235–8.
Eysenck, H. J. and Wakefield, J. A. Jr. (1981) 'Psychological factors as predictors of marital satisfaction', *Advances in Beh. Res. and Therapy*, **3**, pp. 151–92.

# GILBERT REPLIES TO WILSON

My major concern with Wilson's chapter is that it generally does not reflect the size and various possible meanings of Eysenck's careful measurements and does not deal with the limitations of Eysenck's cross-sectional correlational data base. The chapter gives the reader the impression that the correlations of personality with sexual and with marital behaviour may be stronger than they really are. Furthermore, it seems to suggest, without justification, that these correlations are indicative of the causal influences of personality.

*1  Size of correlations*

Eysenck acknowledges the smallness of the correlations of his personality factors with reported sexual and marital behaviour and attitudes. On the other hand, Wilson's chapter generally fails to note the important fact that the correlations he describes rarely account for more than 5 to 10 per cent of the variance.

*2  Implications of correlations*

Wilson's chapter frequently states that extraverts or neurotics are characterized by one type of behaviour or attitude, while introverts or stables are characterized by another type. Such statements can generally not be substantiated since the exact natures of the distributions of the variables contributing to the correlations have not been investigated. The smallness of the correlations leads to the possibility that only a very small percentage of individuals at one extreme of the personality continuum are accounting for the correlations. For example, Eysenck notes the tendency of male subjects with high P scores to wish to do away with marriage, yet only 8 per cent of all male subjects reported such a desire. If 20 per cent of all subjects can be considered to be high on P, and if all subjects who claimed such a desire were in this high P group, one would have to conclude that a majority of high P scorers, 12 out of 20 per cent, did not express such a desire. Eysenck (1976, p. 125) has noted this problem, and has stated that when one says individuals at one extreme of a personality dimension are a certain way, one really means that the relative proportion of people at that extreme is greater than the proportion of people at the other extreme.

Furthermore, I believe that Wilson's chapter errs in that it frequently unjustifiably assumes that the correlations between Eysenck's personality factors and other variables are causal. His conclusion states that he has '...reviewed research by Eysenck and his associates concerning the way personality *influences* our sexual attitudes and behaviour and marital choice and satisfaction. These are important areas of life in which biologically-based personality factors can be seen to manifest themselves.' This question of whether the associations that Eysenck has found are caused by the influence of personality upon the above-noted variables is a matter that is far from clear. It is likely that part of these correlations is caused by common methods variance. Yet longitudinal studies fairly clearly demonstrate that the correlations between personality and marital satisfaction are partly reflective of causal processes (Burgess and Wallin 1953; Terman and Oden, 1947). On the other hand, there is only very weak evidence to support the causal interpretation of the low correlations of personality with sexual satisfaction, attitudes and behaviour.

The weakness of this support has been noted by Eysenck, who has stated that 'there seems to be little doubt that genetic factors are likely to be responsible for many of the individual differences in sexual attitudes and behaviour that we have documented on previous pages; nevertheless, there is very little scientific evidence even for genetic causes of male-female differences other than those directly associated with physical differences' (Eysenck, 1976, p. 192). Eysenck's pioneering work in the genetics of sexual attitudes and behaviour is an important first step in the right direction. However, as Eysenck notes, the number of twins used in his genetic studies was too small to allow definitive answers concerning the relative role of genetics in determining these processes.

## 3   Predictive power and clinical relevance

Wilson argues that clinicians who have a knowledge of the relationship of constitutional personality and sexual tendencies might better understand the sexual problems of their clients. Such an appreciation would probably be of some help, but we need to remember that the mean differences between clients with sex problems and controls rarely exceed three points on any of the Eysenck personality questionnaire scales, while the standard deviation on these scales approximates five points.

## 4   Simplification versus oversimplification: cutting nature at her joints

Wilson is correct in stating that Eysenck's work is valuable in reminding us that certain personality characteristics brought to the marital relationship are predictive of marital unhappiness. However, if personality researchers want to make their models move beyond the r = .30 correlational level to a level of clinical relevance and theoretical sophistication, more complex models of the relationship of personality to marital and sexual behaviour and satisfaction must be developed. It seems reasonable to assume that the more adequate causal models will be based upon the multivariate personality profile of one spouse interacting with that of the other.

## 5   Points of agreement

There is growing evidence that biological and genetic factors play a major role in determining personality and temperament, and that behaviour is generally a function of the interaction of personality with situation. It seems very likely that sexual and marital behaviour and attitudes are also a result of the interaction of the biologically-based temperaments of the individuals involved. It is a great credit to Eysenck that he has flown in the face of the *Zeitgeist* and taken important steps towards understanding the importance of these factors. But it is important that we remember that his steps, though very important, are just the beginning of a long journey towards understanding the enormous complexity of biopsychosocial systems.

## REFERENCES

Burgess, E. W. and Wallin, P. (1953) *Engagement and Marriage*, Chicago, Ill., Lippincott.
Eysenck, H. J. (1976) *Sex and Personality*, Austin, Tex., University of Texas Press.
Terman, L. M. and Oden, M. H. (1947) *The Gifted Child Grows Up: Twenty-Five Years Followup of a Superior Group*, Palo Alto, Calif., Stanford University Press.

# Part X: Smoking and Health

# 17. Smoking, Personality and Health

CHARLES D. SPIELBERGER

Over the course of his enormously productive career, which spans more than forty-five years, Professor Hans J. Eysenck's creative genius has enlightened our understanding of many different areas of psychological science. The *Centennial Psychology Series*, which was established to commemorate the founding of Wilhelm Wundt's laboratory at Leipzig in 1879 and scientific psychology's one-hundredth anniversary, invited distinguished contributors to psychological theory and research to develop a volume that included twelve to fifteen of their most important papers. For his *Centennial* volume, the papers selected by Eysenck (1982) as representing what he considered to be his most significant contributions were in the following four general areas: personality, behaviour therapy, genetics and social psychology.

The tremendous breadth of Eysenck's research interests is clearly reflected in the eight topics of controversy that comprise this volume. In addition to these topics and the four general areas noted in the preceding paragraph, Eysenck's work has included investigations in such divergent fields as 'criminology, psychopharmacology, sexual behaviour, the causes and effects of smoking, experimental aesthetics, the experimental study of reminiscence, learning, memory and conditioning, the psychological basis of ideology, the influence of the media, and many more including the experimental study of extrasensory perception and astrology!' (1982, p. 1).

A deep and abiding interest in the nature, measurement, causes and consequences of individual differences in behaviour is at the root of Eysenck's scientific work, and provides the foundation for his empirical studies. Quoting the Greek philosopher, Theophrastus, Eysenck poses the key question of individual differences as it relates to a number of specific areas that he has himself investigated:

'Why is it that while all Greece lies under the same sky and all the Greeks are educated alike, it has befallen us to have characters variously constituted?' This question, asked two thousand years ago, is still as puzzling and as important for an understanding of human behaviour as it was then. Why is it that one person smokes, while another does not, and yet a third tries without success to give it up?

**305**

Why is one person faithful to his spouse, while another is a philanderer, but a third puritanically avoids all sex? Why do some children respond better to praise, others to blame, in their schoolwork? Why does a given sedative drug improve some people's performance, while impairing that of others? Why do some people condition more quickly than others, or extinguish conditioned responses less quickly? Why, in other words, is there such extreme variability in the responses of human beings (and of animals) to stimulus situations broadly equivalent? (Eysenck, 1982, pp. 1–2).

In seeking answers to these questions, Eysenck adopts a 'typological approach' that recognizes the potential causal influence of both environmental and genetic factors. On the basis of the empirical findings in numerous experimental and correlational studies of many different behaviours and populations, he has delineated three major personality dimensions—introversion-extraversion (E), emotionality or neuroticism (N) and psychoticism (P). The neurophysiological causes and the behavioural consequences and correlates of individual differences in these typological dimensions of personality have been examined extensively and persistently in numerous scientific papers, and in books that have collated and integrated the empirical findings with the scientific literature in many different fields (e.g., Eysenck, 1947, 1952, 1953a, 1953b, 1957, 1960a, 1960b, 1964, 1965, 1967, 1972, 1973, 1975, 1976a, 1976b, 1980, 1982; Eysenck and Eysenck, 1969, 1976; Eysenck and Wilson, 1978, 1979).

Whatever the subject matter, there are four important qualities that characterize Eysenck's scientific work: (a) clearly stated theoretical assumptions, permitting the derivation of factual propositions that can be either verified or falsified; (b) objective and reliable measurement operations for defining and quantitatively assessing his theoretical constructs; (c) comprehensive review and critical analysis of relevant empirical findings from diverse areas of psychology and other disciplines that bear on the particular problem under investigation; and (d) examination of the relative merits and limitations of alternative theoretical explanations. These admirable qualities are complemented by a lucid, informal writing style and enlivened by descriptions of critical experiments and analogies from other scientific disciplines.

Controversy is another facet of Eysenck's work which both justifies and provides the focus for the current volume. In his biography, *Hans Eysenck: The Man and His Work*, H. B. Gibson (1981) notes that while Eysenck's research 'extends into an extraordinary large number of areas, and he has gained a unique reputation for communicating psychological ideas to a wide and varied audience...he has also become a highly controversial figure who has been violently attacked for his supposed views on race and intelligence.' The same is true with regard to his research on smoking and health (Eysenck, 1980), in which he has courageously challenged the official pronouncements of the US Surgeon General, the British Minister of Health, and the British and American medical establishments!

The main goal of this paper is to examine and critically evaluate Eysenck's theoretical views with regard to the relationship between smoking and health. As an experimental psychologist specializing in personality research, Eysenck's interest in what is generally considered a medical problem might seem surprising. But considered in the context of his investigations of the influence and importance of differences in personality for a wide range of social behaviours, his interest in smoking becomes immediately apparent. As Eysenck himself states:

Inevitably, smoking and drinking emerged as suitable topics of investigation—particularly as my theory enabled me to make predictions regarding both the causes and the effects of drug taking in this particular context. It was as a consequence of this rather specialized interest that

I . . . recognized, as had Fisher so much earlier, that while the problems of lung cancer and coronary heart disease are ultimately medical, the epidemiological aspects of these problems are statistical, and closely related to constitutional differences in personality, of just the sort I was studying (1980, p. 12).

Eysenck's position with regard to the relationship between smoking and health is outlined in the next section of this paper. In the following section his model of smoking behaviour is considered, along with the findings in several recent studies by the writer that provide evidence to support Eysenck's view with regard to factors that cause people initially to take up smoking and factors that cause them to continue smoking.

## SMOKING AND HEALTH

On the basis of his analysis of the existing evidence, Eysenck acknowledges a statistical association between smoking and disease. He strenuously objects, however, to the simplistic interpretation of this association as demonstrating that smoking causes lung cancer and coronary heart disease:

Even if we were to take the correlation between smoking and lung cancer seriously as proof of causal connections, we would still have to conclude that smoking was neither a necessary nor a sufficient cause. Roughly speaking, only one heavy smoker in ten dies of lung cancer; thus smoking is not a sufficient cause. One person in ten of those who die of lung cancer is a non-smoker; thus smoking is not a necessary cause (Eysenck, 1980, p.21).

Errors in research design and the statistical analyses of the epidemiological studies on which the 'environmental hypothesis' that 'smoking causes lung cancer' is based were first enumerated by Eysenck in his 1965 book, *Smoking, Health and Personality*. A comprehensive and detailed explication of Eysenck's current views on smoking and health is presented in his recent book, *The Causes and Effects of Smoking* (Eysenck, 1980). In this volume he reviews the criticism previously raised by distinguished statisticians, such as the late Sir Ronald Fisher (1958, 1959) and other leading authorities (Berkson, 1958, 1960, 1962; Berkson and Elveback, 1960; Katz, 1969; Mainland and Herrera, 1956; Reid, 1975; Sterling, 1973), and notes the inconclusive and contradictory nature of much of the evidence that is cited in support of the environmental hypothesis.

In his recent book Eysenck also reviews and evaluates the evidence for 'genetic theories', which attribute both the development of a disease and the maintenance of the smoking habit to genetic or constitutional differences. The genetic theory developed by Professor P. R. J. Burch is considered most promising, and extensive reference is made to Burch's theoretical arguments and his research findings (1974, 1976, 1978a, 1978b, 1978c). In addition, Eysenck reports new evidence of the heritability of smoking and disease based on extensive studies of large samples of twins, adopted children, and their families, on which he has collaborated with Dr Lindon J. Eaves, a professional geneticist. Although Eysenck considers the results of these studies as strongly supporting genetic-constitutional explanations of the relationship between smoking and health, he notes that environmental and genetic theories are not mutually exclusive. On the basis of the available evidence, Eysenck concludes that 'some form of interaction between genetic and environmental factors may be the most promising type of theory to look for in the future' (1980, p. 64).

Some of Eysenck's major criticisms of environmental explanations of the observed associations between smoking and disease are briefly summarized below. This same literature is reviewed and criticized from a genetic perspective by Professor Burch in the following chapter. Burch also examines Eysenck's proposals for needed research that will discriminate between environmental and genetic explanations of the relation between cigarette smoking and disease. Since Burch provides detailed information about his own and other genetic explanations of the association of smoking with lung cancer and ischaemic heart disease, such explanations are not further considered in the present paper.

A major argument in support of the hypothesis that smoking causes lung cancer is based on statistical findings that smokers of a given age and sex die more frequently of a particular disease than do non-smokers. Eysenck (1980, pp. 17–20) describes a US study of nearly 5000 persons in which the 'mortality ratio' of observed to expected deaths due to lung cancer was 10.8, indicating that more than ten times as many smokers died of this disease than would have been expected if none had smoked. But the mortality ratios of smokers to non-smokers for Parkinson's disease, diabetes and alcohol consumption are consistently less than 1.0. Eysenck concludes that it may be equally as wrong to interpret positive ratios as indicating a *causal* effect as it would be to interpret negative ratios as evidence that smoking inhibits the development of a particular disease.

Another major argument in support of the hypothesis that smoking causes lung cancer is based on correlations between cigarette consumption and national death rates from lung cancer in various countries. The environmental hypothesis would require parallel changes over time in annual cigarette consumption and cancer mortality rates, allowing for a delay of approximately thirty years between observations of consumption and mortality rates. Citing an analysis reported by Burch (1976) of cigarette consumption and male death rates from lung cancer in twenty-one different countries, Eysenck observes that the overall relationship was quite weak. Moreover, in a number of countries the correlations between annual national cigarette consumption and age-adjusted death rates from lung and bronchial cancer were actually negative (Stocks, 1970).

The same general point is reflected in the pattern of sex differences in the relationship between cigarette consumption and death from lung cancer. Citing data reported by Rosenblatt (1974) and Passey (1962), Eysenck notes that the relative rate in deaths from lung cancer for males and females has not changed since the nineteenth century when cigarette consumption was minimal. In commenting on these findings, Eysenck (1980, p. 32) states:

> The increase in smoking of the men, as compared with the women, from 1890 to 1920, is not mirrored by any corresponding increase in their proportion of lung cancer cases, and the rapid increase in smoking of the women, as compared with the men, from 1920 to 1940, is not mirrored by any corresponding increase in their proportion of lung cancer cases. . . . If smoking causes cancer, then it should have produced a superabundance of cancers in the men who took up smoking from 1890 to 1920, as compared to the women who did not take up smoking, and similarly the large number of women who took up smoking from 1920 to 1940 should have produced a super-abundance of cancers, compared to the men who hardly increased their smoking of cigarettes during this period.

Clearly, the results do not support the environmental hypothesis, but Eysenck notes that they also pose problems for genetic interpretations. He attributes the overall increase in lung cancer cases largely to improvements in diagnostic accuracy and to the increasing practice of making cancer diagnoses for known smokers. Differences in mortality rates between men and women are attributed to unequal genetic predispositions.

If there is a causal relation between cigarette smoking and lung cancer, heavy smokers should develop cancer more often, and at an earlier age, than light smokers. Citing the research of Passey (1962), who examined the smoking histories of a large group of men with lung cancer, Eysenck observes that the amount smoked is unrelated to the age at which cancer was initially diagnosed. Moreover, light smokers were afflicted with lung cancer at about the same age as heavy smokers. Since no relation was found between the age of onset of lung cancer and either the amount smoked or the age at which smoking began, there appears to be little evidence of a causal 'dose-response' relationship between cigarette smoking and lung cancer.

Eysenck also calls attention to findings related to inhaling cigarette smoke that seem to contradict the environmental hypothesis. Citing the results of an early study by Fisher (1959), Eysenck (1980, p. 43) observes that 'inhalers suffered, on the average, a 10 per cent *lower* incidence of lung cancer among heavy smokers who were inhalers than those who were non-inhalers', and Schwartz, Flamanti, Lellouch and Denoix (1961) reported that the lung cancer risk among heavy smokers who inhaled was only 60 per cent of the risk for heavy smokers who were non-inhalers.

According to the Royal College of Physicians (RCP, 1971), an epidemiological study that compared the mortality rates for British doctors with the general population (Doll and Hill, 1964) provides the strongest possible support for the environmental hypothesis. During the period preceding this study (1953–57), the doctors' cigarette smoking declined about 50 per cent, and the finding that the doctors' death rate declined more than that of the general population was attributed to this reduction in cigarette smoking. In challenging these conclusions, Eysenck refers to a reanalysis of the data by Seltzer (1972), who identified numerous inconsistencies and contradictions in the original study and the RCP report. For example, Seltzer pointed out that both the doctors and the general population showed a similar decline in the proportion of smokers. Moreover, there was little difference in the *total* death rate for the doctors and the general population, the decline in the death rate for 'unrelated causes' in the general population was almost twice as great as for the doctors, and the death rate for coronary heart disease for the doctors actually increased by 8 per cent during a period in which cigarette smoking declined. Nevertheless, despite the inconsistencies and contradictions in their own data that were identified by Seltzer, the RCP continues to maintain that changes in the mortality rate among British doctors provide strong evidence that giving up smoking increases life expectancy.

In examining the array of evidence marshalled to support environmental and genetic explanations of the association between smoking and disease, Eysenck (1980) clearly favours the genetic hypothesis, which attributes cigarette smoking, personality traits and disease to genetic factors. Insisting 'that it is imperative to get away from the simple assertion that "smoking causes disease"', Eysenck contends that the relationship between smoking and disease should be examined separately for coronary heart disease, lung cancer, other forms of cancer, and other causes of death such as accidents and suicides for which relationships with cigarette smoking have also been reported. In the final analysis, Eysenck seems to accept the possibility that cigarette smoking may contribute to the development of diseases such as lung cancer, and that 'some form of interaction between genetic and environmental factors' would be the most promising type of theory to guide future investigations.

In several recent papers Eysenck (1984) has emphasized the importance of stress and personality in the aetiology of lung cancer. He calls attention to evidence from animal research that environmental stress may cause cancer (e.g., Bammer and Newberry, 1981), and that stress in humans may be instrumental in producing both lung cancer and an inclination to smoke for persons with certain personality types. The relationship between stress, smoking and personality is considered in some detail in the following section of this paper.

## EYSENCK'S MODEL OF SMOKING BEHAVIOUR

The controversy on smoking and health has stimulated extensive interest in identifying factors that influence the initiation and maintenance of smoking behaviour. In reviews of research in this field (Matarazzo and Matarazzo, 1965; Evans, Henderson, Hill and Raines, 1979; Leventhal and Cleary, 1980), social influence variables such as parental smoking habits and peer-group pressures have been repeatedly identified with the initiation of smoking. Positive relationships between the smoking habits of parents and the smoking behaviour of their children have been reported in eight studies (Banks, Bewley, Bland, Dean and Pollard, 1978; Borland and Rudolph, 1975; Clausen, 1968; Horn, Courts, Taylor and Solomon, 1959; Merki, Creswell, Stone, Huffman and Newman, 1970; Palmer, 1970; Salber and MacMahon, 1961; Wohlford, 1970); only one study, which was based on a very small sample of college students, failed to find any relationship between these variables (Straits and Sechrest, 1963). Although an empirical relationship between parental smoking habits and children's smoking behaviour seems firmly established, it is not clear whether this relationship reflects environmental or constitutional-genetic influences (see Eysenck, 1980).

Wohlford (1970) has called attention to the importance of examining the differential impact of the smoking habits of fathers and mothers on the smoking behaviour of their sons and daughters. In general, sons were found to be more likely to smoke if their fathers smoked and daughters were found to be more likely to smoke if their mothers smoked (Banks *et al.*, 1978; Horn *et al.,* 1959; Salber and MacMahon, 1961; Wohlford, 1970). Peer-group pressure is also widely recognized as a primary factor in the initiation of smoking (e.g., Eysenck, 1980; Matarazzo and Matarazzo, 1965). Leventhal and Cleary (1980) have recently suggested that peers and parents are both important sources of environmental influence in cigarette smoking, and that older siblings may be even more important than other peers in influencing adolescents to initiate smoking. Consistent with this view, Banks *et al.* (1978) found that junior and senior high school students whose siblings smoked were more likely to be smokers themselves.

In his model of smoking behaviour Eysenck (1973, 1980) distinguishes between factors that cause people to take up smoking and factors that contribute to the maintenance of the smoking habit. Consistent with the research literature, he assumes that the initiation of smoking is determined by environmental pressures, primarily from peer groups, and that genetic factors have a relatively small influence on this process.

A 'diathesis-stress model' is proposed by Eysenck to account for the maintenance of the smoking habit. This model emphasizes genetic predispositions (diathesis), which are related to personality factors. Stress interacts with personality factors in producing the motivational and reinforcement conditions that maintain the smoking habit. The model postulates that the two major motivational causes of smoking behaviour are *boredom* and *emotional strain*. In questionnaire studies, boredom-producing and emotional strain-producing circumstances have been identified as the types of situations in which people are most likely to 'light up'.

The diathesis-stress model assigns personality factors a central role in maintaining the smoking habit. Extraverts are known to show less cortical arousal, as mediated by the ascending reticular formation, than introverts, and are, therefore, more susceptible to boredom. Neurotic, anxious persons have labile autonomic nervous systems and are thus genetically disposed to react with more intense emotional reactions to environmental stress. Because of the underlying neurophysiological processes, persons who are high in extraversion or neuroticism would be expected to smoke more, though for different reasons.

Since men tend to be more extraverted and women are more introverted, Eysenck's model predicts that men will smoke more often from boredom than women, and this has been found to be the case. However, since women tend to be more neurotic than men, it would be expected that women would smoke more often under stressful conditions. It also follows that extraverted men are likely to smoke more when bored, and that the smoking behaviour of neurotic women will be intensified in stressful circumstances that evoke intense emotional reactions (anxiety states).

In a recent development of his model Eysenck postulates a positive relationship between smoking behaviour and individual differences in 'toughmindedness' or 'psychoticism' (P), which refers to aggressive, rebellious types of behaviour that are found at a pathological level in psychotics. Like extraversion and neuroticism, there is a strong genetic factor in psychoticism which disposes persons who are high on this factor to smoke more in expressing these non-conforming social tendencies. Although there are important sex differences, both males and females who are high in psychoticism, for example, criminals, smoke more than individuals who are low on this dimension.

In Eysenck's model, nicotine is the active agent that links individual differences in motivation with smoking behaviour. He posits a complex relationship between nicotine consumption and cortical arousal, in which small amounts provide stimulation that relieves boredom, whereas larger quantities reduce anxiety through a reduction in autonomic (sympathetic) nervous system activity. According to Eysenck's theory, males and extraverts who are frequently exposed to boredom-producing situations are more likely to continue to smoke because the stimulation of smoking actively reinforces them for doing so. For persons high in psychoticism, Eysenck suggests that smoking brings social reinforcement for their non-conforming, independent behaviours. Social factors may also influence the smoking behaviour of extraverts who are motivated to emulate the practices of their peer groups.

Evidence from laboratory studies in support of Eysenck's model of smoking behaviour is now reasonably strong regarding the dependence of smoking on personality factors, situational stress and nicotine. Although the relationships posited by the model with regard to the interactive influence of personality and social factors on smoking behaviour are speculative at the present time, recent empirical findings have been encouraging. The findings of a large-scale study will be briefly described in which we investigated the relations between family smoking habits and personality, and the initiation and maintenance of smoking behaviour (Spielberger and Jacobs, 1982; Spielberger, Jacobs, Crane and Russell, 1983). On the basis of Eysenck's model and previous research findings, siblings were expected to have a greater influence on smoking behaviour than parents, and smokers were expected to score higher than non-smokers on extraversion, neuroticism and psychoticism, as measured by the Eysenck Personality Questionnaire (EPQ).

The EPQ and a fifty-item Smoking Behaviour Questionnaire (SBQ) were administered to a total sample of 955 American college students enrolled in introductory psychology courses. The students were tested in groups of twenty to 100 over a ten-month period. The SBQ was designed to obtain specific information about the students' smoking behaviour and the smoking habits of their families (Spielberger *et al.*, 1983). They were asked to report whether they and their parents and older siblings were current smokers, occasional smokers, ex-smokers, or non-smokers. A current (regular) smoker was defined as 'someone who smokes one or more cigarettes every day'; an occasional smoker was 'someone who smokes cigarettes from time-to-time, but *not* every day'; an ex-smoker was 'someone who was previously either a regular or an occasional smoker, but who currently does *not* smoke.' A non-smoker was defined as 'someone who has never smoked, or has only experimented briefly with cigarettes, but never became a regular or occasional smoker.'

Students whose older brother or sister smoked were much more likely to be smokers than those whose older siblings did not smoke, and older siblings had a much stronger influence on smoking behaviour than did parents. For students whose older siblings were smokers, the smoking habits of their parents seemed to have no added influence on their smoking behaviour. However, students with no older siblings, or with older siblings who were non-smokers, were more likely to take up smoking if one or both parents smoked. These results were generally consistent with Eysenck's (1980) model and the mounting evidence that peer-group pressures are perhaps the single most important influence on the *initiation* of smoking (e.g., Banks *et al.*, 1978). Since no differences were found in the smoking habits of the parents of current, occasional and ex-smokers, nor in the smoking habits of their older siblings, there was little evidence that family smoking habits influenced the *maintenance* of the students' smoking behaviour.

In evaluating the association between personality and the initiation of smoking, current, occasional and ex-smokers were classified as smokers. The results for the total sample indicated that smokers had significantly higher scores than non-smokers on the EPQ Extraversion, Neuroticism and Psychoticism scales, and that females scored significantly higher than the males on Neuroticism and lower on Psychoticism (Spielberger *et al.*, 1983). While these differences were in the same direction for both sexes, the effects were larger in magnitude for the females, except for neuroticism on which comparable differences were found.

The EPQ scores of current, occasional and ex-smokers were compared in evaluating relations between the personality variables and the maintenance of smoking behaviour. Current smokers of both sexes scored higher on extraversion and psychoticism than occasional and ex-smokers, but these differences were not statistically significant. Female smokers had significantly *lower* Neuroticism scores than occasional and ex-smokers; a similar trend for males was not statistically significant, due in part to the fact that the magnitude of the difference was larger for females and the male sample was smaller. Females who smoked regularly also had significantly *lower* scores on the trait anxiety scale of Spielberger's State-Trait Personality Inventory (STPI).

Taken as a whole, the results of this study were generally consistent with Eysenck's model of smoking behaviour, which hypothesizes that smokers will be higher than non-smokers in extraversion, neuroticism and psychoticism, and with previous research in which it has been demonstrated that smokers are more extraverted, neurotic and tense, and have stronger anti-social tendencies than non-smokers. The finding that smokers were higher than non-smokers in neuroticism was also consistent with the conclusions of Matarazzo and Matarazzo (1965) that there are 'a slightly higher number of . . . "neurotic" and "tense" individuals among smokers as compared to non-smokers' (p. 377) and with Eysenck's (1980) hypothesis that females who are high in neuroticism are more likely to take up smoking in order to reduce tension. The finding that female current smokers scored *lower* in both neuroticism and trait anxiety than occasional and ex-smokers further suggested that smoking may be an effective tension reducer for women who smoke regularly.

In addition to the findings that have been described, smokers of both sexes had significantly lower scores on the EPQ Lie scale. Although designed to measure the tendency to dissimulate ('fake good'), recent research suggests that low scores on the Lie scale are associated with non-conforming, rebellious attitudes (Eysenck, 1980). The findings that smokers have significantly lower Lie scores and higher psychoticism scores than non-smokers are consistent with Eysenck's hypothesis that genetic predisposing factors influence both personality development and smoking behaviour. Moreover, the finding that occasional smokers of both sexes had lower Lie scores than current and ex-smokers may indicate that occasional smokers take up smoking as a non-conformist behaviour, but also resist pressure from their peers to become regular smokers.

From the foregoing discussion it is apparent that the relations between smoking and personality, and smoking and health, are exceedingly complex. A simplistic environmental hypothesis that 'smoking causes disease' is clearly untenable. Although a genetic-constitutional interpretation of the association between smoking and health, which attributes both cigarette smoking and disease to predisposing genetic factors, is supported by a great deal of evidence, Eysenck's conclusion that 'some form of interaction between genetic and environmental factors' seems to best fit all of the known facts relating to this association at the present time.

There can be no question that Eysenck's views on smoking and health are strongly at variance with the official pronouncements of governmental agencies and the medical establishments in both the United States and the United Kingdom, but are his views controversial? On the basis of a careful examination of a wide range of research findings and critical analysis of key theoretical issues, Eysenck takes a moderate position with respect to environmental and genetic interpretations of the relation between smoking and disease. Moreover, he calls for more and better research to clarify the relative contributions of these alternative hypotheses and specifies potentially fruitful lines of investigation. Rather than being extreme and controversial, his conclusions seem logical, reasonable and consistent with the available evidence.

## REFERENCES

Bammer, K. and Newberry, B. H. (1981) *Stress and Cancer*, Toronto, C. J. Hogrefe.

Banks, M. H., Bewley, B. R., Bland, J. M., Dean, J. R. and Pollard, V. (1978) 'Long term study of smoking by secondary school children', *Archives of Disease in Childhood*, **53**, pp. 12–19.

Berkson, J. (1958) 'Smoking and lung cancer: Some observations on two recent reports', *Journal of the American Statistical Association*, **53**, pp. 28–38.

Berkson, J. (1960) 'Smoking and cancer of the lung', *Proceedings of the Staff Meeting of the Mayo Clinic*, **35**, pp. 367–85.

Berkson, J. (1962) 'Smoking and lung cancer: Another view', *The Lancet*, pp. 807–8.

Berkson, J. and Elveback, L. (1960) 'Competing exponential risks, with particular reference to the study of smoking and lung cancer', *Journal of the American Statistical Association*, **55**, pp. 415–28.

Borland, B. L. and Rudolph, J. P. (1975) 'Relative effects of low socio-economic status, parental smoking and poor scholastic performance on smoking among high school students', *Social Science and Medicine*, **9**, pp. 27–30.

Burch, P. R. J. (1974) 'Does smoking cause lung cancer?', *New Scientist*, February, **21**, 458–63.

Burch, P. R. J. (1976) *The Biology of Cancer*, Lancaster, Medical and Technical Publishers.

Burch, P. R. J. (1978a) 'Are 90 per cent of cancers preventable?' *FRCS Journal of Medical Science*, **6**, pp. 353–6.

Burch, P. R. J. (1978b) 'Coronary heart disease: Risk factors and ageing', *Gerontology*, **24**, pp. 123–55.

Burch, P. R. J. (1978c) 'Smoking and lung cancer: The problem of inferring cause', *Journal of the Royal Statistical Society*, **141**, pp. 437–77.

Clausen, J. A. (1968) 'Adolescent antecedents of cigarette smoking: Data from the Oakland Growth Study', *Social Science and Medicine*, **1**, pp. 357–82.

Doll, R. and Hill, A. B. (1964) 'Mortality in relation to smoking: Ten years' observations of British doctors', *British Medical Journal*, **1**, pp. 1399–1410 and 1460–7.

Evans, R. I., Henderson, A. H., Hill, P. C. and Raines, B. E. (1979) 'Current psychological, social, and educational programs in control and prevention of smoking: A critical methodological review', *Australian Journal of Psychology*, **23**, pp. 189–99.

Eysenck, H. J. (1947) *Dimensions of Personality*, London, Routledge and Kegan Paul.

Eysenck, H. J. (1952) *The Scientific Study of Personality*, London, Routledge and Kegan Paul.

Eysenck, H. J. (1953a) *The Structure of Human Personality*, London, Methuen.

Eysenck, H. J. (1953b) *Uses and Abuses of Psychology*, London, Penguin Books.

Eysenck, H. J. (1957) *The Dynamics of Anxiety and Hysteria*, London, Routledge and Kegan Paul.

Eysenck, H. J. (Ed.) (1960a) *Experiments in Personality*, London, Routledge and Kegan Paul.

Eysenck, H. J. (Ed.) (1960b) *Behaviour Therapy and the Neuroses*, Oxford, Pergamon Press.

Eysenck, H. J. (1964) *Crime and Personality*, London, Routledge and Kegan Paul; New York, Houghton Mifflin.

Eysenck, H. J. (1965) *Smoking, Health and Personality*, London, Weidenfeld and Nicholson.

Eysenck, H. J. (1967) *The Biological Basis of Personality*, Springfield, Ill., C. C. Thomas.

Eysenck, H. J. (1972) *Handbook of Abnormal Psychology*, 2nd ed., London, Pitman.

Eysenck, H. J. (1973) *Eysenck on Extraversion*, London, Granada Publications.

Eysenck, H. J. (1975) 'Personality and the maintenance of smoking habit', in Dunn, W. L., Jr. (Ed.), *Smoking Behaviour: Motives and Incentives*, Washington, D. C., V. H. Winston and Sons.

Eysenck, H. J. (1976a) *The Measurement of Personality*, Lancaster, Medical and Technical Publishers; Baltimore, Md., University Park Press.

Eysenck, H. J. (1976b) *Sex and Personality*, London, Open Books; Austin, Tex., University of Texas Press.

Eysenck, H. J. (1980) *The Causes and Effects of Smoking*, London, Maurice Temple Smith.

Eysenck, H. J. (1982) *Personality, Genetics, and Behaviour: Selected Papers*, New York, Praeger.

Eysenck, H. J. (1984) 'Stress, personality and smoking behaviour', in Spielberger, C. D., Sarason, I. G. and Defares, P. B. (Eds.), *Stress and Anxiety*, Vol. 9, Washington, Hemisphere Publishing Corporation.

Eysenck, H. J. and Eysenck, S. B. G. (1969) *Personality Structure and Measurement*, London, Routledge and Kegan Paul; San Diego, Calif., R. R. Knapp, Educational and Industrial Testing Service.

Eysenck, H. J. and Eysenck, S. B. G. (1976) *Psychoticism as a Dimension of Personality*, London, Hodder and Stoughton; New York, Crane, Russak.

Eysenck, H. J. and Wilson, G. D. (1978) *The Psychological Basis of Ideology*, Lancaster, MTP Press; Baltimore, Md., University Park Press.

Eysenck, H. J. and Wilson, G. D. (1979) *The Psychology of Sex*, London, J. M. Dent.

Fisher, R. A. (1958) 'Cigarettes, cancer and statistics', *Centennial Review*, **2**, pp. 151–66.

Fisher, R. A. (1959) *Smoking. The Cancer Controversy*, Edinburgh and London, Oliver and Boyd.

Gibson, H. B. (1981) *Hans Eysenck: The Man and His Work*, London, Peter Owen.

Horn, D., Courts, F. A., Taylor, R. M. and Solomon, E. S. (1959) 'Cigarette smoking among high school students', *American Journal of Public Health*, **49**, pp. 1497–511.

Katz, L. (1969) *Hearings on Cigarette Labeling and Advertising*, part 2, US Committee on Interstate and Foreign Commerce, House of Representatives.

Laoye, J. A., Creswell, W. H. and Stone, D. B. (1972) 'A cohort study of 1205 secondary school smokers', *Journal of School Health*, **42**, pp. 47–52.

Leventhal, H. and Cleary, P. D. (1980) 'The smoking problem: A review of the research, theory, and research policies in behavioral risk modification', *Psychological Bulletin*, **88**, pp. 370–405.

Mainland, D. and Herrera, L. (1956) 'The risks of biased selection in forward going surveys with non-professional interviewers', *Journal of Chronic Disease*, **4**, pp. 240–4.

Matarazzo, J. D. and Matarazzo, R. G. (1965) 'Smoking', in Sills, D. L. *et al.* (Eds.), *International Encyclopedia of the Social Sciences*, New York, Macmillan.

Merki, D. J., Creswell, W. H., Stone, D. B., Huffman, W. and Newman, M. S. (1970) 'The effects of two educational and message themes on rural youth smoking behaviour', *Journal of School Health*, **38**, pp. 448–54.

Palmer, A. B. (1970) 'Some variables contributing to the onset of cigarette smoking among junior high school students', *Social Science and Medicine*, **4**, pp. 359–66.

Passey, R. D. (1962) 'Some problems of lung cancer', *The Lancet*, ii, pp. 107–12.

Reid, D. D. (1975) 'International studies in epidemiology', *American Journal of Epidemiology*, **102**, pp. 469–76.

Rosenblatt, M. (1974) 'Lung cancer and smoking—the evidence reassessed', *New Scientist*, 9 May, p. 332.

Royal College of Physicians (1971) *Smoking and Health Now*, London, Pitman.

Salber, E. J. and MacMahon, B. (1961) 'Cigarette smoking among high school students related to social class and parental smoking habits', *American Journal of Public Health*, **51**, pp. 1780–9.

Schwartz, D., Flamanti, R., Lellouch, J. and Denoix, P. F. (1961) 'Results of a French survey on the role of tobacco, particularly inhalation, in different cancer sites', *Journal of the National Cancer Institute*, **26**, pp. 1085–108.

Seltzer, C. C. (1972) 'Critical appraisal of the Royal College of Physicians report on smoking and health', *The Lancet*, pp. 243–8.

Spielberger, C. D. and Jacobs, G. A. (1982) 'Personality and smoking behaviour', *Journal of Personality Assessment*, **46**, pp. 396–403.

Spielberger, C. D., Jacobs, G. A., Crane, R. S. and Russell, S. F. (1983) 'On the relation between family smoking habits and the smoking behaviour of college students', *International Review of Applied Psychology*, **32**, pp. 53–69.

Sterling, T. D. (1973) 'The statistician vis-à-vis issues of public health', *The American Statistician*, **27**, pp. 212–17.

Stocks, P. (1970) 'Cancer mortality in relation to national consumption of cigarettes, solid fuel, tea and coffee', *British Journal of Cancer*, **24**, pp. 215–25.

Straits, B. C. and Sechrest, L. (1963) 'Further support of some findings about the characteristics of smokers and non-smokers', *Journal of Consulting Psychology*, **27**, p. 282.

Wohlford, P. (1970) 'Initiation of cigarette smoking: Is it related to parental smoking behaviour?', *Journal of Consulting and Clinical Psychology*, **34**, pp. 148–51.

# 18. Smoking and Health

PHILIP BURCH

The subject of smoking and health is too broad to be treated adequately in a single chapter of this book. I shall therefore direct most of my arguments to the two associations of outstanding interest: those between smoking on the one hand and lung cancer and coronary heart disease on the other. In terms of notoriety the connexion with lung cancer must be regarded as the more important but, in terms of the supposed numbers of deaths caused by smoking, coronary heart disease claims first place in the Royal College of Physicians (1977) league table. Professor Eysenck and I have both studied the relationships between smoking and these two diseases; our writings on these matters illustrate, conveniently, the similarities and differences in our perspectives.

Opinion on smoking and lung cancer is almost unanimous. In the confident 1971 report of the Royal College of Physicians, *Smoking and Health Now*, we read: 'Many countries have set up authoritative committees and commissions to study the cause of this modern scourge [lung cancer]. All have concluded [nine references given] that it is almost entirely due to cigarette smoking.' To achieve balance the report adds: 'A small number of individuals [ten references given including one to H. J. Eysenck, *Smoking, Health and Personality*, 1965] have challenged these expert conclusions and some have publicised their criticisms. This may explain why nearly nine out of every ten smokers in this country believe that "experts disagree" about this question, and that cigarette smoking has not yet been proved to be the main cause of lung cancer.' Evidently, the dissenters, among whom was R. A. Fisher as well as H. J. Eysenck, were guilty through their lack of expertise of misleading gullible and wishful-thinking smokers.

The most recent report of the Royal College on this subject, entitled *Smoking or Health* (1977), betrays some loss of confidence. Greater efforts are devoted to countering 'The "Genetic" or "Constitutional" Hypothesis' and the authors concede: 'A number of apparent anomalies in recorded deaths from lung cancer in different

**317**

countries, such as very low rates in Japan where cigarette smoking has long been widespread, and unexpected variations in sex ratios, remain unexplained.' We then encounter the strangely cautious statement: 'At present it is safe, and wise from the public health standpoint, to conclude that exposure to tobacco is the main cause of lung cancer, that the greater the exposure to the smoke the greater the risk, and that if a smoker ceases to smoke his increased risk of lung cancer diminishes compared with those who continue.' Is it now only *safe and wise* to conclude that tobacco is the *main* cause of lung cancer? What has become of the earlier certainty? It is fortunate (see later) that the claim about the reduction of risk of lung cancer following the cessation of smoking was made before the publication of the results of randomized controlled intervention trials in London (Rose *et al.*, 1982) and the United States (MRFIT Research Group, 1982).

We cannot accuse the Surgeon General of the United States and his committee of any lack of confidence in their latest (1982) report, *The Health Consequences of Smoking. Cancer*. Among their conclusions we find, without qualification: 'Cigarette smoking is the major cause of lung cancer in the United States.' 'Cessation of smoking reduces the risk of lung cancer mortality compared to that of the continuing smoker.' 'Lung cancer is largely a preventable disease. It is estimated that 85 per cent of lung cancer mortality could have been avoided if individuals never took up smoking.'

Although the Surgeon General allows no doubts to assail him about the causal connection between smoking and lung cancer his views on coronary heart disease (1979) are less emphatic: 'In summary, for the purpose of preventive medicine, it can be concluded that smoking is causally related to coronary heart disease for both men and women in the United States.' Some of us are sceptical enough to wonder whether the purposes of truth always coincide with those of preventive medicine. Eysenck (1980) comments with reference to

> ... errors of methodology, of argument, and of conclusions ... One would have thought, in view of these many defects, that the conclusions drawn by responsible bodies, like the Surgeon General's Committee or the Royal College of Physicians, would be suitably low-key and cautious. What is so impressive, unfortunately, is that only very scant attention is paid to anomalies and criticisms, or to alternative hypotheses. Rather, very strong conclusions are based on weak and contradictory data. Quite generally, evidence apparently indicting cigarette smoking is mentioned prominently, while evidence indicative of lack of causal connection is either not mentioned, or dismissed without discussion or explanation.

Eysenck's criticism is largely justified, but I have drawn attention above to some apparent hesitancy by the Royal College about lung cancer and by the Surgeon General about coronary heart disease. Curiously, the Royal College in its 1977 report appears to be confident where the Surgeon General is hesitant: 'That the association between smoking and heart disease is largely one of cause and effect is supported by its strength and consistency, its independence of the other risk factors, its enhancement in those smokers who inhale, and by the progressive lessening of risk in those who give up, particularly as shown by the experience of British doctors.'

In these reports we see no earnest attempt to adjudicate between alternative hypotheses; it is difficult to avoid the impression that scientific detachment has been displaced by the needs of propaganda. The dangers of such displacement were clearly perceived by R. A. Fisher in a prophetic letter to the Editor of the *British Medical Journal*, 6 July, 1967:

Your annotation on 'Dangers of Cigarette-smoking' leads up to the demand that these hazards 'must be brought home to the public by all the modern devices of publicity.' That is just what some of us with research interests are afraid of. In recent wars, for example, we have seen how unscrupulously the 'modern devices of publicity' are liable to be used under the impulsion of fear; and surely the 'yellow peril' of modern times is not the mild and soothing weed but the organized creation of states of frantic alarm.

I do not suppose for one moment that the committees of the Surgeon General and the Royal College have consciously organized 'states of frantic alarm' but I do get the impression that a preoccupation with health, noble in itself, has so expanded as to obstruct scientific judgment.

## HERESY AND ITS FOUNDATIONS

The essential conclusions of committees of experts have been made clear as has the opposition of two of their main critics, Hans Eysenck and the late Sir Ronald Fisher. With so much intelligence and ability on both sides how has this sharp divergence of opinion arisen? The answer, I suspect, has been given indirectly and in the context of case-control studies by an eminent clinical epidemiologist, A. R. Feinstein, Professor of Medicine and Epidemiology in the University of Yale. According to Feinstein (1979), a 'licensed' epidemiologist '... can obtain and manipulate the data in diverse ways that are sanctioned not by the delineated standards of science, but by the traditional practice of epidemiologists.' Concerning the roots of the divergence Fisher, characteristically, was both subtle and devastating:

My claim, however, is not that the various alternative possibilities [to the causal interpretation of the association between smoking and lung cancer] all command instant assent, or are going to be demonstrated. It is rather that excessive confidence that the solution has already been found is the main obstacle in the way of such more penetrating research as might eliminate some of them ... Statistics has gained a place of modest usefulness in medical research. It can deserve and retain this only by complete impartiality, which is not unattainable by rational minds ... I do not relish the prospect of this science being now discredited by a catastrophic and conspicuous howler. For it will be as clear in retrospect, as it is now in logic, that the data so far do not warrant the conclusions based upon them.

It is remarkable that one of the greatest statisticians who ever lived—some say *the* greatest—should have been so opposed to prevailing attitudes but powerless, it seems, to modify them. How have 'licensed' epidemiologists been able to pursue practices that are not sanctioned by 'the delineated standards of science'? Questions of this kind are not easy to answer; perhaps they would repay study by psychologists with concern for scientific inference and the history of epidemiology.

In a chapter entitled 'The Critics Hit Back' Eysenck (1965) begins by discussing the work of Doll and Hill and of Horn and Hammond. He generously comments: 'I believe that the case which they make out can be criticized but that is merely to say that scientific investigators, even the most eminent, are only human; whatever the truth of the criticisms here presented the work of these investigators will always remain as a fine example of scientific detective work.' He goes on to describe the criticisms of Berkson and Fisher but gives special emphasis to those of Yerushalmy (1962), who discussed the established association between smoking and lung cancer in the following terms: 'The main difficulty in evaluating such association stems from the fact that the individuals observed have made for themselves the crucial decision whether they are smokers, non-smokers or past-smokers. Consequently, the groups lack the comparability necessary for definitive experimentation.' Appropriately enough, Yerushalmy calls this phenomenon of decision-taking, 'self-selection'.

Eysenck (1965) ends his chapter by posing a question similar to those I have asked above: 'And why is it that in spite of these criticisms so many highly qualified people still believe in the causal hypothesis? The answer probably is, as Conant once pointed out, that theories in science are not overthrown by criticism, however well justified; they are overthrown only by better theories.' I suspect that the issue of smoking and health involves not only intellectual competition but also moral and emotional judgments that lie outside the rational process.

## COMMON GROUND AMONG HERETICS

I very much doubt whether Eysenck and I have any substantial differences of opinion about the fundamental scientific issues at stake which are, or ought to be, non-controversial. Given that an indisputable positive association has been established between a habit, or characteristic, *H*, such as cigarette smoking, and a disease *D*, such as lung cancer, then the rules of scientific inference oblige us to consider all of the following hypotheses:

1   The habit *H*, or something very closely connected with it such as the means of lighting cigarettes, pipes and cigars, causes the disease *D*. This is usually called the *causal hypothesis*.
2   *D*, or a connected pre-*D* condition, such as dysplasia or carcinoma *in situ*, causes *H*. I call this the *converse causal hypothesis*.
3   A 'third factor', such as genetic constitution, causes or predisposes to both *H* and *D*. This is often described as the *constitutional hypothesis*.
4   Because hypotheses 1 to 3 are not mutually exclusive then any combination of them might be needed to explain the overall association.

Although some investigators, especially of ischaemic heart disease, give the impression of being unwilling to proceed beyond 1, others are prepared to consider 1 and 3, often treating them (incorrectly) as mutually exclusive alternatives. So far as I am aware, no-one has been able to cope with the demands implicit in 4 where smoking and lung cancer are concerned. Unfortunately, no study of an association can be regarded as fully satisfactory until the relative contributions of 1, 2 and 3 have been properly evaluated, complete with confidence limits, and preferably rather narrow ones.

Studies by Passey (1962) in the UK and by Herrold (1972) in the USA on the age of starting to smoke in relation to the age of onset of lung cancer show that the relative contribution of 2—disease causes habit—is small or negligible. They found that the mean age of onset of lung cancer is effectively independent of both the age of starting to smoke and the level of smoking. (Their findings are implicit in the demonstration that the mortality ratio: death rate from lung cancer in smokers divided by that in non-smokers, is also effectively independent of age.)

My own attempts to assess the relative contributions of 1 and 3 to lung cancer in the England and Wales population have proved abortive largely owing, I fear, to errors of death certification and, to a lesser extent perhaps, in the data for cigarette consumption. These barriers are likely to frustrate most critical analyses for some time to come.

We have to contend, however, with a prior and more elementary difficulty: that of the reproducibility—or lack of it—in the magnitude of the association between smoking and lung cancer. As the Royal College of Physicians recognized, the level of lung cancer in Japan is low although rates of smoking, especially in recent years, have been very high. Furthermore, the mortality ratio in Japanese men (cigarette smokers versus non-smokers) is about 3.8 (Hirayama, 1972) in contrast to a mean of around 10 in studies of European and North American men. We now know that similar divergences are found in other oriental populations. In mainland China, for example, a risk ratio (smokers versus non-smokers, sex unspecified) of only 1.57 has been reported at second hand (Henderson, 1979) which is even weaker than that (3.8) found in Chinese men in Singapore (MacLennan *et al.*, 1977) and comparable with the value (1.74) found among Chinese women in Hong Kong, who have a very high incidence of lung cancer (Ho, 1979; Chan *et al.*, 1979). These and other related observations make it unlikely that hypothesis 1 will provide an exclusive interpretation of these highly variable associations between smoking and lung cancer although it is just conceivable that differences in the mode or duration of smoking, or of the carcinogenicity of tobacco, might account for this seemingly ethnic-related variability. A survey by Hinds *et al.* (1981) of lung cancer among women of Japanese, Chinese and Hawaiian extraction resident in Hawaii provides some measure of control over environmental effects and, perhaps, the types of cigarette and tobacco smoked. For all histological forms of lung cancer they found relative risks (ever-smokers versus never-smokers) of 4.9 for Japanese women, with a 95 per cent confidence interval of 3.2 to 7.3; 1.8 (0.69 to 4.8) for Chinese women and 10.5 (6.1 to 18.3) for Hawaiian women. From this study Hinds *et al.* (1981) concluded, 'cigarette smoking is clearly not the only cause, nor even the major cause, of lung cancer in all populations of women.'

When we turn to associations between cigarette smoking and ischaemic heart disease a very different pattern emerges. Mortality ratios (smokers versus non-smokers) are high at 40–49 years—up to 5.5 for heavy smokers—but decrease with rising age, approaching or going below unity at 70–79 years (Hammond and Garfinkel, 1969). So far as I can discover, this interesting and surprising phenomenon has attracted no quantitative analysis by causationists. If smoking for, say, twenty years is very productive of fatal heart attacks we might expect that smoking for thirty, forty or fifty years would be increasingly, rather than less, dangerous. The initially steep fall in mortality ratios with increasing age from 40–44 years upwards cannot be attributed to the early elimination of a susceptible subpopulation (Burch, 1980a). That smoking at one to nine cigarettes per day by women aged 70–79 years should appear to halve the risk of death, compared with that in non-smokers (Hammond and Garfinkel, 1969), is surely worthy of exploration by causationists; at the least, we require a good explanation for these paradoxes.

It is not without interest that a genetic hypothesis of the association gives a ready explanation of the decline—and the form of the decline—in mortality ratios with rising age, not only for smoking, but also for the other so-called 'risk factors'—hypertension, hypercholesterolaemia and obesity (Burch, 1980a). The prediction (Burch, 1980a) that mortality in very old persons with these 'risk factors' should be *lower* than that in persons without them has now been verified in connexion with hypertension (Rajala *et al.*, 1983).

## CAUSAL AND/OR CONSTITUTIONAL?

This brings me conveniently to a key question: how should we plan to evaluate the roles of causal (especially smoking) and constitutional factors in the aetiology and pathogenesis of disorders such as lung cancer and ischaemic heart disease? It is at this level, I suspect, where Eysenck and I might favour different strategies. Let us first consider the area of agreement. If the constitutional hypothesis is to command serious consideration it is necessary to demonstrate that genetic factors predispose both to the disease in question and, at the least, to some forms of smoking. Granted that these predispositions can be established—as they have been—we then have to find, by direct and indirect methods, the extent of their association and the contribution to the overall connections between smoking habits and disease.

We have both reviewed the voluminous evidence from studies of twins, genetic markers, morphology and personality that testify to the involvement of genetic factors in various forms of smoking (Burch, 1976, 1978; Eysenck, 1965, 1980). Studies of twins show a striking concordance in monozygotic pairs, raised together or apart, for types and levels of smoking (Fisher, 1958a, 1958b). Anthropometric surveys show differences not only between cigarette smokers and non-smokers but also between pipe and cigar smokers (Seltzer, 1963, 1967, 1972). We have to conclude from these several and varied investigations that genes predispose to some or all forms of smoking—and of non-smoking—and that different forms of smoking often entail different genotypes. Ultimately, we shall need to determine which combinations of alleles are involved and their chromosomal locations.

Direct investigations of the genetics of lung cancer have been limited to one large-scale familial study (Tokuhata, 1964, 1976; Tokuhata and Lilienfeld, 1963a, 1963b). However, analysis of the age-patterns of the disease (Burch, 1976) corroborates the conclusions drawn from the familial study. This neglect of the role of genes receives a ready explanation for, in Doll's (1974) words, '. . . few scientists have been sufficiently attracted by the [genetic] hypothesis to mount the effort required to study large numbers of twins.' Nevertheless, it is unfortunate that preconceptions of a distinctly unscientific character have limited the collection of potentially valuable data; the genetics of disease seems to be a subject that is almost as unpopular in some circles as that of genetics and IQ.

Although not designed to do so, the study of Tokuhata and Lilienfeld offers some clues to our main objective: that of an association between smoking and lung cancer genotypes. Tokuhata (1976) determined the frequency of cigarette smokers among the first-degree relatives of (a) smoking and (b) non-smoking probands and controls. When the lung cancer proband (that is, an established case) was a smoker, 41.1 per cent of relatives smoked; when a non-smoker, 40 per cent of relatives smoked. Among controls, 41.8 per cent of the relatives of smoking index subjects were smokers, in contrast to only 30.7 per cent of the relatives of non-smoking index subjects. These findings, and comparable ones for the percentage of smoking offspring, indicate either that some non-smoking lung cancer cases nevertheless had a genetic predisposition to smoking or, more likely, a marked positive association exists between the genotypes for lung cancer and smoking.

## EYSENCK'S PERSPECTIVE

Eysenck outlines his critique of past methods and his strategy for future investigations in *The Causes and Effects of Smoking* (1980), pp. 64–5:

> It seems highly unlikely that the methods of investigation adopted hitherto (i.e. large-scale
> epidemiological studies) will give us results of any great scientific value. Instead what is needed are
> clearly defined and properly controlled experimental studies of specific hypotheses, such as those
> predicting different outcomes for the smoking of different types of tobacco. Equally important
> would be twin studies and half-sib studies which enable us to keep the genetic factor constant while
> varying the smoking factor.

One of the main large-scale methods used in epidemiology and on which causal
hypotheses have been freely erected is the *retrospective case-control* study. Various
habits and characteristics of probands are compared with those of controls matched
for features such as age, sex, occupation and area of residence. If it is found, for
example, that people with heart disease are significantly more often smokers than
their normal controls, then a positive association between the habit and the disease
may be said to exist in the population investigated. Such associations, especially if
they are strong and reproducible, obviously call for further investigation although, in
isolation, they tell us nothing whatsoever about causation.

Retrospective studies tend to be vulnerable to the 'bias of recall'—people with
the disease under investigation might remember episodes suspected of causing it more
readily than healthy persons—and prospective studies aim to defeat such bias. In
*prospective* studies, habits of people are determined in advance of the onset of the
disease(s) in question; the subsequent incidence of the disease(s) in, say, smokers, is
compared with that in control non-smokers and in ex-smokers. Although the bias of
recall is greatly reduced or eliminated the conventional prospective study suffers from
the same fundamental limitations. It is capable of estimating associations, positive or
negative, but just as incapable of estimating causation or prevention.

When Eysenck refers to 'large-scale epidemiological studies' I presume that he
has in mind retrospective case-control and prospective surveys. For my part, I am less
dismissive. For example, large-scale case-control and prospective investigations of the
association between smoking and lung cancer in mainland China would be valuable
because the very weak association reported indirectly (Henderson, 1979) requires
confirmation. Indeed, any significant association discovered in one ethnic group
might, with advantage, be investigated in as many other ethnic groups as possible. If
all other pertinent factors can be suitably controlled, and the strength of the
association still depends on ethnicity, then it is a fair assumption that the association
between the habit and the disease involves a constitutional factor of some kind.

Whether studies of temporal trends of incidence or mortality in whole populations, such as England and Wales, Japan, US Whites, etc. should be regarded as
'epidemiological' is a matter of definition. They are certainly 'large-scale' and they do
determine the distributions of disease, within the limits of diagnostic error and
census-based estimates of population size, by age, sex and calendar year. If we
disregard the usually trivial biases of immigration and emigration we can examine the
trends in the level of disease in relation to those of smoking, for the entire population,
and thereby avoid the potentially dangerous and misleading bias of self-selection.
Comparison of mortality from IHD, say, in self-selected ex-smokers relative to that in
self-selected continuing smokers is a fruitless exercise if we aim to test causal

hypotheses. Ex-smokers have been shown to differ from continuing smokers in many respects before they gave up smoking (Friedman *et al.*, 1979). In making comparisons it is essential to rigorous hypothesis-testing that the two (or more) groups should be as alike as possible in all pertinent respects except for the variable under examination, in this case smoking. If smoking actually causes a particular disease and is more or less linearly related to incidence then a reduction in the mean level of smoking within a national population will be followed, *other things being equal*, by a reduction in the mean level of that disease. In practice, 'other things' are seldom equal but they can sometimes be identified and reliably allowed for and then strong inferences can be drawn from studies of whole populations. Through them I have been able to conclude that the association between smoking and ischaemic heart disease has little or no causal component in various countries, including the United States and England and Wales (Burch, 1980a).

Another form of 'large-scale epidemiological study' of great value is that of the *randomized controlled intervention trial*. In a typical design, smokers satisfying certain admission criteria, for example, of age, sex and freedom from certain diseases, are then allocated randomly (a) to the *special intervention* group and (b) to the *usual* or *normal* care group that acts as a control. The special intervention group is subjected to intense pressure, controlled by the investigator, to quit smoking, while the control group forms part of the general population insofar as exposure to anti-smoking propaganda is concerned. Smoking habits of both groups are monitored and the levels of smoking-associated diseases in the two groups are compared after a suitable interval. If the association is purely constitutional we expect the level of smoking-associated diseases in the two groups to be equal; if the association is purely causal we expect the difference in disease levels to be related to the difference in smoking levels through the causal hypothesis under test. A part-constitutional, part-causal hypothesis makes, of course, intermediate predictions.

In principle, this is another way of defeating the bias of self-selection: through randomization we begin with two effectively comparable groups and then in one group, the intervention group, special pressures are exerted to quit smoking. Such trials, if large enough to yield results of a suitable statistical accuracy, are inevitably expensive and difficult to conduct but, at the fundamental level, suffer only one potentially serious drawback: quitting smoking under pressure might of itself generate other changes of, say, diet and stress. These accompanying changes might then help to cause, or prevent, the disease(s) under investigation. In such circumstances the intervention and normal-care groups would then differ, on the average, with respect to pertinent factors other than the one (smoking) under test. This complication has to be recognized and efforts should always be made to monitor any changes in 'life-style' induced by quitting. If it can be established that such changes are negligible or have little or no consequence then the results of such randomized trials acquire immense scientific value. The outcome of two randomized trials, one carried out in London (the 'Whitehall' study) and another in the USA (MRFIT), is described below.

I have to conclude, in opposition to Eysenck (?), that large-scale epidemiological studies still have an important part to play in unravelling the nature of the links between smoking and diseases. What, then, of 'controlled experimental studies of specific hypotheses'? These are, of course, also immensely important and the randomized controlled intervention trial might well be included among them.

I am not clear as to what particular experiment Eysenck has in mind when he refers to predictions of 'different outcomes for the smoking of different types of tobacco.' In communities where two types of tobacco are freely available—one producing 'acid' and the other 'alkaline' smoke—as in certain provinces in Germany, the phenomenon of self-selection would, I believe, preclude us from drawing reliable conclusions about their relative carcinogenicity. Although a randomized trial of the effects of the two types of tobacco, taken in conjunction with conventional case-control or prospective surveys, would be most illuminating, I fear that practicability, ethical considerations and expense are likely to prohibit such an experiment on a suitably large scale.

I now need to consider the deceptively simple problem of twins studies. An attractive study design relates to series of twins, monozygotic (MZ) and dizygotic (DZ), that are appreciably discordant for smoking habits (Cederlöf *et al.*, 1977). That is to say, one member of a twin pair smokes relatively heavily while the co-twin smokes relatively lightly, or not at all. (This criterion, rather than that of the fully-discordant, smoker versus non-smoker, is adopted because few MZ twin pairs are fully-discordant.) Criteria for discordance are defined and applied equally to MZ and DZ pairs.

For simplicity, suppose that a discordant pair consists of a smoker and a non-smoker, that the average level of smoking in the MZ smokers is the same as that in the DZ smokers, and that the MZ and DZ pairs are matched for age and sex. Suppose that the disease, *D*, is associated with smoking with a relative risk determined in the general, singleton population (smokers versus non-smokers) of *R*, at the average level of smoking found in the two series of twins. Assume that *D* is not associated with either type of twinning and that causal agents other than smoking have the same impact on smokers and their non-smoking co-twins. From these several assumptions a 'pure' causal hypothesis of the association, with relative risk *R*, predicts that the incidence of *D* in the smoking twins of both the MZ and DZ series will be *R* times higher than that in the non-smoking twins. On a 'pure' constitutional hypothesis, in which smoking has no causal action, the incidence of *D* in the smoking members of the MZ series will be the same as that in the non-smoking MZ members. In the DZ series, the incidence of *D* in the smoking members will be greater than that in the non-smoking members but the ratio will be less than *R* because DZ pairs are more alike, genetically, than unrelated individuals in the general population of singletons from which *R* was derived. A part-causal, part-constitutional hypothesis makes intermediate predictions.

Table 1 shows the findings obtained by Cederlöf *et al.* (1977) for mortality from lung cancer, coronary heart disease and 'all causes' in 'present and former smokers', males and females combined, born in the period 1901–25. (This is the largest data set available for all three classifications of disease.)

Numbers are too small for definitive conclusions but it will be seen that the nominal results for lung cancer are, fortuitously, in virtually exact agreement with the predictions of the 'pure' constitutional hypothesis. The nominal ratio of deaths from lung cancer (pooled high group) to (pooled low group) in the DZ series, 10 to 2, is perhaps marginally higher than would be expected, but, for what it is worth, the corresponding 2 to 2 ratio in the MZ series is exactly as predicted by the 'pure' constitutional hypothesis. The findings for coronary heart disease show a higher ratio of deaths (pooled high group) versus (pooled low group) in the DZ than in the MZ series. The ratio in the MZ series is greater than unity, but not significantly so (P = 0.26). These findings are consistent with all three theories, although the

**Table 1**  *Mortality (Numbers of Deaths) from Lung Cancer, Coronary Heart Disease and 'All Causes' in MZ and DZ Twins, Sexes Combined, Born 1901–25 and Discordant ('Low' versus 'High') for Smoking (Series of 'Present and Former Smokers')*

| Cause of death | DZ Twins | | | MZ Twins | | |
|---|---|---|---|---|---|---|
| | Number of pairs at risk | Pooled low* group | Pooled high† group | Number of pairs at risk | Pooled low* group | Pooled high† group |
| | 1487 | Deaths | Deaths | 572 | Deaths | Deaths |
| Lung cancer | 2 | 10 | | 2 | 2 | |
| Coronary heart | 22 | 40 | | 11 | 18 | |
| All causes 1961–75 First deaths in a pair only | 98 | 142 | | 46 | 53 | |

*Source*:  Adapted from Cederlöf *et al.* (1977), Tables 7.10, 7.13 and 7.14.
*Notes*:  \* Relatively low-level smokers.
† Relatively high-level smokers.
(See original paper for criteria.)

nominal ratios favour a mixed hypothesis. On other grounds, with much better statistical power, I conclude that any causal effects are, in fact, small or negligible (Burch, 1980a). Deaths from 'all causes' in the DZ series are very significantly more frequent in the pooled high than in the pooled low group (P = 0.004), but almost identical in the MZ series (P = 0.53). Superficially, the 'pure' causal hypothesis might appear to be rejected but, because of relatively small numbers, the 'high'/'low' ratio for the MZ series (1.15) does not differ significantly from that (1.45) in the DZ series (P $\simeq$ 0.36).

I would like to be able to proclaim an unqualified enthusiasm for studies of twins but Table 1 reveals their main practical limitation, which is the difficulty of obtaining adequate numbers. On theoretical grounds I feel bound to express reservations of a more fundamental character. These mainly concern an assumption, adopted traditionally, about monozygotic twins. One member of such a pair is deemed to be 'genetically identical' to his or her co-twin; indeed, this assumption has acquired the status of an axiom. Few axioms in empirical science, alas, are sacrosanct. In fact, we are only entitled to assume that a monozygotic pair derives from a common zygote; there is no justification for assuming that genetic identity is maintained throughout embryogenesis and foetal life and is present at birth. On the contrary, there are certain clear instances where this assumption is manifestly false. Perhaps the most dramatic is that of discordance for sex (see, for example, Schmidt *et al.*, 1976), but differences in the complement of autosomes in MZ twin pairs are almost as striking and equally significant (Karp *et al.*, 1975; Carakushansky and Berthier, 1976; Pedersen *et al.*, 1980). I interpret cytogenetic discordance in MZ twins as reflecting, in general, a much wider phenomenon: that of an autoaggressive attack on the part of the mother on her germ cells, zygote, or early-stage embryo (Burch, 1968). Attacks on early-stage embryos can result in mosaicism for aneuploidy in both singletons and twins, and in discordance for aneuploidy in twins. Those attacks that result in aneuploidy are readily identified but those that induce gene change (mutation), without gross chromosomal alteration, are more elusive.

If such attacks occur then my unified theory of growth and disease predicts that the probability of their occurrence in relation to maternal age—or paternal age when male germ cells are attacked—will be described by 'autoaggressive statistics' (Burch, 1966, 1968, 1976). The occurrence of many disorders in offspring depends on parental age at conception and hence birth (Mayo *et al.*, 1976). It is particularly interesting that the relative risk of breast cancer (Standfast, 1967)—known to involve genetic predisposition—increases with maternal age, $t$, at birth (corrected for a latent period of 2.5 years), as: $1 - \exp(-kt^2)$, where $k$ is constant. This mathematical relationship suggests that a 'forbidden clone' is initiated in a predisposed female by two random somatic mutations in a growth control stem cell and that products of the forbidden clone attack ova, the zygote, or the early-stage embryo to induce a specific genetic change. The change predisposes the female offspring to breast cancer.

From this standpoint, theory predicts that maternal autoaggressive attacks on early-stage embryonic MZ twins will occur and that, on some occasions, these will render the twins genetically discordant for one or more traits. Such discordances will often depend on maternal age, as described by 'autoaggressive statistics'. (However, when the plateau region of a prevalence curve for an autoaggressive disorder is reached before the menarche no dependence on maternal age will be observed.) Furthermore, when the growth of the initiated forbidden clone in the mother depends on an extrinsic precipitating factor, such as a micro-organism, then theory predicts that the risk of a genetically-based disorder will often depend on the season at conception and hence birth. It is well known that the risk of schizophrenia, for example, is related to the season of birth and hence this and similar phenomena may be interpreted in terms of autoaggressive theory. (The risk of schizophrenia in relation to parental age at birth—maternal and paternal—might repay examination.)

Finally, we cannot disregard the possibility that in either or both members of a twin pair random changes in growth-control genes—the genes that predispose to autoaggressive disease—will also render MZ twins discordant at birth. Both induced and random changes will affect DZ twins but because they derive from genetically-dissimilar zygotes anyway, the consequences are unimportant in our present context.

For the above reasons I believe that the classical assumption of the genetic identity of MZ twins *at birth* has to be treated with great reserve. This is a very inconvenient spanner to throw into the works because, if the reasons advanced are valid, some if not all attempts to calculate 'heritability' become suspect. In general, traditional calculations based on data for twins will be expected to underestimate the importance of the genetic contribution not only to disease but also to traits such as personality and intelligence. Random or maternally-induced genetic changes in MZ twins that render them discordant will be interpreted as environmental effects, as in some sense they are—temporal and maternal. It will be appreciated that the whole concept of 'heritability' needs to be re-examined. In spite of these complications it remains true that MZ twins will generally be much more alike, genetically, than like-sexed DZ twins, although gross chromosomal discordance might, of course, produce drastic phenotypic differences within MZ pairs. On the other hand, the growth-control genes that are involved in predisposition to autoaggressive disorders (including lung cancer and IHD) are extremely mutable, at least in somatic cells (Burch, 1968, 1976), and hence the above complications cannot be ignored in connection with studies of smoking and disease. In connection with the smoking habit, Eaves and

Eysenck conclude: '...there is a suggestion that environmental factors are comparable with genetic factors as far as the causes of twin similarity are concerned' (Eysenck, 1980). According to my arguments, Eaves and Eysenck are likely to have overestimated the role of the environment and to have underestimated that of the genotype.

Although MZ twins reared together or apart are often strikingly concordant for smoking habits (Fisher, 1958a, 1958b) they are sometimes discordant and we are not justified in assuming automatically that discordance cannot sometimes have a genetic basis. If there is a genetic association between smoking and lung cancer—and that seems likely—then we have to consider that a random or an autoaggressively-induced genetic change in one MZ twin might render that twin predisposed both to smoking and to, say, lung cancer, while the co-twin remains non-predisposed. Similarly, a pair that is initially predisposed to both smoking and lung cancer might be converted to discordance for one character.

Because of these possibilities, studies of twins can corroborate the 'pure' constitutional hypothesis—when potential complications are negligible or absent— but, unfortunately, they cannot reject that hypothesis unless it can be established by independent means that the complications discussed here are absent.


## OTHER APPROACHES


As a theoretician I hold, not surprisingly, that an explicit working hypothesis of disease mechanisms is a valuable adjunct to investigations of the causes of disease. Eysenck, I believe, endorses this view. A well-tested theory helps to orient thinking and to expose what might not otherwise be obvious. Needless to say, the ideal theory will be all-embracing and will describe the agents and mechanisms of change whether of intrinsic or extrinsic origin.

When analyzing possible links between the temporal trends in smoking and those of an associated disease, assumptions about the duration and distribution of the lag between the stimulus (smoking) and the response (disease incidence or mortality) need to be made and evaluated. It is helpful if theory, combined if necessary with other evidence, can define the nature of the lag or latent period.

For rigorous tests we need *quantitative* hypotheses both of natural (spontaneous) and of tobacco-induced disease. The failure or inability of dedicated causationists to elaborate a theory of natural and tobacco-induced lung cancer that is consistent with salient features of the evidence constitutes a major weakness of their case. Doll (1971) proposed a theory of lung cancer in which the age-specific incidence in smokers rises much more steeply with age than that in non-smokers. His theory predicts that mortality ratios (lifetime history of cigarette smoking versus non-smokers) should rise from about 3.4 at 40 years of age to 25 at 80 years of age. This prediction is falsified by various observations and notably those of Hammond (1972) who found that mortality ratios remain effectively constant with age. Further and more complicated tests of Doll's (1971) hypothesis, including comparisons of the age-patterns of lung cancer mortality in countries with low and high tobacco consumption, also show it to be untenable (Burch, 1978). A causal hypothesis—my 'precipitator hypothesis'—can be devised, however, that is consistent with the evidence for age patterns and mortality ratios that rejects Doll's (1971) hypothesis.

The precipitator hypothesis can in turn be tested using temporal trends for sex- and age-specific cigarette consumption and lung cancer mortality in England and Wales (Burch, 1980b, 1981a). Changes in recorded mortality, however, bear no consistent relation to those in cigarette consumption; there can be little doubt that many of the more anomalous trends in mortality, particularly from 1950–54 to 1963–67, should be attributed to errors of death certification and their change with time. Necropsy studies to evaluate the accuracy of death certification in this country have demonstrated large errors—false negative and false positive—especially in connection with lung cancer (Heasman and Lipworth, 1966; Waldron and Vicker-staff, 1977). A particularly insidious type of error has been identified by Feinstein and Wells (1974), *detection bias*, in which the physician is more likely to diagnose lung cancer in smokers than in non-smokers and in heavy than in light smokers; the mortality ratio for heavy smokers versus non-smokers based on clinical diagnosis was exaggerated by a factor of 1.45.

Because of the errors of diagnosis and death certification for specific causes of death I have felt obliged to study the relation between the temporal trends in smoking and those of *mortality from all causes* for which death certification is somewhat more reliable (Burch, 1981b). Probably the main limitation in the accuracy of statistics for all causes is the estimate of population size, which can be rather poor in the higher age groups for those years that are remote from a census year. Nevertheless, if the whole of the association between smoking and mortality is causal, changes in mortality following changes in the levels of smoking should have been readily detected in my analysis. No such changes were apparent (Burch, 1981b), which is hardly surprising when it is considered that ischaemic heart disease is the major single cause of death and that its association with smoking appears to be largely or wholly non-causal (Burch, 1980a). The results for 'all causes' can be regarded as corroborating the earlier ones for ischaemic heart disease.

Throughout the period 1950–52 to 1974–76, sex- and age-specific death rates generally fell; the rate of fall tended to be more rapid when rates of smoking were rising than when they were falling. (It does not follow that smoking therefore reduces mortality.) Generally, perturbations in the curves of death rates versus calendar time were common to both sexes, and, up to the age of about 45, the fall in death rates was almost entirely accounted for by the near-eradication of mortality from tuberculosis (Burch, 1981b).

The claims of the US Surgeon General (1979) and Royal College of Physicians (1971, 1977) regarding 'excess deaths' attributable to smoking derive from mortality ratios: the foundations of their calculations would appear to be insecure. The Department of Health and Social Security (1975) concluded, again on the basis of mortality ratios, that in England and Wales, 1971, some 52,000 deaths in the age range 35 to 74 years were caused by smoking. The possible errors in this estimate are not mentioned—a remarkable dereliction in an official publication—and it would be interesting to know how this and similar claims can be reconciled with secular trends.

Another test of the precipitator hypothesis entails analyses of the age-patterns of disease. Whereas it is obvious that temporal (secular) changes in the level of smoking will, for a causal relation, be followed by temporal changes in the level of the associated disease, it has not been so widely appreciated that changes in the rate of smoking with age will also give rise to characteristic distortions of the age-pattern (Burch, 1976, 1980a). To predict the form of the distortion a specific causal hypothesis is necessary. However, in the example of ischaemic heart disease, the age-patterns in the two sexes show no smoking-caused distortions; they are consistent with the hypothesis of no causal effect. Lung cancer presents a more difficult problem because the age-patterns of the several types of lung cancer in men differ markedly from those in women and in a way that is not clearly accounted for by (smoking) causal hypotheses (Burch, 1976). Furthermore, sex- and age-specific trends in mortality from lung cancer and levels of smoking fail to corroborate the precipitator hypothesis (Burch, 1980b, 1981a). (I should add that the secular trends and the age-patterns of oesophageal cancer both corroborate the hypothesis that alcohol helps to cause the disease, though probably through an indirect mechanism; they fail to support the hypothesis that cigarette smoking has an appreciable causal role.)

In the section above, Eysenck's *Perspectives*, I have already indicated my qualified partiality for randomized controlled intervention trials and the results of the studies in London (Rose *et al.*, 1982) and the United States (MRFIT, 1982) bear quoting. The London study intervened with respect only to smoking but the US study entailed, in addition, dietary advice and stepped care treatment for hypertension in the intervention group.

Some 1445 male smokers aged 40–59, and at high risk of cardiorespiratory disease, entered the London ('Whitehall study') trial (Rose and Hamilton, 1978). After three years the average per capita cigarette consumption claimed by men in the intervention group was 6.2 per day as opposed to 15.7 per day in the normal care group. This difference narrowed as the trial proceeded and over the ten years the average reduction in the intervention group was 7.6 cigarettes per day ( − 53 per cent) compared with normal care controls (Rose *et al.*, 1982). The only statistically significant difference in mortality by cause was found in connection with 'cancers at all sites other than lung' which '. . . showed overall a large excess in the intervention group (P = 0.003)' (Rose *et al.*, 1982). However, this test was of a *post hoc* hypothesis and no correction was applied to the P value for the number of statistical tests carried out. That quitting smoking, even if accompanied by psychological stress and dietary changes, might more than double the incidence of these cancers fails to convince. Rose *et al.*, (1982) observed only 'minor' adverse psychological effects and they gave five reasons for attributing this disturbing finding to chance. Their arguments are plausible and it is reassuring that no comparably significant difference was found for this category of cancers in the MRFIT study. Findings for lung cancer and 'all causes' in the Whitehall study are pooled below with those from MRFIT (1982).

The US trial involved 12,866 men aged 35 to 57 years, 59 per cent of whom were current cigarette smokers at randomization; at seventy-two months later, the thiocyanate-adjusted proportions were 46 per cent smokers in the 'usual care' group and 29 per cent in the 'special intervention' group. (Levels of smoking in the two groups were not reported.) The dietary advice and treatment for hypertension given to the intervention group would not be expected to have influenced mortality from lung cancer; these interventions were intended to reduce the risk of coronary heart disease, an important component of overall mortality. On a causal theory deaths from lung cancer should have been lower in the intervention than in the usual care group but the opposite result was found: thirty-four deaths (intervention) versus twenty-eight (usual care). Numbers are too small to reject the causal hypothesis. By pooling the data from these two randomized trials we obtain the best estimate available for the effect of quitting smoking on the incidence of lung cancer. (Studies of self-selected quitters in relation to self-selected continuing smokers are, of course, worthless in this respect.) Adding deaths and registrations for lung cancer in the

Whitehall study (twenty-five, normal care; twenty-two, intervention) to deaths in the MRFIT study, and combining the populations, we obtain the proportion of lung cancer cases in the normal-usual-care groups: $53/7169 = 0.74$ per cent; and in the intervention groups: $56/7142 = 0.78$ per cent. Because of small numbers this superficially striking corroboration of the 'pure' constitutional hypothesis is, of course, fortuitous. When we recall that the MRFIT trial cost over one hundred million dollars it seems unlikely that we shall ever see a randomized trial large enough to discriminate adequately between alternative hypotheses.

Non-significant differences in mortality from coronary heart disease were found in both studies, a result that was particularly disappointing in the US trial in which dietary advice and treatment for hypertension supplemented counselling against cigarette smoking in the intervention group.

Findings for deaths from all causes give the largest available numbers and the pooled data from both trials yield a proportionate mortality of $388/7169 = 5.41$ per cent in the normal-usual-care groups; and $388/7142 = 5.43$ per cent in the combined intervention groups. The rumour that constitutionalist moles have doctored these results is, I believe, without foundation. Be that as it may, the findings do not seem to enjoy much popularity in the medical literature. They do, however, corroborate conclusions drawn from other evidence and independent methods (Burch, 1981b).

### AN OPTIMUM STRATEGY?

Only too often we read in our newspapers and even in the medical and scientific literature that smoking, drinking, oral contraceptives, ionizing radiation, saccharin and a host of other constituents of our diet cause this, that and the other disease, generally one or more types of cancer. The alarmist headlines are frequently based on mere association although findings from cell culture and experimental animals can also achieve prominence. Is there an optimum strategy that we ought to pursue when assessing such claims, preferably before the headlines have dramatized the issue, or, failing that, after the public has been suitably alarmed? It would be interesting to have the views of experts on this important question.

I would be surprised if they could offer us any general solution. Much would depend on the frequency of the disease, the reliability of its diagnosis, the nature and distribution of the supposed noxious agent and a host of other factors. It would obviously be helpful to know the details of the association between agent $A$ and the disease $D$, including any sex- or age-dependence, although a positive association established from case-control and prospective studies would not necessarily imply cause and a negative or neutral association would not reject it. (A strong negative constitutional association could cancel or overwhelm a causal effect.)

If changes in $A$ with time in an effectively closed, for example, national population, were followed in a clearly defined way by changes in $D$, and if comparable changes were observed in different national populations, the causal hypothesis would be greatly strengthened. Because this type of analysis defeats the phenomenon of self-selection, avoids any stresses and changes caused by 'intervention' from the investigator, and involves the largest numbers of people available—entire national populations—it has much to commend it. The collection of reliable sex- and age-specific data for $A$, for example, tobacco consumption, alcohol consumption and animal fat consumption, is the most difficult and expensive part of the exercise given that mortality statistics have to be compiled in any case, for other reasons. Sufficient corroborative evidence for a causal hypothesis from studies of secular trends might be so convincing as to overcome reasonable doubt. In practice, the causal relation between $A$ and $D$ would need to be strong enough and sufficiently definable, especially in its temporal aspect, to overcome the masking effects of errors in the data, random and systematic, together with the interfering effects of other causal or prophylactic agents.

Analysis of the age-patterns of disease $D$ (sex- and age-specific incidence or mortality), in relation to the sex- and age-specific consumption of $A$, shares some of the advantages and disadvantages of studies of secular trends and relies on the same sources of evidence. However, estimates of the distortion of the age-pattern depend on our ability to assess the form of the undistorted age-pattern, in the absence of $A$ and other confounding factors.

Constitutional hypotheses require corroboration from genetic studies, both of predisposition to disease $D$ (or to life-span), and of predisposition to $A$, when $A$ is a habit such as cigarette smoking or drinking. In spite of their limitations, twins and familial studies of the kind pursued by Eysenck and his collaborators are indispensable for this purpose in the absence of direct genetic markers of a biochemical, immunological or physiological character. Eventually, DNA probes should become available to map and define the genotype and much of our current ignorance will doubtless vanish under the onslaught of molecular biologists.

## CODA

Finally, I should like to pay tribute to Professor Hans Eysenck for his long and unswerving devotion to the scientific investigation of human behaviour. A deep distrust of genetic explanations for behaviour and disease permeates many supposedly scientific disciplines as well as the laity; to maintain a rigorous approach in defiance of widespread hostility calls for courage and perseverance, qualities that Hans possesses in abundance.

In this essay I have highlighted certain differences between us but these concern detail and the choice of priorities; I believe that we agree over fundamentals. The implementation of objectives in epidemiology is a task of quite extraordinary and generally underestimated difficulty; it is unlikely that unanimity as to methods will be achieved.

## REFERENCES

Burch, P. R. J. (1966) 'Spontaneous auto-immunity. Equations for sex-specific prevalence and initiation-rates', *J. Theor. Biol.*, **12**, pp. 397–409.
Burch, P. R. J. (1968) *An Inquiry Concerning Growth, Disease and Ageing*, Edinburgh, Oliver and Boyd.
Burch P. R. J. (1976) *The Biology of Cancer. A New Approach*, Lancaster, MTP; Baltimore, Md., University Park Press.
Burch P. R. J. (1978) 'Smoking and lung cancer: The problem of inferring cause' (with discussion), *J. Roy. Stat. Soc. A. (General)*, **141**, pp. 437–77.

Burch, P. R. J. (1980a) 'Ischaemic heart disease: Epidemiology, risk factors and cause', *Cardiovasc. Res.*, **14**, pp. 307–38.

Burch, P. R. J. (1980b) 'Smoking and lung cancer: Tests of a causal hypothesis', *J. Chron. Dis.*, **33**, pp. 221–38.

Burch, P. R. J. (1981a) 'Smoking, lung cancer and hypothesis testing', *Medical Hypotheses*, **7**, pp. 1461–70.

Burch, P. R. J. (1981b) 'Smoking and mortality in England and Wales, 1950 to 1976', *J. Chron. Dis.*, **34**, pp. 87–103.

Carakushansky, G. and Berthier, C. (1976) 'The deLange syndrome in one of twins', *J. Med. Genet.*, **13**, pp. 404–6.

Cederlöf, R., Friberg, L. and Lundman, T. (1977) 'The interactions of smoking, environment and heredity and their implications for disease aetiology', *Acta Med. Scand.*, Suppl. 612.

Chan, W. C., Colbourne, M. J., Fung, S. C. and Ho, H. C. (1979) 'Bronchial cancer in Hong Kong 1976–1977', *Br. J. Cancer*, **39**, pp. 182–92.

Department of Health and Social Security (1975) *Smoking and Health*, London, HMSO.

Doll, R. (1971) ' The age distribution of cancer: Implications for models of carcinogenesis' (with discussion), *J. Roy. Stat. Soc. A*, **134**, pp. 133–66.

Doll, R. (1974) 'Smoking, lung cancer, and Occam's razor', *New Scientist*, **61**, pp. 463–7.

Eysenck, H. J. (1965) *Smoking, Health and Personality*, London, Weidenfeld and Nicolson.

Eysenck, H. J. (1980) *The Causes and Effects of Smoking* (with contributions by L. J. Eaves), London, Maurice Temple Smith.

Feinstein, A. R. (1979) 'Methodologic problems and standards in case-control research', *J. Chron. Dis.*, **32**, pp. 35–41.

Feinstein, A. R. and Wells, C. K. (1974) 'Cigarette smoking and lung cancer: The problems of "detection bias" in epidemiologic rates of disease', *Trans Ass. Am. Physicians*, **87**, pp. 180–5.

Fisher, R. A. (1958a) 'Lung cancer and cigarettes?', *Nature* (London) **182**, p. 108.

Fisher, R. A. (1958b) 'Cancer and smoking', *Nature* (London), **182**, p. 596.

Friedman, G. D., Siegelaub, A. B., Dales, L. G., and Seltzer, C. C. (1979) 'Characteristics predictive of coronary heart disease in ex-smokers before they stopped smoking: Comparison with persistent smokers and non-smokers', *J. Chron. Dis.*, **32**, pp. 175–90.

Hammond, E. C. (1972) 'Smoking habits and air pollution in relation to lung cancer', in Lee, D. K. (Ed.), *Environmental Factors in Respiratory Diseases*, New York, Academic Press, pp. 177–98.

Hammond, E. C. and Garfinkel, L. (1969) 'Coronary heart disease, stroke, and aortic aneurysm. Factors in the etiology', *Arch. Environ. Health*, **19**, pp. 167–82.

Heasman, M. A. and Lipworth, L. (1966) *Accuracy of Certification of Cause of Death. Studies on Medical and Population Subjects, No. 20. General Register Office.* London, HMSO.

Henderson, B. E. (1979) 'Observations on cancer etiology in China', *Natn Cancer Inst. Monogr.*, **53**. pp. 59–65.

Herrold, K. McD. (1972) 'Survey of histologic types of primary lung cancer in US veterans', *Pathol. Annual*, **7**, pp. 45–79.

Hinds, M. W., Stemmermann, G. N., Yang, H-Y., Kolonel, L. N., Lee, J. and Wegner, E. (1981) 'Differences in lung cancer risk from smoking among Japanese, Chinese and Hawaiian women in Hawaii', *Int. J. Cancer*, **27**, pp. 297–302.

Hirayama, T. (1972) 'Smoking in relation to death rates of 265,118 men and women in Japan. A report of five years of follow-up', Handout at American Cancer Society meeting, Florida, 24–29 March.

Ho, J. H-C. (1979) 'Some epidemiologic observations on cancer in Hong Kong', *Natn Cancer Inst. Monogr.*, **53**, pp. 35–47.

Karp, L., Bryant, J. I., Tagatz, G. and Fialkow, P. J. (1975) 'The occurrence of gonadal dysgenesis in association with monozygotic twinning', *J. Med. Genet.*, **12**, pp. 70–8.

MacLennan, R., da Costa, J., Day, N. E., Law, C. H., Ng, Y. K. and Shanmugaratnam, K. (1977) 'Risk factors for lung cancer in Singapore Chinese, a population with high female incidence rates', *Int. J. Cancer*, **20**, pp. 854–60.

Mayo, O., Murdoch, J. L. and Hancock, T. W. (1976) 'On the estimation of parental age effects on mutation', *Ann. Hum. Genet. Lond.*, **39**, pp. 427–31.

MRFIT Research Group (1982) 'Multiple risk factor intervention trial: Risk factor changes and mortality results', *J. Am. Med. Ass.*, **248**, pp. 1465–77.

Passey, R. D. (1962) 'Some problems of lung cancer', *Lancet*, ii, pp. 107–12.

Pedersen, I. K., Philip, J., Sele, V. and Starup, J. (1980) 'Monozygotic twins with dissimilar phenotypes and chromosome complements', *Acta Obstet. Gynecol Scand.*, **59**, pp. 459–62.

Rajala, S., Haavisto, M., Heikinheimo, R. and Mattila, K. (1983) 'Blood pressure and mortality in the very old', *Lancet*, ii, pp. 520–1.

Rose, G. and Hamilton, P. J. S. (1978) 'A randomised controlled trial of the effect on middle aged men of advice to stop smoking', *J. Epidemiol. Comm. Hlth.*, **32**, pp. 275–81.

Rose, G., Hamilton, P. J. S., Colwell, L. and Shipley, M. J. (1982) 'A randomised controlled trial of anti-smoking advice: 10-year results', *J. Epidemiol. Comm. Hlth*, **36**, pp. 102–8.

Royal College of Physicians (1971) *Smoking and Health Now*, London, Pitman.

Royal College of Physicians (1977) *Smoking or Health*, London, Pitman.

Schmidt, R., Sobel, E. A., Nitowsky, H. M., Dar, H. and Allen, F. H. (1976) 'Monozygotic twins discordant for sex', *J. Med. Genet.*, **13**, pp. 64–8.

Seltzer, C. C. (1963) 'Morphologic constitution and smoking', *J. Am. Med. Ass.*, **183**, pp. 639–45.

Seltzer, C. C. (1967) 'Constitution and heredity in relation to tobacco smoking', *Ann. N. Y. Acad. Sci.*, **142**, pp. 322–30.

Seltzer, C. C. (1972) 'Differences between cigar and pipe smokers in healthy White veterans', *Arch. Environ. Health*, **25**, pp. 187–91.

Standfast, S. J. (1967) 'Birth characteristics of women dying from breast cancer', *J. Natn Cancer Inst.*, **39**, pp. 33–42.

Surgeon General (1979) *Smoking and Health*, US Department of Health, Education, and Welfare.

Surgeon General (1982) *The Health Consequences of Smoking. Cancer*, US Department of Health, Education, and Welfare.

Tokuhata, G. K. (1964) 'Familial factors in human lung cancer and smoking', *Am. J. Public Health*, **54**, pp. 24–32.

Tokuhata, G. K. (1976) 'Cancer of the lung: Host and environmental interaction', in Lynch, H. T. (Ed.), *Cancer Genetics*, Springfield, Ill., C. C. Thomas, pp. 213–32.

Tokuhata, G. K. and Lilienfeld, A. M. (1963a) 'Familial aggregation of lung cancer among hospital patients', *Public Health Reports*, **78**, pp. 277–83.

Tokuhata, G. K. and Lilienfeld, A. M. (1963b) 'Familial aggregation of lung cancer in humans', *J. Natn Cancer Inst.*, **30**, pp. 289–312.

Waldron, H. A. and Vickerstaff, L. (1977) *Intimations of Quality. Ante-Mortem and Post-Mortem Diagnosis*, London, Nuffield Provincial Hospitals Trust.

Yerushalmy, J. (1962) 'Statistical considerations and evaluation of epidemiological evidence', in James, G. and Rosenthal, T. (Eds.), *Tobacco and Health*, Springfield, Ill., C. C. Thomas.

# Interchange

## SPIELBERGER REPLIES TO BURCH

Burch presents a logical and coherent analysis of critical theoretical issues that bear on the observed associations between smoking and two major degenerative disorders, lung cancer and coronary heart disease. He also reviews the epidemiological and experimental evidence on which alternative environmental and constitutional-genetic interpretations of these associations are based. Noting numerous discrepancies between the available scientific evidence and the pronouncements by governmental officials and medical authorities that 'smoking causes disease', Burch takes issue with the 'orthodox assessment of the hazards of smoking'. On the basis of impressive evidence favouring a genetic-constitutional interpretation of the association between smoking and disease, he makes a compelling case for his conclusion that there has been 'no earnest attempt to adjudicate between alternative hypotheses', and that 'it is difficult to avoid the impression that scientific detachment has been replaced by the needs of propaganda.'

For the present volume Burch's assignment was to present a 'predominantly negative' evaluation of Eysenck's work on smoking and health. As Burch himself acknowledges, however, there are few if any substantial differences in the positions taken by Burch and Eysenck with regard to fundamental scientific issues in their interpretation of the association between smoking and disease. Indeed, Eysenck explicitly acknowledges Burch's work as 'the major genetic theory in the field of lung cancer [that] has led to certain types of analyses which are very relevant to the proper understanding of the argument' (1980, p. 27). Eysenck also draws extensively on Burch's research to support his own views that genetic factors play an important causal role in predisposing certain individuals to both smoking and disease.

While the views of Burch and Eysenck regarding smoking and health are similar in many respects, they differ in terms of the relative emphasis each gives to environmental and genetic factors as causes of smoking and disease. They also differ in the research strategies each believes will prove most useful in clarifying observed associations between smoking and disease, and in identifying the mechanisms that mediate these relationships. On the whole, Eysenck takes a more balanced position in which both environmental and genetic factors predispose certain individuals to both smoking and disease, whereas Burch places a stronger emphasis on genetic determinants. From the perspective of his theory of autoaggressively-induced genetic change, Burch contends that 'Eaves and Eysenck are likely to have overestimated the role of the environment and to have underestimated that of the genotype.' But Eysenck would certainly have no problem with this argument, and would no doubt welcome data in support of Burch's thesis.

The major differences between Burch and Eysenck are to be found in their convictions with regard to the research strategies that will eventually prove most useful in demonstrating that genetic factors predispose certain individuals to both smoking and disease. Eysenck is sceptical about the potential of large-scale epidemiological studies to give results of much scientific value in clarifying the association between smoking and disease. In contrast, Burch feels that controlled prospective studies of different ethnic groups 'still have an important part to play in unravelling the nature of the links between smoking and diseases.' While Eysenck favours carefully controlled studies of identical twins and families, Burch has reservations about such studies, noting that genetic identity may not be present at birth because of autoaggressive attacks that induce chromosomal alterations and gene mutation. Nevertheless, Burch concludes that 'in spite of their limitations, twins and familial studies of the kind pursued by Eysenck and his collaborators are indispensable ... in the absence of direct genetic markers of a biochemical, immunological or physiological character.'

In summary, it would seem that the positions of Eysenck and Burch on smoking and health are largely complementary rather than opposed. The differences in research strategies that have been noted are more closely related to training and experience than theoretical orientation or interpretation of the available evidence. In the long run, comprehensive understanding of the association between smoking and disease can perhaps be best achieved by simultaneous pursuit of the research strategies recommended by both Eysenck and Burch.

**REFERENCE**

Eysenck, H. J. (1980) *The Causes and Effects of Smoking*, London, Maurice Temple Smith.

## BURCH REPLIES TO SPIELBERGER

In his comments Spielberger delineates the similarities and differences (mainly of emphasis) between the views of Eysenck and myself. I have no need to add to that discussion but I would like to pursue the two-thousand-year-old question posed by Theophrastus and quoted by Spielberger from Eysenck: 'Why is it that while all Greece lies under the same sky and all the Greeks are educated alike, it has befallen us to have characters variously constituted?' The answer to this venerable question impinges directly on our current concern with the associations between behavioural habits, such as the various forms of smoking, and diseases such as lung cancer and heart disease.

Direct observation and the quantitative studies of Eysenck and Spielberger testify to the extreme complexity of the patterns of human behaviour; an analogous complexity is also seen in the apparently infinite variations of personal build and appearance. Even monozygotic twins are not quite identical; their mothers, usually, have little difficulty in distinguishing between them. This example serves, however, to help define the most important factor in polymorphism. Physical resemblances, which persist in monozygotic twins reared apart, would appear to derive from the common zygote and/or the common intra-uterine environment. The often substantial differences between dizygotic twins leave little doubt that a major determinant of not only biochemical, but also physical characters, is genetic inheritance. But how do genes determine morphology?

My unified theory of growth, cytodifferentiation and age-dependent disease deals with this question. From studies of the anatomical specificity of autoaggressive diseases, particularly of clinical dental caries, my collaborator Professor D. Jackson and I infer that a conventional 'tissue', such as odontoblasts lining the pulp cavity of teeth, consists of an immensely complicated set of mosaic elements. A particular mosaic might be present at only one, or at multiple, anatomical sites, depending on genetic constitution. In normal growth, each specific mosaic is identified with effectors from the central system of growth-control by a complex recognition factor which we call a 'tissue coding factor' (TCF). Recognition between effectors—'mitotic control proteins' (MCPs)—and their target TCFs depends on the identity of the MCP-TCF recognition polypeptides. In autoaggressive disease special somatic mutations of genes that synthesize MCPs in central growth-control cells convert the identity relationship into one of complementarity between the mutant MCP and its cognate target TCF. Target cells at one or multiple anatomical sites suffer an autoaggressive attack.

The number of distinctive polypeptides comprising a given TCF in various tissues is at least eight and, in the general population, at least two versions exist of each polypeptide. Hence, at least $2^8$ versions (256) of certain TCFs will be possible in the general population. I have been unable to estimate reliably the number of distinctive TCFs in a given individual but the total number of cells in the human organism is some $10^{14}$ to $10^{15}$ and the number of mosaic elements might well be as high as $10^{10}$ (Burch, 1976). The morphology of an organized tissue derives from the morphology of individual cells and their contact relations (largely TCF-determined) and hence it will be appreciated that the potential for polymorphism—within the same basic organizational plan—is virtually infinite. If we assume that some features of behaviour depend on comparable intercellular relations within the central nervous system then behavioural complexity follows inevitably.

The structure of TCFs is hierarchical ranging from relatively non-tissue-specific major and minor histocompatibility antigens, via classical tissue-specific antigens, to so far undemonstrated but clearly implied polypeptides that distinguish one mosaic from another within a classical tissue. Polypeptides common to TCFs in two or more different tissues—and, of course, to their cognate MCPs—will give rise to positive associations between different diseases. Consequently, this is one biological level at which associations between behavioural characteristics and diseases are to be anticipated. Eventually we should be able to test conclusions about associations drawn from psychological and epidemiological surveys by appropriate biochemical, immunological and genetic analysis.

## REFERENCE

Burch, P. R. J. (1976) '*The Biology of Cancer. A New Approach*', Lancaster, MTP; Baltimore, Md, University Park Press.

# Part XI: Astrology and Parapsychology

## 19. Parapsychology and Astrology

CARL SARGENT

Parapsychology and astrology are highly controversial areas of science, and this chapter will not attempt to cover all areas of research within them, nor all critical literature pertaining to them. Rather, an assessment of major areas of research will be made, and the nature of Hans Eysenck's contributions examined.

## PARAPSYCHOLOGY

Parapsychology may be defined as the study of two basic phenomena, extrasensory perception (ESP) and psychokinesis (PK). ESP may be defined as the non-inferential acquisition of information not mediated by any known sensory process. PK may be defined as the influence of an observer's will on an observable, external material system not mediated by any identified physical agency. It is common for the two phenomena, ESP and PK, to be grouped together and termed 'psi phenomena' since, in many cases, it may not be easy to discriminate between them (e.g., in a case of ostensible telepathy—'thought transference'—it may be the case that one person receives information from another by ESP, or on the other hand another person may affect the thoughts, or brain activity, of another by PK). However, this review will focus on ESP (defined for our purposes in a methodological manner), not least because more systematic data are available from ESP experiments than from PK experiments.

Unless otherwise stated, data to be reported from ESP studies have used forced-choice 'guessing' tasks, where an exact chance success rate can be computed (e.g., 25 per cent in a task in which the stimuli are playing cards and the task for the subject is to 'guess' the card suits), where the stimuli are randomly ordered, and where the stimuli are screened from detection by 'conventional' sensory means. The term 'significant' implies that the result has a two-tailed probability of .05 or less using a conventional statistical test.

## Demonstration Studies

In these studies the aim is to provide a definitive demonstration of ESP. It has been argued that these studies are effectively 'empty', most forcefully by Stanford (1974). Stanford argues that such studies are not scientific, because they cannot (for example) specify the optimal or necessary conditions for ESP to occur. All the experimenter is doing is to state that once upon a time an experiment was conducted in which the obtained result was certainly not due to chance by virtue of a very small P-value. Since science, unlike mathematics, does not deal with 'proof', Stanford's argument appears to this author very strong. While there are some advocates of the demonstration study (e.g., Pratt, 1973) it is noticeable that younger parapsychologists do not favour this approach. It is not a strategy Eysenck has advocated. Perhaps the strongest example, because of the use of multiple experimenters and tightly controlled protocols, is the research with the single subject, Pavel Stepanek, summarized by Pratt (1973); for a discussion of this work and criticism of it see Eysenck and Sargent (1982).

An alternative strategy for ESP research is the search for replicable correlates of ESP test performance. Two major areas of this research will be examined here: research on trait correlates of ESP, and on state correlates of ESP, in which intrasubject factors are examined in relation to ESP test performance.

## Trait Correlates of ESP Performance

*Extraversion and ESP.* Sargent (1981) and Eysenck and Sargent (1982) have provided the most recent reviews of the data, updating an earlier review by Eysenck (1967b). Twelve studies completed since these reviews are known to the present author, so that the total data base comprises approximately sixty-five separate studies (the exact number is uncertain, because some reports exist only in abstract form and provide almost no information at all about method and results). The outcome of the analysis of the extraversion/ESP correlation is unknown in some cases; in all such cases it is assumed that the obtained correlation was within chance limits. Seventeen of the studies used free-response test methods (see below, p. 343) rather than forced-choice tests. The entire reported data base contains twenty-one significant positive ESP-extraversion correlations, and three significant negative correlations. Thus, approximately one-third of the studies reported to date replicate the earliest reports of a positive ESP-extraversion relationship.

It may be argued that this proportion of successful replications is inflated because of non-publication of chance results. This is unlikely to be a substantial effect, since there are many forums for presentation of chance data within parapsychology, and parapsychologists are keenly aware of the need for publishing chance data. However, even if publication of chance data has been suppressed, this would not affect the distribution of significances between the two tails of the normal distribution—significant positive and significant negative. However, as we have seen, there are twenty-one significant positive and only three significant negative results (exact binomial P = .00014). Thus the results reported by numerous experimenters suggest that there is a real positive correlation between extraversion and ESP test performance. This data base has not been the subject of critical review other than those provided by parapsychologists themselves. It may also be noted that this finding has cross-cultural validity, having been reported from the UK, the USA, Sweden and South Africa among other countries (see Eysenck and Sargent, 1982).

Eysenck has suggested (1967b) that this finding is consistent with predictions drawn from his cortical-arousal model of extraversion (Eysenck, 1967a), since extraverts have lower levels of cortical arousal and may therefore detect weak ESP 'inputs' more readily than introverts. Unfortunately, few studies have examined the possible mechanisms underpinning the ESP-extraversion relationship. This is not least because of a strong pressure to replicate basic effects over and over in parapsychology, an unhealthy tendency criticized by Stanford (1974) and Sargent (1979). However, a handful of experiments has examined such mechanisms.

No study has directly examined Rao's (1974) suggestion that the effects of extraversion are social in causation, for example, that extraverts create less formal, more enjoyable test atmospheres. There is, however, evidence that such interpersonal effects do influence ESP (e.g., Honorton, Ramsay and Cabibbo, 1975). A research priority should be a study of such effects in relation to extraversion.

Data from Scherer (1948) and others stress the importance of spontaneity in ESP test performance (for review see Palmer, 1978), and it is possible that studies examining strategy-formation by introverts and extraverts in ESP tasks could show a cognitive basis for the ESP-extraversion relationship, mediated by response-bias effects and differential development of ESP-inhibitory habitual responding in extraverts and introverts (see Stanford, 1977). Such studies are another priority for further research.

Finally, a handful of studies has examined Eysenck's model. Eysenck (1975b), studying precognition in rats, reported results consistent with his model, and a drug study by Sargent (1977) also reported supporting data. Unpublished data from Matthews (personal communication) provide evidence of interactions between state-report arousal levels and extraversion influencing ESP performance which indicate fruitful avenues for further research. On the other hand, direct studies of EEG indices in relation to ESP have provided very inconsistent results (see Eysenck and Sargent, 1982).

*Anxiety and ESP.* Data here have been reviewed by Palmer (1977) and Eysenck and Sargent (1982). Palmer has demonstrated convincingly that two moderator factors may be at work in these data. The first is that data from studies in which subjects have been tested individually have shown a replicable picture of negative ESP/anxiety correlations, while group testing has produced much less consistency. The second factor is that different measures of anxiety have given different patterns of results. For example, data from Cattell's 16PF (Cattell, Eber and Tatsuoka, 1970) have given much more replicable results than data from the Taylor Manifest Anxiety Scale (Taylor, 1953). This could well be due to such factors as the likely tendency for the MAS to pick up repression-based defensiveness rather than only low anxiety at the bottom end of the scale (Lazarus and Alfert, 1964).

Considering studies in which subjects have been tested individually, the author is aware of forty-six studies which have examined the ESP-anxiety correlation. Of these, fourteen have yielded significant negative relationships, and one has yielded a significant positive one. Eleven of these studies have used free-response tests. Two have examined both state and trait anxiety. It may again be argued that the apparent replication rate of 30 per cent is inflated by non-reporting of chance results, but the pressure of fourteen significant negative correlations and one significant positive one (exact $P = .00034$) cannot be explained on the basis of chance causation.

Again, relatively few studies have examined mechanisms underlying this effect. The most substantial literature concerns the interaction of anxiety with stimulus type; it has been reported frequently that the anxiety-ESP correlation is maximized by the use of erotic stimuli (Palmer, 1978). However, in these studies—which typically compare scoring on erotic versus neutral stimuli—a true interaction (with the effect reversing on neutral stimuli) usually occurs, which makes interpretation tricky, since in tests which employ only neutral stimuli the negative correlation with anxiety is the typical pattern of results. There is, in fact, evidence that stimulus-contrast ESP tasks of the type noted produce unusual scoring effects simply by virtue of the contrast itself (Carpenter, 1977) and thus the erotic/neutral stimulus procedure may be providing results more confusing than enlightening due to the overuse of within-subjects designs. More traditional approaches, such as examining anxiety/ESP correlations under conditions of low and high stress, have not been widely employed by parapsychologists. Thus, the interpretation of the anxiety-ESP relationship is uncertain.

*Belief and ESP.* The oldest reported correlation with ESP performance is that of belief in, or at least acceptance of the possibility of the existence of, ESP. Schmeidler (Schmeidler and McConnell, 1958) reported a huge data base from both individual testing (151 subjects) and group testing (1157 subjects) showing what Schmeidler has termed the 'sheep-goat effect'. Data regarding beliefs about ESP were collected initially from interviews and later from questionnaire measures. Data showed that the believers (sheep) scored higher than disbelievers (goats) in the ESP task (for individual tests, $P < .00001$; for group tests, $P < .00003$).

A masterful review of data collected up to 1970 has been given by Palmer (1971), and updated by the same author (1977). Further updating yields a data base of forty-four studies, yielding sixteen significant sheep-goat effects and one 'goat-sheep' effect, i.e., disbelievers scoring higher than believers. However, this single exception (Moss, Paulson, Chang and Levitt, 1970) is a very unusual study. The 'goats' were preselected for previous high scores in an ESP test (!), and so are hardly representative of the goat population. Even if we include this dubious reversal, the existence of sixteen significant confirmations and one significant reversal (exact $P = .00014$) provides strong support for the claim that the sheep-goat effect is a real one.

Palmer (1972) provides further support for this claim. Noting that the initial Schmeidler effect was of small magnitude, and that several subsequent studies had used inadequate sample sizes, he analyzed trend information in insignificant-result datasets and showed that the fit of later data to an expected distribution of results, assuming the Schmeidler data to give a true estimate of the magnitude of the sheep-goat effect, was remarkably close. The reader is urged to consult Palmer's two-part review (1971, 1972).

There is a small body of research examining moderators of the basic effect.

Unfortunately, this author has the impression that most of it is concerned with *post hoc* effects; a notable exception is a report by Schmeidler (1960) in which she showed that the sheep-goat effect was maximized in socially-adjusted subjects. If one makes the reasonable assumption that such subjects may be most comfortable with their beliefs, this makes sense. Also, Stanford (1964) predicted from cognitive dissonance theory that sheep should tend to show a performance decline across a series of test trials, while goats should incline, in the context of a tedious and complex task. Stanford's argument was that goats should show a shift towards higher scoring over time, because compliance with the task in some way implies at least acceptance of the possible validity of what they are doing; but sheep would shift to lower scoring because of boredom. The differential effect was indeed significant. Unfortunately, such explorations of the sheep-goat effect have been unusual. These data will be summarized and discussed below.

### State Variables and ESP

In recent years a major impetus for ESP research has been the use of what may be termed 'altered states of consciousness' in ESP testing, in the hope of stabilizing overall above-chance significant ESP scores with unselected subjects. The range of ASCs employed includes hypnosis, meditation, progressive relaxation, the dream state, the imaginary dream, sensory deprivation and sensory pattern isolation. Since this data base comprises well over 200 studies, it is impossible to survey it here, but certain points may be noted. First, the absolute replication rates for these studies are higher than those for the trait-variable studies, despite the fact that in parapsychology as a whole a greater proportion of reported studies gives chance results for the last decade (state studies in the majority) than for the previous decade (trait studies in the majority). Thus, it would appear that more replicable effects, and larger-magnitude effects, can be obtained with ASC studies than with other techniques. Second, these studies (with the exception of hypnosis research) use free-response tests rather than forced-choice tests; the stimuli employed are typically complex and pictorial in nature, and thus the response is not restricted as it is in forced-choice tests. Statistical assessment in free-response tests is based on blind forced-choice selection by the subject, or independent judges given a transcript of the subjects' responses, from an array of stimuli, one of which is the 'target' stimulus employed in the test trial, and the others of which are 'dummy', control pictures. It may be that forced-choice tasks more readily generate maladaptive, strategy-bound response patterns than free-response tasks, since subjects are unaware of the pool of possible 'target' stimuli in free-response tasks and thus respond more freely and imaginatively. Third, there is evidence that use of ASCs may maximize trait effects (Sargent, 1981)—thus, extraversion effects are more replicable and of greater magnitude with ASC/free-response tasks than with forced-choice/'normal'-state tasks.

A common feature to the 'psi-conducive' ASCs is low arousal level, and thus these data would agree well with Eysenck's (1967a, 1967b) model referred to above. However, it is not certain whether this low arousal is the key feature here; e.g., Casler (1976) argues for a motivational interpretation of hypnosis effects on ESP performance. Further, outside hypnosis studies, control groups have not been employed in ASC studies as often as they should have been. There is also a critical literature on various aspects of ASC research (e.g., Kennedy, 1979; Hyman, 1983). Thus, Hyman

(1983) has argued, in the case of sensory pattern isolation research, that results reporting significantly above-chance ESP scores have more methodological flaws than chance-result studies. However, in turn his critique has a major methodological flaw; he made judgments about flaws alone, with knowledge of the study outcomes. Honorton (1983) has analyzed the same data base and come to opposite conclusions.

### The Study of ESP: Conclusions

The strategy employed here has been to search for regularity in arrays of data in major areas of ESP research, which happen to be those in which Eysenck has taken greater interest. The logic behind this approach is clear; social science does not deal with absolute replicability, only statistical reliability. Eysenck (1983) has been a forceful advocate of this view. As he notes (1983, p. 330), 'many psychological experiments are difficult to replicate.' It is also the case that ESP test scores show a low test-reliability (Palmer, 1977), and that without selected subjects, or special test environments, the magnitude of effect found is typically weak. Therefore, conclusions should be drawn only from broad arrays of data. Also, the strategy of examining both replication rate and contrasting significant outcomes in opposite directions (which are not affected by non-publication of chance data) is one which has been used convincingly elsewhere in experimental psychology (e.g., Rosenthal and Rosnow, 1978, on experimenter expectancy effects). Because of the large number of studies examined, it is impossible to analyze adequacy of method in every case. Here, I have excluded a handful of studies because of invalid statistical procedures, violation of random-stimulus-order requirement, etc. The effect on the conclusions drawn would be very small, and would be to weaken them. Thus I have, for example, excluded two significant positive ESP-extraversion findings (Humphrey, 1951) since the statistical assessment of data does not permit generalization of the results to a wider population (use of $Z$ rather than t, with small subject number and large sample size per subject). It would be safe to conclude that parapsychology has a set of modestly replicable findings relating ESP to the independent variables of belief, extraversion, anxiety and state factors including low arousal components. The absolute replication rates vary between six and ten times chance expectation; whether this is acceptably high depends on one's empirical yardstick for comparison (Honorton, 1976; Sargent 1979). However, internal analyses (e.g., of trend data with the sheep-goat effect—Palmer, 1971, 1972) provide further evidence for a possible lawfulness of these correlational data.

Priorities for further research are:

1   the use of reliable and valid questionnaire measures of trait and state variables (Sargent, 1980; Eysenck and Sargent, 1982);
2   the separation of effects; thus, it is reported that sheep are more extravert than goats (Thalbourne and Haraldsson, 1980), and while the extraversion effect has been reported independently of the sheep-goat effect, the reverse is not true. In this context studies using several predictor variables should be a priority. This has been stressed by Eysenck (1983).
3   research aimed at explicating mechanisms underlying the findings is essential if parapsychologists are not going to be seen as having just a handful of empty correlations. There certainly exist predictive and testable models such

as Eysenck's (1967b) model for the extraversion-ESP relationship which should be the major foci of research. While some research of this kind has been reported, it has not been subjected to enough replication work to be judged supportive or refutational. This author is of the view that no experimental finding means much until at least half a dozen independent experimenters have reported relevant findings. This applies equally to positive findings and to negative ones; in social science, where replication is statistical and not absolute, the risk of premature falsification is considerable.

Perhaps the outstanding feature of Eysenck's contributions to parapsychology—which have included theoretical, methodological and experimental contributions—is the willingness to examine data bases without prior prejudice, and to accept the implications of data collected from methodologically acceptable studies irrespective of whether or not they happen to agree with one's personal prejudices. This laudable and thoroughgoing empiricism is one to which many other scientists have pretensions, but one finds that with controversial areas of science adherence to empiricism suddenly evaporates on grounds which can only be described as irrational and prejudicial. As we shall now see, this thoroughgoing empiricism typifies Eysenck's approach to astrology.

## ASTROLOGY

For the purposes of this review, astrology may be defined as the study of the relationships between human behaviour and the heavens at the moment of an individual's birth. This preliminary definition will require subsequent refinement, and as it stands it excludes some areas of traditional astrology (e.g., effects of planetary positions on plant growth). However, since I shall make no attempt to cover the entire field, the definition will do for our purposes. We do not find in astrology large arrays of independently reported data similar to those examined in parapsychology. For this reason, a different analytic method will be employed here, focusing on a few key areas and attempting to concentrate on methodologically oriented suggestions for improving the quality of research.

### What's Your Sign?

A number of studies, reviewed by several authors (Eysenck and Nias, 1982; Kelly and Saklofske, 1982), have examined the relationship between personality variables and the sun-sign (the sign of the zodiac in which the sun is located at the time of birth; since the sun takes twelve months to progress through the twelve signs of the zodiac, this factor is easily computed for individuals if the birthdate is known). The study by Mayo, White and Eysenck (1978) was the first to spark off major interest here. With a large sample (N = 2324), they tested the predictions drawn from classical astrology (1) that extraversion scores would be higher for the 'positive' signs (Aries, Gemini, Leo, ...) than for the 'negative' signs (Taurus, Cancer, Virgo, ...), and (2) that neuroticism scores would be higher for the Water signs (Cancer, Scorpio, Pisces) than for the Fire, Air and Earth signs. The extraversion prediction clearly follows from astrological theory, although the neuroticism prediction is not so obvious (to this author, at any rate). They found confirmation of both predictions, the extraversion effect being larger than the neuroticism effect. Later studies have confirmed this pattern insofar as the extraversion effect has been more replicable than the neuroticism effect (Nias and Dean this volume).

There is a major problem with this methodology. It is clearly open to a sceptic to argue that positive effects could be attributed to one or both of two mundane factors. The first is that subjects involved in an experiment on astrology and personality might bias replies to a questionnaire measure of personality in order to conform to astrological stereotypes. The second is that social learning could affect personality; if someone knows they are a Libran, and Librans are supposed to have certain traits, they may tend (even if only slightly) to emphasize those traits in their behaviour.

The first problem (response bias) can be overcome in several ways. One is not to employ questionnaires, but criterion measures (occupation, etc.) which are not subject to the same bias. The literature on seasonality of birth uses this type of procedure (see below). A second is to collect the birthdate data separately from the questionnaire data, so that subjects are not alerted to the nature of the experiment. Retrospective studies are an example of this approach. The second problem (social learning) might be countered by studying relative magnitude of effect in adults and children, but there are two problems here. The first is that questionnaire measures with children are known to have poorer reliability (and hence validity) than with adults (Cattell, 1970), and the second is that the nature of this social learning process is unspecified, so one does not know what age group of children to study in order to test the sceptical claim.

However, it is clear that studies which have attempted to use one or more methodological improvements of the type suggested have yielded chance results as opposed to the significant results yielded from the basic (Mayo *et al.*) design. For example, Eysenck and Nias (1982) and Mohan, Bhandari and Sehgal (1982) have tested large child samples—Eysenck and Nias also using retrospective analysis. Both found chance results, and this combined with data showing that sun-sign/personality correlations only hold for knowledgeable adult subjects suggests an artifactual basis for the significant outcomes. Mayo (cited in Eysenck and Nias, 1982, pp. 58–9) reported that this 'labelling effect' appeared strongest for somewhat knowledgeable subjects, weaker for largely ignorant subjects, and weakest for highly knowledgeable subjects; Pawlik and Buse (1979) found strongest effects with subjects who were inclined to believe in astrology, weaker effects for those who strongly believed in astrology, and weakest effects for disbelievers. This suggests that response bias is complexly determined. Nonetheless, summary studies to date have not provided any clear support for a link between sun-sign and personality.

A related literature is more interesting; that on season of birth in relation to extreme criterion group membership (e.g., eminent individuals and mentally ill individuals). Pioneer research by Huntingdon (1938) showed that there was a considerable surplus of births of highly eminent people (selected in a manner similar to Gauquelin; see below, pp. 348–52) in winter/spring months as opposed to summer/autumn months. His massive research programme has been replicated by Kaulins (1979), though there is some sample overlap. This research appears to have isolated a genuine effect.

An even more interesting effect is the clear surplus of births of later schizophrenics in the December-April period, reported by many authors (e.g., Hare, Price and Slater, 1973; Barry and Barry, 1961). These data are reviewed by Watson, Kucala,

Angulski and Brunn (1982) and in part by Eysenck and Nias (1982). Unfortunately, Eysenck and Nias accept at face value an erroneous critique by Lewis and Griffin (1981) which seeks to explain this effect in terms of a combination of artifacts, of which the two most important are the age-prevalence (AP) and age-incidence (AI) effects. The AP effect is simply that people born early in any given year will be at greater cumulative risk for schizophrenia than people born later in the year by simple virtue of being older. The AI effect is subtler; people born early in the year will be in a higher-risk period for schizophrenia than people born later in the year, if one is dealing with a sample with an age distribution below the median onset age for schizophrenia. Lewis and Griffin argue that existing data can be explained by these artifacts.

In accepting this critique at face value, Eysenck and Nias (1982) miss an obvious piece of sleight-of-hand by Lewis and Griffin (1981). They order their years from December to November owing to reluctance to break up the winter season; but this procedure, which they employ in their analyses, is meaningless since other researchers have employed January-December years. Lewis and Griffin appear to have done this because there is a clear December birth peak in most of the studies on season birth and schizophrenia (Watson, Kucala, Angulski and Brunn, 1982), which flatly contradicts their claim that the AP and AI artifacts can explain the seasonality effects. These artifacts should produce a clear trough in December births of future schizophrenics.

A second feature of existing data inexplicable by Lewis and Griffin (1981) is internal and contrast effects, of which one example will be given here (one must presume that Eysenck and Nias (1982) were unaware of this research). Kinney and Jacobson (1978) have analyzed data from the classic American-Danish adoption studies of schizophrenia (Kety, Rosenthal, Wender, Schulsinger and Jacobson, 1975). They found that while the January-April birth rate for schizophrenics who had at least one afflicted biological relative (genetic high-risk group) was 21 per cent, for schizophrenics without any genetic risk (phenocopies) the rate was 70 per cent. The differential is significant (P = .019). This differential, and others like it, cannot be accounted for in terms of the artifacts suggested by Lewis and Griffin (1981). The reader is urged to consult also Watson, Kucala, Angulski and Brunn (1982).

In summary, there is evidence that season of birth is related to such factors as eminence, schizophrenia and also manic-depressive psychosis, and perhaps other extreme subgroups (Eysenck and Nias, 1982). The relation to traditional astrology is unclear since researchers employ calendar month divisions and not sun-sign divisions. Also, some correlations have obvious possible physical intermediaries (perhaps obstetric complications for schizophrenics (McNeil and Kaij, 1978), though this cannot be the whole story). Others (e.g., eminence) would not be so obvious.

## The Dynamics of Astrology

The sun-sign has received much attention not because it is the major factor in a horoscope but simply because it is easily assessed. Other factors such as the position of the planets in the zodiac and their interrelations, and the sign rising over the eastern horizon at the moment of birth, have received much less attention. What data exist have been painstakingly compiled and analyzed by Dean and Mather (1977). I think it would not be unfair to term this literature a nightmare. It consists almost entirely of one-off studies of isolated factors, or interactions between two or three factors, and their effects on sometimes questionable dependent measures of behaviour, occupation, etc.; the exception is the Gauquelin research (see below). Almost nothing can be concluded from this research, since independent replications with standardized procedures are wholly lacking.

For a sound research programme which does justice to the complex and dynamic interplay of horoscope factors which traditional astrologers emphasize, it would be necessary to use multivariate analytic measures. It would be necessary to poll astrologers on which predictor variables would best predict a limited range of criterion variables (e.g., extraversion, aggressiveness, manifest anxiety, etc.), select those predictors for which greatest communality of agreement is present, and use multiple regression techniques for criterion prediction from the predictors, comparing predictive power with that achieved by 'dummy' predictors in separate multiple regressions, using random predictor variables. At present such a research programme has not been implemented.

### Cosmic Clocks: The Research of the Gauquelins

The most systematic body of research on astrology has been conducted by Michel and Françoise Gauquelin (hereafter MG and FG). For summaries of this work see Gauquelin (1974) and Eysenck and Nias (1982); the full technical summaries are by Gauquelin and Gauquelin (1970–79). Their research strategy has been the selection of extreme criterion groups of distinguished individuals such as sports champions, war generals, members of the French Academy of Medicine, etc., using prespecified and non-variant criteria, coupled with an examination of the position of the planets at birth in their birth charts. Pilot data showed that certain occupation/planetary position patterns of striking symmetry emerged. The Gs' technique is as follows. Since the earth rotates, planets will appear from an earthly viewpoint to rise and set just as the sun and moon do. The path of the planet is divided by the Gs into twelve sectors (similar to, but not the same as, the traditional 'houses' of astrology). The expected occurrence of a planet in any sector is readily calculated, and indeed the Gs have calculated theoretical expectations taking relevant astronomical and demographic factors into account, using very large random-selection groups to validate their computations empirically. What they have found is that certain occupations show an elevated frequency of certain key planets in sectors 1 and 4 (just past the rising and culminating points) and, to a lesser extent, in sectors 7 and 10 (just past the setting point and lower culmination). They have repeatedly replicated the central effects, so questions of probability pyramiding through overanalysis (Neher, 1967) which are scarcely relevant even to the pilot work in view of the significance of the results are irrelevant to the replications. Working with European continental samples, they have been able to obtain exact birth-time data for their subjects through years of painstaking research. Two points may be noted here. The first is that errors in recording birth time would, of course, create only random error variance. The second is that the effects hold (see below) for natural births but not for induced births.

Among the relationships the Gs have reported are: Saturn emphasized in the births of scientists, Jupiter for actors, the Moon for writers and artists, Mars and Saturn for doctors, and Mars for generals and sportsmen. There are also avoidance effects; e.g., artists avoid being born with Saturn in the key sectors. The effects are typically not large (e.g., the frequency for Mars in sectors 1 and 4 for sportsmen is around 22 per cent as opposed to chance expectation of 17.1 per cent), and the effects are reported only for very eminent individuals, but the theoretical significance is enormous. Note that the effects of planets are not modified by the background zodiac sign, and therefore our original definition of astrology (above, p. 345) needs modifying to accommodate this 'neo-astrology'.

A first independent replication of the Gs' research, examining the Mars effect in sportsmen, was conducted by the sceptical Belgian Comite Para, who after several years issued a report on their research (Dommanget, 1976). They replicated the Gs' effect exactly, finding a Mars effect of slightly greater magnitude. Incredibly, they declined to accept the validity of the Gs' findings on the grounds that the 17.1 per cent theoretical expectation for Mars in sectors 1 and 4 was erroneous. There are two points to note about this. The first is that everyone else, including critics of the Gs, agrees on the 17.1 per cent figure (see below on the 'Zelen Test'). The second is that, despite repeated challenges, Dommanget has never published his theoretical expectation values and justified them. This extraordinary state of affairs is highlighted by a recent statement by de Marre (1982), who resigned from the Comite Para on this issue, in which he states that the lag to publication was caused by a desperate search for any way of explaining away the effect, and he states that various control tests (such as sliding the birth-hour data as a function of the alphabetical order of the sample) 'showed beyond all dispute that Gauquelin's theoretical (expected) frequencies were correct' (de Marre, 1982, p. 72). Since the Comite Para collected a new sample of sports champions for their analysis, there is no doubt that their study represents an independent replication of the Gs' work. The continued denial of the validity of the Gs' theoretical sector frequencies by Dommanget (1982) is virtually beyond belief.

A second committee of sceptics, the so-called Committee for the Scientific Investigation of Claims of the Paranormal (CSICOP), has also attempted to study the Mars effect. Their first involvement was the 'Zelen Test', proposed by CSICOP member Zelen as a challenge to the Gs (Zelen, 1976). The procedure agreed upon with CSICOP members was simple. The Gs would supply a random subset of 303 of their sports champions (since 300 is about the minimum number one needs to show a significant effect given the magnitude of the Mars effect) and a large, randomly selected control group of individuals born in close spatiotemporal proximity to the members of the champion group. It is crucial to remember in what follows that Zelen referred to this test as 'an objective way for unambiguous corroboration or disconfirmation' (Zelen, 1976). Actually, this is false, since as CSICOP Fellow Dennis Rawlins has pointed out (Rawlins, 1981), it presumes a 'clean' sample of sports champions (i.e., one unaffected by subjective sampling bias). However, it is still relevant to the very dubious *post hoc* data-splitting CSICOP were to indulge in later.

Results were reported by Kurtz, Zelen and Abell (1977). One interesting feature of their study was that they deleted nine female sports champions from the sample *post hoc*, and they have at different times given at least three different and conflicting reasons for doing this (Curry, 1982). Be this as it may, it is worthy of note that they did not inform the reader that of these nine, three showed a Mars effect (Mars in sector 1 or 4). The control sample clearly validated the Gs' theoretical frequency for Mars in sectors 1 and 4, and this is not disputed by any of the investigators. The champions showed a 20.8 per cent Mars effect, which was significantly different from the control group with P = .04.

Did the CSICOP members accept the outcome of their 'unambiguous' study? The reader, primed by the account of the Comite Para's behaviour, will know the answer. Kurtz, Zelen and Abell (1977) demurred to accept the obvious verdict on two grounds. The first was that the effect was barely significant and that if just one champion fewer had shown a Mars effect the result would have been insignificant. This is, of course, irrelevant; with a sample of 303 champions only a marginal effect would have been expected. If Kurtz et al., were looking for P = .001 effect, they would have needed a larger sample. This is a simple issue in mathematics. The second concern was that the Paris subgroup of birth data showed a significant control/champion difference, while the French (less Paris) and Belgian samples did not. Thus, Kurtz et al. (1977) imply that the sample heterogeneity casts doubt on the generalizability of the effect. This is a notably defective argument, because comparison *across* subgroups shows that the variance between them is well within the bounds of chance, and if one is talking about sample heterogeneity this type of analysis is the appropriate one, not individual comparisons. Adding to this elementary statistical error the fact that this subgroup splitting was not part of the original protocol, one can have little faith in the statistical expertise or general objectivity of the CSICOP researchers.

Unfortunately, the same CSICOP researchers then conducted their own test of the Mars effect using American-born sports champions (this test did not have a control group, since the 17.1 per cent theoretical frequency for sectors 1 plus 4 combined was accepted by all concerned). The design of this study doomed it to failure. The warnings of CSICOP Fellow Rawlins that the test must have written protocols agreed in advance and impartial judges (Rawlins, 1981) were ignored. Kurtz has claimed that the Gs agreed to the protocol in discussions (Kurtz, Zelen and Abell, 1979–80b). The Gs deny this (Gauquelin, 1980) and in the absence of written proof one way or the other it is impossible to know the answer for sure. However, certain features of the data make it extremely unlikely that the Gs would have accepted the sample used as a valid one. Thus, 10 per cent of the sample were born after 1950, and would have included many induced births. More importantly, it is clear that many of the 'champions' used were not within pre-set criteria for the Gs' selection process, and as we shall see below there is evidence that this factor is influential in the CSICOP sample.

Further, a disturbing aspect of the CSICOP data is that one individual, Paul Kurtz, and his two assistants had complete control over the selection of data, and these were sent to Rawlins for analysis. A first subsample of 128 showed a Mars effect of 19.5 per cent and, according to Rawlins, Kurtz insisted on receiving feedback about data at various stages of analysis. The second subsample sent by Kurtz showed a Mars effect of 12 per cent, and a third subset a Mars effect of only 7 per cent. It is interesting that, while Kurtz, Zelen and Abell (1977) quarrelled with the Gs over heterogeneity in the sample of 303 sports champions the Gs sent (which, as we have seen, is not present), they remain rather quiet about this extreme heterogeneity within their own sample. MG maintains that the declining rate is clearly related to Kurtz having selected progressively fewer eminent sportsmen, and the Gs have reported a Mars effect of 31.3 per cent in a sample of American Olympic champions (Gauquelin and Gauquelin, 1979–80). One final point is in order. Dennis Rawlins, having repeatedly notified other senior members of CSICOP of his misgivings about both the Zelen test and the American sample and their handling, was dropped from the CSICOP board of Fellows without warning, and without a ballot being taken (Rawlins, 1981; Curry, 1982). It is essential to realize that Rawlins was a CSICOP founder member, and remains a non-believer in the Mars effect. The full account by Rawlins of the CSICOP debacle (Rawlins, 1981) puts into perspective the competence of this organization as de Marre's noted statement (1982) does for the Comite Para. It is impossible not to agree with Curry's conclusion, after surveying the entire history of critical examinations of the Gs' research:

> I don't think I need to stress how badly the Committee (CSICOP) has handled the investigation of the Mars effect; the facts above speak for themselves. Their work could now best function as a model and a warning of how not to conduct such investigations. Given the ample internal (Rawlins) and external (Gauquelin) warnings that went suppressed or ignored, it is even difficult to accept protestations of 'good faith' and 'naivete' (Abell, 1981). Rawlins and Gauquelin are in fact the only two major figures to emerge with scientific credibility intact. It seems to me that this situation must call into question any further (unrefereed, at least) CSICOP involvement in research on the Mars effect, and possible other 'paranormal' areas (Curry, 1982, p. 49).

Eysenck has expressed complete agreement with this summary (Eysenck, 1982). In addition to cited references, the reader should consult Kurtz, Zelen and Abell (1979–80a), Gauquelin and Gauquelin (1979–80) and Gauquelin (1982).

With some relief one may turn from this abject critical literature and examine some more puzzle pieces in the Gauquelin schema. Two further findings are of note. If planetary effects are related to occupation, presumably personality factors mediate this effect. The Gs have shown (Gauquelin, 1974) that (e.g.) the Mars effect is much more marked in 'iron-willed' sports champions than in ones not so described by their biographers, and this research has been put on a sound footing by studies in which the Gs have abstracted all adjectives used by biographers of their subjects and sent them to Sybil Eysenck, who (blind) fitted them into positive and negative loading adjectives related to extraversion, neuroticism and psychoticism (see Gauquelin, Gauquelin and Eysenck, 1979, 1981; Eysenck and Eysenck, 1969, 1976). Clear effects emerged for extraversion (Mars +, Jupiter +, Saturn − effects), weaker effects for psychoticism, and none for neuroticism. These data bore out prior predictions and have been replicated. Second, Gauquelin (1966) has analyzed the birth information for 25,000 parents and children and found a remarkable effect; what he terms 'planetary heredity'. A child born to a parent with a particular planet in sectors 1 or 4 has a higher than chance likelihood of being born with the planet in the same position; moreover, this effect is increased in size if both parents have the same planetary placement. This is a remarkable datum. Added to the fact that this only holds for natural, and not induced, births, the clear implication is that some genetic factor predisposes the foetus to respond to some signal from a key planet and contribute to the initiation of its own birth.

## Astrology: Conclusions

The outstanding data here are those of the Gauquelins. They have withstood critical attack, and the Gs have behaved throughout in a manner which contrasts sharply with that of their severest critics. One independent replication, by the Comite Para, is clearly supportive of their results. The other (CSICOP) replication is worthless for assessing anything other than, as Curry (1982) notes, how not to do research.

Research into sun-sign effects has yielded no clear support for traditional astrology; study of other horoscope factors has been too crude and inconsistent to provide any indications of the validity, or otherwise, of astrological theory.

## PARAPSYCHOLOGY AND ASTROLOGY: STATUS AND PROSPECTS

These two youthful sciences differ in many respects. Parapsychology has large data arrays of acceptable quality which contain numerous independent replications, showing modest repeatability. Models for interactions between psi and psychological factors exist, notably Eysenck's (1967b) model for the ESP/extraversion relationship. Further, models of how ESP may occur at the physical level, which are testable, also exist (e.g., Mattuck and Walker, 1979). There is at least some acceptance of parapsychology among other scientists; thus the Parapsychological Association was affiliated to the American Association for the Advancement of Science in 1969. Astrology, on the other hand, has only one published data set of real worth: the Gauquelin data, though this is of exceptional quality. Mechanisms for the observed effects at the physical level are non-existent. Hence, astrology appears less developed than parapsychology.

The major feature of Eysenck's contributions to both young sciences is his refusal to prejudge with prejudice. This is an unusual, indeed exceptional, attitude, and one which this author suspects is characteristic of most truly great scientists. Further, Eysenck has not taken one easy escape route: to admit the effects noted exist, but to state that they are of weak magnitude (which they are) and thus pragmatically uninteresting (the present author, indeed, respects this as the most powerful of all sceptical arguments). Eysenck notes that:

> Only a dozen years before the explosion of the first atomic bomb, both Einstein . . . and Rutherford . . . put forward statements which said that the disintegration of the atom would never lead to any practical consequences! If such great scientists . . . can be wrong . . . on matters on which they were the greatest living experts, how would anyone dare to predict what might or might not be the importance of parapsychology in the future? (Eysenck, 1983, p. 335).

Indeed, Eysenck has been a positive support for scientific researchers in parapsychology and astrology, being in particular a notable champion of the Gauquelins (e.g., Eysenck, 1975a, 1982). If these sciences are to develop, they will owe a great deal to Hans Eysenck and the very few others like him who treat data on their merits without prior prejudice.

## REFERENCES

Barry, H. and Barry, H., Jr (1961) 'Season of birth; An epidemiological study in psychiatry', *Archives of General Psychiatry*, **5**, pp. 292–300.
Carpenter, J. C. (1977) 'Intrasubject and subject-agent effects in ESP experiments', in Wolman, B. (Ed.) *Handbook of Parapsychology*, New York, Van Nostrand Reinhold, pp. 202–72.
Casler, L. L. (1976) 'Hypnotic maximization of ESP motivation', *Journal of Parapsychology*, **40**, pp. 187–93.
Cattell, R. B. (1970) *The Scientific Analysis of Personality*, Harmondsworth, Penguin.

Cattell, R. B., Eber, H. W. and Tatsuoka, M. M. (1970) *Handbook for the Sixteen Personality Factor Questionnaire*, Champaign, Ill., Institute for Personality and Ability Testing.

Curry, P. (1982) 'Research on the Mars Effect', *Zetetic Scholar*, **9**, pp. 34–53.

de Marre, L. (1982) 'Critical commentary', *Zetetic Scholar*, **9**, pp. 71–2.

Dean, G. A. and Mather, A. C. M. (1977) *Recent Advances in Natal Astrology: A Critical Review 1900–1976*, Perth, Analogic.

Dommanget, J. (1976) 'Report', in *Nouvelles Breves*, September.

Dommanget, J. (1982) 'Critical commentary', *Zetetic Scholar*, **9**, pp. 73–4.

Eysenck, H. J. (1967a) *The Biological Basis of Personality*, Springfield, Ill., C. C. Thomas.

Eysenck, H. J. (1967b) 'Personality and extra-sensory perception', *Journal of the Society for Psychical Research*, **44**, pp. 55–71.

Eysenck, H. J. (1975a) 'Planets, stars and personality', *New Behaviour*, pp. 246–9.

Eysenck, H. J. (1975b) 'Precognition in rats', *Journal of Parapsychology*, **39**, pp. 222–7.

Eysenck, H. J. (1982) 'Critical commentary', *Zetetic Scholar*, **9**, pp. 61–3.

Eysenck, H. J. (1983) 'Parapsychology: Status and prospects', in Roll, W. G., Beloff, J. and White, R. A. (Eds.), *Research in Parapsychology 1982*, Metuchen, N. J., Scarecrow Press, pp. 328–35.

Eysenck, H. J. and Eysenck, S. B. G. (1969) *Personality Structure and Measurement*, London, Routledge and Kegan Paul.

Eysenck, H. J. and Eysenck, S. B. G. (1976) *Psychoticism as a Dimension of Personality*, London, Hodder and Stoughton.

Eysenck, H. J. and Nias, D. K. B. (1982) *Astrology: Science or Superstition?*, London, Temple Smith.

Eysenck, H. J. and Sargent, C. L. (1982) *Explaining the Unexplained*, London, Weidenfeld and Nicolson.

Gauquelin, M. (1966) *L'Hérédité Planetaire*, Paris, Denoel.

Gauquelin, M. (1974) *Cosmic Influences on Human Behaviour*, London, Garnstone Press.

Gauquelin, M. (1980) 'The Mars Effect: A response from M. Gauquelin', *Sceptical Enquirer*, Summer, pp. 58–62.

Gauquelin, M. (1982) 'Critical commentary', *Zetetic Scholar*, **9**, pp. 54–61 and 75–7.

Gauquelin, M. and Gauquelin, F. (1970–79) *Birth and Planetary Data Gathered since 1949, Series A–D*, Laboratory for the Study of Relationships between Cosmic and Psychophysiological Rhythms.

Gauquelin, M. and Gauquelin, F. (1979–80) 'Star U. S. sportsmen display the Mars effect', *Sceptical Enquirer*, Winter, pp. 31–40.

Gauquelin, M., Gauquelin, F. and Eysenck, S. B. G. (1979) 'Personality and position of the planets at birth: An empirical study', *British Journal of Social and Clinical Psychology*, **18**, pp. 71–5.

Gauquelin, M., Gauquelin, F. and Eysenck, S. B. G. (1981) 'Eysenck's personality analysis and position of the planets at birth: A replication on American subjects', *Personality and Individual Differences*, **2**, pp. 346–50.

Hare, E. H., Price, J. S. and Slater, E. (1973) 'Mental illness and season of birth', *Nature*, **241**, p. 480.

Honorton, C. (1976) 'Does science have the competence to confront claims of the paranormal?' in Morris, R. L., Roll, W. G. and Morris J. D. (Eds.), *Research in Parapsychology 1975*, Metuchen, N. J., Scarecrow Press, pp. 199–223.

Honorton, C. (1983) 'Response to Hyman's critique of psi ganzfeld studies', in Roll, W. G., Beloff, J. and White, R. A. (Eds.), *Research in Parapsychology 1982*, Metuchen, N. J., Scarecrow Press, pp. 23–6.

Honorton, C., Ramsay, M. and Cabibbo, C. (1975) 'Experimenter effects in extra-sensory perception', *Journal of the American Society for Psychical Research*, **69**, pp 135–49.

Humphrey, B. M. (1951) 'Introversion-extroversion in relation to scores in ESP tests', *Journal of Parapsychology*, **15**, pp. 252–62.

Huntingdon, E. (1938) *Season of Birth: Its Relation to Human Abilities*, New York, Wiley.

Hyman, R. (1983) 'Does the ganzfeld experiment answer the critics objections?', in Roll, W. G., Beloff, J. and White, R. A. (Eds.), *Research in Parapsychology 1982*, Metuchen, N. J., Scarecrow Press, pp. 21–3.

Kaulins, A. (1979) 'Cycles in the birth of eminent humans', *Cycles*, **30**, pp. 9–15.

Kelly, I. and Saklofske, D. (1982) 'Personality and Sun-sign', *Correlation*, **2, 1**, pp. 17–21.

Kennedy, J. E. (1979) 'Methodological problems in free-response experiments', *Journal of the American Society for Psychical Research*, **73**, pp. 1–15.

Kety, S. S., Rosenthal, D., Wender, P. H., Schulsinger, F. and Jacobson, B. (1975) 'Mental illness in the biological and adoptive families of adopted individuals who have become schizophrenic: A preliminary report based upon psychiatric interviews', in Fieve, R., Brill, H. and Rosenthal, D. L. (Eds.), *Genetics and Pyschopathology*, Baltimore, Md., Johns Hopkins.

Kinney, D. and Jacobson, B. (1978) 'Environmental factors in schizophrenia: New adoption study evidence', in Wynne, L., Cromwell, R. and Matthysse, S. (Eds.), *The Nature of Schizophrenia*, New York, Wiley, pp. 38–51.

Kurtz, P., Zelen, M. and Abell, G. O. (1977) 'Is there a Mars effect?', *The Humanist*, November–December, pp. 36–9.

Kurtz, P., Zelen, M. and Abell, G. O. (1979–80a) 'Results of the U.S. test of the "Mars Effect" are negative', *Sceptical Enquirer*, Winter, pp. 19–26.

Kurtz, P., Zelen, M. and Abell, G. O. (1979–80b) 'Response to the Gauquelins', *Sceptical Enquirer*, Winter, pp. 44–63.

Lazarus, R. S. and Alfert, E. (1964) 'The short circuiting of threat by experimentally altering cognitive appraisal', *Journal of Abnormal and Social Psychology*, **69**, pp. 195–205.

Lewis, M. S. and Griffin, T. A. (1981) 'An explanation for the season of birth effect in schizophrenia and certain other diseases', *Psychological Bulletin*, **89**, pp. 589–96.

McNeil, T. F. and Kaij, L. (1978) 'Obstetric complications in the development of schizophrenia: Complications in the births of preschizophrenics and in reproduction by schizophrenic parents', in Wynne, L., Cromwell, R. and Matthysse, S. (Eds.), *The Nature of Schizophrenia*, New York, Wiley, pp. 401–29.

Mattuck, R. and Walker, E. H. (1979) 'The action of consciousness on matter: A quantum-mechanical theory of psychokinesis', in Puharich, A. (Ed.), *The Iceland Papers*, Amherst, Essentia Research Associates, pp. 111–59.

Mayo, J., White, O. and Eysenck, H. J. (1978) 'An empirical study of the relation between astrological factors and personality', *Journal of Social Psychology*, **105**, pp. 229–36.

Mohan, J., Bhandari, A. and Sehgal, M. (1982) 'Astrological factors and personality: Cross-cultural validation in children', *Correlation*, **2, 1**, pp. 10–16.

Moss, T., Paulson, M. J., Chang, A. F. and Levitt, M. (1970) 'Hypnosis and ESP: A controlled experiment', *American Journal of Clinical Hypnosis*, **13**, pp. 46–56.

Neher, A. (1967) 'Probability pyramiding, research error, and the need for independent replication', *Psychological Record*, **17**, pp. 257–62.

Palmer, J. (1971) 'Scoring in ESP tests as a function of belief in ESP. Part I. The sheep-goat effect', *Journal of the American Society for Psychical Research*, **65**, pp. 373–408.

Palmer, J. (1972) 'Scoring in ESP tests as a function of belief in ESP. Part II. Beyond the sheep-goat effect', *Journal of the American Society for Psychical Research*, **66**, pp. 1–26.

Palmer, J. (1977) 'Attitudes and personality traits in experimental ESP research', in Wolman, B. (Ed.), *Handbook of Parapsychology*, New York, Van Nostrand Reinhold, pp. 175–201.

Palmer, J. (1978) 'Extrasensory Perception: Research findings', in Krippner, S. (Ed.), *Advances in Parapsychological Research, Vol. 2: Extrasensory Perception*, New York, Plenum.

Pawlik, K. and Buse, L. (1979) 'Selbst-attribvierung als differentiell-psychologische moderatorvariable', *Zeitschrift für Sozialpsychologie*, **10**, pp. 54–69.

Pratt, J. G. (1973) 'A decade of research with a selected ESP subject', *Proceedings of the American Society for Psychical Research*, **30**, pp. 1–78.

Rao, K. R. (1974) 'Psi and personality', in Beloff, J. (Ed.), *New Directions in Parapsychology*, London, Paul Elek.

Rawlins, D. (1981) 'Starbaby', *Fate*, October.

Rosenthal, R. and Rubin, D. B. (1978) 'Interpersonal expectancy effects: The first 345 studies' *Behavioural and Brain Sciences*, **1**, pp. 377–86.

Sargent, C. L. (1977) 'Cortical arousal and psi: A pharmacological study', *European Journal of Parapsychology*, **1, 4**, pp. 72–9.

Sargent, C. L. (1979) 'The repeatability of significance and the significance of repeatability', paper delivered at Third International Conference of the Society for Psychical Research, Edinburgh.

Sarggent, C. L. (1980) *Exploring Psi in the Ganzfeld*, New York, Parapsychology Foundation.

Sargent, C. L. (1981) 'Extraversion and performance in "extra-sensory perception" tasks', *Personality and Individual Differences*, **2**, pp. 137–43.

Scherer, W. B. (1948) 'Spontaneity as a factor in ESP', *Journal of Parapsychology*, **12**, pp. 126–47.

Schmeidler, G. R. (1960) *ESP in Relation to Rorschach Test Evaluation*, New York, Parapsychology Foundation.

Schmeidler, G. R. and McConnell, R. A. (1958) *Extrasensory Perception and Personality Patterns*, London, Oxford University Press.

Stanford, R. G. (1964) 'Differential position effects for above-chance scoring sheep and goats', *Journal of Parapsychology*, **28**, pp. 155–65.

Stanford, R. G. (1974) 'Concept and psi', in Roll, W. G., Morris, R. L. and Morris, J. D. (Eds.), *Research in Parapsychology 1973*, Metuchen, N. J., Scarecrow Press, pp. 137–62.

Stanford, R. G. (1977) 'Conceptual frameworks of contemporary psi research', in Wolman, B. (Ed.), *Handbook of Parapsychology*, New York, Van Nostrand Reinhold, pp. 823–58.

Taylor, J. A. (1953) 'A personality scale of manifest anxiety', *Journal of Abnormal and Social Psychology*, **48,** pp. 285–90.

Thalbourne, M. and Haraldsson, E. (1980) 'Personality characteristics of sheep and goats', *Personality and Individual Differences*, **1,** pp. 180–5.

Watson, C. G., Kucala, T., Angulski, G. and Brunn, C. (1982) 'Season of birth and schizophrenia: A response to Lewis and Griffin', *Journal of Abnormal Psychology*, **91,** pp. 120–5.

Zelen, M. (1976) 'Astrology and statistics: A challenge', *The Humanist*, January-February, pp. 32–6.

# 20. Astrology and Parapsychology

DAVID K. B. NIAS AND GEOFFREY A. DEAN

All argument is against it; but all belief is for it (Dr Johnson)

## ASTROLOGY

The literature of astrology, totalling some 200 shelf-metres of Western-language books and periodicals, is so unsatisfactory that most of it (but not all) is hard to take seriously. Much of the writing abounds with inconsistent and even contradictory assertions, and nobody should be surprised to learn that the hardest things to find in astrology are facts. Depending on your point of view, these qualities make astrology irresistibly fascinating or irrevocably worthless.

Nevertheless, astrology has a solid core of testable traditional ideas. It was this important quality of testability, plus the apparent positive results of relevant tests, that first attracted Eysenck's attention. The same was true of parapsychology. In both cases the result was a confrontation between a learned 'man of facts' and areas where facts are hard to come by. In other words, our story is largely about what happens when unstoppable rationality meets immovable irrationality. As we shall see, the results tell us a little about astrology and parapsychology, and a lot about human nature. Some current areas of research in astrology, including those to which Eysenck has made original contributions, are shown in Table 1. Eysenck's most important writings are discussed in the text; for completeness the rest are listed at the end of the reference section.

### Eysenck's First Involvement with Astrology

Eysenck's active involvement with astrology began with his investigation of the

**Table 1**  *Some Current Areas of Research in Astrology*

*Tests involving people*

| Area | Test | Question asked |
|---|---|---|
| Individual factors | Aspects<br>Harmonics<br>Houses<br>Signs | Does the factor correlate with personality independently assessed by ratings, biographies or personality questionnaires? |
| Whole chart | Discrimination | Can the subject tell authentic interpretations from controls? |
|  | Interpretation | Are astrologers' interpretations correct? |
| Specific claims | Events | Does the birth chart correlate with events in a person's life? |
|  | Gambling | Can the birth chart predict successful times to gamble? |
|  | Heredity | Are there links between the birth charts of parents and children? |
|  | Relationships | Do contacts between birth charts correlate with compatibility? |
|  | Time twins | Are people born together in time more alike than those born apart? |

*Tests involving phenomena*

Can these be predicted:

Business cycles
Chemical reactivity
Plant growth
Radio propagation quality
Rainfall
Solar activity

findings of French psychologist Michel Gauquelin. Gauquelin and his wife, Françoise, had painstakingly obtained from registry offices the birth data for many thousands of eminent professionals, and had confirmed Gauquelin's original observation that at the birth of eminent professionals certain planets tended to cluster just past the rising point and just past the midheaven. The amount of clustering was typically 10 to 25 per cent more than expected and was highly significant (P typically .0001). The planets concerned were those predicted by astrology (and by no other theory), but surprisingly the areas emphasized were those where most astrologers would have predicted a lack of emphasis. In a review of this research in the magazine *New Behaviour*, Eysenck (1975a) described how the Gauquelins were presenting objective evidence, including the raw data, that strongly supported their claim. Moreover, he described how their results for Mars and sports champions had been replicated by the sceptical Belgian Committee for the Scientific Study of Paranormal Phenomena. Because of the factual basis of the Gauquelin evidence, together with the Belgian replication, Eysenck with his policy of 'letting the facts speak for themselves' could not fail to be impressed.

In the same article Eysenck (1975a) took issue with Karl Popper's argument that astrology, like psychoanalysis, is no more than a pseudo-science since it consists of assertions not definite enough to be proved false. Eysenck argued that, on the contrary, astrology makes a number of testable assertions such as those linking planetary positions and personality (see Table 1), hence 'there should be no difficulty in arranging an experiment to test the hypothesis quite unambiguously.' In giving Gauquelin's research as an example Eysenck went so far as to say, 'I think it may be said that, as far as objectivity of observation, statistical significance of differences, verification of the hypothesis, and replicability are concerned, there are few sets of data in psychology which could compete with these observations.' This is a good illustration of Eysenck's insistence on the facts, and nothing but the facts.

In his article Eysenck also observed that the personality descriptions extracted by Gauquelin from the professionals' biographies could be related to E, N and P. The outcome of this observation was a joint study by the Gauquelins and Sybil Eysenck that compared planetary positions at the birth of these famous professionals with their biographical descriptions expressed in terms of the three major personality dimensions. The results were clear-cut: there was a tendency for famous people classified as extraverted or high on psychoticism to be born under Mars or Jupiter, and for those classified as introverted or low on psychoticism to be born under Saturn (Gauquelin *et al.*, 1979). These results were subsequently replicated using an independent sample of 497 eminent Americans (Gauquelin *et al.*, 1981).

### The Mayo Study

At the time of his *New Behaviour* article Eysenck was also becoming involved in a comparison of sun-signs with EPI scores. In 1971 the British astrologer Jeff Mayo had sent Eysenck the results of a study that compared the sun-signs for 1795 subjects with their scores on Mayo's own extraversion questionnaire. The comparison showed a zig-zag pattern completely in accordance with astrology. Eysenck was intrigued and made the EPI (Form B) available to Mayo for further tests. Then in 1973, quite independently of Mayo, the British sociologist Joe Cooper showed Eysenck a comparison of sun-signs with EPI scores for Bradford University students. This comparison showed the same zig-zag pattern.

The outcome of all this was the publication in 1978, in the *Journal of Social Psychology*, of a paper by Mayo, White and Eysenck detailing the EPI results for 2324 subjects, and a paper by Smithers and Cooper detailing EPI results for 559 students. In each case the result was a zig-zag pattern in agreement with astrology. However, the difference in mean E score between odd and even signs was only 0.7, which is very small compared to the mean E score of about 13 and is much smaller than the claims of sun-sign astrology would suggest. These two papers were accompanied by a third from US psychologist H. W. Wendt suggesting an explanation based on seasonal effects.

Just before the Mayo study appeared there was published *Recent Advances in Natal Astrology* (Dean *et al.*, 1977), the first critical scientific review of the research basis to astrology. To ensure accuracy it involved a total of fifty-four collaborators, one of whom was Eysenck, who assisted with the sections on personality and psychology. This review took seven man-years to prepare, surveyed many hundreds of books and articles, and documented over 150 experimental studies by astrologers and over twenty by psychologists. (To date new studies and previously missed studies bring these totals to about 200 and fifty respectively.)

The availability of this review and the encouraging results of the Gauquelin, Mayo and Cooper studies prompted Eysenck to do two things. One was to facilitate the use of the Institute of Psychiatry by astrologers and psychologists for a joint weekend research seminar in May 1979; for a description and critical comments see Gibson (1981). The seminar was a success and has been repeated several times since. The other was to prepare with David Nias an overall investigation of the scientific evidence for astrology aimed at a more general readership than was *Recent Advances*. The result was the book (Eysenck and Nias, 1982) described next.

## Astrology: Science or Superstition?

Among other things this book covers astrological principles, sun-signs, marriage, illness, suicide, appearance, time twins, season of birth, terrestrial and solar cycles, radio propagation, earthquakes, lunar effects and the work of the Gauquelins. Because it addresses a complex unfamiliar field characterized by a large and unsatisfactory literature, the text was submitted in whole or in part to a total of nine experts for comments. Such consultation is essential when writing in a diverse and unfamiliar field, and in this case it greatly improved accuracy and balance. Despite the availability of *Recent Advances*, the original literature was accessed wherever possible; the result was a stack of photocopies two feet high. This illustrates the care taken to be independent and to get the facts right. Also new material was discovered with about 40 per cent of the book's 230 references being additional to those appearing in *Recent Advances*.

Apart from reviewing the evidence for astrology, Eysenck and Nias made some original and important refutations. First, the Mayo zodiac effect was shown in two separate studies to be an artifact of prior knowledge. This conclusion has been confirmed by Pawlik and Buse (1979) and by Mohan *et al.* (1982). Also as further confirmation Dean (1983c) has shown that the magnitude of the effect is consistent with the general level of belief in astrology as determined by opinion polls. Second, the claims of John Nelson (1951, 1978) that planetary positions can be used to predict sunspots and radio interference with about 90 per cent accuracy were investigated in a small-scale study. After comparing some of his forecasts with what actually happened, it was concluded that his claims probably rest on nothing more than an artifact in calculating the accuracy rate. This refutation has been confirmed by Dean (1983a,b), who showed that for a total of 5507 of Nelson's daily forecasts the mean correlation between forecast and outcome in terms of radio propagation quality was 0.01 or almost exactly chance. Nelson's claims have long been quoted by astrologers as evidence for aspects, and with their refutation a major pillar of support for astrology has disappeared.

So what were the overall conclusions of the book? Eysenck and Nias concluded that, with the exception of Gauquelin's positive findings, there was precious little evidence to support any of astrology's claims. This conclusion is essentially in agreement with that of Dean *et al.* (1977) and of other well-informed critics such as Kelly (1979). Of course, this does not mean that later research may not produce positive results, but only that positive results have so far not been forthcoming.

In the book Eysenck and Nias fully supported Gauquelin's findings. Furthermore, for the reasons discussed in the next section, they rejected fraud as extremely unlikely. Fraud has been the favourite explanation among hostile critics, but in this case it can be further ruled out by Gauquelin's offer to pay the hotel expenses of any scientist who wishes to check his files on the sole condition that the conclusions are published (Gauquelin, 1982). We might add that one of us has personally inspected Gauquelin's files and has been impressed by their meticulous organization. The possibility of inadvertent error has also become even more remote since Gauquelin (1984) has re-checked by computer all the many thousands of original hand calculations and obtained essentially the same results.

### Response by Scientists

Some workers have criticized Eysenck for premature publication of his work with Mayo, because the results turned out to rest on an artifact. If a parallel is drawn with the reporting of other unexpected discoveries, then it may be noted that Michelson and Morley in their classic attempt to measure the absolute speed of the earth in space repeated their experiments many times before declaring their result in print as correct. Similarly, Joseph Rhine was very cautious and waited years before publishing the results of his first ESP experiments at Duke University.

Eysenck's defence in immediately communicating the results of the Mayo study would presumably be that 'science is a self-correcting process'. The paper did provoke numerous replications and the false nature of the original claim was probably demonstrated all the sooner as a result. Moreover, Eysenck had warned in the paper that a possible 'weakness of the study' was that the data were collected from people interested in astrology. When later sending out reprints he often enclosed an accompanying note inviting the reader to suggest how the results might have come about. These tactics illustrate Eysenck's faith in factual evidence and his emphasis on correctly interpreting the exact meaning of such evidence.

Responses to Eysenck's support of Gauquelin's findings have been of a different quality. Like the zodiac effect, the 'planetary effect' is based on a large amount of data and has been replicated, but unlike the zodiac effect there is no plausible mechanism that can explain it. As a result, rather than resign themselves to the facts and await further developments, critics have resorted to emotional arguments and allegations of fraud. For example, in a review entitled 'Eysenck's Folly', the noted debunker of pseudo-science and a member of the US Committee for the Scientific Investigation of Claims of the Paranormal, Martin Gardner (1982), implies that Gauquelin's results are due to errors and artful selectivity. This view blatantly disregards the fact that CSICOP chairman Paul Kurtz personally examined part of Gauquelin's files for supposed errors (and found none), that Gauquelin's original data were taken from biographical dictionaries without any selection at all, and that his results for sports champions were replicated by the sceptical Belgian Committee. Such a response, and that of the CSICOP generally (Curry, 1982), shows that scientists all too often have precisely those irrational biases of which their training supposedly makes them free.

In a different class are the thoughtful comments of Gibson (1981) in his biography of Eysenck. He devotes a whole chapter to ESP and astrology noting 'that instead of criticising the topic [ESP] with the same vigour with which he had criticised psychoanalysis, he defended those who treated the subject seriously and castigated its critics!'. In outlining Eysenck's main work in these fields, Gibson raises the question of why Eysenck became involved when there was a danger of giving 'a gloss of scientific respectability to something [astrology] which is regarded by a large number of scientists as wholly regrettable and a mark of the growing superstition and irrationalism of our age.' After considering whether Eysenck was being naive in believing some of the claims made for astrology to the extent of becoming actively involved, Gibson rejects naiveté as a likely explanation. Instead he suggests that Eysenck was pursuing the course of 'Socratic irony—not to reject propositions out of hand (which is the attitude of most scientists to astrology) but to entertain them to the extent of active participation, but finally to expose their weaknesses by further investigation of crucial issues.' Gibson gives the Mayo study and its subsequent refutation as an example of this strategy.

## Response by Astrologers

To some astrologers Eysenck has brought to astrology a long-deserved respectability. For example, the Mayo study was welcomed as a scientific demonstration of a basic astrological truth in the astrology journal *Phenomena* (1977), where it was described as 'possibly the most important development for astrology in this century', a comment that probably owed as much to Eysenck's eminence as it did to the actual results! But of course Eysenck is not pro-astrology, only pro-facts. When the facts conflict with astrological beliefs, as they did when Eysenck reported to the 1979 astrology research seminar that their acclaimed zodiac effect was all due to an artifact, 'there was a strong feeling among some of the astrologers that Eysenck had first beguiled them with his patronage, and then betrayed them by bringing forward some ugly facts' (Gibson, 1981).

A reading of astrological magazines suggests that most astrologers have a negative opinion of Eysenck's conclusions along the lines of I-know-that-astrology-works-so-who-cares-what-scientists-say. For example, in response to an article by Eysenck (1982) on research methodology in astrology, the astrologer Ellis (1982) comments:

> I am puzzled why some astrologers...feel a need to be accepted by self-styled sole proponents of rationality. Why should one particular discipline have to justify itself in alien terminology? ...An organic dimension of truth, dealing in dynamic wholes and specialising in the rhythms of the universe, cannot be confined within dogmatically formulated compartments.... Astrology, I find, attempts to pin down experiences, not people.

Scientists will of course dismiss these points as a mixture of *non-sequiturs*, straw men and holy writ. But astrologers will see them as perfectly logical, simply because they view birth charts not in terms of scientific validity but as a tool for personal development and self-understanding. The crucial point here is that the popularity of chart reading leaves astrologers in no doubt that clients find charts to be personally valid. Hence astrologers are persuaded that astrology works, and are unmoved by considerations of scientific evidence. The same was true of phrenologists, and only time will tell whether astrologers will share their fate.

## Conclusion

In being the first to champion Gauquelin's cause, Eysenck has aroused scientific interest in the possibility that astrology may contain elements of truth. Eysenck has argued that, according to the facts, reliable evidence already exists in support of an inexplicable effect. The results of Gauquelin point to a planetary correlation with personality, and to planetary links between parents and children. If satisfactory replications continue to be made of Gauquelin's main findings, and if detailed checks of his raw data continue to rule out error and fraud, then scientists will be forced into the dilemma of accepting evidence that is counter to their established principles. There should be no problem in doing this since the history of science provides many examples of phenomena being accepted even though at the time they were inexplicable. Gravity and electricity are still very much a mystery as regards a full understanding of their nature, and the infinity of space may be seen as a concept that defies human understanding. Astrology if it does prove to contain elements of truth will have to come under a similar category if no physical mechanism emerges to explain it.

So is there a plausible mechanism to explain Gauquelin's planetary effects? To date all those who have attempted to come up with one have retired defeated. In short, nobody has the faintest idea what might be happening. Unlike the Mayo zodiac effect, it cannot be explained in terms of knowledge of astrology and self-fulfilling prophecies. Very few people know the position of the planets at the moment they were born and, in any case, the emphasized position is not what astrology would predict. In attempting to arrive at testable hypotheses, we have a number of observations to bear in mind. According to results so far, the planetary effect disappears if the birth is induced, the effect is enhanced if geomagnetic activity is high at birth, the effect on personality (but not on parent-child links) disappears if the subjects are less than eminent, and so on. Any one of these might provide a clue as to the next step to be taken. But rather than attempt speculations as to possible mechanisms, Eysenck has been content so far to limit his endeavour to establishing that the planetary effect is genuine. If it does survive as genuine, then Eysenck's main contribution was in recognizing that the research was scientific and in urging that academics should take it seriously.

As for the astrological claims that have been disproved, Eysenck's contribution may be seen in terms of demonstrating the power of science in refuting false claims. It is too early yet to say what influence Eysenck has had on the development of astrological research generally, although it may be noted that his policy of taking seriously all positive claims—however unlikely they may appear—and then attempting to disprove them is in the best traditions of the scientific spirit.

## PARAPSYCHOLOGY

Parapsychology is similar to astrology in that its alleged effects have no obvious explanation. However, there are two important differences. First, parapsychology has a much larger body of research than astrology (perhaps 100 times as many studies) and many more competent researchers. Second, many of the alleged psi effects are precisely those simulated by mental magicians. Indeed, a large number of alleged psychics have been found to be using nothing more than trickery in their acts. In other words parapsychology is at once much more professional, and much more open to trickery and fraud. Nevertheless, it does have testable hypotheses, and as with astrology it was this testability, plus the apparent positive results of relevant tests, that first attracted Eysenck's attention.


## Eysenck's Early Writings on Parapsychology

A chapter on 'Telepathy and Clairvoyance' in *Sense and Nonsense in Psychology* (1957) formed Eysenck's first writings on this subject. In it he outlined the state of knowledge at that time, and concluded that psi is a reality. He also concluded that it is not universally accepted by scientists because as soon as they leave the field in which they have specialized they 'are just as ordinary, pig-headed, and unreasonable as anybody else.' The question of fraud as an explanation of psi results was discounted in the now famous quote:

> Unless there is a gigantic conspiracy involving some thirty University departments all over the world, and several hundred highly respected scientists in various fields, many of them originally hostile to the claims of the psychical researchers, the only conclusion the unbiased observer can come to must be that there does exist a small number of people who obtain knowledge existing either in other people's minds, or in the outer world, by means as yet unknown to science.

In further considering the question of fraud, Eysenck described how trickery has often been used to produce apparently psychic phenomena. In warning researchers to be on their guard against trickery on the part of their subjects, he pointed out that 'a few hours' instruction in elementary conjuring should enable any reasonably adept person to produce most of the alleged psychical phenomena seen at séances.' Unfortunately researchers have not heeded this warning, nor similar warnings by others, with (as we shall see) dire results!

Ten years later Eysenck (1967) responded to the suggestion of Rao (1966) that 'there is no intrinsic reason why personality differences should help or hinder psi if it is like other abilities such as perception or memory.' Eysenck argued that, on the contrary, if psi is a primitive form of perception, evolving before higher forms of perception based on the cortex, then cortical arousal and its associated personality traits (i.e., introversion) should hinder the ability. Psi would thus be the opposite of the other senses, and so be truly *extra*-sensory! He pointed out that experimental evidence indicated that (1) psi scores tend to decline during test sessions (the 'decline effect') suggesting a monotony factor; (2) introducing novelty in testing sessions helps; and (3) subjects typically perform better under spontaneous rather than rigidly controlled conditions, all of which is consistent with extraverts performing better than introverts. He then showed that a survey of the limited literature at the time supported this. As an aside Eysenck argued that the association with extraversion constitutes evidence against faking because presumably 'the investigators did not know of the hypothesis in question.'

Eysenck also pointed out that psi researchers had not followed the standard practice of calculating reliabilities. This guards against subjects who consistently score above chance being counter-balanced by others who consistently score below chance, a situation which is suggested by his argument for personality effects. Hence individual reliabilities 'should always be calculated as a matter of routine.' However, for some reason most psi researchers have not taken this advice.

The latest edition (15th) of *Encyclopedia Britannica* includes a review by Eysenck (1974) on psi. Here he points out that 'the very existence of parapsychological phenomena is still very much in dispute', probably because critics fail to present arguments 'supported by a survey of all the known facts'. The common practice of citing isolated studies is not enough—it is the balance of evidence that must be considered. After describing how recent psi experiments have been investigated by the American Psychological Society and the American Statistical Society, without any adverse criticisms being made, Eysenck concluded that 'the evidence for ESP is stronger than that for many tenuously supported psychological phenomena.' He also warned again about the dangers of trickery: 'Investigators who cannot explain every trick performed by stage magicians should consider themselves barred from investigating alleged psi phenomena.'

## The Precognition Experiment

In an attempt to 'highlight certain methodological and theoretical considerations which have hitherto played very little part in parapsychological work', Eysenck (1975b) tested the precognitive ability of rats by seeing if they could anticipate randomly-generated electric shocks. The results seemed to show that rats did have precognitive ability. But because the equipment had a tendency to go wrong, Eysenck organized a more extensive experiment using more reliable equipment (Hewitt *et al.*, 1978). Unfortunately none of the results was significant, and it was concluded that the earlier results were spurious. This again illustrates the power of science in being a 'self-correcting process'.

## Eysenck's Recent Writings

*Explaining the Unexplained: Mysteries of the Paranormal* (Eysenck and Sargent, 1982) was written at the same time as *Astrology: Science or Superstition?*, but it did not involve consultation with outside experts and as we show the result is far less balanced. Among other things the book covers card guessing, dreams, faith-healing, mediums, poltergeists, reincarnation, remote viewing, and the effects of hypnosis, personality and meditation. In it Eysenck and Sargent give an overview of the positive evidence for psi, and attempt to show that (1) psi effects seem to conform to recognizable laws, and (2) psi effects interact with variables like personality in ways that make sense. In particular they attempt to show how a good theory (such as E. H. Walker's based on quantum considerations) can begin to make sense out of apparent disorder and lead to new tests, and the emphasis of their book is on various theories and how they stand up to testing. Because the various theories are testable every inch of the way, nobody who reads Eysenck and Sargent's account can fail to be impressed by the progress being made.

Eysenck and Sargent criticize the critics of psi for failing to take into account all the evidence. They also point out that the noted critic C. E. M. Hansel has committed many errors of fact, and that while some of these have been corrected in his later writings others have not. Unfortunately they themselves are selective in the evidence they cite. For example, they do not balance the picture by mentioning that although Hansel was attacked by nearly every leading parapsychologist for suggesting in 1966 that the experiments of S. G. Soal were falsified, it was shown incontrovertibly in 1978 that Hansel was right. They devote seven pages to D. D. Home, concluding that 'no-one has ever equalled his feats', but the magician Milbourne Christopher (1970) has provided plausible explanations, has found evidence of sleight-of-hand and has managed to duplicate Home's more baffling feats including levitations. They devote eight pages to Helmut Schmidt, whose experiments left them 'highly impressed' but do not mention that Schmidt works virtually alone, that no-one so far has had access to the raw data and that he changes the equipment too frequently to allow the continuity necessary for proper assessment. They report favourably on the Targ and Puthoff experiments in remote viewing, but say nothing about the critique of Marks and Kammann (1980) who, after a detailed investigation, concluded that the reported effect was 'nothing more than a massive artifact of poor methodology and wishful thinking'. Most importantly they give no hint of the various prizes offered for convincing evidence of psi, such as the 10,000 dollars offered by the late Joseph Dunninger, the 10,000 dollars currently offered by James Randi and the 100,000 dollars currently offered by Australian millionaire and sceptic Dick Smith, none of which has been successfully claimed.

Despite Eysenck's early warnings about trickery and fraud, there is scarcely any mention of these topics in the book, and neither appears in the index. This is unfortunate, because trickery and the credulity of parapsychologists have formed the main thrust of recent criticism, and a rather devastating literature is accumulating, as anybody who reads through the back issues of the *Skeptical Inquirer* will discover. In other words Eysenck is not following his own advice regarding the need for a balanced view of all the facts.

The need for a balanced view is even more apparent in Eysenck and Sargent's (1984) second book, *Know Your Own Psi-Q*. The objection of sceptics is perhaps best illustrated by Randi (1984). He describes the book as 'a disaster in every way except one: it may provide us with an accurate picture of just how naive the authors are in designing proper protocol for testing psi-powers. If their book correctly expresses the standards of parapsychologists in general, it is no wonder that the rest of the scientific community scoffs at their efforts.' Randi points out that they cite Delmore and Girard as psi-stars even though each is known to employ sleight-of-hand, and that the two-and-a-half pages of their bibliography contain not a single sceptical work. He concludes that their book gives 'a totally one-sided view of the subject'.

In his latest article Eysenck (1983) reviews the status and prospects of psi, and again asserts its reality. Because of the rigour of design, statistical analysis and interpretation of recent work he suggests that 'experiments in parapsychology are at least as rigorous as most of those published in psychological journals in more "reputable fields", and probably more so.' However, as we shall now see, for at least some experiments this is demonstrably untrue.

**Fraud, Trickery and Credulity**

Gibson (1979) argues that researchers who devote their lives to psychic research are strongly motivated to obtain significant results, otherwise they are wasting their time and are shown up to be fools! He describes cases where the subjects may have used trickery in producing their results, of experimenters who have been naive enough to use sloppy methods and of experimenters who have actually been shown to have cheated. Gibson suggests that the positive evidence for psi reveals nothing more than 'the human propensity to deceive oneself and others'. Further, he argues that research in psi has not increased human knowledge 'one iota', but has wasted the time of able researchers and fostered the suspicion of fraud in scientific research generally.

The most cited example of sloppy research methods probably concerns Rhine's early work at Duke University. A rumour started that the Zener cards used in his ESP experiments were heavily printed to the extent that some subjects were able to see the symbols through the backs of the cards. Kennedy (1938) decided to investigate this possibility and with the commercially available cards tested subjects until he found one who consistently scored above chance level. Since this subject did not admit to being aware of using visual cues, it seemed to be a case of subliminal perception (the subject could score above chance only when actually looking at the cards). Kennedy next found that he too was able to obtain extra-chance scores by practising tilting the cards against a light and looking for a faint impression of the symbols. Finally, he was able to train a student with particularly good eyesight to correctly 'guess' all twenty-five of the cards in the Zener pack! Following this demonstration, Rhine was of course careful to screen the cards from view and so the criticism does not apply to his later experiments. But it does suggest that he was not as careful as he might have been, although to his credit he had delayed publication of his early work which he saw more in terms of developing techniques than of demonstrating ESP. Even so, this is an unfortunate story since the rumour has persisted and the reputation of Rhine's pioneering research programme has suffered as a result.

In contrast to Eysenck (1974) who argued that 'the question of cheating is not capable of rational discussion', Rhine (1977) saw it as 'an entirely proper question' to ask whether psi researchers have been trustworthy. He described the safeguards he used to avoid depending on any one person, such as always having two experimenters and suspending judgment until there has been an independent replication. He then cites the discovery of the 'decline effect' in data collected before the effect was discovered as the 'kind of proof that allows no question of experimenter honesty to arise... I can conceive of no stronger evidence of psi, even today after 30 years have passed.' Unfortunately Rhine and parapsychologists in general write as if the decline effect was discovered in 1944, whereas it was first reported over fifty years before by the French physiologist and Nobel laureate, Charles Richet (1889)—a fact that obviously weakens their argument.

People who read about magic and conjuring may well see it as a challenge to see if they can fool an academic researcher, especially as such books often describe psychic ability in terms of clever trickery. For example, Fulves (1979), in describing sixty-seven mind-reading tricks, defines psychic ability as magic and the supernatural combining 'to produce mental magic, telepathy and clairvoyance, the ability to see the future and read minds.' The last of his sixty-seven tricks is described as 'a staggering demonstration of paranormal ability, an overwhelmingly positive test that ESP exists'! Fulves also observes that 'the mentalist has an advantage that the magician does not.... His experiments in extrasensory perception are accepted as real magic. The audience wants to believe that the mentalist has paranormal powers.'

Magicians understandably refuse to reveal secrets on which their living depends, but they have always been ready to reveal basic techniques. For example, in a reference book on mental magic intended for both magicians and parapsychologists,

Kaye (1975) includes an annotated bibliography of 120 books and articles on mental magic, and explains dozens of tricks that to the uninitiated are totally baffling. One would therefore expect researchers to be aware of mentalist techniques, and to involve magicians when designing their experiments.

Unfortunately quite the opposite situation prevails, as was cleverly demonstrated by magician James Randi (1983). Having been told repeatedly over the years that parapsychologists had no use for magicians and were perfectly capable of detecting trickery, Randi persuaded two young magicians to pose as psychics and infiltrate the psychical research programme at Washington University in St Louis, whose psychical research laboratory had been established by a half-million-dollar grant from the McDonnell Foundation. During three years of testing the researchers were fully persuaded that the magicians had genuine psychic powers. They also ignored all the precautions that Randi had suggested, and for two years continually rejected his offers of help. Randi provides a series of amusing stories of the activities of his team, and the mixed reactions of researchers exposed as naive or incompetent. Some researchers have even shown signs of ingratitude at being enlightened in this way! As might be expected, Randi's experiment has raised considerable controversy (a full discussion of the issues appears in *Zetetic Scholar*, 12, 1984); nevertheless it demonstrates in no uncertain way the unbelievable credulity of some parapsychologists.

A similar credulity has been documented by Brandon (1983) in a survey of spiritualists in the nineteenth and twentieth centuries. She notes that attempts to expose fraud tend to be futile, saying that 'it is like punching a feather pillow...an indentation is made, but soon refills, and the whole soft, spongy mass continues as before.' Clearly the failure of Eysenck and Sargent's books to cover trickery and credulity is a serious deficiency.

### Conclusion

Henry Sidgwick elected to be the first President of the Society for Psychical Research in 1882, expressed the following aim: 'We must drive the objector into the position either to admit that the phenomena are inexplicable, at least by him, or to accuse the investigators either of lying or cheating or of a blindness or forgetfulness incompatible with any intellectual condition except absolute idiocy' (Sidgwick, 1882). In the light of Randi's research and the reactions of informed sceptics such as Hansel and Gibson, the aim to incite accusations has finally been achieved!

How can we reconcile the positive findings reported by Eysenck and Sargent (1982) with the fraud, trickery, credulity and general negative findings claimed by the critics? Such a reconciliation is essential if other scientists are going to be expected to take seriously the claims of parapsychology. The case of the critics does seem to be strong enough to demand an answer. It is clear then that the next step must be a full-scale response to their challenge.

Eysenck with his willingness to examine controversial areas without prior judgment has always balanced this with an insistence on a full survey of all the facts. The pity is that his recent surveys have fallen short of achieving this ideal. It remains to be seen whether he was right in advocating that there is something in the claims of parapsychology worthy of investigation.

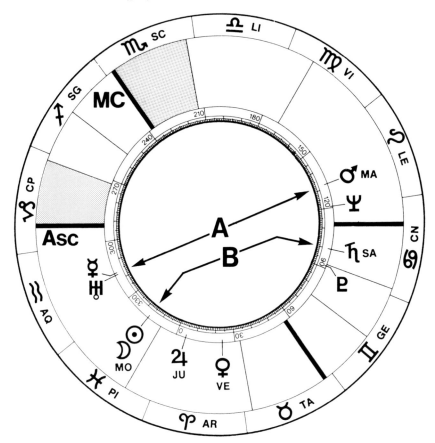

**ASTROLOGICAL BIRTH CHART OF HANS EYSENCK**

The inner and outer rings show the signs of the zodiac. The middle ring shows the planets and Placidus houses, with Gauquelin's five significant planets identified by abbreviations. The chart is calculated for 5 am (4 am GMT) 4 March 1916 at Berlin (data from Eysenck's birth certificate). Eysenck is precisely the kind of eminent scientist for whom Gauquelin observed significant planetary effects. So to what extent does Eysenck's birth chart support the claims of Gauquelin and astrology?

To find out, we first searched Gibson's (1981) biography of Eysenck and valedictory articles (*Bethlem and Maudsley Gazette*, Spring 1983) for descriptions of Eysenck's personality. The result was over fifty short statements of two to twelve words each, which were then sorted into clusters according to their common meaning. The main clusters, with number of contributing statements in brackets, were as follows: quiet and reserved (7); placid, rarely gets upset (6); helpful, easy to get on with (8); self-willed (6); very self-confident (9); determined, provokes confrontation (12). In short a strong-minded, stable introvert. Gibson points out that Eysenck's quiet, soft-spoken personal manner is nothing like his public image of extreme tough-mindedness.

How does this compare with Gauquelin's findings? Gauquelin found that at the birth of eminent scientists and introverts Saturn tended to occupy the houses shown shaded, and to a lesser extent the opposite houses, while Jupiter (characteristic of extraverts and actors) tended to avoid these positions in favour of intermediate positions. Because the chart is drawn in terms of space, the houses differ in size, whereas in terms of time (which is the viewpoint involved here) they are equal. When this distortion is allowed for, Eysenck's chart is clearly in agreement with both findings. The probability of this arising by chance is about one in ten.

In view of Eysenck's prodigious writings it is interesting that the moon (characteristic of imaginative writers) is not emphasized. However, Eysenck has told us that he is no good at *imaginative* writing and poetry, in which case there is no conflict with Gauquelin's findings.

In astrological terms the chart has a Pisces sun and moon, a Capricorn ascendant, and is dominated by the two configurations marked A and B. A is a close conjuction between Mercury and Uranus that is opposed to Mars, indicating self-will and outspokenness. B is an unusually exact (to the minute) conjunction between the sun and moon that is trine to Saturn, indicating reserve and self-control. At first sight this appears to be an uncanny match to the contrasting public and personal sides mentioned by Gibson. However, if as a control we take the exactly opposite personality, namely loud, outgoing, easily upset, submissive and lacking in confidence, inspection of astrology textbooks shows that the first three traits are exactly matched by A, and the rest by B—especially as the sun and moon are in Pisces, indicating sensitivity and passivity. Therefore, Eysenck's chart reveals little about traditional astrology other than its ability to describe almost anything in retrospect!

## REFERENCES

Brandon, R. (1983) *The Spiritualists: The Passion for the Occult in the Nineteenth and Twentieth Centuries*, New York, Knopf.

Christopher, M. (1970) *ESP, Seers and Psychics*, New York, Crowell.

Curry, P. (1982) 'Research on the Mars effect', *Zetetic Scholar*, **9**, pp. 34–53.

Dean, G. A. (1983a) 'Shortwave radio propagation non-correlation with planetary positions', *Correlation*, **3, 1**, pp. 4–37.

Dean, G. A. (1983b) 'Forecasting radio quality by the planets', *Skeptical Inquirer*, **8, 1**, pp. 48–56.

Dean, G. A. (1983c) 'Can self-attribution explain sun-sign guessing?', *Correlation*, **3, 2**, pp. 22–7.

Dean, G. A., Mather, A. C. M. and 52 others (1977) *Recent Advances in Natal Astrology: A Critical Review 1900–1976*, Perth, Analogic.

Ellis, S. (1982) 'Eysenck methodology' (letter), *Astrological Journal*, **24, 3**, pp. 198–200.

Eysenck, H. J. (1957) *Sense and Nonsense in Psychology*, Harmondsworth, Penguin.

Eysenck, H. J. (1967) 'Personality and extrasensory perception', *Journal of the Society for Psychical Research*, **44**, pp. 55–71.

Eysenck, H. J. (1974) 'Theories of parapsychological phenomena', *Encyclopedia Britannica*, 15th ed.

Eysenck, H. J. (1975a) 'Planets, stars and personality', *New Behaviour*, 29 May, pp. 246–9.

Eysenck, H. J. (1975b) 'Precognition in rats', *Journal of Parapsychology*, **39**, pp. 222–7.

Eysenck, H. J. (1982) 'Methodology in astrological research', *Astrological Journal*, **24, 2**, pp. 76–83.

Eysenck, H. J. (1983) 'Parapsychology: Status and prospects (The J. B. Rhine Lecture)', in Roll, W. G., Beloff, J. and White, R. A. (Eds.), *Research in Parapsychology*, Metuchen, N. J., Scarecrow.

Eysenck, H. J. and Nias, D. K. B. (1982) *Astrology: Science or Superstition?* London, Temple Smith.

Eysenck, H. J. and Sargent, C. L. (1982) *Explaining the Unexplained: Mysteries of the Paranormal*, London, Weidenfeld and Nicolson.

Eysenck, H. J. and Sargent, C. L. (1984) *Know Your Own Psi-Q*, New York, World Almanac.

Fulves, K. (1979) *Self-Working Mental Magic: 67 Foolproof Mind-Reading Tricks*, New York, Dover.

Gardner, M. (1982) 'Eysenck's folly' (review of *Astrology: Science or Superstition?*), *Discover*, October.

Gauquelin, M. (1982) 'A proposal', *Zetetic Scholar*, **10**, pp. 72–3.

Gauquelin, M. (1984) 'Profession and heredity experiments: Computer re-analysis and new investigations on the same material', *Correlation*, **4, 1**, pp. 8–24.

Gauquelin, M., Gauquelin, F. and Eysenck, S. B. G. (1979) 'Personality and position of the planets at birth: An empirical study', *British Journal of Social and Clinical Psychology*, **18**, pp. 71–5.

Gauquelin, M., Gauquelin, F. and Eysenck, S. B. G. (1981) 'Eysenck's personality analysis and position of the planets at birth: A replication on American subjects', *Personality and Individual Differences*, **2**, pp. 346–50.

Gibson, H. B. (1979) 'The "Royal Nonesuch" of parapsychology', *Bulletin of the British Psychological Society*, **32**, pp. 65–7.

Gibson, H. B. (1981) *Hans Eysenck: The Man and His Work*, London, Peter Owen.

Hansel, C. E. M. (1966) *ESP: A Scientific Evaluation*, London, McGibbon and Kee.

Hansel, C. E. M. (1980) *ESP and Parapsychology: A Critical Re-evaluation*, London, McGibbon and Kee.

Hewitt, J. K., Fulker, D. W. and Eysenck, H. J. (1978) 'Effect of strain and level of shock on the behaviour of rats in psi experiments', *Psychological Reports*, **42**, pp. 1103–8.

Kaye, M. (1975) *The Handbook of Mental Magic*, New York, Stein and Day.

Kelly, I. W. (1979) 'Astrology and science: A critical examination', *Psychological Reports*, **44**, pp. 1231–40.

Kennedy, J. L. (1938) 'The visual cues from the backs of the ESP cards', *Journal of Psychology*, **6**, pp. 149–53.

Marks, D. and Kammann, R. (1980) *The Psychology of the Psychic*, Buffalo, N. Y., Prometheus.

Mayo, J., White, O. and Eysenck, H. J. (1978) 'An empirical study of the relation between astrological factors and personality', *Journal of Social Psychology*, **105**, pp. 229–36.

Mohan, J., Bhandari, A. and Sehgal, M. (1982) 'Astrological factors and personality: Cross-cultural validation in children', *Correlation*, **2, 1**, pp. 10–16.

Nelson, J. H. (1951) 'Shortwave radio propagation correlation with planetary positions', *RCA Review*, March, pp. 26–34.

Nelson, J. H. (1978) *The Propagation Wizard's Handbook*, Peterborough, N. H., 73 Inc.

Pawlik, K. and Buse, L. (1979) 'Selbst-Attribuierung als differentiell-psychologische Moderatorvariable: Nachprüfung und Erklärung von Eysencks Astrologie-Persönlichkeit-Korrelationen', *Zeitschrift für Socialpsychologie*, **10**, pp. 54–69.

Randi, J. (1983) 'The Project Alpha experiment', *Skeptical Inquirer*, **7, 4**, pp. 24–33; **8, 1**, pp. 36–45; and **8, 2**, pp. 102–3.

Randi, J. (1984) 'Mirror on naive protocol' (review of *Know Your Own Psi-Q*), *Skeptical Inquirer*, **8, 2**, pp. 180–2.

Rao, K. R. (1966) *Experimental Parapsychology*, Springfield, Ill., C. C. Thomas.

Rhine, J. B. (1977) 'Extrasensory perception', in Wolman, B. B. (Ed.), *Handbook of Parapsychology*, New York, Van Nostrand.

Richet, C. (1889) 'Further experiments in hypnotic lucidity or clairvoyance', *Proceedings of the Society for Psychical Research*, **6**, pp. 66–83.

Sidgwick, H. (1882) 'Presidential address', *Proceedings of the Society for Psychical Research*, **1**, pp. 1–12.

## Additional Articles by Eysenck Not Cited in the Text

Eysenck, H. J. (1978) 'On Jerome's *Astrology Disproved*', *Phenomena*, **2, 2**, pp. 9–11.

Eysenck, H. J. (1979) 'Biography in the service of science: A look at astrology', *Biograph*, **2, 1**, pp. 25–34.

Eysenck, H. J. (1979) Review of *Recent Advances in Natal Astrology*, *Zetetic Scholar*, **3/4**, pp. 85–6.

Eysenck, H. J. (1979) 'Astrology: Science or superstition?', *Encounter*, December, pp. 85–90.

Eysenck, H. J. (1980) 'Telepathy: Sense or nonsense?', *Bethlem and Maudsley Gazette*, Spring.

Eysenck, H. J. (1981) 'The importance of methodology in astrological research', *Correlation*, **1, 1**, pp. 11–14.

Eysenck, H. J. (1982) 'Critical commentary on the Mars Effect', *Zetetic Scholar*, **9**, pp. 61–3.

Eysenck, H. J. (1982) 'The Vernon Clark experiments', *Astro-Psychological Problems*, **1, 1**, pp. 27–9.

Eysenck, H. J. (1983) 'Response to Kurtz's review of *Astrology: Science or Superstition?*', *Skeptical Inquirer*, **8, 1**, pp. 89–90.

Eysenck, H. J. (1983) 'You, the Jury: Are astrologers also prejudiced?', *Astro-Psychological Problems*, **1, 2**, pp. 4–9.

Eysenck, H. J. (1983) 'Happiness in marriage', *Astro-Psychological Problems*, **1, 2**, pp. 14–24; and **1, 3**, pp. 15–19.

Eysenck, H. J. (1983) 'Methodological errors by critics of astrological claims', *Astro-Psychological Problems*, **1, 4**, pp. 14–17.

Eysenck, H. J. (1984) 'The Mars Effect and its evaluation', *Astro-Psychological Problems*, **2, 2**, pp. 22–6.

## Note

*Astro-Psychological Problems* is available from BP 317, 75229 Paris, France.

*Correlation* is available from 98 Hayes Road, Bromley, Kent BR2 9AB, England.

*Phenomena* is now discontinued.

*Recent Advances in Natal Astrology* is available from Temple Field, Anvil Green, Waltham, Kent CT4 7EU, England.

*Zetetic Scholar* is available from Department of Sociology, Eastern Michigan University, Ypsilanti, Michigan 48197, USA.

# Interchange

## SARGENT REPLIES TO NIAS AND DEAN

I should first like to correct some serious errors and misrepresentations on the parts of Nias and Dean.

First, their discussion of the decline effect in psi research is erroneous. They claim that Rhine and other parapsychologists assert that the decline effect was discovered in 1944; but this confounds the PK decline effect (reported in 1944 by Rhine) with the ESP decline effect, reported in his own work by Rhine in his 1934 monograph. Had Nias and Dean bothered to read that monograph, they would have found that Richet is cited *eleven* times (including citations in the context of the decline effect) and that other previous decline effects (e.g., Estabrooks) are reported also. Second, their insinuation that Rhine adopted superior test methods including screening test cards from view *after* Kennedy's demonstration is false, since the 1934 monograph reports tests with such procedures as the DT (Down Through) test, in which the pack of cards is sealed and the subject must guess all twenty-five straight off; only then is the deck opened and checked. Reader beware! Rhine was much more knowledgeable and intelligent that Nias and Dean give him credit for.

I shall also take issue with Nias and Dean's claims about selective citation in my collaborations with Eysenck. No reference was made to Christopher's book because it is irrelevant; of course it is possible to simulate some of Home's effects under circumstances which bear no relation to those in which the effects were originally shown. So what? Nias and Dean's discussion of Schmidt ignores the replications which Eysenck and I cited in our book, and the fact that some of the data reported by Schmidt were collected in his absence by other researchers. Anyone who has read *Explaining the Unexplained* will know that the remote viewing research was mentioned briefly and only *en passant*. If we had been going into detail, we would have mentioned Marks and Kammann, and Targ and Puthoff's reply in *Nature* (23 July 1981), *and* Tart's reanalysis of the data, *and* the very impressive and strongly significant independent replications by Bisaha, Schlitz and Gruber, and the Jahn team at Princeton, none of which Nias and Dean mention. We did not bother to mention the absurd 'challenges' cited by Nias and Dean because we know what they mean in practice; as Dennis Rawlins claims about Randi's 'challenge', Randi stated to him, 'I always have an out'—i.e., the conditions are *very* carefully thought out. We saw no reason to doubt Rawlins' claim on this matter. Finally, Randi's misunderstanding of the *Psi-Q* book is presumably wilful and for polemical purposes, though I cannot see why Nias and Dean were taken in by it; this book was no more meant as a manual of laboratory research methods than Eysenck's *Know Your Own IQ* was meant as a manual of intelligence research experimentation. This is not to say that the designs included are not adequate for amateur research and they include full protections against sensory cues, randomization errors, etc. when this is not so, this is clearly stated. The computerized tests would be sound for experimental research, of course. However, since this book is a manual of *method* it should frankly be obvious that the research findings reported are only a backdrop to this; *of course* we didn't go into detail on the research with Girard and Delmore, since we dealt with such work in the first book!

Everyone is selective in what they cite; Eysenck and Nias, for example, almost completely ignored John Addey's research on harmonics in astrology. Some selection is inevitable. What we objected to was the kind of selection indulged in by Hansel, who in the 1981 edition of his sceptical work cites less than half-a-dozen of the near-hundred experiments on the sheep-goat effect and extraversion, with only one reference more recent than 1953!

Nias and Dean would have done well to temper their critical assertions about parapsychology; their clanger on the decline effect betrays a very basic lack of knowledge of this subject.

We turn finally to Nias and Dean's claim that it is necessary that fraud be eliminated in the search for psi and astrological effects. They effectively suggest doing this at the level of the individual experiment; but this is impossible for obvious reasons. Presumably, one needs watchers checking the experimental participants. But who are they to be? Sceptics? Surely the involvement of CSICOP in astrology has given dire warning in this respect. *And who watches the watchers?* After all, Hansel and other sceptics have felt quite free to indulge in conspiracy theory. One ends up in an infinite regress. Even worse, even if *at the time* everyone agrees that the design is watertight, sceptics have an infinite period of time after the event to invent some loophole *somewhere*. Pellinore had a better chance with his quest than anyone who is foolish enough to search for the fraud-proof experiment. There is no such thing. Have Nias and Dean learned nothing from the Soal debacle? The whole point about this work is that everyone agreed that the protocol was the best in existence; so much for the watertight experiment. Incidentally, Markwick's discovery proved Hansel right in much the same way that the discovery of Neptune proved the researchers who predicted its position on the basis of an entirely fanciful, even absurd, set of principles right. But one can see, in this context, why Eysenck states that the problem of fraud is not capable of rational discussion. Within the context of the search for the illusory fraud-proof experiment, research itself is not capable of rational discussion.

The *only* protection is to stimulate independent replication. Even this is not perfect, but it is all we have, and arguments against it are arguments against the central epistemology of social science, so they had better be deployed with great care.

# REFERENCE

Eysenck, H. J. (1962) *Know Your Own IQ*. Harmondsworth: Penguin Books.
Eysenck, H. J. and Sargent, C. L. (1982) *Explaining the Unexplained*, London, Weidenfeld and Nicolson.

# NIAS AND DEAN REPLY TO SARGENT

We are in substantial agreement with Sargent about the evidence and Eysenck's influence in the case of astrology. However, we have two main criticisms regarding his presentation of the evidence for parapsychology.

First, as in his article (1981) and book with Eysenck (1982), Sargent exhibits the common fault of meta-analysts and cites only significance levels. Hence we have no idea of how big the effects are. But effect size is crucial to a proper assessment because the long runs favoured by researchers can inflate trivial effects to impressive significance. For example, one's astonishment at a test of 40,000 coin tosses that produced evidence of psi at the .001 level might well evaporate on our learning that for every 100 tosses it required averaging 50.8 heads instead of the 50 expected by chance. Furthermore, and this is the important point, if the effect is small, then so is the amount of trickery (conscious or otherwise) needed to produce it.

Second, Sargent's chapter suffers from the same one-sidedness that exists in his books with Eysenck. Thus not a single critical work such as Hansel (1980) appears in the references, and the reader is given no hint that there is another side to the story. As to the evidence that psi increases with increasing extraversion, we would add to Sargent's list of possible mechanisms the observation that the propensity for practical jokes also increases with increasing extraversion! Obvious questions like how many tricksters among the subjects would be needed to produce the same results, and whether this is compatible with the incidence of magicians and practical jokers in the general population, are conveniently ignored. The point is not that the opposing view is right or wrong, but that Sargent's viewpoint is one-sided in an area which can least afford it. Presumably Sargent is fully conversant with the view of the critics and has an answer to it, in which case he must put his side of the story. Extraordinary claims demand extraordinary evidence or, in the words of Laplace, 'the weight of the proofs must be suited to the oddness of facts.'

## REFERENCES

Eysenck, H. J. and Sargent, C. L. (1982) *Explaining the Unexplained*, London, Weidenfeld and Nicolson.
Hansel, C. E. M. (1980) *ESP and Parapsychology: A Critical Re-evaluation*, London, McGibbon and Kee.
Sargent, C. L. (1981), 'Extraversion and performance in "extra-sensory perception" tasks,' *Person. and Individual Differences*, **2**, pp. 137–43.

# Part XII: Concluding Chapter

# 21. Consensus and Controversy: —Two Types of Science

H. J. EYSENCK

It is never worth a first class man's time to express a majority opinion. By definition, there are plenty of others to do that. (G. H. Hardy)

Gordon Allport and I did not always see eye to eye on theoretical matters. I remember very well him telling me that he thought every psychologist should write his autobiography at the end of his life, to see the unities that emerged in his conduct over a lengthy period of time. This idiographic point of view contrasted very much with my own nomothetic one, and at the time I paid little attention to it. Now, half a life-time later, I can see what he was driving at, and can also see the possible importance of such consistencies of behaviour in one's own life.

Related to scientific achievement, it would be obvious to anyone that my work and my writings have given rise to controversy more than would be true, perhaps, of any other psychologist. My writings on Freud and psychotherapy, on conditioning and behaviour therapy, on intelligence and genetics, on the biological basis of personality, on smoking and disease, on social attitudes and sexual behaviour, on astrology and parapsychology, and even on the experimental study of art have all aroused strong emotions and extended controversy. Why should this be so?

John Ray suggests a personal delight in controversy and the infighting usually associated with it. We do not, of course, always know the motivational forces that drive us to do things, but I think I must disillusion him (and others who have thought alike) on this point. I would much prefer to have my theories and experiments accepted by the scientific community, and I would be quite happy if no controversy ever resulted from my publications! Cambridge University once introduced the following question into their Bachelor's examination: 'If Freud had not lived, Eysenck would have had to invent him', suggesting that intellectual battle of this kind was a necessity for me. This is not so. I would have been quite happy if Freud had never existed, and we did not have to battle strenuously to eliminate the evil effect of his

**375**

teaching, and substitute good methods for bad in the treatment of neurotic and other mental patients.

It was not amusing to me, when I came to the University of Birmingham to give a lecture on intelligence, to see walls of the university daubed in gigantic letters with what must be the ultimate example of an oxymoron: 'Fascist Eysenck has no right to speak—Uphold genuine academic freedom'! I did not enjoy being beaten up by bully boys at the London School of Economics to prevent me from giving a lecture on the biological basis of intelligence. I did not appreciate having to flee across the roof of the University of Sydney, where I was giving a talk on 'The History of Behaviour Therapy', while a mob of 200 protesting students broke down the very stout gates at the bottom of the building and beat up other students who were trying to keep them away. I was not amused when I tried to give a talk on personality and education at the University of Melbourne, when 150 police had to protect the building, and a raging mass of students inside kept shouting *Sieg Heil*, and raised their right hands in the Hitler salute all through my lecture. I am not complaining, but I would like to point out to John Ray that to imagine that anyone would actually *enjoy* this kind of 'controversy' would be to suggest a degree of masochism to which I would plead not guilty.

On a more mental plane, I have not particularly enjoyed controversy in scientific journals either, largely because it has been rather unfruitful, and has given rise to heat rather than light. Mostly this has been because many opponents have criticized statements I never made, or perhaps assumed that I held certain opinions when in fact my views were exactly the opposite. A few examples must suffice. In my 1952 paper on 'The Effects of Psychotherapy', I was careful to state that the evidence did not support the view that psychoanalysis and psychotherapy were efficacious methods of treatment; I was very careful not to say that the evidence *disproved* their efficacy, yet every one of the many critics who wrote papers castigating my stand criticized me for saying the latter, and went on from there to conclude that I was wrong. This is understandable, but not amusing. Similarly in my book on *Race, Intelligence and Education* I very carefully pointed out that there were not in existence any methods for demonstrating along biological lines that the differences in IQ between members of different racial groups were due to genetic causes. In spite of this explicit statement, practically all reviewers and critics have chastised me for holding the opposite view! I could go on giving many other examples but there would be little point. I do not believe that these errors occur because I cannot express myself clearly enough; I think anyone reading the books and articles in question will see that my statements are quite categorical and clear cut. It will be clear from what I have said that I do not particularly enjoy controversy, and would much prefer an unemotional, rational debate on the issues involved, without the adoption of an adversary position implied in the very term 'controversy'.

Perhaps we can gain some insight into the mystery by considering two kinds of science, or two approaches to science, which psychologists and philosophers of science have discriminated in their discussions. A well-known German chemist, W. Ostwald, once wrote a book on the two types of scientist he considered to be representative of alternate ways of doing science; he called them the 'romantics' and the 'classics'. The romantics were the more extraverted, creative types of scientist, constantly producing new ideas, innovative and original; the classical type of scientist was more likely to be introverted, concentrating on single issues, and trying to achieve perfect closure. This theme was taken up by the German psychiatrist, E. Kretschmer, in his book on genius. Following his theories of personality and body build, he postulated two extreme types of genius, the cyclothyme (extraverted) and the schizothyme (introverted). His description of these two types is not too dissimilar to that given by Ostwald. Last but not least, we have the distinction made by the philosopher of science, Thomas S. Kuhn, whose theories postulate a clear-cut division between *ordinary* science and *revolutionary* science, with the former resembling Ostwald's classical and Kretschmer's schizothyme types, and the latter Oswald's romantic and Kretschmer's psychothyme types.

Clearly my own contribution has been of the romantic, cyclothyme, revolutionary variety, and this perhaps inevitably had led to a considerable amount of misunderstanding and controversy escalating in the manner described above to physical assaults and verbal misrepresentations. Thus Allport was probably quite right in looking for uniformities in one's behaviour; these uniformities would seem to be reducible to personality traits and thus presumably to genetic causes.

It is not only in science that I have shown this tendency to depart from orthodoxy, and to voice views uncongenial to the majority. When I was still a pupil at school in Germany, there was great support for Hitler and the Nationalist-Socialist Party; indeed, in the school I attended practically all the boys were vehemently pro-Hitler, with the obvious exception of the few Jewish boys. My own stand was strongly anti-Hitler, outspokenly so, and I would surely have suffered the fate of all school boys who voice unpopular opinions had it not been for the fact that I was always big and strong, and good at sports. You don't beat up someone who is on all the school teams, whether football, handball, hockey, tennis or whatever! Nevertheless, this was my first essay in controversy, and while I did not get beaten up it afforded me good experience in rational argument and tolerance of misrepresentation, and encouraged me to maintain an independent position.

The fact that I am, as it were, on the 'revolutionary' side of science, rather than the 'ordinary' side, immediately suggests that while my contributions may be original in many ways, they are unlikely to be correct in every detail. It is, as Kuhn has pointed out, characteristic of revolutionary ideas that at the time they arise they have comparatively little support, they confront an established array of facts which have to be reinterpreted (not always to the delight of those who have worked with them along traditional lines!), and they are liable to change very quickly under the impact of the new facts that are being unearthed as a result of the presentation of the new theories. I never had any illusions that the new ideas I was putting forward, and the new theories I was elaborating, would be 'correct' even in the rather limited sense which philosophy allows to apply to scientific theories. They were usually, if not always, in the right direction, part of what Imre Lakatos, a well-known philosopher of science, called 'a progressive problem shift', as opposed to a 'degenerative problem shift', i.e., programmes of research that advance knowledge, rather than programmes of research that fight a rear-guard action by *ad hoc* explanations of anomalies which proved destructive to the programme.

I am thus in the fortunate position of not having to engage in controversy with rational critics, such as those contributing to this book; their criticisms, in fact, are eminently useful in furthering the advance of science, by pointing out the inevitable weakness in my theories and experiments, and suggesting ways of improving both. I have no hesitation in admitting these weaknesses; only a fool would believe that original contributions to science are sacrosanct, and do not admit of improvement. I am only too aware of the improvements needed for my own theories, and am grateful to critics who do not reject the whole approach on ideological grounds, but take it seriously enough to look at specific anomalies, and suggest ways and means of getting rid of these.

There are only two contributions to this book where I would take a slightly different line, and argue that the critics are fundamentally mistaken. These contributions are from Arnold Lazarus and Paul Kline. Before turning to the others, to discuss at least briefly their contributions, I will therefore try and point out why I believe that these two are fundamentally mistaken in their views.

## 1   Behaviour Therapy

Arnold Lazarus makes a contribution to the book which is characterized most of all by an inability to understand both the aims and the claims I would put forward on behalf of my research. As the philosopher Collingwood once pointed out, it is impossible to talk about a person's achievement without knowing what he was trying to achieve. Lazarus writes from the point of view of what he calls 'scientist-practitioner', although there is more evidence of the practitioner than of the scientist in his writings. He advocates an eclectic point of view, which by definition means an anti-scientific point of view: eclecticism has always been the enemy of scientific understanding.

My concern has been with the definition and explanation of a variety of disorders usually called 'neurotic', and the elaboration of a successful treatment for these disorders based upon this theory. Now it is, of course, true that the term 'neurosis' is used in many different ways by many different people; this does not suggest to me that it should be abandoned, but rather that its meaning should be clarified and restricted to a rather unified group of disorders. This is the usual practice in science; remember Newton's words regarding the concept or 'mass'; he points out that the term is used in ordinary language in a different way to the way in which he defines it, but he goes on to say that he is not concerned with the common herd. I think to introduce any kind of order into this Augean stable is certainly a difficult task, but neither an impossible nor an unnecessary one. The eclectics, of course, are happy to live in a world of confused images and undefined terms, and see no need for such clarification; the scientist on the other hand does.

It seems possible to delineate a large area of problems which seem to originate with Pavlovian conditioning and are curable by Pavlovian extinction; it also seems reasonable to call this area by the name 'neurosis'. It does contain, after all, the majority of disorders commonly so-called—anxiety states, phobias, obsessive compulsive neuroses, etc. I find it difficult to follow Lazarus' arguments concerning this point—indeed, he does not seem to have considered the methodology which I have adopted in his writings.

To say that Pavlovian conditioning (based undoubtedly on genetic factors predisposing the individual) is the principal causal factor in neurotic disorders, and that Pavlovian extinction is the basis of all curative efforts, is to put forward a theory which can certainly be disproved empirically. Let me point out first of all that the theory does not pretend that in neurotic disorders other factors may not also play a part. Instrumental conditioning may embed the neurosis more firmly; cognitive factors may lead to many false interpretations, and other factors (family reaction, financial needs, insurance claims, etc.) may also play a part. All this is obvious, but irrelevant;

we are concerned at the moment not with what the practitioner would have to do in order to treat, but with the essence of the patients' disorders.

Let us consider a simple case from general medicine, namely the dentist who excavates a tooth afflicted with caries, and who provides a filling. He knows what is the cause of the disorder, and he knows how to treat it. However, as regards the actual method of treatment, many other factors are also involved. He has to allay certain anxieties on the part of the patient, he has to be adept at giving the appropriate injections to dull the pain of the drilling, he has to try and make the patient refrain from eating too many sweets, he has to try and make him brush his teeth regularly, he has to make him return regularly for inspection, etc. All these things are part of the duty of the dentist, but they are not directly relevant to the scientific problems of the origin and treatment of caries!

Nowhere does Lazarus attempt to discuss the large-scale experimental evidence I have adduced to support my theory; instead he seems to rely on quotations from others, taken out of context, which themselves are not based on such an examination. Indeed, it is clear from his own chapter that he completely misunderstands my theory. He maintains that 'Eysenck has provided a tenable theory to account for persistent maladaptive behaviours and emotional disturbances that stem from traumatic events.'

The whole tenor of my theory has been to point out that this is true of Watson's original hypothesis, but that recent work has rendered this hypothesis untenable. I have tried to show that there is good empirical evidence for the *incubation of anxiety*, that this is related to Pavlovian B conditioning, not to Pavlovian A conditioning as used to be thought, and that a complete restructuring of the original theory was required. This I attempted to do, but Lazarus shows no signs of having read the new theory, or of finding any explicit criticisms to make of it. In the absence of such criticism it would be pointless to go on with the discussion of my theory; if Lazarus has read and understood it, he has certainly given no indication of this, and the reader who is interested in it must be referred to my 1982 paper, which he mentions. Far be it from me to say that the theory is adequate; all I am claiming is that it enables us to conceptualize remarkably well a large number of facts in the area of the origins and treatments of neurosis, and at present there is no alternative theory which even begins to approach it in this respect. If Lazarus knows of one, he certainly shows no evidence of it.

Lazarus makes a particular point of stressing the practicality of theories— 'theories that fail to generate techniques which meet the needs of a wide spectrum of the clinical population will soon fall into disfavour.' He also seems to favour conceptions concerned with 'expectancies', 'encoding', 'plans', 'values' and 'self-regulatory systems', and makes large claims for cognition, typically undefined. He maintains that Eysenck 'constantly extrapolates from animal studies to human functioning, seemingly unaware that the complexity of human interaction renders infrahuman research a pale, if not sterile, paradigm of human learning.' Does all this bear the slightest resemblance to the facts? I venture to doubt it.

Let me give just one example. It is well known that obsessive-compulsive hand-washing behaviour is extremely difficult to treat; Rachman and Hodgson (1980) quote the well-known psychoanalyst D. Malan as witness to the fact that psychoanalysis is powerless as far as this disorder is concerned. Other methods of psychotherapy, such as ECT, leucotomy, etc. have been tried on a large scale and failed. We may say, therefore, that this disorder is extremely persistent and difficult to treat.

In my early book with Rachman (Eysenck and Rachman, 1965) I drew attention to the analogue to obsessive compulsive hand-washing presented by Solomon's work on dogs in a shuttle box, suggesting that the method of treatment there used could be used with humans also. Briefly, the dogs are conditioned to jump from compartment A to compartment B, and *vice versa*, to a conditioned stimulus by giving them shocks shortly after the oncoming of the CS. Soon the dogs learn to jump to the conditioned stimulus alone, and the electric supply is disconnected so that they never receive another shock. Nevertheless they continue to jump to the CS for a long time. Just as the human patient washes his hands all the time to reduce the anxiety produced by contamination, so the dog jumps in order to reduce the anxiety produced by the CS. The dogs are cured by a method of 'flooding' and response prevention; the hurdle that divides the two compartments is raised so high that the dog cannot jump over it, and he is then exposed to the CS. He shows a great deal of fear and anxiety (in other words, he is 'flooded' with emotion), but he is prevented from escaping from the situation. Gradually his anxiety dies down (extinction), and after a few repetitions he is cured.

We introduced the same method into the treatment of obsessive-compulsive patients, with results reported by Rachman and Hodgson (1980): to cut a long story short, 80 to 90 per cent of the cases were cured by means of this very simple method. Lazarus typically fails to mention this outstanding example of the application of an animal-model-based conditioning-extinction procedure to human subjects, in a condition previously known to be extremely difficult to treat. His whole tirade is consequently far removed from a factual discussion of the actual effectiveness of the type of therapy advocated by me, and based on the kind of theory I have always put forward. Instead, he makes meaningless claims for so-called 'cognitive' procedures which have not in the past shown the slightest signs of helping the obsessive-compulsive hand-washer to reduce his anxieties, or his symptoms.

Indeed, it is obvious that all the claims made by Lazarus are unsubstantiated by empirical research. This again is typical of the eclectic therapist. Making no testable statements, and not submitting himself to any proof of the efficacy of his treatment, he is able to appear in a completely safe and uncriticizable position—as he is not saying anything positive, he cannot be wrong! At the same time, however, such a position makes any progress impossible—we have no theories to test, we have no specific statements to investigate, we have no experiments to replicate, we have nothing! Such a position may satisfy some practitioners: I hope it does not satisfy all. If progress is to be achieved, we need theories that are testable and falsifiable. My own may have no other advantage but that of being testable and falsifiable, but that certainly is the beginning of scientific wisdom. I would claim a little more for them; I think they point a way to the construction of better and more efficacious theories, as in the case of the flooding with response prevention treatment for obsessive-compulsive disorders. It seems a pity that Lazarus didn't concentrate on criticizing on a factual basis those specific theories which I have put forward: that would have been useful, and might lead to progress. As it is, his comments are misdirected, not based on any apparent knowledge of my theories, and largely irrelevant to what I have had to say. His contribution illustrates *par excellence* the difficulties of making psychotherapy scientific—so many practitioners don't want to be bothered by science, and prefer vague, eclectic words they find reassuring, like cognition, expectancy and coping mechanisms. If these concepts really have a contribution to make to the treatment of patients, I would only be too ready to look at experiments, such as that reported by

Rachman and Hodgson on obsessive-compulsive hand-washing, to demonstrate the effectiveness of therapies so based as compared with others, such as those based on my own conception. In the absence of such proof I can only say that these concepts have not yet entered the realm of scientific discussion, and are left to swirl about in cognitive miasmas of cosmic irrelevance.

## 2  Psychotherapy

Paul Kline's admirable work on *Fact and Fantasy in Freudian Theory* (1972, 1981) is more critical than any other examination of the experimental evidence relating to Freudian theories, but even so it is more optimistic than I think is justified. The reason, as Eysenck and Wilson (1973) have shown, is Kline's refusal to consider alternative hypotheses to the Freudian. In his contribution to this book he makes an interesting point which illustrates very well the consistent failure of Freudians in their attempts to be scientific. In science one must assume a particular hypothesis or stand, throughout one's dealing with a particular topic. Freudians often make contradictory statements, both of which cannot be true, but both of which are used in different places to answer specific criticisms. Kline in his book is quite definite that the Freudian opus does not constitute a unified theory, but that the different types of hypotheses which are put forward have to be tested in separation. This is a perfectly well argued point of view, and I would essentially agree with it. But look now what he has to say in his contribution to this book. He maintains that: if we have twenty experiments, each apparently confirming different parts of psychoanalytical theory, is it more elegant, more in accord with Occam's razor to regard each as confirming the relevant aspect of psychoanalysis, or to produce, as do Eysenck and Wilson (1973), twenty *ad hoc* hypotheses (more strictly *post hoc*) tied to no theory of any kind other than to reject any confirmation of psychoanalysis?'

I will not here comment on his erroneous notion that the counter-hypotheses used by Eysenck and Wilson are 'tied to no theory of any kind'; this is obviously untrue, as even the most cursory reading of our book will show. Our counter-hypotheses are usually derived from learning theory, or some other aspect of academic psychology, thus disconfirming Kline's belief. But most of all, note that he now claims that his own treatment is superior to ours because the twenty experiments which apparently confirm different parts of psychoanalytic theory are in some way unified by being relevant to that theory. But as he has maintained in his book, there is no such general theory! In the book he maintains that each theory has to be judged on its own, and treated in separation from all others; now when it is more convenient to hold the opposite view, he suddenly accepts this view. This is not a scientific type of argument nor a logical one, and it must make one doubt the value of his contribution.

I will not here go into the details of all the experiments that Kline mentions in his paper; to do so would require more space than I have at my disposal. I will, however, briefly comment on just one or two, to indicate how far I believe the alleged 'proofs' are far from being even marginally relevant to Freudian theory. Kline mentions the fact that menstrual taboo might be interpreted in Freudian terms as reflecting the intensity of castration anxiety felt by the men in a given society. Castration anxiety as such is not mentioned in the anthropological literature (very wisely—there is no way of quantifying it after all!), so instead certain hypothetical antecedents and consequences were rated across seventy-two societies together with a measure of menstrual taboo. Amongst such hypothetical antecedents were *post partum* sex taboo, severity of masturbation punishment, strictness of father's obedience commands, etc. It appears that all of these were related to the menstrual taboo scale in the expected direction. But would anyone have expected anything different? All the items relate to a kind of Victorian morality, authoritarian, anti-sex, and restrictive. There is no glimmer of evidence to link this with such a far-fetched concept as castration anxiety! Yet Kline claims that: 'This study is impressive support for the Freudian claim that castration anxiety originating in the Oedipal situation is a widespread phenomenon!' One can only say, in the immortal words of the Duke of Wellington who, walking down the street in his Marshall's uniform, was addressed by a man who said, 'Mr Smith, I believe', to which Wellington replied, 'If you believe that you'll believe anything!'

I have one further remark. Kline, like many other defenders of the psychoanalytic religion, grasps at straws which will not stand a proper scrutiny. In his 1980 study Kline put forward ten hypotheses regarding the so-called oral personality; he found that seven of these were disproved, while three of the results were positive. He claims that 'although more hypotheses failed than did not, these results do confirm, to a surprising degree, the link between personality traits and oral behaviours, as claimed in psychoanalytic theory.' But we cannot, of course, as Kline does, treat each of these predictions in isolation. Statistically each constitutes part of a sample of predictions, and consequently the application of simple statistical criteria of significance to each separately is not feasible. Overall I think the verdict must be that little if any statistical significance attaches to the results as a whole; there is certainly no evidence I would consider as significant here favouring Freudian theories. Similar criticisms to those advanced in relation to these two studies, concerning either interpretation or statistical treatment, can be made of the other studies, but it must be left to the reader to discover for himself the reasons for regarding these experiments as inadmissible from the point of view of evidence.

### 3   Parapsychology and Smoking

I am treating these two topics together, not because there is any relationship between them, but because in relation to both even friendly critics have felt that I had gone a little too far. Iconoclasm, so it might be said, is all very well, but the scientist should not have anything to do with astrology and parapsychology, subjects which are clearly beyond the pale, and have nothing in common with science. Neither should he throw doubt publicly on theories such as those linking smoking with lung cancer and coronary heart disease; such conduct is considered to be irresponsible in view of the possible harm it may cause. Let me take these issues separately.

Unlike most of the critics who dismiss astrology and parapsychology altogether, I have taken great care to read the large literature that has accumulated around these topics, with particular reference to experimental studies and methodological and statistical issues arising therefrom. This itself is sometimes criticized, and it is said that one should not waste time on topics which are obviously absurd, and can have no empirical basis. I do not believe myself that *a priori* judgments of this kind are admissible in science; scientists have been wrong too many times in making explicit statements of this kind to be considered infallible. In any case, the time that is wasted is mine, and to waste it by reading the literature on astrology and parapsychology is probably better spent than in watching pornographic films, or becoming a football hooligan!

I have a strong interest in metrology, i.e., the study of measurement as a scientific problem, and have always been particularly concerned with the application of measurement to matters that seem at first sight to be very intractable, such as intelligence, personality, aesthetics, and later on astrological and parapsychological predictions. I cannot see why the standard methods of statistical analysis cannot be applied to these fields, and I have been very much concerned with attempts to do so. All this may be a waste of time, but it is also possible that some positive results may emerge; only the future can tell in these cases.

As regards parapsychology, I have carried out only one large-scale experiment, dealing with precognition in rats (Hewitt, Fulker and Eysenck, 1978). This followed up two reported experiments, claiming positive results. It had been suggested that when put in a shuttle box, i.e., a box divided in two, with the two compartments being separately linked to an electric supply, so that an electric shock could be given to the feet of the rat either in one or the other, a rat with precognition could anticipate the random application of these shocks, and go to the safe compartment more frequently than chance would allow. I determined to test this hypothesis, doing so on a fairly large scale, with different strains of rats and different severities of shock. The outcome was almost embarrassingly negative, being closer to chance than one might have expected on a chance basis! (It is interesting to note that the write-up of this study was turned down by the *Journal of Parapsychology*, on rather spurious grounds of inadequate statistical treatment; the statistical treatment used was in fact the best and the most extensive that was appropriate to the experiment, as recommended by some of the best statisticians in Great Britain, and the suggested changes and additions would have made no difference to the result whatever. The article was finally published in an orthodox psychological journal instead.)

In spite of this individual failure, I became convinced by the relatively small number of outstanding experiments published in the literature that there was evidence for extrasensory perception, and even for psychokinesis. I am not enthusiastic about this, and I am quite willing to agree that I may be wrong in my estimation; to err is human, and I would certainly not consider myself infallible! But I do feel that those who criticize my stand should at least be familiar with the literature and spend as much time as I have on checking these statistics, trying to look at the precise details of the methodology used, and consider possible sources of error. Without such a background. I consider criticism inappropriate, as I would in any other scientific endeavour.

As far as astrology is concerned, I came to the conclusion (in my book with D. Nias) that with the solitary exception of the work of Michel and Françoise Gauquelin there was very little evidence in favour of astrology, although there were many intriguing but not replicated empirical findings. I have known the Gauquelins personally, and collaborated with them, and find it impossible to discover any source of methodological or statistical error in their work. This is not without trying: I have spent a good deal of time in my attempts to find such errors because I was convinced on *a priori* grounds that the results could not be true. It only seems honest for me to admit this failure, and to apply the same standards of evidence to their work as I would apply to anybody else's work in psychology, or in physics, or in astronomy.

I could, of course, simply have refrained from writing on the topic at all, but this seemed to me an act of cowardice. I believe that the Gauquelins are right and that they have been treated extremely shabbily by orthodox scientists. The future will tell whether I am right in this, or whether I have been soft-headed and suggestible. I do not enjoy being in a minority in this, and I do not enjoy having to defend empirical findings which go counter to my own instinctive beliefs. I would much rather be in a position to disprove all parapsychological and astrological claims: life would be so much easier if we could cosily go to sleep in the shadow of orthodox science! However, I find that I cannot do this, that the evidence that I have looked at is so convincing that I simply cannot deny it. So much for these areas. Parapsychology and astrology will no doubt attract a good deal of attention in the future, and more and better research will soon show whether I was right or wrong in my estimates. I certainly did not come to positive conclusions in these matters simply in order to annoy orthodox scientists, or to play the *enfant terrible*; to claim such motivations would be quite incorrect. Perhaps strong innate feelings for the underdog have something to do with it; I believe that these fields have been decried by orthodox scientists without specialist knowledge of what was been done in them, and this I consider to be insupportable.

As regards the point made in my book on *The Causes and Effects of Smoking*, namely that the evidence for a causal relationship between smoking cigarettes, on the one hand, and the development of cancer and coronary heart disease, on the other, had not been proven, I can only advise the reader to go to my book and read it. I think the facts support my case, which is not that the relationship had been *disproved*, but simply that the evidence was not strong enough to prove it beyond any reasonable doubt.

I have been far more interested in a positive type of argument, rather than the simple negative one that the orthodox opinion here was wrong. The positive argument, going back to my early work with Kissen, relates to the influence and importance of personality in developing lung cancer, and other types of cancer. We had found that stable and extraverted people develop lung cancer much more readily than do neurotic and introverted people, and there is much evidence now to support this view. The best evidence probably comes from an as yet unpublished prospective study, carried out in Yugoslavia, in which large numbers of subjects were followed up over a period of years, and the causes of death noted (Grossarth-Maticek *et al.*, in press). For this group it was known how much they smoked, and also the type of personality, on the basis of a questionnaire which measured essentially a combination of neuroticism and introversion. Both the smoking and the personality variables were subdivided in three, and chi square values calculated for different causes of death. For lung cancer the chi square for smoking was 69, for personality it was 84! For other cancers it was 11 for smoking, 211 for personality! For coronary heart disease it was 3 for smoking and 70 for personality! For all causes of death it was 5 for smoking and 232 for personality. I find it very difficult to resist the conclusion that orthodox medicine, which completely disregards personality and the genetic factors related to it, and concentrates exclusively on smoking, is wrong, and that my own approach, emphasizing the relevance of personality, has something important to contribute. I would suggest that the evidence is now overwhelming in indicating the importance of personality factors, and theories are now being developed to link personality with underlying hormonal factors. I believe this a very important line of development and Figure 1 shows in diagrammatic form the kind of theory my colleagues and I are developing in this field.

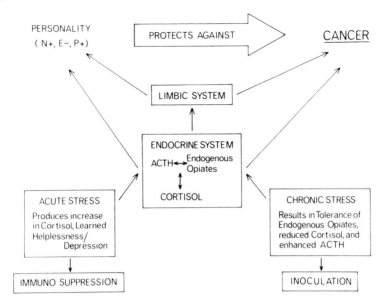

**Figure 1** *Hormonal Factors in Relation to Personality and Cancer*

It is perfectly possible, of course, that the two sets of theories, those emphasizing the influence of smoking, and those emphasizing the influence of genetics and personality, may be complementary rather than contradictory. In the Yugoslav study it was found, for instance, that *all* cases of lung cancer occurred when *both* the appropriate personality *and* smoking were present; there was not a single case in the other three quadrants! Here is an area of great ignorance, where unorthodox hypotheses and suggestions are easily ridiculed and dismissed from serious consideration, and the research money goes entirely in predictable and not very fruitful directions. This seems to me a pity, and I am quite willing to endure the vilification which has been my portion in this field, as a result of my writings, if only in due course this results in more research effort being directed into genetic and personality factors, and their underlying biochemical and hormonal constituents.

It is natural that the further you depart from orthodoxy, the more likely you are to be mistaken, and my views on these matters may be regarded in the future simply as evidence of Eysenck's folly. This is a risk one has to run: remember Newton's belief in a peculiar form of religious fantasy, Kepler's belief in astrology and the 'music of the spheres', or Marx's belief in the infinite improvability of mankind. However, the history of science contains many instances where orthodoxy dismissed as absurd and idle speculation ideas which in the long run were found to be valuable and indeed indispensible: as one example note the mathematics of multidimensional geometry. The Russian mathematician Lobachewski was declared to be insane, and dismissed from his post, for working out such a geometry, and even the great Gauss was afraid of communicating his calculations on this topic, and left them to be published after his death! Again only time will tell.

One last word may be said on the topic of practical usefulness. Even if it were true, as I believe, that personality is at least as important, probably more so, than smoking in relation to various medical diseases, the objection has often been made that while we can do something about smoking, we can do nothing about personality.

This, of course, is true, although the most intriguing work of Grossarth-Maticek (unpublished), the Yugoslav prospective study on the effects of behaviour therapy on cancer of the breast, has shown that in terminal cases of this disease behaviour therapy can be as effective as chemotherapy in delaying death (while psychoanalysis actually causes death to come significantly more quickly!).*

However, I am not concerned with this particular line of argument at the present time. I would rather put it this way. At the moment we know that even if smoking were to be considered to have a causal influence on death from lung cancer, it is neither a necessary nor a sufficient cause. Out of ten people who die of lung cancer, one is a non-smoker: hence smoking is not a *necessary* cause. Out of ten heavy smokers only one dies of lung cancer: hence smoking is not a *sufficient* cause. If we could pin-point (as apparently we now can) certain personality configurations which much more than others are susceptible to smoking in producing cancer, then we could isolate the individuals at risk and help them give up the smoking habit much more successfully than can be done at the moment. At present all we can do is to suggest to a given individual that there is a one-in-ten chance that in due course he may contract lung cancer and die of it. Given his personality profile, we could say with much greater assurance that he is almost certain to contract lung cancer in due course if he goes on smoking. (I am assuming here that smoking is in fact the causal agent in producing lung cancer, which is doubtful. I am simply assuming this to be so in order to demonstrate the power of the argument.) Few people when confronted with the certainty of a painful death if they continue to smoke would refuse to give it up and we have worked out much better methods along behaviour therapy lines which, by making use of personality and motivational differences, enable us to help people to give up the habit much more successfully than was possible before. It is along these lines that I think our research could be medically important in reducing the rate of lung cancer at the present time.

## 4   The Psychology of Politics

This is one area in which there has been much criticism of my work, although, as John Ray acknowledges, much of this has been ideologically inspired, and is of no scientific interest. He acknowledges the essential correctness of my major proposition, namely that there are two great dimensions in this field, one going from Right-wing Conservatism to Left-wing Radicalism, the other, rather less easy to identify, but perhaps collinear with the Authoritarianism-Liberalism division, although I still prefer my own terms, tough-minded versus tender-minded. As he also points out, the idea of Left-wing Authoritarianism, or Left-wing Fascism, was highly unpopular at the time the book was written, and this probably accounted for much of the bitterness with which it was criticized.

There are many difficulties with research in this area, and I will mention only a few. In the first place, when I studied members of the Communist Party it became quite clear that there were two radically different types of people involved. On the one hand

---

*As one listener to a lecture I gave on this topic remarked, in relation to the relatively greater influence of personality, as compared with smoking, on death from cancer or coronary heart disease: 'I think I'll give up personality!' One can only wish that life were that easy.

we had the largely working-class membership, deeply committed to revolution, to the support of Russia and Stalin, and to Marxist-Leninism. On the other hand there was a fair number of idealistic students and other intellectuals, who had little idea of what they were letting themselves in for, and who usually left the party within a year or two after joining, highly disillusioned. This division was well recognized by long-term members of the party, who used to regard the antics of the idealistic students with humorous disdain. My own research was done on long-term members of the party, mostly working-class, but also middle-class, but not students or intellectuals. I found it very amusing that some American critics, having tested a few idealistic student members, considered that the results they achieved contradicted mine: such naïveté would be too laughable to mention, were it not for the fact that American psychologists not knowing the position in England took the criticism seriously.

Another obvious difficulty is this. When the social forces in a given society favour the Right or the Left-wing, Conservatism or Radicalism, then the adherents of the favoured group readily resort to violence, intimidation and other non-democratic methods of behaviour if they are on the authoritarian side of the great divide. When my research was done society was essentially conservative in England, and hence it was the Right-wing authoritarians who were more inclined to violence, and Left-wing authoritarians who preferred to lie low and use argument rather than violence. My theory predicted the emergence of Left-wing Fascism, a prediction then very much ridiculed: when the pendulum started to swing Leftwards, however, it became only too clear that Left-wing Fascism was a reality, and the excessive violence now shown in England by the 'Militant Tendency' and other authoritarian Left-wing organiz-ations makes it only too clear how right my prediction was. It is amusing to recall that the violent attack on me at the London School of Economics marks the beginning of this phase of Left-wing politics; I could have wished for no clearer indication that I had been right all along!

John Ray has indicated another difficulty in the study of social attitudes, namely that Left-wing authoritarians are less ready than Right-wing authoritarians to admit on questionnaires their authoritarian tendencies. Ray has also criticized me for using largely sex-related questions in order to identify Left-wing authoritarianism. He clearly has not read Grossarth-Maticek (1975), whose large-scale work in Germany has indicated the intimate relationship between undisciplined sexuality and Left-wing tough-mindedness! Whether Grossarth-Maticek is right in his causal analysis is a question difficult to answer; that a relationship of the kind posited by me exists, his work seems to leave little doubt.

Much more needs to be done in this field before we can begin to feel that we have reached a satisfactory answer to the problem. Indeed, the precise nature of the problem, and therefore the precise answer, may be constantly changing from year to year. I have already indicated that this may be so with respect to the overt violence preached and offered by Right- and Left-wing authoritarians respectively; this is one problem. Another is the constantly changing nature of the particular social problems that emerge, and towards which Right and Left, tough and tender, have to orient their positions. It is reassuring that the questions originally selected for my inventory of social attitudes in the early 1950s still give rise to similar or identical factors (Hewitt *et al.*, 1977), and it seems little short of miraculous that these items also give rise to similar factors in other nations and other cultures (Eysenck and Wilson, 1978). Yet in spite of this consistency it would be useful if a large-scale study, preferably using a quota sample, could be done using a much extended base of attitude questions to identify these two factors more closely, and to investigate in detail some of the problems raised by Ray and by Brand. In addition, such a survey should be repeated every two years, in order to see to what extent the attitude structure remained steady, and to what extent it changed with time.

All in all, I would agree with most of Ray's criticisms, and Brand's alternative suggestions. There is considerable room for improvement in the details of the theory, there are obvious weaknesses in the choice of items, there is insufficient evidence concerning the relationship with personality and there are many other weaknesses that only future research can remedy. Nevertheless, I do feel that the general theory is along the right lines, and that it encompasses modern political structures much more readily than do alternative hypotheses. When we add to this the very high degree of genetic determination found in this field (Eysenck and Wilson, 1978; see also the chapter by Martin and Jardine in this volume), it is difficult not to feel that here we have a very real and very important slice of the action, and that the earlier theories of Jaensch and Adorno, who would have allied all the desirable human qualities with either Right-wing or Left-wing political dogmas, were mistaken, and that my more even-handed hypothesis is more likely to survive.

One more word may be necessary to deal with an issue that is at first sight rather puzzling. My theory has dealt with Right-wing and Left-wing politics in democratic countries, and it cannot be assumed that what is true there would also be true of politics in Communist countries. In democratic countries people have a free choice whether to join a given party, whether Communist, Fascist, Labour, Liberal or Conservative; in an authoritarian country there is little such choice. Preferment, or even the availability of jobs altogether, may depend on membership of the ruling party, and hence such membership, not being freely chosen by a given person, cannot carry the same meaning as it does in a free society. Similarly, attitudes of Communists in a democratic country must differ very considerably from those of Communists in a Communist country, simply because in the latter they constitute the government, whereas in the former they constitute a small minority intent upon upsetting the government and preaching revolution. Thus typical civil servants find no place in the Communist Party in England, but they would be suited for membership of the Communist Party of the Soviet Union. It is difficult, and may be impossible, to study attitude structures in dictatorships; the one thing that seems fairly obvious is that one cannot necessarily extrapolate from structures observed in a free society to those that may exist in Communist or Fascist countries. It is not impossible to formulate hypotheses that might apply there also, but it is not my intention to do so here.


## 5   Personality

It is interesting from the historical point of view to see the changes in attitude to my work on personality which have taken place over the years. At first my insistence on the importance of major dimensions of personality, such as extraversion-introversion, or neuroticism-stability, was regarded as a retrograde step; it was thought that the usefulness of such major descriptive variables had been fairly thoroughly disproved, and that multiple factor analysis had suggested rather a plethora of traits, such as Cattell's sixteen personality factors. Gradually it became clear to most personality theorists that these primary factors were either difficult or impossible to replicate, lacked reliability and showed little practical usefulness, as for instance Cattell's sixteen PF. Alternatively, primary factors were very circumscribed, and often consisted essentially of variations in the formulation of a single question. In either case it became clear that there were high correlations between these factors, and that analysis had to proceed to a higher order, using the intercorrelations between primary factors to discover higher-order factors, which in the vast majority of cases turned out to be the despised neuroticism and extraversion typologies!

I am not here concerned particularly with the discussion of the descriptive aspects of personality research; this has been extensively reviewed elsewhere (Eysenck and Eysenck, 1985), and the results show quite clearly that when factor analyzed practically all existing questionaires which cover larger fields than just one or two traits give rise to superfactors analogous to extraversion and neuroticism, and frequently psychoticism. Furthermore, these factors emerge in many different cultures, not only the Western one: they are highly heritable, as shown in the Martin and Jardine chapter in this book; and they tend to persist over long periods of time. I regard this chapter as effectively closed, and my interest over the last few years has been centred on the *causal* elements, biological in nature (i.e., physiological or hormonal), which lie at the base of these three major dimensions of personality. I believe that the theories I have advanced regarding extraversion-introversion have been shown to be along the right lines; that my theories concerning neuroticism are probably also along the right lines, but contain some mysterious anomalies as far as empirical research is concerned: and that theories concerning psychoticism, as Gordon Claridge has pointed out in his chapter, are still relatively weak. Again I would like to stress that I am not concerned to defend any of these theories as being ultimately 'right'. The research programme is a progressive one, not a degenerative one: it is this aspect of my work I am concerned with. In a rather novel field early theories are never correct, and to hope that mine are would be sheer delusion.

Let me take as an example the contribution made by John Dalton, the father of modern chemistry and the originator of our modern conceptions of the atom. All that Dalton said about atoms—apart from the bare fact of their existence, which wasn't novel—was wrong. They are not indivisible nor of unique weight; they need not obey the laws of definite or multiple proportions; and anyway his values for relative atomic weights and molecular constitutions were for the most part incorrect. Yet in spite of all this, John Dalton, more than any other single individual, was the man who set modern chemistry on its feet. As one scientific historian pointed out on the occasion of Dalton's two-hundredth birthday: 'For in devising a general scientific theory, the important thing is not to be right—such a thing in any final and absolute sense is beyond the bounds of mortal ambition. The important thing is to have the right idea.'

It is in this sense that I would like my contribution to be understood. Perhaps, or even probably, no single element of my theory will remain unchanged in the long run: nevertheless, I firmly believe that the theory points in the right direction, and that what Kuhn calls 'the ordinary business of science' will successfully improve the theory where it is wrong, supplement it where it is weak, and lead to a better theory than is at present available.

It may be relevant to add that I have tried very carefully to avoid the temptation of founding a 'school', as unfortunately so many other psychologists have done. A school essentially assumes the correctness of a given individual's views whether they be those of Freud, Skinner or whomever else one may associate with a given school. I have attempted instead to indoctrinate my students with the firm belief that their job was not to agree with me, but to disagree; not to rest content with my formulations, but to go on and improve them. It is one of my proudest boasts that there are no 'Eysenckians' trying to spread a certain message around, regardless of its truth, or regardless of any contrary evidence. Instead, we have people like Gordon Claridge, Jeff Gray and many others who, while acknowledging that their work may follow similar lines to mine, yet emphasize the weaknesses and anomalies in my theories, and attempt to improve upon them. That, to me, is the right scientific spirit, and in that way alone, I believe, will we ever come nearer to solving the important problem of human personality. To try and found a school is to ossify the process of discovery, and nothing could be further removed from generating genuine scientific advances.

For many people my theories in this field seem simplistic, or indeed oversimplified; how can you encapsulate the whole rich tapestry of human personality and individual differences within the confinement of three major factors? Indeed, this would be impossible, but of course the aim of science is different from that of the playwright or the novelist. What we are trying to discern are *uniformities* in nature; once these have been identified and measured, we can see to what extent they account for observations within the given discipline, and what proportion of the variance they account for. Dalton started with just a few elements; we now have well over a hundred, and we know a great deal more about atoms than Dalton ever dreamed about. Nevertheless, a beginning had to be made somewhere, and Dalton made the right beginning; he too was accused of being overly simplistic, and oversimplifying a difficult and complex field. Nevertheless, it was this simplistic beginning that led to great advances; the complex ideas and overly ambitious attempts made by others led nowhere. I firmly believe that the same is true in the field of personality. We cannot start with overly complex schemes, such as the Freudian, because there is no way in which we can test their validity, or measure their components. Only by the obviously humdrum methods of slow and piecemeal advance can we subjugate this complex field, and the beginning along these lines must inevitably appear unsatisfactory and oversimplified to those whose ambitions soar into the empyrean. Science does not hold with such ambitions: it proceeds step by step, making sure at each point that it is not running into a quagmire, but rests on firm ground.

This it has been my intention to do, and if I can boast of one thing, it is that my theory has been eminently testable and falsifiable. As I once pointed out, if somewhat tongue in cheek, my personality theory is the only one, parts of which have ever been disproved! This may sound a curious boast, but for a scientist it is a sign that the theory is indeed scientific, and not purely visionary or speculative.


*6   Intelligence*

In reading through the chapter by Carlson and Widaman, I found little to criticize; from their point of view, all their comments are reasonable and justified. I think where they go wrong is in failing to understand that the term 'intelligence' has several meanings, and that apparent controversy may arise when these meanings are not kept separate. As Hebb, Vernon and others have pointed out, we are dealing with at least three different concepts of intelligence. Intelligence A is the biological basis of all cognitive behaviour, genetically determined and presumably capable of being reduced to a physiological basis (Eysenck, 1982). Intelligence B is the application of this fundamental, biological intelligence to everyday life problems, e.g., problem-solving, learning, comprehension, memorizing, the formation of judgments, reasoning, adaptation to the environment, information processing, the elaboration of strategies and the three noe-genetic functions specified by Spearman: apprehension of experience, eduction of relations and eduction of correlates. Intelligence A plays a vital part in all this, but other factors enter into it also, mainly of an environmental kind. Third, we have Intelligence C, i.e., measurement of intelligence by means of IQ tests. There are many different types of IQ tests, some (culture-fair tests) relating more to Intelligence A, others (linguistic tests) correlating more with Intelligence B. IQ itself has been shown not to be unitary, but can be broken down into three independent factors: mental speed, error checking and continuance (or persistence) (Eysenck, 1982).

Figure 2 shows the scheme in rough diagrammatic form. The biological basis which would seem to underlie all these complex interactions is error-free transmission of information through the cortex; the more errors occur in this transmission, the lower the IQ, and the lower Intelligence B. This, at least, is the general scheme I have put forward (Eysenck, 1982), based on the theoretical and experimental work of Alan and Elaine Hendrickson, and it would seem that Carlson and Widaman are more concerned with Intelligence B, whereas my concern is with Intelligence A. There is nothing right or wrong in these concerns; clearly both need understanding and research, and in particular we require more information about the interrelations of Intelligence A, Intelligence B and Intelligence C. My interest in Intelligence A is due to the fact that it is much more fundamental than the other concepts of intelligence, that relatively little work has been done in relation to it, as compared with Intelligence B and Intelligence C, and that recent advances in psychophysiological measurement have enabled us to gain a much clearer understanding of Intelligence A than was possible hitherto. I believe that on this basis we could come to a better understanding of some of the issues raised by Carlson and Widaman.

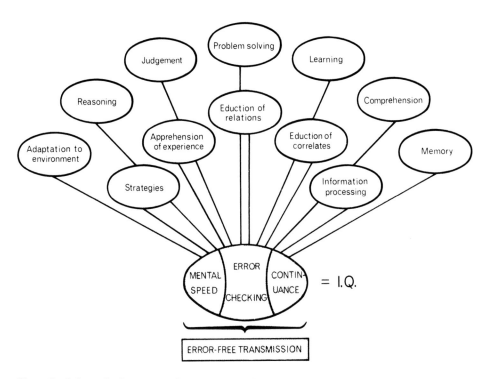

**Figure 2**   *Relationship between Intelligence A, IQ and Intelligence B*

There are one or two points on which I think there is disagreement. I believe that our new model of Intelligence A resolves the issue between Spearman and Thompson; certainly no-one would nowadays believe that there is any physiological basis to the kind of conception that Thompson advocated. It is possible to argue this point, but I think future research will show its justification.

The authors doubt the evidence that general intelligence is in fact unitary. Admittedly factor analytic studies can never prove the point because we can always allocate the variance in different ways, as caprice dictates. It is much more difficult to dismiss the fact that when we correlated the *g* loadings on the eleven Wechsler subtests which we had correlated with our evoked potential measure of intelligence, the two sets of correlations (factor loading on one hand, correlations with evoked potential on the other) correlated .95! It is very difficult to interpret this in any other way but as evidence for a general factor in intelligence which is measured with very great accuracy by the evoked potential measure (Eysenck and Barratt, 1985).

Carlson and Widaman suggest that Piaget's approach might present an alternative picture to the one I have presented. As they say: 'For example, it is conceivable that no 6-year-old child would pass any presentation of a particular type of Piagetian task and that all 8-year-old children would pass every presentation.' Conceivable perhaps, but quite untrue to the facts of the case; no such test has ever been found, and just to be able to imagine it is no argument against my theory. The evidence against Piaget's notions, based as they are on the study of very few children, carried out in a very rough-and-ready manner and without proper controls, does not really support his views, nor does it contradict mine (Modgil and Modgil, 1982).

Carlson and Widaman take me to task for suggesting that our national intelligence may be declining, and 'that some sort of selective breeding would be of positive social value.' As regards the former point, Cattell's (1983) recent book might suggest to them that possibly there is some value to the suggestion, and as regards selective breeding (on a strictly voluntary basis, of course) I do believe that we might get rid along these lines of many inherited diseases, both psychiatric and medical. The question of whether we should breed for certain types of behaviour (non-criminal, pro-social, peaceful rather than aggressive) is one I have never discussed, and on which I have not voiced any opinion one way or the other. It is, however, a question I believe *ought* to be discussed by people better qualified to do so than I am.

Carlson and Widaman, in another connection, state that: 'Eysenck's view that genetic factors are largely responsible for Caucasian-Negro differences in measured IQ is neither demonstrable nor refutable.' This is precisely the conclusion I came to in my book on *Race, Intelligence and Education*: I pointed out explicitly that there was no method of biological experimentation which could conclusively decide this question. I pointed out that all the evidence inevitably had to be circumstantial, and tried to give as fair an account of this circumstantial evidence as I could. To ascribe to me a view which in that form I do not hold is not uncommon, but is not commensurate with the careful academic scrutiny that the authors have given to my theories elsewhere in their paper.

On a later page Carlson and Widaman argue that personality and other factors are related to IQ performance, and that such performance can be improved by suitable teaching. All this is perfectly true, and I would not doubt it for one minute; it is for this reason that I have interested myself more in Intelligence A than in Intelligence C, which, in spite of its considerable practical importance and relevance, is obviously subject to interference by non-cognitive factors, among which I have explicitly named personality.

Last, Carlson and Widaman discuss our measure of evoked potential as a direct test of Intelligence A, and consider exogenous factors. 'Evidence implicating a specific exogenous factor comes from the apparent fact that stimuli of *only* 85 decibels will elicit the pattern of waves which will yield correlation with psychometric *g*. Accordingly, the relationship could be artifactual.' It is not true that only auditory stimuli of 85 decibels produce results showing correlations with *g*: it is merely that more intense stimuli than that result in startle responses, muscle movements and other types of artifact, while stimuli less intense than that sometimes allow subjects to go to sleep. Correlations are of course found with stimuli more or less intense than 85 decibels, but the correlations are lower. We have reported correlations between .7 and .8 for visual stimuli also, for instance, thus the hypothesis of artifactuality is very far-fetched. It is difficult to see how an artifact could generate correlations of .83 between Wechsler intelligence and a psychophysiological measure! One can only say that it would be nice to come across such artifacts more frequently!

It would be possible to go into much greater detail concerning some of the arguments put forward by Carlson and Widaman, but there seems little point in prolonging unduly this part of the chapter. Many of the points raised are genuine matters of concern, and it is hoped that future research will settle them once and for all. Obviously new advances in this field such as those relating to the measurement of intelligence by means of evoked potentials (Eysenck and Barrett, 1985) cannot settle all questions at issue; such innovation is likely to raise more questions than it can answer. It does, however, produce a genuine challenge to historically dominant theories, such as those associated with Binet; only the future will tell how this challenge will be resolved (Eysenck, 1985).

## 7 Genetics

My contributions to behavioural genetics have been substantive rather than theoretical or methodological, although I have made one or two theoretical suggestions which I think might be helpful. Thus I originally suggested the need to use factor scores rather than individual test scores in the analyses of genetic and environmental factors, for the simple reason that factor scores are purer measures than single test scores can ever hope to be. I believe this is a very important point, unfortunately disregarded by most behavioural geneticists.

Another suggestion of mine which I believe to be important, but which has been generally neglected, is the need to correct obtained estimates of heritability for *attenuation*. The idea is not one which comes natural to geneticists because usually they work with very precise measurements, such as the number of bristles on the leg of a fruit fly. Clearly these can be precisely enumerated, and no correction for errors of measurement is needed. However, psychological measurements are inherently more liable to such errors, and it would be psychologically and genetically meaningless to increase the environmental variance contribution by the amount of measurement error, as is usually done! It has taken me a long time to convince my geneticist friends of this, and even now they seem to regard the process with much suspicion.

In looking back at the devolopment of genetic theories of personality and mental disorder, many people nowadays will find it difficult to realize quite the degree of total environmental dominance that was characteristic of the years between 1950 and 1970. Here, for instance, is a quotation from a widely used text book by Redlich and Freedman (1966) on *The Theory and the Practice of Psychiatry*. This is their one comment on the importance of genetic factors in mental disorders: 'The importance of inherited characteristics in neuroses and sociopathies is no longer asserted except by Hans J. Eysenck and D. B. Prell' (p. 176.). The statement is, of course, not true: there was a certain amount of work going on even at that time, but certainly psychologists and psychiatrists, as well as criminologists and many others, simply took no account of it, and refused to pay any attention to the results which were emerging. This general *Zeitgeist* made it very difficult or indeed impossible to obtain grants for research in this area; it was assumed that the last word had been spoken on the subject, and that genetics simply did not influence individual differences generally, and mental disorders specifically. It was in this sort of climate that my early work was done, and it would be hard to overstate the difficulties which were encountered at every step.

Loehlin comments on some of this early work, namely the Eysenck-Prell study, quoting a comment of mine to the effect that: 'It would seem useful to repeat the Eysenck-Prell study with suitable technical improvements, in order to throw some further light on the relative importance of the factors in question.' He quotes me as stating that: 'Such studies would support the results of the original paper.' He then goes on to state: 'What he does not even hint at is that such a study had already been attempted in his laboratory, and that it had failed to yield such results'. His account of what happened is second-hand, and quite inaccurate. Interested readers are referred to Blewett's (1953) PhD thesis; here let me merely give a very brief account of the research.

It had been intended to conduct a replication of the Eysenck and Prell study, and to add various measures of intelligence, of autonomic functioning and of extraversion, in the hope of getting some ideas of the interrelations between these factors. Two Canadian PhD students were willing to undertake this work, but unfortunately the University of London intervened and drew attention to certain regulations which forebade two or more students to cooperate on a project. Thus the programme of testing had to be curtailed very badly, and instead of replicating the Eysenck-Prell study only a very small number of the many tests they had used could be incorporated, including suggestibility and ataxia tests which had in the previous and other studies proved themselves as good marker variables for neuroticism. Because of the very small number of tests involved, it proved difficult if not impossible to obtain a satisfactory neuroticism factor, although a suggestive factor with high loadings on suggestibility and ataxia was found, which gave a $h^2$ of .44. I was doubtful about the interpretation of this factor, because it did not correlate with ratings of emotional instability: we did not know then that such ratings of children are so invalid as to produce little by way of correlation with neuroticism as measured by objective tests. However that may be, it is quite incorrect that a repetition of the Eysenck-Prell study had been done, and that it had failed. Circumstances made it impossible to mount such a replication, and the interpretations of the rudimentary data we were able to obtain were too subjective to publish in any detail.

Loehlin's major criticism appears to be that he feels I have overestimated the importance of genetic factors in both intelligence and personality. This is a criticism in which he is joined by Carlson and Widaman, in whose chapter in this book the same criticism occurs. It would be idle to go into technical detail here; I have tried to do this in very great detail elsewhere (Eysenck, 1979), where I have analyzed (with D. Fulker) all the available evidence regarding intelligence. A similar summary had been made by Fulker (1981) for all material then available in the personality field. I still believe that my estimate of about two-thirds of the 'true' variance being due to genetic factors, one-third to environmental ones would be found to be an acceptable rough-and-ready guide to the situation in Western countries; recent work on intelligence in Russia, Poland and East Germany suggests that the figure as far as intelligence is concerned is not very different there either.

But I fully recognize that the point is debatable, that there are many arguments concerning correction for attenuation and other factors which are required, and that many of the data are of doubtful value. I am myself not at all convinced that the data on adoption studies, particularly when black children are concerned, can be given very much weight. It is almost inevitable that successful adoptions will be reported and that the parents involved will volunteer, whereas unsuccessful ones will try to keep out of the limelight. It is difficult to prove such points, and even more difficult to assign a quantitative value to them, for the purpose of calculation. Thus I fully acknowledge the points made by Loehlin, and I can only hope that in the future better designed studies on a larger scale will settle the issues between us.

## 8 Sex and Marriage

In this field I believe I have made three interesting and possibly important contributions. The first is the demonstration that there are strong genetic components, probably mediated through personality, of sexual behaviour, both with respect to libido and with respect to sexual satisfaction. As far as I know there was very little evidence on this point, and I think the analyses done by Dr Martin and myself were the first to throw any real light on this topic.

My second contribution, I would say, is the demonstration that personality is related to sexual behaviour in a predictable fashion. Gilbert is right in saying that relationships are not particularly strong, and might be due to common methods variance. It does not seem likely to me that this is so, and I do not believe that one would have expected very high correlations in a field where there are so many possible sources of error which would attenuate the true relationships. My main point in answer to Gilbert would be that the relations are not just accidental findings of large-scale correlational studies; they are predicted in the strictest sense, and every one of our predictions has in fact been verified, not only by us, but also by other writers. I think this is an important point which is not given sufficient consideration by Gilbert. It should also be noted that at the same time the findings in this field strengthen the conception of personality developed on the basis of other more experimental findings.

It should also be noted that some of our findings in the sexual field have been experimental, so that common method variance would not account for them. As an example, consider some (unpublished) work done by Dr E. Nelson in my department. I had predicted, on the basis of my general theory of personality, that extraverts would extinguish (habituate) responses to sexual stimuli more quickly than would introverts. For this experiment we developed nine four-minute films of a uniform character, by cutting out of pornographic films certain sequences. Thus one of the nine films would portray intercourse in the missionary position; another film would only contain portrayals of fellatio, or of cunnilingus; another film would show only 'sixty-nine'; etc. The measure of reaction was a penis plethysmograph suitably calibrated in terms of maximum expansion.

Subjects were chosen to fit the four quadrants of the extraversion-neuroticism scheme, i.e., high extraverted-high neurotic, low extraverted-high neurotic, high introverted-high neurotic, and low introverted-low neurotic. Subjects were tested on three days, and on each day three four-minute films were presented in random order, with four-minute rests between films. The hypothesis of habituation-extinction was tested (1) within films, (2) between films on a single day, and (3) between days. For all three comparisons extraverts habituated or extinguished more quickly than did introverts, as predicted, with neuroticism playing a very minor role. Thus it is possible to make predictions of a testable kind which can be verified in the laboratory, and are not subject to Gilbert's criticism.

The third contribution I think our work has made is in relation to the importance of personality for a happy marriage. We have demonstrated the relatively unimportant contribution that similarity and complementarity make in this respect, in spite of the considerable amount of attention that has been paid to these variables in the past. Our main contribution has been the theory of *asymmetry*, which comes out very clearly from the results, and which I believe is entirely new. Note also our findings that the personality of the proband himself or herself exerts a powerful influence; this too is a finding not previously emphasized by other writers.

To say this does not mean that I would disagree with Gilbert that multimethod, multitrait longitudinal studies that evaluate personality profile interactions will be required to determine the contribution of personality to marital satisfaction. Such studies are certainly desirable, and indeed necessary if we are to progress in this field. However, such studies require strong financial support, and a large group of investigators to carry out the follow-ups and the testing required. My own studies were done entirely by myself, without any financial support; if such support were forthcoming, I would gladly undertake the more complex type of work envisaged by Gilbert, and I hope that others will be able to do what was impossible for me, due to circumstances.

Having now dealt with some of the criticisms and points made by various contributors, I may perhaps say a few final words to put my work in perspective. I mentioned at the beginning that much of this has been of the 'revolutionary' variety, as Kuhn would call it; yet it is possible to look upon it from a different point of view. It has always seemed to me that much of what I had to say was so obvious that it should hardly have needed saying. Can any sensible person really doubt that personality is an important variable in determining people's behaviour and reactions? Can anyone really doubt that genetic factors play an important part in personality and intelligence differences between people? Is it not obvious that Right-Left differences in social attitudes have to be supplemented by something like the kind of dimension I call tough-versus tender-minded? Can anyone look at the evidence concerning the effects of psychotherapy and seriously maintain that it works? Can anyone seriously maintain that the set of speculations offered by Freud is really a scientific system in the sense which the term is normally used by scientists? On these and many other issues I feel that I have really acted the part of the child in the fairy-tale of the Emperor's new clothes, pointing out, for instance, in the case of Freudian psychoanalysis that the Emperor really had no clothes on at all!

Thus we have the odd position that I will seem to claim two contradictory achievements. On the one hand, I believe that the general tenor of my theories has simply been an extension of common sense, in agreement with beliefs which practically everyone in society holds anyway, or at least which follow directly from the reading of the relevant literature. On the other hand, I have claimed that much of my work has been novel and revolutionary, pointing in directions different from, and opposite to, those pursued by most psychologists. Can both these claims be correct?

I think the answer is that they can, and that the reason for this is that most psychologists have steadily averted their faces from common sense, and have marched resolutely in a position opposite to that which I believe is correct psychology. My belief is that psychology is a science in the same sense that physics, or chemistry or astronomy are sciences. I believe that psychology should follow the same path as other sciences, namely the construction of theories, the deduction of consequences from these theories, and the testing of these deductions, followed by improvements in the theory, where necessary, new deductions, etc. In other words, I believe that we must follow the hypothetico-deductive method of all the other sciences if we are to prosper.

Experimental psychologists would almost certainly agree with this proposal, but those working in the clinical, social, educational and other 'soft' areas seem to have set their faces firmly against such a proposal, preferring idiographic methods, Freudian speculations and unproven methods of therapy to the arduous work of providing actual proofs for their veiws.

When those general literary and anti-scientific tendencies combine with ideological beliefs and indeed political fanaticism, as they often do, we find an actual unwillingness to search for facts, or accept these facts as ultimate arbiters of our theories. T. H. Huxley talked about the ultimate tragedy of science—the slaying of a beautiful theory by an ugly fact. Most psychologists in the 'soft' areas refuse to countenance this unhappy event; when there is a conflict between fact and theory, they firmly reject the fact and cling to outmoded theories.

How true this is can be seen by anyone who looks at modern textbooks of personality. He will not find therein the cogent discussion of theories and experiments, in an attempt to bring together what is known about personality; he will usually find separate chapters eponymously entitled and dealing with the given authors' theories, without critical discussion, and usually without any attempt to form a judgment on the basis of published experiments. Thus the student is left in the position of making a choice on the grounds of personal preference, untrammelled by factual and general scientific considerations.

This, to me, is a scandal, and it does not speak well for psychology as a science. My own attempts, however humble, have been to try to introduce the methods of the hard sciences into this field, and to refuse resolutely to take seriously anything short of proper proof; to disregard idle speculation, offered to us on the ground that it provides 'insights' of a pseudo-religious character; and to try and steer research in a more empirical theory-related direction. It may be impossible to succeed in such an endeavour, but the effort has to be made, and it is from this perspective that my work should be judged. It can only point the way; future generations must take from it what proves to be of value, and let fall by the wayside that which isn't.

## REFERENCES

Blewett, D. B. (1953) 'An experimental study of the inheritance of neuroticism and intelligence', Unpublished PhD thesis, University of London.

Cattell, R. B. (1983) *Intelligence and National Achievement*, Washington, D. C., Cliveden Press.

Eysenck, H. J. (1979) *The Structure and Measurement of Intelligence*, New York, Springer.

Eysenck, H. J. (1982) *A Model for Intelligence*, New York, Springer.

Eysenck, H. J. (1985) 'The theory of intelligence and the psychophysiology of cognition', in Sternberg, R. J. (Ed.), *Advances in the Psychology of Human Intelligence*, Vol. 5, London, Lawrence Erlbaum.

Eysenck, H. J. and Barratt, P. (1985) 'Psychophysiology and the measurement of intelligence', in Reynolds, C. R. and Willson, V. (Eds.), *Methodological and Statistical Advances in the Study of Individual Differences*, New York, Plenum Press.

Eysenck, H. J. and Eysenck, M. W. (1985) *Personality and Individual Differences*, New York, Plenum Press.

Eysenck, H. J. and Rachman, S. (1965) *The Causes and Cures of Neurosis*, London, Routledge and Kegan Paul.

Eysenck, H. J. and Wilson, G. (1973) *The Experimental Study of Freudian Theories*, London, Methuen.

Eysenck, H. J. and Wilson, G. (1978) *The Psychological Basis of Ideology*, Baltimore, Md., University Park Press.

Fulker, D. W. (1981) 'The genetic and environmental architecture of psychoticism, extraversion and neuroticism', in Eysenck, H. J. (Ed.), *A Model for Personality*, New York, Springer, pp. 88–122.

Grossarth-Maticek, R. (1975) *Revolution der Gestörten*, Heidelberg, Quelle and Meyer.

Grossarth-Maticek, R., Bastiaans, Z. and Kanazir, D. T. (in press) 'Psychosocial factors as strong predictions of mortality from cancer, ischaemic heart disease and stroke: The Yugoslav prospective study'.

Hewitt, K., Eysenck, H. J. and Eaves, L. (1977) 'The structure of social attitudes after 20 years replication', *Psychological Reports*, **40,** pp. 183–8.

Hewitt J. K., Fulker, D. W. and Eysenck, H. J. (1978) 'Effect of strain and level of shock in the behaviour of rats in PSI experiments', *Psychological Reports*, **42,** pp. 1103–8.

Kline, P. (1981) *Fact and Fantasy in Freudian Theory*, 2nd Ed. London, Methuen.

Modgil, S. and Modgil, C. (Eds.) (1982) *Jean Piaget: Consensus and Controversy*, Eastboune, Holt, Rinehart and Winston.

Rachman, S. and Hodgson, R. (1980) *Obsessions and Compulsions*, Englwood Cliffs, N. J., Prentice-Hall.

Redlich, F. C. and Freedman, D. (1966) *The Theory and Practice of Psychiatry*, New York, Basic Books.

# Author Index

# Subject Index

AB scales
   *see* adaptive behaviour scales
ability testing, 104–5
abnormal psychology, 75, 87
   *see also* psychology
activation
   of central nervous system, 76–9
adaptive behaviour (AB) scales, 105
adoption studies, 395
AEP
   *see* average evoked potential
aesthetic preference, 64
age
   and conservatism, 142
   and extraversion, 42
   and individual differences, 42
   and intelligence, 133–4
   and neuroticism, 42
   in twin studies, 25–7, 42
age-incidence (AI) effect, 347
age-prevalence (AP) effect, 347
AI
   *see* age-incidence effect
altered states of consciousness (ASCs), 343–4
American Association for the Advancement of
   Science, 352
American Psychiatric Association, 248
American Psychological Society, 365
American Statistical Society, 365
'anal' character concept, 147, 194, 199
analogical reasoning, 111–12
androgen, 276–7
*Annual Review of Psychology*, 56
anthropology
   data of, 219–20
anxiety, 16–17, 20–9, 37–40, 41, 44, 78–9, 264–5,
   341–2, 344, 378–81
   *see also* neuroticism
   and extrasensory perception, 341–2, 344
   and sexual behaviour, 264–5
AP
   *see* age-prevalence effect
arousal
   of central nervous system, 76–9
ASCs
   *see* altered states of consciousness
Association for Advancement of Behaviour
   Therapy, 8, 235, 252, 258, 260, 261
assortive mating, 289–90

astrology, 5, 345–52, 357–63, 382–3
   areas of research in, 358
   and birth in relation to eminence, 346–7,
     348–9, 359, 369–70
   and birth in relation to group membership,
     346–7, 348–9, 359, 369–70
   and birth in relation to group membership,
     346–7, 348–51, 358–9, 369–70
   and birth in relation to schizophrenia, 347
   and cosmic clocks, 348–51
   definition of, 345
   dynamics of, 347–8
   methodology for research on, 346, 348, 350
   and parapsychology, 339–55, 357–71, 372–4
   and personality, 359–63, 369
   prospects for, 352
   as science, 360–1
   and sun-signs, 345–8, 352, 359–63, 369–70
   and traits, 359, 369–70
*Astrology: Science or Superstition?*, 5, 365
*Astro-Psychological Problems*, 371
attenuation, 393, 395
attitudes
   and behaviour 168–9
   and genetics, 14–44
Australia
   twin studies in, 9, 13–47, 59–61
Australian Army, 165
*Authoritarian Personality, The*, 158–9, 160, 161,
   164, 174
authoritarianism, 140–1, 142–3, 148–9, 150–2,
   159, 160, 165, 166, 167–9, 176, 177, 386–8
autism, 248, 258
autoaggressive disorders, 326–8, 335, 337
average evoked potential (AEP), 97–8, 114
   121–3, 145
   *see also* evoked potential

Balaam, 6
Balak, 6
behaviour
   clusters of, 240
behaviour therapy, 7–9, 233–61, 378–81
   *see also* conditioning
   definition of, 234–5, 252–3
   relationship of research and clinical practice in,
     236–7 as science, 236–7, 260
   and symptomatic treatment, 250
   theory in, 237–8, 258–9